American Christianities

American Christianities

A History of Dominance and Diversity

Edited by

CATHERINE A. BREKUS

and

W. CLARK GILPIN

THE UNIVERSITY OF

NORTH CAROLINA PRESS

Chapel Hill

Publication of this book was supported in part by funds from
the University of Chicago Divinity School, the Yale University
Department of Art History, and the School of Historical,
Philosophical, and Religious Studies at Arizona State University.

Set in Minion and Meta types by Rebecca Evans

The paper in this book meets the guidelines for permanence
and durability of the Committee on Production Guidelines for
Book Longevity of the Council on Library Resources.

The University of North Carolina Press has been a member
of the Green Press Initiative since 2003.

Library of Congress Cataloging-in-Publication Data
American Christianities : a history of dominance and
diversity / edited by Catherine A. Brekus and W. Clark Gilpin.
p. cm.
Includes bibliographical references and index.
ISBN 978-0-8078-3515-9 (cloth : alk. paper)
ISBN 978-0-8078-7213-0 (pbk : alk. paper)
1. Christianity—United States. I. Brekus, Catherine A.
II. Gilpin, W. Clark.
BR515.A48 2011   277.3'08—dc23   2011020423

cloth 15 14 13 12 11   5 4 3 2 1
paper 15 14 13 12 11   5 4 3 2 1

For our teachers

Jerald C. Brauer

Jon Butler

Martin E. Marty

Harry S. Stout

Contents

American Christianities

CATHERINE A. BREKUS & W. CLARK GILPIN

Introduction

Christianity—like electricity—is simultaneously omnipresent and invisible in the modern United States. It so thoroughly permeates American sensibilities about space and time, right and wrong, us and them, that many citizens find it remarkable only when it does something unexpected, spectacular, and potentially dangerous: the cultural equivalents of a power failure or lightning on the golf course. But in the more usual course of everyday life, a department store manager may possess scanty knowledge of the Christian liturgical year yet, nonetheless, presuppose its dominance over her marketing strategy. Pervasive invisibility punctuated by spectacular attention tacitly narrows the working definition of Christianity, for scholars and citizens alike, to points of public controversy, such as the teaching of evolution in the public schools. Consequently, both the immense variety of Christian thought and practice and the manifold, frequently surprising influences of Christianity in the broader sweep of American history are too easily overlooked. In response to this state of affairs, this book, *American Christianities*, takes its title seriously. By considering the topic of American Christianity in the plural as well as the singular, we hope to give both general readers and scholars a more sophisticated understanding of the varieties of Christianity in America and the reciprocal influences that have shaped the churches and the nation.

Throughout American history, extraordinary numbers of men and women have identified themselves as Christian, 78.4 percent of the American public according to a 2008 survey by the Pew Forum on Religion and Public Life.[1] But the term is a big tent that accommodates a stunning variety. Today, hundreds of religious groups trace their roots back to Jesus of Nazareth, including (to name just a few) Korean Presbyterians, Latino Pentecostals, Southern Baptists, Missouri Synod Lutherans, Nazarenes, Mormons, Catholics, Greek Orthodox, Disciples of Christ, African Methodists, Episcopalians, and Congregationalists. Not surprisingly, given these numbers of individuals and organizations, there is hardly a feature of American life—including politics, foreign policy, literature, science, sexuality, gender, race,

1

violence, pacifism, warfare, the media, and capitalism—that has not been influenced by some aspect of the Christian tradition. Yet American Christians have often disagreed sharply over religious practice and its implications for their lives as citizens and have adopted strikingly different postures toward the wider culture on matters ranging from service in the military to forms of popular entertainment. So much is this the case that persons advocating "the Christian position" have taken stances on *every side* of contested public issues, from the abolition of slavery to women's rights. Whereas some Christians speak in ways that make it hard to separate what is "Christian" from what is "American," others regard a clear distinction between these two loyalties as a primary test of Christian authenticity. Should Old Glory hang in the sanctuary? Don't expect a Christian consensus.

As these few sentences suggest—and as the essays in this book will demonstrate—the diversity of American Christianities and the power of the Christian presence in American history are factors that need to be considered together. At first blush, diversity of belief and collective social influence might not seem to go together. One might more readily suppose that a single, unified message would have greater social influence than a diverse, frequently contentious argument. But a half century ago, American cultural historian R. W. B. Lewis explained how diversity and debate can powerfully shape a culture. Every culture, Lewis proposed, seems gradually "to produce its own determining debate over the ideas that preoccupy it: salvation, the order of nature, money, power, sex, the machine, and the like." From Lewis's perspective, a culture achieves its characteristic form not so much through the ascendancy of one particular set of convictions as through debate about the meaning of these preoccupying ideas.[2] American Christians have never been completely unified in their opinions, but their debates have revolved around a set of common issues that have never lost their potency: for example, the possibility of moral progress and the meaning of America's claim to be a "city on a hill."

Christians have infused American society with an extensive repertoire of stories, symbols, and ethical ideals that have been among the defining terms of American cultural debate. Over time, Americans have drawn selectively from this repertoire, combined its themes with economic and political values, and mobilized (or resisted) social reforms around the potency of its symbols. For centuries, for example, Americans have debated over whether the story of Eve's sin in the Garden of Eden means that women should be subordinate to men, and they have debated just as fiercely about what it means to "love thy neighbor as thyself." Many contested issues and questions in American politics—including freedom of conscience, the limits of institutional authority, and the sanctity of human life—have drawn their energy from long-standing controversies within the Christian tradition. A Christian accent frequently inflects American political debate, advocacy for social reform, and proposals for the renewal of public education, even when that accent is unrecognized or unacknowledged. As a result, the sizable diversity of Christianity in America is not neatly contained under the steeples of its churches or in the governing bodies of its denominations but has, in addition, extended out into other sectors of society. It frequently requires concentrated attention to spot its variegated presence in the cadence of a presidential oration or the plot of a Hollywood film. We intend *American Christianities* to hone that skill of recognition.

There is a further—extraordinarily important—reason for scholars, students, and citizens to acquire this particular skill of recognition. Although Christianity is clearly an important part of America's religious history, it is by no means the entirety of American religion. Yet, as we will discuss later in this introduction, American religious history was written for many decades as if Christianity, especially white Protestantism, were its sole topic of concern. And this near equation of *Christianity* with *religion* remains a commonplace when citizens or journalists discuss American society, as in such phrases as "the religious right." In response to these problems, the past thirty-five years of scholarship by American religious historians has labored to broaden the field of American religion to include non-Christian traditions like Islam, Hinduism, and Buddhism in order to do justice to the nation's pluralism. The importance of this scholarship cannot be overstated: it has greatly enriched our understanding of American religious dynamism in both the past and the present.

We fully share the desire to create new, more inclusive narratives of American religion, and we are convinced that both scholars and the general public need to be better educated about the nation's full religious diversity. That said, we are also convinced that this wider research into America's religions not only creates the opportunity for a critical reevaluation of the concept of American Christianity but in fact requires it. On the one hand, scholarly and public awareness of the nation's religious diversity enhances the ability to recognize the distinctive forms and influences of Christianity in the United States. On the other hand, unless we critically examine the ways in which Christianity has shaped the term "religion," our understanding of America's religious pluralism will almost certainly be skewed by Christianity's tacitly privileged place in the American religious canon.

By bringing to bear on Christianity the insights from the "new religious history," *American Christianities* aims to stimulate a new conversation about America's dominant religious tradition. Given the powerful but variegated role that Christianity has played in shaping all aspects of American life, its history requires fresh, rigorous, serious attention.

The One and the Many

Even though Christianity has been the nation's largest religion, most Americans are unfamiliar with its internal variety and tend to define Christianity in narrow terms according to their own upbringing or what they have seen and heard in the media. This lack of awareness of Christian diversity is not merely because the public has not been "paying attention." Rather, the predominant Christian groups of each era have tended to submerge or marginalize alternative versions of Christianity in order to stake a claim to their own orthodoxy, centrality, and power. The pluralistic narrative of American Christianities that this book explores therefore requires actively probing below powerful, long-standing narratives of oneness that have obscured the many that have been there all along.

Embedded within Christianity, as Catherine Albanese points out in her essay for this volume, is a claim to unity that makes pluralism a problem. Jesus and his followers spoke of one God, one way to heaven (a "narrow way"), and one true church. Ever since the first century, however, Christianity has taken multiple forms, and the persistent disjunction between rhetoric and reality has meant that Christians usually identify "manyness" as a failure. Christians believe that in the ideal world, the tradition is supposed to be singular, and rather than confronting its plurality, they have usually chosen to identify their own part of it with the whole. Catholics, for example, tend to define Christianity in their own distinct language of sacrament, saints, and the mass, while Fundamentalists equate it with a belief in biblical inerrancy. Their understandings of Christianity are "partial" in two senses of the word: they are not only incomplete—they are partisan. Despite their ecumenical titles, for example, both the *Christian Century* (a liberal Protestant magazine) and *Christianity Today* (an evangelical one) approach Christianity with a singular identity in mind. The word "Christian" in the *Christian Century* points toward Protestant ecumenism, tolerance, and progressive politics; the same word in *Christianity Today* connotes Protestant biblicism, missionary zeal, and political conservatism.

Although the term "heresy" has fallen out of the American religious lexicon, many ways of narrowing the scope of Christianity amount to distinctions between "true" and "false." Most religious surveys and polls have asked questions about how people identify themselves (Christian, Muslim, Jewish, for example), but not what they mean by the label they choose. It is clear from interactive websites, however, that ordinary Christians have strong opinions about how to define their faith. For example, on About.com, a popular website that offers information about everything from "action figures" to "depression," the entry on "Christianity" has turned out to be controversial. Mary Fairchild, the author of the Christianity section, is an evangelical, and much of the material on her site has an evangelical slant. Yet because she was raised as a Catholic, she not only decided to include the "Roman Catholic Church" in her list of Christian denominations but also to provide links to books about Catholicism. In response, a disgruntled user posted a comment objecting to her decision to include Catholics as Christians. " I am really perplexed," the man wrote.

> I came upon your interesting site today and have been checking things out, with profit. When I noticed all of the links to Catholic lists and sites, I was perplexed. When I went to the list of 10 books on Catholicism, I was shocked to discover that they were promoting the Catholic Church. . . . It has been called the largest cult in the world. . . . How can you promote a church that is literally filled with false teachings, false beliefs, false ways . . . ? Instead of leading the visitor to the truth, all of those links will only lead him or her astray. I'm concerned and dismayed for I thought that this might be a helpful site.

To defend herself, Fairchild insisted that her intention on the website was "not to promote any church denomination," and she invited users to post their thoughts in a forum entitled "Are Catholics Christians?" The response was divided. On the one hand, "Jen" claimed that there should be limits to who can claim to be truly Christian. "I believe like this," she wrote; "just because a person calls themself a 'Christian' doesn't mean that they are." On the other hand, "Clothesgrl" retorted, "this sort of fruit sorting just really riles me up. Who ever it is, don't they have something better to do? What pin heads."[3] It isn't clear whether "Clothesgrl" is a practicing Christian or not, but her exasperation is shared by those who worry when the word "Christian" becomes explicitly partisan.

One version of the distinction between true and false Christianity has been an especially persistent feature of the nation's religious history. In the seventeenth century, the Puritans sharply contrasted their own ardent Christianity, with its stress on a "new birth" in conversion, to what they denounced as the merely nominal Christianity of those who conformed to the established practice of the Church of England. Continuing this contrast in the eighteenth century, revivalists like Jonathan Edwards and George Whitefield insisted that "true" Christianity involved a heartfelt experience of divine grace, not simply an intellectual assent to doctrine, and they condemned many other Protestant ministers as "pharisees." According to Gilbert Tennent, preachers who had never experienced conversion were no better than "dead dogs that can't bark."[4] This stereotypically Protestant distinction between authentic inward faith and perfunctory public practice has had a long and extraordinarily influential life in American society, not only as a strategy for narrowing the definition of Christianity but also as a working definition of religion in its entirety. It is presupposed in the classically American dismissal of "organized religion" and by those who declare themselves "spiritual, but not religious." And, in perhaps the most famous definition of religion ever proposed by an American, William James emphasized "feelings" over ritual or practice: religion "shall mean for us the feelings, acts, and experiences of individual men in their solitude, so far as they apprehend themselves to stand in relation to whatever they may consider the divine." From this indispensable core of personal religious experience, James argued, "theologies, philosophies, and ecclesiastical organizations may secondarily grow."[5]

During the nineteenth century, when scholarly ministers began to write general histories of Christianity in America, they ingeniously excluded and homogenized in order to fabricate a semblance of Christian unity from the already numerous and rapidly proliferating denominations. Robert Baird, a Presbyterian minister who published *Religion in America* in 1844, divided his subject into two categories: "evangelical churches" and "unevangelical churches." The first category included Congregationalists, Baptists, Methodists, and Presbyterians, who were supposedly linked together by their commitment to social reform, orderly worship, and learning. Because older Puritan prejudices had waned by the mid-nineteenth century, Baird favored Quakers and Episcopalians with the label "evangelical" as well. (The boundaries between religious "insiders" and religious "outsiders" have never been stable in American history.) In contrast, "unevangelicals" were a motley assortment of Deists, Unitarians, Jews, Atheists, Mormons, Catholics, and Shakers, who supposedly did not understand the gospel. Besides claiming that the Catholic Church had "buried the truth amid a heap of corruptions of heathenish origin," Baird denounced the Mormons as "a body of ignorant creatures." Perhaps not surprising, he believed that his own Presbyterian denomination was responsible for the best features of America's religious character, and he praised the "evangelical churches" for being part of "one great Presbyterian family."[6]

The Reverend Daniel Dorchester, a Methodist, believed that Methodism, not Presbyterianism, represented the purest form of Christianity, but like Baird he saw Protestantism as the apex of the Christian tradition. In his 1888 book *Christianity in the United States*, Dorchester created a slightly more complicated classification of American Christianity, dividing it into three categories rather than two: "Protestantism," "Romanism," and "Divergent Elements." But by using the pejorative term "Romanism" for Catholicism and disparaging Unitarians, Shakers, Spiritualists, and Swedenborgians as "divergent elements," he made his value judgments clear. Catholics seemed especially threatening, to Dorchester's way of thinking, because their allegiance to the pope took precedence over loyalty to the nation. Associating Catholics with immigration and crime, Dorchester feared that they had "retarded" the nation's moral progress.[7] (His other books had titles like *The Liquor Problem in All Ages*, *Romanism versus the Public School System*, and *The Problem of Religious Progress*.) Yet even though Dorchester lamented that the republic had been "invaded" by Romanism, he still believed that the "majestic unfolding of Providence" would lead to the ultimate triumph of Protestantism.[8] The divine plan was for the United States to be a Christian nation—and by "Christian" he meant Protestant.

Dorchester's conviction that "real" Americans were Protestant was widely shared in the nineteenth century. Even though the First Amendment guaranteed the separation of church and state, Protestantism was the nation's unofficial religion. As Kathleen Flake, Jonathan Sarna, David Kling, and Tracy Fessenden show in their essays for this volume, state governments frequently proclaimed days of fasting and thanksgiving in Jesus' name, Congress designated public lands for the building of churches, the nation's calendar was organized around Christian holidays like Christmas and Easter, and the King James Version of the Bible was read aloud in public schools. When Catholics complained about Protestant influence, they were not only accused of trying to subvert "the civil and religious liberties of the United States" (supposedly as part of a papal plot) but they were even portrayed as enemies of the true Protestant faith.[9]

American Catholic leaders resented the charge that they were not really Christian, but instead of trying to make the term more inclusive, they responded by claiming the word entirely for themselves. The 1908 *Catholic Encyclopedia*, published in part to counter what were regarded as anti-Catholic articles in the *Encyclopedia Britannica*, included an entry on "Christianity" that dismissed Protestantism as a heresy undeserving of recognition. As the author explained at the beginning of the entry, "The Christianity of which we speak is that which we find realized in the Catholic Church alone; hence, we are not concerned here with those forms which are embodied in the various non-Catholic Christian sects, whether schismatical or heretical."[10] On the one hand, the author admitted that Protestantism was part of the Christian tradition, but on the other hand, by lumping all Protestant denominations together as "sects" he portrayed them as marginal and deviant.

Protestant worries about a "Christian America" suggest another historically important strategy for delimiting the scope of the term "Christian": the boundaries of Christianity incorporated those churches that directly promoted the values of citizenship and civic culture. In 1955, shortly before the nation elected its first Catholic president, the sociologist Will Herberg wrote *Protestant-Catholic-Jew*, a widely influential book in which Herberg concluded that being a Protestant, a Catholic, or a Jew was understood "as the specific way, and increasingly perhaps the only way, of being an American and locating oneself in American society." In Herberg's judgment, these represented the "three great branches or divisions of 'American religion,'" and most Americans regarded them as "three diverse representations of the same 'spiritual values,' the 'spiritual values' American democracy is presumed to stand for."[11] Focusing attention on the centrist, culture-affirming varieties of Christianity, Herberg made only passing mention of African American Christianity and ignored the public presence of Billy Graham, Harold Ockenga, and other self-described "neo-evangelicals."

Terms such as "mainline" or "mainstream" nicely capture the popular perception during the 1940s and 1950s that American culture had a unified Protestant center. Mainline Protestant churches were large, politically active, mostly white, and theologically liberal, and although they probably never made up more than 60 percent of the Protestant churchgoing population, they loomed large in the public imagination because of their social prominence.[12] When a scholar examined the religious affiliations of all the people included in the 1931 edition of *Who's Who*, he found that "among 16,600 who listed a preference, fully 7,000 were either Episcopalians or Presbyterians. Congregationalists, despite the small size of that denomination, numbered an equally astounding 2,000."[13] Because so many business leaders, university professors, politicians, journalists, diplomats, and public intellectuals belonged to the Protestant "establishment," they seemed to represent the dominant form of American religion. When magazines or newspapers wanted to write about American religion, they did not interview Pentecostals or Fundamentalists but instead mainline Protestant leaders like Reinhold Niebuhr or William Sloane Coffin.

Today, however, mainline Protestantism is no longer synonymous with words like "American" and "Christian," and in a development that would have stunned earlier generations of Protestant leaders, evangelicalism has taken its place. The transformation began in 1976 when Jimmy Carter, a Southern Baptist, ran for president. Because Christianity was still associated with mainline leaders like Reinhold Niebuhr (who had died a few years earlier), many politicians and journalists were confused by Carter's claim to have been "born again," and they treated evangelicalism as if it were a strange new discovery that had to be explained to the public. John Coyne Jr., a former speechwriter for Gerald Ford, wrote an editorial for the *Los Angeles Times* in which he invoked Freudian language to try to make sense of Carter's religious experiences: "What, for example, is the average voter to make of this Carter remark at a recent question-and answer session: 'In 1967, I had a profound religious experience that changed my life. . . . I accepted Christ into my life.' Unless he—like Carter—is a member of American Protestantism's growing 'evangelical' wing, the voter will probably be in the dark, for the Democratic presidential front-runner is a born-again believer, one of those people who believed they have been transformed by what Sigmund Freud called an 'oceanic' experience." With surprise, Coyne explained that "apparently millions of Americans have undergone a similar awakening."[14]

Although evangelicals seemed odd and perhaps not quite "Christian" to the media in the mid-1970s, the situation had changed by 1980 because of their crucial role in the election of Ronald Reagan to the presidency. Two magazine covers tell the story. In 1948, *Time* magazine featured Reinhold Niebuhr on its cover, but twenty-eight years later, in 1976, the cover of *Newsweek* was emblazoned with the words, "Born Again: The Evangelicals." The article inside announced that 1976 was "The Year of the Evangelical."[15] Historian William Hutchison's description of the "mainline" during the 1950s could easily have been written about evangelicals in the 1980s, 1990s, and the early twenty-first century: "The Protestant churches felt responsible for America: for its moral structure, for the religious content of national ideals, for the educative and welfare functions that governments could not (or, was thought, should not) carry out. The agents of the Protestant establishment went on to ask, implicitly or otherwise, Who will do these things if we do not? Who else can run America?"[16]

In short, perceptions have shifted over time concerning which part of Christianity represents the whole. Changing identification of insiders and outsiders has periodically moved the boundaries of acceptable Christian belief and practice. Ongoing debates between Christian patriots and Christian critics of governmental policy have regularly reconfigured the relationships of American Christianities to the state. And, as the nineteenth-century historians Baird and Dorchester emphasized, socially unacceptable economic or family practices quickly cast Owenites, Shakers, or Latter-day Saints beyond the pale of consensus about what was properly American and Christian. An urban telephone directory usefully indicates the diversity of American Christianities, but it fails to capture the definitional debates—and occasional physical violence—that went into composing the list.

Given our emphasis on Christian pluralism, readers might well wonder whether we think American Christians share anything at all. In response, we recall an aphorism from a leading Catholic theologian of the twentieth century, John Courtney Murray: Disagreement is a hard thing to achieve.[17] Without shared scriptures, shared narratives of autobiography and history, and shared traditions of ethics and personal identity, American Christians would have little to talk about, let alone dispute. Whatever else it involves, Christianity is a religion of redemption; it envisions a humanity that has "fallen" from its proper place in the cosmos and must be saved from this fate by Jesus Christ and the redemptive community that extends his person and work through history—the church. This narrative of salvation has taken diverse forms in American history, from aspirations for a just social order, redeemed from corrupting greed, to steps toward release from alcohol addiction, whether through a constitutional amendment or an intimate support group. These narratives of transformation address profound and difficult issues concerning the conduct of personal and social life. Precisely by virtue of their difficulty and importance, they are not only a source of Christian diversity in America but also have shaped a wider debate about national purposes and ideals.

Non-Christians in America (including Jews, Hindus, Buddhists, Muslims, and secular humanists) have never doubted that American Christians share something—and that something is power. Those who stand outside of the Christian center have been acutely aware of the way that American Christians have shaped the nation in their own image. Despite their disagreements, American Christians have created informal coalitions with one another that have deeply influenced the nation's identity. In the nineteenth century, for example, Protestant denominations put aside their theological differences in order to support Sunday laws and Prohibition, and more recently, Mormons, Catholics, and evangelical Protestants have been willing to overlook long-standing antipathies in order to join forces against abortion and same-sex marriage. (Given the fact that these groups used to despise one another, their détente is one of the most remarkable features of modern Christianity.) Even though American Christians have never spoken with a single voice, their strategic alliances have given them the appearance of acting as a unified bloc. Even if Christians have been too occupied with their own internal debates to recognize it, they have always occupied a privileged place in the nation, and they have often used their collective power to create or to resist change.

Christianity amid America's Many Religions

American Christianities contributes to a field of scholarship known as "American religious history." This field has undergone a major expansion in the past thirty-five years, an expansion that reflects contemporary public and academic recognition of the prominent role that religions have played in the development of American culture. It also reflects heightened awareness of the amazing religious diversity within this nation of immigrants. In our judgment, this attention to the scope and variety of religious influences in the history of the United States is—along with the study of race and gender—one of the pivotal recent advances of American historical scholarship. Why, then, within a field that addresses the many religions of the United States, produce a book that addresses only one? To answer this question requires a brief excursion into the "pre-history" of the academic field of American religious history. This, as it turns out, is no merely academic question. Instead, the story of Christianity's place within the academic study of religions in America casts light on a whole array of public confusions and conflicts regarding the role of religions in American civic life.

From the later decades of the nineteenth century until the 1960s, most scholars of American religion taught in theological seminaries, in departments of theology in church-related universities such as Notre Dame or Fordham, or in divinity schools connected to nondenominational private universities such as Yale, Harvard, or Vanderbilt. Since a constitutive purpose of these institutions was education for Christian leadership, scholars wrote in service to churches as well as the academy, and their work had a theological aim: to understand the development of the church as an expression of providential history. Presidential addresses to the leading professional organization in the field, the American Society of Church History, consequently focused on the overarching theological purposes of historical study. As James Hastings Nichols explained in his 1950 presidential address, "Our task is to trace the actualization of the Gospel in human history, to discern and describe the signs of the Kingdom, to reveal the subtle indications of the presence of the Risen Christ to his adopted brethren." Unlike secular historians, who offered economic, political, and social explanations for historical events, church historians were supposed to ask additional questions about providence and divine revelation. Leonard Trinterud, who was elected to the presidency of the American Society of Church History in 1955, acknowledged the "baffling variety" of Christianity in America, but he argued that the "task of the church historian" was "to show how this strange religious history is somehow the redeeming work of God through Christ."[18]

Given these theological and educational purposes, historians' principal concern was "church history" or the history of Christianity as a whole, and especially prior to World War I, the religious history of the United States was a relatively minor enterprise within this much larger investigation. But the balance began to shift in the 1920s and 1930s, significantly expanding scholarship on Christianity in the United States. Without denying the importance of research on the general history of Christianity, an increasing number of church historians began to specialize on the United States and focus their attention on the social and environmental factors that gave distinctive shape to American Christianity. Explaining that he wanted to "develop an entirely new field of history," William Warren Sweet, professor of American church history at the University of Chicago from 1927 to 1946, effectively created the field of *American* religious history by viewing the churches through the lens of Frederick Jackson Turner's frontier thesis. Turner, in a famous address to the American Historical Association in 1893, had argued that "the peculiarity of American institutions" had arisen from adaptation to the distinctive conditions of the frontier and westward expansion. "The advance of the frontier" had created a society independent from European models, according to Turner, "and to study this advance, the men who grew up under these conditions, and the political, economic, and social results of it, is to study the really American part of our history."[19] Instead of asking questions about how God had revealed himself in history, Sweet followed Turner's lead and devoted his career to explaining how European churches were transformed into American churches by their work of settling (and civilizing) the American West. Despite Sweet's efforts to refrain from theological speculation, however, he was still influenced by the Protestant orientation of the field, and his own Methodist religious sympathies were clear. Besides remarking that it was a "strange anomaly" that Catholics had been responsible for the founding of Maryland, the first colony to espouse religious liberty, he attributed the rise of the Millerites, Mormons, and Spiritualists to a tendency toward "fanaticism" in the New England "blood."[20] Nevertheless, by asking new questions about the way that Christianity had both shaped and reflected American society, he helped to build the foundation for the modern field of American religious history.

By the late 1960s, historians of Christianity in America had not only distanced themselves from theological readings of history but had generally concluded that the old Protestant model could not—and should not—withstand the pressures of social and religious change.[21] The Immigration Act of 1965 (which led to a wave of non-European immigrants), the civil rights movement, the women's rights movement, and the Vietnam War all had a profound effect on the academy. Confronted with new questions about race, ethnicity, class, gender, and religious diversity, historians challenged the traditional assumptions of their field. Speaking at a meeting of the American Society of Church History in 1969, Yale's Sydney Ahlstrom declared, "Pluralism has asserted itself. The supreme court, a no-longer-anti-Catholic electorate, the Black revolution, the war in Southeast Asia, moon shots, the student protest movement, the Beatles, the radical theologians, the so-called 'new morality,' and assorted other manifestations of a similar nature have ushered in a post-Puritan, post-Christian, post-WASP America."[22] In a groundbreaking 1968 book entitled *Reinterpretation in American Church History*, Jerald C. Brauer argued that "the assumptions on which the church historian used to function are no longer valid." Instead of viewing the church as "a unique institution grounded in the supernatural and fulfilling a transcendent will in history," most historians now treated it as the product of human decisions, and as Brauer saw it, they were more interested in examining its relationship to politics or economics than in searching for evidence of God's providence.[23] Although Brauer shared the common concern that church history had lost its distinctiveness (he worried that it might become a minor subfield of secular history), he exhorted his colleagues to look forward instead of backward. Influenced by the work of comparativist historians of religion like Joachim Wach and Mircea Eliade, he argued that historians of Christianity should carve out a distinctive discipline by asking questions about religious experience, symbols, and rituals.

Brauer's vision of a more comparative approach, which placed the history of Christianity within a larger inquiry into the global history of religions, converged with broader social and academic currents in the 1960s and 1970s. In the wake of the Supreme Court decision in the 1963 *Abington v. Schempp* case, which argued that public schools could teach about religion as part of a liberal education (though they could not teach any particular religion as the truth), many colleges and universities—including public universities—created religious studies departments. The new discipline of religious studies was built on the premise that religion should be studied as a product of human cultures, not as revelation or dogma. In order to distinguish themselves from church historians and theologians, scholars of religious studies resolved to withhold judgment about the truth claims embedded in particular traditions, instead approaching religion theoretically and comparatively. As a result of this upheaval in the academic study of religion, religious studies departments insisted that no single religion should be given pride of place in the curriculum. As the Religious Studies Department at Indiana University explains on its website, "Religious studies does not aim to promote or undermine any particular religion or world view; the academic study of religion seeks to examine religion from outside the framework of any particular belief system."[24] Of course, as Jonathan Z. Smith has commented, no one practices "religion" but only a particular kind of religion— for example, Methodism or Orthodox Judaism—but the word "religion" proved attractive precisely because of its neutral, abstract quality.[25]

The desire for neutrality, however, has come at a price. Because American religious historians have sought to separate themselves from both the partisan scholarship of the past and the political controversies of the present, they have frequently preferred the more detached-sounding word "religion," even when the actual topic of their research is Christianity. Given the fact that American religious historians have been admirably sensitive to the complexities and ambiguities embedded in words like "American" or "female," it would be easy to criticize them for failing to subject the category of "Christianity" to the same critical analysis. Yet the truth is that most of the contributors to this volume—and its two editors—have been guilty of the same mistake. The result is that the word "Christianity" has been one of the least examined terms in the field of American religious history. Sometimes it is treated as a synonym for mainline Protestantism or evangelicalism; sometimes it is taken for granted, as if readers automatically know what it means;

and sometimes it is subsumed under the larger category of religion as if it has no unique meaning of its own. Ironically, this relative silence about Christianity frequently, if inadvertently, perpetuates its privileged place in historical narratives by implying that religion and Christianity are virtually synonymous. It is hard to imagine a scholar of Buddhism, Islam, or Hinduism claiming to write about all of American "religion," but historians of American Christianity implicitly make this claim on a regular basis. For example, when Leonard I. Sweet published a collection of essays about religion and the media, he entitled it *Communication and Change in American Religious History* even though it contains only one essay (out of thirteen) that does not focus specifically on American Protestants. Similarly, Robert R. Mathison's *Critical Issues in American Religious History* is an impressive collection of 151 essays and documents about American religion, but only nine focus on non-Christian topics, including two on Judaism, one on Islam, one on Zen Buddhism, and three on Native Americans. Both Joanna Brooks's book, *American Lazarus: Religion and the Rise of African-American and Native American Literatures*, and Edward J. Blum's *Reforging the White Republic: Race, Religion, and American Nationalism, 1865–1898* advertise themselves as books about religion, but both are studies of Protestantism.[26]

Textbooks about American religion are marked by the same linguistic choices. Even though most of them are tacitly organized around Christian themes (with chapters about other religions "tacked on"), they seldom identify their main topic as American Christianity. In *A Religious History of the American People*, Sydney Ahlstrom notes that "Christianity is by no means the only current in American religious history, although it has been the major one," but despite his desire to be as inclusive as possible, he relegates non-Christian religions to separate chapters that are disconnected from the main narrative. His discussion of Judaism, for example, appears in a section entitled "Countervailing Religion" (a term that is reminiscent of Daniel Dorchester's "Divergent Elements"). Similarly, John Corrigan's *Religion in America* (a revision of Winthrop Hudson's 1965 textbook) focuses almost entirely on Christianity until the end of the book, when he discusses "the fracturing of Protestantism" and "world religions in America."[27]

Use of the generic term "religion" obscures what turns out to be a focus on Christianity, and more specifically on Protestantism. Many of the books that claim to be about American "religion" exclude Jews, Buddhists, Muslims, Sikhs, and Hindus—and even Catholics. Since the Catholic Church is one of the nation's largest religious communities, making up 23.9 percent of the population, according to a 2008 survey by the Pew Forum on Religion and Public Life, it is surprising that historians have not recognized it as a more important presence.[28] For example, Ahlstrom's book examines Catholics in separate chapters that seem removed from the main story. In parts 2, 3, and 4 he focuses exclusively on Protestantism, and in part 7 he writes about Catholicism in only one of eight chapters. Because of his conviction that the main theme of American religion should be the "Puritan ethic," he seems to have found it difficult to integrate Catholics into his narrative. It was not until the 1960s, he argues, that the "Puritan Epoch" came to an end. In contrast, Corrigan tries to integrate Catholics more fully into his narrative, but his longest discussions of them take place in separate chapters on early missionary endeavors and their twentieth-century "maturity."[29]

As these examples suggest, traces of the older Protestant hegemony still linger. Although historians who write about Catholics and Mormons usually signal their topics in their book titles, historians of Protestantism feel comfortable describing their work in the neutral language of the study of "religion." Whereas John McGreevy's book *Catholicism and American Freedom* announces its focus on American Catholics in the title, Leigh Eric Schmidt's book *Hearing Things: Religion, Illusion, and the American Enlightenment* purports to be about "religion," even though it focuses entirely on Protestants. To mention another example, Frederick Sontag published a book about Protestant thought with the title *The American Religious Experience: The Roots, Trends, and Future of American Theology*, while Patrick W. Carey's book about Catholic theology has the less sweeping title of *American Catholic Religious Thought: The Shaping of a Theological and Social Tradition*. Even the two scholarly societies that are devoted to studying the history of Christianity reveal this Protestant tendency to appropriate the more encompassing term. The American Society of Church History, founded in 1888, was largely a Protestant organization until 1969, when it elected its first Catholic president, John Tracy Ellis. (Jay Dolan, the organization's second Catholic president, was elected eighteen years later, in 1987.)[30] Yet the society has never explicitly defined itself as a Protestant organization, and the word "church" in its title sounds ecumenical. In contrast, the American Catholic Historical Association, founded in 1919, announced its Catholic identity in its title because it could not make a claim to being neutrally Christian.

As the academic study of American religious history properly expands its purview to investigate the nation's full religious diversity, the *explicit* identification of Christian ideas, institutions, and practices therefore becomes more important, not less. Much work remains to be done in order to interpret the religions in their rich diversity and to make religion a genuinely comparative category that does not skew interpretation by tacitly employing Christian assumptions. *American Christianities*, by explicitly examining Christian variety in the American context, aims to contribute to this broader endeavor of American religious history.

American Christianities

Christianity is an old, complex, and global religion. It has adapted—and is constantly adapting—to many different social environments. Through immigration, this multiplicity of cultural forms is a major source of Christian diversity in the United States. Once arrived, some individuals and communities then recombined Christian ideas and symbols in order to launch new Christian denominations in the United States. These many arrivals and formations have produced a history of "border encounters" between different Christian groups and between Christians and other religious traditions, especially African American and Native American. Some of these encounters have included sustained and tragic violence, and many have involved jostling for social influence. Comprehensively considered, such encounters have led Christians not only to demarcate sharp boundaries of religious difference but also to engage in religious borrowing, appropriation, exchange, and negotiation, which have tended to make each group a hybrid of distinctively combined beliefs and practices. In other words, the long American experiment with religious freedom and the separation of church and state has created an American religious environment of voluntary affiliation, institutional flexibility, and self-directed development in which Christians, as well as other religions, have learned to operate and cooperate. In this setting, Christian denominations have rarely prospered by withdrawing into cultural cocoons or by assimilating into an undifferentiated "melting pot." Instead, they may be thought of as embroiled in a long, sometimes fractious cultural debate about the possibilities for being appropriately both Christian and American.

As suggested in our earlier discussion of American Christian diversity, this variety of Christian relationships to the American nation has troubled some adherents. As a result, they have not only sought to impose a narrowed definition of Christianity but have also insisted that the United States can be imagined in only one way: as a "Christian nation" founded by God. This has been especially true when the nation's future has looked bleak or uncertain. During the Civil War, a group of Protestants proposed an amendment to the Constitution identifying the United States as a Christian nation. They did not succeed, but others continued the crusade during the late nineteenth century because of anxieties about immigration, intemperance, and immorality.[31] More recently, Christians concerned about both "secular humanism" and immigration have claimed that despite the Constitution's secular language, the Founders were divinely inspired when they wrote it. According to a story frequently recounted in evangelical textbooks and homeschooling materials, the Founding Fathers were deadlocked about the Constitution until Benjamin Franklin proposed that they begin each meeting with daily prayer. Once they allowed God to guide them, they quickly put aside their conflicts and wrote a document that should be understood as sacred writ. Like the Bible, the Constitution is God's word, and hence the United States is not just one of many nations but God's *favored* nation. As historians have pointed out, however, this story about prayer at the Constitutional Convention is mostly a myth. Franklin did indeed make a resolution to begin each day with prayer, but his motion was tabled, and the Founders mentioned God only once in the Constitution: when they dated it "anno domini 1787."[32] Some Christians have claimed that this small Latin phrase, "in the year of our Lord," should be seen as significant, but it seems far more significant that God is not invoked anywhere else. "We forgot," Alexander Hamilton supposedly said.[33] Most of the Founders were Deists who were skeptical about Christ's divinity (but who believed in God), and they were strongly committed to religious freedom. In a famous letter to Newport's Jews in 1790, George Washington assured them that they would always enjoy "liberty of conscience." As he wrote, "For happily the Government of the United States, which gives to bigotry no sanction, to persecution no assistance, requires only that they who live under its protection, should demean themselves as good citizens."[34] Nevertheless, many groups of Christians in American history have argued that the republic cannot survive without a religious foundation.

These power struggles over Christian and American identity are a major theme of this book. When we focus on American "Christianities" instead of American "religion," we not only see the de facto Protestant establishment that dominated the United States for much of its history but also the struggles of other Christians—Catholics, Fundamentalists, Pentecostals, Mormons, Christian Scientists, and many others—to make their voices heard. On the one hand, it would be a mistake for historians to underestimate the power of Protestants to shape the republic in their own image. As Jonathan Sarna reminds us in his essay on the relationship between Christians and Jews, nineteenth-century Protestants often tried to use state power to advance their own religious agenda, and as Tracy Fessenden argues, they have played a disproportionate role in defining who is "religious" and who is "American" and even how religion itself should be defined.[35] The "American" idea that religion should be a matter of individual conscience, not public enforcement, has distinctly Protestant roots. On the other hand, however, neither mainline Protestants in the past nor evangelical Protestants in the present have been able to stifle alternative voices, and other Christians have offered other understandings of both selfhood and the nation. In the nineteenth century, for example, Catholics strongly objected to the American emphasis on individualism, arguing that the corporate good should take precedence over individual freedom.[36]

Our argument is not simply that a majority of Americans have been Christian, an observation that would tend to limit Christianity's influence to the private realm. Nor do we want to make the opposite argument, that Christianity is so deeply woven into the institutional structures of the nation that its precepts make up the guiding presuppositions of government. Instead, we want readers to understand how Christianity—in multiple forms—has actively participated in civil society, "the many forms of community and association that dot the landscape of a democratic culture."[37] As the middle space between individual citizens and the government, civil society includes a wide range of voluntary organizations that link people together in a common cause: civil rights groups, philanthropic agencies, and political parties, as well as churches. It is within this democratic civic space, perhaps, that American Christianities have exerted their most formative influence on national public culture.

As a pluralistic tradition, Christianity has had multiple and often contradictory effects on American civil society—sometimes for good, sometimes for ill. As Curtis Evans, Timothy Lee, and Michael McNally show in their essays, Christianity was implicated in slavery, in the forced removal of Native Americans from their lands, and in exclusionary immigration laws that were designed to keep Asians out of the United States. But as they also show, African Americans, Native Americans, Latinos, and Asians developed their own distinctive Christian traditions to resist oppression and discrimination. McNally thus argues that Native American religion represents a fusion of Christian and indigenous practices that is virtually impossible to disentangle. Similarly, Ann Braude illustrates that Christian language permeates both the feminist and the antifeminist movements, meaning that for some

Americans the struggle over women's rights is at least partially a struggle over biblical interpretation. Taken together, the essays in this volume reveal that Christianity has influenced American attitudes toward war, science, education, social reform, literature, gender, capitalism, sexuality, and the nation itself. This influence usually occurred not because Christians agreed on these topics but because their disagreements tended to shape the broader social debate around Christian categories.

The effects of American culture on Christianity have been similarly profound. Suburbanization, for example, by relocating congregations from urban political and economic centers into residential communities, has played a pivotal role in the long process by which Christianity and religion generally have become identified with the private sphere and domestic life. Similarly, the American drive to develop new media technologies has affected the way that Christians experience their faith. As Stewart Hoover argues, the rise of transnational media networks has resulted in greater religious syncretism and a climate of individual seeking. At the same time, the American appetite for consumer goods has encouraged the growth of new Christian churches that celebrate wealth. The "prosperity gospel," as Catherine Brekus argues, should be understood as the fusion of capitalism with Pentecostalism, the Holiness movement, and New Thought.

Because Christianity is so deeply entwined with American civil society, its influence has often been invisible; but for that reason it has been especially potent. As Kristina Bross shows in her essay, American literature has been saturated with Christian themes that are no longer identified specifically as Christian but only as American. From darkness to light, from captivity to freedom, from crucified Jesus to resurrected Christ—this is the story that Christians have always told about themselves, and it permeates American culture even when it has been disconnected from its Christian roots. In his book *The Redemptive Self: Stories Americans Live By*, Dan McAdams argues that many Americans frame their life stories around the theme of redemption, emphasizing that they have overcome suffering on the way to productive, successful lives. Being an American, like being a Christian, has meant believing in the possibility of self-transformation.[38] Our goal in this volume is to bring these reciprocal influences to light, exposing the way that Christianity has interacted with virtually every aspect of American public and private life.

As we have searched for the right language to discuss this American style of practicing Christianity, we have settled on the term "American Christianities," a phrase that means both more and less than what readers might expect. Precisely because the word "Christianity" is a fraught one in American culture, we have decided to define it as broadly as possible. Our criteria for defining Christianity are not doctrinal or theological but practical: we have treated as Christian any group that identifies itself as such. This will undoubtedly trouble some readers, but after reading the work of historians like Robert Baird and Daniel Dorchester, we prefer to investigate the debates over who deserves the label "Christian" instead of making judgments in advance. The term "American" is, perhaps, even more contested than "Christianity," but we have decided to use it. First, its multiple and conflicting symbolic connotations fit well with our interest in accentuating the contentious history of Christian ideas about "the meaning of America." Second, our use of the term "American" invites, we hope, future comparative scholarship about Christianity in the *Americas*, a crucial topic toward which Mark Noll's essay points.

American Christianities is divided into four sections: "Christian Diversity in America," "Practicing Christianity in America," "Christianity and American Culture," and "Christianity and the American Nation." Throughout, we are concerned with both Christian diversity and the reciprocal influences between Christianity and American culture. In addition to providing readers a general overview of important topics in American Christian history, the book seeks a finer-grained understanding of influential people, ideas, and practices. Our aim is not comprehensiveness but texture. We have not sought inclusion in the sense of covering every aspect of a topic, but we have sought inclusion in the sense of being particularly alert to the many ways that diverse American Christians have shaped both America and Christianity.

NOTES

1. See the results of the 2008 U.S. Religious Landscape Survey by the Pew Forum on Religion and Public Life. The results are available on the Pew Forum's website: http://religions.pewforum.org/reports (accessed August 28, 2009).

2. R. W. B. Lewis, *The American Adam: Innocence, Tragedy and Tradition in the Nineteenth Century* (Chicago: University of Chicago Press, 1955), 1–2.

3. See http://forums.about.com/n/pfx/forum.aspx?tsn=1&nav=messages&webtag=ab-christianity&tid=18307 (accessed May 28, 2009).

4. Gilbert Tennent, *The Danger of an Unconverted Ministry* (1740), reprinted in *The Great Awakening: Documents on the Revival of Religion, 1740–1745*, ed. Richard Bushman (Chapel Hill: University of North Carolina Press, 1969), 91.

5. William James, *The Varieties of Religious Experience: A Study in Human Nature* (New York: Longmans, Green, 1902), 31 (italics deleted).

6. Robert Baird, *Religion in America; or, an Account of the Origin, Progress, Relation to the State, and Present Condition of the Evangelical Churches in the United States, with Notices of the Unevangelical Denominations* (New York: Harper, 1844), 288, 286, 266.

7. Daniel Dorchester, *Christianity in the United States* (New York: Phillips and Hunt, 1888), 771.

8. Ibid., 752, 759.

9. *Address of the Board of Managers of the American Protestant Association* (Philadelphia, 1843), 42; Philip Hamburger, *Separation of Church and State* (Cambridge: Harvard University Press, 2002), 219–29.

10. Joseph Keating, "Christianity," in *Catholic Encyclopedia* (New York: Robert Appleton Company, 1908), retrieved May 28, 2009, from New Advent: http://www.newadvent.org/cathen/03712a.htm; Thomas E. Woods, *The Church Confronts Modernity: Catholic Intellectuals and the Progressive Era* (New York: Columbia University Press, 2004), 6.

11. Will Herberg, *Protestant-Catholic-Jew: An Essay in American Religious Sociology* (Garden City, N.Y.: Doubleday, 1955), 52–53.

12. William R. Hutchison, "Protestantism as Establishment," in *Between the Times: The Travail of the Protestant Establishment in America, 1900–1960*, ed. William R. Hutchison (New York: Cambridge University Press, 1989), 5.

13. Ibid., 11.

14. John R. Coyne Jr., "Shedding Some Light on 'Born-Again' Carter," *Los Angeles Times* (1886–Current File), May 27, 1976, http://www.proquest.com.proxy.uchicago.edu (accessed May 29, 2009).

15. *Time*, March 8, 1948; *Newsweek*, October 25, 1976.

16. William R. Hutchison, "From Protestant to Pluralist America," preface to Hutchison, *Between the Times*, viii.

17. John Courtney Murray, S.J., *We Hold These Truths: Catholic Reflections on the American Proposition* (New York: Sheed and Ward, 1960).

18. James Hastings Nichols, "The Art of Church History," *Church History* 20, no. 1 (March 1951): 9; Leonard J. Trinterud, "The Task of the American Church Historian," *Church History* 25, no. 1 (March 1956): 14.

19. Frederick Jackson Turner, *The Frontier in American History* (New York: Henry Holt, 1920), 1–4; William Warren Sweet, "Every Dog Has His Day," *University of Chicago Magazine* 39 (February 1947), quoted in Sidney E. Mead, "Prof. Sweet's Religion and Culture in America, *Church History* 22, no. 1 (March 1953): 33. On Sweet, see also James L. Ash Jr., "American Religion and the Academy in the Early Twentieth Century: The Chicago Years of William Warren Sweet," *Church History* 50, no. 4 (December 1981): 450–64.

20. William Warren Sweet, *The Story of Religions in America* (New York: Harper, 1930), 113, 396.

21. David W. Lotz, "The Crisis in American Church Historiography," in *The Writing of American Religious History*, ed. Martin E. Marty, vol. 1 of *Modern American Protestantism and Its World* (New York: K. G. Saur, 1992), 95–105.

22. Sydney E. Ahlstrom, "The Problem of the History of Religion in America," in ibid., 24–25.

23. Jerald C. Brauer, "Changing Perspectives on Religion in America," in *Reinterpretation in American Church History*, ed. Jerald C. Brauer (Chicago: University of Chicago Press, 1968), 20.

24. See http://www.indiana.edu/~relstud/index.shtml (accessed March 14, 2011).

25. Jonathan Z. Smith, *Imagining Religion: From Babylon to Jonestown* (Chicago: University of Chicago Press, 1982).

26. Leonard I. Sweet, ed., *Communication and Change in American Religious History* (Grand Rapids, Mich.: Eerdmans, 1993); Robert R. Mathison, *Critical Issues in American Religious History* (Waco, Tex.: Baylor University Press, 2006); Joanna Brooks, *American Lazarus: Religion and the Rise of African-American and Native American Literatures* (New York: Oxford University Press, 2003); Edward J. Blum, *Reforging the White Republic: Race, Religion, and American Nationalism, 1865–1898* (Baton Rouge: Louisiana State University Press, 2005).

27. Sydney E. Ahlstrom, *A Religious History of the American People* (New Haven: Yale University Press, 1972), xiii; John Corrigan, *Religion in America*, 7th ed. (Upper Saddle River, N.J.: Pearson/Prentice Hall, 2004).

28. See http://religions.pewforum.org/reports.

29. Ahlstrom, *A Religious History of the American People*, 1095; Corrigan, *Religion in America*.

30. See Henry Warner Bowden, *A Century of Church History: The Legacy of Philip Schaff* (Carbondale: Southern Illinois University Press, 1988), appendix A, 355, 360.

31. Gaines M. Foster, *Moral Reconstruction: Christian Lobbyists and the Federal Legislation of Morality, 1865–1920* (Chapel Hill: University of North Carolina Press, 2002).

32. For a discussion of this story, see Mark A. Noll, "Evangelicals in the American Founding and Evangelical Political Mobilization Today," in *Religion and the New Republic*, ed. James H. Hutson (Lanham, Md.: Rowman and Littlefield, 2000), 137–38.

33. Ron Chernow, *Alexander Hamilton* (New York: Penguin, 2004), 235. In May 2009, Congressman Randy Forbes of Virginia submitted a resolution to designate the first week of May as "America's Spiritual Heritage Week." His resolution was prompted by President Barack Obama's 2009 speech in Turkey in which he argued that America was not a "Christian nation." Forbes responded: "I wish he had asked and answered two questions when he did that. The first question was whether or not we ever considered ourselves a Judeo-Christian nation, and the second one was, if we did, what was the moment in time where we ceased to be so? If asked the first question, Mr. Speaker, you would find that the very first act of the first congress in the United States was to bring in a minister and have congress led in prayer, and afterwards read four chapters out of the bible. . . . When our constitution was signed, the signers made sure that they punctuated the end of it by saying, 'in the year of our lord, 1787,' and 100 years later in the supreme court case of Holy Trinity Church vs. United States, the Supreme Court indicated, after recounting the long history of faith in this country, that we were a Christian nation." The

full text of his speech is available at http://forbes.house.gov/judeochristiannation (accessed August 31, 2009). The phrase "Judeo-Christian nation" is a twentieth-century invention that is designed to sound inclusive. Forbes's speech, despite his inclusion of the word "Judeo," focused entirely on America's Christian character. Forbes points out many examples of the nation's privileging of Christianity (especially Protestantism), without acknowledging contrary evidence. For example, the 1796 Treaty of Tripoli, which was signed by President John Adams, declared that "the government of the United States of America is not, in any sense, founded on the Christian Religion." The full text of the treaty is available on the website of the Avalon Project at Yale Law School: http://avalon.law.yale.edu/18th_century/bar1796t.asp (accessed August 31, 2009). For a balanced discussion of the Founders' religious convictions, see Jon Meacham, *American Gospel: God, the Founding Fathers, and the Making of a Nation* (New York: Random House, 2006).

34. "George Washington's Letter to the Jews of Newport, Rhode Island," 1790, can be found on the website of the Jewish Virtual Library. See http://www.jewishvirtuallibrary.org/jsource/US-Israel/bigotry.html (accessed July 9, 2009).

35. On this theme, see Tracy Fessenden, *Culture and Redemption: Religion, the Secular, and American Literature* (Princeton: Princeton University Press, 2007).

36. John T. McGreevy, *Catholicism and American Freedom: A History* (New York: W. W. Norton, 2003).

37. The definition of the term "civil society" comes from Jean Bethke Elshtain, *Democracy on Trial* (New York: Basic Books, 1995), 6.

38. Dan P. McAdams, *The Redemptive Self: Stories Americans Live By* (New York: Oxford University Press, 2006). As McAdams points out, all religions are ultimately about redemption (p. 18), but given the powerful influence of Christianity on American culture, it seems likely that in the American context, this redemptive language springs at least partially from Christian sources.

PART I
Christian Diversity in America

The amazing diversity of Christianities in the United States has numerous sources. Many traditions arrived in the cultural luggage of immigrants, from Europe or Asia, from Ethiopia, or from the Caribbean. Other groups, including the Assemblies of God and the Latter-day Saints (Mormons), arose as new Christian movements in the United States. Still others emerged in the aftermath of controversies over doctrines, ethnic differences, or regional tensions such as those that fractured Methodists, Baptists, and Presbyterians in the years preceding the Civil War. On some occasions, church unions have temporarily reduced the number of different Christian denominations, only to see them expand again when clusters of congregations refused to go along with the merger. Nor has Christian diversity followed neatly along denominational lines. A Presbyterian in the eighteenth century might likely have embarked from Edinburgh, but today a Presbyterian immigrant is more likely to have arrived from Seoul. As this implies, since late antiquity Christianity has been peripatetic, with borders that are porous and potentially creative when it encounters other traditions, including both other forms of Christianity and other religions. Hence, as Michael McNally demonstrates with respect to Native American Christianities, along with the tragic violence of colonialism, cultural assimilation, and missionary encounter, "it is also important to register just what Native peoples, with considerable resolve and resourcefulness, have *made of* the missionaries' message." This opening section of *American Christianities*, beginning with an overview from historian Catherine Albanese, provides readers with a historically informed perspective on the sources and extent of this variety.

These various Christian groups continuously face decisions about how they will relate to one another, to non-Christian religions, and to the wider society. Through these decisions, Christians and other religious communities situate themselves in what Jonathan Sarna calls "the marketplace of

1 Fort George	6 The Prifon.	11 Old Dutch Church	16 Quaker's Meeting
2 Trinity Church	7 New Brick Meeting	12 Jew's Synagogue	17 Calvinist Church
3 Presbyter. Meeting	8 King's College	13 Lutherian Church	18 Anabaptist Meeting
4 North D. Church	9 St. Paul's Church	14 The French Church	19 Moravian Meeting
5 St. George's Chapel	10 N. Dutch Cal, Church	15 New Scot's Meeting	20 N. Lutheran Church
			21 Methodist Meeting

American religion," a civic setting in which many forms of cooperation and coexistence are possible but which can be threatened when any specific group attempts to enlist governmental support for its version of religion. This section therefore illustrates and analyzes the historical processes by which specific Christian groups have resisted, adapted, and borrowed from their religious and social environment in order to develop a distinctive understanding and practice of Christianity. These distinctive practices fashion communal identity at many levels. They may meld Christian rituals and symbols with specific ethnic or racial traditions. They may counterbalance the hostile or exclusionary practices of more powerful groups. They may accentuate a group's separate or elect status, but they may also celebrate religious experiences or ethical commitments that transcend institutional and ethnic boundaries. As James Bennett points out in the concluding chapter of this section, "relations among American Christians have moved along a continuum ranging from intense and even violent conflict at one end to remarkable cooperation at the other." Given these variables, part 1 of *American Christianities* includes chapters that approach Christian and other diversities from a general and comparative perspective as well as chapters that offer illustrative case studies of Native American, Asian, Latino, and African American Christianities.

Finally, within the religious marketplace, where adaptation, reinvention, and borrowing are constant features of active religious life, Christians—whether self-consciously or not—make decisions not only about relationships to other religious and social groups but also about the relationship to their own religious past. Tradition undergoes constant changes of emphasis, style, and interpretation. As many chapters in this section illustrate, "Christian Diversity in America" includes variation and change over time as well as diversity across geographic space and social location. Indeed, Christian groups frequently find variation over time more troubling than the diversity among their Christian neighbors, since the continuance of cherished rituals from generation to generation and the stable transmission of authoritative texts, beliefs, and institutions are close to the core of religious society. As with all of the four parts of *American Christianities*, the intent is not to "cover"—even if that were possible—every form of Christian diversity but rather to select and interpret especially important illustrations of the social and historical processes that have generated that diversity.

Understanding Christian Diversity in America

Christianity shapes people to think in terms of oneness. Ideologically, there is one God over all nations, and there is one Great Commission from Christ to the nations. Historically, there has been one "true church"—whether conceived in material form as in medieval Europe or understood spiritually as in post-Reformation theologies. Historiographically, generations of American religious historians (originally, church historians) played off all of this as they wrote this nation's religious history. Their story line proclaimed Protestant consensus and, with the passage of time, increasing departures from it (unhappily, in the view of the earliest consensus historians). Moreover, the departures kept impinging in increasingly noticeable ways. By 1972 and the last great monument of the consensus school—Sydney Ahlstrom's *A Religious History of the American People*—the story and its ideological center were growing more suspect. For its part, the Ahlstrom work ended in lament for a Puritan center that was no longer holding and organizational puzzlement over how to chart events and movements still unfolding. The next decades brought consensus historiography down—first in an avalanche of postmodern protest against grand narratives and then in plural and postplural paradigms that alternately emphasized conflict, toleration, or religious blending.[1]

To a great extent, however, the emerging story line(s) stressed two points. The first—found in older work in the field—contrasted a Christian center with a "sectarian" Christian periphery and then moved past it to discover even greater Christian diversity. As early as 1937, for example, Elmer T. Clark's *Small Sects in America* was making the point about difference. And as late as a year after the publication of Sydney Ahlstrom's work, Edwin Gaustad's *Dissent in American Religion* (1973) appeared and became a small classic.[2] But by that time, historians (including Ahlstrom) had already modified the narrative as they moved toward greater notice of diversity, and the church-sect model increasingly broke down. Historians were pointing to the large presence of a Catholic population, to immigrant and black Christian expression, to the post–Civil War bifurcation of Protestants into liberal and conservative camps, and to a series of other topics that suggested Christian variety.[3] Thus, by the 1980s, difference was beginning to be construed as normal, not exceptional. Consider, for instance, Richard Pointer's *Protestant Pluralism and the New York Experience*, produced at a time (1988) when pluralism had become a feature of American religiosity to be admired and celebrated.[4] In keeping with the new paradigm, Pointer found colonial New Yorkers not only tolerating one another's religious differences (mostly Protestant) but even modifying their views to accept the situation as positive and beneficial.

The second point of the story line, however, went further than noticing major features of American Christian diversity. A new historiographical consciousness about American religion grew out of the encounter of the old Christian center with non-Christian people and commitments. Moving past domestic Christian pluralism, what now came through as strikingly different for American religious historians was all those non-Christian others—Asians and the Fiji Islanders, Lebanese and Syrian Muslims, denizens of new non-Christian American religious movements, Native American traditionalists, Hindus and Buddhists and Sikhs. But what of intra-Christian pluralism? Had historians delved deeply enough and come sufficiently to terms with the multiplied forms in which American Christianity had thrived and proliferated? Had they encountered the full landscape of diversity or only its largest, most undeniable landmarks and formations? Arguably, despite the nods to pluralism within Christian ranks, it is worth asking whether the diversity within American Christianity itself had been less than fully examined as it evolved in new locations and situations. And it is worth asking what happens to the narrative of American religious history if the question is answered affirmatively.

Hence, in what follows, I offer evidence—as do the other essays in this volume—for an underexamined story of Christian diversity in America. It is a story more complex than the tale of curious "sects" and "also-rans," or of noticeably unusual variations, or of a few large bodies or social situations that stand out from the crowd. As I hope this essay demonstrates, it is time to pay more attention to a body of historiographical material that has not been sufficiently examined or seen in relationship to other accounts. Looking at this story in this way, in fact, has precedents, especially in the work of recent interpreters of "global Christianity."[5] Here in the United States, however, at least three historiographical myths (in the colloquial sense) about the unity of American Christianity and its decline have percolated through standard assessments. Myth One asserts that the Christian story, especially before the Civil War, is mostly about Europeans. Myth Two declares that the Protestant Christianity of European settlers was, at its beginnings, virtually monolithic. Finally, Myth Three views Christian pluralism as a late-breaking development, a post–Civil War and especially twentieth-century and later phenomenon.

Describing Difference
The Horizontal Axis

If we conceptualize differently, however, we can look at the more-nuanced account that these myths obscure and also attend to a story of variety and difference that developed in a series of ways. In brief, if we examine American Christian diversity as a reality with both horizontal and vertical vectors, we can glimpse the outlines of a rich and productive narrative. We can render a fuller account of how modern Christianity in America became so diverse.

What are these "horizontal" and "vertical" vectors? One way to think about the horizontal in Christianity is to see it as a spatial or typological or denominational set of proclivities. Where, geographically, can we locate different kinds of Christianity in America? In comparative terms, can we identify types or variants that are meaningful? In organizational terms, what are the institutions that embody these different forms? In other words, leaving aside changes that came with time, what have been the regional, ideological, and structural religious possibilities for Christian expression? On the other hand, thinking in terms of the vertical dimension, how can we factor in the developments as the American Christian story—or, better, stories— unfolded through time? Old-country forms of Christianity came with cultural baggage attached but encountered strangers' forms of Christianity and bounced off them. So old forms changed, even as they sparked newer, separate versions of Christianity in a plethora of new denominations, sects, and movements. How do we tell the story/stories, when most religious things, it seemed, were up for grabs and modifications?[6]

Turning to the horizontal axis first, regional forms of Christianity flourished from the time of the first settlers, and later developments served to encourage regional enclaves. Even a cursory glance at early American Christian history highlights the presence of separate groups of Christian believers in different sites. British presence dominated in New England and Virginia, but in New York it was tempered by the Dutch Reformed presence that came with the colony's initial days as New Amsterdam. In Pennsylvania and New Jersey, Scandinavian Protestants—Lutheran and sometimes sectarian—had preceded the inauguration of the Quaker colony. A strong German Lutheran and sectarian cohort could be witnessed especially in eastern Pennsylvania and in its burgeoning new city of Philadelphia. Maryland was established initially by the Catholic Lords Baltimore and was only subsequently upstaged by Protestant rule.

Meanwhile, outside the British North Atlantic colonies, in what is now the state of Florida, French and Spanish forces vied for control until the Spanish founded the city of St. Augustine in 1565. Catholic Christian presence had been established. By the end of the sixteenth century, the Spanish had also taken control of New Mexico, and the Franciscan friars began their ministry there. The Jesuits appeared in the present state of Arizona by 1700. In eighteenth-century California, the fabled mission system, organized by Franciscan Father Junipero Serra, included, at its height, some twenty-one stations designed to be model Indian settlements. A century and more earlier, French Jesuits had already fanned out across the upper Midwest to convert Huron peoples and had ventured further east to missionize the Iroquois. At the same time, French Huguenots planned to settle Nova Scotia, even as French Catholics in Quebec dug in.

Each settlement made its mark with its own version of Christian belief and practice. None became normative, and in the breakaway British colonies—as the religious tolerance of the Revolutionary War era and the new Constitution of the United States reflects—plural versions of Christianity were the order of the day. The later history of the United States would be similar. At any point in its evolution, it is easy to notice regional Christian communities with distinctive characteristics and marks. We can nod to Russian Orthodox believers in Alaska and Greek Orthodox ones in New York City and parts of New England; Catholics in California and East Coast cities and in southern cultural enclaves such as New Orleans and Miami; Amish sectarians in central Pennsylvania; Hutterites in the upper Midwest; Anglicans-become-Episcopalians in post-Revolutionary Virginia and New York; Quakers in Pennsylvania and New Jersey; Moravians, Dunkers, and German Pietists in Pennsylvania and elsewhere; Baptists and Presbyterians in Philadelphia and later in the New West; African American slaves in the "hush harbors" of the pre–Civil War American South; English nonconformists, assorted other Protestants, and Dunkers in Southern Appalachia; *curanderismo* culture in Christian/Catholic forms of Latino spiritism in the

Southwest; New Thinkers in New England, Illinois, and California; and so forth—in seemingly endless local variations.

If regionalism brought old- and new-country forms of Christianity together on the historical stage, ideological characteristics inherent in religious expression across cultures also influenced the Christianity of the new nation. It is possible to identify, in numbers of religious traditions, the presence of different spiritual proclivities, and American Christians were not shy about demonstrating such. As Jon Butler has so carefully shown, from the first, three forms of belief and practice ran through the Christian cultures of the colonies and continued on after their demise.[7] Butler identified the first as organized Christianity along the lines of the state-church traditions of Europe and the second as evangelical Christianity in an endemic, if less organized, form of religious expression. He pitted these two against the third form—what he called the "occult," but an occult that wove itself into Christian culture and could not be completely separated from it, as the lived reality of Christians (their beliefs, behaviors, and libraries) showed.[8] For our purposes here, we can modify Butler's categories to acknowledge the full Christian expression of the third form, suggesting thus the strong and growing presence of three (not two) forms of Christianity from early colonial times. Denominational Christianity can be identified easily, and so can the evangelical Christianity spread by the revivals. Finally, metaphysical Christianity has hardly been an add-on but, rather, a distinct and robust form of Christian belief and behavior from the first.

It is important to add here that all three forms of Christian expression—organizationally predominant, evangelical and emotion-oriented, and metaphysical and characterized by ideas and practices related to "mind" and its correspondence with ultimate realities—reflect types of religiosity available outside American Christianity. It takes only a short sociological detour to the classic work of Ernst Troeltsch to begin to suggest the dimensions of a larger phenomenological picture. Troeltsch's "church, sect, and mysticism" roughly parallel the religious differences I am attempting to identify, and the three categories also point the way toward comparative religious phenomena.[9] To say this, of course, is to undercut estimates of Christian exceptionalism, but it is also to bring Christianity, and especially American Christianity, into the tapestry of the world's religions. And it is to understand the inherent diversity among American Christians in ways that move well beyond simple divisions between centrists and odd others or affirmers of and dissenters from a putative mainstream. What do these comparative categories for religiosity do in sorting out American Christianity? They illuminate the spiritual impulses behind external forms. They acknowledge that institutionalists, evangelicals, and metaphysicians were always part of the story—all three—and will continue to be so for any future that we can foresee.

The institutionalists might be characterized, to use Weberian language, as "priests," happiest in social centers with structure and definition surrounding them. They could be Catholic or Episcopalian, Greek Orthodox or Seventh-day Adventist, Presbyterian or Lutheran or Methodist, all believing members of groups that officially prefer organization over excitement and stability over continuing change. They have been concerned about creating good order in their personal and social worlds, and so their work has at times extended toward social ethics and social action. By contrast, the evangelicals come through as more movement-oriented. They have been "heart" Christians, for whom devotion and piety trump structure, however much they may feel comfortable with the latter. They might be Southern Baptist or Methodist or Episcopalian, following the evangelical wing of their respective denominations. Or they could be devotees of Calvary Chapel or the Vineyard Christian Fellowship, or members of any number of parachurch organizations. Often, too, to invoke Max Weber again, they have functioned as "prophets," since their call to mission urges them toward the transformation of the neighbor and the neighbor's society. Beyond these, the metaphysicians—neither priests nor prophets in the missionary sense but rather "exemplars" or perhaps "exemplary prophets"—have preferred a networking style of association, more freewheeling than priestly institutionalists, less effervescent than prophetic evangelicals with their emissary consciousness. They might be Christian Scientists or students of the Unity School of Christianity. Or they could be old-fashioned Christian Spiritualists or Swedenborgians in the Church of the New Jerusalem or newer-model adherents to mainstream or evangelical churches who, alongside the theologies of their respective groups, are given to metaphysical views and practices. They have been adept, like the New England Transcendentalists, at cultivating a heightened sense of self in relation to perceived higher realities.[10]

On the social terrain of the nation, though, ideology has interwoven with the external scaffolding of organization. Religions have had addresses and phone numbers, not to mention—in recent times—websites. Regional sites and spiritual forms took shape in what we can roughly call the Christian denominations. In the strict sociological sense, some of these have been highly organized and politically powerful; others have been more separatist in their smaller, sectarian consciousness; and still others have been so ephemeral that their passional intensity is matched to the brevity of their duration. Whatever the characteristics and the endurance qualities of Christian groups, it is their manyness that needs to be noticed in the American situation. Telling the story/stories of the emergence of that manyness leads us directly into the vertical dimension and the historical narrative.

At the same time, identifying differences between Christian groups that consider themselves "the church" and others that happily proclaim themselves small and separate communities invites us to go further. The camouflaged questions are, What groups count as Christian, and who gets to decide? No professional historian today would straightaway demand theological orthodoxy for a group to be labeled Christian. On the other hand, simple platitudes—such as calling a group Christian if members say they are—can force us into bizarre definitional places.

As a nuanced instance of the problems with either stance, take, for example, the introductory work on the Mormons produced by Claudia Lauper Bushman and Richard Lyman Bushman. *Mormons in America* appeared originally in 1998 as part of the Religion in American Life series edited for Oxford University Press by Jon Butler and Harry S. Stout. Aimed at a high school and junior college audience, it began by declaring that "Mormonism, one of the world's fastest-growing Christian religions, doubles its membership about every 15 years." In a searching and generally positive review of the Oxford series, Stephen Prothero noticed the problematic nature of the assertive first sentence, since it forestalled the question of whether Mormons were Christians or not. This, obviously, was a strong call on the issue. But given Jan Shipps's memorable work announcing that Mormonism is a new religious tradition, it was hardly unfair. And given the extra-Christian metaphysical proclivities of Joseph Smith and early Mormons, there was yet more to notice.[11] So readers needed to fuss with the question of how Mormons counted as Christian (if they did), not simply be told that they were.

It is also true that the Mormon case is especially rich since both theological and social identity norms mix there in interesting ways. It is not simply that Mormons proclaim themselves Christians, and have done so increasingly in late twentieth-century and early twenty-first-century times. Nor is it the case that theological strictures can be discarded since, after all, the Latter-day Saints have placed a second authoritative text, the Book of Mormon, alongside the Christian Bible. In the shadow of American evangelicalism, recent Latter-day Saints have understood themselves in increasingly Christian terms, *and* they can point to the continuing centrality of Jesus the

Christ to their belief structure. After all, they are officially the Church of *Jesus Christ* of Latter-day Saints.

What all of this suggests is that definitional issues loom especially large as we near the margins of what popularly gets counted as Christianity and that these issues will not easily go away. Rather than invoke a rigid template for application, historians need to exercise their contextual and critical skills in each case as it comes their way. This is what the stuff of history is about, and this is the core of what it means to tell a story in ways that resonate with past and present time. It is why revisionism keeps historians gainfully employed and why, in every age, historians find ways to tell new stories.

Surveying Diversity
The Vertical Narrative

So far, elements of the story of Christian diversity could have been meaningfully applied elsewhere in the world. Regionalism is hardly just an American phenomenon. Spiritual styles—establishment, evangelical, metaphysical—can be traced elsewhere among Christian believers; and Christian groups, in the contemporary era, run the gamut from churches and denominations to sects and movement-style groups abroad, as well as at home. Boundaries and margins are not peculiarly American. But historians set up their stories—new or old—on vertical lines. In other words, they attend to chronology, and they search for resemblance and change from past to present. It is in the midst of these chronological labors and related accounts of novelty—and its explanations—that a specifically *American* story of Christian diversity begins to emerge. As I have already noted, many of the pieces of the story have been with us for a while, but putting them together as a major part of explaining American Christian difference can be a powerful assist.

A good place to begin the vertical narrative is with the denominations of colonial America (here I count Catholicism among them). Theological differences surely explain them in part, but the social story of a church's rise and continuance was never far behind. Meanwhile, national origins and ethnic identities remained important parts of the social story. Lutherans from the German Palatine, for example, formed different religious groupings from, say, Finnish Lutherans. By the same token, any account of colonial and nineteenth-century American Catholics has to notice the friction between national groups, so well detailed in the older work of Jay Dolan.[12] Among Protestants, from the first, two major branches would yield, by the nineteenth century, to a plethora of new denominations. On the one hand, the Puritan branch—Congregationalists, Presbyterians, Baptists, Quakers, to cite the most prominent—made its blended Calvinist-Anabaptist (gathered-church) mark on the public culture of its time and continued to inform the public religion of the emerging United States. On the other, the Anglican branch, largely subsumed by the early nineteenth century into Methodism, brought its "warmer" style. Evangelicalism would draw on both branches in intricate and varied permutations. Indeed, the way that Calvinist- and Methodist-leaning denominations often intertwined with each other in the American context became a major organizational source of diversity. Earlier historiography stressed the Calvinist churches, but in recent times we are gaining a richer, fuller view of the role of Methodism.[13]

If we think of Christians in more than Protestant terms, a contemporary Christian denominational "tree" in America would branch and leaf out in prodigal display.[14] To the right would be Orthodox and other Eastern Christians—Greek and Russian Orthodox (the latter in at least three separate divisions), Ukrainian Orthodox in at least three groups, the Syrian Orthodox in two, and in single groups a series of different national churches that understand themselves as Orthodox. Other Eastern Christians who had been separated into their own religious enclaves before the Orthodox–Roman Catholic split of the eleventh century made their way to the United States, among them Coptic Christians and Armenian Apostolic Church members. And still other Eastern Christians—Uniates—have claimed loyalty to the pope of Rome even as they maintain distinctive national rites and clerical protocols. It has been an Eastern Christian picture of manyness, indeed, and chronicles of church life in cities like Pittsburgh, Pennsylvania, and Worcester, Massachusetts, reveal the uneasy alliances and conflictual tensions that have continued among these churches.[15]

Mentioning Eastern Uniates takes us to a second huge branch of Christianity in the United States—that of Catholicism. We might, in fact, think of Uniates as participating in the worlds of both Eastern Christianity and main-branch Catholicism. American Catholics, of course, consider themselves Roman Catholic for the most part. Yet even here, other forms of Catholic Christianity may be cited. Probably the most well-known of these, outside the various Uniate groups, is the Polish National Catholic Church, formed in Scranton, Pennsylvania, in 1904. Meanwhile, throughout the nineteenth century and on, ethnic tensions bedeviled the Catholic Church—accommodated first through national parishes but then camouflaged in a stricter territorial diocesan system. The negotiations between Irish and German Catholics (with their Cahenslyism—see below) form the stuff of any account of American Catholic history, as do later Irish-Italian conflicts, the Polish ones that resulted in a separate church, and, more recently, strains between Latinos and the Irish Catholic leadership and African Americans and, again, the Irish Catholic hierarchy (see below).[16]

But other Catholic spin-offs and almost-spin-offs can also be noted. To the right of the Vatican, we can point to Father Leonard Sweeney's Slaves of the Immaculate Heart of Mary from the 1950s and the more recent followers of Veronica Leuken, who has claimed visions of a Virgin Mary with apocalyptic predictions and has garnered a decided frown from the diocese of Brooklyn. Or, in contrast, we can notice a series of liberals-turned-radical. Here have been feminist nuns such as those in the Immaculate Heart of Mary order, who refused obedience to James Cardinal McIntyre of Los Angeles in the early 1970s and were laicized. And here are Catholics who dispute Vatican injunctions against a gay lifestyle and participate in the Dignity movement within their church today, in clear tension with the official institution. Here, too, are members of the Voice of the Faithful, who contend with bishops in local dioceses in support of the victims of pedophilic priests. Boundary questions abound: Do we, for example, consider Women-Church to be Catholic, since it is a radical feminist group that encompasses now not only Catholics but many Protestant women? And what about Latino incarnations of liberation theology, such as the militant Católicos por la Raza of the late 1960s? Does the Imani Temple movement (the African American Catholic Congregation) count in the Christian camp—begun as it was by former black Catholic priest George Stallings and attractive to Afro-Caribbean immigrants for its African dancing and chanting?[17]

Exploring the branches of the tree toward the center and the left, if manyness was the order of the American day for Orthodox Christians and Eastern and Western Catholics, the American Protestant story could be called the same, only more so. Colonial Anglicans had become Episcopalians and, in growing numbers, Methodists by the late eighteenth century. A century later, with important influence from Reformed (Calvinist) believers in a series of denominations, they turned to Holiness religion and then Pentecostalism. These movements, in their turn, spawned a series of denominations with nuanced differences in theology and practice. Some Methodists, by contrast, became involved with the New Thought movement, as did numbers of rank-and-file Presbyterians and other evangelicals. Others practiced complex marriage, male continence, mutual criticism, and even Christian Spiritualism in the sanctified perfectionism of the Oneida Community in upper New York State. In still another major branch of the "tree," Lutherans—in some twenty-four different national churches by the early twentieth century—kept on merging. By a century later, the liberal Evangelical Lutheran Church in America claimed the bulk of Lutheran believers, and the Fundamentalist-oriented Lutheran Church–Missouri Synod held a sizable half as many.

The Calvinist-Anabaptist-Anglican blend of early Puritans gave way to a series of nineteenth-century American evangelical denominations—the Congregationalists, Presbyterians, Baptists, and Quakers have already been cited. These, in turn, had their own stories of fission and fusion to tell. By the end of the twentieth century and on, the liberal United Church of Christ could look back on its mixed ancestors, prominent among them the Puritans-turned-Congregationalists of old New England. Others who came out of the old New England Congregationalist stock had moved so left of center that, from 1961 as the Unitarian Universalist Association, they had embraced the Humanist Manifesto of the 1920s. By the end of the century, Unitarians also included neo-pagan followers of the Goddess, Zen Buddhist devotees of Thich Nhat Hanh, and some who still followed Christian ritual order.

Presbyterians had their own narrative of evolution and change throughout their American history. Old and New School Presbyterians, from the time of the First Great Awakening, saw each other as, at the very least, unfortunate in the patent falsity of their views—until, in the mid-nineteenth century, they healed their controversies in the direction of the New Siders. Earlier, the restorationist movement had grown strong throughout Presbyterian ranks, and some championed a primitivist New Testament theology and eschewed any label but "Christian." But ironically, by the time of the Civil War, the "Christians" existed in a northern version as the Disciples of Christ and in the South as the Churches of Christ, with a schism between them. In the early twentieth century, it was among Presbyterians that major sources of Fundamentalism could be found, even as by the end of the century the main body of Presbyterians in the Presbyterian Church (U.S.A.) formed one of the more liberal Protestant denominations.

Meanwhile, Baptist believers branched off through a plethora of forks and limbs. The most recent edition of Abingdon Press's *Handbook of Denominations in the United States* (2005) found it important to list some thirty-one different Baptist bodies.[18] From the nineteenth century and earlier, Missionary and Anti-Mission Baptists contended for the hearts and minds of Christian believers, as revival calls to mission (and East Coast provision of missionary societies) ran up against old predestinarian beliefs about divine election. The widespread (especially in the South) Landmark movement among Baptists complicated things even more, tying into restorationism with the cry of "old landmarks" and rejecting other churches with their "fashion" for religious union.

Nor were these the only major sources of Baptist sub-branching. By 1860, remnants of the old Millerite movement—which had been disappointed in its predictions of the Second Coming of Jesus in 1843 and again in 1844— would be forming, with Seventh Day Baptists, the Seventh-day Adventist Church. Before the century was out, another major Adventist group—the Jehovah's Witnesses—had come on the scene. The great split in 1845 between Northern and Southern Baptists over the issue of slavery also yielded splits between more liberal and more conservative Baptist branches. Indeed, Fundamentalism arose not in the American South but in the context of disagreements in the North among Baptists and Presbyterians.[19] Even further, among the top ten American denominations today are the (African American) National Baptist Convention, USA, Inc., and National Baptist Convention of America, Inc.

American Quakers likewise branched off in directions that, by the nineteenth century, brought many of them close in sentiment to Protestant evangelicals and others among them to a radical edge that in places merged with a growing Christian Spiritualism.[20] More thoroughly receptive than other Reformed Christians to entanglements with the Anabaptist, or Radical, Reformation and its branch of the "tree," Quakers embodied, especially, mystical forms of Anabaptism. At the same time, they took injunctions against hierarchies and an elevated, separate clergy as far as they could. When the Spirit said different things to different people, Quakers moved enthusiastically in radical but opposite directions. They became major sources of both metaphysical religion within Christianity (and sometimes outside it) *and* a social-action agenda that challenged more orthodox liberal Protestant churches. Still others who adhered strictly to Anabaptism or the Radical Reformation preserved their separate branch from outside influence insofar as they were able. English Shakers with their numerous American converts in their celebrated nineteenth-century communities could be counted among them.[21] Radicals, too, were often immigrants from the European continent, forming small ethnic groups, such as those of the Mennonites, the Amish, and the Hutterites. Yet even here, diversity flourished aplenty; Abingdon's *Handbook of Denominations in the United States* lists among them eleven separate major groups.[22]

Explaining Change

Given the branches and sub-branches of this Christian tree in all of its profusion of religious forms and distinctive views and practices, how—in the question behind this essay—do we explain the diversity? How can we account for an American Christian manyness the dimensions of which we have only partially explored? What got the tree growing in so many extravagant ways? A place to begin is with the governmental arrangements that dominated the nation from its inception. The phenomenon that I have elsewhere called "public Protestantism" found strong expression in the Constitution of 1789 with its disestablishment of religion. What Roger Williams in the mid-1640s called "the hedge or wall of separation between the garden of the church and the wilderness of the world" had become by 1802 for Thomas Jefferson "a wall of separation between Church and State."[23] Effected in the constitutional era more for practical than for ideological reasons (unlike the earlier ideas of Williams), religious disestablishment encouraged the growth of voluntaryism and, so, denominationalism. Nobody in the national government (and soon in all state governments as well) was paying clerical salaries or demanding conformity to a church. Volunteers had to do what establishments did, or Christian religion would not happen. Voluntary societies flourished. Middle-level leaders, set free from state interference and buttressed by the new ideology of democracy and power to the people, tweaked the Christian message to their liking to form new versions of old Christian groups and sometimes more radically different groups.[24]

The religious activism of volunteers brought with it, in the heady atmosphere of the new republic, a disregard for inherited forms. History and tradition were out and newness was in, as the Great Seal of the United States proclaimed with its motto *Novus ordo seclorum.* A new order it was, indeed. Spurred by the cultural practice of revivalism and by beliefs about the importance of the individual and the requirements, always, of answering first to divine, not human, law, Christian diversity grew apace. Alexis de Tocqueville was surely right in observing that Christianity became a social requirement in the new United States even as it lost its establishment status.[25] In other words, neighborly expectations, and then their public echo in media, schools, and other community organizations, set a context of societal approval and "reward" for joining up with a church. However, the particular version of Christianity was ever a contested artifact.

Contested yes, but at the same time the general milieu invited a combinativeness in which groups, aware or not, borrowed from one another, even as they customized their Christianity to their needs. Given the overall combinativeness—a function not only of the manyness of immigrant groups but also of church disestablishment and religious freedom, the activism of generations of volunteers, and the democratic ethos of the land—it is not surprising that we can chart the emergence, on these shores, of new forms of Christianity. The general cultural ideology of "newness" provided a nurturing matrix for such developments, and a series of new Christian movements cropped up seemingly everywhere.

Ethnicity and race became important markers for many of the new forms. Either as indigenous peoples, as nonvoluntary (black) immigrants in a land of volunteers, or as willing immigrants, new and old Americans dwelled in ethnic and racial enclaves even as growing cities and towns began to break them apart.[26] Native American Christians came together in New England from the seventeenth century in experiments like John Eliot's Praying Towns and Thomas Mayhew Jr.'s work in Martha's Vineyard and Nantucket. In the Middle Colonies among the Delaware, Presbyterian David Brainerd and his brother John both worked, even as the Quaker government of Pennsylvania encouraged a climate of tolerance and interchange. The Great Awakening encouraged Indian conversion, and some Natives became Methodist or Baptist as the evangelical denominations made their way among Native peoples.

For their part, the Spanish and French brought their priests, as we have already seen. By the nineteenth century, both Catholic Indian mission communities and Protestant missionary experiments had fallen away, and a new reservation system became the order of the American day. Denominations—among them noticeably the Mormons in the West—created mission outposts on the reservations, often several of them vying for the loyalty of mission subjects. Among the Cherokee, for example, Moravians appeared in 1801 to begin a center and school. Presbyterians followed, and then Baptists, Methodists, and Congregationalists were allowed to come by Cherokee leaders. For most of the Cherokee, all of this missionary work did not prevent their trek along the Trail of Tears in 1838 to the Oklahoma country. But Indian assent to Christian teaching and practice did mean, for the Cherokee and other groups, a visible nuancing of belief and behavior so that it melded more easily with Indian tradition. As Indians converted to Christianity, in other words, greater Christian diversity resulted.

To gain one view of what this could mean, consider the late twentieth- and early twenty-first-century Catholic case. With evolving ideas about inculturation on the part of Catholic missionaries, a new openness to Native symbols and rituals in the official services of the church could be seen.

Perhaps no more visible symbol of this combinative Christianity exists in our time than Blessed Kateri Tekakwitha, a seventeenth-century Mohawk woman who converted to Catholic ways and is now on a path to Catholic sainthood. Using Tekakwitha as an icon, annual Kateri Tekakwitha conferences and smaller Kateri circles thrive in the Indian Catholic world. Led by Native priests, the conferences also feature Native languages, musical instruments, and prayer accoutrements such as feathers, sacred pipes, materials for smudging, and the like. Vestments display Native designs, and inherited Indian ritual traditions are part of the new Catholic ceremonial world.

We can go further, too, and enter the same world of boundary phenomena that we touched for the Mormons. As individual Indian nations or tribal cultures saw their ranks being decimated and their ways growing weaker, many came together spiritually in new pan-Indian forms of belief and ceremony. In the late nineteenth century, the most striking of these was the Ghost Dance. In the twentieth and twenty-first centuries, it has been Peyotism. At first glance, neither of these are forms of Christianity. Yet deeper scrutiny reveals the amalgam of Christian and Native elements that have given these movements their magnetism and power in a new time. The Ghost Dance featured a millennialism in which the old world conquered by whites would end and a new one bequeathed to the Indians would rise up. It also featured a spiritism—talking to the spirits of the ancestors—that drew from Christian as well as from Native themes. In Peyotism, Christian elements seem still more central. With all-night communion rituals that feature the ingestion of peyote (considered to be a deity) and with a peyote "road" to travel in a moral and upright life that involves the rejection of alcohol, gambling, womanizing, and the like, the peyotist arguably is on a blended path that combines Native with Christian elements.

Among blacks, a richly varied story of the Christian meeting with African elements can likewise be told. Blacks never took to Christianity en masse throughout the colonial period and the nineteenth century, and in the twentieth and beyond, their spiritual attractions moved in more-than-Christian directions—toward Islam, for example, or toward non-Christian versions of metaphysics. When they did convert to Christianity in noticeable numbers, the forms they embraced were those that resonated with the West African past. Thus, early Anglican attempts to convert black slaves failed miserably. This was not simply because slave masters wanted their property working plantation fields. It was also because a religion of the book—of the printed Bible and catechism and prescribed prayers for recitation—sat poorly with West Africans. Either they had been Muslims in the lands of their birth—

with a strong oral tradition of Qur'anic recitation and prayer, or, for most of them, they had followed indigenous religious ways that stressed community with one another and the spirit world—including their own quasi-divine ancestors—and they saw "worship" as a transformation of consciousness through possession by gods and spirits. Here were deities that got off scot-free in theodicy because divinities were supposed to alter private consciousness, not interfere in the world. Blacks were not being punished for their sins, and no God was being hard and pitiless toward his subjects.

Hence, when blacks embraced Christianity—at first in the Great Awakening and then in continuing years—they were attracted to revival forms among Methodists and Baptists. In the evangelical ritual of conversion and in the shouts and tears and ecstasies that came after, they felt some of what their traditions had given them—intense and memorable inner experience that changed consciousness without altering historical situations. For most of those who turned to Christianity, this was sufficient—whether they were southern slaves or free blacks in the North. And, as the classic work of Albert J. Raboteau has shown, the sin consciousness that white preachers tried so hard to instill in blacks did not catch on.[27] Religion was about joy and elation, not about wailing for one's offenses in stealing from the master or working slow time.

African Americans were already customizing Christianity in the South during slavery times, as the creation of new ritual and the evolution of a new preaching style of call and congregational response testify. In the South, too, in New Orleans and environs, blacks turned to Catholic forms of Christianity and inflected them with Africanisms, supported in this endeavor by the presence of refugees from Afro-Caribbean regions. Border phenomena abounded—as in voodoo, which combined West African spirit deities with Catholic saints. By the twentieth century, the Spiritual Churches of New Orleans brought together a Holiness-Pentecostal worship style with Catholic saints and the Native American hero Black Hawk. Prophecy, healing, and voodoo elements mixed and mingled in a new metaphysical form of Christianity with women in charge. And later in the century, in East Coast cities, more Afro-Caribbean blended religious forms could be found. Now there was *vodou*, as distinct from New Orleans–style voodoo, and there was Afro-Cuban *santeria*—again with Catholic saints incorporated into borderline rituals that combined Christian with African and metaphysical worlds.

These later developments can, in the end, probably be called extra-Christian. But they do tell us how diverse the diversity had become. Meanwhile, even in the North, free blacks as well as slaves inflected their Christian practice their own way, as the work of William Piersen has shown.[28] After the Civil War, in Holiness and then in Pentecostal congregations, the black Jesus and his dark-skinned mother appeared in church representations. The spirituals that had found voice in the hush harbors of slave times incorporated blues and jazz in the new form of gospel music accompanied by drums and tambourines. Other churches with evolving worship styles grew and flourished. The huge (Pentecostal) Church of God in Christ brought Christian and metaphysical forms together (and blacks and whites together, too), even as its charismatic founder-leader Charles H. Mason encouraged followers to think of him in terms that underlined his more-than-ordinary status. The black God appeared again and more explicitly among the Garveyites with their African Orthodox Church, Anglican in background but shaped to foster racial pride and the creation of a black Israel. Meanwhile, the more conventional African American churches found their own Christian ways to preach the religion of blackness—as the theological witness of black liberation theology and the social witness of Martin Luther King Jr. and his legacy demonstrate.

If Indians and African Americans found in their Christian expression ways to incorporate difference, a larger story of difference may be told of the European immigrants. From colonial times, English, Germans, Dutch, Scandinavians, Scotch-Irish, and even French from Quebec and Nova Scotia found homes in what later became the United States. Each ethnic group had found its own way to inflect belief and behavior, as Anglicans, Lutherans, Presbyterians, Reformed Christians, and others mixed their denominational forms with national customs and characteristics. Tensions between Christian "nations" already existed before the Revolution, and by the nineteenth century they were a continuing feature of the American landscape.

Among Catholics, as an example, trusteeism—the bid for lay power to hire and fire clergy—interwove itself with ethnic tensions by the late eighteenth century. Germans disputed Anglo-Catholic leadership, and French bishops also experienced endemic conflict with the Irish. Then a huge Irish immigration in the 1840s brought an influx that particularly grated on Germans. After the Civil War, an Irish Catholic hierarchy bemoaned the "Italian problem," which could not be brought to an Italian pope. Italians were taking to the streets in *feste*, marrying off their sons and daughters instead of encouraging them to celibate lives in the church, and disdaining much financial support for the institution.

On another Catholic immigrant front, Polish rough edges with the official church grew sharper, as Poles aimed to preserve their language in churches and schools. The Poles brought new and distinctive devotions with them, as their fabled Black Madonna of Czestochowa attests. The National Polish Catholic Church was one result of tensions that pointed, in the end, to Christian difference. Meanwhile, German struggles with the Irish American hierarchy over similar issues of language and culture had already come to a head in Cahenslyism (named for German businessman Peter Paul Cahensly, who founded a society to aid German emigrants). Here *national* Catholicism in old-country terms became the path to salvation, and pressures on the Vatican led to repercussions in the United States. The Americanist crisis and its "phantom heresy" of the late nineteenth century were not unrelated, as the official church of Rome acted against a one-size-fits-all brand of American Catholicism, which looked, to Vatican eyes, ever more Protestant.

By contrast, the separate ethnic expressions of Catholic piety embodied traditions reflecting the old European Catholic world. Ironically, it was Americanists, with their phantom heresy, who clashed especially strongly with efforts by the Vatican to consolidate and regularize doctrine and practice, even as Vatican policy discouraged national (for example, Polish, German, Irish, Italian) parishes in America. Standardization was to be desired, said the Vatican, but *not* standardization into a Protestantizing mold. Ethnic Catholics in America seemingly had not heard the news, cherishing their differences from one another *and* not overly concerned about becoming like their Protestant neighbors.

American immigration law also heavily influenced the Catholic Christian presence in America—and that of other Christian groups from Southern and Eastern Europe (and from Asia and other lands as well). After 1924, the Johnson-Reed Act replaced an older quota act from 1921 with a new version that generally limited immigration to 2 percent of nationals from any country who were living in the United States at the time of the 1890 census. According to the law, this limit would be replaced in 1927 by a quota derived from 1920 data on the ratio of specific national groups in the country. The law specifically aimed to discourage Southern and Eastern European immigration and to buttress the older immigration from Western Europe and Scandinavia. It did what its makers intended, and by the Depression era new results showed an altered immigration pattern. It would not be until 1965 and its Hart-Celler Act that the old quota system would be abolished in favor of a new, more evenhanded one. With its provision for no "national limitations" on immigrants from the Western Hemisphere, Southern and Eastern Europeans found themselves welcomed for their skills and professions rather than their lands of origin. More than that, as we will see, the act provided for 170,000 immigrants annually from outside the West (later raised to 270,000), with 20,000 allowed for each separate country.[29] Later changes tweaked immigration law still further, but the 1965 decisions revolutionized immigration patterns and the nation's religious complexion in ways that continue.

In the twentieth century and on, Latino versions of Christian practice came increasingly to the fore. Early in the century, Mexican presence in Texas, California, and the Southwest grew by leaps and bounds. By midcentury, the Puerto Rican population of New York City was becoming noticeable, and, after 1959 and the Cuban revolution, Miami became home to large numbers of refugees from the Caribbean island. Haitians, too, were continuing to come. Catholicism—the culture religion of all of these groups—functioned as the largest Christian denomination among Latinos, but Pentecostals, Jehovah's Witnesses, and evangelicals in general began to make large inroads. The Catholic base kept on eroding. This, however, is hardly the only story of Latino diversity that can be told. Among Mexicans and Mexican Americans, to take one example, Latino Christianity had developed its own distinctive marks. Devotion to the Virgin of Guadalupe was central, but prominent, too, were the rituals that surrounded the Day of the Dead (November 2, or All Souls' Day) and the relationships cultivated between godparents and godchildren. At the same time, Mexicans combined their Catholic practice with spiritism and herbalism in another border phenomenon—the pervasive healing work of *curanderismo*. Here a distinctive form of French spiritism (based on the work of Allan Kardec) blended its metaphysics with Native American influences and the ever-present Catholicism.

Asian Christians, too, added to the nation's Christian manyness. Noticeable numbers of East and Southeast Asians were converted already in the lands of their origin by French Catholic missionaries to Indochina or by American Protestants, especially Presbyterians, in China and Korea. Add to this the belief that one route to acculturation for Chinese and Japanese immigrants in a hostile white environment could be Christian conversion. In America, by 1877, a San Francisco Gospel Society, formed by Japanese immigrants, began, and it was subsequently admitted to the California Conference of the Methodist Episcopal Church. Soon Presbyterians, Congregationalists, and Baptists were turning their attention to Asian immigrants, and by 1892 eleven denominations were at work among the Chinese American population.[30]

For more recent times, according to Thomas Tweed and Stephen Prothero, approximately half of the post-1965 Asian immigration (after the changed law) has been Christian, with most Filipinos Catholic and the largest number of Koreans Protestant. And in the early twenty-first century, according to more conservative data extrapolated from the *American Religious Identification Survey 2001* (the work of the Graduate Center of the City University of New York), probably 21 percent of all Asian Americans in the United States have been Catholic, with not only Filipinos but also Vietnamese immigrants the largest contributors to these numbers. At the same time, Protestants have constituted well over 9 percent (with Baptists clearly the largest group among them) of Asian Christians, and other Christians make up nearly 6 percent of the Asian American population.[31]

Again, denominational overviews and data provide only a small part of the story. There are worlds of difference to be searched in the lived religiosity of each Asian Christian community, even if there is not space to discuss them here. It is important, though, to ask questions about what the influx of immigrants—foundational to this nation's history—means for American Christian diversity. It is surely the case that each distinct group contributed its part to any narrative of Christian manyness. But arguably, this is just the tip of the proverbial iceberg. Members of different Christian groups met one another and were influenced by one another. They often married one another. They learned from one-on-one encounters, from group interactions, and from the sheer presence of multiple groups who thought about and did things in their own distinctive ways. So combinativeness was everywhere the Christian rule, and even those with sectarian leanings who chose to stand apart developed distinctive Christian practice in and through their separateness. People who dance alone alter their dance patterns, however slowly and subtly.

On another front, if we return to early America and its Anglo-Protestant settlers, stern Calvinist theologies of predestination gave way as urban Protestants grew more liberal, founding nineteenth-century Unitarianism while their country cousins became Universalists.[32] Liberalism grew in new directions as it became perfectionism. Meanwhile, other new directions flourished in restorationism and millennialism. The liberal (and perfectionist) story begins with Arminianism, the Dutch "heresy" that crept slowly into American pulpits as hellfire and damnation gave way to homilies on virtue and its possibilities. Thus, when Arminian teachings of human freedom began to take hold, they eroded beliefs about the inscrutable God whose judgments brooked no questioning. From the other side, as the Old Testament God made his way into the nineteenth-century evangelical world, he increasingly yielded to his gentler, milder son.[33] Jesus of Nazareth and his New Testament teaching took on new cogency. Judgment and rebuke seemed less compelling messages than the word from the God of love who embraced and saved all. Whether humans were too good to be damned or God was too good to damn them, hellfire gave way, for many, before universal salvation. Still more, with humans too good to be damned, perfectionism grew apace, expressed in still other new religious movements that invoked sanctification as a second work of the Holy Spirit after conversion. Holiness and Pentecostalism rode the wave out of the nineteenth century and into the twentieth and on. Other new religious movements—like Mormonism and Christian Science—blended Christian elements with metaphysical ones, new revelations, and new and authoritative writings.

Some perfectionists—such as, to some extent, the early Mormons and, more explicitly, the Oneida Community of Perfectionists with its Methodist roots—chose to live communally, embracing a millennial perfection lived out in the present moment. Communes, in general, looked to the millennium as the inspiration for a perfected lifestyle in their own utopian moment. Shakers, after all, were the United Society of Believers in Christ's Second Appearing. Nor were the communal movements confined to an English-speaking population. As early as 1697, German perfectionists with Hermetic (metaphysical) views, led by Johannes Kelpius, formed the Society of the Woman in the Wilderness just outside Philadelphia in Germantown. Their millennial orientation could be read in the name the community adopted, even as they blended their Christianity with Jewish and pagan ideas. And in the early nineteenth century, German Pietist and metaphysician Georg Rapp echoed perfectionist millennial views in his formation of the Harmony Society in western Pennsylvania and then, in 1819, in the town of New Harmony in southern Indiana. Indeed, the history of new American Christianities can be read in solid part as the narrative of perfectionist Christian communes of both American and foreign origin that enjoyed their moment in the inviting matrix of the New World.[34]

The search for perfection was on in other quarters as well. If some Christians chose utopian space as the means to impeccability and full realization, others looked forward and backward in time. We have already noticed millennialists in good supply among Christian communalists, but their message of the imminence of the Second Coming pervaded American culture and lent it a particular heady enthusiasm for things religious and for religious experiment. Seventeenth-century American Puritans already expected the millennium in their lifetimes, and America's putatively greatest theologian, Jonathan Edwards, in the eighteenth century thought that the millennial kingdom would be situated in America. In like vein, we have met the nineteenth-century Millerites and later American Adventists who so strongly put their premium on the nearness and perfection of the end.

Others, especially in the nineteenth century and thereafter, honed their millennialism to what became known as postmillennial views. Here they beheld an advancing perfection brought on by their own labors that prepared the way for the Second Coming of Christ. Postmillennialism encouraged a general culture of Protestant moralism and pushed it toward a series of social reform movements, from antislavery and abolitionism (freedom for the slaves now), to protests against Indian Removal, to antiwar and peace efforts, to women's rights, to temperance work before and after the Civil War. By the end of the nineteenth century, the Social Gospel was proclaiming the kingdom of God on American soil through the efforts of Christian activists. Charles Sheldon's famous question, "What would Jesus do?" grew more sophisticated and corporate, and some Social Gospelers began to see the need to change the social structures that bred sin and dis-ease.[35] By the late twentieth century, their legacy could be found in the civil rights movement of the 1960s and the second-wave feminism of the same period and on.

Even as the Social Gospelers advanced their cause in largely postmillennial terms, premillennialists were creating yet other forms of Christian community. Especially as allied with John Nelson Darby's dispensationalism, with its teaching about distinct ages/dispensations in Christian history and distinct divine injunctions for each, premillennialism became a major movement in American Protestant culture. Here Jesus would come *before* the millennium, and so signs of crisis and catastrophe—not hard to find in any age—were occasions for hope. Spread among Protestant clergy by a series of annual Bible conferences at Niagara, Ontario, from 1868, the new views swept through church leadership in the United States and became, by the twentieth century, a major source of the Fundamentalist movement. The Scofield Reference Bible of 1909 propagated dispensationalist beliefs, even as these beliefs turned Christian teaching into a prophetic charter for an imminent and traumatic future. In the scenario that developed, Rapture, Tribulation, the coming of the Antichrist, and the Second Coming itself became fixed points in a familiar and vicariously lived drama. By the late twentieth century and after, popular works such as Hal Lindsey's *Late Great Planet Earth* (1970) and then the sixteen *Left Behind* novels of Tim LaHaye and Jerry Jenkins (1995–2007) continued to fuel premillennial dispensationalist belief.

The point is that different forms of millennialist belief and behavior advanced still more diverse Christianities for American consumption, as they wove themselves in and out of various denominations and groups and in and out of the general culture. Nor did futurism hold an edge on Christian diversity. Some Christians with perfectionist leanings looked to the past as the time of fullness. Restorationism, with its yearning for primitive New Testament times and practices, erased history as thoroughly as millennialism did, and it brought new forms of Christian witness to the fore. The Disciples of Christ tradition, already noted, had made restoration the mark of Christian difference, but so had Landmark Baptists and some early Methodists. By the latter part of the nineteenth century, groups as diverse as Christian Scientists and Pentecostalists sought to restore early-church practice. And as Jan Shipps has shown for the Mormons, restorationists could seek to return to Old Testament belief and practice as well.[36] Ironically, the attempt to efface history by living out of one privileged moment in Christian time brought new diversity to that history. By the 1920s, in fact, restorationists would launch what was probably their largest American success, in the birth of Fundamentalism—an American Christian product that continues into the present time. As comparative history shows, again ironically, restoring the old simply brought more of the new. There were more (and more compelling) choices for Christian seekers to make.

Perhaps the presence of diversity itself spawned yet more diversity in these millennial and restorationist forms. If history was being eradicated in both, maybe it was because a plural present was just too frightening, too overwhelming for Christian believers to live with easily. They needed to flee into worlds of difference that could provide comfort zones for the confused, places of refuge in a world grown—even within the Christian order—too various. So patterns of fragmentation and reconnection became nearly normative. Christians could choose to be just about anybody, to belong to just about any group, and to affiliate with those whose beliefs and behaviors resonated with their own. This was perhaps nowhere more apparent than in the huge rifts that developed among Christians in the crisis occasioned by slavery and the Civil War. C. C. Goen, in a memorable work in 1985, argued that the division of the nation at the time of the Civil War was preceded by the divisions of the major Protestant churches over the issue of slavery.[37] Baptists, Methodists, Presbyterians, and—in their own way—Episcopalians divided into northern and southern factions. Among Baptists, the Southern Baptist Convention mediated the culture religion of the South and continues to do so. Other denominations healed their divisions after the war, but local enclaves of difference lingered on. Meanwhile, the aftermath of the Civil War brought a series of new African American denominations, created by the opportunities that freedom brought, by the desire of blacks for religious autonomy and their self-segregation from white churches, and by the frosty welcome the white churches gave to blacks.

The aftermath of the Civil War brought, too, increasing liberal and conservative strains. The war was only one sign of a changed America. New intellectual developments emanating from Western Europe, and especially from Germany, gave American Christian leaders the "higher criticism" (as it was called) of the Bible. The higher criticism called into question literalist views and advanced sophisticated notions about layering in biblical texts and the work of a series of biblical editors—with distinctive theological and social concerns that expressed their own time and place in history. As liberal thinkers grew increasingly confident, they became modernists, arguing for a Bible that needed to yield before the knowledge and science of modern times whenever the Bible conflicted with modernity. At the same time, the growth of scholarship in comparative religions worked to render Christian teaching more relative. Still further, the new authority of scientific evolutionism—with Charles Darwin's case for evolution and natural selection in his *Origin of Species* (1859)—became, by the first decades of the twentieth century, a popular rallying point to distinguish modernist Christians from emerging Fundamentalists. The Scopes trial of 1925 inaugurated a nearly century-long time of science-religion controversies, connections, and almost-connections.[38]

The Fundamentalists, whom George Marsden in 1980 identified as champions of "militantly anti-modernist Protestant evangelicalism," brought their own versions of Christian manyness.[39] After the Scopes trial, they flourished in cultural enclaves in which separate schools, conferences, publications, and even summer camps brought them together. But they also began to feel the strain of more and then less conservative belief, and by the early 1940s the American Council of Christian Churches and the National Association of Evangelicals had given institutional form to earlier Fundamentalist differences. Moderates were wearing new dress as evangelicals. New sources of Christian diversity, new American Christianities, were noticeably on the scene.

Even more, both new and old forms of conservative Christianity were moving away from previous patterns of separation from the "world." By the 1980s, the old separatists had discovered the political order, and they began to dream of transforming it. Whereas older forms of civil and public religion had worked to unify the nation under one banner of nationalism with strong Christian overtones, the newer civil religion of the Christian Right was ironically working to ensure Christian diversity. Its strident arguments against abortion, feminism, and same-sex relationships, its endorsement of public law and constitutional amendment to legislate its theological ethic, its militant views on national defense to preserve a pure and Edenic America against godless forces in the world—all these brought controversy more than unity to the nation. And yet again, the Christian Right breached its own wall of separation. Now instead of condemning papists, the evangelicals of the Right embraced Catholics as fellow travelers. And instead of denouncing Mormons and Orthodox Jews for their lack of Christianity, they welcomed alliances with these others, who, after all, had their ethics right.

It was additionally ironic and also somewhat appropriate that an ecumenical movement would arise in this twentieth-century-and-continuing world of plural Christianities, where red states and blue states reflected strikingly different versions of Christian belief. Even before a world missionary conference at Edinburgh, Scotland, in 1910 putatively began a worldwide ecumenical movement, Americans had begun to dream of Christian union as a way to advance their postmillennial Social Gospel agenda. Organizations formed throughout the twentieth century to spawn an ecumenical movement, but somehow they never got off the ground as mass movements in the way that perfectionism, restorationism, and millennialism had. At least part of the reason for the formation of the National Association of Evangelicals in 1942 had been concern over perceptions that the ecumenical (American) Federal Council of Churches was engaging in exclusionary practice in keeping Fundamentalists out of broadcasting. So the quest for unity itself was contributing to Christian diversity, and ecumenists were helping to spread plural versions of Christianity as much as the unity they sought.

By the second half of the twentieth century, older-style ecumenism was joined by a series of denominational mergers, as, notably, Lutherans, Methodists, and Presbyterians tried to simplify their denominational lives. And again the ironic upshot was that mergers could themselves bring more diversity when holdouts continued in separate churches or formed new ones. Factions, it seemed, were everywhere in Christian America, and the only constant was change and diversity. Meanwhile, in the American Catholic Church, which had largely navigated an organizational unity in the midst of its own ethnic diversity and the pluralist imperative of the nation, the twenty-first century would bring postmodern fractures to the historic bastion of unity. A conservative movement swept the world church with Vatican leadership under Pope John Paul II and then Pope Benedict XVI. In the United States, it became increasingly easy to find a Latin mass in a city of any size. At the other end of the ideological spectrum, in 2002, sympathetic liberal Catholic bishops ordained the first Catholic women—on the Danube River and therefore in no one's jurisdiction. The Womenpriest movement took off, so that by 2011, as part of an international movement, U.S. female priests and bishops (ordaining other female priests) could be found across the nation, condemned by Rome but thriving.[40]

Conceptualizing American Christianities

By the twenty-first century, perhaps the state of Christian belief and behavior in these United States had become part of what Reinhold Niebuhr had over a half century before called the "irony of American history."[41] At first glance, from a theological perspective it surely looked that way. The worldwide Christian church, including versions with a "one-true-church" mentality, had gone to seed in a profusion of local expressions and corrupted forms. From another point of view, though, the spendthrift prodigality of Christian forms and expressions reflected the exuberant religious pluralism and postpluralism of a once-Christian nation. It told not merely of tolerance of different views and a culture of allowance but of cross-fertilization and vibrant growth in many new species and forms. Americans could talk about their Christianities and feel good about them, even as increasing numbers of them self-consciously followed different religious paths. Understanding Christian diversity means not only explaining but also intuiting the power and persuasiveness of the new paradigm and its multiple messages.

NOTES

1. Sydney E. Ahlstrom, *A Religious History of the American People* (New Haven: Yale University Press, 1972); R. Laurence Moore, *Religious Outsiders and the Making of Americans* (New York: Oxford University Press, 1986); Diana L. Eck, *A New Religious America: How a "Christian Country" Has Now Become the World's Most Religiously Diverse Nation* (San Francisco: HarperSanFrancisco, 2001); Thomas A. Tweed, ed., *Retelling U.S. Religious History* (Berkeley: University of California Press, 1997); Catherine L. Albanese, *America: Religions and Religion*, 4th ed. (Belmont, Calif.: Wadsworth Publishing, 2007).

2. Elmer T. Clark, *The Small Sects in America* (Nashville: Cokesbury Press, 1937); Edwin Scott Gaustad, *Dissent in American Religion* (Chicago: University of Chicago Press, 1973).

3. See, for example, Winthrop S. Hudson, *Religion in America*, in its first edition (New York: Scribner, 1965); Edwin S. Gaustad, *A Religious History of America* (New York: Harper and Row, 1966), also in its first edition; and the later Martin E. Marty, *Pilgrims in Their Own Land: Five Hundred Years of Religion in America* (Boston: Little, Brown, 1984).

4. Richard W. Pointer, *Protestant Pluralism and the New York Experience: A Study of Eighteenth-Century Religious Diversity* (Bloomington: Indiana University Press, 1988).

5. See, for example, David Chidester, *Christianity: A Global History* (San Francisco: HarperSanFrancisco, 2000); Dale T. Irvin and Scott W. Sunquist, *History of the World Christian Movement* (Maryknoll, N.Y.: Orbis, 2001); Martin E. Marty, *The Christian World: A Global History* (New York: Modern Library, 2007); Rebecca Moore, *Voices of Christianity: A Global Introduction* (Boston: McGraw-Hill, 2006); and Frederick W. Norris, *Christianity: A Short Global History* (Oxford, UK: Oneworld, 2002). For Pentecostalism, there is Donald E. Miller and Tetsunao Yamamori, *Global Pentecostalism: The New Face of Christian Social Engagement* (Berkeley: University of California Press, 2007). For Methodism, there is David Hempton, *Methodism: Empire of the Spirit* (New Haven: Yale University Press, 2005). Among Catholics, a recent Theology in Global Perspective series has appeared at Orbis Books. Meanwhile, Vietnamese American Catholic theologian Peter Phan has been distinguishing Asian versions of Christianity in a prolific number of works. Peter Phan has also, with Diana Hayes, edited a volume on diversity within U.S. Catholicism: Peter C. Phan and Diana Hayes, eds., *Many Faces, One Church: Cultural Diversity and the American Catholic Experience* (Lanham, Md.: Rowman and Littlefield, 2005). For a more general edited collection that leans toward the United States, see Mary Farrell Bednarowski, ed., *Twentieth-Century Global Christianity*, vol. 7 of *A People's History of Christianity* (Minneapolis: Fortress Press, 2008). I am grateful to Ann Taves for her input in developing this list.

6. For a recent reflection on this process from a world historical and theological perspective, see Gary Macy, "Diversity as Tradition: Why the Future of Christianity Is Looking More Like Its Past," The Santa Clara Lecture (Santa Clara, Calif.: Santa Clara University, 2007).

7. Jon Butler, *Awash in a Sea of Faith: Christianizing the American People* (Cambridge: Harvard University Press, 1990).

8. See, for example, Butler's discussion of Thomas Teackle's Virginia library in 1697, in ibid., 48–49, 77–78, 80. Recent historiographical practice, especially among historians of esotericism, reserves the term "occult" for developments from 1875 on—with the efflorescence of a literary, artistic, and metaphysical confluence of which the Theosophical Society was an important part.

9. Ernst Troeltsch, *The Social Teaching of the Christian Churches*, 2 vols., trans. Olive Wyon (1911; Chicago: University of Chicago Press, 1976). For an exploration of the comparative dimensions of these categories, with an eye to American experience, see Catherine L. Albanese, ed., *American Spiritualities: A Reader* (Bloomington: Indiana University Press, 2001).

10. For the Weberian distinctions between priests, "ethical" prophets, and "exemplary" ones, see Max Weber, *The Sociology of Religion*, trans. Ephraim Fischoff, from the 4th ed. (1922; Boston: Beacon Press, 1963), esp. 28–31, 55–57.

11. Claudia Lauper Bushman and Richard Lyman Bushman, *Mormons in America* (New York: Oxford University Press, 1998), 11 (the book appeared again in 2001 in a new version aimed at a university and more general audience, as *Building the Kingdom: A History of Mormons in America*); Stephen Prothero, "Readin', Writin', and Ideas about God," Religion & Values in Public Life, *Harvard Divinity Bulletin* 8, no. 1 (Spring 2000): 13–14; Jan Shipps, *Mormonism: The Story of a New Religious Tradition* (Urbana: University of Illinois Press, 1985); Catherine L. Albanese, *A Republic of Mind and Spirit: A Cultural History of American Metaphysical Religion* (New Haven: Yale University Press, 2007), 136–50.

12. Jay P. Dolan, *The Immigrant Church* (Baltimore: Johns Hopkins University Press, 1975).

13. See, for example, Russell E. Richey, *Early American Methodism* (Bloomington: Indiana University Press, 1991); A. Gregory Schneider, *The Way of the Cross Leads Home: The Domestication of American Methodism* (Bloomington: Indiana University Press, 1993); Ann Taves, *Fits, Trances, and Visions: Experiencing Religion and Explaining Experience from Wesley to James* (Princeton: Princeton University Press, 1999); and Hempton, *Methodism.*

14. For a graphic representation of a large part of the discussion that follows, see Albanese, *America*, 122.

15. For a useful recent history, see John H. Erickson, *Orthodox Christians in America: A Short History* (New York: Oxford University Press, 2008).

16. See Jay P. Dolan, *The American Catholic Experience: A History from Colonial Times to the Present* (Garden City, N.Y.: Doubleday, 1985); James T. Fisher, *Communion of Immigrants: A History of Catholics in America* (New York: Oxford University Press, 2002); and, more recently, James M. O'Toole, *The Faithful: A History of Catholics in America* (Cambridge: Belknap Press of Harvard University Press, 2008).

17. See, for example, Robert Connor's account of the Slaves of the Immaculate Heart of Mary, founded by Father Leonard Sweeney, *Walled In* (New York: New American Library, 1979); see also Daniel Wojcik, *The End of the World as We Know It: Faith, Fatalism, and Apocalypse in America* (New York: New York University Press, 1997), 60–96; Michael W. Cuneo, *The Smoke of Satan: Conservative and Traditionalist Dissent in Contemporary American Catholicism* (Baltimore: Johns Hopkins University Press, 1997); Charles A. Meconis, *With Clumsy Grace: The American Catholic Left, 1961–1975* (New York: Seabury Press, 1979); Robert S. Ellwood, *The Sixties Spiritual Awakening: American Religion Moving from Modern to Postmodern* (New Brunswick, N.J.: Rutgers University Press, 1994), 223, 300–301; Rosemary Radford Ruether, *Women-Church: Theology and Practice of Feminist Liturgical Communities* (San Francisco: Harper and Row, 1985); and Albanese, *America*, esp. 72–73.

18. Frank S. Mead, Samuel S. Hill, and Craig D. Atwood, *Handbook of Denominations in the United States*, 12th ed. (Nashville: Abingdon, 2005), 181–217.

19. See the account in Ferenc Morton Szasz, *The Divided Mind of Protestant America: 1880–1930* (University: University of Alabama Press, 1982).

20. See Thomas D. Hamm, *The Transformation of American Quakerism: Orthodox Friends, 1800–1907* (Bloomington: Indiana University Press, 1988), on Orthodox and Gurneyite (evangelical-leaning) Quakers; and Albanese, *Republic of Mind and Spirit*, 180–81, for Hicksite and still more radical Quakers and Spiritualists.

21. See Stephen J. Stein, *The Shaker Experience in America: A History of the United Society of Believers* (New Haven: Yale University Press, 1992), 5.

22. Mead, Hill, and Atwood, *Handbook of Denominations*, 148–59.

23. See Roger Williams, "Mr. Cotton's Letter," and Thomas Jefferson, "Letter to Messrs. Nehemiah Dodge, Ephraim Robbins, and Stephen S. Nelson," as quoted in John T. Noonan Jr., *The Believer and the Powers That Are: Cases, History, and Other Data Bearing on the Relation of Religion and Government* (New York: Macmillan, 1987), 66, 130–31.

24. See Nathan O. Hatch, *The Democratization of American Christianity* (New Haven: Yale University Press, 1989).

25. Alexis de Tocqueville, *Religion in America*, ed. J. P. Mayer, trans. George Lawrence (Garden City, N.Y.: Doubleday, Anchor Books, 1969), esp. 290–301.

26. I have summarized and restated most of what follows from Albanese, *America*.

27. Albert J. Raboteau, *Slave Religion: The "Invisible Institution" in the Antebellum South* (New York: Oxford University Press, 1978); see also Albert J. Raboteau, *Canaan Land: A Religious History of African Americans* (New York: Oxford University Press, 2001).

28. William D. Piersen, *Black Yankees: The Development of an Afro-American Subculture in Eighteenth-Century New England* (Amherst: University of Massachusetts Press, 1988), 49–86.

29. See http://www.thenagain.info/webchron/usa/ImmigrationAct.html for a succinct summary of the Hart-Celler Act of 1965. For a useful discussion of its effects, especially on Asians, see Raymond Brady Williams, *Religions of Immigrants from India and Pakistan: New Threads in the American Tapestry* (Cambridge: Cambridge University Press, 1988), 15–16.

30. See David K. Yoo, "Asian-American Protestants," in *Dictionary of Christianity in America*, ed. Daniel G. Reid et al. (Downers Grove, Ill.: InterVarsity Press, 1990), 84–86.

31. Thomas A. Tweed and Stephen Prothero, *Asians in America: A Documentary History* (New York: Oxford University Press, 1999), 9. Much of the work on Asian American religion (and Christianity) is recent. See, for example, Jane Naomi Iwamura and Paul Spickard, eds., *Revealing the Sacred in Asian and Pacific America* (New York: Routledge, 2003); Pyong Gap Min and Jung Ha Kim, eds., *Religions in Asian America: Building Faith Communities* (Walnut Creek, Calif.: AltaMira Press, 2002); and Peter C. Phan, *Christian-*

ity with an Asian Face: Asian American Theology in the Making (Maryknoll, N.Y.: Orbis, 2003). And for the extrapolated survey data, see http://www.asian-nation.org/religion.shtml.

32. For Unitarianism, see Conrad Wright, *The Beginnings of Unitarianism in America* (1955; Hamden, Conn.: Archon Books, 1976); and Conrad Wright, *The Liberal Christians: Essays on American Unitarian History* (Boston: Beacon, 1970). For Universalism, see Albanese, *Republic of Mind and Spirit*, 150–60.

33. See Stephen Prothero, *American Jesus: How the Son of God Became a National Icon* (New York: Farrar, Straus and Giroux, 2003), esp. 43–86.

34. See accounts in William Alfred Hinds, *American Communities: Brief Sketches* (Oneida, N.Y.: Office of the American Socialist, 1878); Mark Holloway, *Heavens on Earth: Utopian Communities in America, 1680–1880*, 2nd ed. (New York: Dover, 1966); Charles Nordhoff, *The Communistic Societies of the United States: From Personal Visit and Observation* (1875; New York: Hillary House, 1960); and John Humphrey Noyes, *History of American Socialisms* (1870; reprint as *Strange Cults and Utopias of Nineteenth-Century America*, New York: Dover, 1966).

35. Charles M. Sheldon, *In His Steps* (1896; New York: Odyssey Press, 1966). For a classic theological expression of the Social Gospel, see Walter Rauschenbusch, *A Theology for the Social Gospel* (1917; Nashville: Abingdon, 1945).

36. Shipps, *Mormonism*, 67–85. On restorationist themes in American Christian history in general, see Richard T. Hughes and C. Leonard Allen, *Illusions of Innocence: Protestant Primitivism in America, 1630–1875* (Chicago: University of Chicago Press, 1988); and Richard T. Hughes, ed., *The American Quest for the Primitive Church* (Urbana: University of Illinois Press, 1988).

37. C. C. Goen, *Broken Churches, Broken Nation: Denominational Schisms and the Coming of the American Civil War* (Macon, Ga.: Mercer University Press, 1985).

38. See Szasz, *Divided Mind of Protestant America*, 1–10, 109–13, 128–29; and Edward J. Larson, *Summer for the Gods: The Scopes Trial and America's Continuing Debate over Science and Religion* (Cambridge: Harvard University Press, 1997).

39. George M. Marsden, *Fundamentalism and American Culture: The Shaping of Twentieth-Century Evangelicalism, 1870–1925* (New York: Oxford University Press, 1980), 4.

40. On Womenpriests, see the website: http://www.romancatholicwomenpriests.org.

41. Reinhold Niebuhr, *The Irony of American History* (New York: Charles Scribner's, 1952).

The Practices of Native American Christianities

Only recently have scholars begun to traverse the disciplinary boundaries that have prevented their fuller apprehension of the wide range and complex texture of the practices and theologies of Native American Christians. Specialists of indigenous religions largely have left the story of Native Christianity to missions historians. Historians of missions, in turn, lacking the linguistic and ethnographic training to otherwise interpret the subtleties, have understood Native Christianity largely as the straightforward product of missionary intentions and efforts. But this has begun to change. Informed by a number of important recent studies, I aim in this essay to examine what Native communities have variously done with the Christianity presented by missionaries. How they improvised locally on the missionary tradition such that the Christian tradition thus engaged bears consideration not simply as a subset of missions history or church history but as a Native American religious tradition among other Native American religions. In this regard, this volume's attention to Native American Christians adds not only important cases to enlarge American Christianity's larger narrative but refines it by questioning assumptions common to the history of Christianity and the history of "religion" generally. We must consider the distinctive contours of indigenous religious practices—specifically the relationship between practice and belief, between religion and culture, between sacred and profane—for the Native Christianities that emerged from missionary encounters often drew on these indigenous religious idioms in ways that defy conventional analytic frameworks of conversion and acculturation.

From the point of view of many Native people and no small number of professional historians and anthropologists, the story of Native American Christianity, associated as it must be with conquest, colonialism, and cultural assimilation, has been set in a context of tragedy. It is as true of Francis Jennings's *The Invasion of America: Missionaries, Indians, and the Cant of Conquest* as it is of Osage scholar George Tinker's *Missionary Conquest: The Gospel and Native American Cultural Genocide*.[1] Even as it is important to lay claim to the lived experience of those tragedies and the profound losses—human, linguistic, and cultural—that can be tied to missionary encounters and their legacy of assimilation policy, it is also important to examine just what Native peoples, with considerable resolve and resourcefulness, have *made of* the missionaries' message. In this, the story of Native American Christians cannot content itself with a consideration of what Christian missionaries, along with other forces of colonialism, tragically did to Native people, but it must examine what Native Christians were able to do, albeit often within tight confines of colonialism, with that Christian tradition. Of course, a consideration of what Native people have done with the Christian tradition must include consideration of the colonial context and the tragic legacies of the missionary encounter. But it must also reckon fully with how Native Christians remade missionary Christianity not simply through a process of *translation* but through a creative and complex *transposition* through Native religious idioms of practice and belief.

The Varieties of Native American Christian Practice

If their connection to the Christian tradition unites such a wide range of instances, the first word in any careful consideration of Native American Christians must be "diversity," for Native Christianities reflect three different sources of variation: the dynamics of indigenous religions, the varieties of missionaries and the contexts of their encounters with Native people, and finally the artful creativity of Native Christians themselves.

It may seem counterintuitive, given the position of many Christian missionaries—that they were bringing the gospel to peoples without religion—but Native peoples' own aboriginal religions did much to equip them to make something of missionary Christianity. Native religions have differed greatly across more than 500 recognized tribes speaking over 200 languages and informing economies and cultural ecologies tied to landscapes ranging from Alaska's tundra to Florida's swamps. For some, the circle is sacred; for others, the square is sacred; for some, the salmon or the whale are sacred; for still others, wild rice or the cultivated corn plant are sacred.

Still, the many religious traditions indigenous to North America share the distinctive dynamics of, first, orality and, second, profound connections to specific landscapes and lifeways tied to living well on those landscapes. These shared characteristics produce a rich variety of highly sophisticated traditions of religious belief and practice, but they also produce religious traditions that are highly—make that profoundly—local, and thus set in sharp contrast to the universalizing claims of missionary Christianity. Joseph Epes Brown called the ethos of religious relativism that belongs to many indigenous traditions "non-exclusive cumulative adhesion," a term whose very awkwardness suggests the ill fit between wooden analytical abstractions of systemic religion and supple indigenous traditions of practice.[2] Sam Gill and others have noted that Native religions proceed more in terms of the logic of religious practice than they do in terms of the logic of insistence on orthodoxy or theological consistency. These approaches each suggest in their own ways that aboriginal religions have predisposed Native people to regard missionary Christianity as a resource among others rather than as the all-or-nothing tradition that missionaries so consistently proffered.[3]

Secondly, the diversity of Native American Christianity owes much to the variety of encounters with missionaries representing the whole gamut of American Christendom: Roman Catholics, Protestants, Russian Orthodox, Moravians, Mormons, Pentecostals, and others. Missionaries represented the great variety of distinctions their respective denominational traditions carried in terms of doctrine, ritual, and ethos. Added to denominational variables are those of historical context, and especially of the particularities of the relationship between missionaries and the agencies of political, economic, and cultural colonialism extended over nearly 400 different treaties and successive waves of U.S. Indian policy.

What resulted when diverse peoples with varying aboriginal religions encountered a diverse group of Christian missionaries is a bewildering range of idiosyncratic Native Christianities, but as recent case studies have emphasized, the array is no mere product of the variables of Native religions meeting different denominations; it also results from the resourceful and creative capacity of Native Christians to make of the missionaries' beliefs and practices something new. In this respect, as a number of recent studies have ably shown, the story of Native Christianity is not only irreducible to missionary history; it often meaningfully begins only after the missionaries (not to mention their prodigious correspondence) have left, and along with them the historical record.[4] Bonnie Sue Lewis tracks the religious history of Christianity among Dakota and Nez Perce communities following the 1862 Dakota uprising, on the one hand, and the 1847 death of the Presbyterian Whitmans in Oregon Territory, on the other. Mission historians have frequently taken such events as emblematic of "missionary failure," but Lewis takes them as the starting points for her history of the creative process by which Native clergy struggled to produce and maintain a faithful Christianity of their own. She begins with the religious revivals led by indigenous

FIGURE 1. *Ojibwe Family at Daughter's First Communion, ca. 1920–30. This photograph was taken in Wisconsin to commemorate a young Ojibwe woman's First Communion. A Franciscan priest is seated at the center. Courtesy of the Department of Special Collections and University Archives, Marquette University Libraries.*

Christians that followed closely on the heels of these purported "failures" and traces the indigenization of Christianity through the 1930s. "While missionaries were at the forefront of bringing Christianity," Lewis writes, "it was the Indians themselves who established Christianity among their own people."[5] If Lewis's observation seems rather unsurprising, the evidence to support it has demanded much of historians, often requiring facility with oral tradition and the fieldwork and community relationships upon which access to such oral tradition typically depends. But in paying attention to how they made the Christian tradition their own, one finds that these communities often have drawn resourcefully on their indigenous traditions and idioms not so much to translate Christianity as to transpose its narratives and practices into the distinctive idioms and structures of Native religions, oftentimes in ironic relation to the intentions of European American missionaries. If consideration of the fuller diversity and texture of Native Christianities can be no mere coda to the history of missionary encounters and exchange, it certainly cannot but begin there, for the variations on Christian belief and practice of previous generations and efforts on the part of indigenous intellectuals to articulate sovereign theologies and theologies of sovereignty reckon in no small part with an experience common to Native American communities in all their diversity: that of the close, often symbiotic relation between Christian missions and colonialism.

Missionary Encounters and Colonialism

The details could vary in terms of the particular stance of particular missionaries to particular instances of colonization, but Christian missions were conjoined if not united with European and American presumptions to dominate indigenous peoples economically, politically, and culturally. Missionaries could construe their work as reform and often expended their own political capital in behalf of what they took to be Native American interests against other colonizing forces, like traders and military leaders. Similarly, some missionaries were more invested than others in yoking cultural revolution to adherence to Christian practices, beliefs, and communities. Still, as George Tinker has importantly observed in *Missionary Conquest*, whatever their intentions, missionaries of all denominations were "partners" in cultural "genocide," complicit in, if not directly responsible for, "the effective destruction of a people by systematically or systemically (intentionally or unintentionally in order to achieve other goals) destroying, eroding, or undermining the integrity of the culture and system of values that defines a people and gives them life."[6]

Indeed, the history of Christianity in North America is intricately related to the story of the dispossession of Native American lands, languages, and cultures, and a consideration of what Native Christians made of Christianity that makes full sense must begin with that larger story. In sixteenth-century New Spain, for example, conquest was rendered morally sound by means of reading to indigenous people (in a language they could not understand) of the *requirimento*, a document which gave indigenous peoples an opportunity to convert on the spot or else be immediately vulnerable to conquest and enslavement. The close relationship between Christianity and colonialism became perniciously ensconced through a legal "doctrine of discovery," which was sutured to U.S. law in the Supreme Court decision *Johnson v. McIntosh*, in which two Euro-American men vied for the recognition of their respective titles to land in the Midwest, the one having purchased it outright from Indians, the other having received title from the United States, following its conferral from Indians by treaty. The latter prevailed in that 1823 decision, and in the difficulty of basing his decision on something solid, Chief Justice John Marshall turned to the colonial legal discourse justifying the claims of various European nations to the "New World" with the declared absence of religion among indigenous peoples and with the papal conferral of title to European sovereigns claiming lands in the name of Christendom. No Indians, by the way, were represented in the proceedings, and their claims, like those of other indigenous peoples, were delimited to claims of "aboriginal title," an extinguishable right to occupation and use of land but ultimately subordinate to the former.[7]

As can be seen in the following four examples, missionaries have themselves been agents of the colonization process. By the early 1600s, Franciscans connected with military invaders of the portion of New Spain that is now the American Southwest had established networks of missions on the upper Rio Grande and along the coast of California. These missionaries baptized many, to be sure, but often through strategies of division, even as diseases and compulsory labor were fracturing Native communities. Native people responded in a variety of ways, including an anticolonial military movement in the 1680s under Popé, a visionary prophet, which destroyed missions and drove the Spanish from the upper Rio Grande region for some time. Although the missionaries, the soldiers, and their discipline returned, missionaries from the mid-eighteenth century until the region's absorption into the United States in 1848 paid less attention to Northern New Spain, and later Northern Mexico, meaning that the Pueblo and other Native Christians were relatively free of clerical control. Native peoples were able to fold Christian practice and belief into their own religious idioms of architecture, healing, music, dance, and economic practices.

In the region claimed as New France, Roman Catholic missionaries worked among a wide range of Native communities from the 1630s on. To be sure, the Jesuits, who wrote prodigious *Relations* of their mission in New France, were influenced by assumptions about savagery and civilization, but they also paid disciplined attention to Native languages and customs, accommodating many indigenous practices in their effort to bring Native people under their sacramental and catechetical influence. With time, Jesuits came to view such aboriginal traditions more as obstacles than mediators to the Christian faith, but at the time that the Jesuits were expelled from

North America in 1763, Native communities enjoyed considerable autonomy in the shaping of their faith. The disciplinary efforts of returning Roman Catholic missionaries in the nineteenth century had to reckon with indigenized forms of practice. Christopher Vecsey has recently documented the varieties of Catholic practice that have resulted.[8]

Along the north Pacific Coast, in the fur-trading region claimed as New Russia, Orthodox priests promoted a form of Christianity with even more pronounced liturgical emphases among the Tlingit and other peoples. Orthodox priests drew their lines between Christianity and what they considered to be pagan, to be sure, but their efforts (in a fur trade encounter relying on traditional ways of life) were less about cultural revolution than about incorporating Native people into a sacramental view of Christian community.

In the lands claimed as New England, missionaries took a Protestant theological view, one more consistent with the interests of settler colonization—that to become Christian must involve inward transformation, which would result not simply in sacramental participation but in demonstrable cultural conversion. As was particularly clear among Moravians, Mennonites, and Quakers, Protestant missionaries could take a wide range of positions on the appropriate relationship between Christian faith and cultural revolution, but they could agree that true religion required a rigorous inner religious life and practices of piety often tied to cultural practices.

There are many examples of Native people encountering Christianity in the context of colonization and dispossession, but formal U.S. policies of cultural assimilation in the last decades of the nineteenth century until 1934 were especially flagrant in this regard. Beginning with the "reforms" of President Grant's "Peace Policy" in the late 1860s, missionary boards were, among other things, charged with overseeing the administration of treaty payments and the appointments of field agents of the federal Indian Bureau.[9] Missionaries not only played enormous roles at the level of policy making but more immediately through their local influence on reservations, especially in English-only boarding schools expressly designed to root out the Indianness of Native children, extracting these from the fabric of kin, language, and land. Missionaries in this era were also broadly supportive of religious crimes codes, directives within the administrative apparatus of the Indian Bureau, which criminalized the Sun Dance, ceremonial give-aways and potlatches, and other indigenous practices deemed inimical to civilization. Such have been the conditions under which Native American peoples have engaged the Christian tradition.

Native Transformations of Christianity

If there was little room available under such circumstances to make mission-ary Christianity their own, Native people were remarkably deft in practicing a Christianity that could stand out in relief from what missionaries origi-nally intended in their conversion.

Indeed, as we learn from Kenneth Morrison, we ought to question the adequacy of "conversion" as an interpretive term in the first place. Morrison examines how, in seventeenth-century New France, Montagnais/Naskapi, Micmac, and Huron/Wendat people were changed by their encounter with the Jesuits, and how their new religious practices led to tensions with fel-low Native people. The workings of power mattered more to them than the orthodoxies of abstract theology. But Native religious idioms that focused on the cosmological centrality of sacred power led to a transformed construal of the sacraments, especially baptism and last rites, and the notion of God conveyed in the Jesuits' preaching. Here, a concept of "religious change," not conversion, better accounts for the way that the power accessed through Christianity was embraced by those left with "religious uncertainty" in light of disease and concomitant social chaos.[10]

In the American Southwest, developing as it did largely outside the disci-pline of Euro-American clergy, Catholicism in the upper Rio Grande Pueb-los brought traditional seasonal corn dances and ceremonials into hybrid forms intermingled with devotion to saints. For example, on the feast day of St. Bonaventure, July 14, the members of Cochiti Pueblo hold a complex of dances and celebrations collectively referred to as the Pueblo's "feast," which defy clear distinctions between Native and Christian. One could argue that the entire Pueblo of Cochiti, centered around its plaza and continuously oc-cupied for centuries, is a sacred precinct, but the Pueblo honors two differ-ent kinds of particularly sacred architecture: the Roman Catholic Church and the kiva. Both buildings draw on the same organic shapes and the earthen color of the adobe. Cochiti's kivas are round buildings with a ladder opening through the roof—sacred buildings whose design reiterates Pueblo emergence from an underworld and where initiates receive proprietary cer-emonial knowledge.

On the feast day, St. Bonaventure's image leaves the church to preside in an arbor at the end of the rectangular plaza, accompanied by Franciscan brothers as well as various elders and dignitaries seated under the arbor. On its front, the arbor includes multiple heads of deer as well as evergreens. Dancers in two large parties emerge from their respective kivas in full ceremonial dance regalia and take their places in a complicated series of dance steps lasting hours, with music and singing and drums.

If there are distinctions between traditions rooted in Cochiti Pueblo sacred narratives and ritual knowledge and those traditions associated with Roman Catholic narratives and practices—and there are—the visitor gets the distinct impression that more than 400 years of Pueblo Christian practice have recast those distinctions in terms of a Pueblo idiom. In practice and lived experience, the respective traditions are so intertwined that one might not know where the Pueblo traditions end and the Catholicism begins.

Among Native peoples whose principal encounters were with Protestant missionaries, such transformations in practice are typically subtler, emerging over time through the cracks of the missionary discipline. Still, Native Protestants could assert considerable agency in the creation of their own traditions. Given the intentions of Baptist and Methodist missionaries among the Mississippi Choctaw, historian Clara Sue Kidwell finds it ironic that mission churches and schools became havens for the sustained public practice of distinctive Choctaw traditions and core values. "Choctaws took advantage of mission churches," she writes, "as places where they could congregate and be themselves, where they could speak their own language and visit and play stickball, with its attendant gambling and drinking."[11] Similarly, as David Silverman has shown, the organization of the Wampanoag of Martha's Vineyard off Cape Cod into Christian congregations became a lasting and crucial medium for distinctive community identity, continuity, and coexistence with non-Native peoples.[12]

Among Minnesota's Ojibwe people, a tradition of hymn singing reveals how Native people can make something quite their own from the materials of missionary Christianity. Translations of Protestant hymns into the Ojibwe language were promoted by nineteenth-century missionaries as sharp tools in their campaign to root out the communal structures, indigenous ideas, and seasonal rhythms of Ojibwe lifeways. But with time, the translated hymns took on their own life in the oral tradition. Today, the ritualized singing of these hymns, usually at all-night funeral wakes, has become, for many Ojibwes at least, emblematic of who they are as a distinctive people. This appears to be the case regardless of whether those gathered at a wake identify as Christian. The elders who travel the North Woods to sing the hymns are neither emissaries for evangelical Christianity nor "hymn singers" per se. Instead, they are known as "Ojibwe Singers," elders who sing "Ojibwe songs."

The story did not begin this way. In the mid-1800s, missionaries promoted translated hymns as part of a concerted effort to instill Anglo-

American Protestant ways of valuing self, land, and community. Contemporary educational theorists taught that hymns were effective didactic tools for inculcating values in children. Missionaries carried that logic into their work among peoples whom they considered to be like children. Of course, missionaries were ever frustrated that the cultural revolution never came as fully as they hoped. But when they heard Native hymn singing, they considered it nothing less than the *sound of civilization.* "I am deeply touched by their singing," wrote an Episcopal bishop while on a visit to the White Earth reservation in 1881: "The *wild* Indian voice is harsh. Nothing could be more discordant than their wild yell and hideous war song. The religion of Christ softened this; their voices became plaintive, and as they sing from the heart their hymns are full of emotion. All sing, and you are taken afar to think of the multitude no man could number."

The bishop was right in some respects. Hymn singing gained momentum in the 1870s, when Minnesota Ojibwes were confined to reservations, where disease and dispossession increased Ojibwe dependence on the mission and the Indian agent for survival. Under such circumstances, hymn singing mattered in the same way that cultivating land mattered, keeping Sabbath mattered, and cutting one's hair mattered. The hymns proceeded according to Western tunes and involved the conspicuous absence of the drum, which had always accompanied Ojibwe sacred music.

Yet, as some Ojibwes came to embrace it, hymn singing was no mere performance of civilization. Under the religious leadership of elders, in candlelit shacks and wigwams far from the mission house, performances were ritualized to make room for the practice of alternative values. The songs came within the province of certain singing groups, which resembled the old societies associated with particular drums. Hymns were associated with certain occasions, especially nightly prayer meetings and funeral wakes. The Ojibwe songs were sung slowly like laments, more the chanting of syllables than the conveyance of discursive meaning. Music was regularly punctuated by the ceremonial speech of elders.

In these contexts, hymn singing was less about the performance of other people's songs than about the way of life required of those who were entrusted to sing them. Hymn societies became primary social networks through which age-old values of reciprocity, subsistence, and the seasonal round were negotiated within the demands of the new life on the reservation. And today, it is in and through such practices as hymn singing that a distinctive Ojibwe Christian identity coheres. By the late twentieth century, on certain Minnesota reservations, both Christian and non-Christian

Ojibwe could consider such ritualized hymn singing by groups of elders as a "traditional" rite of mourning, fully Christian but also fully Ojibwe.[13] For although Native people can disagree—sometimes contentiously so—about what makes up the "traditional," it is hardly the case that Christian practices and beliefs are perforce "untraditional."

Tlingit people in southeast Alaska also sing Native language hymns associated with Presbyterian missionaries from the late nineteenth and early twentieth centuries. But well before the Presbyterians came, most Tlingit had been incorporated into Christianity by Russian Orthodox priests, whose emphasis on the church as a community engendered through liturgy made them—in sharp contrast with the subsequent Presbyterians—relatively unconcerned about requiring a cultural revolution as part of professing the Christian faith. Indeed, the Orthodox priests stressed continuities between Christian liturgy and traditional Tlingit ritual practices, like the funerary complex known commonly as the "potlatch."

For Tlingit people, whose elaborate potlatches offered the ceremonial focal point for their culture's emphasis on proper reciprocal exchanges with ancestors, the elaborate Russian Orthodox practices that ritualize death, mourning, and the ongoing relations between the living and the dead, were compelling indeed.[14] As Sergei Kan found, the Tlingit could assign "their own meanings to Orthodox symbols" and were able to make Orthodoxy "meaningful to them without deviating in any major way for the Orthodox ritual practice."[15] That the respective belief systems to which these practices referred in Russian Orthodoxy and Tlingit tradition could vary so did not go unnoticed by Orthodox clergy as they directed catechetical efforts to interpret the proper meanings of the performances. But by the very logic of practices, these religious actions could not be fixed airtight in meaning or performance, no matter how hard missionaries might have tried to rein in the range of those meanings and those performances. By the late twentieth century, even non-Orthodox Tlingit would consider the elaborate Orthodox ceremonies of the forty-day funerary feast to be *traditional* Tlingit activities.[16]

Conceptualizing Native Transformations of Christian Practice

Sherman Hall, a Congregationalist missionary among Wisconsin Ojibwes in the 1830s, was not alone in his concern for the "backsliding" of Native converts. "An Indian is as unstable as water," Hall complained. "He will profess to wish for instruction one day, but tomorrow he may be engaged in a heathen dance."[17] Hall's moralizing is clear enough, but he was onto something, for the fluid, processual image of culture is more fitting to indigenous idioms of religion. If they look unstable, well that's in the eye of the bewildered beholder. Rather than looking for how something familiar—Christianity qua "religion"—has been *translated* into the vernaculars of Native communities, we ought to consider how the Christian tradition has been *transposed* into a very different religious idiom, where religion is not a discrete segment of culture but an integrative force in the entirety of a lifeway, an idiom where multiple religious traditions can be viewed as potential resources for living. The key shift in religious idiom here is from system to bricolage, from belief to practice.

According to Cherokee theologian William Baldridge, "Doing theology is a decidedly non-Indian enterprise. When I talk about Native American theology to many of my Indian friends, most of them just smile and act as if I hadn't said anything. And I'm pretty sure that as far as they are concerned I truly hadn't said anything."[18] If we are to appreciate how Native people have inflected the cultural practices of colonizers and missionaries in order to enact indigenous ways of valuing land, community, and the sacred, we will find it in practices more than we will find it in declarative statements of theology. This is tricky ground for the historian, since it requires the interpretation of the shifting ground of actions and behavior, which may be only partly conscious—and certainly much less plainly available in textual sources.

Nonetheless, there are resources for the interpretation of practices, especially the ritual theory rooted in the work of social theorists Pierre Bourdieu and Michel de Certeau.[19] To Bourdieu, scholarly understanding of practices does not come easily, because practices proceed according to a logic all their own, a pragmatic logic that favors tangible, practical results instead of the quest for coherent, consistent, systematic meaning on which discursive endeavors like theology depend. But it is for this very reason that religious practices are equipped to do all kinds of important cultural work, especially in the tight spaces of colonization, for both missionaries and the missionized.[20]

Because practices can "go without saying," it is difficult for the powers-that-be to succeed in entirely disciplining their meanings. Because the detailed elaboration of a practice's meaning in so many words is unnecessary (even impossible) in their performance, practices are nimble, capable of holding together a wide range of meanings and uses. Religious practices, then, demonstrate a remarkable capacity for negotiating differences in the social field and can sometimes undermine putative boundaries between religious systems. Moreover, because practices have a certain taken-for-granted quality to them, they are equipped to smuggle in all sorts of new (or old) ways of configuring what is real and of value in the world and, in our case, of clearing room for the practice of indigenous ways of valuing land and community.

Practices can help navigate social tensions, not only by enabling people to assign their own inner meanings to them but also by performing them in ways that render the practices relevant, useful, and beautiful to them. The logic of practice allows for the suspension of contradictions or inconsistencies that might obtain if people were required to spell out the theological meanings of their practices in so many words. In this sense, the history of Native Christians must be told not only in terms of what Christian signs have meant to Native people in translation but also in terms of what work, cultural and social, they have done in practice.

There is no one term in Ojibwe that cleanly translates to the modern Western meaning of "religion." So how did Ojibwe people express in their language the concept of Christianity when missionaries introduced it as a religion? The answer is key to our purposes here: in Ojibwe, the word is *Anamiawin*, prayer or praying, and those who identified as Christians called themselves by the related word *Anamiajig*—"those who pray." Actually the root word is less a noun than a substantive form of the verb and is perhaps better rendered as "how we pray." Note the stress on the practice of prayer, not on its content, its object, or the system to which it refers. Ojibwe Christianity is a way of praying.

If missionaries erected boundaries around Christianity as a belief system and tried to maintain those boundaries by disciplining its meanings among Ojibwe converts, the practice of *Anamiawin* did not always recognize those boundaries. For some Ojibwes, this was enough to claim the Christian tradition as their own. The practice of *Anamiawin* was an instance of neither pure resistance nor pure accommodation, but a real-world mix of the two in the struggle of a people for whom *making meaning* and *making do* had become part and parcel of the same religious project.

One can go too far in this interpretive direction, however, by exaggerating indigenous agency in missionary encounters and ignoring the many Native voices that have decidedly rejected the capacity of Christian narratives and practices to encompass Native traditions. Many missionaries forbade (and continue to forbid) any Native continuities of Christian practice.

Native American Christian Theologies

As crucial as it is to understand the history of Native Christianities in terms of practice, it would of course be a mistake to reduce that history to a history of practice that excludes the history of ideas. Although there is today an emerging body of consciously postcolonial theological writing by Native scholars, historians and literary scholars have recently appreciated anew the distinctively Native intellectual and theological positions of a number of nineteenth-century Native Christian writers, including William Apess, George Copway, and Sarah Winnemucca, whose work previously had been written off as mere evidence of the denaturing aims of assimilation and missionization.[21]

Influenced by this long Native tradition of writing about community well-being, including economic and political well-being, Native thinkers have begun in earnest to engage the practices of writing theology to address the "Native" and "Christian" problematic, making formal theological room for distinctively Native religious idioms of belief, which indigenized liturgical practices had done for Native idioms of practice. But these efforts typically have not resembled "formal" theological writing; they have often been local, collaborative endeavors, found in dialogues between Christian and "traditional" spiritual leaders or rooted in indigenous theological institutes.[22]

In 2001, Clara Sue Kidwell, Homer Noley, and George Tinker collaborated on *A Native American Theology*. Besides revisiting categories of traditional systematic theology, like creation, Christology, sin, and eschatology, they proposed new ones, such as "land" and "trickster," in order to "create a dialogue in which Indian people can speak as equals to Christians." They not only encouraged Native people to "recognize the uniqueness of their practices with regard to Christianity," but they also challenged "Indian people to examine their beliefs," whereby "some may reaffirm their faith" and "others may decide to abandon churches in order to maintain their national ceremonial traditions in lieu of participation even in Indian Christianity."[23] More recently, Tinker has continued to articulate what he terms an American Indian "theology of sovereignty," one which seeks to decolonize Native Christian thought and practice and draw on its liberating message as a resource for indigenous assertions of sovereignty.[24] Tinker's theological position is notably nourished by its conversation with others in the global indigenous movement, bringing the articulation of ethics and theology into a critique of modern nation-states and global capitalism and distinguishing itself from other liberation theologies in its insistence on the moral standing of nonhuman life in the liberation process. But it retains the "communitist" vision that Jace Weaver identified as the distinguishing mark of earlier Native Christian writing by Apess and others, exhibiting intellectual dexterity and drawing on both Native and Christian ethical traditions in the service of community well-being. Native Christian theology of the sort that Tinker represents is also distinctive in the way that it draws on solidarity and deliberation with other postcolonial voices, even while it insists on the particularities of different indigenous traditions of belief and practice.

Native Christianity and Christians Today

As Tinker's theological position traverses putative boundaries between the "Christian" and the traditional "Native," so too do the reported leanings of Native Christians generally. Until recently, scholars have had only anecdotal knowledge of the reach of Christianity in Native communities or sociological evidence at the extreme margins of surveys of contemporary religion generally. Eva Garroutte and her colleagues have recently undertaken an important first step in filling in that knowledge. They surveyed more than 3,000 residents of two reservation communities—one in the Southwest and the other on the Northern Plains—in order to gauge the salience of religious beliefs pertaining to aboriginal, Christian, and Peyotist Native American traditions. What they found was stunning on two counts: first, on these two reservations, fully one-third of the respondents assigned "high salience to the beliefs of Christianity" and another third noted the importance of the beliefs of the Native American Church, or the Peyote movement, which has in many local variants incorporated elements of Christianity into its ceremonial practice and ethical teachings.[25] Second, Garroutte and her colleagues found that one-half of the respondents assigned salience to aboriginal beliefs. That the numbers add up to well over 100 percent indicates the continued ways in which Native peoples can construe religion in general, and no less Christianity, as one among a number of religious resources that are not necessarily mutually exclusive.

Beyond statistics, the annual gatherings of Catholic Native devotees of Kateri Tekakwitha, the beatified Mohawk woman, provide evidence for this texture of Native Christianities. Such conferences bring together local circles of devotion, including clerical leaders, who unite in gratitude and devotion to Blessed Kateri and resolve to further her cause in sainthood. But they are also remarkably colorful and vibrant displays of and interchanges among the various tribal languages, cultures, and religious traditions presently joined together under the rubric of Native Catholicism. Just where the indigenous and Roman Catholic traditions begin and end is a question that is not easily answered. And given the priority of practices in the indigenous idioms of Native American religions, one wonders whether it is, from the perspective of the Native Christians gathered, a question worth asking at all.

NOTES

1. Francis Jennings, *The Invasion of America: Indians, Colonialism, and the Cant of Conquest* (Chapel Hill: University of North Carolina Press, 1975); George Tinker, *Missionary Conquest: The Gospel and Native American Cultural Genocide* (Minneapolis: Fortress Press, 1993).

2. Joseph Epes Brown, *The Spiritual Legacy of the American Indian* (New York: Crossroad, 1984). "Ethos of religious relativism" is a turn of phrase associated with John and Jean Comaroff, *Of Revelation and Revolution: Christianity, Colonialism, and Consciousness in South Africa* (Chicago: University of Chicago Press, 1991).

3. Sam Gill, *Native American Religious Action* (Columbia: University of South Carolina Press, 1987).

4. See, for example, Ann Fienup-Riordan, *The Real People and the Children of Thunder: The Yup'ik Eskimo Encounter with Moravian Missionaries John and Edith Kilbuck* (Norman: University of Oklahoma Press, 1991); and Bonnie Sue Lewis, *Creating Christian Indians: Native Clergy in the Presbyterian Church* (Norman: University of Oklahoma Press, 2003). See also Christopher Vecsey's three-volume study of Native Catholicism: *On the Padres' Trail* (Notre Dame: University of Notre Dame Press, 1996); *The Paths of Kateri's Kin* (Notre Dame: University of Notre Dame Press, 1997); and *Where the Two Roads Meet* (Notre Dame: University of Notre Dame Press, 1999).

5. Lewis, *Creating Christian Indians*, 7.

6. Tinker, *Missionary Conquest*, 4, 6.

7. *Johnson v. McIntosh* 21 U.S. (8 Wheat.) 543 (1823). See also Robert Williams, *The American Indian in Western Legal Thought: The Discourses of Conquest* (New York: Oxford University Press, 1990).

8. Vecsey, *Paths of Kateri's Kin*, 23–26.

9. See Frederick E. Hoxie, *A Final Promise: The Campaign to Assimilate the Indians, 1880–1920* (Lincoln: University of Nebraska Press, 2001).

10. Kenneth Morrison, *The Solidarity of Kin: Ethnohistory, Religious Studies, and the Algonkian-French Religious Encounter* (Albany: State University of New York Press, 2002), 131, 145.

11. Clara Sue Kidwell, *Choctaws and Missionaries in Mississippi, 1818–1918* (Norman: University of Oklahoma Press, 1995), 183.

12. David J. Silverman, *Faith and Boundaries: Colonists, Christianity, and Community among the Wampanoag Indians of Martha's Vineyard, 1600–1871* (New York: Cambridge University Press, 2005).

13. Michael D. McNally, *Ojibwe Singers: Hymns, Grief, and a Native Culture in Motion* (2000; St. Paul: Minnesota Historical Society Press, 2009).

14. Sergei Kan, *Memory Eternal: Tlingit Culture and Russian Orthodox Christianity through Two Centuries* (Seattle: University of Washington Press, 1999), 404–54.

15. Ibid., 419.

16. One should also note a wide range of important religious transformations that drew on and improvised Christian practices and beliefs (especially those concerning heaven and hell) in light of indigenous traditions, but distinctively, through the authority of visionary prophets such as Handsome Lake (1735–1815) among the Seneca and Smohalla (ca. 1815–95) among the peoples of the Plateau in Washington Territory, whose Indian Shaker religion continues to this day, and in the Peyotist traditions of the Native American Church. Appropriately, these movements ought to be classified as new religious movements rather than as Native Christianity, given that their center of gravity lay not in Christian narratives and institutions but in the charismatic authority of prophets or in the transformative power of ritual, as in the Peyotist traditions.

17. Sherman Hall to Laura Hall, February 4, 1835, American Board of Commissioners for Foreign Missions Correspondence, in Grace Lee Nuts Collection, box 3, folder 9, Minnesota Historical Society, St. Paul.

18. William Baldridge cited in James Treat, *Native and Christian: Indigenous Voices on Religious Identity in the United States and Canada* (New York: Routledge, 1996), 112.

19. Pierre Bourdieu, *Outline of a Theory of Practice*, trans. Richard Nice (Cambridge: Cambridge University Press, 1987); Michel de Certeau, *The Practice of Everyday Life*, trans. Stephen Rendall (Berkeley: University of California Press, 1984).

20. John and Jean Comaroff's work on the missionization of southern Africa is particularly attentive to the complex transformations, domination, and resistance effected through practices. See *Of Revelation and Revolution*.

21. See, for example, Jace Weaver, *That the People Might Live: Native American Literatures and Native American Community* (New York: Oxford University Press, 1997).

22. See, in particular, Treat, *Native and Christian*; Jace Weaver, ed., *Native American Religious Identity: Unforgotten Gods* (Maryknoll, N.Y.: Orbis, 1998); and Marie Therese Archambault, Mark G. Thiel, and Christopher Vecsey, eds., *The Crossing of Two Roads: Being Catholic and Native in the United States* (Maryknoll, N.Y.: Orbis, 2003).

23. Clara Sue Kidwell, Homer Noley, and George Tinker, *A Native American Theology* (Maryknoll, N.Y.: Orbis, 2001), 3–4.

24. George Tinker, *American Indian Liberation: A Theology of Sovereignty* (Maryknoll, N.Y.: Orbis, 2008).

25. One suspects that the proportion of responses indicating the salience of Christianity would be even higher on many reservation communities in, say Oklahoma, or in urban communities. Eva Garroutte, Janette Beals, Ellen Keane, et al., "Religiosity and Spiritual Engagement in Two American Indian Populations," *Journal for the Scientific Study of Religion* 48, no. 3 (September 2009): 480–500.

From the Coercive to the Liberative

Asian and Latino Immigrants and Christianity in the United States

In his essay "Liberty, Coercion, and the Making of Americans," Gary Gerstle argues that the coercive has been no less operative than the liberative in the history of immigrants in the United States.[1] Gerstle finds the locus classicus for the liberative motif in *Letters from an American Farmer*, written in 1782 by the French immigrant Hector St. John de Crèvecoeur, who wrote: "What then is the American, this new man? . . . He is an American who, leaving behind him all ancient prejudices and manners, receives new ones from the new mode of life he has embraced, the government he obeys, and the new rank he holds. . . . Here individuals of all nations are melted into a new race of men, whose labours and posterity will one day cause great changes in the world."[2] Crèvecoeur's liberative motif, Gerstle argues, was a myth that influenced well into the twentieth century the historiography on European immigration to the United States.

This myth, according to Gerstle, resonates with experiences of certain groups of immigrants to North America. On the other hand, scholars have found it problematic since it elided the unromantic and hardscrabble aspects of immigration experiences. Thus Robert E. Park criticized the Crèvecoeurian assumption that it had been easy for European immigrants to adjust to their new life in the United States.[3] Oscar Handlin objected to it by pointing out that America did not prove to be a single melting pot that accommodated all immigrants and that for many immigrants Americanization was more an alienating experience than a liberative one.[4] Moreover, Frank Thistlewaite and others have shown that, contrary to the myth, new immigrants often did not care to be assimilated into America and resented being coerced into doing so.[5]

These scholars' researches have focused on European immigration experiences, but their unsentimental observations apply all the more to Asian and Latino immigrants, given the marginalized status they have occupied in the racialized society that is the United States.[6] Gerstle himself has applied the coercion-liberation analysis—coercion in both its exclusionary and its assimilative modes—not only to Europeans but also to Asian and Latino immigrants. He also differs from Park, Handlin, and Thistlewaite in that he regards race as a key constraint in the making of Americans. After all, Crèvecoeur's famous question, "What then is the American, this new man?," was followed immediately by "He is either an European, or the descendant of an European, hence that strange mixture of blood, which you will find in no other country."[7] The mixture, of course, may have been strange, but not strange enough to include the blood of Native Americans, Africans, Chinese, and Mexicans. "Race," Gerstle asserts, "even more than class and gender, still limits the options of those who seek to become American."[8]

The coercion-liberation rubric is useful in examining Latino and Asian immigrants' interaction not only with U.S. society at large but also with Christian churches in the United States. Scholars such as Sang Hyun Lee and Moises Sandoval, who have produced insightful studies on Asian and Latino Christians, have demonstrated the fruitfulness of such inquiry.[9] Thus far, however, scholars have shied away from studying Latino and Asian immigrant experiences under the same rubric—understandably so, given the risk of overgeneralization inherent in it. Notwithstanding the risk, this essay makes a foray into such study, with the assumption that examining Latino and Asian immigrants side by side will yield insights that may be hard to gain if each is studied alone. The twofold argument this essay seeks to make is this: Before 1965, coercive experiences loomed large in the way Asian and Latino immigrants related to U.S. Christian churches—looming (though not only) as exclusion for the Asians, more ambiguously as exclusion-cum-assimilation for the Latinos, with the Cuban case adding a nearly exceptive twist. After 1965, liberative experiences came to the fore, as Latinos and Asians pressed for justice within their churches and as the European-American leadership embraced their cause, spurred on to do so by the progressive climate of the times. The year 1965 was pivotal. This was the year the Voting Rights Act was passed. Just as important—if not more important for the immigrants, especially those from Asia—this year also saw the passing of the Immigration and Nationality (Hart-Celler) Act, which enabled Asians to immigrate to the United States on equal footing with their European counterparts, leading to the increased diversification of society and churches.

Asian Immigrants and Christian Churches

Asians were present in America as early as 1763, when a band of Filipino sailors jumped ship and formed a community in the bayous of Louisiana.[10] Their community, however, was eclipsed by the Chinese, who began arriving in large numbers in the 1840s to work in the sugarcane plantations in Hawaii, in the gold mines of northern California, and on railroad construction further east.[11] They were followed by Japanese and Koreans.[12] Filipinos began arriving in large numbers after the end of the Spanish-American War in 1898 when the Philippines was annexed by the United States.[13] South Asians began arriving in the early 1800s and especially since the turn of the twentieth century.[14] Vietnamese and other Southeast Asians arrived in the mid-1970s, after the end of the Vietnam War.[15]

Because of immigration restrictions, the number of Asian Americans before 1965 was small. The largest Asian group was the Japanese, who numbered around 150,000 at the start of World War II. The Chinese reached a peak of 107,000 in 1890 before declining to 70,000 by 1940. In that same year, the Filipinos numbered 40,000 and the Koreans 14,000.[16] Asian Indians did not immigrate in large numbers till the late twentieth century. One record has it that 13,607 persons emigrated from India between 1820 and 1960, with many later returning to their native places.[17] After 1965, with the passage of the Hart-Celler Act, Asians from various nations immigrated in much larger numbers, becoming one of the fastest growing segments of the population.

Unlike Latino arrivals, such as Cubans and Puerto Ricans, who were already Christians and faced the expectation that they would assimilate into the existing ecclesial structure, most Asian immigrants were not Christians and became objects of missionary endeavors by various denominations. Presbyterians were the first to approach them. The first Presbyterian mission for Asians was established among the Chinese in San Francisco in 1852. A Japanese mission was founded in San Francisco in 1869,[18] followed by a Korean mission in Los Angeles in 1906.[19] Methodists established their first Asian mission among the Chinese in 1867 in Sacramento, California;[20] among the Japanese in 1879 in San Francisco;[21] among the Koreans in 1903 in Honolulu;[22] among the Filipinos in 1912 in Honolulu;[23] and much later among Asian Indians in 1973 in Chicago.[24] The Baptists' first Asian mission was also established among the Chinese in San Francisco in 1870.[25] The Disciples of Christ were likewise involved: their endeavor will be examined in more detail later. The U.S. Catholic mission was active also, establishing its first Asian American congregation among the Chinese in San Francisco in 1903.[26]

FIGURE 1. *Occidental School of the Presbyterian Chinese Mission, 1887. The school was founded in 1853 in San Francisco as part of the Presbyterian Church's evangelism to Chinese immigrants. After it began receiving state tax money, it became a public school for Chinese children, who were not allowed to attend any other public school. Courtesy of the Bancroft Library, University of California, Berkeley.*

The importance of churches for European immigrants has been well documented. For them, the church has functioned as a centering institution and a conduit to the mainstream society.[27] The churches provided succor to Asians as well, but not so much in the way of mainstreaming them. This was largely due to the anti-Asian attitude that existed in the dominant society, which saw Asians as not being capable of assimilating. Such an attitude was reflected in the exceptions Will Herberg made to his triple melting pot in *Protestant-Catholic-Jew*: "But, by and large, in the America that has emerged with the third generation, the principle by which men identify themselves and are identified, locate themselves and are located, in the social whole is neither 'race' (except for Negroes and those of Oriental origin) nor ethnic-immigrant background (except for recent arrivals [such as Latinos]) but religious community."[28]

Immigration Laws and Asian Immigrants

From 1790 until 1965, a series of racialized laws discriminated against Asian immigrants, treating them as a monolithic entity. Among the most important of these laws was the Naturalization Act that Congress passed in 1790. It specified that only persons of the white race were qualified to become American citizens. The law considered inhabitants of the Western Hemisphere, that is, Latinos, "white."[29] After the Civil War, in 1870, the right of naturalization was extended to African immigrants as well, leaving Asians as the only major continental group denied the right. Also important was the Chinese Exclusion Act, passed in 1882, the first of a series of laws aimed at preventing Asians from entering the country.[30] In the Immigration Act of 1924 (also known as the National Origins Act), Asians were categorically barred from entry, as the law stipulated that only those qualified to be naturalized could immigrate. The law also severely limited immigration from Eastern and Southern Europe. In 1952, the racist Naturalization Act was finally repealed for all Asians, but the number of Asians who could immigrate was still extremely limited. In 1965, Congress passed a new immigration law—the Hart-Celler Act—that finally did away with race and national origins as qualifications for immigration.[31] Despite adjustments made to it, the 1965 act has since served as the basis of U.S. immigration policy.

Asian Immigrants and Christian Churches

Sentiments embedded in racialized immigration laws were more often than not condoned, if not shared, by U.S. Christians. U.S. Christian churches, therefore, presented an ambiguous face for Asian immigrants. On the one hand, they appeared to advocate fellow feeling based on a universal gospel: Asian souls were deemed worthy of saving. Conversion, however, did not assure Asians that they would be spared the experience of exclusion. Inclusive-minded leaders of some denominations, such as Congregationalists, sought to rectify the situation by encouraging white Christians to, in the words of Timothy Tseng, demonstrate "Christian love over 'caste' prejudice. This strategy was only partially successful, however, for many white congregations resisted accepting converted Chinese into membership."[32]

Indeed, a minority of white Christians supported the bigoted laws. For example, leading the efforts to drive Chinese away from the West Coast were Irish Catholics, especially Irish Catholic laborers, who regarded the Chinese as competitors. Sometimes this bigotry was abetted by their religious leaders—like Father James Bouchard, S.J., a popular mission preacher on the West Coast, who in 1873 delivered a speech at a church in San Francisco. In the speech, titled "White Man or Chinamen—Which?," he stated: "But suppose that these Chinese that come into our country are all free; could come and sojourn in our country and become citizens if they wished—and Christians too, if they like—still I maintain that they are an inferior race of people and consequently cannot be a safe class (that is, if introduced in any considerable number) of people in our country. Their immigration should therefore be opposed. . . . 'Tis the white race we want."[33] Some white Protestants matched Father Bouchard in their demagoguery against Chinese immigrants. Jennifer C. Snow writes of one of them, a certain Congregationalist minister named Starr: "Israel, he [Starr] noted, was frequently warned to destroy the heathen, not to co-exist in peaceful communities with them. . . . Deeply concerned with the evils of 'race-mixing' and 'mongrel half-breed' . . . Starr nonetheless accused the Chinese of being 'a nation of Sodomites' who sent 'eunuched' men and prostitutes 'deprived of their womanly parts' to America."[34]

One way to examine the coercion experienced by Asian immigrants before 1965 and their liberative experiences afterward is to focus on the experiences of a particular Asian Christian group, such as those in the Disciples of Christ.[35] Before 1965, Disciples had eight Asian immigrant congregations. The earliest one was founded as a mission by members of the First Christian Church of Portland, Oregon, in collaboration with the Christian Woman's Board of Missions. It was for a while led by Chinese pastors trained at Drake College in Des Moines, Iowa, before they returned to China. The success of this mission led to the founding in 1907 of the Chinese Christian Institute in San Francisco. In 1908, the first Japanese Disciples Church was founded in Los Angeles. Three other Japanese Disciples communities were established in California—in San Bernardino, Imperial Valley, and Berkeley—and one more was established in Rocky Ford, Colorado.[36] In 1933, collaboration between Anglo Disciples and Filipino immigrants resulted in the founding of a Filipino Disciples congregation in Los Angeles.[37]

These churches served as centers of their respective communities, often reaching out to more than their immediate members—orienting Asians to the divine, caring for the weak and the elderly, educating the young, and providing solace and meaning. But the Asians were in a marginalized position, forced to be dependent on the dominant church. The flow of power was clear—missionary work was done to the Asians by well-meaning white

Disciples, usually represented by the United Christian Missionary Society, an institution incorporated in 1920 upon the amalgamation of various missionary enterprises belonging to the Disciples. The organization often made decisions that the Asians were powerless to refuse. This state of affairs became painfully clear when the church bowed to societal forces that discriminated against Asians. Such connivance eventually led to the dissolution of seven of the eight Asian Disciples churches before 1965.

The closure of Portland Chinese Mission was the subject of the following announcement, which appeared in the February 1924 issue of *World Call*, the leading Disciples magazine of the time. A local advisory board entrusted with supervising the Chinese congregation made the announcement:

> On account of peculiar conditions among the Chinese, such as the decreasing Chinese population, the inability to secure trained native leadership . . . and the consequent small attendance at religious services we do not feel it wise to spend so much missionary money for the results obtained. . . . In view of the existing conditions among the Chinese of Portland, Oregon, and the policy and program under which we seem compelled to carry on the work of our mission among them, we recommend to the home department of the United Christian Missionary society as follows: . . . That the Chinese Mission at Portland, Oregon, be discontinued, effective February 1, 1924.

The most important of the "peculiar conditions" left unspecified in this notice was stated forthrightly in a United Christian Missionary Society pamphlet: "Chinese exclusion laws and bitter race prejudice caused the depletion of the Chinese community. Therefore, in 1923, it seemed best to close the mission."[38] In time, San Francisco's Chinese Institute also closed. Another moment of coercion occurred for Asian Disciples two decades later, in February 1942, after the bombing of Pearl Harbor, when President Franklin D. Roosevelt issued Executive Order 9066, which forcibly interned 110,000 persons of Japanese descent, two-thirds of whom were U.S. citizens. During this time, all of the Japanese Disciples communities were disbanded.[39] Only the Filipino church escaped closure.

Given the denomination's passivity in the face of the coercion dealt to the Asians, one would hardly have expected Asian Disciples to thrive after 1965. Yet by 2006, eighty-three Asian American and Pacific Islander churches were identified as Disciples—representing eleven different ethnic groups.

This growth came about because during the fifty years after 1965, the Disciples leadership sought out and included Asians (and other racial-ethnic minorities) within its structure.

This is not to say that between 1945 and 1965 the white Disciples establishment actively helped the Asians to reestablish their communities. In fact, Asian Disciples were subjected to another kind of coercion as the denomination pressured them to assimilate into white churches. Thus, when Japanese Disciples who returned from the internment camps sought to reestablish their communities, they were discouraged from doing so by the denomination, which instead urged them to join the established Euro-American churches.[40] The pressure to be assimilated into white churches was felt by Asians in other denominations as well. Among the Methodists, this pressure led to the disbanding of provisional conferences that had specifically served Asian Americans.[41] Similarly, Tseng writes, "during the 1940s and 1950s, the American Baptists embraced the civil rights vision for racial integration and gradually emphasized the dissolution of ethnic-specific ministries."[42] Eventually, many of the Asian American leaders who had initially supported "color-blind" assimilationist policy became disillusioned, realizing that the policy would eliminate their ethnic identity without erasing racism.[43] As a result, these leaders took a different tack—that of actively advocating for an autonomous sphere within the context of their denominations.

In implementing this advocacy, Asian leaders were aided by the progressive atmosphere that prevailed in the country, engendered by the civil rights movement and especially by the 1965 Immigration Act, which enabled the long-overdue influx of immigrants from all corners of Asia. In the Disciples Church, these influences led to the initiation of an urban emergency program aimed at addressing issues of racism and urban poverty at a denomination level. In 1972, this program was made permanent as a Ministry of Reconciliation.[44] The denomination also empowered a number of its leaders to work toward building a more multicultural community where racial-ethnic minorities such as Asians could find equality. As a result, in 1979, American Asian Disciples (later renamed as North American Pacific Asian Disciples) became an official group within the denomination. And in 1992, the position of executive pastor for North American Asian Ministries was established to provide sustained leadership for Asian American and Pacific Islander churches in the denomination. This liberative development was accompanied by the growth of over eighty new Disciples churches of Asian and Pacific Island backgrounds.

Asians in other denominations followed similar trajectories. A historic move for Asian American Presbyterians was the formation of the Asian Presbyterian Caucus in 1972, which sought "to be the vehicle to assure the 'full self-hood and cultural integrity' of Asian American Presbyterians."[45] The United Methodist Church formed the Commission on Race and Religion in 1968 to assist racial ethnic groups in the denomination. This led to the founding in 1971 of the Asian American Caucus of the United Methodist Church, with the aim of "liberation from the elements of racism within the United Methodist Church and society."[46] The Baptists were likewise involved, forming in 1971 the Asian American Baptist Caucus in the American Baptist Convention.[47] The Catholic Church was slower to respond institutionally, but in 1990 it issued "Recommendations to the Catholic Church at National and Local Levels from National Hearings of Asian Catholic Communities in the United States." One of the recommendations was "the naming of an Asian Bishop in the U.S."[48] That recommendation was finally met, in January 2003, when Ignatius Wang became San Francisco auxiliary bishop. He was followed in February 2004 by Oscar A. Solis, a Filipino American, who became auxiliary bishop of Los Angeles.[49] A 2001 study estimates that 43 percent of Asian Americans are Christians—Christians who, along with their Latino counterparts, help to de-Europeanize American Christianity.[50]

Latino Immigrants and U.S. Christian Churches

Latinos were not subjected to exclusionary immigration laws, but they too experienced coercive treatment by U.S. society and churches. Latino immigrants do have a tradition of joining Protestant churches, with their participation in the Pentecostal movement especially noteworthy.[51] But most are Catholic. A 2007 study by the Pew Hispanic Center found that 67.6 percent of Latinos were Catholic and 19.6 percent were Protestant.[52] Thus this section will focus on the relationship between Latino immigrants and the Catholic Church. The focus is further narrowed by examining only the Mexican, Puerto Rican, and Cuban experiences, if only because these three constitute the vast majority of Latinos in the United States—the three combined constitute 71.6 percent (25.2 million) of the entire Latino population in 2000 (35.3 million). Mexican Americans made up 58.5 percent (20.6 million), Puerto Ricans made up 9.6 percent (3.4 million), and Cuban Americans made up 3.5 percent (1.2 million).[53]

Cuban Immigrants and the U.S. Catholic Church

Of the histories of Latino immigrants, that of the Cubans stands out. This distinctiveness has much to do with the peculiar circumstances in which their mass migration occurred—at a time when the United States was locked in a hegemonic struggle with the Soviet Union. Before 1959, when the Fidel Castro–led communist revolution occurred, about 35,000 Cubans lived in the United States; since then, tens of thousands have arrived.[54] "In all, taking into account clandestine immigration between 1960 and 1985, 875,000 left Cuba."[55]

The Cuban exiles, especially the early ones, tended to represent the middle and upper classes of Cuban society. They were overwhelmingly white, as Michelle A. Gonzalez notes: "The mass exodus of primarily white Cubans to the United States brought about the construction of a white Cuban-American community identity. In this sense, Cuban-Americans are at odds with other U.S.-based Latino/a groups that are defined as brown or as people of color."[56] The exiles likely shared racial prejudices that prevailed among whites in Cuba.[57] Thus, Cuban exiles' values meshed with those of middle-class America. As a group, they tended to be more religious than the general Cuban population, and they arrived with their own priests and nuns.[58] In pre-Castro Cuba, only about 10 percent of the population was observant Catholic, but observant Catholics constituted about 80 percent of the 100,000 Cubans that arrived between 1960 and 1961.[59]

The Cuban exiles were welcomed by Bishop (later Archbishop) Coleman F. Carroll of the Miami diocese. Under his leadership, between December 1960 and October 1961 the Cubans received more than $875,000 in goods and services from the diocese.[60] With Coleman's support, the exiles also founded religious institutions in southern Florida like the ones that they had left behind in Cuba. This included Belen Jesuit Preparatory School, established in Miami in August 1961, an influential alumni association called Agrupación Católica Universitaria (Catholic University Association), and St. Thomas University, established in northern Miami.[61]

The Catholic Church, represented by Bishop Coleman, won accolades for its support of the Cuban immigrants. This is not to say that the church was blameless. Coleman was an advocate of integrationism (that is, assimilation), which was an influential policy among the Catholic leadership in mid-century. He urged expatriate Cuban priests to apply themselves to learn English, assigning many of them outside of Miami in English parishes, thus separating them from the Cuban community. Coleman also was against the establishment of nationality (ethnicity)-based parishes, which had been prevalent among earlier Catholic immigrants from Europe. In the end, however, his policy failed. Cuban immigrants congregated in particular parishes where they felt at home, leading Coleman to relent and designate two churches in his diocese for Latinos, particularly Cubans: the St. John Bosco parish and the Shrine to Our Lady of Charity.[62] The assimilationist policy was dealt another blow with the passage of the Bilingual Act of 1968. Spanish now became an alternative language in the Miami–Dade County public schools, with full support of the Cuban exiles.[63] All in all, the Cuban immigrant experiences have been exceptional, as noted by Jay P. Dolan: "Cubans are welcomed into the United States as political refugees, victims of Castro and communism. Few immigrant groups have had such a welcome mat awaiting them when they arrived in this country."[64]

Puerto Ricans and the U.S. Catholic Church

The United States took over Puerto Rico after the Spanish-American War of 1898, placing it under military government for the first two years. In 1900, thanks to a congressional act, Puerto Ricans became American nationals, though they had no collective say in the matter. Against this political background, Puerto Rican Catholics' experience on the mainland was one of a struggle against coerced assimilation.

With the U.S. occupation of the island, the Puerto Rican church came under the direct oversight of the Vatican—before this time it had been supervised by Santiago de Cuba. Even so, the Holy See invited U.S. clergy to provide ministry to Puerto Ricans—which they did by striving to remake the Puerto Rican church in the image of their home church. Such assimilationist policy paralleled the U.S. government's efforts to Americanize the island—exemplified in the law that the public school system use English as the medium of instruction, a law that was on the books as late as 1950.[65] In 1917, Congress unilaterally declaring Puerto Ricans to be U.S. citizens evoked little enthusiasm among the people—it was regarded as another imposition, one that made the independence of Puerto Rico all the more difficult.[66] Jaime R. Vidal captures the psychological significance of this legislation for the Puerto Ricans who had migrated to the mainland: "But citizenship was a purely legal identity. At the emotional level the Puerto Ricans thought of 'Puerto Rican' and 'American' as two distinct nationalities, each with its own homeland, language, culture, and flag. To leave the island for the mainland was to leave one's country and emigrate to a foreign country—of which, by an anomaly of fate, one happened to be a citizen."[67]

Puerto Ricans' ambiguous status and their struggle with coerced assimilation continued when they migrated to the mainland, which did not happen in large numbers until 1945. By 1930, about 45,000 Puerto Ricans lived in New York City, by far the largest Puerto Rican community in the country. Between 1945 and 1965, in a movement of people known as the Great Migration, tens of thousands migrated. They settled mainly on the eastern seaboard, centering on New York, and then spreading farther west in the 1970s to Ohio and the Midwest, especially Chicago. By 1950, the total number of Puerto Ricans on the mainland had risen to 301,375; by 1970 the number was 1,429,396; and by 2000 it was 3.4 million.[68]

Just as they felt ambivalent toward the country, Puerto Rican migrants felt ambivalent toward the U.S. Catholic Church. They appreciated the ministry extended to them but preferred to worship in churches ministered to by their own priests. But the paucity of Puerto Rican priests precluded that, a paucity stemming from Puerto Rican Catholics' long-standing eschewal of institutional Catholicism.

This situation posed a particular challenge for the New York archdiocese, where Puerto Ricans became the majority Latino population as early as 1930.[69] Initially, the church sought to solve the problem by having Puerto Ricans worship in specially designated churches with Spanish priests. This was hardly a satisfactory arrangement, given the cultural differences between the Spanish and the Puerto Ricans.[70] Yet it at least allowed them to worship in Spanish. The arrangement, however, was abandoned as the New York archdiocese embraced the assimilationist policy.[71]

As was the case in Miami among the Cubans, the New York archdiocese promoted the assimilationist policy with good intentions. Ethnicity-based parishes seemed to segregate ethnic groups and promote the notion that the Catholic Church was foreign. Thus Francis J. Spellman, archbishop of New York from 1939 to 1967, insisted that Puerto Ricans be integrated into the mainstream—that they join parish churches. These churches would be supplied with bilingual priests, so that Spanish would be available where it was indispensable, such as in sermons or confessions. The bilingual arrangement was considered a temporary measure, lasting perhaps a generation, until Puerto Ricans became sufficiently assimilated.

For Puerto Ricans, however, the assimilationist approach was problematic for at least two reasons. It assumed that they would eventually give up their language and culture, an unacceptable assumption given Puerto Rican ambivalence toward the U.S. establishment and the deep bond with the Spanish language and Spanish folkways. The assimilationist approach also denied the Puerto Ricans the benefits of an ethnic parish. Ethnic parishes had provided, as an example, German immigrant Catholics a place of their own, where they could be at home and solidify their individual and collective identity and from which they could venture into the mainstream society with confidence and integrity. Such benefits were denied the Puerto Rican immigrants.[72]

Spellman and the Catholic establishment sought in their own paternalistic ways to accommodate the Puerto Ricans. In addition to the bilingual arrangement, they created the Office of Spanish Catholic Action of the Archdiocese of New York in March 1953. Its task was to coordinate ministry to Puerto Ricans. Also important was the establishment of the Fiesta of St. John the Baptist, which the church sought to use as a vehicle to unite not only Puerto Ricans but all Latino Catholics in the city. The fiesta was especially important to the Puerto Ricans—St. John the Baptist was the patron saint of their homeland. The fiesta thrived well into the 1960s, at which time the church discouraged its becoming singularly identified with the Puerto Rican community.[73] But David A. Badillo observes that "Puerto Ricans in New York City passively resisted Americanization, holding on to their language and culture rather than integrating into parish communities."[74] Though this statement was made with respect to Nuyoricans, it could very well have been said for Puerto Ricans in general.

Mexicanos and the U.S. Catholic Church

Mexican immigrants' relationship with the U.S. Catholic Church has been complex. This is not surprising given the long history of Mexican presence in the church and in the border regions, predating the U.S.-Mexican War (1846–48), which resulted in the United States acquiring a vast territory, which includes California, Colorado, Arizona, New Mexico, and Texas. For many decades after the war, the border between the two countries remained quite open. But Mexicans did not immigrate to the United States in large numbers until the twentieth century, when the Mexican civil war (1910–20) forced thousands out of the country.[75] During this time and well into the early 1950s, as people moved across the border, the distinction between Mexican immigrants and native Mexican Americans remained rather blurry, especially in the Southwest, where most resided. For this reason, this discussion will use the term "Mexicano" to refer to both groups of people.[76] Whichever label is used, Mexican immigrants and native Mexican Americans were often lumped together by the dominant white society, which excluded them from structures of power even as it sought to assimilate them. Mexicanos themselves made the distinction among themselves.[77]

U.S. immigration policy toward Mexican migrants was self-serving: welcoming them when their labor was in demand and discouraging them at other times. Mexican migrants were in demand between 1882 and 1930, when the country was short of labor as a result of the anti-Asian immigration laws and the 1924 National Origins Act.[78] During this period, a great many Mexican migrants settled in the United States, but many came and went as seasonal workers. In the 1930s, during the Depression, thousands were forcibly returned to the border.[79] Their labor, however, was indispensable. Between 1942 and 1947 and again between 1951 and 1964, the U.S. government operated the *bracero* program, involving hundreds of thousands of legal temporary workers from Mexico.[80] But many *braceros* remained illegally when their contracts expired. And the U.S. labor market attracted other Mexicans who arrived and worked without proper documents. In the 1950s, from 500,000 to 1 million illegal migrants entered California alone.[81] In 1954, concerns about illegal Mexican immigration led the Immigration and Naturalization Service to launch Operation Wetback, which became notorious for its abusive treatment of Mexicanos living along the border, documented or not.[82] But Operation Wetback did not stop the movement of the poor in search of jobs in the United States. And in 1986, as a result of the Immigration Regulation and Control Act, over 2 million Mexicans who had been in the country without documents became legal citizens. This proved to be a temporary measure as undocumented Mexican migrants continue to arrive, helping to fuel the national debate over immigration.

As was the case with the Puerto Ricans, the treatment Mexicanos received by the larger society was paralleled by the treatment they received by the Catholic Church. At the end of the U.S.-Mexican War, ecclesial jurisdiction of the Southwest transferred to the U.S. church. The church then sought to Americanize Mexicano communities in the region, sending non-Latino bishops to Texas, New Mexico, and California. The clergy focused on serving Anglo Catholics in the regions and expected the 80,000 or so Mexicans who had now become American citizens to forsake their folkways and assimilate into the new structure.[83]

When Mexican priests protested, they were unceremoniously suspended or defrocked.[84] One such priest was Father Antonio José Martínez. And the person against whom—and with whom—he lodged his protest was the Frenchman Jean Baptiste Lamy, the first bishop (and later archbishop) of the Santa Fe diocese, who had suspended several Mexican priests and had made tithing mandatory, as opposed to the free will offering that had been the custom in the region. In his protest letter, Martínez wrote:

> Does your excellency propose to treat me as he has other defenseless clergymen whom he accused without recourse. . . . First you broke up his parish [the parish of Father Juan Felipe Ortiz, pastor of Santa Fe], completely ignoring church law as regards the division of parochial boundaries. Then you suspended him, a penalty that he continues to suffer despite his innocence and meritorious service. I omit making mention of other discredited clergymen. . . . As regards the fifth rule, I challenge the validity of the following clause: "To the faithful of this Territory. . . . Be aware that we have forbidden priests to administer the sacraments and officiate at religious burials for heads of families who refuse to comply with mandatory tithing." As it stands, this clause suspends pastors in perpetuity and excommunicates the heads of families who do not comply with mandatory tithing.[85]

For his protest, Martínez was excommunicated by Lamy.

Mexicanos were excluded from the leadership of the church and were significantly poorer than their Anglo counterparts—which partly explains why their material contributions were comparatively less than those of the Anglos. But such extenuating circumstances were not considered by the church, as its pastoral focus followed where the power and money were. For example, in 1930, the largely Mexicano Corpus Christi diocese had about 113,000 more faithful than the diocese of Galveston, which was largely Anglo. Yet Corpus Christi had only three-fourths as many priests as Galveston.[86] Given the church's neglect of them and its disparagement of their popular religiosity, most Mexicano Catholics felt alienated from it. Indeed, they were compelled to construct an alternative society within the Catholic Church, much the way African American Protestants had done within U.S. Protestantism.[87] Such a situation persisted well into the middle of the twentieth century.

By mid-century, however, the church began to be more attentive to Mexicanos, partly because of the threats of proselytization from Protestant churches. But a number of Mexicano and Anglo Catholics began to provide leadership to right the unjust circumstances. Conspicuous among the latter was Robert E. Lucey, archbishop of San Antonio from 1941 to 1969, who actively pursued social justice ministry among Mexicanos under his jurisdiction.[88] And there was the collaboration between Anglo and Latino clergy to create the Spanish Mission Band, an itinerant ministry to *braceros* and other migrant workers from Mexico.[89] In the 1960s, migrant workers in California organized the United Farm Workers Union, led by the devout Catholic César Chávez, to press for their basic rights. The church was slow to support them, for fear of alienating white Catholic growers. Consequently, when Chávez organized a boycott march in 1966, he was supported by several conscientious priests and Protestant and Jewish organizations, but not by the Catholic hierarchy. By 1973, however, the hierarchy came around to support the boycotters—some bishops even stood on the picket line—influenced by the farmworkers' nonviolent persistence, outcries of Latino rights groups such as Católicos por la Raza (Catholics for the Race), and the Second Vatican Council.[90]

Latinos and the U.S. Catholic Church since 1965

As the activities of Chávez and Católicos por la Raza attested, since the mid-1960s Mexicanos in particular and Latinos in general have openly challenged structures that had coerced them into marginality. In doing so, they were aided not only by the pronouncements of the Second Vatican Council but also by the broader civil rights movement of the period and the liberationist theology that arose in Latin America.[91] Influenced by such developments, numerous institutions were formed to further the rights of Latino Catholics. One of the more conspicuous was PADRES (Padres Asociados por los Derechos Religiosos, Educativos, y Sociales—Priests Associated for Religious, Educational, and Social Rights), the first nationwide organization for Mexican American priests. Formed in October 1969, one of its avowed goals was the "promotion of a Mobile Team Ministry to try to maximize the limited resources for the extended needs of Spanish-speaking people."[92] Las Hermanas was a parallel institution formed among Latina nuns, started by Mexican Americans but including Latinas from other ethnicities, lay and religious. Its declared goal was "to meet the needs of the Spanish-speaking people of God, using our unique resources as Spanish-speaking women."[93]

The Secretariat for Hispanic Affairs is another important institution for Latino Catholics. It was organized in 1945 as the Bishops' Committee for the Spanish Speaking under the leadership of Archbishop Lucey. It was to be an ad hoc committee to provide spiritual and social care for Latino Catholics in the Southwest; in 1964, its scope became national.[94] In 1969, it was upgraded to become the Division for the Spanish Speaking in the National Catholic Welfare Center in Washington, D.C. In 1974, it was elevated once more to become the Secretariat under the National Conference of Catholic Bishops/United States Catholic Conference. In 1988, it became a permanent committee of the church. Under the auspices of this office, four Encountros, gatherings of church leaders working among Latinos, were held between 1972 and 2000. In the very first Encountro, held in 1972, Latino participants recommended that the church renounce the policy of assimilation in favor of multiculturalism.[95] A watershed moment occurred on December 12, 1983, when that recommendation was accepted and formally publicized by the National Conference of Catholic Bishops in a pastoral letter. In it the bishops stated: "Respect for culture is rooted in the dignity of people made in God's image. The Church shows its esteem for this dignity by working to ensure that pluralism, not assimilation and uniformity, is the guiding principle in the life of communities in both the ecclesial and secular societies. All of us in the Church should broaden the embrace with which we greet our Hispanic brother and sisters and deepen our commitment to them."[96] As Moises Sandoval states, "The pastoral signaled an end to the policy of assimilation or Americanization. From then on, Hispanics would have their own place in the Church."[97] Meanwhile, Latinos have been gaining ground in the hierarchy of the church. In 1970, a Mexican American, Father Patricios Flores, became the first Latino bishop, as an auxiliary of Archbishop Francis J. Furey of San Antonio, succeeding to Furey's archbishopric upon his death in 1979. Twenty-two other Latinos were ordained bishops between 1970 and 1992, almost half of whom were immigrants or Puerto Ricans. As of 2007, forty Latino bishops have been ordained in the United States—twenty-seven of whom remain active, ten of whom are in retirement—constituting 6 percent of the total number of U.S. Catholic bishops.[98] That Latinos' influence in the Catholic Church will continue to increase in the future is almost certain, given the large number of Latinos in the church. As of 2000, Latinos constituted over a third of the U.S. Catholic population. By 2050, that figure is likely to be more than half—the year when European Americans are projected to no longer constitute the majority of the U.S. population.[99]

This essay began by noting Gary Gerstle's argument that the coercive has been no less operative than the liberative in the history of American immigration, an argument provoked by Hector St. John de Crèvecoeur's *Letters from an American Farmer*, a letter that celebrates America's liberative potential for European immigrants even as it elides the coercive underside of that potential, especially the denial of liberation to nonwhites. Until about 1965, race-based coercion characterized the experiences of Asian immigrants and most Latino immigrants in the United States, in society and in churches—coercion in both exclusionary and assimilative forms, with Asians experiencing it chiefly in its exclusionary form and Latinos mainly in its assimilative form.

Such experiences of coercion were also had by African American Christians, whose experiences provide an instructive contrast. In the mid-1960s, neither Asian Americans nor Latino Americans were as numerous or as intimately integrated with their churches as were African Americans. This situation made it difficult for Asians and Latinos to work for justice through their churches. Could one imagine Martin Luther King Jr. as a civil rights leader outside of the African American church? To be sure, there was César Chávez, whose advocacy for exploited farmers certainly received wide support from Latino Christians. But as has been noted above, in the early years of his activist career, he was opposed by his church—and without the church's blessing, Latino Catholics could not mobilize their resources to support Chávez, as African American Baptists did to support King. The Asian churches were then too small in numbers, too vulnerable vis-à-vis their white counterparts, and too diverse among themselves to constitute a cohesive and effective social force.

After 1965, however, Asian and Latin American Christians took charge of their liberative process much more vigorously. In doing this, they were encouraged by the African American example, vindicated by the Second Vatican Council and liberation theology, and bolstered by the influx of immigrants from Asia and Latin America. In the meantime, race's saliency as a constraint has abated, even though it is premature (if it is ever mature) to sound the death knell for racism in America.[100] In a climate where race is less a constraint—where the son of an African sojourner could become president of the United States—Latino and Asian immigrants are not only injecting new vitality into American Christianity but they are also helping it to liberate itself from European captivity.[101]

NOTES

1. Gary Gerstle, "Liberty, Coercion, and the Making of Americans," in *The Handbook of International Migration: The American Experience*, ed. Charles Hirschman, Philip Kasimitz, and Josh Dewind (New York: Russell Sage Foundation, 1999), 257–93; see also Gary Gerstle, *American Crucible: Race and Nation in the Twentieth Century* (Princeton: Princeton University Press, 2001).

2. Cited in Gerstle, "Liberty, Coercion, and the Making of Americans," 275.

3. Robert E. Park and Herbert A. Miller, *Old World Traits Transplanted* (New York: Harper, 1921).

4. Oscar Handlin, *The Uprooted: The Epic Story of the Great Migrations That Made the American People*, 2nd ed. (Boston: Little, Brown, 1973).

5. Frank Thistlewaite, "Migration from Europe Overseas in the Nineteenth and Twentieth Centuries," in *Population Movements in Modern European History*, ed. Herbert Moller (New York: Macmillan, 1964), 73–92; Gerstle, "Liberty, Coercion, and the Making of Americans," 276. Gerstle states (276): "To these new and radical historians [such as Thistlewaite], Americanization was a coercive process forced on the newcomers who preferred maintaining their old cultures to becoming 'new,' exploited men." It is apparent that by "coercion," Gerstle does not simply—or even primarily—mean the threat of physical force but "to compel to an act or choice," which is the second definition of "coerce" in *Merriam-Webster's 11th Collegiate Dictionary* (2003). It is in this sense that "coerce" and its cognates are used in this study. The notion of coercion is familiar to scholars working on Asian American and Latino Christian experiences. For example, Sang Hyung Lee, a professor of systematic theology at Princeton Theological Seminary, has made it a key concept in his analysis of Asian American experiences, be it Christian or not. See Sang Hyung Lee, "Marginality as Coerced Liminality: Toward an Understanding of the Context of Asian American Theology," in *Realizing the America of Our Hearts: Theological Voices of Asian Americans*, ed. Fumitaka Matsuoka and Eleazar S. Fernandez (St. Louis: Chalice Press, 2003); see also Sang Hyung Lee, *From a Liminal Place: An Asian American Theology* (Minneapolis: Fortress Press, 2010). As will be noted below, in scholarship on U.S. Latino Christians—especially Puerto Ricans and Mexican Americans—coercion emerges even more prominently. See Moises Sandoval, *On the Move: A History of the Hispanic Church in the United States*, 2nd rev. ed. (Maryknoll, N.Y.: Orbis, 2006), especially part 3, "American Conquest and the Melting-Pot Church."

6. Ronald Takaki, *Strangers from a Different Shore: A History of Asian Americans*, rev. ed. (Boston: Little, Brown, 1989); David A. Badillo, *Latinos and the New Immigrant Church* (Baltimore: Johns Hopkins University Press, 2006); Roger Daniels, *Coming to America: A History of Immigration and Ethnicity in American Life*, 2nd ed. (New York: Perennial, 2002).

7. Gerstle, "Liberty, Coercion, and the Making of Americans," 287.

8. Ibid., 288.

9. See their works cited in note 5.

10. Marina E. Espina, *Filipinos in Louisiana* (New Orleans: A. F. Laborde, 1988), xv.

11. Fenggang Yang, *Chinese Christians in America: Conversion, Assimilation, and Adhesive Identities* (University Park: Pennsylvania State University Press, 1999); Kenneth J. Guest, *God in Chinatown: Religion and Survival in New York's Evolving Immigrant Community* (New York: New York University Press, 2003).

12. Brian Masaru Hayashi, *For the Sake of Our Japanese Brethren: Assimilation, Nationalism, and Protestantism among the Japanese of Los Angeles, 1895–1942* (Stanford: Stanford University Press, 1995); Ho-Youn Kwon, Kwang Chung Kim, and R. Stephen Warner, eds., *Korean Americans and Their Religions: Pilgrims and Missionaries from a Different Shore* (University Park: Pennsylvania State University Press, 2001); David K. Yoo and Ruth H. Chung, *Religion and Spirituality in Korean America* (Urbana: University of Illinois Press, 2008).

13. Steffi San Buenaventura, "Filipino Religion at Home and Abroad: Historical Roots and Immigrant Transformations," in *Religions in Asian America: Building Faith Communities*, ed. Pyong Gap Min and Jung Ha Kim (Walnut Creek, Calif.: AltaMira Press, 2002), 143–83; Fred Cordova, *Filipinos: Forgotten Asian Americans, a Pictorial Essay: 1763–circa 1963* (Dubuque, Iowa: Kendall, 1983).

14. Man Singh Das, "Sojourners in the Land of the Free: History of Southern Asian United Methodist Churches," in *Churches Aflame: Asian Americans and United Methodism*, ed. Artemio R. Guillermo (Nashville: Abingdon, 1991), 19–33; Raymond Brady Williams, *Christian Pluralism in the United States: The Indian Immigration Experience* (Cambridge: Cambridge University Press, 1996).

15. Peter C. Chan, *Vietnamese-American Catholics* (New York: Paulist, 2005). In the past two decades, a considerable number of works have been published on Asian American religions, especially on Christianity. In addition to those already mentioned, see Tony Carnes and Fenggang Yang, eds., *Asian American Religions: The Making and Remaking of Borders and Boundaries* (New York: New York University Press, 2004); Jane Naomi Iwamura and Paul Spickard, eds., *Revealing the Sacred in Asian and Pacific America* (New York: Routledge, 2003); Russell Jeung, *Faithful Generations: Race and New Asian American Churches* (New Brunswick, N.J.: Rutgers University Press, 2005); Thomas A. Tweed and Stephen Prothero, eds., *Asian Religions in America: A Documentary History* (New York: Oxford University Press, 1999); and David K. Yoo, ed., *New Spiritual Homes: Religion and Asian Americans* (Honolulu: University of Hawaii Press, 1999). See also Peter C. Phan and Jung Young Lee, eds., *Journeys at the Margin: Toward an Autobiographical Theology in American-Asian Perspective* (Collegeville, Minn.: Liturgical Press, 1999); and Jonathan Y. Tan, *Introducing Asian American Theologies* (Maryknoll, N.Y.: Orbis, 2008).

16. Timothy Tseng, "Baptist Ethnic and Immigrant History—Part III: Polity, Theology, and Ethnicity: Three Factors in the History of Asian-American Baptists in Twentieth-Century America," in *Baptist History Celebration—2007: A Symposium on Our History, Theology, and Hymnody*, ed. Baptist History Celebration Steering Committee (Springfield, Mo.: Particular Baptist Press, 2008), 489–96.

17. Williams, *Christian Pluralism in the United States*, 30.

18. Michael J. Kimura Angevine and Ryo Yoshida, "Contexts for a History of Asian American Presbyterian Churches: A Case Study of the Early History of Japanese American Presbyterians," in *The Diversity of Discipleship: The Presbyterians and Twentieth-Century Christian Witness*, ed. Milton J. Coalter, John M. Mulder, and Louis B. Weeks (Louisville: John Knox, 1991), 280–311.

19. Joseph H. Ryu, "Korean Immigrant Churches and the PC(USA)," in *Korean American Ministries*, ed. Sang Hyung Lee and John V. Moore (Louisville: General Assembly Council–PC(USA), 1993), 25–36; Sang Hyun Lee, "Korean American Presbyterians: A Need for Ethnic Particularity and the Challenge of Christian Pilgrimage," in Coalter, Mulder, and Weeks, *The Diversity of Discipleship*, 312–30.

20. "Strangers Called to Mission: History of Chinese American United Methodist Churches," in Guillermo, *Churches Aflame*, 65–89.

21. Lester E. Suzuki, "Persecution, Alienation, and Resurrection: History of Japanese Methodist Churches," in Guillermo, *Churches Aflame*, 113–34.

22. Key Ray Chong and Myung Gul Son, "Trials and Triumphs: History of Korean United Methodist Churches," in Guillermo, *Churches Aflame*, 47–63; Yŏng-ho Ch'oe, "History of the Korean Church: A Case Study of Christ United Methodist Church, 1903–2003," in *Korean-Americans: Past, Present, and Future*, ed. Ilpyong Kim (Elizabeth, N.J.: Hollym International, 2004), 38–97.

23. Artemio R. Guillermo, "Gathering of the Scattered: History of Filipino American United Methodist Churches," in Guillermo, *Churches Aflame*, 91–112.

24. Man Singh Das, "Sojourners in the Land of the Free," in Guillermo, *Churches Aflame*, 28.

25. Horace R. Cayton and Anne O. Lively, *The Chinese in the United States and the Chinese Christian Churches: A Statement Condensed for the National Conference on the Chinese Christian Churches* (New York: National Council of the Churches of Christ in the United States of America, 1955), 40.

26. Jeffrey M. Burns, Ellen Skerrett, and Joseph M. White, eds., *Keeping Faith: European and Catholic Immigrants* (Maryknoll, N.Y.: Orbis, 2000), 230.

27. There is a plethora of literature on this subject. See, for example, Handlin, *The Uprooted*; Jay P. Dolan, *The Immigrant Church: New York's Irish and German Catholics, 1815–1865* (Notre Dame: University of Notre Dame Press, 1977); Charles P. Lutz, ed., *Church Roots: Stories of Nine Immigrant Groups That Became the American Lutheran Church* (Minneapolis: Augsburg, 1985); and J. J. Mol, *Churches and Immigrants: A Sociological Study of the Mutual Effect of Religion and Immigrant Adjustments* (The Hague, Albani: Research Group for European Migration Problems, 1961). See also Martin E. Marty, ed., *Modern American Protestantism and Its World: Ethnic and Non-Protestant Themes* (New York: K. G. Saur, 1993); and in particular, Timothy L. Smith, "Religion and Ethnicity in America," 3–33; and Martin E. Marty, "Ethnicity: The Skeleton of Religion in America," 33–50.

28. Will Herberg, *Protestant-Catholic-Jew: An Essay in American Religious Sociology* (1955; Chicago: University of Chicago Press, 1983), 36.

29. Daniels, *Coming to America*.

30. R. D. McKenzie, *Oriental Exclusion: The Effect of American Immigration Laws, Regulations, and Judicial Decisions upon the Chinese and Japanese on the American Pacific Coast* (Chicago: University of Chicago Press, 1928).

31. "Under this law, the Eastern Hemisphere was allotted 170,000 immigration visas, with each country [receiving] no more than 20,000; the Western Hemisphere was allotted 120,000 on a first-come, first served basis." Roger Daniels, *American Immigration: A Student Companion* (New York: Oxford University Press, 2001), 148.

32. Timothy Tseng, "Ministry at Arm's Length: Asian Americans in the Racial Ideology of American Mainline Protestants, 1882–1952" (Ph.D. diss., Union Theological Seminary, 1994), 83.

33. Burns, Skerrett, and White, *Keeping Faith*, 233.

34. Jennifer C. Snow, *Protestant Missionaries, Asian Immigration, and Ideologies of Race in America, 1850–1924* (New York: Routledge, 2007), 63. Snow does not provide Starr's full name.

35. There is no particular reason for choosing this denomination over others for a closer look—I am just more familiar with it than with others. Focusing on, say, the Presbyterians or the Methodists would have served just as well. For a thumbnail overview of Asian Americans in the Stone-Campbell Movement (of which the Disciples are a part), see Geunhee Yu, "Asian American Disciples," in *The Encyclopedia of the Stone-Campbell Movement*, ed. Douglas A. Foster, Paul M. Blowers, Anthony L. Dunnavant, and D. Newell Williams (Grand Rapids, Mich.: Eerdmans, 2004), 40–41.

36. Ben E. Watson, *A Story of the Japanese Christian Churches in the United States as Adventures, Discoveries, Achievements, Aspirations* (published under the auspices of the Home Department of the United Christian Missionary Society, n.p., n.d.).

37. Royal F. Morales, *Makibanka 2: The Pilipino American Struggle*, 2nd ed. (Laoag City, Ilocos Norte, Philippines: Crown Printers, 1998), 216.

38. Jessie M. Trout, "Where We Have Shared" (Indianapolis: United Christian Missionary Society, 1953). Trout was a former missionary to Japan who in the 1950s worked at the denominational headquarters in Indianapolis.

39. Sumio Koga, comp., *A Centennial Legacy: History of the Japanese Christian Missions in North America, 1877–1977* (Chicago: Nobart, 1977), 1:244.

40. In 1948, the disbanded Japanese Christian Church was reconstituted as West Adams Christian Church (Disciples of Christ). Joe Nagano, one of the original members, recollects: "And only after considerable pleading was our church allowed to begin as the West Adams Christian church." Joe Nagano's letter to Dr. Geunhee Yu (ca. 1996), in the file of the North American Pacific Asian Disciples Ministries, Division of Homeland Ministries, Christian Church (Disciples of Christ), Indianapolis.

41. Jonah Chang, "Movement of Self-Improvement: History of the National Federation of Asian American United Methodists," in Guillermo, *Churches Aflame*, 138.

42. Tseng, "Baptist Ethnic and Immigrant History," 492.

43. Timothy Tseng et al., *Pulpit and Pew Research on Pastoral Leadership: Asian*

American Religious Leadership Today, a Preliminary Inquiry (Durham: Duke Divinity School, 2005), 14.

44. "Recommendations Concerning Reconciliation Mission," in *Share the Feast: 2007 General Assembly of the Christian Church (Disciples of Christ)* (Indianapolis: General Assembly of the Christian Church [Disciples of Christ], 2007), 291–93.

45. Angevine and Roshida, "Contexts for a History of Asian American Presbyterian Churches," 280–81.

46. Chang, "Movement of Self-Improvement," 141.

47. Tseng, "Baptist Ethnic and Immigrant History," 492.

48. Burns, Skerrett, and White, *Keeping Faith*, 306. For a special issue on Asian American Catholics, see *U.S. Catholic Historian* 18, no. 1 (Winter 2000).

49. Jerry Filteau, "As New Year Begins, a Look Back at 2003," *Georgia Bulletin: The Newspaper of the Catholic Archdiocese of Atlanta (Online Edition)*, January 1, 2004; Ellie Hidalgo, "Auxiliary Bishop Oscar Solis Becomes First Filipino American Bishop," *Tidings Online* (February 20, 2004)(accessed on November 28, 2008).

50. Tseng et al., *Pulpit and Pew Research on Pastoral Leadership*, 50.

51. On Latino Protestants, see Paul Barton, *Hispanic Methodists, Presbyterians, and Baptists in Texas* (Austin: University of Texas Press, 2006); Daisy L. Machado, *Of Borders and Margins: Hispanic Disciples in Texas, 1888–1945* (New York: Oxford University Press, 2003); and Larry L. Hunt, "Hispanic Protestantism in the United States: Trends by Decade and Generation," *Social Forces* 77, no. 4 (June 1999). See also Pew Hispanic Center, *Changing Faiths: Latinos and the Transformation of American Religion* (Washington, D.C.: Pew Hispanic Center, 2007); and Sonya Geis, "Latino Catholics Increasingly Drawn to Pentecostalism," *Washington Post*, April 30, 2006.

52. Pew Hispanic Center, *Changing Faiths*, 7.

53. U.S. Census Bureau, *The Hispanic Population: Census 2000 Brief*, issued May 2001.

54. Jay P. Dolan and Jaime R. Vidal, eds., *Puerto Rican and Cuban Catholics in the U.S., 1900–1965* (Notre Dame: University of Notre Dame Press, 1994).

55. Sandoval, *On the Move*, 135.

56. Michelle A. Gonzalez, *Afro-Cuban Theology: Religion, Race, Culture, and Identity* (Gainesville: University Press of Florida, 2006), 72. According to a 2002 census, the racial composition of Cuba was as follows: white, 65.1 percent; mulatto and mestizo, 24.8 percent; and black, 10.1 percent. Central Intelligence Agency: The World Fact Book, https://www.cia.gov/library/publications/the-world-factbook/geos/cu.html (accessed March 15, 2011).

57. At the turn of the twentieth century, white Cubans' prejudice toward their black counterparts was blatant, even in the Catholic Church, as noted by Aline Helg: "The Catholic church continued to enforce the principle of *limpieza de sangre* (purity of blood) in its seminaries, which amounted to excluding Afro-Cubans. Some Catholic parishes still registered whites and *pardos y morenos* [mulattoes and blacks] in two separate books listing births, marriages, and deaths, and only whites' names were preceded with the appellation Don or Doña." Aline Helg, *Our Rightful Share: The Afro-Cuban*

Struggle for Equality, 1886–1912 (Chapel Hill: University of North Carolina Press, 1995), 99. According to Gonzalez, "Race became an unresolved category for the Cuban people, and its connection with nationhood was contentious. The 1959 revolution brought some progress in the struggle to overcome racism, but race is far from being a nonissue in Cuba." Gonzalez, *Afro-Cuban Theology*. See also Eugene Robinson, "Cuba Begins to Answer Its Race Question," *Washington Post*, November 12, 2000, A01; and Susan D. Greenbaum, *More Than Black: Afro-Cubans in Tampa* (Gainesville: University Press of Florida), 204–5.

58. Dolan and Vidal, *Puerto Rican and Cuban Catholics in the U.S.*, 191.

59. Sandoval, *On the Move*, 135.

60. Dolan and Vidal, *Puerto Rican and Cuban Catholics in the U.S.*, 195.

61. Ibid., 198–206.

62. Ibid., 196.

63. Ana Maria Diaz-Stevens and Anthony M. Stevens-Arroyo, *Recognizing the Latino Resurgence in U.S. Religion: The Emmaus Paradigm* (Boulder: Westview, 1998), 15.

64. Jay P. Dolan and Allan Figueroa Deck, eds., *Hispanic Catholic Culture in the U.S.: Issues and Concerns* (Notre Dame: University of Notre Dame Press, 1994), 443.

65. Jaime R. Vidal, "Citizens Yet Strangers: The Puerto Rican Experience," in Dolan and Vidal, *Puerto Rican and Cuban Catholics in the U.S.*, 143; Ana Maria Diaz-Stevens, *Oxcart Catholicism on Fifth Avenue: The Impact of the Puerto Rican Migration upon the Archdiocese of New York* (Notre Dame: University of Notre Dame Press, 1993).

66. Vidal, "Citizens Yet Strangers," 22.

67. Ibid., 62.

68. Dolan and Vidal, *Puerto Rican and Cuban Catholics in the U.S.*, 56; Bureau of the Census, New Release, May 10, 2001.

69. Badillo, *Latinos and the New Immigrant Church*, 54.

70. Moises Sandoval, *Fronteras: A History of the Latin American Church in the USA since 1513* (San Antonio: Mexican American Cultural Center, 1983), 274.

71. Dolan and Vidal, *Puerto Rican and Cuban Catholics in the U.S.*, 72.

72. Ibid., 134.

73. Ibid., 95.

74. Badillo, *Latinos and the New Immigrant Church*, 83.

75. Sandoval, *Fronteras*, 316–17.

76. The *Oxford English Dictionary* defines the term "Mexicano" as referring to both Mexicans (therefore potentially Mexican immigrants) and Mexican Americans. On the complexity of the Mexicano population in particular and of the Latino population in general, see Joan Moore, "The Social Fabric of the Hispanic Community since 1945," in Dolan and Deck, *Hispanic Catholic Culture in the U.S.*

77. See, for example, Joan Moore's discussion of Manitos or Hispanos (descendants of Spanish settlers of the seventeenth and eighteenth centuries) in New Mexico and Colorado, in Moore, "Social Fabric of the Hispanic Community," 6–49.

78. Sandoval, *On the Move*, 42.

79. Jeffrey M. Burns, "The Mexican Catholic Community in California," in *Mexican Americans and the Catholic Church, 1900–1965*, ed. Jay P. Dolan and Gilberto M. Hinojosa (Notre Dame: University of Notre Dame Press, 1994), 129–233.

80. *Bracero* literally means "one who swings his arms." Daniels, *American Immigration*, 192.

81. Burns, "The Mexican Catholic Community in California," 141.

82. *The Border* (PBS): http://www.pbs.org/kpbs/theborder/history/timeline/20.html (accessed November 28, 2008).

83. Dolan and Hinojosa, *Mexican Americans and the Catholic Church*, 21.

84. Ibid., 19–20.

85. Antonio José Martínez's letter to Jean Baptiste Lamy, April 13, 1857, in Timothy Matovina and Gerald E. Poyo, eds., *Presente: U.S. Latino Catholics from Colonial Origins to the Present* (Maryknoll, N.Y.: Orbis, 2000), 69.

86. Dolan and Hinojosa, *Mexican Americans and the Catholic Church*, 39.

87. Dolan and Deck, *Hispanic Catholic Culture in the U.S.*, 454.

88. Dolan and Hinojosa, *Mexican Americans and the Catholic Church*, 115.

89. Ibid., 210–11.

90. Sandoval, *On the Move*, 119–25; Matovina and Poyo, *Presente*, 209.

91. For a good overview of these developments, see Sandoval, *On the Move*; and Philip E. Lampe, ed., *Hispanics in the Church: Up from the Cellar* (San Francisco: Catholic Scholars Press, 1994).

92. Juan Romero, "Mexican American Priests: History of PADRES, 1969–89," in Lampe, *Hispanics in the Church*, 71–94.

93. Yolanda Tarango and Timothy M. Matovina, "Las Hermanas," in Lampe, *Hispanics in the Church*, 95–120.

94. Dolan and Deck, *Hispanic Catholic Culture in the U.S.*, 135.

95. Sandoval, *On the Move*, 99.

96. National Conference of Catholic Bishops, *The Hispanic Presence: Challenge and Commitment (A Pastoral Letter on Hispanic Ministry)* (Washington, D.C.: Office of Publishing and Promotional Services, United States Catholic Conference, 1984), 5.

97. Moises Sandoval, "The Organization of a Hispanic Church," in Dolan and Deck, *Hispanic Catholic Culture in the U.S.*, 152.

98. Ibid., 150. http://www.nccbuscc.org/comm/backgrounders/hispanic.shtml (accessed on March 14, 2010).

99. "Executive Summary—Latino Catholics: Presence, Participation, and Leadership in the Catholic Church," http://www.latinoleadership.org/research/reports/latino-catholics.html (accessed April 18, 2010); Jeff Guntzel, "Between Two Cultures: Catholic Church Must Meet Challenges of Ministry to Hispanic Youth, Report Says, or 'Risk Losing a Significant Portion of the Faithful for Generations to Come,'" *National Catholic Reporter*, January 30, 2004. Jay P. Dolan and Gilberto M. Hinojosa conjecture that Latinos may compose half of the U.S. Catholic population by 2010. See Dolan and Hinojosa, *Mexican Americans and the Catholic Church*, 1. The U.S. Census Bureau estimates that

by 2050 the total U.S. population will be 439 million; it further estimates that 54 percent (235.7 million) will be nonwhite. Among the nonwhites, it estimates that 132.8 million (30 percent) will be Hispanic, 65.7 million (15 percent) will be black, and 40.6 million (9.2 percent) will be Asian. U.S. Census Bureau News, August 14, 2008.

100. William Julius Wilson, *The Declining Significance of Race: Blacks and Changing American Institutions*, 2nd ed. (Chicago: University of Chicago Press, 1980).

101. Joseph Mitsuo Kitagawa, *Christian Tradition: Beyond Its European Captivity* (Philadelphia: Trinity Press International, 1992).

African American Christianity and the Burden of Race

It may be necessary to note why we treat "black Christianity" in a separate category from other Christianities in America. The facts of American history will come to mind for most literate Americans: slavery, legal segregation, and informal and formal customs of keeping blacks out of neighborhoods and positions of power. All of these factors have served to distance African Americans from whites in terms of both geographic proximity and issues of positions of power and cultural authority. It is within black churches that the most salient differences emerged between blacks and whites. Consider the following: African American Christians and white evangelical Protestants (especially in the South) make up two of the most active churchgoing populations in contemporary America, yet their views of social justice, their voting records, and their general conceptions of the American nation's ideals and history are very different. How is it that two groups of people in the same country with a shared Christian tradition who read the same Bible can have such fundamentally different practices and beliefs? Understanding the formation and evolution of black Christianity in the United States provides a major clue to this enigma.

The question of black religion as a site of resistance and a social space of difference has perennially occupied scholars. Much of this scholarship has been nearly obsessed with a reified notion of "the black church" as a unified institution that has historically faced the behemoth of American racism. Scholars have posed the question of whether the black church has been an instrument of reform that promotes civil rights and social justice for blacks and other Americans or a mode of accommodation advocating an otherworldly ideology that counseled blacks to accept their lot meekly and gather whatever crumbs their white oppressors threw their way. This approach to scholarship has implicitly incorporated a false concept of unity among African Americans that flattens out the nuance and complexity of their history. Historians have labored under deep background assumptions about the need for a progressive or prophetic black church that can heroically do for blacks what no other institution can do or has done. By focusing on four moments in African American Christian history—the pre–Civil War period, the "free" North in the early nineteenth century, the rural South in the 1930s, and modern America in the late twentieth century—I hope to demonstrate how black churches have been required to take on a range of duties and responsibilities. By attending to local contexts and different periods, we also get some sense of the diversity and complexity of African American Christianity.

African American Christianity has of necessity been exceptional, even though black Christians share beliefs, practices, and a history with white Christians, particularly in the South. Black religion more generally has played a unique role in black communities and in American culture. Historical circumstances have placed a distinct burden upon African American Christianity that cannot be compared to the experience of whites in America. This does not, however, suggest that "the black church" is an actual reality or institution. African American Christians, even though there are obvious differences among them in terms of class, gender, and geography, have been compelled to imagine themselves as a collective body of people experiencing suffering and solidarity against seemingly ubiquitous racial oppression. It is this social imaginary and this sense of living against a common enemy that has made possible the scholarly construct of "the black church."

Yet on the ground, blacks have had to deal in very particular and local ways with living in a world of economic, social, and political oppression. Ironically, the emergence of new technologies and media (most notably newspapers, radio, and television) made possible a gradual formation of a public sphere, which allowed blacks to imagine themselves as a collective, even as black migration and diversity increased. These technologies and a shared history of racism enabled blacks to be lifted from their particular circumstances into a broader "racial" imaginary that confronted common problems. Indeed, from the very origins of independent black churches, blacks have perceived their churches as reflections of a shared experience and condition. As James Campbell writes about the rise of independent black churches in the late eighteenth century: "These humble institutions both reflected and fostered an emerging sense of peoplehood, of membership in an 'imagined community' of black people, transcending barriers of time, space, and condition."[1] It is this evolutionary process of becoming an imagined community that made possible a Jeremiah Wright, pastor of Trinity Church in Chicago, Illinois, the former church home of President Barack Obama, who cast critics' attacks against him as a frontal assault against "the black church." This crucial thread of subsuming black churches and their particular struggles under the rubric of "the black church" structures this essay. I argue that the peculiar history of blacks in America has made possible both the scholarly monolith and a popular conception of "the black church," which has burdened black Christianity with unrealistic expectations in light of persisting heroic and progressive conceptions of a unified black church. This notion of the black church hinders individual self-expression within black communities, implicitly reinforces older notions of racial essentialism and unity, and imposes a static scholarly abstraction on a pulsating, diverse, and complex reality. This essay deconstructs this notion of the black church in order to give both historians and black Christians a more fruitful and critical understanding of African American Christianity.

Becoming Christians in the American South

The very introduction of Christianity to Africans in the British North American colonies by Anglican missionaries, who held a near monopoly in southern colonies in the eighteenth century, placed a special burden and duty on the shoulders of African converts. Unfortunately, we do not know how Africans saw or experienced this burden because most of the evidence we have are the carpings of missionaries, angered over slave owners' refusal to put more effort into converting their slaves. It may seem rather naive to us that missionaries and evangelists were caviling with slave owners about their lack of effort in converting slaves, as though slave owners did not need to worry about the effects of introducing the Christian faith to a population held in bondage for labor. But missionaries assured slave owners that Christianity would make slaves more docile and loyal and ever more dedicated as faithful servants of their earthly masters. As a public testimony to masters, slaves, and God, in 1709, Francis Le Jau, an Anglican missionary to St. James Parish at Goose Creek, South Carolina, required his slave converts to confess the following: "You declare in the Presence of God and before this Congregation that you do not ask for the holy baptism out of any design to free yourself from the Duty and Obedience you owe to your Master while you live, but merely for the good of Your Soul and to partake of the Graces and Blessings promised to the Members of the Church of Jesus Christ."[2] Le Jau proposed to slaves and their owners that baptism had no effect on slaves' civil or outward condition and that the harsh system of slavery as it existed in South Carolina did not detract from blessings bestowed on those slaves who joined the church. For Le Jau and other Anglican missionaries, Christianity transformed the soul and brought inward freedom and did not abolish unequal relations in society, because these conditions were ordained by God.

Anglicans failed in their attempts to convert slaves in significant numbers to Christianity. African slaves were introduced to a Christianity that required its hopeful converts to learn a detailed and abstruse theology that conveyed an implicit assumption that Africans were dunces incapable of becoming a part of this tradition. When reading missionary reports, one gets the sense that missionaries and slave owners were worried that blacks' intellectual capacities stood as barriers to their Christianization because of their moral condition of superstition and heathenism. By their own missionary techniques, Anglican Christians gave the impression that it was for the limited and literate few. More generally, Africans noticed the intertwining of class, racial prejudice, and Christianity in their first encounter with this alien religion.[3] Christian inequality and class privilege deepened in the following century of enslavement by Christian masters.

There were, of course, other factors at work that help explain why Anglicans failed in their attempts to convert slaves. Linguistic and cultural barriers, limited contact because of insufficient missionaries, and geographic distance were among the factors inhibiting sustained attempts at Christianization of the constantly incoming African population. Methodist and Baptist evangelicals had several advantages over Anglicans, one being a slave population that was gradually learning enough English to communicate, though many pockets of freshly arrived Africans throughout the South always stood as a potential barrier to communication and conversion attempts. Freedom from the common practice of being mostly tied to one parish or church also helped evangelical attempts at slave Christianization. Baptists and Methodists were fervent itinerants and charged into frontier populations seeking new converts. Then there was the conversion experience: a radical visceral transformation, a bodily sensation attesting to an inward change, and a sense of release from one's former life. Albert Raboteau stresses that there is some continuity (in the "patterns of motor behavior preceding and following the ecstatic experience") between West African traditions of spirit possession and the evangelical emphasis on the indwelling of the Holy Spirit.[4] Clearly, a radical new cognitive meaning was given to possession of the person in the Christian tradition, but the connection of bodily movement and sensation with spiritual transformation and new life must have resonated with Africans, whose religious traditions placed strong emphasis on gods and spirits inhabiting the bodies of devotees.

Tactile experience and contact with the body are crucial in understanding the conversion of Africans to evangelical Christianity. To a people who had been branded, poked, prodded, whipped, and examined as specimens on the auction block, tender human contact in the emotional context of church services must have been a powerful experience. Donald Mathews notes the importance of social rituals of physical contact among early evangelicals: the anointing of the sick with oil, the laying on of hands for ordination, the right hand of fellowship, the kiss of charity, and the washing of feet.[5] These were powerful physical and symbolic gestures of spiritual communion. Africans could surely "read" these gestures for what they meant, and we should not overlook their effect in promoting Africans' conversion to Christianity. Similarly, public confession of sin and the sharing of spiritual struggles among blacks and whites in early evangelical churches created both community and unusual intimacy.[6]

Experience and practice are crucially important in religions, but did Africans understand the concepts and theology of this new religion of Christianity? What did they believe and what did they accept and practice? Is there any credence to complaints by northern critics like Frederick Law Olmsted, who argued as late as the 1850s that Africans in the South had accepted only a vulgarized version of Christianity? Here interpretation is difficult to disentangle from racially tinged description and culturally obtuse observation. Olmsted and other observers noted the unique emphases of slave religion: visions of apostles and Jesus, trance, catalepsy, altered states of consciousness, and possession by the Holy Spirit or tempting words whispered in the ear by the devil. Olmsted remained convinced, however, that there were so many restrictions against and reservations about instructing slaves in the South that attempts at Christianization often resulted in furnishing a "delusive clothing of Christian forms and phrases to the original vague superstition of the African savage."[7] We must read Olmsted's comments with caution because his instrumentalist notion of slave religion was based on whether it produced the right kind of laboring subjects. He deemed slaves' religious experience to be inauthentically Christian to the extent that it did not resemble his normative notion of Christianity. Yet his attention to difference is worth pondering. Emotion and feelings as dominant expressions of black

Christianity were almost universally commented upon by white observers, who varied in their assessments of these qualities. Blacks fell to the ground during worship and revival services, shouted and fainted, were possessed by the Spirit, groaned until they found release from sin or particular troubles, and fully engaged the body in their religious experiences. Their Christianity put the body and its emotions at the very center of worship and looked quite different from the Christianity of whites in the South and the North.

Eugene Genovese argues that slaves did not accept original sin and an attendant sense of personal guilt.[8] Observers during and after slavery argued that blacks did not have a sense of having wronged a holy God and were not as deeply troubled or as guilty about certain sins (adultery and stealing, for example) as whites. Cultural myopia and racism can explain much of this attempt to portray black religion as divorced from ethics, but there is evidence that the experience of slavery made it difficult for blacks to bear the weight of original sin. Apparently, this was a burden too heavy to sustain. Yet the irony is that—although slave marriages were not legally recognized in the South, children were forcibly separated from their parents, and slavery as an institution allowed white masters to physically and sexually assault slave women with virtual impunity—white Christian moralists, even abolitionists, criticized black Christians for allegedly failing to honor the sacredness of marriage or to uphold proper sexual morality. The experience of slavery led blacks to emphasize less the judgment of God than his love, which irked white critics working among them even after the Civil War. Slaves and their descendants found solace in visions of and conversations with figures in the Old Testament and with Jesus and the apostles in the New Testament. God walking with them through their times of hardship and earthly difficulty was much more real than a sovereign and exacting God dispensing judgment to sinful humans. For white southern evangelicals, it was not simply slaves' family lives that were seen as deficient; their enchanted world densely populated with ancient biblical figures, angels, and demonic personages was regarded as too superstitious. White evangelicals did not want their religion to be too similar to the faith of an enslaved black population. Religion often functioned as a signal quality of difference for white Americans and blacks, and though evangelicals were by no means Enlightenment advocates in a critical or anti-Christian sense, they were aware enough of the force of arguments for religion as a civilizing force to want to distance themselves from the excesses of slave religion, especially if it in any way seemed tainted with African superstition.

Black Christianity in the North

Black Christians in the northern states found themselves facing common problems of discrimination, segregated schools, and general mistreatment in a society that viewed all blacks, slave or free, as inferior. Scholars are still revising origin narratives about black churches in the United States, but there remains general agreement that the opening of Richard Allen's African Methodist Episcopal Church in Philadelphia in 1794 signaled the formation of a new independent movement among "African churches" in the North.[9] Under the auspices of Methodists, Allen had worked patiently alongside Francis Asbury and other white leaders, studying the teachings of Christianity under their tutelage. But it was discrimination in the church and the refusal to grant equal status to blacks that led to the founding of a new movement of black churches.

These northern churches demonstrated at their very founding the impossibility of black churches preaching solely or primarily about individual salvation. Although Allen was an ideal candidate for this kind of preaching—with his strong emphasis on personal morality, uplift, and decorum—his encounter with white racism in the form of colonization, aspersions against blacks during the yellow fever epidemic in 1793, and a backlash against free blacks after the Revolution indicated the future direction of black Christianity in the North. Out of Allen's Bethel Church formed the strongest opposition to colonization, plans for uplift of the race, and a collective identity of blacks as an oppressed group in America. Black churches of necessity had to deal with the broader problems of society from the pulpit because these so directly affected the prospects of blacks merely remaining in the United States. What scholars have come to call the "prophetic function" of black churches should perhaps be seen less in heroic terms than as a moral necessity or burden imposed on black churches and leaders because of the problem of racial oppression in America. (This observation does not diminish the courage demonstrated by leaders such as Allen.) How could Allen avoid talking about and confronting head-on the racism of the American nation when a considerable and influential number of white citizens in the American Colonization Society wanted to remove free blacks like him from the country and ship them off to Africa? As the convention notes of the American Society of Free Persons of Color (over which Allen presided) stated in 1830: "In the nineteenth century of the Christian era, laws have been enacted in some states of this great republic, to compel an unprotected and harmless portion of our brethren, to leave their homes and seek an asylum in foreign

FIGURE 1. *Bishops of the African Methodist Episcopal Church, 1876. In 1876, the African Methodist Episcopal Church commemorated the fiftieth anniversary of its founding. This engraving depicts the Reverend Richard Allen (1760–1831), the founder of the church, surrounded by ten bishops. The other scenes depict the educational and missionary endeavors of the church, including the Payne Institute, Wilberforce University, and the sending of missionaries to Haiti. Courtesy of the Prints and Photographs Division, Library of Congress.* LC-DIG-pga-03643.

climes."[10] Allen realized that his very own being as an American citizen and his continuing livelihood as a minister depended on his "mixing" religion and politics to counter pernicious forces at work to remove free blacks from America.

Many northern black clergymen led churches that became hotbeds of abolition. Allen, Alexander Crummell, and Henry Highland Garnet are a few examples of such activist clergy. These leaders emphasized racial uplift and moral reform, both personal and social. They defended human equality by citing scripture and by invoking foundational American documents like the Declaration of Independence and the Constitution. Their sermons evinced deep anger over the enslavement of their southern brethren, the discrimination blacks faced in the North, and the widespread denigration of black intellectual and moral capacities. Yet these men differed in their assessments of the American nation. Some despaired of America and yet continued to call the nation to account for its sins. Others were more optimistic about the future end of slavery and the place of blacks in the nation. They saw themselves as not only ministers and servants of God but as moral agents entrusted with representing the race and articulating the strivings and hopes of America's disgraced African slaves. Even so, many of their sermons were devoted to moral or spiritual growth, traditional doctrines of Christianity, and the narratives and teachings of scripture. In this regard, they shared a common heritage with white Christians; yet it was marred by a deep racial divide and profoundly different experiences as (non)citizens of the nation.

Black Christians in the Land of Egypt

Like the ancient Hebrews, who expressed joy and excitement over their deliverance from Egypt, African Americans interpreted the end of slavery as answered prayer and deliverance by God from the house of bondage. Separation and consolidation were the two marked qualities of black religion in the post–Civil War South. Black churches and white churches were almost completely segregated by the late 1870s. Primarily because blacks preferred their own preachers, desired to govern their own affairs, and were tired of second-class treatment, they formed their own churches. Black churches became the center of black life: they were the primary institutions controlled and owned by blacks, and they operated for the most part outside of the purview of direct white supervision.

Black churches also went through a sorting-out process before they could become consolidated. Doctrinal, denominational, class, and cultural differences and geography were all factors in the consolidation of black churches into mostly black Baptist and Methodists churches, with a smattering of Episcopalian, Presbyterian, Congregationalist, Lutheran, and Catholic churches in various parts of the South and the North. In the South, Methodists and Baptists dominated. Consolidation coexisted with denominational cooperation, even though many blacks were fiercely loyal to their own denomination. Black political leaders emerged principally from the churches.[11] Several reasons account for this development. Churches were among the few voluntary institutions that blacks owned, and those leaders who rose to positions of power had practical experience with church government and the kind of politicking that few other environments would provide. Respect and symbolic authority attached to church leaders, and such men were usually already held in high esteem by their peers and parishioners. The church also put black leaders into intimate and sustained contact with the everyday problems, aspirations, and concerns of African Americans. In turn, the churches provided a community of support and affirmation for aspiring leaders. Black leaders developed a sense of communal identity and connection with blacks in the context of the churches. No other institution functioned in this way for blacks in the late nineteenth century.

Although the period from 1880 to 1920 has been referred to as the nadir of race relations by some historians, Evelyn Brooks Higginbotham argues that it was during this period that black women within the National Baptist Convention, the largest black denomination, broadened the public arm of black churches and made them into the most powerful institutions of self-help in the black community. Within a broader social context in which blacks were losing political power, black churches became not only centers of collective worth and human dignity but also sites of public debate. Black women formed the Women's Convention within the National Baptist Convention in 1900. With a membership of over 1 million women, the Women's Convention governed its own agenda, elected its leaders, and developed criteria that won the respect and emulation of other women. Black women developed a discourse of resistance, a feminist theology that critiqued not only the racism of the broader society but also gender restrictions within black churches. Higginbotham describes this double burden for black church women: "Black women found themselves in the unique position of being at once separate and allied with black men in the struggle for racial advancement while separate and allied with white women in the struggle for gender equality."[12] At least for these elite black women, the churches served as communities that provided a public venue for protest against the racism of American society and sources of frustration because of gender restrictions against women in the churches.

Between 1915 and 1918, half a million black southerners relocated to the North. In the 1920s, another 700,000 went north looking for jobs and seeking to escape racial oppression. The Great Migration transformed black life in several ways. It placed blacks in a more fluid social environment and made possible the proliferation of diversity within the black Christian community and movement beyond Christianity; it caused blacks to develop a heightened racial consciousness and a sense of belonging to a larger community; and it thrust the churches into an industrial environment with secular and rival organizations that forced black churches to practice a Christianity that addressed more than individual salvation or personal morality, as was so common among many migrants from the rural South. A social Christianity emerged in this context—but also a self-conscious Christian community more aware of its need to evangelize and reach an audience that it could no longer take for granted. Blacks had entered modernity in the North, and efforts were now made to learn the psychology of a new audience, to increase not only the churches' numbers but also the very viability and cultural authority of black Christianity in a new and alien environment.

The urbanization of black life increased expectations for black churches. Ministers were expected to concern themselves with a wide range of secular activities: political action, protest against discrimination, advice on finding jobs, and the encouragement of black businesses.[13] Ministers now argued that if they did not attend to the "needs" of their congregants, their churches could not survive. In their massive study of black life in Chicago in the late 1930s and early 1940s, sociologists St. Claire Drake and Horace Cayton noted that because the segregation of blacks from whites at the congregational level was "almost absolute," black churches were especially subject to criticism to the extent that they did not express "race loyalty." Churches were charged with "advancing the race," and black ministers were in fact freer to engage a range of issues because they were not dependent on whites, as were civic leaders. It was precisely because of their "freedom" that they were expected be "real race men" who supported the interests of the community.[14] The burden placed upon black churches thus increased in the urban context.

Urbanization was a long-term and sporadic process. Prior to the 1960s, many blacks continued to live in the South. For those who remained in the South, especially in its rural hinterlands, the possibilities of change and progress seemed distant. Black churches often served as places that softened the pain of the daily grind of working in the cotton fields and experiencing slights from a hostile white world. Many sermons focused on heaven as the ultimate freedom from the hardships of this life. A minister in a church in Indianola, Mississippi, in the 1930s preached about those who "may be rich in earthly wealth, but poor in heavenly treasures." He judged them "rich for [earthly] time, but poor for eternity."[15] Was this a veiled critique of wealthy planters who made their livings on the backs of overworked and underpaid black field hands? Perhaps. But the sermon was mainly intended to comfort weary black sharecroppers. They were reminded that "the earth is a little isle, eternity the ocean around it." In this situation, they should not despair, because the "Christian is rich in the things which money cannot buy—a contented mind, [and] peace of heart."[16] Time was short. One should set one's mind on things above. These kinds of messages are precisely the reason that scholars and those outside the church criticized black churches in the rural South for being "otherworldly." Even Hortense Powdermaker, the anthropologist who transcribed this sermon, argued that the church served as "an antidote, a palliative, an escape." She believed that it helped blacks to endure the status quo by relieving and counteracting the discontent that would usually make for rebellion against injustice.[17] Yet Powdermaker also noted that churches allowed blacks to freely exercise their talents and powers and to contribute to their sense of self-respect. Black churches helped shape a culture that worked on black subjects by enabling them with great difficulty to attempt to vanquish bitterness in their hearts against whites who insulted, degraded, and murdered them.[18] This cathartic function of black religion is often undervalued or overlooked by writers on "the Negro church," who are generally preoccupied with questions about how the church engages in political reform or attempts to change the social system. But a more complex analysis of the variety of ways in which churches functioned in the everyday lives of black Americans, especially in the rural South, allows us to move beyond such a generalized and sterile debate about the function of "the black church."

The pervasive violence against blacks in the South was noted by observers in the 1930s, especially in local studies of Sunflower County, Mississippi. John Dollard, a social psychologist, observed that the "threat of lynching is likely to be in the mind of the Negro child from earliest days." Dollard reported many conversations with blacks whose memories of "such events came out frequently" in his life history studies. He concluded that every "Negro in the South knows that he is under a kind of sentence of death."[19] In the midst of these harsh circumstances, Powdermaker noticed frequent calls from black church pulpits to "love one another" and one's neighbors, which included white plantation owners and those who oppressed blacks.[20] Although she noted that younger blacks were becoming impatient with these religious doctrines and passive approach to oppression, she felt that many blacks still accepted and tried to live by these Christian beliefs:

These Negroes are believing Christians who have taken very literally the Christian doctrine that it is sinful to hate. Yet on every hand they are faced with situations which must inevitably produce hatred in any normal human being. These situations run the scale from seeing an innocent person lynched to having to accept the inferior accommodations on a Jim Crow train. The feeling of sin and guilt is frequently and openly expressed. In a Sunday-school class in a southern rural colored church a teacher tells the tale of a sharecropper who had worked all season for a white planter, only to be cheated out of half his earnings. The teacher's lesson is that it is wrong to hate this planter, because Christ told us to love our enemies. The members of the class say how hard it is not to hate but that since it is sin they will change their hate to love. They regard this as possible, though difficult.[21]

It was within this social and historical context that Benjamin Mays and Joseph Nicholson's *The Negro's Church* (1933) made the compelling case that within the churches African Americans felt as though they were "somebody" and experienced themselves as full human beings. Here blacks found the "freedom to relax" and a place where they could temporarily cease looking at themselves through the eyes of others, "of measuring one's soul by the tape of a world that looks on in amused contempt and pity."[22] We may note the social and psychological buffers that churches provided African Americans without overstating their ability to protect blacks from actual violence and racial oppression in the South. Black churches continue to be significant, in part because of their important role in helping blacks through one of the most difficult times of their history.

African American Christianity in Contemporary America

As in most varieties of American Christianity, women have made up the bulk of the membership in black churches. Women have not usually occupied positions of formal authority within churches but have often served in a variety of less than public roles, though women ministers have become more common, in response to feminism, urbanization, and the drift of men away from the churches. Women have contributed time, money, and expertise to church boards, missionary endeavors, educational and Sunday school projects, and the general morale of the church. As early as the 1930s and 1940s, women had become so dominant in black churches that studies of the urban North complained about the dearth of men and its implications. Black men did indeed drift away from churches in significant numbers, composing less than a third of church membership among Chicago's working- and lower-class blacks (the majority of blacks) in 1945. The reasons varied: the

increasing availability of other forms of recreation; complaints about the ir-
relevance of church to modern living and its alleged effeminacy, especially
among black youth; identification with radical political and "racial" movements; and the desire to "get ahead," which left little time for church attendance.[23] Even before the widespread influence of new technologies, the face
of black Christianity was mostly female and thus had to address the issues
that black women faced.

In the late twentieth century, televangelists had a significant influence
on the practice of African American Christianity, especially among black
women. Televangelists de-emphasize race, preach a form of individualism,
and heighten hopes for material success and prosperity if one has faith and
believes the right things.[24] Though it is difficult to make a causal connection—and certainly many other forces are at work— the continued exposure
to this kind of preaching has partly destabilized the salience of race even as
it makes possible greater involvement in a particular "church" away from
actual church services (through television, the Internet, audio cassettes, CDs,
and DVDs). African American preacher T. D. Jakes, for example, has reached
a vast audience of black women through his conferences and workshops. He
has addressed many difficult issues such as rape and domestic abuse in his
books, television broadcasts, and sermons.[25] The growth of megachurches
like Jakes's Potter's House (Dallas) and Bryon Brazier's Apostolic Church
of God (Chicago), which sponsor activities throughout the week, does not
simply indicate their success at catering to a niche market, as a crass and
reductionistic economic model would suggest. Rather, the continuing vitality of multipurpose churches in black neighborhoods reflects a historical
heritage of churches providing entertainment, social services, and spiritual
and psychological aid to members.

Because sociologists have demonstrated that interracial churches are quite
small in number and that various attempts at racial reconciliation have not
been successful in the long term, there is no indication that the separation
of Christians in America will end anytime soon.[26] Thus black Christianity
for the foreseeable future is likely to remain *black*, which means that black
Christians will continue to be seen as part of a black church while whites
will be rightly seen as a diverse religious lot. However, the salience of race is
slowly declining as the historical memory of injury and oppression gradually erodes. Thus black churches face the same challenges of other Christians
in contemporary America: trying to remain authentically Christian (vari-

ously defined by different groups) in a consumer culture that co-opts and tames modern religion. Yet geography and history still impose unique duties on the shoulders of black churches. In urban areas, we can expect to see churches like Jeremiah Wright's continuing to take on gang violence, broken schools, and inequality, all the more so as government infrastructure sags because of a weak tax base and low public concern about mostly black and immigrant neighborhoods. Black Christians' overwhelming support for social programs and policies that seek to address these historical inequalities is one reason that white evangelical Christians, who in significant numbers reside in suburban communities, differ politically from black Christians. African American Christians know that in reality they can only do so much to address the problems that continue to mainly affect black communities, no matter what others may say about "the black church" and its range of duties. President Barack Obama's lauding of the emphasis on individual *and* "collective salvation" in black churches signifies one of the major fault lines in religion in modern America, with many conservative Christians criticizing him for failing to emphasize exclusive personal faith in Jesus. (Of course, this is not simply a racial fault line. Many white liberal Protestants, Catholics, and progressive Jews also share these political and social values espoused by Obama and black churches.) It remains to be seen whether the race line can be resolved or dissolved by Christianity. We have yet to see if W. E. B. Du Bois's prediction for America in the twentieth century remains a prophecy for the churches in the twenty-first century: the persistence of the problem of the color line in American Christianity.

NOTES

1. James T. Campbell, *Songs of Zion: The African Methodist Episcopal Church in the United States and South Africa* (Chapel Hill: University of North Carolina Press, 1998), 20.

2. Francis Le Jau, *The Carolina Chronicle of Dr. Francis Le Jau, 1706–1717*, ed. Frank W. Klingberg (Berkeley: University of California Press, 1956), reprinted in *Slavery: A Documentary History in North America*, ed. Willie Lee Rose (Athens: University of Georgia Press, 1999), 29.

3. Sylvia R. Frey and Betty Wood, *Come Shouting to Zion: African American Protestantism in the American South and British Caribbean to 1830* (Chapel Hill: University of North Carolina Press, 1998), 63–79.

4. Albert J. Raboteau, *Slave Religion: The "Invisible Institution" in the Antebellum South* (New York: Oxford University Press, 1978), 64–65.

5. Donald G. Mathews, *Religion in the Old South* (Chicago: University of Chicago Press, 1977), 42.

6. Ibid. See also Christine Heyrman, *Southern Cross: The Beginnings of the Bible Belt* (Chapel Hill: University of North Carolina Press, 1997), 46.

7. Frederick Law Olmsted, *The Cotton Kingdom: A Traveller's Observations on Cotton and Slavery in the American Slave States*, ed. Arthur M. Schlesinger (1861; New York: Modern Library, 1984), 462.

8. Eugene D. Genovese, *Roll, Jordan, Roll: The World the Slaves Made* (New York: Vintage Books, 1976), 246–47.

9. For the most recent work on Allen as a "founding father," see Richard S. Newman, *Freedom's Prophet: Bishop Richard Allen, the AME Church, and the Black Founding Fathers* (New York: New York University Press, 2008).

10. *Constitution of the American Society of Free Persons of Color, for Improving Their Condition in the United States, for Purchasing Lands, and for the Establishment of a Settlement in Upper Canada; Also, the Proceedings of the Convention, with Their Address to the Free Persons of Color in the United States* (Philadelphia: I. W. Allen, 1831); found in Dorothy Porter, ed., *Early Negro Writing, 1760–1837* (Baltimore: Black Classic Press, 1995), 179.

11. Eric Foner, *Reconstruction: America's Unfinished Revolution, 1863–1877* (New York: Harper and Row, 1988), 93.

12. Evelyn Brooks Higginbotham, *Righteous Discontent: The Women's Movement in the Black Baptist Church, 1880–1920* (Cambridge: Harvard University Press, 1993), 80.

13. St. Claire Drake and Horace Cayton, *Black Metropolis: A Study of Negro Life in a Northern City* (1945; Chicago: University of Chicago Press, 1993), 428, 653–54.

14. Ibid., 424, 427–28.

15. Hortense Powdermaker, *After Freedom: A Culture Study in the Deep South* (1939; Madison: University of Wisconsin Press, 1993), 393.

16. Ibid. 394.

17. Ibid., 285.

18. Ibid., 247.

19. John Dollard, *Caste and Class in a Southern Town* (1937; Garden City, N.Y.: Doubleday Anchor Book, 1957), 359, 331.

20. Powdermaker, *After Freedom*, 247.

21. Hortense Powdermaker, "The Channeling of Aggression by the Cultural Process," *American Journal of Sociology* 48 (May 1943): 754.

22. Benjamin Elijah Mays and Joseph William Nicholson, *The Negro's Church* (1933; New York: Arno Press, 1969), 281–82. I have taken the liberty of using the last clause in the above sentence from W. E. B. Du Bois's "Strivings of the Negro People" (1897), which became part of his *Souls of Black Folk* (1903). See Brook Thomas, ed., *Plessy v. Ferguson: A Brief History with Documents* (Boston: Bedford, 1997), 143.

23. Drake and Cayton, *Black Metropolis*, 612.

24. Marla Frederick, *Between Sundays: Black Women and Everyday Struggles of Faith* (Berkeley: University of California Press, 2003), 140–42.

25. See Shayne Lee, *America's New Preacher: T. D. Jakes* (New York: New York University Press, 2005).

26. Brad Christerson, Korie L. Edwards, and Michael O. Emerson, *Against All Odds: The Struggle for Racial Integration in Religious Organizations* (New York: New York University Press, 2005), 3–6. The authors regard churches as segregated if 90 percent or more of a congregation is of one race.

Christians and Non-Christians in the Marketplace of American Religion

On September 9, 1844, South Carolina governor James H. Hammond issued the following Thanksgiving Day Proclamation to the citizens of his state:

> Whereas, it becomes all Christian nations to acknowledge at stated periods, their dependence on Almighty God, to express their gratitude for His past mercies, and humbly and devoutly to implore His blessing for the future:
>
> Now, therefore, I, James H. Hammond, Governor of the State of South Carolina, do, in conformity with the established usage of this State, appoint the first Thursday in October next, to be observed as a day of Thanksgiving, Humiliation and Prayer, and invite and exhort our citizens of all denominations to assemble at their respective places of worship, to offer up their devotions to God their Creator, and his Son Jesus Christ, the Redeemer of the world.[1]

Most South Carolinians paid no attention to Hammond's proclamation. They were Christian, he was Christian, and the proclamation, which claimed to be "in conformity with the established usage of this State," expressed sentiments that, as Christians, they found unremarkable. But the proclamation did catch the attention of non-Christians, who noted that the document identified the state, indeed the nation as a whole, as a Christian one, relegating them to outsider status. The document also assumed that "citizens of *all* denominations" would offer up devotions to "Jesus Christ, the Redeemer of the world." This left them to wonder what their status was in the State of South Carolina, and whether, in the governor's eyes, they remained full citizens or not.[2]

Governor Hammond's proclamation highlights a key aspect of the relationship of Christians to non-Christians in the United States, that is, the use of state power to advance Christianity in the marketplace of American religion, to the disadvantage of non-Christians. Government proclamations at Thanksgiving and especially at Christmastime were for many decades tinged with Christianity. As recently as 1962, President John F. Kennedy proclaimed, triumphantly, that "Moslems, Hindus, Buddhists, as well as Christians pause from their labors on the 25th day of December to celebrate the birthday of the Prince of Peace. There could be no more striking proof that Christmas is truly the universal holiday of all men."[3] Wherever the state has publicly exercised and displayed its authority, from the public square to the public school and from the armed forces to correctional institutions, the faith of the majority has tended to win a recognition that minority faiths are denied. In realms where the state has not intruded, by contrast, competition operates more freely. There, amid the thrusts and counterthrusts of majority and minority faiths, both are transformed.

In the case of Governor Hammond's 1844 proclamation, Jews, then the largest and most visible of America's non-Christian faiths, felt particularly aggrieved. South Carolina was home to approximately 1,000 Jews, among them cultural and political figures of renown and individuals of substantial wealth and influence. Jews had resided in South Carolina since colonial days and gloried in being what the dramatist, editor, and educator Isaac Harby had called "a portion of the people." In Charleston, where the bulk of the state's Jews lived and where the majority of inhabitants were black slaves, Jews' skin color and multilayered ties to the community's elite had, for some time, rendered them political insiders. Now Governor Hammond's proclamation called this vaunted status into question.[4]

Some Jews wrote to the governor to complain. His own political advisers urged the governor to apologize for an "oversight" and make amends. But the proud governor, who did not much like Jews and considered their complaints "insolent" and "impertinent," obdurately refused. In response, Jews kept their synagogues closed on Thanksgiving Day of 1844; they felt that they had no other choice.[5]

A memorial, signed by 110 members of the Charleston Jewish community, set forth what would become a standard response from non-Christians to the claims of those who excluded them. Quoting from the constitutions of the state and the federal governments, the Jewish petitioners demanded their rights as citizens: "We propose to test the position you have assumed, by that constitution, which you have sworn to support. From that alone do you derive your present authority. Thank God, sir, that noble instrument, together with the Constitution of the United States, presents a glorious panoply of defence against the encroachments of power, whether its designs be bold or insidious. Under its universal and protecting spirit, we do not sue for *toleration*, but we *demand our rights*."[6] In addition, Jews warned, as they would on most such occasions, that to exclude them would be to create a dangerous precedent: "The *Catholic*, the *Unitarian* . . . and numerous other sects may find their privileges *discriminated* away, and their most cherished opinions crushed or slighted by a gubernatorial preference." The issue, as they saw it, came down to minority rights. "The constitution," they declared in a later "report" published in the press, "has nothing to do with the relative numbers of the citizens—with popular or unpopular modes of faith." What affected them now "might at another time be fatal to the rights of other minorities."[7]

Governor Hammond, whose term in office was ending, viewed the Jewish complaint as an affront to his authority. "I answered it pretty sharply, refused to make an apology, and defended my Proclamation," he reported to his diary.[8] That defense, notwithstanding its sarcastic language and intemperate tone, offered a significant Christian counterthrust to the arguments put forth by the Jews. It won him "a good many compliments" at the time and set forth arguments that, worded differently, would continue to echo down to the present day.[9]

First, Hammond insisted that America was culturally and self-consciously Christian. Even an avowedly poor Christian like himself—"I am not a professor of religion; nor am I specially attached by education or habit to any particular denomination"—still "always thought it a settled matter that I lived in a Christian land!"[10]

Second, he questioned whether religiously neutral prayers were either possible or desirable. "A Proclamation for Thanksgiving which omits to unite the name of the Redeemer with that of the Creator is not a Christian Proclamation," he explained, "and might justly give offense to the Christian People."[11]

Third, he countered Jewish claims concerning threats to minority rights by warning against minority group imposition: "If in complaisance to the Israelites and Deists, his [Jesus'] name must be excluded, the Atheists might as justly require that of the Creator to be omitted also; and the Mahometan or Mormon that others should be inserted."[12]

Finally, he pointed to other laws and institutions of the state that were "derived from Christianity," notably legislation forbidding labor on Sunday, the Christian Sabbath. Would these too, he wondered, now be called into question? Where Jews had pleaded for minority rights, he now made a forceful case for the Christian majority, "ninety-nine hundredths of my fellow citizens."[13]

The Jewish community was taken aback by Hammond's response. At a well-attended meeting, Jews made clear that what they actually sought was inclusive language, a proclamation addressed, as many earlier ones had been, to "our Christian fellow-citizens" as well as to members of "all other denominations." Rather than continuing an intemperate debate, they resolved to publish all of the correspondence in the press, allowing "public opinion of the country" to decide the issue.[14]

The issue, of course, was never decided. Instead, Hammond's clash with the South Carolina Jewish community reflected *ongoing* themes in the confrontation between the Christian majority and the non-Christian minority in the United States. It posed the same intractable and explosive questions that would forever after characterize these confrontations: questions concerning the role of Christianity in American life, the relationship of the state to Christianity, the prerogatives of the Christian majority versus the rights of the non-Christian minority, and linkages between the rights of particular groups of non-Christians and the rights of every American. In later years, Mormons, Muslims, Buddhists, members of new religions, and atheists would, when confronting the Christian majority, face questions of a parallel kind. All would have occasion to wonder whether the marketplace of American religion is truly free, open, and competitive or whether, in reality, Christianity enjoys state protection and support that non-Christian faiths are denied.

Confrontations in the Public Square

Confrontations resulting from questions like these generally played out in one of four tension-filled arenas where state power is exercised and displayed: the public square, the public school, the armed forces, and correctional institutions. These spaces, where citizens of different faiths (and no faith) meet and engage one another, individuals are formed and reformed, and civic culture is exhibited, are perennial scenes of conflict. Disputes over the character of these spaces reflect, at the deepest level, contending visions of American society as a whole.

The first of these arenas, the public square, was once self-evidently Christian. The Christian calendar, with its Sunday-Sabbath and major winter and spring holidays, prescribed its settled rhythms. Church spires in close proximity to city hall shaped its sacred landscape. Government laws and proclamations articulated its highest values. Even where no particular form of Christianity was "established," the public square marked time, regulated space, and bolstered values in accordance with Christian religious norms. Non-Christians, who observed different days of rest, celebrated unfamiliar religious holidays, upheld alternative values and lifestyles, and worshiped in places other than Christian churches, threatened those norms.[15]

Jews, as members of perhaps the largest and most visible non-Christian faith in the United States, were parties to many of these disputes. They took the lead, for example, in battling against "Sunday laws," regulations ("blue laws") designed to protect the sanctity of the Christian Sabbath and to guarantee all workers a day of rest and the freedom to attend church. Since Jews observed the seventh rather than the first day of the week as Sabbath, they found such laws oppressive and sought either to repeal them or to gain exemption from them.[16]

Jews likewise waged war against Christian missionaries who sought to convert them. As a beleaguered minority, they viewed missionizing as a violation of their religious liberty, recalling that the Northwest Ordinance of 1787 had promised that "no person, demeaning himself in a peaceable and orderly manner, shall ever be molested on account of his mode of worship or religious sentiments." They strove not only to rebut the missionaries but also to strengthen communal defenses and to shore up communal weak spots that missionaries sought to exploit.[17] Later, Jews battled to keep the public square free of sectarian Christmas decorations, such as nativity scenes. The state, they insisted, had no business employing its power to promote Christian holidays that non-Christian Americans neither recognize nor celebrate.[18]

Jews, of course, were not alone in challenging Christian control of the public square. Bans on the religious use of peyote, efforts to prevent *santeria* ritual slaughter, and restrictive zoning regulations that function to exclude non-Christian houses of worship from religiously mixed neighborhoods reflect similar, albeit more recent, disputes over the control and character of publicly shared spaces. What the character of the public square should be—avowedly Christian, entirely stripped of religious symbols, or opened up to the widest array of religious symbols and practices—remains an unresolved American dilemma.

The Public Schools—Temples of Liberty?

The character of America's public schools has long posed a similar dilemma, and schools have therefore served as another arena of conflict between

Christians and non-Christians. In the late nineteenth century, Jews imagined that the public schools were to be, in the words of the Cincinnati Jewish merchant and communal leader Julius Freiberg, "temples of liberty," where "the children of the high and low, rich and poor, Protestants, Catholics and Jews, mingle together, play together, and are taught that we are a free people, striving to elevate mankind, and to respect one another. In them we plant and foster the tree of civil and religious liberty."[19] In real life, though, schools often fell far short of that ideal. William Holmes McGuffey's *Third Eclectic Reader* (1836–37) taught a generation of public schoolchildren that "the Scriptures are especially designed to make us wise unto salvation through Faith in Christ Jesus." The "Old Testament," according to that reader, was the Jews' "own sacred volume" and contained "the most extraordinary predictions concerning the infidelity of their nation, and the rise, progress, and extensive prevalence of Christianity."[20] Many a public schoolteacher read out uncomfortable passages from the New Testament to her charges. "On Good Friday," the Jewish lawyer Louis Marshall recalled, "the reading always related to the crucifixion and the . . . word 'Jew' was mentioned in such a manner as to convey the idea not only of contempt, but also of hatred. This was always followed during the recess and for several days after by the most hostile demeanor on the part of the Christian boys and girls of the school, some of whom resorted to physical violence."[21] No wonder Rabbi B. H. Gotthelf of Louisville detected a "sectarian and missionary spirit, that governed the teachers and was manifested in the schoolbooks" of the public schools.[22]

The twentieth century brought with it no resolution to this problem. Fueled in part by mainstream Protestants who saw public schools as a vehicle for Americanizing the immigrants and beating back competing faiths, pressure to strengthen the religious component of state-sponsored education heightened. Jewish and Catholic pupils suffered particularly acutely, for both prayers and Bible readings tended to be cast in a Protestant mold. Nor did released-time programs, which took youngsters out of school for religious training, solve the problem. "Practices employed by over-enthusiastic religious groups in many communities," the *American Jewish Year Book* reported in 1947, "not only involve the public schools as a co-partner in the enforcement of their own sectarian instruction, but employ public school facilities." Teachers in some communities pressured students to attend Protestant religious classes; in others, Jewish students were taunted for studying apart from everybody else. In one unhappy incident, all children were asked to pledge allegiance to a "Christian flag" as a mark of their "respect for the Christian religion."[23] The dilemma for Jews and other religious minorities was whether, given these abuses, *all* released-time programs should be opposed, even at the risk of angering the Christian majority and being charged with "godlessness," or whether in the interests of goodwill and interfaith harmony, only the abuses themselves should be attacked, not the program as a whole. The Supreme Court, in a series of decisions, resolved that dilemma. Not only did it declare released-time programs unconstitutional in the public schools, but it went on to outlaw school prayer and devotional readings of the Bible as well. This, however, by no means resolved all issues concerning the place of Christianity in the public schools. In short order, debates arose over curricular issues, holiday celebrations, team prayers, and religious invocations at graduation exercises. In the public school, as in the public square, majority rule and minority rights seemed perennially in conflict.[24]

Religious Liberty versus Military Discipline

The military represents a third arena where Christians and non-Christians have repeatedly clashed. Military tradition inevitably privileges conformity and discipline: as a result, non-Christians, even in early America, frequently faced discrimination. Uriah Phillips Levy, who entered the U.S. Navy in 1812 and fought his way up through the ranks, was court-martialed half a dozen times by those who opposed him as a Jew. In a celebrated 1857 appeal against efforts to strike him from the navy's roll, officers admitted that many of Levy's problems stemmed from prejudice and hostility toward his religion. "What is my case today, if you yield to this injustice, may tomorrow be that of the Roman Catholic or the Unitarian, the Presbyterian or the Methodist, the Episcopalian or the Baptist," Levy warned the court, echoing the Jewish response to Governor Hammond. A panel of inquiry restored him to service.[25]

Three years later, however, the government's military chaplaincy law kept alive the tradition of discrimination against non-Christians. It stipulated that a regimental chaplain be a "regularly ordained minister of some Christian denomination." In the face of Jewish protests, one evangelical paper warned that "Mormon debauchees, Chinese priests, and Indian conjurors" would stand next in line for government recognition, tacit admission that the central issue under debate concerned non-Christians' religious rights. Those rights were only restored indirectly by construing the words "some Christian denomination" in the original law to mean "some religious denomination."[26] Today, over 130 different faiths and denominations, including Jews and Buddhists, have military chaplains of their own, but Don Larsen, a chaplain who applied to become the first Wiccan chaplain in the armed forces, was denied, reputedly out of a concern for "good order and discipline."[27] Arguments based on military discipline similarly underlay the U.S. Air Force's concerted and ultimately unsuccessful effort (1981–86) to prevent an Orthodox Jewish officer from covering his head with a skullcap (yarmulke) in keeping with his religious beliefs.[28] Reconciling the military's interest in discipline and uniformity with minority-group religious practices that are (by definition) nonconforming has never been easy.

Reconciling Majority Rule and Minority Rights

For similar reasons, correctional institutions have witnessed complex confrontations between Christians and non-Christians. Nonconforming foodways, such as kosher food and halal food; nonconforming calendars with different rest days and holy days; and nonconforming prayer requirements of Orthodox Jews and Muslims scarcely jibe with prison regimens designed around Christian norms. "Faith-based" Christian programs to fight substance abuse and transition prisoners back into society raise, for members of minority faiths, the same kinds of questions posed, as we have seen, since pre–Civil War days: Is it appropriate for the state to use its power to recognize and advance the majority's faith? What should be the appropriate role of Christianity in American life? Where do the prerogatives of the Christian majority end and the rights of the non-Christian minority begin? What is the domino effect of injustices against non-Christian minorities? How do they ultimately affect the rights of other minorities, and of Americans generally?

Whatever issue occasions a confrontation between the Christian majority and non-Christian minorities—a governor's proclamation, a school textbook, a Christmas crèche, a menorah in the public square, a faith-based program for incarcerated prisoners, or something else—the question lurking behind the scenes inevitably concerns the character of the country as a whole. Strident debates over church-state separation and the meaning of the First Amendment to the Constitution evoke so much passion because they hit upon fundamental questions of power and social position. Much is at stake in how these volatile issues are resolved. In effect, they determine who is a "protected" insider, who is a "suppressed" outsider, and how majority rule and minority rights are to be reconciled.

The Competitive Religious Marketplace

Many public encounters between Christians and non-Christians do not, of course, involve the government. They reflect the ordinary workings of the competitive religious marketplace, free of state interference. A year after Governor Hammond's confrontation with the Jews of his state, for example, Isaac Leeser, the "minister" (hazan) of Congregation Mikveh Israel in Philadelphia and editor of the monthly *Occident*, America's first successful Jewish periodical, called upon American Jews to unite in forming "a Jewish Publication Society." "No effort is spared," he complained, "to diffuse false views concerning our faith among the Gentiles." In response, he urged Jews to emulate Christian publishers in preparing "suitable publications to be circulated among all classes of our people." "This is, in fact, the plan adopted by our opponents," he declared, "and shall we not profit by them?"[29]

The Jewish Publication Society that Isaac Leeser and his supporters soon established did closely emulate its Christian counterparts. Among Christians, the press had become, in Nathan Hatch's words, "the grand engine of a burgeoning religious culture, the primary means of promotion for, and bond of union within, competing religious groups,"[30] and Leeser felt that the same could happen among Jews. He had already demonstrated the power of the press through his books and journal, but now he set about publishing Jewish religious tracts, each about 125 pages long. Some contained stories based on the Bible and Jewish legends; others presented "affecting tales," heavily Victorian in tone, designed to combat missionaries, prevent intermarriage, and foster observance of the Sabbath; still others, like Leeser's own *The Jews and Their Religion*, treated more academic subjects. All were cheaply produced and printed as part of a series entitled *The Jewish Miscellany*, the very title recalling the *Tract Magazine and Christian Miscellany*, which the Jewish series aimed to counter. Some fourteen different booklets appeared over the next five years, but the series never achieved commercial success. On the night of December 27, 1851, fire swept through the building where most of the stock was stored, and the whole enterprise went up in smoke.[31]

While it lasted, Leeser's Jewish Publication Society competed with its Christian counterparts by borrowing tactics and employing them to Jewish ends. In the free marketplace of religion, where non-Christians did not have to contend with state power arrayed against them, ordinary competition determined success. Nothing prevented Jews and others from studying the methods of the majority and employing them to buttress their own minority positions. Indeed, by selectively emulating the Christian majority, non-

Christian faiths became stronger—better able to preserve their religious integrity.[32]

The Jewish Sunday school, begun by Rebecca Gratz in Philadelphia in 1838, illustrates this phenomenon. Founded to "follow the example of other religious communities" and in the very city where the Christian Sunday school movement was centered, it openly sought to adapt the Protestant model of American education to Judaism.[33] The Sunday school provided Jewish boys and girls with knowledge of the Bible, as Jews understood it, and with catechistic answers to basic questions of faith from a Jewish perspective. The goal was to ensure that "there shall not be a Jewish child ignorant [of] *why* he is a Jew."[34] Children who might not otherwise have known how to respond to challenges from their Christian peers were fortified by their Sunday school lessons. One popular textbook, for example, taught that "God is but one . . . we do not worship any being besides him." It also warned children that "should any designing persons . . . attempt to seduce us from our religion, we must resist such temptation with the firm resolution to live and die in the religion of our forefathers."[35] For all that it emulated its Protestant namesake, the Jewish Sunday school thus basically aimed to compete with Protestant teachings. Its goal was to keep Jews Jewish.

When Protestants, beginning in 1864, established free "mission schools" in Jewish immigrant areas, ostensibly to offer instruction in the Hebrew language but with the clear aim of converting their charges, Jews similarly countered by establishing "free schools" of their own, with great success. "If there had been no 'Jewish missions' in New York, we should have had no Hebrew Free Schools with nearly 3,000 children as pupils," the *Jewish Messenger* admitted in 1888; "the conversionists are our benefactors."[36] Whenever public schools preached Christianity, Jews expressed anger, for that pitted them against the forces of the state and called into question their status as equal citizens. Mission schools, by contrast, received no government support. Jews, as a result, competed with them on a level playing field where they felt much more confident.

Many similar examples could be adduced. Jewish hospitals, Jewish philanthropy, and Jewish orphanages all were stimulated and shaped, at least in part, by competitive pressures from the Christian majority.[37] More broadly, Judaism, like many other non-Christian faiths, democratized and opened up new roles for women in response to Protestant pressures.[38] Where once, for example, synagogue seating was stratified by class and separated by gender, most synagogues over time adopted the patterns of free seating and mixed (family) seating common in American churches. Even in Orthodox synagogues, where men and women continued to be separated by a partition, their seating areas came more and more to be equalized.[39]

Toward a Religious Free Market

Harvey Cox has observed that "few faiths ever escape modification when they collide or interact with others. Most profit from such encounters."[40] This, of course, holds true for American Christianity no less than for its minority counterparts. Indeed, just as Christian religious outsiders like Christian Scientists and Pentecostals "have been an indispensably dynamic force in American religious history," so too non-Christian outsiders.[41] The music and dance of African religions, the meditations and mysticism of Asian religions, the culture and philanthropy of Judaism—all have enriched American Christianity. American Christianity, for its part, has likewise enriched the religions that it has touched.

The relationship between Christianity and non-Christian religions in America has thus been a reciprocal one. In the face of a state power that distorts the functioning of the religious marketplace, competition serves as a restorative. Where the Christian majority and non-Christian minorities in the United States compete freely, they learn from one another, borrow from one another, and strengthen one another.

NOTES

1. *Occident* 2 (1845): 500–10; reprinted in Jonathan D. Sarna and David G. Dalin, *Religion and State in the American Jewish Experience* (Notre Dame: University of Notre Dame Press, 1997), 113.

2. Ibid., 112–21, reprints Hammond's exchange with the Jewish community. For background, see Drew Gilpin Faust, *James Henry Hammond and the Old South: A Design for Mastery* (Baton Rouge: Louisiana State University Press, 1982), 249.

3. *Public Papers of the Presidents of the United States: John F. Kennedy, 1962* (Washington D.C.: Government Printing Office, 1962), 888. For other examples of such Christological Christmas messages, see Jonathan D. Sarna, "Is Judaism Compatible with American Civil Religion? The Problem of Christmas and the 'National Faith,'" in *Religion and the Life of the Nation: American Recoveries*, ed. Rowland A. Sherrill (Urbana: University of Illinois Press, 1990), 155–56. For an 1812 Thanksgiving Proclamation that met with Jewish protests, see *Occident* 1 (1844): 435; and for other examples, see *Publications of the American Jewish Historical Society* 13 (1905): 19–36; and 20 (1911): 133–35.

4. For South Carolina Jewish history, see Barnett A. Elzas, *The Jews of South Carolina* (Columbia: University of South Carolina Press, 1905); Charles Reznikoff and Uriah Z.

Engelman, *The Jews of Charleston* (Philadelphia: Jewish Publication Society of America, 1950); James W. Hagy, *This Happy Land: The Jews of Colonial and Antebellum Charleston* (Tuscaloosa: University of Alabama Press, 1993); and Theodore Rosengarten and Dale Rosengarten, eds., *A Portion of the People: Three Hundred Years of Southern Jewish Life* (Columbia: University of South Carolina Press, 2002). The Harby quote is found in ibid., xv, 75.

5. See Carol Bleser, ed., *Secret and Sacred: The Diaries of James Henry Hammond, a Southern Slaveholder* (New York: Oxford University Press, 1988), 94, where Hammond refers to the brother of Moses Cohen Mordecai as a "miserable Jew." For other quotes, see ibid., 125–26; and Faust, *James Henry Hammond*, 249.

6. Sarna and Dalin, *Religion and State in the American Jewish Experience*, 114.

7. Ibid., 115, 119–20.

8. Bleser, *Secret and Sacred: The Diaries of James Henry Hammond*, 126.

9. Ibid., 138.

10. Sarna and Dalin, *Religion and State in the American Jewish Experience*, 116.

11. Ibid. Privately he recorded in his diary that "whatever may be my religious doubts, I could not conscientiously omit the name of Jesus Christ in my public worship." Bleser, *Secret and Sacred: The Diaries of James Henry Hammond*, 138.

12. Sarna and Dalin, *Religion and State in the American Jewish Experience*, 116.

13. Ibid., 116–17.

14. Ibid., 118–21. "This will be a three days talk for the public," Hammond predicted in his diary after reading the Jews' report. "It has drawn on me the everlasting and malignant hostility of the whole tribe of Jews, which is very unpleasant in many ways." Bleser, *Secret and Sacred: The Diaries of James Henry Hammond*, 126. Hammond's successor, Governor William Aiken, made a point just one day after his inauguration of issuing a new Thanksgiving Proclamation, which disavowed Hammond's principles and (much to the latter's disgust) carefully employed language inclusive of the Jewish community. Ibid., 137–38.

15. Richard John Neuhaus, *The Naked Public Square: Religion and Democracy in America* (Grand Rapids, Mich.: Eerdmans, 1984), depicts the changing public square and what he sees as the consequences of those changes.

16. Sarna and Dalin, *Religion and State in the American Jewish Experience*, 139–65; Naomi W. Cohen, *Jews in Christian America: The Pursuit of Religious Equality* (New York: Oxford University Press, 1992), 58–64, 72–79, 214–39; Morton Borden, *Jews, Turks, and Infidels* (Chapel Hill: University of North Carolina Press, 1984), 103–29.

17. Jonathan D. Sarna, "The American Jewish Response to Nineteenth-Century Christian Missions," *Journal of American History* 68 (June 1981): 35–51; Jonathan D. Sarna, "The Impact of Nineteenth-Century Christian Missions on American Jews," in *Jewish Apostasy in the Modern World*, ed. Todd M. Endelman (New York: Holmes and Meier, 1987), 232–54; Yaakov Ariel, *Evangelizing the Chosen People: Missions to the Jews in America, 1880–2000* (Chapel Hill: University of North Carolina Press, 2000).

18. Sarna, "Is Judaism Compatible with American Civil Religion," 152–73.

19. Lloyd P. Gartner, "Temples of Liberty Unpolluted: American Jews and Public Schools, 1840–1875," in *A Bicentennial Festschrift for Jacob Rader Marcus*, ed. Bertram W. Korn (New York: Ktav, 1976), 157–89 (quote is from p. 180); Cohen, *Jews in Christian America*, 79–87.

20. John H. Westerhoff, *McGuffey and His Readers: Piety, Morality, and Education in Nineteenth-Century America* (Nashville: Abingdon, 1978), 138–39. See Neil Baldwin, *Henry Ford and the Jews: The Mass Production of Hate* (New York: Public Affairs, 2001), 1–7, for McGuffey's influence on Henry Ford.

21. Louis Marshall to William Fox, December 2, 1927, as quoted in Gartner, "Temples of Liberty Unpolluted," 175–76. Since Marshall was born in 1856, he was presumably describing experiences dating back to the 1860s or the early 1870s.

22. Gartner, "Temples of Liberty Unpolluted," 175.

23. *American Jewish Year Book* 49 (1947–48): 32; *Central Conference of American Rabbis Yearbook* 53 (1943): 80.

24. Sarna and Dalin, *Religion and State in the American Jewish Experience*, 16–27, 190–226; Cohen, *Jews in Christian America*, 115–22, 159–213.

25. Melvin I. Urofsky, *The Levy Family and Monticello, 1834–1923* (Monticello: Thomas Jefferson Foundation, 2001), 81; Marc Leepson, *Saving Monticello* (New York: Free Press, 2001); Abram Kanoff, "Uriah P. Levy: The Story of a Pugnacious Commodore," *Publications of the American Jewish Historical Society* 39 (1949): 1–66. See, for more broadly on anti-Semitism in the military, Joseph W. Bendersky, *The Jewish Threat: Anti-Semitic Politics of the U.S. Army* (New York: Basic, 2000).

26. Bertram W. Korn, *American Jewry and the Civil War* (New York: Atheneum, 1970), 56–97, esp. 64; Jonathan D. Sarna, *American Judaism: A History* (New Haven: Yale University Press, 2004), 119–20.

27. Alan Cooperman, "For Gods and Country: The Army Chaplain Who Wanted to Switch to Wicca? Transfer Denied," *Washington Post*, February 19, 2007, C01, at http://www.washingtonpost.com/wp-dyn/content/article/2007/02/18/AR2007021801396_pf.html (accessed September 28, 2008).

28. On the 1986 case of *Goldman v. Weinberger*, see Sarna and Dalin, *Religion and State in the American Jewish Experience*, 278–81. An act of Congress, in 1987, overturned the Supreme Court decision in the military's favor and granted members of the armed forces the right to wear religious apparel, such as a skullcap, so long as it was "neat and conservative."

29. [Isaac Leeser], "Address of the Jewish Publication Committee to the Israelites of America," preface to *Caleb Asher*, no. 1 of *The Jewish Miscellany* (Philadelphia: Jewish Publication Society of America, 1845), 1–4; reprinted in Paul Mendes-Flohr and Jehuda Reinharz, *The Jew in the Modern World*, 2nd ed. (New York: Oxford University Press, 1995), 461–62. Leeser was particularly incensed by the publication in 1845 of *The Jew at Home and Abroad* (Philadelphia: American Sunday-School Union, 1845).

30. Nathan O. Hatch, *The Democratization of American Christianity* (New Haven: Yale University Press, 1989), 126.

31. Jonathan D. Sarna, *JPS: The Americanization of Jewish Culture, 1888–1988* (Philadelphia: Jewish Publication Society, 1989), 1–4; Lance J. Sussman, *Isaac Leeser and the Making of American Judaism* (Detroit: Wayne State University Press, 1995), 152–54.

32. See Lance J. Sussman, "Isaac Leeser and the Protestantization of American Judaism," *American Jewish Archives* 38 (1986): 1–21; and for a broader evocation of this theme, see Gerson D. Cohen, "The Blessing of Assimilation in Jewish History," in *Jewish History and Jewish Destiny*, ed. Gerson D. Cohen (New York: Jewish Theological Seminary of America, 1997), 145–56.

33. Joseph R. Rosenbloom, "Rebecca Gratz and the Jewish Sunday School Movement in Philadelphia," *Publications of the American Jewish Historical Society* 48 (1958): 71–78 (quote is from p. 71); on Gratz and the Sunday school, see Dianne Ashton, *Rebecca Gratz: Women and Judaism in Antebellum America* (Detroit: Wayne State University Press, 1997), esp. 121–69.

34. Isaac Leeser, *The Claims of the Jews to an Equality of Rights* (Philadelphia: C. Sherman, 1841), 86.

35. Salomon Herxheimer, *Doctrines of Faith and Morals for Jewish Schools and Families*, 2nd ed. (Louisville: Terrell, Dietz, 1874), 17–18, 54.

36. *Jewish Messenger*, May 18, 1888, p. 4; for sources that echo this theme, see Sarna, "The Impact of Nineteenth-Century Christian Missions," 252n43.

37. Sarna, "The Impact of Nineteenth-Century Christian Missions," discusses this theme.

38. Jonathan D. Sarna, "The Democratization of American Judaism," in *New Essays in American Jewish History*, ed. Pamela S. Nadell, Jonathan D. Sarna, and Lance Sussman (forthcoming, American Jewish Archives).

39. Jonathan D. Sarna, "The Debate over Mixed Seating in the American Synagogue," in *The American Synagogue: A Sanctuary Transformed*, ed. Jack Wertheimer (New York: Cambridge University Press, 1987), 363–94.

40. Harvey G. Cox, *The Seduction of the Spirit: The Use and Misuse of the People's Religion* (New York: Simon and Schuster, 1973), 121.

41. R. Laurence Moore, *Religious Outsiders and the Making of Americans* (New York: Oxford University Press, 1986), 21. Moore considers Jews in his volume but focuses mostly on Christian "religious outsiders."

Tensions Within

The Elusive Quest for Christian
Cooperation in America

Christians in America have struggled to get along with one another from the moment the colonial impulse first arose. Only a year after Columbus sailed to the Americas, Pope Alexander VI had to issue the 1493 bull *Inter Caetera* to resolve the competing colonial claims of Portugal and Spain and thereby protect the harmonious expansion of Christendom in the New World. Over the next century, the Protestant Reformation intensified the link between colonization and conflict, as Protestant and Catholic states raced to claim territory for their respective religions. The proliferation of Protestant sects only increased religious conflict in Europe, leading some of the persecuted to flee to the Americas for refuge. In 1564, a band of French Protestants, known as Huguenots, settled in Florida in search of freedom to practice their Calvinist form of Protestantism. Yet even in the New World, religious conflict proved hard to escape. Spain's king ordered the colony destroyed the year after the Huguenots arrived. The Spanish admiral who carried out the massacre posted a sign identifying the Huguenots' religion, rather than their ethnicity or politics, as the cause of their suffering: "I do this, not as to Frenchmen, but as to Lutherans."[1]

Religion remained a primary category by which Americans measured each other, even as colonial dominance shifted from Catholic Spain to Protestant England in the seventeenth century. Religious conflict also continued as an impetus to colonization. Pilgrim leader William Bradford explained that rather than opposition from "heathens," it was "the persecutions . . . of the Christians one against [an]other" that forced the Pilgrims to flee from England.[2] Like the English Pilgrims—and the French Huguenots and the Spanish Catholics before them—most immigrants to America have been Christian. But from the very beginning, those immigrants have been anything but unified in their religious beliefs and practices, as Catherine Albanese's survey of Christian diversity in America makes clear. As a result, American Christians have constantly renegotiated their relationships with one another as they have encountered an ever-expanding variety of Christian expression.

Relations among American Christians have moved along a continuum ranging from intense and even violent conflict at one end to remarkable cooperation at the other. These interactions have occurred at every level of society, from governmental enforcement of exclusion and toleration, to denominational competition and cooperation, to local and even individual acts of persecution and compassion. Four periods of American Christian history illustrate many of the ways that American Christians have related to one another: seventeenth-century Puritan New England, the Second Great Awakening of the early nineteenth century, the Modernist-Fundamentalist controversy of the early twentieth century, and the ecumenical movement of the mid- to late twentieth century. From the first of these eras, American Christians were aware of the presence of Jews in their midst, and in subsequent centuries new waves of immigration led to interactions with increasing numbers of Buddhists, Hindus, Muslims, and other non-Christians. Still, even in the context of this ever-expanding religious pluralism, what was true for Bradford's Pilgrims has remained so ever since: tensions from within the faith have influenced the shape of American Christianity more than threats from without.

Constructing and Challenging Puritanism in Colonial New England

Settlers to the earliest American colonies embarked with a vision of a religiously homogeneous society. Whether it was Spanish Florida, Anglican Virginia, or Puritan Massachusetts, these first colonists replicated the European state-church model: Government prescribed the way Christians related to one another through its powers to suppress religious dissent and to exclude nonconformists.[3] Protected by the power of the state, colonists would not have to interact with traditions that might threaten the ideal societies they hoped to create. Nowhere was this hostility to competing forms of Christianity more evident than in Puritan New England. American Puritans covenanted themselves into religiously homogeneous ecclesiastical and civil communities in hopes of redeeming both church and society according to their Calvinist principles. Understanding themselves to be "knit together in this work as one man," the communal dimension of their endeavor was essential. To that end, they brooked no dissent. In Dedham, Massachusetts, town members signed a covenant "to profess and practice one truth" and to prevent discord by the promise that "we shall by all means labor to keep off from us all such as are contrary minded, and receive only such unto us as may be probably of one heart with us." The quest for uniformity across the entire colony was evident in a 1631 Massachusetts law requiring all voters to belong to a Puritan congregation. The statute concerned more than ensuring civility within the state. American Puritans understood themselves to be on a divinely ordained mission to settle New England. Their ability to get along harmoniously was one measure of their faithfulness, which would determine the extent to which God would continue to bless the Puritan enterprise.[4]

New England Puritans took seriously the preservation of a pure and religiously conforming society that would ensure God's continued favor. Quakers were early targets of religious persecution in New England. Mary Fisher and Ann Austin were the first Quakers to arrive in the American colonies when they landed in Boston in 1656. The two women were immediately imprisoned, accused of witchcraft, and strip-searched for evidence. Their books were burned, and their prison cells were boarded to prevent their having conversation with or receiving food from Bostonians. Five weeks after their arrival, they were deported back to Barbados from which they had sailed. A mere two days after their departure, eight more Quakers arrived by ship and received the same treatment. Following these incidents, the Massachusetts Bay Colony passed laws ensuring that subsequent Quaker arrivals would face the already established pattern of arrest, whipping, and expulsion and that ship captains who transported Quakers to the colony would be fined. As Quaker missionaries devised new ways to reach Massachusetts, the colony responded with harsher punishments, culminating in the hanging death of four Quakers between 1659 and 1661. Although King Charles II ordered an end to the hangings, Puritans persisted in the pattern of arresting and expelling Quaker interlopers.[5]

The Puritan response to Quaker missionaries is also an example of how disagreement concerning women's roles has been a source of conflict in American Christianity. Quaker doctrines of equality before God scandalized Puritans because they enabled women such as Mary Fisher and Ann Austin to become preachers and missionaries, speaking in public and traveling alone. Although Puritan theology acknowledged a wife's spiritual equality, it nonetheless limited that equality to the privacy of the home and subjected it to the authority of male ministers. As a result, the relative freedom accorded Quaker women to preach and to speak publicly led Puritans to punish them as both theological heretics and threats to the social order. Puritans routinely characterized religious dissenters, including Quakers, as feminine, using the same language of weakness and vulnerability to describe both women and any person (male or female) susceptible to theological error. The accusations of witchcraft, the need to strip-search, and the emphasis on isolating Quakers—all suggest the gendered overtones that characterized the Puritan response to Quakers. Just as women were responsible for the Fall, now women and feminine religions threatened the purity of New England. As with the Quaker missionaries, the continuing conflicts surrounding gender in American Christianity have stemmed as much from the presence of women as public voices as from the content of their speech.[6]

Catholicism was another threat to New England's religious purity. To prevent contamination, a 1647 Massachusetts law threatened prison for the first offense and death for the second to any "Jesuit, or spiritual or ecclesiastical person ordained by the authority of the Pope, or See of Rome [who] shall henceforth at any time repair to, or come within this jurisdiction."[7] Colonial anti-Catholicism perpetuated the fundamental Protestant-Catholic divide of European Christianity and laid the foundation for America's most enduring religious conflict. Protestants did not consider Catholics to be Christian. They were, however, superstitious and anti-intellectual, sexually perverse, and conspiratorially working for the political and religious domination of the world. Cotton Mather's 1702 history of New England, *Magnalia Christi Americana*, claimed that a prime reason many Puritans migrated to New England was to "raise a bulwark against the kingdom of anti-Christ, which the Jesuites labor to rear up."[8] Puritan New England did not have a monopoly on anti-Catholicism, as Catholic settlements in French Canada and in Maryland elevated the sense of urgency for Protestants throughout the colonies. Fears of Catholic missionary success among Natives heightened the sense of crisis among Protestants, who recognized that Native appropriations of rival forms of Christianity would make already difficult Native-colonial relations even harder. By 1700, eleven of the original thirteen colonies had laws restricting both the civil and the religious liberties of Catholics. Even Maryland, originally established as a haven for English Catholics, gave way to a Protestant majority that imposed legal restrictions on Catholic worship and civic participation. Anglicans and Puritans joined together to destroy Catholic churches, deport priests, and attack the Catholic governor, Lord Baltimore, when he supported the Catholic-leaning king rather than the Protestant Parliament during the English civil war. By 1702, Anglicans had legally established the Church of England in Maryland and passed laws forbidding Catholics from worshipping in public.[9]

Hatred of Catholics united otherwise disparate Protestants into a common cause.

In other colonies, the relations between competing forms of Christianity, including Catholicism, were less conflicted. The founders of Rhode Island and Pennsylvania instituted varying degrees of state-mandated toleration, thereby ensuring that Christians of diverse traditions could live together, even when they did not agree. Rhode Island was founded by Roger Williams, a Puritan who had been expelled from Massachusetts in 1635 for his critique of Puritan inconsistencies. Religious dissenters in Rhode Island retained their civil and religious rights, a freedom unmatched by any other colony. It quickly became a haven for a wide variety of Christian expression. Anne Hutchinson joined Williams in Rhode Island after the Boston General Court expelled her in 1638 for overstepping acceptable bounds as a female religious teacher. Hutchinson, whose followers included Mary Dyer, who later experienced persecution as a Quaker missionary in Massachusetts, stands among the earliest examples of the ways gender could threaten Puritan orthodoxy. Further south, William Penn founded Pennsylvania as a refuge for persecuted Quakers but also opened his colony to Christians of all kinds, including Catholics. Penn believed "liberty of conscience" to be a God-given right that people of faith must honor in their relations with one another.[10] Neither Williams nor Penn suggested that Christians must seek theological unity to act civilly toward one another. Nor did a commitment to toleration lead either man to abandon claims of his own tradition's superiority. Williams engaged Quakers in a public and tense four-day debate, which was later published as an anti-Quaker tract—even as he continued an increasingly exclusive search for pure Christianity, which took him from Puritan to Baptist, finally to become a spiritual seeker independent of any church. By the time of Williams's death in 1683, the American colonies had established models for Christian interaction that ranged from homogeneous exclusivism to broad toleration.[11]

Christian Cooperation and Challenges to Protestant Hegemony in Antebellum America

The nineteenth century began with a wave of revivals known as the Second Great Awakening. The revivals were interdenominational affairs, drawing leaders and participants from across the spectrum of evangelical Protestantism. The newly converted swelled the ranks of a broad range of Christian churches. The Awakening continued for three decades, significantly increasing not only the number of Christians but also their diversity and the variety of traditions to which they adhered. Out of the Second Great Awakening emerged new opportunities for cooperation, even as the widespread revivalism furthered existing tensions and created new ones.

Evangelism of the new nation's western territories and frontier was among the driving forces of the Second Great Awakening. The nineteenth century had opened with one of the first explicitly ecumenical and cooperative efforts, the 1801 Plan of Union between Congregationalists and Presbyterians, which helped realize the new desire for missions and signaled the cooperative ethos of the new century. Putting aside their differences, which were rooted in regional and organizational differences rather than theology, the two denominations agreed to cooperate in their mission efforts in the Old Northwest. A shared concern that an unconverted frontier threatened the nation's Christian (meaning Protestant) character had prompted the denominations to move from a competitive and even conflicted relationship into a cooperative one. The union lasted thirty years before it fell prey to internal conflicts among Presbyterians. Nonetheless, memories of the Plan of Union lived on as it became a frequently invoked precedent for twentieth-century ecumenical efforts to forge cooperative agreements between denominations.[12]

Missions to slaves were another evangelical focus emerging from the Second Great Awakening. Following modest success in converting slaves during the previous two centuries, the revivals of the early nineteenth century resulted in a substantive expansion of slave Christianity. The revivals of the earliest years were often radically inclusive, featuring both gender and racial mixing, not only among participants but even among preachers. But the brief moment of cooperation transcending race and gender quickly gave way to traditional hierarchies. Nonetheless, the floodgates had opened, and no degree of control by white masters or plantation missionaries could stop the emergence of a distinct slave Christianity that emphasized biblical narratives of deliverance and apocalypse over and against white efforts to teach Christianity as obedience to earthly masters, which would result in freedom only in the afterlife. At the same time, free blacks in the North formed independent congregations and denominations to escape their unequal treatment in predominantly white denominations and to worship without the restrictive interpretations imposed upon them. Despite repeated attempts by African Americans and a few sympathetic whites, the line separating black and white churches would outlast slavery, and it continues today as a visible division in American Christianity. Native American Christians experienced similar exclusion, as conversion to Christianity neither prevented the loss of land nor enabled their inclusion as equals in church or society. Both the promise and the failures of the Second Great Awakening reveal the extent to which race has been a fundamental and often impassible barrier to cooperation in American Christianity.

The missionary movements directed toward Indians, slaves, and settlers in the American West were just one part of a whole range of cooperative reform efforts that emerged from the Second Great Awakening. Collectively known as the Benevolent Empire, these societies brought like-minded Christians together into voluntary societies, each committed to purging the nation of a particular ill or converting those not yet saved within the evangelical Protestant framework that dominated the era. Besides missions and education, these Protestant alliances directed their attention to a variety of other issues, including literacy, Sabbath-keeping, temperance, prostitution, and slavery. So pervasive were the organizations that one critic complained that "a peaceable man can hardly venture to eat or drink, to go to bed or get up, to correct his children or kiss his wife, without obtaining the permission and the direction of some moral or other reform society."[13]

The Benevolent Empire's mostly lay leadership came from a variety of Protestant traditions, which warned that the work was too important to suffer from sectarian divisions. The American Bible Society declared in its founding constitution that "sectarian littleness and rivalries can find no avenue of admission."[14] The leaders of the Benevolent Empire signaled a new era of interdenominational cooperation as they moved beyond even the bilateral cooperation of the Plan of Union to welcome the participation of Protestants from a multitude of backgrounds. The voluntary societies also increased the number of people able to participate because their membership came from all interested individuals rather than just from denominationally appointed representatives. The resulting alliances advanced Protestant cooperation by subordinating denominational differences to the shared essentials of faith. As Presbyterian minister and social reform advocate Albert Barnes explained, "The church of Christ is not under the Episcopal form, or the Baptist, the Methodist, the Presbyterian or the Congregational form exclusively; all are, to all intents and purposes, to be recognized as parts of one holy catholic church."[15]

Even as the Second Great Awakening fostered cooperation among some Christians, it heightened tensions between others. One corollary to the growing Protestant collaboration was an expanded campaign against Catholics. The Benevolent Empire's voluntary societies played an important role in spreading anti-Catholic views, especially through their vast array of publications. Antebellum Protestants stoked the embers of anti-Catholic sentiment in response to the waves of immigration that would make Catholicism larger than any single Protestant denomination by the mid-nineteenth century. (Protestants as a whole continued to outnumber Catholics.) The united animosity of Protestants against Catholics was also evident in schools, especially in conflicts over Bible reading. Catholics repeatedly complained about the use of the Protestant King James Version of the Bible. Without acknowledging the irony, Protestants responded that accommodating Catholic concerns would introduce sectarianism. Conflicts over the Protestant character of public schools led many Catholics to withdraw and erect their own private schools. Others did not give up so easily, though they paid a heavy price. In Boston, a school official spent half an hour bloodying a Catholic schoolboy's hand with a stick for refusing to read a Protestant version of the Ten Commandments. A Jesuit in Maine was tarred, feathered, and run out of town following a dispute over Bible reading in the schools. In Philadelphia, the bishop's request that schoolchildren be allowed to read a Catholic translation of the Bible was one cause of that city's 1844 riots, which left fourteen dead and was the nation's deadliest outbreak of anti-Catholic violence.[16] Watching these conflicts unfold, children absorbed lessons that would ensure subsequent generations of suspicion and hostility.

As nineteenth-century Protestants intensified their assaults on American Catholics, they amplified themes that stretched back through the colonial era to the Protestant Reformation. Protestants railed against the dangers of Catholicism to both Christianity and the American nation in every format conceivable, from scholarly theological critiques to periodicals such as *The Protestant* and from poetry to fiction to illustrations in popular magazines such as *Harper's Weekly* and the *Atlantic Monthly*. Regardless of the context in which it appeared, the outlines of anti-Catholicism were the same. Catholicism manifested every possible evil and theological error, marking it as the anti-Christ and the "Whore of Babylon," who signaled impending apocalypse. Nor could Catholics be good Americans, since their loyalty to Rome inhibited the ability to act democratically or patriotically. Protestants also remained suspicious of Catholic motives in the United States. Lyman Beecher, an esteemed minister and president of Lane Seminary in Cincinnati as well as Harriet Beecher Stowe's father, published a fund-raising letter warning of a papal conspiracy to subvert the United States via a new Catholic headquarters in the Mississippi Valley.

Voyeuristic sexual exposés joined political conspiracies as another popular anti-Catholic theme. Protestants found Catholic celibacy fascinating and frightening, reacting with confusion and suspicion to priests and nuns and their departure from Protestant constructions of gender. Priests failed to become heads of households, while nuns were unable to achieve the ideals of feminine piety best expressed through domesticity. These gender anxieties pervaded anti-Catholic materials, which often depicted priests as feminine and nuns as "manly," and suggested that the sisters hid evidence of their deviant sexual practices under their garb and behind the walls of their convents. Maria Monk's *Awful Disclosures of Maria Monk* (1836) purported to unveil the secret sexual debauchery of priests and nuns, including babies buried in a tunnel between the convent and the priests' seminary. Like most tales of salacious nuns and predator priests, Monk's volume was patently false. Nonetheless, the novels could have deadly consequences. Those who deviated from the dominant Protestant expectations for women continued to attract persecution and create tensions in American Christianity. A mob burned a convent to the ground when parts of Rebecca Reed's forthcoming *Six Months in a Convent* were leaked in conjunction with false rumors that the same Charlestown, Massachusetts, Ursuline convent was holding a nun against her will.[17]

The only other religious conflict that approached the virulence of anti-Catholicism was against Mormonism, which was just one of many new religious expressions to emerge from the revivals of the Second Great Awakening. Protestants drew on many of their anti-Catholic themes to articulate their new conflict with Mormons. Anti-Mormons pointed to tyrannical leaders whose demands for loyalty ran counter to the American system separating church and state, and Latter-day Saint teachings that the United States was home to the New Jerusalem seemed evidence of a subversive plot. The Mormon preference for distinct communities apart from those they considered "gentiles," as well as secret rituals conducted in temples closed to the public, only fueled the conspiratorial fires. Once Joseph Smith announced his revelation permitting polygamy, Mormon sexual deviance became the primary evidence for the threat that Mormonism posed, not just to Christian principles but also to the moral fabric necessary for the preservation of a democratic society. Some opponents argued that such practices made Latter-day Saints non-Christian (the Saints understood themselves to be the only expression of true Christianity), and others denied that Mormonism was a religion at all. Alexander Campbell, a revivalist preacher and founder of the Disciples of Christ denomination, declared Smith an atheist.

Denying Mormons the status of a religion would also exempt them from claiming religious protection under the First Amendment. Incredulity about Smith's claims of conversing with God and angels and of translating golden plates into the Book of Mormon led many to believe he was a charlatan in pursuit of worldly gain. Accordingly, opponents focused on exposing Mormonism as counterfeit, prominently featuring words such as "exposed" and "unveiled" in the titles of their anti-Mormon tracts.[18]

But Mormonism's rapid growth suggested that written persuasion was not enough to stop the movement Joseph Smith had launched. Protestant antagonists turned to more direct forms of confrontation, which further elevated the tensions with Latter-day Saints. Some ministers were not content to speak from their pulpits, choosing instead to go into the community and engage Saints, challenging them privately and in public debates. More confrontational were those who disrupted Mormon meetings to present charges of religious heresy and fraud. As with anti-Catholicism, the hostile relationships could turn violent. Real or threatened hostilities from surrounding communities and the repeated imprisonment of Smith and other leaders forced the Latter-day Saints to move frequently in the 1830s. The 1838 Mormon War in Missouri left twenty-one Mormons dead and led to the departure of nearly 10,000 Latter-day Saints for Illinois. In Illinois, the violence culminated in the murder of Joseph Smith and his brother in 1844 and the expulsion of the entire Mormon community two years later. Though opposition followed the Mormons to Utah, it subsided as slavery and the Civil War took center stage on the national agenda. In the 1870s and 1880s, conflict with Mormonism reemerged in the antipolygamy campaign. In this latter phase, antipolygamists turned to the federal government for support, recalling colonial models in which civil authorities rather than individuals or religious bodies structured and enforced religious conflict and cooperation. With the 1890 Woodruff Manifesto, which ended polygamy, Christian perceptions of Mormons began a slow and still uncompleted transformation from objects of scorn to potential partners in matters of common concern.[19]

Conservatives and Liberals
The Great Divide in Twentieth-Century Christianity

The opening of the twentieth century continued the contradictory impulses in American Christianity, simultaneously pointing toward both conflict and cooperation. The divisive dimension was most evident in the Modernist-

Fundamentalist controversies. Reflecting the progressive spirit of the age, Modernists were confident that God was guiding human progress. Accordingly, Modernists adapted religious thinking to the advances they saw in contemporary culture. They embraced new modes of learning as consistent with faith, including the scientific theory of evolution and the new methods of biblical scholarship known as "higher criticism." The Modernist movement stressed the goodness of humanity and a confidence in progressive ideals, which worked together to move society toward the kingdom of God. Tests of orthodoxy and confessional conformity distracted from their progressive goals, so Modernists rejected them in favor of religious toleration.[20] Fundamentalism emerged as an aggressive rejection of Modernism, emphasizing the inerrancy and literal truth of scripture in all matters, including history and science. Fundamentalists stressed belief in the Virgin Birth, Jesus' bodily resurrection, and the literal truth of miracles to underscore their supernatural as opposed to scientific view of the world. They also emphasized human sinfulness and the imminent destruction of the world—in contrast to Modernist optimism about human nature and progress. A series of booklets entitled *The Fundamentals*, which lent the movement its name, set forth the uncompromising points of doctrine. From a Fundamentalist perspective, anyone who disagreed was not a Christian. Modernists agreed that their conflict with Fundamentalists left no room for compromise.[21]

Still, this was a disagreement among white Protestants. The early twentieth-century Modernist-Fundamentalist controversy revealed the extent to which long-standing divisions between Protestantism and Catholicism, and between black and white Protestants, remained dividing lines within American Christianity. Both Catholics and black Christians read and interpreted the Bible differently than their feuding counterparts, avoiding both the literalism and the new biblical scholarship that was dividing white Protestants.

The clash between Fundamentalists and Modernists in the first quarter of the twentieth century created a fault line that has shaped much of American Christianity ever since. Admittedly, Fundamentalists failed in both parts of their initial assault on Modernism: they neither gained control of denominational leadership and institutions nor did they overturn the teaching of evolution. The denominational battles played out among northern Presbyterians and Baptists, while the battle over evolution culminated in the 1925 Scopes trial. Although Fundamentalists technically won the battle to convict Scopes, they lost the larger cultural war as the trial played out before the American public. But subsequent reports of Fundamentalism's demise were greatly exaggerated. Although some retreated into schismatic denominations, many remained in their more liberal churches. They stayed connected to one another and their conservative ideals through a variety of interdenominational associations, which included Bible colleges such as Moody Bible Institute in Chicago and BIOLA University in Los Angeles, summer gatherings such as the Niagara Bible Conferences, and a sophisticated use of media including radio and television. Starting in the 1970s, and with increasing vigor ever since, this expanding alliance of Fundamentalist, evangelical, Holiness, and Pentecostal Christians, reentered the public square to challenge their liberal opponents. Women's rights, the sexual revolution, the antiwar movement, the outlawing of prayer in schools, and the legalization of abortion were among the problems that conservatives believed were undermining the nation's moral foundation. Racial integration as an infringement on local and individual rights was another issue motivating conservatives, highlighting the continued divisiveness of race in American Christianity. With alliances between religious and political conservatives evident in the 1980 election of Ronald Reagan, the resurgence was complete.[22] The crevice that emerged in the Modernist-Fundamentalist controversy had become a gaping canyon that reconfigured the nation's religious landscape.

By the last quarter of the twentieth century, the gap that separated conservative and liberal Christians had replaced denominationalism as the prism through which American Christians most often viewed each other. Denominationalism had been on the decline as rising educational and income levels erased socioeconomic distinctions between church traditions. At the same time, church members increased the frequency with which they changed denominations, a result of geographic mobility and rising rates of marriage across denominational lines. As the differences between denominations diminished, affiliation with a particular tradition no longer predicted how people would stand on religious and moral issues. These changes transformed the way Americans looked for churches, emphasizing compatibility along the conservative-liberal divide more than the name on the sign out front. The gap in American Christianity had become so wide that it better characterized the differences within denominations than the divisions between them. That is, a liberal Congregationalist, Methodist, and Lutheran—and even a Catholic—now have more in common with each other than with conservative members of their same denomination. Each side views the other as the primary opponent—even more than secularism—making the tension between them rather than the division itself the fundamental dynamic of the new religious topography. Surveys reveal how pervasive the bifurcation has become: church members report that increased interaction and familiarity with the other side leads to elevated levels of dislike and mistrust.[23] Still, as has so often been the case in the history of American Christianity, race complicates any effort to reduce divisions into simply binaries. Black churches and denominations often split the conservative-liberal divide, more closely allying with conservatives on theological issues even as they side with much of the social agenda of liberal Christians.

Ecumenical Expansion in the Twentieth Century

But conflict is only half the story of twentieth-century American Christianity. While some began the century digging trenches of division others were building bridges of cooperation. The year 1908 saw the birth of the modern ecumenical movement, as thirty-three Protestant denominations entered into a formal relationship with one another in the Federal Council of Church of Christ in America (FCC). The participating denominations constituted the majority of American Protestantism, including African American Baptist and Methodist denominations, with Southern Baptists and Lutheran communions the most conspicuous absences. Among the FCC's early successes were supporting striking workers and bolstering the military chaplaincy during World War I. The FCC's role was advisory only; it claimed no authority over its member churches nor any desire to create common creeds, polity, or worship. Unity of effort and purpose, rather than organic union into a single church, was its aim. This broadly construed intent facilitated the inclusion of Russian, Syrian-Antioch, Romanian, and Ukrainian Orthodox churches into the FCC before mid-century. The FCC also played an important role in the 1948 formation of the World Council of Churches, the largest international ecumenical organization.[24]

In 1951, the National Council of Churches of Christ in the U.S.A. (NCC) became the successor to the FCC and eleven other interdenominational agencies. The NCC has remained the nation's largest ecumenical council since its founding and has maintained a broad membership, retaining several African American denominations as well as most of the Eastern Orthodox communions in the United States. The NCC has a variety of agencies that address, for example, race, gender, war, poverty, education, evangelism, and ecumenism. The NCC also coordinated the biblical translation work that led to the 1952 Revised Standard Version of the Bible and then the New Revised Standard Version in 1989. The 1952 translation was the first English translation to become more widely used than the 1611 Authorized (King James)

Version. The NCC pointed to acceptance of the new translations among Protestant, Orthodox, and Catholic congregations, as well as its advocacy in areas such as race and women's rights, as evidence of what ecumenical endeavors could achieve. At the same time, these perspectives on scripture, race, and gender continued as a crucial dividing line that kept more conservative traditions from joining the NCC. Holiness, Pentecostal, Fundamentalist, and other traditionally conservative denominations have not been a part of the NCC, just as they did not participate in the FCC that preceded it. Many conservative Protestants disagreed with the NCC's agenda, and this dissent fueled the growth of the National Association of Evangelicals (NAE), which has functioned like an ecumenical organization, with agencies dedicated to education, evangelism, missions, and moral issues from an evangelical perspective.[25]

Upheavals in Roman Catholicism introduced a new ecumenical partner in the 1960s. The decade opened with the election of Catholic John F. Kennedy as president, signaling a new acceptance of Catholicism within the majority Protestant nation. During the post–World War II years, many American Catholics had moved out of insular ethnic neighborhoods as a product of rising education and income levels. With the resulting suburbanization and professional diversification of the Catholic population, Protestant and Catholic encounters became more common and less threatening, helping transform Catholics from demonized others into acceptable partners for cooperation in religion, no less than in business or recreation. Most significant for Catholic ecumenical relations were the transformations emanating from the Second Vatican Council (1962–65). Catholic doctrine had officially banned participation in ecumenical endeavors until Vatican II's "Decree on Ecumenism." American Protestants constituted over a third of the delegate observers at the 1964 discussion of the ecumenical decree, which created a Secretariat for Christian Unity, recommended cooperation among all Christians, encouraged dialogue on matters of both faith and practice, recognized Christians of other communions as brothers and sisters in faith rather than as "erring schismatics," and tempered Catholic claims to exclusive truth.

Americans immediately experienced the changes emanating from Vatican II. In 1965, a newly created Catholic Bishops' Commission for Ecumenical Affairs inaugurated ongoing dialogues with a variety of Protestant and Orthodox traditions to explore theological commonalities and opportunities for cooperation. The Bishops' Commission also worked with the NCC, which soon had several Catholic priests and nuns on its staff. Other institutional manifestations of the Catholic ecumenicity included the entrance of

Catholic theological centers into the nation's leading interdenominational academic consortiums in places like Berkeley, Boston, Chicago, and Washington, D.C. But not all Catholics agreed with the changes. The Second Vatican Council's tolerance for dissenting voices created space for these critics to voice their concerns and to establish special-interest organizations that inflected American Catholicism with the same conservative-liberal divide that characterized the nation's Protestant denominations.[26]

Still, neither the successes nor the failures of these relations between denominations reveal the extent of Christian cooperation over the last century. Even as ecumenical task forces debated the nuances of polity and theology, interdenominational associations in local communities across the nation brought Christians together to cooperate in common tasks that transcended the theological and bureaucratic minutia that often preoccupied national councils. These local expressions of Christian cooperation drew in a broader denominational diversity than did the FCC and NCC. The longing for Christian cooperation was especially evident in the wake of Vatican II. Within a month of the council's close, Catholics and Protestants initiated interfaith meetings to deal with race. Others participated in a program called "living room dialogues," which brought together Catholic and Protestant neighbors for conversation in homes. There were over 150,000 dialogue guides in circulation within three years of the program's start. The manuals themselves were an ecumenical endeavor, jointly produced by the NCC and the Catholic Paulist Press. Protestants and Catholics also gathered for Bible study, in prayer groups, and for joint worship, in which they shared all but the Eucharist. Local church councils and ministerial associations experienced an influx of Catholic members. Even mixed marriages between Protestants and Catholics became more common and accepted. Fifteen years after the close of Vatican II, Catholic historian and Jesuit James Hennesey claimed that a mere two decades earlier the extent of interdenominational cooperation would have been "far beyond the wildest imaginings."[27]

Into the Future
Cooperation and Conflict in the Twenty-first Century

Twenty-first-century Christians continue to traverse the continuum between conflict and cooperation in ways that both repeat and innovate on the patterns of four centuries of Christian history in North America. The increasing breadth of ecumenical endeavors suggests a yearning for Christian unity, even as many interdenominational organizations organize and operate in ways that reinforce rather than transcend divisions. The proliferation of nondenominational megachurches suggests a postdenominational age, even as these churches create organizations that function much like the denominations and councils about which they proclaim such cynicism. Meanwhile, both the media and partisans in the religious divide often miss moments when conservatives and liberals confound traditional dichotomies and find new ways to work together on issues such as the environment, HIV/AIDS, peace, and poverty. The increasing racial and ethnic diversity of American Christianity, alongside continuing debates about the role of women, complicate and transcend points of cooperation and conflict. Nor have traditional denominations disappeared, despite the significant realignments that have taken place. Denominational Christians still fight vigorously over the leadership, institutions, and future of their communions. In recent years, debates over homosexual marriage and ordination have become a flash point, dividing Christians in typical patterns within and across denominations. The conflict dominates national gatherings of many denominations, and some, including Presbyterians and Episcopalians, have endured schism as conservative factions withdraw into alternative ecclesial organizations. Dissenting Episcopalians have aligned with like-minded Anglican communions in Africa and South America, pointing to the international dimensions of the conflicted and cooperative ventures of American Christians. The changing face of worldwide Christianity, whose adherents in the Global South now outnumber those in the Global North, suggests that American Christians' relations with other Christians will increasingly play out on a global stage, where they will undoubtedly discover new sources of conflict and new opportunities for cooperation.[28]

NOTES

1. Kenneth C. Davis, *America's Hidden History: Untold Tales of the First Pilgrims, Fighting Women, and Forgotten Founders Who Shaped a Nation* (New York: Smithsonian Books, 2008), 7–9.

2. William Bradford, *Of Plymouth Plantation, 1620–1647* (New York: Random House, 1981), 2.

3. Chris Beneke, *Beyond Toleration: The Religious Origins of American Pluralism* (New York: Oxford University Press, 2006), 17–19.

4. John Winthrop, "A Model of Christian Charity," in *The American Puritans: Their Prose and Poetry*, ed. Perry Miller (New York: Columbia University Press, 1956), 79–84; Kenneth A. Lockridge, *A New England Town: The First Hundred Years* (New York: W. W.

Norton, 1970), 4–5; Jon Butler, *New World Faiths: Religion in Colonial America* (New York: Oxford University Press, 2007), 52.

5. Sydney E. Ahlstrom, *A Religious History of the American People* (New Haven: Yale University Press, 1972), 178–79; Thomas D. Hamm, *The Quakers in America* (New York: Columbia University Press, 2003), 22–23; "Austin, Ann," "Fisher, Mary," and "Friends, The Religious Society of (Quakers)," in *Dictionary of Christianity in America*, ed. Daniel G. Reid (Downers Grove, Ill.: InterVarsity Press, 1990).

6. Marilyn J. Westerkamp, "Puritan Women, Spiritual Power, and the Question of Sexuality," in *The Religious History of American Women: Reimagining the Past*, ed. Catherine A. Brekus (Chapel Hill: University of North Carolina Press, 2007), 51–72.

7. *The Laws and Liberties of Massachusetts: Reprinted from the Unique Copy of the 1648 Edition in the Henry E. Huntington Library* (San Marino, Calif.: Huntington Library, 1998), 26.

8. Cotton Mather, *Magnalia Christi Americana; or, The Ecclesiastical History of New England* (1702; Hartford, Conn.: Silus Andrus and Son, 1855), 69.

9. Jay P. Dolan, *The American Catholic Experience: A History from Colonial Times to the Present* (Garden City, N.Y.: Doubleday, 1985), 84–85, 89; John Tracy Ellis, *American Catholicism*, 2nd ed. rev. (Chicago: University of Chicago Press, 1969), 19–32; James Hennesey, S.J., *American Catholics: A History of the Roman Catholic Community in the United States* (New York: Oxford University Press, 1981), 36–54.

10. William Penn, "A Persuasive to Moderation to Church Dissenters, in Prudence and Conscience" (1686), in vol. 2 of *The Select Works of William Penn*, 4th ed. (London: William Phillips and George Yard, 1825), 507–42.

11. Edwin S. Gaustad, *Liberty of Conscience: Roger Williams in America* (Grand Rapids, Mich.: Eerdmans, 1991); Beneke, *Beyond Toleration*, 15–48.

12. Catherine L. Albanese, *America: Religions and Religion*, 3rd ed. (Belmont, Calif.: Wadsworth, 1999), 125–26; Ruth Rouse and Stephen Charles Neill, eds., *A History of the Ecumenical Movement*, vol. 1, *1517–1948*, 2nd ed. (Philadelphia: Westminster, 1967), 233–34; Peter W. Williams, *America's Religions: Traditions and Cultures* (Urbana: University of Illinois Press, 1998), 329, 331.

13. Orestes A. Brownson, "Ultraism," *Boston Quarterly Review* 1 (July 1838): 349; Robert H. Abzug, *Cosmos Crumbling: American Reform and the Religious Imagination* (New York: Oxford University Press, 1994); Ahlstrom, *A Religious History of the American People*, 422–28; Williams, *America's Religions*, 176–78.

14. *Constitution of the American Bible Society* (New York: American Bible Society, 1816), 16.

15. Barnes quoted in John Corrigan and Winthrop S. Hudson, *Religion in America*, 7th ed. (Upper Saddle River, N.J.: Pearson–Prentice Hall, 2004), 163; Rouse and Neill, *A History of the Ecumenical Movement*, 1:235–36; Daniel Walker Howe, *What God Hath Wrought: The Transformation of America, 1815–1848* (New York: Oxford University Press, 2007), 192.

16. Ray Allen Billington, *The Protestant Crusade, 1800–1860: A Study of the Origins*

of American Nativism (Gloucester, Mass.: Peter Smith, 1963), 220–37; Dolan, *American Catholic Experience*, 266; Hennesey, *American Catholics*, 122–24; John T. McGreevy, *Catholicism and American Freedom: A History* (New York: W. W. Norton, 2003), 7–11, 19–42, 115–18; Mark A. Noll, *The Old Religion in a New World: The History of North American Christianity* (Grand Rapids, Mich.: Eerdmans, 2002), 87–88, 269.

17. Albanese, *America*, 92, 505–7; Ahlstrom, *A Religious History of the American People*, 559–62; Billington, *Protestant Crusade*, 53–84, 118–41, 345–79; David Brion Davis, "Some Themes of Counter-Subversion: An Analysis of Anti-Masonic, Anti-Catholic, and Anti-Mormon Literature," *Mississippi Valley Historical Review* 47 (September 1960): 217–18; Dolan, *American Catholic Experience*, 201–2; Jenny Franchot, *Roads to Rome: The Antebellum Protestant Encounter with Catholicism* (Berkeley: University of California Press, 1994); Hennesey, *American Catholics*, 119–22, 182.

18. Davis, "Some Themes of Counter-Subversion," 212, 216; Kathleen Flake, *The Politics of American Religious Identity: The Seating of Senator Reed Smoot, Mormon Apostle* (Chapel Hill: University of North Carolina Press, 2003), 64; Terryl L. Givens, *The Viper on the Hearth: Mormons, Myths, and the Construction of Heresy* (New York: Oxford University Press, 1997), 47; J. Spencer Fluhman, "Anti-Mormonism and the Making of Religion in Antebellum America" (Ph.D. diss., University of Wisconsin, 2006), 2–62, 145, 205, 220; Jan Shipps, *Sojourner in the Promised Land: Forty Years among the Mormons* (Urbana: University of Illinois Press, 2000), 69, 71–72; Jan Shipps, "Difference and Otherness: Mormonism and the American Religious Mainstream," in *Minority Faiths and the American Protestant Mainstream*, ed. Jonathan D. Sarna (Urbana: University of Illinois Press, 1998), 85, 88.

19. Flake, *Politics of American Religious Identity*, 1–9, 157; Fluhman, "Anti-Mormonism," 80, 142–43, 155–56, 171–72, 212; Jan Shipps, *Mormonism: The Story of a New Religious Tradition* (Urbana: University of Illinois Press, 1985); Shipps, "Difference and Otherness," 86.

20. William R. Hutchison, *The Modernist Impulse in American Protestantism* (Durham: Duke University Press, 1992).

21. George M. Marsden, *Fundamentalism and American Culture: The Shaping of Twentieth-Century Evangelicalism, 1870–1925* (New York: Oxford University Press, 1980); James Davison Hunter, *Culture Wars: The Struggle to Define America* (New York: Basic Books, 1991), 82–83.

22. Albanese, *America*, 369–88; Hunter, *Culture Wars*, 82–83; Robert Wuthnow, *The Restructuring of American Religion: Society and Faith since World War II* (Princeton: Princeton University Press, 1988), 184, 202, 211; Williams, *America's Religions*, 355–60.

23. Hunter, *Culture Wars*, 77, 91–92; Robert Wuthnow, *The Struggle for American's Soul: Evangelicals, Liberals, and Secularism* (Grand Rapids, Mich.: Eerdmans, 1989), 24; Wuthnow, *Restructuring of American Religion*.

24. Ahlstrom, *A Religious History of the American People*, 803, 894, 889–90, 908; Samuel McCrea Cavert, *The American Churches in the Ecumenical Movement, 1900–1968* (New York: Association Press, 1968); Robert Lee, *The Social Sources of Church Unity: An*

Interpretation of Unitive Movements in American Protestantism (Nashville: Abingdon, 1960), 79; Rouse and Neill, *A History of the Ecumenical Movement*, 1:256–58, 621–23; Harold E. Fey, ed., *A History of the Ecumenical Movement*, vol. 2, *1948–1968* (Philadelphia: Westminster, 1970), 24; Williams, *America's Religions*, 331.

25. H. George Anderson, "Ecumenical Movements," in *Altered Landscapes: Christianity in America, 1935–1985*, ed. David W. Lotz (Grand Rapids, Mich.: Eerdmans, 1989), 92–105; Cavert, *American Churches in the Ecumenical Movement*, 70, 204–9, 225; Rouse and Neill, *A History of the Ecumenical Movement*, 1:624; Fey, *A History of the Ecumenical Movement*, 2:24, 82, 97, 99, 100.

26. Cavert, *American Churches in the Ecumenical Movement*, 235–38; Dolan, *American Catholic Experience*, 424–27, 433; Ellis, *American Catholicism*, 180–85; Hennesey, *American Catholics*, 309–10, 316, 325–26; Noll, *Old Religion*, 173–74; Williams, *America's Religions*, 54, 60–62.

27. Cavert, *American Churches in the Ecumenical Movement*, 238; Corrigan and Winthrop, *Religion in America*, 411; Hennesey, *American Catholics*, 325; Martin E. Marty, *Pilgrims in Their Own Land: 500 Years of Religion in America* (New York: Penguin, 1984), 466.

28. Philip Jenkins, *The Next Christendom: The Coming of Global Christianity* (New York: Oxford University Press, 2002); Todd M. Johnson, "Christianity in Global Context: Trends and Statistics," in "The Coming Religious Wars? Demographics and Conflict in Islam and Christianity," *Pew Forum on Religion and Public Life*, May 18, 2005, at http://www.pewforum.org/events/?EventID=82 (accessed February 16, 2009).

PART II
Practicing Christianity in America

Alasdair MacIntyre, in his historically attuned study of moral theory, *After Virtue* (University of Notre Dame Press, 1981), emphasized that "every action is the bearer and expression of more or less theory-laden beliefs and concepts; every piece of theorizing and every expression of belief is a political and moral action." Taking its lead from MacIntyre, Part II of *American Christianities* examines Christian theology and Christian practice as interdependent and interpenetrating. "Theory-laden" rituals, such as baptism, the images of gravestones or religious statuary, and the potent narratives of the Bible, convey, at least implicitly, Christian ideas about the factors that enhance or threaten human flourishing, about the relationship of human societies to the natural order, and about the ultimate environment of forces shaping human life. Through these various practices, Christianity seeks to instill and advocate a way of life, replete with messages of personal and social transformation, that will guide and motivate action in society, ranging from domestic social reform to international missions.

But symbols, rituals, and evocative, authoritative texts have all been understood differently in different times and places. Christian individuals and entire Christian groups "change their minds" about the meaning of specific practices and ideas over the course of their personal or corporate lives, and Christians from different ethnic communities or social classes perceive rituals and symbols in light of their particular experiences. The biblical narrative of the Exodus out of Egypt thus resonated quite differently for Puritans in colonial New England than it did for African American preachers in the aftermath of the Civil War. The continuities of Christian practice are impressive, but no more so than the transformations. Change and diversity in Christian practices stimulate critical reflection on the wisdom about living that is purportedly conveyed through these practices. How does one assess the validity of a Christian way of life? When is it necessary to change

153

an inherited practice? And why? In making such judgments, as MacIntyre asserted, "theorizing"—the Christian practice of theology—becomes a political and moral action of social diagnosis and Christian self-appraisal.

To MacIntyre's categories—concept and action—a third should be added: emotion. Rituals, spiritual disciplines, hymnody, and church architecture are all aimed, in part, to bind loyalties and affections among church members and between church members and the divine from which they take their bearings. Theological concepts, likewise, are not primarily an abstract system but, far more important, a persuasive rhetoric employed in liturgy, sermon, poetry, and song to inculcate basic narratives of the self and Christian society. Hence, the great theologian of colonial New England, Jonathan Edwards, concluded that, although the nature of true religion had evoked a "variety of opinions" that "divide the Christian world," he would demonstrate that true religion primarily consisted of "holy affections," the "more vigorous and sensible exercises of the inclination of the will of the soul." Two and a half centuries of American Christian revivals, First Communions, and marriages, together with national thanksgivings and tragedies, lend some credence to Edwards's view.

The ways that Christians have told their life stories, imagined sacred space and time, testified to their beliefs through evangelism, or mourned the death of family and neighbors are all instances of the theory-laden practice of Christianity. The following essays explore the history and varied forms of these practices in the United States.

Redeeming Modernity
Christian Theology in Modern America

"In what sense, if in any," Harvard philosopher Josiah Royce asked in 1912, "can the modern man consistently be, in creed, a Christian?"[1] The efforts of Catholic and Protestant theologians to resolve Royce's question about the connection between modernity and Christian ideas shaped the task and methods of theology in the United States for a full century, from the 1860s to the 1960s, from the Civil War to the civil rights movement, from the First Vatican Council to the Second. "Modern" is, of course, a capacious term, and as a consequence, the beginning of the modern age has been variously dated in every century since the fourteenth![2] But whatever the century, when any present time becomes "modern times," it carries the sense that the world looks different now and stands in marked contrast to preceding ages in general and the immediately preceding era in particular. "Modern" announces change and implies discontinuity. Hence, any judgment about the beginning of the modern age depends on which social phenomenon is regarded as its organizing or constitutive feature. As Royce put it, when persons speak of the "present age," their own interests and purposes determine its length and scope by identifying "some unity which gives relative wholeness and meaning to this present."[3]

American theologians, who wrestled with Royce's question and increasingly recognized its complexity, concluded that the phenomenon that gave "relative wholeness and meaning to this present" was modern historical consciousness. For modern persons to hold Christian ideas, and hold them "consistently," they needed to understand how theological ideas interpreted and affirmed lives, thoughts, and actions carried out within the this-worldly flux of nature and history, in which human powers create whatever meaning human life on earth may achieve.[4] This essay explores three dimensions of modern historical consciousness—historical change, contingency, and choice—and their consequences for theological interpretations of tradition, revelation, and transcendence. When these three components of the modern sense of history converged after the Civil War, they constituted the common problem for Christian theology in this century-long epoch. But since the theologians approached the issue of modern historical consciousness from different intellectual perspectives and denominational traditions, their substantive interpretations of the relationship between faith and history varied widely and sometimes clashed dramatically.

Royce's way of posing the question of modernity reflected a widespread presumption among American intellectuals at the beginning of the twentieth century: historical change had brought about some substantial difference of outlook that separated modern persons from the inherited formulations of Christian doctrine. For some, this gap between modernity and tradition provided indisputable evidence of a secular society's fall into worldliness; for others, it represented an indictment of traditional Christianity for failure to keep pace with the progressive unfolding of divine truth. In either case, rapid change seemed to characterize the institutions and ideas of society, pressing theologians to decide how, if at all, Christian ideas were also changing and developing. The effort to construe the relation between Christian ideas and historical change shaped not only the content of theology but also its formal methods. Issues surrounding the continuity of tradition amid changing times were felt with special force in the years from the 1880s to the 1930s, but the question of the historical change of doctrine was by no means settled at any point in the American century of modernity. Thus, John Courtney Murray, the American Jesuit who was among the leading theological advisers at the Second Vatican Council (1962–65), considered the concept of the historical "development of doctrine" as "*the* issue under the issues" facing the council in its deliberations.[5]

Royce had presented the development of ideas in the modern epoch as the present stage in a larger "education of the human race."[6] As Royce himself recognized, and as others would argue more emphatically, this melioristic and progressive image of historical change was called into question by another aspect of historical consciousness: the modern sense of the historical contingency of all things human. By the 1930s, "the myth of progress" was under attack among American theologians and their contemporaries in other disciplines, and this eclipse of progressive theories of historical change demarcated a second major phase in the era of modernity, one that ran from the 1930s to the 1960s. Theologically, if processes immanent to history bore no evident traces of divine direction, then the meaning of revelation needed to be rethought in relation to historical contingency. Two broad theological movements, Protestant neo-orthodoxy and a scholastic revival or neo-Thomism among Catholics, pursued comparable strategies in this reassessment, and engagement with the issue of contingency, like the issue of historical change, brought about a significant shift in theological method.[7]

Finally, when confronted by the contrast between Christian ideas and modern thought, a "modern man" might elect to discard theology. The denizens of modernity, so Royce supposed, perceived the creed of a Christian as one possible option among several comprehensive interpretations of the world. Choice, and the personal freedom choice implied, constituted modernity's underlying theory of human nature, instantiated, on the one hand, in the sufficiency of human reason to shape the physical environment to human needs and, on the other hand, in the freedom to pursue preferences within a consumer culture. But if this was the case, where within human historical experience did one encounter the transcending purposes and providence of God? Hence, as the twentieth century unfolded, theologians tended increasingly to map the gap between Christian beliefs and "modern man" as the movement from a religious to a secular culture. Thinking through the theological development of the twentieth century, Protestant theologian Langdon Gilkey observed that if secular moderns tended to experience life and its meanings as the consequences of human choices, little space seemed to be left for the notion that human fortunes were "dependent upon a transcendent ruler of time and history." To the extent that this was the case, traditional God-language had become meaningless, in the sense that its assertions did not relate to concrete life experiences and therefore were "not possible modes of understanding experience."[8]

Royce's reference to the "creed" of modern persons should not be taken to imply that theological concerns during this one-hundred-year era were abstractly doctrinal. To the contrary, American theologians throughout this period oriented their work toward ethics and religious practice, what Ralph Waldo Emerson had earlier called "the conduct of life." As they saw it, whatever else it involves, Christianity is a religion of social and personal transformation—indeed, of redemption. It envisions a humanity that has "fallen" from its proper place in the cosmos and must be saved from this fate by Jesus Christ and the redemptive community that extends his person and work through history, the church. Although the concept of redemption has taken many forms in the history of Christianity, during this period Catholic and Protestant theologians defined redemption and the redemptive community in reciprocal relation to definitions of modernity and the modern world. Responding adequately to Royce's question in these three dimensions of change, contingency, and choice was urgent and fateful for the intellectual cogency of theology because, apart from such a response, Christianity had no interpretation of the church's purpose in relation to modern society and the meaning of personal faith for "modern man." Theologians therefore took up the task of redeeming modernity as a time and place in which a person could be "consistently, in creed, a Christian."

The nineteenth- and twentieth-century theologians who grappled with the implications of Royce's question were a diverse lot. Some came from recently immigrated families; others could trace a lineage into the colonial era. Most were clergy, but lay intellectuals also made pivotal contributions. They represented various Protestant and Catholic theological traditions, and especially prior to World War I, they tended to write and think within denominational borders. Indeed, until the 1960s, sustained theological dialogue between exponents of alternative visions—whether Catholic and Protestant or liberal and conservative Protestant—proved relatively infrequent. When Catholic and Protestant theologians sized up the proper mission of the church in the modern world, each all too frequently concluded that the other was one of the principal impediments to that mission. As Richard P. McBrien has recently summarized the situation, "Catholic and non-Catholic theology moved along parallel paths in the decades prior to the Second Vatican Council. Catholics, on the one hand, and Protestants, Anglicans, Orthodox, and other separated Eastern Christians, on the other, generally did not read one another's writings. Catholic students of theology (mostly in seminaries) were warned against reading works by non-Catholic authors."[9] When this intellectual distance closed in the 1960s, the vigorous interdenominational theological discussion that ensued was one piece of evidence for the conclusion of the modern era of American theology.[10]

Perhaps the most consequential development for Christian theology in the century following the Civil War was the professionalization of theology as a specialized academic discipline, to be pursued, in university departments and graduate theological schools, by scholars of Christian scripture, doctrine, and history.[11] As will become apparent, these academic theologians concerned themselves not only with educating future generations of clergy but also with advancing scholarly knowledge of Christianity through literary, philosophical, and historical research. Although usually ordained to the ministry, they served their respective religious communities less through the direct proclamation of Christian teaching or the celebration of Christian liturgy than through systematic reflection on the meaning and coherence of these teachings and rituals. Theology was a Christian practice, but it was also a critical reflection on that practice. During the modern era of American theology, such reflection required a judgment about whether and how to use the academic disciplines, including history, psychology, and sociology, to advance theological understanding. The question of the place of theology in the university was therefore parallel to the general question of the place of Christianity in modern society, and higher education became a highly contested setting for the broader theological project of "redeeming modernity."

Change

"As traumatic wars do," remarks Louis Menand, "the Civil War discredited the beliefs and assumptions of the era that preceded it." It not only "swept away the slave civilization of the South," but also "the whole intellectual culture of the North." Responding to this traumatic disruption, American intellectuals sought during the following half century to fashion "a set of ideas, and a way of thinking that would help people cope with the conditions of modern life."[12] Surveying the developments of the nineteenth century, some marked the boundaries of modern life through the emergence of its characteristic social forms: the establishment of modern republics, exercising an assertive nationalism; the maturation of modern science, especially the evolutionary biology associated with the name of Charles Darwin; and the expansion of capitalist economy, centralized in the industrial city and epitomized by the mass production of consumer goods. Others emphasized the modern qualities of mind that seemed to inhabit these institutional forms: individualism, liberalism, democracy, and the authority ascribed to empirical observation. American intellectuals found all these aspects of modern life converging in the aftermath of the Civil War, and Menand's book, *The Metaphysical Club*, recounts the impact of this modern convergence on the formation of the American philosophical tradition of pragmatism, from Charles Peirce and William James to John Dewey. Among American theologians who were contemporaries of the pragmatists, intellectual developments of comparable scope occurred in the content and method of theology. The changes they identified as modern not only generated arguments about the relation of theology to new ideas and institutions but also evoked reflection on the nature of change itself.

In the very titles of their books, Protestant and Catholic theologians conveyed their sense of confrontation with dramatic social change. John Ireland, Catholic archbishop of St. Paul, collected his most recent lectures and addresses in 1896 under the title *The Church and Modern Society*, announcing that "in no other epoch of history, since the beginning of the Christian era, did changes so profound and so far-reaching take place." Ireland, whom historian John McGreevy has characterized as the foremost Catholic liberal of the late nineteenth century, believed that a "natural alliance" existed between the church and "the freedom-giving democratic institutions of America," and, despite conservative detractors, Ireland envisioned the church and modern America "drawn into bonds of warm amity, laboring for the progress and happiness of humanity." He therefore waxed optimistic about the church's redemptive mission in the United States: "With the new order have come new needs, new hopes, new aspirations," and, if the church hoped "to conquer the new world to Christ," she must "herself be new, adapting herself in manner of life and in method of action to the conditions of the new order, thus proving herself, while ever ancient, to be ever new, as truth from heaven is and ever must be."[13] A decade later, Shailer Mathews, a prominent leader among the Northern Baptists and a theologian at the University of Chicago Divinity School, wrote similarly, in *The Church and the Changing Order*, that citizens of the age "are growing increasingly alive to the fact that we are facing remarkable social changes in the immediate future." Mathews concluded from this that "the old order is indeed changing, yielding place to the new." Like Archbishop Ireland, Mathews declared that when the church confronted this new and changing social order, it found itself "face to face with the formative influences which are making tomorrow." In such a circumstance, "the church must face the vital decision as to what part it shall have in producing the new world."[14]

Ireland and Mathews typified turn-of-the-century theologians who deliberately accentuated the distinction between the traditions of the church and the "formative influences" shaping the "new order" of the modern age. Although the term "secular" had not yet achieved the prominence it would hold among mid-twentieth-century theologians, a compartmentalization had occurred, which presupposed a gap between Christianity and the secular. Furthermore, the secular domain itself was differentiated into independent spheres of science, politics, and economy, operating without recourse to explicitly religious ideas and institutions. As Shailer Mathews put it, the "division of labor that characterizes society to-day" entailed "special duties," distinctive to each social institution, including "the school, the state, the bank," alongside the church.[15] This social differentiation most immediately affected theologians through the rise of the modern research university, beginning with the founding of Johns Hopkins in 1876 and organized around academic departments whose aim was to extend knowledge through original research in such newly constituted social scientific disciplines as psychology, sociology, anthropology, and education. Denominational leaders and theologians immediately saw the parallels between the church's relationship to a compartmentalized modern society and theology's relationship to a departmentalized modern university. In order to argue an intellectual path forward, Catholic and Protestant thinkers had to interpret both the central witness of the church and the most consequential features of modernity and then explain how, if at all, one should relate to the other. Theology had the task of locating itself—or perhaps relocating itself—among the differentiated and increasingly specialized fields of modern knowledge, not simply as academic disciplines but also as the governing ideas of a changing social order.

For turn-of-the-century thinkers whose attention had been captured by the modernization of society, the relationship of the church to modernity required a decision. They wrote in order to call the church to action. Theology stood in the closest possible connection to social ethics and evangelistic mission. Hence, when they contrasted tradition and the modern world, they did so not as detached observers recording social data. Instead, they actively shaped this duality, placing traditional ideas on one side of the ledger and a set of ideas deemed modern on the other, in order to generate an agenda for action. The persuasive power of theology drew motivational energy from this tension between tradition and the modern world, precisely in order to mobilize religious audiences to pursue the course of action the theologian recommended.

But when theologians moved past broad distinctions between faith and modernity to propose specific arguments for the church's response, important differences began to appear, and they provoked polemic and controversy between religious conservatives and various advocates of liberal and "modernist" theological adaptation.[16] Among theological liberals, the standard trope for dramatizing the intellectual challenge of modernity was first to remind the reader that the contemporary church was "living in the midst of the most extraordinary intellectual transition that the world has ever seen" and then to present a seemingly impossible choice between modern knowledge of the world and an unaltered theology. "When," Mathews declaimed, "the church insists that in order to become one of its members one must assent to a series of doctrines embodying the cosmology, the psychology and the philosophy of the New Testament taken literally, it inevitably sets up a test which will compel a man under the influence of to-day's scholarship to abandon not only a life of evil thinking and of evil action, but also the results of his education."[17]

As implied, however, by Mathews's parable of a self divided between an outmoded cosmology and "the results of his education," theologians frequently posited the modern credibility gap precisely in order to overcome it. Having drawn a sharp line between theology and modernity, they immediately crossed the line, by identifying points of continuity or congruence between the affirmations of the church and the aspirations of modernity. From this perspective, the principal theological agenda of the early twentieth century was to devise strategies for intellectual unification, to exposit, according to the title of Mathews's most famous book, *The Faith of Modernism*. Consequently, their stories of the divided self were frequently accompanied by autobiographic narratives of the successful passage from inherited modes of thought into modern faith. In *Sixty Years with the Bible*, for instance, liberal Baptist theologian William Newton Clarke recounted his own intellectual evolution "from the old view of the Bible to the new." It had occurred to him, Clarke wrote in 1909, that he had lived through "the crisis of the Nineteenth Century" with respect to the historical study of the Bible and "that if I were to tell the story of my own life in the single character of a student, lover, and user of the Bible, exhibiting the mental processes through which the change in my own attitude toward the Bible has come to pass," this spiritual autobiography "might be an enlightening and encouraging thing to many a perplexed and anxious soul."[18]

Some theologians, of course, would have none of it. Conservative thinkers did not doubt that society was undergoing remarkable institutional and intellectual changes, but they rejected the notion that the core depository of faith was subject to these same historical dynamics of change. For conservative Protestants, that history-transcending core was the Bible; for Catholics, it was the church. Among conservative Protestants, Princeton Theological Seminary's Benjamin B. Warfield found that the "leaven of agnosticism underlying much of modern thought" had shifted the object of theology away from God toward a historical inquiry into the developing religious consciousness of the church. But this historical science of human religiosity, Warfield concluded, was "something radically different from systematic theology," and for him the authentic sources for knowledge of God culminated in Christian scripture. He posed a rhetorical question: "Do the Scriptures contain a special revelation of God; or are they merely a record of religious aspirations and attainments of men—under whatever (more or less) divine leading?" Beginning with the famous essay "Inspiration" that he wrote with his colleague Archibald Alexander Hodge in 1881, Warfield argued in behalf of "the entire agency of God in producing the divine element which distinguished Scripture from all other writings" and accounted for "the absolute infallibility of the record in which the revelation, once generated, appears in the original autograph" of the biblical text.[19] With this elevation of Christian scripture beyond the flow of historical change, conservative biblical interpreters turned away from both the historical method of biblical criticism presupposed among liberal theologians and exegetes and the broader historicism of scholarship in American universities. Consequently, writes historian Mark Noll, "conservative evangelicals, either locked out of or alienated from the academy, turned for support to non-scholars who shared similar theological convictions," established independent evangelical seminaries insulated from the universities, and would not succeed in strategies for engagement with modern university scholarship until the 1960s and 1970s.[20]

Among Catholics, the papacy's long nineteenth-century struggle with European democratic revolutions, culminating in the decade of the 1860s, placed traditional doctrine in an adversarial relation to such modern institutional innovations as the separation of church and state and, especially, conceptions of the church that made its constitution subject to historical change, as was the case for simply human institutions. In an encyclical letter (*Testem benevolentiae*, 1889) on "Americanism" addressed to James Cardinal Gibbons, archbishop of Baltimore, Pope Leo XIII observed that controversy had occurred over new opinions about "the manner of leading a Christian life," which proposed that "the Church ought to adapt herself somewhat to our advanced civilization, and, relaxing her ancient rigor, show some indulgence to modern popular theories and methods." Leo reminded the American bishops that "the doctrine of faith" was not simply a philosophical proposal but, as summarized by the Vatican Council, "a divine deposit delivered to the Spouse of Christ to be faithfully guarded and infallibly declared." Of course, in maintaining this faith, the papacy had "never disregarded the manners and customs of the various nations which it embraces" when "modifications" to the rule of life proved necessary to the salvation of souls. But, Leo emphasized, such modifications were "not to be determined by the will of private individuals" but instead "ought to be left to the judgment of the Church." Leo XIII perceived an even greater danger to Catholic doctrine and discipline in the idea that individuals should be free to exercise personal liberty of opinion in imitation of "that liberty which, though quite recently introduced, is now the law and foundation of almost every civil community." This modern notion ignored precisely the point on which Leo insisted, that is, "the difference between the Church, which is of divine right, and all other associations, which subsist by the free will of men."[21] Leo's successor, Pius X, extended this conception of the church in his 1907 encyclicals and decrees condemning Catholic "modernism." Among the errors Pius identified was the idea that "the organic constitution of the church is not unchangeable, but is subject to perpetual evolution, just as human society is," and that "dogmas, sacraments, and hierarchy are nothing but evolutions and interpretations of Christian thought."[22] Whether or not such "modernism" fully and accurately described the theological position of any Catholic theologian of the era, nonetheless Catholic bishops in the United States were "profoundly conservative" on such fundamentals as the nature of the church, and even the progressive Archbishop Ireland "penned ringing defenses against the Modernists of the reality of the supernatural and of the dogmatic authority of the papacy."[23]

Protestant and Catholic theologians representing a wide spectrum of opinion thus attempted to retrieve, retain, or accentuate specific aspects of the tradition as the ones that led the way into the church's engagement with the critical features of modernity—sometimes as bulwarks against the modern and sometimes as adaptations to it. They propounded different senses in which the church embodied or established the ideals toward which society should strive, if it was to approach its own best possibilities. Two general models of adaptation to modernity emerged, the first of which is well illustrated by Archbishop Ireland's 1893 address "The Church and the Age." Ireland lamented that a widespread apprehension that "the Church and the age are at war" was, in fact, a misapprehension. He blamed both the church and the age for this mistake. Neither the church nor the age had penetrated to the "essentials" of the other, Ireland judged, and serious intellectual rapprochement had too frequently been replaced by indiscriminate endorsements or wholesale repudiations. Amid this confusion, modernity, repelled by "the isolation and the unfriendliness of the Church," had become "hardened in its secularism, and taught itself to despise and hate religion." Ireland found in such times an opportunity "to bridge the chasm separating the Church from the age," in order "to Christianize its aspirations, and to guide its forward march." In Ireland's view, the present age represented "one of the mighty upheavals which, from time to time, occur in humanity, producing and signalizing the ascending stages in its continuous progress. Humanity, strengthened by centuries of toil and reflection, nourished and permeated by principles of Christian truth, is now lifting its whole mass upward to higher regions of light and liberty, and demanding full and universal enjoyment of its God-given rights."[24]

Within the context of this narrative of human progress, Ireland presented a classic argument, frequently employed in Protestant as well as Catholic versions, in which the task of theology consisted in the *application* of a permanent, supernatural truth to an ever-changing world, adapting the "outward features" of this eternal message so that it might be appropriately heard at a given historical moment. "The Church, created by Christ for all time, lives in every age and is of every age," Ireland declared. Furthermore, since the supernatural represented the true goal of the natural order, the church's responsibility was not merely to rebuke the defects of the age but to identify and promote all that was "holy and legitimate" in modern ideals. Modernity's quest for knowledge, democracy, social justice, and material progress represented steps toward the church's "own most sacred principles of the equality, fraternity, and liberty of all men, in Christ and through Christ." And this complementarity of faith and modern ideals was by no means surprising, Ireland concluded, because "the Catholic Church proclaims that all truth, natural as well as supernatural, is from God." Especially in the democratic polity of the United States, Ireland found that "the Catholic Church, the church of the people, breathes air most congenial to her mind and heart." In short, the only real danger was posed by modern ideologies that artificially separated nature from the supernatural, such that "natural truth is made a protest against revealed religion," and that through this separation misdirected "all that is good and true" in modern social movements toward "things false and pernicious."[25]

Walter Rauschenbusch, the leading expositor of the Protestant Social Gospel, articulated a second general model for the theological interpretation of historical change. Rauschenbusch emphasized not simply the changing mind and temper of the age, to which the church must apply the perennial wisdom of Christian faith, but, drawing on ideas from Germany's liberal Protestant tradition, he argued that theology too underwent historical development. Continuous change in the course of history was a fundamental property of theology itself. Indeed, a theologian's greatest intellectual error would be the idea that the church's doctrine was an unchanging deposit of truth. "If we seek to keep Christian doctrine unchanged," he summarily concluded, "we shall ensure its abandonment." According to Rauschenbusch, the spirit of Christ was developing and extending its influence as an organic principle immanent to history, and he therefore warned that the central religious responsibility of theology was to engage the ethical imperatives of present-day life: "The Church is halting between two voices that call it. On the one side is the voice of the living Christ amid living men to-day; on the other side is the voice of past ages embodied in theology."[26] By no means would every theologian accede to Rauschenbusch's interment of traditional theology in the tomb of the past. But Rauschenbusch's formulation dramatized his strategy for resolving the tension between theology and modernity.

Rauschenbusch numbered "social solidarity" among the dominant ideas of the age, and it certainly was the dominant idea driving his synoptic theological work of 1918, *A Theology for the Social Gospel*. The book proceeded through the classic doctrines of Christianity—sin, salvation, kingdom of God, Holy Spirit—and reworked each in light of this governing idea of social solidarity: "That sin is lodged in social customs and institutions and is absorbed by the individual from his social group is so plain that any person with common sense can observe it, but I have found only a few, even among the modern hand-books of theology, which show a clear recognition of the theological importance of this fact." Hence, a theology for the Social Gospel would need to interpret the doctrine of original sin in its social dimension, recognizing that "it runs down the generations" by social assimilation and that the doctrine therefore addressed "the spiritual authority of society over its members."[27] To counteract such powerfully institutionalized forms of sin, among which Rauschenbusch enumerated religious bigotry, political corruption, militarism, and a class system of prideful contempt for the poor, he argued that the church's message of redemption must therefore be restated in the "solidaristic" terms first enunciated by the Old Testament prophets and Jesus.

Like many Catholic and Protestant thinkers in the first decades of the twentieth century, Rauschenbusch believed that the most significant threat of modernity in America came from its individualism, which distorted community in a competitive struggle for power and wealth.[28] Rauschenbusch further thought that a major burden of responsibility for this threat rested on the individualistic message of traditional Protestantism, which, because of its emphasis on personal salvation, had not evoked faith in the "power of God to redeem the permanent institutions of human society from their inherited guilt of oppression and extortion." In contrast to the pervasive individualism of American culture, Rauschenbusch derived a model for socially oriented faith from the scriptural narratives in which prophets "received their prophetic mission." In none of these accounts did the prophet "struggle for his personal salvation as later Christian saints have done. His woe did not come through fear of personal damnation, but through his sense of solidarity with his people and through social feeling; his hope and comfort was not for himself alone but for his nation." The Social Gospel, Rauschenbusch concluded, "creates a type of religious experience corresponding closely to the prophetic type." He argued that Jesus Christ, in continuity with this prophetic God-consciousness, had "set in motion a new beginning of spiritual life within the organized total of the race," and the church, although "faltering, sinning, and defiled," had maintained this "collective personality" in the course of its social development through its embodied ideal of human solidarity, the kingdom of God.[29]

By these two broad strategies, illustrated through representative writings of John Ireland and Walter Rauschenbusch, theologians in the half century from the 1880s to the 1930s sought to redeem modernity by "Christianizing the social order." Despite clear differences regarding the issue of doctrinal change and development, these strategies shared an evangelistic and ethical commitment to the church's role as the spiritual and moral guide of modern society.[30] They emphasized tensions between Christianity and modernity not in order to isolate the church but instead to urge it to take up its responsibility to capture and direct the progressive social energies of the age. Religiously attuned intellectuals, such as social settlement pioneer Jane Addams, shared their hopeful idealism about the socially redemptive possibilities of modernity. In her 1907 book, *Newer Ideals of Peace*, Addams described her perception that "in the immigrant quarters of a cosmopolitan city" the commingling of diverse peoples, who were "unlike each other in all save the universal characteristics of man," not only required but was in fact producing new powers of association, altruism, and justice. "Because of the many nationalities which are gathered there from all parts of the world," urban immigrants recognized that both equity and self-preservation required them to move past "tribal" antagonisms toward the common good, and they were "really attaining cosmopolitan relations through daily experience." In Addams's appraisal, as these social forces actively refashioned the social morality of the pluralistic city, "they would, in the end, quite as a natural process, do away with war."[31] Addams and her theological fellow travelers thus envisioned historical change, aided and abetted by Christian ideals, as socially redemptive progress.

By interpreting the characteristics of modernity and taking a stance toward them, theologians not only shaped the content of theology but also its method and formal structure. The classical task of theology had been—and remained—a systematic presentation of the interconnections among the teachings of scripture and tradition. Its aim was not a "proof" of Christian doctrine so much as it was an internally coherent statement of communal belief. When the Christian community largely coincided with society as a whole, such a statement functioned as the systematic exposition of the common faith regarding human nature, destiny, and conduct. But when, as in modernity, Christian teaching was not coincident with general social perspectives on the human condition, a second basic task of theology emerged. Systematic theology now became not only the systematic ordering of Christian teaching but also the systematic exposition of that teaching in relation to other domains of modern thought, sociology, anthropology, the natural sciences, and so on. Shailer Mathews, to cite him yet again, provided a succinct interpretation of this second basic task of theology: "Theology in the final analysis is the result of an attempt of the thinkers of an age to make religion intelligible to their fellows. It is the *correlation* of the facts of religion with the other things they know."[32]

Correlation, to the extent that it could be achieved, thus aimed at cultural synthesis; it was the intellectual analogue to the ethical aim of John Ireland and Walter Rauschenbusch to "Christianize" the highest aspirations of American society. Theologians differed over whether the accent should fall on a cohesive exposition that was appropriate to the tradition or on a systematic correlation with the various branches of modern knowledge. "It is not easy so to state the Christian gospel as at once to preserve its continuity with the past and its living touch with the present," explained William Adams Brown of Union Theological Seminary, but "the office of Christian theology is not fully accomplished until it has fulfilled this double task."[33]

Contingency

The historical consciousness of the twentieth century included not simply attention to historical change but also an acute awareness of historical contingency, the idea that events occurred as they did from specific, dependent, chance interactions with other events and that personal and social life was entirely situated within this indeterminate flow of events. Among the many implications of this awareness of contingency, perhaps the most consequential for theology was the idea that a person's sense of the wholeness, form, and meaning of "the world" represented a specific and limited perspective, assembled out of a society's existing stock of ideas and personal motives and the immediate pressures of the environment. This idea of the historically contingent, purposive production of meaning was a cornerstone of the pragmatic philosophies of William James and John Dewey. Writing from this perspective about the religious dimension of human experience, Dewey observed in his book from 1934, *A Common Faith*, that "there actually occurs extremely little observation of brute facts merely for the sake of the facts." Instead, humans observed their environment "with reference to some practical end and purpose, and that end is presented only imaginatively." Such imaginatively represented ends lent direction to the self by incorporating immediate objectives within ever-more-inclusive goals, thereby attaining "the unification of the self throughout the ceaseless flux of what it does, suffers, and achieves." Through this process of active, purposive interpretation, "the idea of a whole, whether of the whole personal being or of the world, is an imaginative, not a literal idea. The limited world of our observation and reflection becomes the Universe only through imaginative extension."[34]

By the time Dewey offered this interpretation in 1934, some version of historical contingency had deeply affected most theologians working in academic environments. Yale Divinity School's H. Richard Niebuhr, for instance, asserted that modern "historical relativism" affirmed the historical contingency of human subjectivity even more than the contingency of the objects that subject observed: "Man, it points out, is not only in time but time is in man." Even more significantly, continued Niebuhr, "the time that is in man is not abstract but particular and concrete; it is not a general category of time but rather the time of a definite society with distinct language, economic and political relations, religious faith and social organization." Hence, both societies and persons erred when they identified their historical reasonings with universal reason or appealed to the "apparent innateness, clarity or inescapability" of their concepts, "since the ideas commonly accepted in a society always appear to its members to be self-evident and inevitable."[35]

Leading Protestant and Catholic theologians of the 1930s and 1940s found the idea of historical contingency, in differing ways and to differing degrees, useful to their attack on the ideals of progress that had characterized the preceding era. The criticisms they directed against the proponents of universal ideals received pithy summation from Reinhold Niebuhr, professor of Christian ethics at Union Theological Seminary in New York City. Brother of Richard Niebuhr and perhaps the most publicly renowned American theologian of the twentieth century, Reinhold Niebuhr argued that whenever humans pursue more inclusive ideals and loyalties, those ideals are invariably shaped by power and material interest. Further, as he elaborated the point in *Moral Man and Immoral Society* (1932), this insinuation of interest into every ideal, especially when it occurs in the behavior of human collectives such as social classes and nations, bends these ideals with a force that is difficult to restrain. Hence, he concluded, hypocrisy was "perhaps the most significant moral characteristic of a nation," which in times of crisis invariably enlisted the loyalty of its citizens by representing the nation as their "own special and unique community and as a community which embodies universal values and ideals."[36] In 1935, Niebuhr observed upon the close link between idealism and armed conflict:

> One reason why modern social conflicts are more brutal than primitive ones is that the development of rationality has actually imparted more universal pretensions to partial social interests than those of primitive men. . . . The consequence is that modern men fight for their causes with a fury of which only those are capable who are secure in the sense of their righteousness. Thus all modern social conflicts are fought for "Kultur," for democracy, for justice, and for every conceivable universal value. A rereading of the pronouncements of men of learning and philosophers, as well as of the statesmen and politicians, who were involved in the world war, fills the reader with a depressing sense of the calculated insincerity of all their pretensions.[37]

Such insights into the ways that power shaped hegemonic ideas and the ways that theology was enlisted in support of wider systems of social and political power had not, of course, been utterly invisible to those members of American society who lacked such power. At the close of the nineteenth century, while male Protestant theologians divided over historical critical interpretation of the Bible, Elizabeth Cady Stanton, who had lost none of the outspoken clarity with which she had led the American movement for women's rights for half a century, enlisted a group of women to publish *The Woman's Bible* (1895), with new translations and commentaries on those passages of the Bible that addressed the condition of women. Stanton was by no means reluctant to argue that the church as a whole had used the authority of the Bible to sanction an immoral collusion with the most oppressive features of society. She introduced *The Woman's Bible* with the observation that ever since "the inauguration of the movement for woman's emancipation the Bible has been used to hold her in the 'divinely ordained sphere,' prescribed in the Old and New Testaments." Appeals to scriptural authority sanctioned the rankest injustices, she concluded, and "church property all over this broad land is exempt from taxation, while the smallest house and lot of every poor widow is taxed at its full value. Our Levites have their homes free, and good salaries from funds principally contributed by women, for preaching denunciatory sermons on women and their sphere."[38]

Forty years later, Howard Thurman faced a difficult decision over whether to take a leave of absence from his position as dean of Rankin Chapel and professor of theology at Howard University in order to accept an invitation from the international Student Christian Movement to lead a delegation of African Americans to India, where he would meet with Gandhi. Thurman's crisis of conscience revolved around whether he could go to India "as a representative of the Christian religion as it was projected from the West, and primarily from America. I did not want to go to India as an apologist for a segregated Christianity." Thurman finally decided to make the trip during the 1935–36 academic year. Even then, he found that white missionaries, including the renowned E. Stanley Jones, had circulated certain expectations about the style of African American Christianity—"We were to be singing, soul-saving evangelists"—which made Thurman determined to "steer clear" of roles "defined for us by other Christians" in order to "give the Indian people free access to our feeling about ourselves and our idiom." Years later, Thurman recalled Gandhi's response to a question about obstacles to the spread of Christianity in India: "Christianity as it is practiced, as it has been identified with Western culture, with Western civilization and colonialism. This is the greatest enemy that Jesus Christ has in my country—not Hinduism, or Buddhism, or any of the indigenous religions—but Christianity itself."[39]

This tendency, vividly identified by Stanton and Thurman, for social ideals to sanction or disguise social injustices led Niebuhr to assert that "the bourgeois idealists" were completely unconscious of the degree to which "their own interests and perspectives insinuated themselves into the conception, and even more into the application of their timeless ideals." Hence, the deep fault of the liberal tradition, in politics and theology, was not that it had grown complacent with the status quo but instead that it failed to acknowledge its own historical contingency and attributed false universality to the ideals toward which it aspired: "Religion, declares the modern man, is consciousness of our highest social values. Nothing could be further from the truth. True religion is a profound uneasiness about our highest social values."[40]

This insistence on historical contingency did not mean that Protestant neo-orthodox theologians like the Niebuhr brothers did not have a profound appreciation for the importance of history to theological interpretation. Quite the contrary, within the contingent flux of human events, they were "neo-orthodox" in the sense that they turned to the history of Christianity for resources to mount a cultural critique of the prevailing assumptions of their time. A key text in this regard was H. Richard Niebuhr's book from 1941, *The Meaning of Revelation*. Niebuhr began by affirming the critical capacity of historical retrieval. Upheavals in religious and moral thought, Niebuhr wrote, have often begun from serious historical "search in the common memory for the great principles which lie back of accustomed ways." And since society's accustomed ways were "perversions as well as illustrations" of these great principles, historical retrieval and reinterpretation "can be a very radical and pregnant thing." Even if historical perspective did not have this revolutionary potential, however, the observer's historical point of view still must be considered when appraising or advancing a rational argument, Niebuhr proposed, simply because "no observer can get out of history into a realm beyond time-space; if reason is to operate at all it must be content to work as an historical reason." What, then, could count as *revelation*, when all ideas incorporated the standpoint, principles, and institutions that have grown out of the history of a particular society? Niebuhr responded that revelation occurred when members of a society discerned a "rational pattern" in an event that served to illuminate "our personal and communal history." A revelatory moment "illuminates other events and enables us to understand them." It was an "intelligible event which makes all other events intelligible." Through revelation, historically and socially conditioned in this way, "a pattern of dramatic unity becomes apparent with the aid of which the heart can understand what has happened, is happening and will happen to selves in their community." It was, all in all, a model of revelation that was profound primarily in its modesty, since to think within historically relative contexts meant that

> we navigate the oceans and skies of our world by dead reckoning, computing our position from a latitude and longitude determined nineteen hundred years ago, using a log that is in part undecipherable and a compass of conscience notoriously subject to deviation. Objections arise in the crew not only because other vessels claim to possess more scientific apparatus for determining where they are and whither they are going, but because revelation, if it be revelation of God, must offer something more immovable than the pole star and something more precise than our measurements of the winds and currents of history.[41]

Up through the 1930s and 1940s, the neo-scholasticism that pervaded American Catholic thought strongly resisted the incorporation of modern ideas of historical contingency into the framework of theology. Historian Philip Gleason has commented that "the system itself was intrinsically antihistoricist in that it ruled out altogether the possibility that the passage of time and changing circumstances might require any *essential* modification of St. Thomas's synthesis of natural knowledge and supernatural revelation. Truth was truth and remained the same, despite changing outward circumstances." At least with respect to contingency, this stance gave neo-scholastic argument a strongly antimodernist cast, not in the sense that Catholic theologians pined for a lost medieval culture of Thomas Aquinas but that they had mounted, in his name, a formidable intellectual rebuttal of the historicist presuppositions of modernity.[42] Despite its antihistoricist argumentation, however, the Catholic retrieval of Thomas was accompanied by a massive, erudite, and influential historical scholarship by Etienne Gilson, Marie-Dominique Chenu, Henri de Lubac, and others on medieval philosophy, theology, and exegesis; this searching return to the sources would offer a basis for both churchly reform and cultural critique.

In the middle decades of the century, neo-scholastic and neo-orthodox thinkers, from their differing positions on historical contingency but their common appreciation for historical retrieval, began to converge on two points. First, both groups of theologians emphasized the nature of the church as a distinctive culture with a communal history that placed it in critical tension with modernity, especially what they regarded as modernity's fatal tendency toward an anthropocentric confidence in human reason's sufficiency to chart its own course. Such internationally known thinkers as philosopher Jacques Maritain, a convert to Catholicism who frequently lectured in the United States, argued that modern humans had been utterly misled by their own mythology of rational and technological self-sufficiency: "Having given up God so as to be self-sufficient, now man is losing track of his soul, he looks in vain for himself, he turns the universe upside-down, trying to find himself, he finds masks, and behind the masks death." In 1939, Maritain wrote, "the tragic wheel of rationalistic humanism" had brought humanity to the brink of catastrophe by opening it to "lower powers" in the modern cults of war, race, and blood, "through the concentration camps, and the new ghettos where thousands of Jews are condemned to a slow death, through the cities of China and Spain eviscerated by bombs, through Europe maddened in an armament race and feverishly preparing for suicide." In response, he called upon Christianity to offer a new "integral humanism" that would define the human not through individualism but by discovering, through "its openness to the world of the divine and super-rational," a fuller sense of "the dignity of the human person, so that man would re-find himself in God refound."[43] The following year, John Courtney Murray offered a similar appraisal, concluding that "the essential idea upon which a democratic culture must be erected, the idea of the dignity of human nature and of man's spiritual freedom," had been debased into a superficial right to materialistic economic grasping. To rescue the "essential idea," it must be brought "once more into contact with its sources in Christian history and Christian truth," thereby "redeeming our culture from its soulless mechanism" and establishing an authentic humanism.[44]

Second, whatever their ultimate goals for the relation of church and society, these revisionist theologians understood the present situation of the churches in the democratic West as an inescapable religious pluralism. In his best-known book, *We Hold These Truths* (1960), Murray famously wrote: "Religious pluralism is against the will of God. But it is the human condition; it is written into the script of history. It will not somehow marvelously cease to trouble the City."[45] In fact, however, Murray's book was built around the idea that pluralistic argument over first principles was the foundation of civil society. In this civic argument, he proposed that Catholic culture had vital things to say about "the American proposition," because Catholics, like the American Founders, based their social and political ethic in a theory of natural law. Democracy proceeded by debate over the diverse implications of common convictions, and Christianity lent indispensable voices to this civic argument.

Together, these two points led mid-century theologians to accentuate the task of theology as the critical interpretation of cultural forms and social movements—that is, they conceived the theological tradition as a diagnostic tool for appraising the cultural assumptions of the age from a perspective, both historical and philosophical, that potentially provided insight because it did not coincide with general cultural assumptions. Yale's John E. Smith, a historian of philosophy who was well acquainted with the relations between philosophy and theology, from Jonathan Edwards to the pragmatists, has written that "the key to understanding the content of any faith" will be discovered in its method for making a "diagnosis of the human predicament."[46] In the diagnostic methods employed by Maritain, Murray, and both Niebuhrs, the church as a coherent and distinctive cultural tradition applied critical leverage to modern culture by viewing it from long historical perspectives that tellingly transcended the truisms of present-day sensibility, even when they left ambiguous the meaning of their insistence (in Reinhold Niebuhr's phrase) that "the centre, source and fulfillment of history lie beyond history."[47]

Choice

The philosopher Charles Taylor has recently characterized the epoch from around 1800 to the 1960s as "the age of mobilization," reflecting the growing sense in modernity that institutions were human fabrications, expressive of human aspirations, interests, and power. The age of mobilization presupposed, says Taylor, that any political, social, or ecclesial structures to which humans aspired had to be "mobilized into existence." That is, members of nations, professions, churches, and increasingly even of families did not conceive of themselves as embedded in institutions that were ordained by God and integrated in a comprehensive order of the cosmos but instead as independent individuals, who voluntarily "associate together" in "a society structured for mutual benefit."[48] Whatever their formal teachings about the nature of the church, Christian communities in the United States have, in fact, participated in this larger framework of activism and choice. Personal adherence to a church became a choice during the age of mobilization, and adherents experienced their religious communities as institutionally flexible, voluntary, and self-directed, emphasizing personal choice and the need for adaptive innovation. This mobilization was, in many respects, spectacularly successful in its innovation of new religious forms, raising religious adherence and practice in the transatlantic world and especially in the United States. And in relation to the wider public, America's voluntarily constituted churches and parachurch organizations justified their continuing importance to civic life in terms of their mission to instill the values and ideals that made for responsible citizens.

But whatever the consequences for other institutions, the age of mobilization had far-reaching, largely unforeseen consequences for the voluntary church because it raised a distinctly theological problem. Having generated an elaborate set of adaptive institutional forms, which stimulated and organized a long era of numerical growth for the American churches, the social process of founding, joining, and voluntarily sustaining these institutions raised a question about their specifically religious status as bearers of transcendence—as the Church, with a capital C. If religious community was based on personal decisions to affiliate and personal commitments to spiritual ideals, what social experience supported the common assumption that religion represented an alignment of life with transcending powers or a claim upon the self that originated from beyond the self? How would persons experience transcendence when the most immediate experience of religious participation arose from personal choice and agency? How did the divine make its appearance or seem to exert its power within this "mobilized" sociology of religion?

Summarily stated, the three dimensions of modern historical conscious-ness—change, contingency, and choice—had disrupted the grand narratives of providence and progress out of which the project of redeeming modernity had arisen in American theology at the close of the nineteenth century. In the course of multiple wars, class conflict, and racial violence, the providen-tial progress of society, guided by an immanent God toward a fulfilling king-dom, appeared to be not merely slowed but thoroughly derailed. Theological ideas long regarded as disclosures of transcendent or universally applicable ideals were seen as having sanctioned highly contingent collective interests. And the sociological experience of religion in the age of mobilization as an optional choice of behavior and belief created a theological problem for Christian ideas of divine presence and transcendence.

The disruption of this grand narrative, which had provided the frame of reference for the conduct of individual lives, reverberated at the personal level for significant numbers of American Christians during the 1960s in the erosion of meaning in theological language about the experience of God. As systematic theologian Schubert M. Ogden wrote in 1966, the "reality of God" had become the central theological problem, and it would not be resolved without "casting aside the supernaturalistic conception of his re-ality, which is in fact untenable, given our typical experience and thought as secular men."[49] Although this crisis of transcendence and therefore of God-language emerged with special clarity in the 1960s and early 1970s, it had been slowly building throughout America's century of modernity, as theo-ries of history shaped around the distinction between the natural and the supernatural gave way under the pressure of historical sensibilities strongly marked by change, contingency, and choice. As Reinhold Niebuhr stated the problem, an adequate Christian theory of history must affirm naturalistic ideas of human existence "inasfar as they insist on the meaningfulness of historical existence" but must refute them "inasfar as they believe that the temporal process explains and fulfils itself." Given this judgment about the insufficiency of purely naturalistic conceptions of history, how were mod-ern theologians to redeem the dialectical conviction represented in what Niebuhr called "the biblical view of life," which both affirmed the meaning of human historical existence and insisted that "the centre, source and fulfill-ment of history lie beyond history?"[50]

The theological response to this slowly building crisis of transcendence took shape in two reinterpretations of the Christian narrative of history that were more attuned to modern historical consciousness: tragedy and irony. Both forms of narrative sought to interpret historical situations and processes, to recall Richard Niebuhr's discussion of revelation, through events that suggested patterns of dramatic unity. Both tragedy and irony presupposed contingent human choices but then went on to describe how those choices were overwhelmed by their own unforeseen or unintended consequences. Both avoided identification with a quasi-divine viewpoint and, instead, suggested that the patterns of divine agency were only recognizable retrospectively. In this way, tragedy and irony, as modes of theological reflection, interpreted personal and social history through narratives in which a presumptuously self-sufficient human rationality confronted its limits in forces that transcended its control, opening a this-worldly space to *the presence*, or as Ogden put it, *the reality* of God.[51]

The tragic element in modern American theology related most closely to the broad liberal tradition, illustrated in this essay particularly from theologians working in the period from the 1890s to the 1920s. The liberals had emphasized religion's role in cultivating the ideals toward which societies and individuals aspired. Tragedy arose when nations or persons faced a choice between conflicting ideals, when they committed evil for the sake of the ideal, or when they lost their way toward the ideal. In *The Problem of Christianity*, Josiah Royce elucidated the tragic sense of history through the extreme case of betrayal of an ideal, a circumstance that raised both "the problem of the traitor" and the possibility of "tragic reconciliation." In Royce's thought, communities were constituted and selves given overarching direction through loyal identification with a cause. A person who was "deliberately false to his cause" thereby betrayed the defining loyalty of personal identity and committed a kind of moral suicide. Further, the deed concerned "not himself only, but the community whereof he was a voluntary member," and, likewise, the possibility of reconciliation concerned "not only the traitor, but the wounded or shattered community." Treason had plunged both individual and community into a "hell of the irrevocable," in which mere remorse could not undo the tragic consequences of the act. But in Christian tragedies of this type, the full meaning of the tragedy included its aftermath: the "tragic reconciliation" or atonement that "transforms the meaning of that very past which it cannot undo." Royce therefore proposed that "atoning deeds are the most creative of the expressions which the community gives, through the deed of an individual, to its will that the unity of the spirit should triumph, not only despite, but through the greatest tragedies,—the tragedies of deliberate sin."[52]

In his view of tragedy and reconciliation, as in his interpretation of "the beloved community," Martin Luther King would later draw on and extend ideas from Royce's philosophy. In his 1963 "Letter from a Birmingham Jail," to take only one example among many, King responded to charges that he was an outside agitator and an extremist by reciting a litany of "creative extremists" from religious and political history—Jesus, Amos, Paul, Martin Luther, John Bunyan, Abraham Lincoln, and Thomas Jefferson—who had loyally devoted themselves to causes of justice, conscience, and equality. Those who now willingly "went to jail for conscience's sake" stood in that line of creative extremism and effected a tragic reconciliation of a nation whose racism had betrayed its own ideals of equality and freedom: "One day the South will know that when these disinherited children of God sat down at lunch counters they were in reality standing up for the best in the American dream and the most sacred values in our Judeo-Christian heritage, and thusly, carrying our whole nation back to those great wells of democracy which were dug deep by the Founding Fathers in the formulation of the Constitution and the Declaration of Independence." It was a *tragic* reconciliation because the betrayal of the dream could not be undone; it was a tragic *reconciliation* because "creative extremists" seized the historic moment to reinscribe the ideals of democratic justice, despite "the long and tragic story of the fact that privileged groups seldom give up their privileges voluntarily."[53]

Irony received its most creative interpretation as a theological narrative of history during the middle decades of the twentieth century, illustrated here through the writings of the neo-orthodox and neo-Thomist thinkers. The year 1952 was, perhaps, irony's signal moment, with the publication by Reinhold Niebuhr of *The Irony of American History* and by Dorothy Day of her autobiography, *The Long Loneliness*. Irony, for Niebuhr, disclosed the subtler shapes of history by calling attention to the unintended and unpredictable consequences of human action:

Irony consists of apparently fortuitous incongruities in life which are discovered, upon closer examination to be not merely fortuitous. . . . If virtue becomes vice through some hidden defect in the virtue; if strength becomes weakness because of the vanity to which strength may prompt the mighty man or nation; if security is transmuted into insecurity because too much reliance is placed upon it; if wisdom becomes folly because it does not know its own limits—in all such cases the situation is ironic.

Recognition of irony might teach the virtue of humility, and Niebuhr found that modern persons were singularly lacking in "the humility to accept the fact that the whole drama of history is enacted in a frame of meaning too large for human comprehension or management." Tracing the ironic elements in American history, Niebuhr counseled that they could be overcome "only if American idealism comes to terms with the limits of all human striving, the fragmentation of all human wisdom, the precariousness of all historic configurations of power, and the mixture of good and evil in all human virtue."[54]

Irony and humility were also integrated in Dorothy Day's carefully crafted account of the death of Peter Maurin, her inspiration and co-laborer in the founding of the Catholic Worker movement. Maurin was an ascetic as well as a visionary: "Peter was the poor man of his day. He was a St. Francis of modern times. He was used to poverty as a peasant is used to rough living, poor food, hard bed." Single-mindedly devoted to his apostolate of service, Maurin had "stripped himself throughout life." He had stripped himself of all external comforts, but, as he neared death, Day wrote,

> there remained work for God to do. We are to be pruned as the vine is pruned so that it can bear fruit, and this we cannot do ourselves. God did it for him. He took from him his mind, the one thing he had left, the one thing perhaps he took delight in. He could no longer think. He could no longer discuss with others, give others in a brilliant overflow of talk his deep analysis of what was going on in the world; he could no longer make what he called his synthesis of cult, culture, and cultivation.[55]

God, in a poignant irony, had perfected Peter Maurin in his long search for humility.

And thus it was that the century-long project of redeeming modernity, which had originated in confidence that earnest labor toward Christian ideals could effect God's will on earth, ended with narratives of history's contingency, in which ideals were overwhelmed by tragedy, unanticipated ironies suggested purposes beyond the merely human, and theology offered the counsel of humility to an idealistically self-righteous nation. As Reinhold Niebuhr concluded in 1944, when history is understood as the flux of time in which human powers create whatever meaning human life on earth may achieve, then "history is creative but not redemptive."[56]

NOTES

1. Josiah Royce, *The Problem of Christianity* (Chicago: University of Chicago Press, 1968), 63.

2. Louis Dupré, *Passage to Modernity: An Essay in the Hermeneutics of Nature and Culture* (New Haven: Yale University Press, 1993).

3. Josiah Royce, *The World and the Individual*, 2 vols. (New York: Macmillan, 1901), 2:130.

4. My phrasing of the traits of modern historical consciousness is indebted to Langdon Gilkey, *Naming the Whirlwind: The Renewal of God-Language* (Indianapolis: Bobbs-Merrill, 1969), 61–62. For more on the concept of historical consciousness and its implications for biblical interpretation, see Grant Wacker, "The Demise of Biblical Civilization," in *The Bible in America: Essays in Cultural History*, ed. Nathan O. Hatch and Mark A. Noll (New York: Oxford University Press, 1982), 121–38.

5. Cited by John W. O'Malley, *What Happened at Vatican II* (Cambridge: Harvard University Press, 2008), 9, 39.

6. Royce, *Problem of Christianity*, 63–65.

7. For the intellectual parallels between neo-orthodoxy and neo-Thomism, see David Tracy, *Blessed Rage for Order: The New Pluralism in Theology* (Minneapolis: Winston-Seabury Press, 1975), 27–31.

8. Gilkey, *Naming the Whirlwind*, 39, 18.

9. Richard P. McBrien, *The Church: The Evolution of Catholicism* (New York: Harper-Collins, 2008), 130.

10. Theologians were regularly employing the term "postmodern" to describe the theological situation in the mid-1960s; see, for example, Schubert M. Ogden, *The Reality of God and Other Essays* (New York: Harper and Row, 1966), 6–13.

11. I have described the history of the academic study of theology in the United States in *A Preface to Theology* (Chicago: University of Chicago Press, 1996).

12. Louis Menand, *The Metaphysical Club: A Story of Ideas in America* (New York: Farrar, Straus and Giroux, 2001), ix–x.

13. John Ireland, *The Church and Modern Society: Lectures and Addresses*, 2nd ed. (Chicago: D. H. McBride, 1897), 88–89, 100, 110–11; John T. McGreevy, *Catholicism and American Freedom: A History* (New York: W. W. Norton, 2003), 120–23.

14. Shailer Mathews, *The Church and the Changing Order* (New York: Macmillan, 1907), 2–3.

15. Ibid., 157.

16. William R. Hutchison, *The Modernist Impulse in American Protestantism* (Cambridge: Harvard University Press, 1976); R. Scott Appleby, *"Church and Age Unite!" The Modernist Impulse in American Catholicism* (Notre Dame: University of Notre Dame Press, 1992).

17. Mathews, *The Church and the Changing Order*, 13, 17.

18. William Newton Clarke, *Sixty Years with the Bible: A Record of Experience* (New York: Scribner, 1909), 3–9.

19. Benjamin B. Warfield, "The Task and Method of Systematic Theology," *American Journal of Theology* 14 (1910): 192–205; Mark A. Noll, ed., *The Princeton Theology: 1812–1921* (Grand Rapids, Mich.: Baker Book House, 1983), 220–21.

20. Mark A. Noll, *Between Faith and Criticism: Evangelicals, Scholarship, and the Bible in America* (San Francisco: Harper and Row, 1986), 7, 36–38, 125, 190–91.

21. John Tracy Ellis, ed., *Documents of American Catholic History* (Wilmington, Del.: Michael Glazier, 1987), 2:539–41.

22. Cited in McBrien, *The Church*, 120.

23. Thomas E. Woods, *The Church Confronts Modernity: Catholic Intellectuals and the Progressive Era* (New York: Columbia University Press, 2004), 18–19.

24. Ireland, *Church and Modern Society*, 90–93.

25. Ibid., 94–95, 97–102, 104.

26. Walter Rauschenbusch, *A Theology for the Social Gospel* (New York: Macmillan, 1918), 7, 8.

27. Ibid., 60–61.

28. For Catholic critique of American individualism in this period, see McGreevy, *Catholicism and American Freedom*, 111, 131, 136–39, 153–54.

29. Rauschenbusch, *Theology for the Social Gospel*, 5, 14, 20, 70, 143–44, 264–65.

30. Woods, *Church Confronts Modernity*, 20.

31. Jane Addams, *Newer Ideals of Peace* (New York: Macmillan, 1907), 3, 11–12, 14–18.

32. Mathews, *The Church and the Changing Order*, 11–13 (emphasis added).

33. William Adams Brown, "The Task and Method of Systematic Theology," *American Journal of Theology* 14 (1910): 215.

34. John Dewey, *A Common Faith* (New Haven: Yale University Press, 1934), 18–19.

35. H. Richard Niebuhr, *The Meaning of Revelation* (New York: Macmillan, 1941), 10–11.

36. Reinhold Niebuhr, *Moral Man and Immoral Society: A Study in Ethics and Politics* (New York: Scribner, 1932), 95.

37. Reinhold Niebuhr, *An Interpretation of Christian Ethics* (New York: Harper, 1935), 223–24.

38. Elizabeth Cady Stanton, *The Woman's Bible: A Classic Feminist Perspective* (1895, 1898; Mineola, N.Y.: Dover Publications, 2002), Part 1: 7, 110.

39. Howard Thurman, *With Head and Heart* (San Diego: Harcourt Brace, 1979), 103–4, 116, 135.

40. Reinhold Niebuhr, *Beyond Tragedy: Essays on the Christian Interpretation of History* (New York: Scribner, 1937), 28, 34.

41. H. Richard Niebuhr, *Meaning of Revelation*, 4, 10–11, 15, 40, 69, 80.

42. Philip Gleason, *Keeping the Faith: American Catholicism Past and Present* (Notre Dame: University of Notre Dame Press, 1987), 25–30.

43. Jacques Maritain, "Integral Humanism and the Crisis of Modern Times," *Review of Politics* 1 (1939): 2–8.

44. John Courtney Murray, S.J., *Bridging the Sacred and the Secular*, ed. J. Leon Hopper, S.J. (Washington, D.C.: Georgetown University Press, 1994), 102–10.

45. John Courtney Murray, S.J., *We Hold These Truths: Catholic Reflections on the American Proposition* (New York: Sheed and Ward, 1960), 23.

46. John E. Smith, *The Analogy of Experience: An Approach to Understanding Religious Truth* (New York: Harper and Row, 1973), 63.

47. Reinhold Niebuhr, *Beyond Tragedy*, ix.

48. Charles Taylor, *A Secular Age* (Cambridge: Harvard University Press, 2007), 423–72.

49. Ogden, *Reality of God*, 1, 19.

50. Reinhold Niebuhr, *Beyond Tragedy*, ix.

51. My discussion of irony and tragedy as theological narratives is indebted to Martin E. Marty, "Irony (Fig.) and (Lit.) in Modern American Religion," *Journal of the American Academy of Religion* 53 (1985): 187–99.

52. Royce, *Problem of Christianity*, 165–86, 208.

53. Martin Luther King Jr., *I Have a Dream: Writings and Speeches That Changed the World*, ed. James M. Washington (San Francisco: Harper, 1992), 87, 94, 100.

54. Reinhold Niebuhr, *The Irony of American History* (New York: Scribner's, 1952), vii–viii, 88, 133.

55. Dorothy Day, *The Long Loneliness* (New York: Harper and Row, 1952), 273–75.

56. Reinhold Niebuhr, *The Children of Light and the Children of Darkness: A Vindication of Democracy and a Critique of Its Traditional Defense* (New York: Scribner's, 1944), 132.

Hearts and Stones
Material Transformations and the Stuff of
Christian Practice in the United States

American Christian practice in past and present is intimately engaged with stuff, as inherently sensory and material as it is textual. Studies of the subject might effectively consider how Christianities look, feel, smell, taste, and sound, as well as what Christian practitioners say and write. The density of "religious" things with which many Christians daily surround themselves makes this a truly voluminous subject, spatial as well as pictorial and material. It includes buildings, landscapes, and yard assemblages as well as house blessings; dish towels and wall plaques printed with biblical mottoes and pictures; religious paint-by-number kits and embroidery patterns; illustrated Sunday school literatures; crosses and crucifixes; stained glass windows; objects of domestic, ecclesiastical, and liturgical pieties; clothing such as special garments worn for First Communions, baptisms, or confirmations; home altars and pocket shrines; and wall and desk calendars with religious images and text.

Although historians and critics have often drawn sharp distinctions between Protestant and Catholic sensory cultures, some of which surely pertain, the overstated case for binary difference has tended to lump together all Protestants in visual and material opposition to all Catholics, rather than to notice more finely grained similarities and differences within and across individuals and groups. Striking a meaningful balance is a difficult thing. These binary oppositions have gained substantial momentum, moreover, from Protestantism's own narrative of origins, its inception and self-conception, as the product of "iconoclastic" rupture and transformation, as a definitive "conversion," or so Protestant reformers claimed, of Christianity itself to right belief and practice.[1] But "iconoclasm," Reformation and otherwise, represents a particular strategy of substitution and replacement, a mechanism of change in the appearance or interpretation of the visual or material field, not a general or absolute prohibition.[2] Sometimes the same objects, and even similar activities around them, persist and flourish, perhaps in new locations and with different beholders and handlers developing new vocabularies of description and signification to produce and mark distinctions important to them.[3] At the most basic level, Christian adherence to a theology of incarnation mobilizes the material world; here divinity assumes a material body, invisible grace is rendered in visible signs, the most holy sacraments (despite disagreements about their numbers and specific meanings) take shape as divine investments in sensory communication.[4]

Scholarship on these subjects would benefit from a reconfiguration of categorical relations among things "visual" and "material." The distinction as it stands, while useful in some respects, is in others decidedly off the mark, communicating more about disciplinary genealogies and past constructions of sensory hierarchies than about actual sensory experiences and practices. Although each sense operates differently (physiologically and culturally), in the embodied experience of human perception the activation of any one sense elicits others too. The use of images and objects in religious practice, for example, is never simply about sight—and certainly not simply about the physical operations of seeing—but consistently choreographs expanded sensory and imaginative interrelationships as well.[5]

As subjects of this short essay, a rather arbitrarily selected constellation of artifacts underscores a set of larger themes concerning Christian visual and material practices. The essay's title, "Hearts and Stones," immediately signals its interest in several interrelated and emphatically cumulative avenues of inquiry. This investigation first asserts the literal and figurative significance of materiality, in general terms but also as secured by the character of particular materials, substances, or media. The treatment of hearts and stones stands in for, and introduces, this larger engagement—and points toward a reciprocity between materiality and human embodiment. The essay simultaneously shows some ways that Christian scriptural analogies and metaphorical imagination generate visual, material, and hermeneutic connections across a wide array of Christian pictures, objects, and practices—and the ways various audiences understand these connections to instantiate points of heightened access to spiritual realities. Second, it pursues the *material* construction of religious life stories, stories that frequently appropriate these scriptural analogies and illuminate the "lives" of objects and their social relations. Third, the essay offers a few observations about the ways visual and material Christian practices intersect with and shape the terms of commodification in the United States, the relations of religion and commerce. And finally, it concludes with remarks about Christian stuff and material transformation.

Analogical Materialities

This essay begins with seventeenth- and early eighteenth-century Puritan colonists, for whom hearts and stones (but not hearts and stones alone) had special religious significance.[6] Colonial Puritans did not relinquish to Catholicism the use of images in devotional practice; they simply reworked the terms within which they understood the spiritual utility of visual and material practice. What animated this Protestant aesthetic was the analogical language of Christian scripture and its interpretation in ways that pointed explicitly to the qualities of material substances and their relations and transformations. Many forms of Puritan visual and material culture might be fruitfully examined in this regard. I focus attention here on gravestone carving.

Puritan Richard Baxter described the aim of his personal religious practice as a matter of knowing the appearance and disposition of his heart. The scriptural foundation for this commitment featured hearts in company with stones: the righteous have God's laws inscribed on their hearts instead of on tablets of stone (Ezekiel 11:19, Jeremiah 31:33, Hebrews 8:10 and 10:16). The reference asserted the importance of internalizing divine law, the transition from seeing words written on stone tablets in the exterior world to subjective bodily incorporation. Calling his spiritual autobiography his "Book of Heart Accounts," Baxter searched himself to see or "trace the workings of the spirit upon [his] heart."[7] A number of gravestones reiterate precisely this action on the part of the artisan, who made his designs by *tracing* letters and other signs *upon a heart (fig. 1)*. The gravestone carver, cutting a heart into cold, hard stone, rehearsed a transformation Puritans expected deity to accomplish in a different medium: God would write and draw on the living, beating human heart. It was not coincidental, though also by no means exclusive to Puritan New Englanders, that burial markers generally replicated the shape of a single tablet of stone and even explicitly reiterated the twin tablets of the Decalogue (the Ten Commandments). In this context, the common expression "tables [that is, tablets] of our hearts" made the connection even more direct and informed pictorial expression on, for example, the Lydia Peaslee stone (fig. 2), where the heart and the tablets of the Decalogue become one. Peaslee, the picture on her stone asserted, had fully incorporated divine law within her heart.

These gravestones were, perhaps most essentially, about metamorphosis—about the transformation of the self from one state to another, an orthodox and beneficent form of image-magic. Hearts of stone became hearts

FIGURE 1. *Sarah Long stone, Charlestown, Massachusetts, 1674.*
Photo: Sally M. Promey.

of flesh—and then hearts of spirit. From a Puritan theological perspective, on and in such hearts the self-ish image of the self was relinquished, to be replaced by the image of Christ in the self. In an important sense, God's perfect law was analogous to God's image: in writing his own law upon the soul of believers, the divine portrait, banned from Puritan churches, was reinscribed on the Puritan heart. Poet and preacher Edward Taylor explicitly articulated this process: "The transplendent Glorious Image of the Son of God in Sparkling-glorious Colours is portrayed again upon the Soule."[8] The objective of pious self-examination, that most characteristic of Puritan devotional activities, was eventually to discern or discover this image of Christ in the self. This was a sort of Protestant pictorial *imitatio Christi*. "My Heart shall be thy [Christ's] Chrystall looking Glass," Taylor wrote.[9] In the space of mediation and encounter offered by the "mirror of election," the Puritan sought not his or her own image but Christ's image. Use of this "*Prospective-Glass for Saints*" transformed the self into the image of Christ.[10] Again, the source was a scriptural one, taken from 2 Corinthians 3:18: "We all with open face beholding, as in a glass, the Glory of the Lord; are changed into the same image."[11] This exercise of self-examination allowed the practitioner to imagine the self as Christ and to bring the self into conformity with a true

image and a true icon. In this way, Richard Sibbes maintained, "Christ is alive" in the world "in the hearts of gracious Christians, that carry the picture and resemblance of Christ in them."[12]

The connection between the stone medium, shaped and carved by the artisan, and the scriptural insistence upon stone as a meaningful spiritual metaphor emphasized an evocative set of associations not lost on Puritans engaged in meditative self-examination in the burying grounds, a practice recommended in contemporary devotional manuals. The heart or soul (and thus the gravestone that represented it) was both canvas and reflective surface, the looking glass that "displayed" the image of Christ. God, the ultimate artist, was a portraitist who painted, drew, and inscribed his image and the image of his divine son/self on lively stones and human hearts *as* the believer's own true portrait. Gravestones themselves thus functioned as, among other things, spiritual "portraits" or representations of saintly individuals. Furthermore, through a theology of resemblance in which all saints, in looking "like" Christ, also looked "like" one another, carvings that sought to represent one saint, one deceased believer, offered a perfect pattern for a survivor to follow. Walking among the tombs in the burial grounds, believers might find "looking glasses" that brought their own "reflections" into

conformity with the image of the godly saint and in which they were expected to imagine their own names inscribed. Beholding the "mirror" of the represented saint, the believer saw his or her own sanctified self looking back. The Reverend Silas Bigelow's stone (fig. 3) offered an especially compelling spiritual portrait of this believer, showing him preaching from the pulpit in the earthly meetinghouse in a manner that also figured his pastoral presence in God's spiritual temple. Bigelow's portrait in stone literally marked his spatial and spiritual transition from one "place" to the other. An "angel"-shaped negative space around Bigelow's body gave him wings, demonstrating the anticipated ascent of his soul from earth to heaven, marking the moment of this transformation, and inviting beholders to imagine their own spiritual flights.

In these visual and material practices, Puritan aesthetics embraced Christian scripture as pattern book and style guide, mining the text for typological content, for the mind-set of exuberant metaphorical redundancy that informed the aesthetic constellation Puritans called "plain style." Puritan plain style, in pictures as in texts, concerned neither artlessness nor hypersimplicity. Instead, the key to Puritan "plainness" was correlation with the stylistic conventions of Christian scripture.[13] Overlapping metaphors and interconnected narratives, verbally and visually expressed, contributed to the "plainness" of plain style—"plain" in the sense of clarity achieved by reiteration. The tension between uniformity and variety animated this artistic vocabulary: lining up a variety of objects and images (stones, hearts, mirrors, pillars, tablets, temples, and so on), practitioners demonstrated that these consistently communicated the same set of interrelated spiritual messages.

Turning these scriptural analogies over and over, pulling them into proximity, coming at them from a variety of perspectives, Puritan exegetes reiterated the intimacy of the believer's relations with the divine; and Puritan stone carvers, artists, and artisans represented these relations materially in a variety of media. According to this metaphysical calculus, apparent opposites (heart and stone, warm and cold, alive and dead) were not perpetually opposites, and objects (like gravestone carvings) that offered sensory access to these assertions affirmed the possibility of transformation, one to the other. Relations among "objects" multiplied through processes of analogy and metamorphosis. Stone could become flesh, flesh could become spirit; far from being static, these were materials capable of transformation. Adjectives favored among Puritan divines made explicit the changes they anticipated. Hearts that were "hard" or "stony" would become pliable, yielding, "soft," "melting," "waxy." These descriptions elicited not just material substances but also substances that retained the memory of temperature and thus of vitality. Stone was cold; hearts were warm; in order to melt, wax needed also to be warm. Explicitly evoking and inviting the sense of touch as well as sight, clergy and laity mined the capacities of materials to represent desired qualities and to engage sensory imagination.

Other American Christians across time and space appropriated scriptural heart imagery too. Mid-nineteenth-century Shaker communitarians in the First Order at New Lebanon, New York, came to worship one Sunday morning in June 1844, in a period of spiritual efflorescence, to find dozens of pink, blue, and white heart cut-outs, one for each of the 148 members of the order, arrayed on the white cloth covering a large rectangular table, or altar, at the front of the meetinghouse. The size of a human heart and the shape of a valentine, these intricately decorated papers also represented the culture of sentiment that saw the rapid rise of commercially produced valentine cards at just about the same time. The Shaker hearts, however, in the context of the visionary experiences that informed them, represented the pictorial visualization of each individual's own heart. Visually consuming this pictorial "sacrament," each Shaker could see and evaluate this personal heart as through deity's eyes, could read the words of approbation and see the emblems of faith that made spiritual ornaments of each believer. Hearts on paper were far more ephemeral than hearts on stone; but hearts on paper could be more intimately saved and treasured by individuals, to be read and reread, as a form of celestial love letter, an assertion of grace already conferred. Shaker hearts validated affect as well as conviction, made of religious feeling a tangible object, rendering it an item that the believer could literally carry with her, a testimony to others who witnessed its reception, a personal reminder of spiritual community and connection, and an assertion of anticipated transformations already under way.[14]

At about the same time that American Puritans first carved hearts into stone, early modern versions of Catholic devotions to the sacred heart of Jesus and the immaculate heart of Mary took initial shape across the Atlantic. The visionary ascetic practices of Marguerite Marie (also called Margaret Mary) Alacoque (1647–90), a French Visitationist nun, assisted in inaugurating these recalibrations of earlier medieval traditions and Christian heart pieties. Over the years, the complicated institutional and extrainstitutional histories of visual and material devotions to the physical hearts of Jesus and Mary yielded a proliferation of pictures and statuary in many variations, scales, and media. Although Rome gave official precedence to Jesus, the sacred and immaculate hearts implied one another and often appeared in pairs, appealing to the gendered bodies of believers and mirroring each other, signifying the love of God for humanity (sacred heart) and the love of humanity for God (immaculate heart).

A widely (and materially) disseminated aspect of one of Alacoque's visions concerned the promise she claimed Jesus made to her: "I will bless every *place* where an image of my heart shall be exposed and venerated [italics added]." This spatial emphasis elicited practices keyed to either particular locale or miniaturized mobility. Thus, by the second half of the nineteenth century and continuing throughout the twentieth century to the present day, in the United States and elsewhere, Catholics formally and informally dedicated various places (geographical, institutional, and domestic) to these hearts and sent miniature heart representations of various sorts (holy cards, pocket shrines, medals, scapulars, badges, pins, and jewelry) for the personal bodily protection of relatives and friends who lived far away and, in wartime especially, of those who served in the armed forces.[15] Heart devotions came to incorporate, furthermore, a long set of traditions relating hearts and homes, where practitioners understood the sacred hearts to offer shelter and protection, to surround them as they took responsive ref-

FIGURE 4. *Sacred Heart house blessing, mid-twentieth century. Photo: Sally M. Promey.*

I will bless every home where an image of my Sacred Heart is exposed and honored

uge in divine love. This specifically domestic hermeneutics of the sacred and immaculate hearts contributed to the popularity of various kinds of house blessings (fig. 4), handmade and manufactured, that pictured or referenced one heart or the other or both. Sometimes these household benedictions modified the standard sacred heart of Jesus text to suit the new context: "I will bless every *home* where an image of my heart shall be exposed and venerated [italics added]." Often the picture alone sufficed.

Artifacts of this sort, generally replicating a sentimental idiom, asserted familial religious feeling and demonstrated the dedication and skill of those who decorated the domestic interior. That women were responsible for the ornamentation of homes, that they purchased or made most of these things, that these altars and shrines were theirs for the keeping, that they spent more time around them than male members of the family, that they wrote more letters and sent more holy cards, marks a significant aspect of the modern consumption of Christian material culture, in this case and in others. The process of conceiving, producing, selecting, inscribing, and presenting religious objects contributed to and shaped reception and significance. Here domestic practitioners labored over decisions about acquisition of appropriate objects, maintained home shrines and their floral embellishments, stitched religious embroideries of various sorts, hand-painted chalkware statues of saints and biblical figures, neatly inscribed gift items, distributed them in domestic or familial "rituals," or recorded family religious histories in photo albums, Bibles, and scrapbooks. In such practices, women situated material production in "slower" meditative spaces, retarding the usual chronological pace of life while also claiming or recommending a set of desired spatial, material, and bodily transformations.[16]

I pause here to say a few words about important aspects of my subject that occupy little or no space in these pages but that claim considerable attention in my larger project on these topics.[17] What is missing in this present essay is an account of the substantial violence, conflict, and loss (loss well beyond that incurred by the situation of mere human mortality) perpetuated in this Christian sensory imaginary and especially in the Christology of material transformation. "Desired" transformations are not always benign. As one example (and there are many others), over time a racist politics of whiteness has appealed to and conflated a series of binaries mined from scriptural sources and metaphors concerning dark and light, black and white, stained and clean. The same politics recommended a unidirectional "salvific" movement in each case from the former to the latter. Hearts numbered among the objects modified by these pairs of adjectives. This insistent framework of valuation informed Christian moral narratives of spiritual purity, in their Enlightenment and post-Enlightenment versions especially, and resonated throughout American religious and cultural ideologies of "material" transformation.[18] It is easy to push this point too far—it is easier still to push it not far enough. The problem was neither human pleasure and security in sunlight nor the mere use of white or black. The problem lay, rather, in deep, and deeply racist, linguistic, metaphoric, and evaluative practices that paired these sets of signifiers and connected them to one another, linking light, pigment, and notions of physical cleanliness with social, moral, and spiritual values.

In the process of reifying conversion from darkness to light, as in the power dynamics of the imperative to remake the heart, visual religious practices replicated and instantiated dominant race and gender politics. This was especially clear in material evangelization and missionary activity and unmistakably inscribed in domestic pieties as well. Ubiquitous representations of light-complexioned religious figures, saintly and divine, in two and three dimensions, as pictures and figural sculptures, gazed down

FIGURE 5. *Gordon Parks, Washington, D.C.,* Dresser in the bedroom of Mrs. Ella Watson, a government charwoman, *August 1942. Library of Congress, Prints and Photographs Division, FSA/PWI Collection, LC-USF34-013443-C.*

compassionately from altars, walls, shelves, and pedestals of other sorts, visibly claiming to regulate the prescribed Christian "imitation" of the biblical figures they represented, implying that "looking like" Jesus or Mary or John suited some more "naturally" than others. Ella Watson, a Washington, D.C., member of the Reverend Vondell Verbycke Gassaway's Protestant, predominantly African American, Verbycke Spiritual Church, constructed a bedroom shrine using a large rosary and six chalkware statues of the sort easily acquired from a Catholic supply store.[19] In this photograph (fig. 5) by Gordon Parks, the Protestant Watson, seen in her dresser mirror, reads from the Bible that she has just taken up from its usual central place on this domestic altar (complete with flowers, candles, crucifix, and two small elephants). A pictorial sacred heart blessing hangs on the wall adjacent to the bureau, at its proper right. Of the eleven pictorial personages visible in her display—from left to right: 1) Jesus of the sacred heart in the print on the wall, 2) St. Therese of Lisieux, 3) Our Lady of Lourdes, 4) Joseph holding the

5) small child Jesus, 6) the crucified body of Christ on the rosary that hangs down the center of the mirror, 7) the statue of St. Martin de Porres, 8) the one of St. Anthony of Padua also holding 9) the Christ child, 10) the body of Jesus on the small standing crucifix, and 11) Our Lady of Grace—only one, St. Martin de Porres, has comparatively dark skin.[20] The photograph underscores and compounds this numerics of complexion: the dresser mirror doubles four of the statues, including St. Martin, but Watson appears only once, as reflection. The language and media of artistic production are by no means ideologically neutral in social and cultural conditions of racism obsessed with skin color. Each of Watson's six full-figure statues (two of them representing two holy persons each) was made of chalkware—the use of this common plaster medium replicated the "color" of marble, alabaster, and porcelain and further instantiated whiteness as the normative material "appearance" of Christianity.[21] Often flying below the level of conscious awareness or recognition, the visual and material qualities of artistic media aid and abet the ritualization of racism, reiterating processes of selection and representation that "naturalize" racist assumptions and projections. Without question, material objects operate to constrain memory and imagination as well as to evoke them.

Social and Sensory Relations of (Religious) Things

Among the material items that might occupy the late nineteenth- or early twentieth-century American Catholic home, regardless for the most part of the occupant's ethnicity or familial nation of origin, the viaticum or last rites cabinet asserted a powerful daily and nightly presence. Located almost always in the bedroom, these pictorial objects stored utensils to provide for the journey at the time of death from this world to the next and, over the course of a lifetime, reminded beholders of the religious care of human bodies; of associations with the physical pains suffered by Jesus; of divine sustenance in time of illness, trial, and death; and of the hope of bodily resurrection. By this time, viaticum cabinets took several shapes, some intended to be installed in or hung from the bedroom wall (fig. 6), others designed to sit on top of a bureau or dresser, in either case creating a home shrine or altar. Common iconographies for both versions of these objects included, in the upper portions, either the Holy Family (child Jesus with exposed heart, Mary, and Joseph) or the Pietà (in a form appropriated from Michelangelo); and on the lower, either the paired hearts of Jesus and Mary or a Last Supper

FIGURE 6. *Viaticum Cabinet, early twentieth century. Photo: Sally M. Promey.*

BLESSED BE THY HOLY NAME

that replicated Leonardo da Vinci's famous, and widely reproduced, Milan fresco. The subject of the Last Supper, as viaticum ornamentation, anticipated the final sacramental meal to be offered by a visiting priest at bedside and then consumed by the bedroom's occupant. In this space, it thus called to mind a multisensory and intersensory ritual experience, involving taste, touch, smell, and sound as well as sight; it also secured the location of the home in a larger pastoral geography.

Protestant homes, too, accommodated abundant material evidence of domestic pieties in numerous forms and media, handmade as well as manufactured. By the first third of the nineteenth century, for example, a thriving Protestant market in domestic prints responded to emerging liberal theologies that linked salvation to Christian nurture, pressing domestic spaces into the service of Christian familial evangelism and requiring that the home be properly decorated for the important task of growing Christians. In this context, contemporary religious advisers claimed, pictures displayed on the walls of living spaces exerted a gentle influence in shaping believers, quietly transforming hearts, bringing little ones to Jesus, and reminding parents of Christian familial roles and duties. Over the course of the century and beyond, print companies like the one founded by Daniel Wright Kellogg (1807–74) in Horace Bushnell's own Hartford, Connecticut, and the now better-known Currier and Ives produced images that cultivated Christian values at home. (Printers catered to Catholic as well as Protestant markets. Currier and Ives offered paired prints of the sacred and immaculate hearts as well as of other "Catholic" subjects.) In the second half of the nineteenth and early years of the twentieth centuries, some publishing and print houses distributed catalogs and "magazines" that modeled uses of pictorial reproductions, inexpensive religious sculptures, and a range of scripture plaques or gospel mottoes, in church, school, and home.[22]

Despite frequent assertions to the contrary, Protestants as well as Catholics make, buy, and otherwise consume material objects for their affinities with properties that might be labeled "magical."[23] One recent example, from the late twentieth century and the first decade of the twenty-first, explicitly evokes transformative engagement with hearts and stones. In these years, various parties mounted a series of legal and constitutional challenges to the public display of the Ten Commandments, often protesting the granite monuments originally planted in front of city halls and other civic buildings at mid-twentieth century by the Fraternal Order of Eagles, in collaboration with Paramount motion pictures' promotion of Cecil B. DeMille's *Ten Commandments*. In responses to proposals to remove these monuments, an assortment of conservative and evangelical Christian individuals and groups, initially in the nation's South and Midwest, recommended visible protest, focusing attention on the front lawns and churchyards of constituents who pounded metal or durable plastic facsimiles (fig. 7) of the Decalogue, in forms otherwise resembling signs used to sell real estate, into their yards and gardens, challenging on "private" property the assault they perceived on public space.

Here the medium (plastic or metal) did not need to replicate the "original." For some promoters, in fact, it was better if it did not. The "heart" of the matter here was, in fact, the transformation of medium: laws carved into stone becoming laws written on the heart. Most important for at least one evangelical commercial distributor of the yard signs was the potential for public conversion presented in this scenario: the "publicness" of display in private yards would effect a silent but certain visual transmission of the message, ensuring that a Christian version of divine law was powerfully "inscribed," by sight, on the hearts of unsuspecting passersby, making America, through a sort of magical sensory coercion, a "Christian" nation.

Hearts and stones: the material flow, from one to the other, worked in both directions and could be turned inside out to suggest alternate meanings.[24] Not only did the heart accommodate divine law (a transformation of

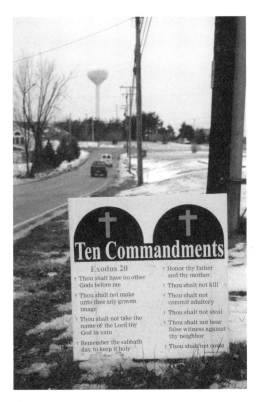

FIGURE 7. *Ten Commandments yard sign, Louisville, Ohio, 2005. Photo: Sally M. Promey.*

stone to human flesh), but that bodily organ was also God's spiritual temple (set in stone, built of and on solid rock). This metaphoric set of devotional associations produced positive resonance for stones or rock as well as hearts and yielded its own related proliferation of objects, pictures, and edifices (fig. 8), emphasizing permanence, firmness of conviction, and sturdiness of foundation, as well as love and vitality. Both hearts and stones, as Christian symbolic objects, reiterate this metamorphic movement and dynamic, back and forth, from one material to the other. As "houses," as containers or receptacles, both hearts and temples also have an inside and an outside and operate as synecdoche, scripturally and otherwise, for the whole human being, the whole human body.

Sociologist Colin Campbell maintains that it has been only in early modern times, a chronology especially relevant for the development of Protestantism and the colonization of America, that emotions have "come to be located 'within' individuals as opposed to 'in' the world." As emotions were subjectified in this fashion, he argues, as they were figured "as states which

emanated from some internal source" rather than from external forces or situations, "there is a sense in which the disenchantment of the external world required as a parallel process some 'enchantment' of the psychic inner world."[25] This process, closely related by Campbell to the modern development of "self-consciousness," focused considerable attention on the dynamics of "inner" and "outer." The inner enchantment on which Campbell remarks was surely facilitated by Calvinism's insistence on the inadequacy and inefficacy of "outside" acts and objects, by John Calvin's demand that these be supplanted by attention to the inner dispositions of the heart.[26] Literary critic Susan Stewart, in an essay titled "Remembering the Senses," joins Campbell in making similar note of engagements between "inner" and "outer." For Stewart, the *senses* "have often been considered as a philosophical problem appearing on a boundary between what we refer to, perhaps for lack of better terms, as internal and external phenomena."[27] In this construction, sensory experience then mediates between "feelings" or emotions (newly located "inside" the modern human person) and the external world, between inner dispositions and outer objects. This historical dynamic is immediately significant for the subject at hand, eliciting new ways of materially parsing long-standing Christian concerns.

The dynamic here, however, is not unidirectional. Material objects, especially religious ones, do not simply facilitate "taking in" the outer world but seek frequently to represent some aspect of the "interior" in "exterior" form, the "invisible" in "visible." As products of human ideation and ingenuity, material objects are themselves "abstractions." They demonstrate external evidence of the quality and character of internal life. They reify this inner/outer boundary and relation in such a way as to render significant, and fairly ubiquitous, an attachment to forms that replicate this relation (for example, boxes, houses, hearts, and other "receptacles"), forms that bring "inner" and "outer" into symbolic proximity. These include 1) objects that substantiate an interior state or emotion (as Shaker hearts, for example, displayed attachment to their godhead and the affect appropriate to that attachment); 2) objects that provide a sensible form to physically insensible things (as gravestones pictured the soul ascending and devotional items gave shape to the sacred heart); and 3) objects that "shelter," protect, and collect special classes of "religious" articles.[28]

Among the latter, manufactured boxed sets of items concerning the "Remembrance of First Holy Communion" offer a compelling illustration and provide a small but focused glimpse of the dense and elaborate material cultures attending Christian (Protestant and Catholic) sacraments and rites of passage, as well as the religious formation of children and youth. Catholic supply houses continue to produce similar "Remembrances" today, and some precedents belong to the mid-nineteenth century. The examples that figure here, however, date in production from the 1930s and 1940s (fig. 9). These boxed sets had several overt uses: they authenticated the experience of the first sacrament itself, recording the details of its liturgical transaction and offering tangible evidence of its observance; they related the experience to individual and communal spiritual biographies; and they provided a material souvenir that replicated an important aspect of the sacrament, reiterating the biblical and liturgical injunction to "Do This in Remembrance of Me." From the start, these commercially made items were both certificates of the event *and* collections of religious objects that sustained additional uses as well. The cardboard boxed set generally contained a child's missal, rosary, scapular, and miniature souvenir lapel pin, sometimes in the shape of a heart. The sets, initially presented by a family member, were augmented over time, as holy cards and other pictures and texts (for example, memorial cards for deceased family members and friends, many of these dated and thus signaling the span of time, tokens of a priest's ordination, religious medals, clippings of religious pictures, small photographs of people and places) were assembled for safekeeping inside the boxes, along with the original contents (which sometimes also included pressed flowers from the day of First Communion or, in the case of boys, the white armbands worn by many to mark the observance). Inscriptions from individuals representing family and church personalized these manufactured items; some items among the additions were handmade, special gifts intended for the new communicant. The boxes themselves were elaborately decorated, inside and out, with certificates that gave the child's name and the date and pictures communicating the event's significance. These images most often asserted Christ's own presence in the mass, showing him in the priest's place, offering the host to a child or group of children. The pictures were arranged not just on the box's outside but also inside the lid, so that the open box made a small shrine or altar, displaying tokens of the day and its lasting significance for the child's religious life narrative. In numerous cases, as surviving archival evidence demonstrates, individuals kept their boxed communion sets, adding items of significance over the course of their lifetimes.

Pictures associated with First Communion referenced and animated other ecclesiastical objects. In the case of some pictures common to children's missals, as well as holy cards and greeting cards designed for this occasion, the representational animation was especially literal, as transubstantiation (the host becoming the living body of Christ) took pictorial place, right before the eyes of the beholder. In the color picture on the frontispiece of a missal titled *Come into My Heart*, presented in 1942 to Elinor McKeon of St. Peter's Church in Worcester, Massachusetts, Jesus, here with sacred heart exposed, offered himself to a child, seated on the altar, who approached the tabernacle door with a gesture of worshipful supplication. This picture, in its prominent location at the book's beginning, invited the youthful communicant to venture further into the book, encouraged her to enjoy this access to the most sacred tabernacle, to enter into intimate communion with Jesus, in consuming the host to welcome Jesus into her own heart—and to imagine shelter in the divine heart in the process. Very similar representations of this liturgical moment appeared on the covers of other children's missals and within the pages of these volumes. These images modeled the use of religious pictures as vehicles for communication with the divine. Often the inside front covers of the missals contained a "compartment" for a crucifix, with a prayer to be said before it printed on the facing page, thus making of the missal itself a portable shrine or "place" of prayer and sacramental imagination.[29]

In their small scale (approximately three-and-a-half inches high by two-

FIGURE 9. *Remembrance of First Holy Communion, box produced by Edward O' Toole Company, 1930s, contents reassembled. Photo: Sally M. Promey.*

and-a-half inches wide by half an inch thick), their attractive colors, and their smooth surfaces, the objects themselves directly appealed to the senses and especially to the sense of touch. They felt good in the palm of the hand, fit neatly within a child's grasp, and could be tucked into a pocket or small handbag for easy transport. Celluloid covers achieved popularity in the decades under consideration; this material manifested bright, eye-catching colors, a shiny, luminous, appearance, and a consistent, finely "polished" tactility that warmed comfortably in the hand when in use. Collections of missals demonstrate that these volumes were well used and almost always personalized in some way—with the addition of an inscription or a hand-decorated bookmark or the insertion of clippings and holy cards. Elizabeth Keener's missal included a 1925 notation from her Irish American grandfather, who gave her the small manual of prayers and useful liturgical information. In the blank pages at the back, furthermore, Elizabeth wrote her own prayer, copied out in pencil, in a hand new to cursive writing: "God, Bless, Daddy and Mother, and [everybody], please God." Likely some years after his 1932 First Communion at age ten, a boy of German ancestry, at St. Francis Xavier's Church in Medina, Ohio, wrote neatly in pen: "Remembrance of my First Holy Communion—May 29, 1932." At some point, he added to his missal a hand-decorated bookmark made of pink grosgrain

FIGURE 10. *Historic Ebenezer Baptist Church, Atlanta, Georgia, 2011, showing River Jordan mural in sanctuary. Courtesy of Ebenezer Baptist Church; courtesy of National Park Service; used by permission.*

ribbon and a die-cut chromolithographic token of the child Jesus seated on a lamb. Neelan Giaquinta, of Malden, Massachusetts, later affixed her own typewritten prayer list to the inside front cover of her 1930s missal. Inside the missal's back cover she glued a similarly typed sheet of paper with a favorite poem-prayer and her own name and address. Barbara Stajszczak's "souvenir" registers—in the familial names it records, in the Polish language printed and written by hand on some of its items, and in the patron saint of the church—the presence of the Polish immigrant community that shaped St. Adalbert's, the second Polish parish founded in the Lagrange Street district of Toledo, Ohio.[30]

Pictures closely attended Protestant sacraments, rites of passage, and religious formation too—and especially Protestant baptism, with variations on visual and material form marking distinctions between those churches that observed infant baptism and those that baptized youth and adults. Denominations of the latter sort frequently show baptismal pools or fonts,

FIGURE 11. *Indian Run Christian Church, East Canton, Ohio, 2009, showing River Jordan mural in sanctuary. Photo: Betty Oyer; used by permission.*

often placing them behind the altar or communion table, on the principal visual axis of the worship space. One noteworthy type of decoration in these often-evangelical Protestant houses of worship pictorially differentiates this space by situating a large-scale painting of the River Jordan, at the front of the sanctuary, above the baptismal pool, re-creating the scene of Jesus' own baptism. This is the case, for example, at Martin Luther King Jr.'s Ebenezer Baptist Church in Atlanta, Georgia (fig. 10), and at Indian Run Christian Church in East Canton, Ohio (fig. 11).[31] These pictures turned sanctuaries into sacred stage sets, mentally transporting congregants to the Holy Land (or it to them) and inviting those looking on to populate the scene, in their imaginations, with their own images and those of their neighbors in the pew. Baptismal certificates sometimes bear similar representations of this sacred geography. These Protestant baptismal examples underscore again the degree to which material religious practices are multisensory. The sensations of cold water and clinging, clammy fabric, of breath sucked in quickly

FIGURE 12. *First Holy Communion photo, 1950s. Private collection.*

and held in anxious anticipation, mark memories of full-immersion baptisms witnessed and experienced and the reception of pictorial certificates and photographs of these observances.

As objects, photos of religious rites of passage mediate a whole set of social relations, asserting their own material capacity to document individual observance and to call to mind related observances and events. In their demonstration of the status newly attained by the photographic subject, these images also carefully stage the mediating contributions of other material objects and ritual accoutrement, the "stuff" of baptism or First Communion.[32] Conventions for First Communion photographs (fig. 12), for example, often show children standing near chalkware religious statues or overseen by religious figures (usually Jesus or angels) that decorated the photographer's studio props or that could be added in the process of developing the film. These images generally depict the communicant holding items of the sort included in Remembrance of Holy Communion sets, especially missals or prayer books and rosaries. Much about these events and the photographs that document them reveals a careful, and carefully gendered and raced, choreography for these rites of initiation. Eight- and nine-year-old girls in frilly white "bridal" dresses and veils and boys in suits with white armbands demonstrate practiced gestures in holding their prayer books, often clasped between prayerful hands, the books frequently oriented to display the pictures of fair-skinned divinities and saints on the front covers. Photographs from the 1950s suggest the degree to which the longer practice of clothing female First Communicants as brides of Christ was assimilated, at this time, to other contemporary practices of childhood costuming such as Christmas pageants, Easter parades, and Halloween.[33]

Among Protestants as well as Catholics, Bibles and Bible boxes have assumed some functions similar to Catholic Remembrance of First Communion boxes. The Bibles themselves, especially larger ones, act as a kind of shrine or receptacle for family genealogies, with names literally inscribed "within the faith" represented by the object, its sacred text, and its own recitations of spiritual genealogies.[34] The pages of Bibles, furthermore, often became repositories—for small religious pictures; clippings of religious poetry and snippets of religious prose; small die-cut chromolithographs intended for Victorian scrapbooks; photographs of baptisms, confirmations, weddings, and family members or family gatherings; single pressed wedding flowers; memorial cards, death notices, or obituaries; and here and there a four-leaf clover. Over time, items like the boxed souvenir sets and family Bibles or Bible boxes came to "house" a personal religious life story, to contribute to the shape of Christian subjectivities.[35] In repetitive practices of accumulation and review, these souvenirs were consumed not just once but time and again, re-collecting both the original event and its related emotions and sensations and re-imagining that event in relation to other people and places and observances represented by the items subsequently assembled in the box interiors or within the Bibles' pages.

Such objects, despite their ephemerality and interpretive plasticity, number among those items most likely to pass from one generation to the next, to remain part of familial "archives," occupying space in cupboards and drawers, chests and attics, as the material remains of people's lives are sorted and redistributed among descendants. These objects gain and lose particular meanings over time, their specific material shape perhaps readjusted as various descendants value some aspects of the "collection" over others, discarding items whose "connections" to the ancestor or themselves or a mutually significant religious or life narrative they no longer recognize, dispatching to trash bins items irreparably worn or broken by repeated handling. In this process, the original objects become increasingly untethered, unmoored, from initial significance and take on new associations. They constitute, in Jeffrey Hamburger's phrasing about images more generally, "a flexible matrix open to a range of meanings and formulations."[36] Sometimes cut loose altogether from families of origin, they float in the commercial spaces of flea markets and eBay, reentering the marketplace as another sort of "collectible."

Christian Commodity and Material Transformations

The subject of commodity culture, as interpretive construct in relation to American religions and as a product of American religious imaginings and practices, hums a steady tune in the background throughout this essay. The manufactured objects examined here could be easily acquired from shops and mail order catalogs. Many of those produced by hand derived from patterns made available in commercial venues and serial publications. A part of the objects' spatial and interpretive mobility they owed to their commercial accessibility. Parishes and congregations participated in commodifying religious time and space in the packaging and selling of such items; these included souvenirs of First Communion manufactured, by the 1950s, in purse and wallet as well as box forms. Commerce might use the moral currency of religious institutions to more effectively market wares, or at least so the editors of the Catholic *Benziger Magazine* claimed in 1912, as they sought to build their own advertising base by attracting manufacturers with assertions that consumers would know the magazine for its sterling ethical reputation and thus be more inclined to buy from companies with ads in its pages. Various commercial enterprises used an even more direct approach to Christian religious sensibilities. "Hires' Improved Root Beer" offered, "as a Souvenir to the patrons" of its product, the premium of a chromolithograph of *The Parting of Ruth and Naomi*. With its sentiment of heart reaching out to heart, the manufacturer insisted that the print retained "all the pathos of this touching episode of Scripture." By the early twentieth century, similar religious, often biblical, pictures adorned the surfaces of many sorts of inexpensive useful items (fans and thermometers, for example) to advertise the services of such widely varying enterprises as funeral homes and welding companies.

Domestic spaces and practices operated not in opposition to the more "public" space of the market but in constant interchange and overlap with it. Beginning around the middle of the nineteenth century, a religious deco-

FIGURE 13. *Currier and Ives, The Word and the Sign, 1877, hand-colored print, detail. Photo: Sally M. Promey.*

rating trend took hold that would link floral ornamentation in American homes to similar forms in American churches and, shortly thereafter, in shop windows and department stores, an especially direct representation of the ongoing association and reciprocal formation of religion and consumer culture in the United States.[37] The latter third of the century would see American picture manufacturers producing hand-colored prints and chromolithographs as a kind of facsimile of these altar decorations (fig. 13). The domestic display of such prints created "home altars" in Protestant houses that were not so dissimilar from Catholic home altars dedicated to the sacred heart(s) or to particular saints.

Various sorts of floral and vernal arrangements involving hearts, crosses, and Bibles were among the most frequently reproduced. Visually, it might be argued, the cross as scriptural "Rock of Ages" (with the close hymnic/poetic assertions of the "Old Rugged Cross" and "Simply to Thy Cross I Cling") became at this time a kind of Protestant version of the crucifix in substituting the female body of the Protestant believer ("clinging" to the cross, hiding or sheltering herself in this rock) for the body of the crucified Christian savior. (Catholic households consumed these images too.) The anecdotal historical record for the "Rock of Ages" hymn has its self-proclaimed "Calvinist"

FIGURE 14. *Rock of Ages chromolithograph, late nineteenth to early twentieth centuries. Photo: Sally M. Promey.*

author, the Reverend Augustus Toplady (1740–78), writing the verses as he took shelter in a cave during a furious storm on England's rocky coast. Despite this story of origins, it was nearly always a woman who clung to the cross in the hymn's melodramatic and widely reproduced, often eroticized, visual representations (fig. 14).

The material demands of American commerce and American Christianities are strikingly similar in some important respects, at least two of which are immediately relevant here. First, commodification necessitates an aesthetic of both standardization and variety, producing apparently endless variations of still necessarily recognizable objects. This commercial aesthetic conforms fluently with the stylistic and substantive operations of biblical metaphor, thus providing a larger cultural frame and interpretive rationale for the manufacture of Christian items that elicit a richly evocative, analogical vocabulary from within their own scriptural parameters but that occupy a more static, apparently superficial and even trivial visual and material register from the perspective of differently situated audiences. Second, the desire for transformation is by no means an exclusively Christian phenomenon but a commercial, and deeply cultural, one. Commodification, like Christianity, is also aimed, paradoxically, at transformation and dematerialization; capitalism connects its material products to "inner" abstractions and to promises/fantasies of transcendence. Under conditions of use, objects of the marketplace may be ultimately no less objects of the heart.

If part of the narrative and theoretical/theological work of both modernization and Reformation concerned a process of disenchantment of the material universe in favor of "spiritual" transformation, with god(s) resident in believing hearts rather than external objects, then both Reformers and Enlightenment thinkers framed Catholic "priestcraft" to suggest a closer relation to the material engagements of other "crafts" (including, for example, "witchcraft," gendered in such a way as to suggest the mediate position of women, as well as the "more primitive" religious practices of colonized "others," especially those imagined as subjects for Christian mission).[38] The beginnings of Protestantism as a break with this "more material," "medieval," "Catholic" past, aligned aspects of Reformed self-understanding more closely with the secularization theory of modernity, the weight of which settled disproportionately on the material practice of religion: what was "primitive," what was "outmoded," what was superseded by modernity, was not just religion, but especially material religion ("fetishistic" religion), religion that activated objects. Secularization theory made of religion, so far as concerned materiality, what Protestantism made of Catholicism. Both modernity and Protestantism strove to distance themselves from this reputedly fetishistic and idolatrous past, construed in modernity's case as "religious" and in Protestantism's as "Catholic."[39] As this essay has suggested, the protestations of the reformed and the enlightened in this respect attained a measure of success not so much in diminishing material practice but rather in diverting attention from continued engagement with a generally modified but no less material set of involvements among both Protestants and "moderns." While various Protestantisms and modernities have each had much to say about the ways people *should* (and should not) practice objects, from the start these narratives have been insufficient to contain the ways people *actually* do so.

The construction and reiteration of Christian subjectivities and affective registers takes place in intimate, sensory interaction with material objects, the engagement with which actively contributes to this process. The analogical interpretation and elaboration of materials accomplishes the work of modeling transformation as significance toggles back and forth from one substance to another: stone to heart; heart to temple; temple to foundation stone; foundation stone to Rock of Ages; Rock of Ages to Bible or to cross— not one after the other, but simultaneously, in constant oscillation, each reinforcing the other, each suggesting its own metamorphic potential. In content and practice, this "motion" suggests the possibility of similar transformation for persons, an ultimate transformation of exterior to interior and flesh to spirit. The material, it turns out, is part and parcel of the equation—the material encodes, signifies, shapes, and constrains the construction of Christian subjectivities and the processes of their transformation. In a cultural system that tends to produce and replicate binary patterns of thought, dematerialization always implies its opposite, and constant oscillation renders many contradictions functionally irrelevant—pulling linear developments back into cyclical motions and forms, asserting material bodies as the ineluctable medium of the human condition, and signaling a fundamental reticence to let them go.

NOTES

I dedicate this essay to the memory of my father, George Herman Louis Promenschenkel, to whom it would have had special significance.

1. See, for example, Bruno Latour, *We Have Never Been Modern*, trans. Catherine Porter (Cambridge: Harvard University Press, 1993); and Webb Keane, *Christian Moderns: Freedom and Fetish in the Mission Encounter* (Berkeley: University of California Press, 2007).

2. For just one historical American example from among a great many, see Sally M. Promey, *Spiritual Spectacles: Vision and Image in Mid-Nineteenth-Century Shakerism* (Bloomington: Indiana University Press, 1993). See also Bruno Latour and Peter Weibel, eds., *Iconoclash: Beyond the Image Wars in Science, Religion, and Art* (Cambridge: MIT Press, 2002).

3. See, for example, Mia Mochizuki, *The Netherlandish Image after Iconoclasm, 1566–1672* (London: Ashgate, 2008).

4. Susan Ridgely Bales, *When I Was a Child: Children's Interpretations of First Communion* (Chapel Hill: University of North Carolina Press, 2009), 73.

5. Sally M. Promey and Shira Brisman, "Sensory Cultures: Material and Visual Religion Reconsidered," *Blackwell Companion to Religion in America*, ed. Philip Goff (Wiley-Blackwell, 2010), 177–205.

6. Sally M. Promey, "Mirror Images: Framing the Self in Early New England Material Piety," in *Figures in the Carpet: Finding the Human Person in the American Past*, ed. Wilfred M. McClay (Grand Rapids, Mich.: Eerdmans, 2007), 71–128.

7. Richard Baxter, *The Mis-Chiefs of Self-Ignorance, and the Benefits of Self-Acquaintance* (London, 1662), 304; Richard Baxter, *Reliquiae Baxterianae: or, Mr. Baxter's Narrative of the Most Memorable Passages of His Life and Times* (London: T. Parkhurst, 1696), 6.

8. Edward Taylor, *Christographia*, ed. Norman S. Grabo (New Haven: Yale University Press, 1962), 97.

9. Edward Taylor, Meditation 132, line 32, in *Edward Taylor's God's Determinations and Preparatory Meditations: A Critical Edition*, ed. Daniel Patterson (Kent, Ohio: Kent State University Press, 2003), 452 (Taylor as quoted in David H. Watters, *"With Bodilie Eyes": Eschatological Themes in Puritan Literature and Gravestone Art* [Ann Arbor, Mich.: UMI Research Press, 1981], 173).

10. Phrases quoted from Sacvan Bercovitch, *Puritan Origins of the American Self* (New Haven: Yale University Press, 1975), 14; Bercovitch quotes Richard Baxter, William Dell, and Richard Mather.

11. Richard Mather, *The Summe of Certain Sermons upon Genes[is] 15:6* (Cambridge, Mass.: Samuel Green, 1652), 23 (referring to 2 Corinthians 3:18).

12. Richard Sibbes, *The Excellency of the Gospel above the Law* (London, 1639), reprinted in *Works of Richard Sibbes*, vol. 4, ed. Alexander B. Grosart (Cambridge: Cambridge University Press, 2001), 264.

13. Compare to Bercovitch, *Puritan Origins*, 29–30.

14. See Leigh Eric Schmidt, *Consumer Rites: The Buying and Selling of American Holidays* (Princeton: Princeton University Press, 1995); and Barry Shank, *A Token of My Affection: Greetings Cards and American Business Culture* (New York: Columbia University Press, 2006); on Shaker hearts, see Promey, *Spiritual Spectacles*.

15. Archive of correspondence, private collection.

16. See Geoffrey Batchen, *Forget Me Not: Photography and Remembrance* (Princeton: Princeton Architectural Press, 2006), on similar processes in decorated photographs.

17. The working title of this larger project is "Written on the Heart: Sensory Cultures of American Christianities."

18. See, for example, Nell Irvin Painter, *The History of White People* (New York: W. W. Norton, 2010); and Kathleen M. Brown, *Foul Bodies: Cleanliness in Early America* (New Haven: Yale University Press, 2009). I am grateful to Tracy Fessenden and Kathryn Lofton for careful reading and shared insights on these subjects and to Traci C. West for encouraging me to think further about visual and material ritualizations of racism. That Protestant Christians in the United States played instrumental roles, as Protestant Christians, in the production and commodification of soap products, with names like "Ivory," advertising close to absolute (99.44 percent) purity, was also no accident; see Kathryn Lofton, "Purifying America: Rites of Salvation in the Soap Campaign," in *How Purity Is Made*, ed. Udo Simon and Petra Rösch (Wiesbaden: Harrassowitz Publishing House, 2010).

19. Colleen McDannell, *Picturing Faith: Photography and the Great Depression* (New Haven: Yale University Press, 2004), 260.

20. Importantly, Gassaway also founded a "school of metaphysical study" that he named "St. Martin's Spiritual Center" (ibid.), likely after the dark-complexioned St. Martin de Porres; St. Martin's met in the church building. Despite this recognition of St. Martin, almost all of the church's religious statues had white features, a characteristic of the statuary available in contemporary church supply catalogs. Verbycke Church's statues represented a selection of saints similar to the one on Watson's dresser.

21. If various print media facilitated the spread of two-dimensional devotional and religious educational images, chalkware figured prominently among media that made possible the wide dissemination of religious statues and wall plaques. This medium is the subject of an essay-in-progress, tentatively titled "Material Complexions: Chalkware and the Shape of Christian Devotions, 1880–1960."

22. Benziger Brothers, for example, produced for and marketed to American Catholic constituencies, and Perry Pictures sold to predominantly Protestant audiences.

23. Protestants as well as Catholics made use of what we might call "activated objects," objects that asserted a kind of agency, things connected to the sorts of "magical thinking" purportedly dispelled in modernity. See also, for example, David Freedberg, *The Power of Images: Studies in the History and Theory of Response* (Chicago: University of Chicago Press, 1989); and David Morgan, ed., *Icons of American Protestantism: The Art of Warner Sallman* (New Haven: Yale University Press, 1996).

24. On supersessionary thought, see Kathleen Biddick, *The Typological Imaginary: Circumcision, Technology, History* (Philadelphia: University of Pennsylvania Press, 2003).

25. Colin Campbell, *The Romantic Ethic and the Spirit of Modern Consumerism* (Oxford, UK: Blackwell, 1987), 72–73. Historian Barry Shank, building on Campbell's now-classic study, reiterates the fascination of "the modern self" with "relationships between the inside and the outside;" Shank, *Token of My Affection*, 23.

26. Paradoxically, perhaps, Protestants have deployed objects to assist in their own "disappearance" or transformation to something else, their own ultimate transcendence of material mortality, their own spiritualization. But this very liminality, this balancing on the edge of metamorphosis, was part of what constituted the attraction, interiorizing and therefore "magically" dematerializing the object, "subjectifying" the material, and informing the conditions of reception and interpretation. Image/object "magic" in a late capitalist market economy is fully consistent with these Christian theoretical and theological assertions.

27. Susan Stewart, "Remembering the Senses," in *Empire of Sense: The Sensual Culture Reader*, ed. David Howes (Oxford, UK: Berg, 2005), 59.

28. In addition to different sorts of sacramental and liturgical boxes or "containers," this category might include such things as shrines, home altars, and reliquaries.

29. See also Thomas Lentes, "As Far as the Eye Can See": Rituals of Gazing in the Late Middle Ages," in *The Mind's Eye: Art and Theological Argument in the Middle Ages*, ed. Jeffrey F. Hamburger and Anne-Marie Bouche (Princeton: Princeton University Press, 2006), 360.

30. See the parish website at http://www.stadalbertsthedwig.org/. Religious suppliers marketed these boxes in multiple languages in the United States, Europe, and elsewhere, for diversely ethnic Catholic audiences.

31. Material evidence demonstrates that Protestants were no strangers to church decoration, despite claims to the contrary. As with the pictures of the River Jordan, twentieth-century Protestants, for example, frequently display imagery in the most visible locations of their worship spaces.

In selecting the name "Ebenezer," incidentally, this church (and others) laid claim to the host of biblical rock and stone analogies to which this essay points. See 1 Samuel 7:12: "Then Samuel took a rock . . . and named it Ebenezer, for he said, 'This far the Lord has helped us.'" See Ebenezer Baptist Church's use of this interpretive foundation on its website: www.historicebenezer.org/Home.html.

32. See also anthropologist Alfred Gell on "social relations in the vicinity of objects mediating social agency," in *Art and Agency: An Anthropological Theory* (Oxford, UK: Oxford University Press, 1998), 7.

33. In one image in my private collection, the First Communicant in "bridal" garb was photographed with her little sister, clearly not about to be upstaged, in her own angel costume.

34. Christian scriptural understanding of the person of Jesus Christ as at once both "true image" and "true word" asserts the intimate connection of the three (image, word, and being). Word is embodied in visual and material form, in the body of Jesus and in the scriptural Word of God equated with him. The scriptural Word—the Christian Bible—itself is a visual and material object and, as such, an object frequently represented in pictorial and material iterations and subject to decoration, illustration, devotion, and display.

35. See also Susan Stewart, *On Longing: Narratives of the Miniature, the Gigantic, the Souvenir, the Collection* (Durham: Duke University Press, 1993).

36. Hamburger, "Introduction," in *The Mind's Eye*, 6.

37. See Schmidt, *Consumer Rites*.

38. Until very recently, most of the items considered in this essay have counted for scholars neither as "art" nor as "piety." On the contrary, these things have suggested to many experts the material vestiges of earlier cultural or biological "primitivisms," either the lingering remnants of "folk" practices (with "folk" here taking the form of the "primitive within" contemporary culture) or the youthful, not yet mature, "magical" Christianity of children still in the nascent stages of their own religious formation. See Freedberg, *Power of Images*; see also Webb Keane on the "moral narrative of modernity," in Keane, *Christian Moderns*.

39. Liberal Protestantism in the mid-twentieth century moved to secure a high art (and high commodity) of transcendence and to claim interiorization and spiritualization of religion for that art; see Sally M. Promey, "Taste Cultures and the Visual Practice of Liberal Protestantism, 1940–1965," in *Practicing Protestants: Histories of the Christian Life in America*, ed. Laurie Maffly-Kipp, Leigh Schmidt, and Mark Valeri (Baltimore: Johns Hopkins University Press, 2006), 250–93.

A Contested Legacy
Interpreting, Debating, and Translating the Bible in America

If, as the editors of this volume observe, Christianity is everywhere in America, the same may be said of its sacred text, the Bible, the nation's best-selling book. Each year, Americans purchase 20 million new Bibles, with annual sales generating between $425 million and $650 million.[1] A perusal of the religion section in national chain bookstores turns up more Bibles or books about the Bible than any other single work on the shelves. Guests in a hotel often find a Gideon Bible or, if in a Marriott-related hotel, the Book of Mormon in the nightstand. John 3:16 banners continue to be unfurled at televised professional football games. Of course, one need not leave home to locate a Bible; more than 90 percent of American households contain at least one copy. According to a 2008 Harris Poll, the Bible is America's favorite book among adults.[2] Biblical words and phrases are embedded in the culture: "the blind lead the blind" (Matthew 15:14); "eye for an eye" (Exodus 21:24); "out of the mouth of babes" (Psalm 8:2); "sin of the fathers" (Exodus 20:5); "two-edged sword" (Hebrews 4:12); "ye of little faith" (Matthew 8:26)—to mention a few.[3] Media reports invoke biblical allusions: legal decisions require "the wisdom of Solomon"; the magnitude of natural disasters (for example, Hurricane Katrina) approach "biblical proportions";[4] a person who aids another is hailed as "a good Samaritan." Continuing a near-century of Bible-based, Bible-themed, box office hits going back to Cecil B. DeMille are a spate of recent films—*The Passion of the Christ*, *Lord of the Rings*, and *Narnia*.

The Bible is sold, cited, and exhibited—it is ubiquitous—but unlike the attributes identified with the divine character, omniscience does not attend omnipresence. Americans revere the Bible but are biblical illiterates. A Gallup survey found that less than half of Americans can name the first book of the Bible, only a third know that Jesus delivered the Sermon on the Mount, and 60 percent cannot name half of the Ten Commandments.[5] Yet despite this current knowledge deficit, the Bible remains the central book of America's cultural and intellectual heritage. If one were pressed to argue for a single factor that has defined American Christianities, a strong case could be made for the influence of the Bible. To understand American Christianity, even American history, is to understand the history of the Bible in America. With its multiple uses, interpretations, and translations, the Bible provides a wide-angled lens by which to view the panorama of Christianities in America.

In their introduction to *The Bible in America* (1982), a volume that signaled the beginning of increased scholarly attention to the subject, Nathan Hatch and Mark Noll observe that although scripture has been "nearly omnipresent in the nation's past," "the actual use of the Bible in American life has been attended with considerable complexity and decided ambiguity."[6] Their observations were borne out in the essays that followed, as well as by an increasing number of studies devoted to aspects of the Bible in American life. Nearly coincident with the Hatch and Noll volume, the Society of Biblical Literature launched a six-volume series, The Bible in American Culture, with a view to the Bible's formative influence in popular culture, the arts, law, politics, education, and social reform.[7] Since then, a variety of monographs and specialized studies have focused on the history of the Bible in America,[8] the production and sale of the Bible,[9] American disputes over translations of the Bible,[10] critical engagement with the Bible,[11] *American biblical hermeneutics*,[12] the Bible and slavery,[13] the Bible's impact on American presidents,[14] denominational understandings of the Bible,[15] the biblical hermeneutics of important theologians such as Jonathan Edwards,[16] and the appropriation of the Bible from the perspective of feminists and racial and ethnic minorities.[17]

The following essay takes into account this ever-expanding body of scholarship with the express purpose of demonstrating that American Christianities have been shaped by rival interpretations, applications, and translations of the Bible.[18] As I will discuss shortly, this arena of contestation was made possible by two developments: initially, the predominance of Protestantism with its twin emphasis on the elevation of the Bible and the right of individual interpretation, followed by disestablishment, which accelerated these characteristics in Protestantism. To illustrate the contested place of scripture in American Christianities, I focus on three issues: the appropriation of the biblical theme of Exodus, debates over the place of the Bible in public education, and controversies over English translations of the Bible.

The Text and Nothing but the Text

The significance of the Bible in America attests to the overwhelming influence of Protestantism in America's founding. Uplifting the doctrine of *sola scriptura*, Protestants undercut traditional forms of Catholic authority and made the Bible the "last word" on matters of faith and morals. The cultural consequences of this move were far-reaching, as is seen best in the biblicism of the Puritans, a people who, in Sacvan Bercovitch's words, "discovered America in the Bible."[19] Their Bible-drenched culture permeated Americans' view of their place in the world, ensuring that America would become a nation shaped primarily by a text, not by tradition.

If the biblical text is the guiding principle, then people must be taught to read. Hence the colonists passed laws requiring that youth "attain at least so much, as to be able to read the Scriptures."[20] The *New England Primer* (for example, "A" = "In Adam's fall we sinned all") and other reading aids promoted a biblically literate people. If the Old Testament supplies a blueprint for New England's "Bible Commonwealth," then its civil laws must be enacted. Hence the Massachusetts authorities heeded the injunction of Leviticus 20:5 ("and if a man lie with a beast, he shall surely be put to death: and you shall slay the beast") in executing William Hackett of Salem in 1642, who was found "in buggery with a cow upon the Lord's Day."[21] Similarly, if Puritan authorities were to fulfill the role of Israel's kings, then they must punish by whipping, imprisoning, banishing, and even hanging those who threatened the civil peace and religious orthodoxy of the colony.[22] If, as the Puritans reasoned, the Bible was to be read figuratively, typologically, and corporately, then there must be some connection between God's covenantal promises to the nation of Israel and God's faithful remnant in New England. Hence the Puritans viewed themselves as the new Israel, the chosen people of God, prophetically engrafted into the history of redemption with a divine mandate to build "a city on a hill."[23] Finally, if the Bible records the origin and dispersal of the human race, then the peoples of other lands, such as the Native Americans, must have a biblical heritage. Hence, John Eliot, the "apostle to the Indians," concluded that the Native Americans were descendants of the Ten Lost Tribes of Israel (though many other Puritans viewed them as minions of Satan). In every area of life, private and public, the Puritans, more than any other group in American history, governed their lives by the Bible.

To be sure, attention to the Bible was not confined to the Puritans or to Protestants in general. Well over a century before the Puritans, bibliocentric cosmographies influenced the views of Catholic explorers to the Americas. Eliot's conclusions about the Native Americans' origins derived from a sixteenth-century world of millennial fervor shared by Catholics and Protestants alike. Convinced from his reading of scripture that the end times were imminent, devout Catholic Christopher Columbus invoked the prophet Zephaniah (2:11) in support of converting the Indians through conquest and coercion.[24] A very different approach was taken by Dominican Bartolomé de Las Casas, who arrived in Hispaniola ten years after Columbus. He witnessed firsthand the destructive consequences of physical and spiritual conquest and became a tireless defender of the rights and dignity of the Indians. In his *In Defense of the Indians* (ca. 1550), Las Casas appealed to the words and life of Jesus, who brought a consoling message of freedom to the captives and sight to the blind. Evangelization required patience and persuasion, not punishment and coercion.[25]

Conflicting views over how to apply the Bible to contemporary affairs were nothing new to Catholics. "What the Bible says" (and some would argue "what the Bible *is*") had been problematic since the writers of scripture put quill to parchment, and yet church authorities and theologians reined in heterodox interpretations and developed an orthodox consensus regarding the church's basic teachings.[26] The uncertain relationship between the divinely authored text and its fallible human interpreters was clarified by the successors to Christ and the apostles and the pope and his teaching magisterium. Protestantism, however, defied the Catholic hierarchy's claim that the Bible is the *prima fidei regula*, the primary authority among others (for example, ancient creeds, rulings of church councils, living authorities) and elevated the Bible as the *sola fidei regula*, the only authoritative voice of God.

During the colonial period, individual or subjective interpretation was generally (there are notable exceptions) held in check by deference to, or the imposition of, clerical interpretation backed by civil authorities. As well, confessional traditions among Anglicans, Lutherans, Congregationalists, and Presbyterians safeguarded individual interpretation of the Bible within their own communities. Catechisms—the Westminster Shorter Catechism (1647) within the Reformed bodies, the Smaller Catechism among Lutherans, and the Book of Common Prayer in Anglican communions—were taught, printed, circulated, and memorized. But the very fact of these rival traditions with their own catechisms or divine liturgies pointed to a historical reality: the Protestant Reformation unleashed multiple and often conflicting interpretations of the sacred text.

In a democratic environment of religious freedom, where common people carried the right of private interpretation to its logical conclusion, interpretive chaos ("democratization" is too mild) and the proliferation of revised and translated Bibles ensued, particularly among religious minorities. The legacy was a Protestant America wracked by controversy, violence, and even bloodshed over contrasting interpretations of the Bible. In the theological debate over slavery, for example, northerners and southerners piled up biblical proof text upon proof text before settling their argument on the battlefield.[27]

Whose Exodus, Whose Promised Land?

Among the biblical stories that have profoundly shaped Christianities in America is the Exodus account, "one of America's central themes."[28] This theme is certainly not unique to America, but its multiple invocations over the centuries by various groups, be they Jewish or Christian, Irish, English, Asian, or African, is perhaps distinct. In the early eighteenth century, for example, the Presbyterian clergy of Ulster "bellow[ed] from their pulpits" that "God has appointed a Country [America] for them to Dwell in," a place where they would be free from "the Bondage of Egipt and goe to ye land of Canaan."[29] More than two hundred years later, in the very different context of World War II, the pastor of a Japanese Episcopal Church in Los Angeles likened his parishioners' internment to Israel's in the Exodus. So powerful was the application of this story that after the war, a stained glass window of Moses and the Exodus was installed in the church.[30]

In applying the Exodus episode to their collective histories, no two groups better illustrate the polarities of interpretive conclusions than New England Puritans, expatriates from England, and African Americans, forced migrants from Africa. Each drew upon the Exodus story to make sense of their histories, but in radically different ways. To Puritans, America was the Promised Land and they were its chosen people. To African Americans, America was their Egypt and they were its enslaved people. Blacks derived sustaining hope from the Exodus narrative, but as Dwight Callahan has observed, the Bible had "the power to curse and cure"—it was "a healing balm and a poisonous book."[31]

Such sharply divergent interpretations of the Exodus event define the contrast between black and white views of America. "The meaning of the Exodus story for America," notes Albert Raboteau, "has remained fundamentally ambiguous." Echoing the question of W. E. B. Du Bois, he asks,

"Is America Israel, or is she Egypt?"[32] For John Winthrop, the Massachusetts Bay Colony's first governor, America was indeed Israel, though he recognized the conditional nature of remaining in God's good graces. If the Puritans fulfilled their covenantal obligations, he announced to his fellow voyagers on the deck of the flagship *Arabella* in 1630, then God would bless the creation of a godly commonwealth; if they did not, "the Lord will surely break out in wrath against us."[33]

This typological mold, casting America as the new Israel (a conjoining of biblical typology and American nationalism) persisted through the Revolutionary era and well into the period of nation building. As Puritan views of human depravity and the conditional nature of the covenant gave way to more optimistic appraisals of human ability and American destiny, a decided shift in Anglo-American self-perception occurred. America was envisioned as the site where "another Canaan shall excel the old."[34]

With independence achieved, the rhetoric of the Exodus took on a decidedly nationalist emphasis that expressed the myth of chosenness and destiny. A New England Congregationalist minister observed, "It has been often remarked that the people of the United States come nearer to a parallel with Ancient Israel, than any other nation upon the globe."[35] Both peoples were the unique recipients of divine favor. When this notion of the nation as God's new Israel merged with the powerfully popular idea that America would become the inaugural site of the fast-approaching millennium, one is not far from the nineteenth century's nationalist ideology of Anglo-Saxon expansionist Manifest Destiny having messianic, mercenary, and racist implications.

Although U.S. presidents have never explicitly identified the nation with God's chosen people, they have reiterated the idea that God providentially directs history and has especially used the United States to carry out a special mission in the world. Two very different presidents in the twentieth century, John F. Kennedy and Ronald Reagan, referred to America using the familiar language of exceptionalism. In his address to the Massachusetts General Court on January 9, 1961, President-Elect Kennedy quoted Winthrop's "city on a hill sermon," and Reagan, who declared 1983 "The Year of the Bible," went so far as to liken the legacy of his two terms in office to the "brilliant vision of America as a Shining City on a Hill."[36] Nearly two decades later, George W. Bush explained that his decision to run for the presidency was inspired by the call of a reluctant Moses to assume the mantle of leadership. More than any other recent "faith-based" president (going back to the Carter era), Bush envisioned America "as a kind of new Israel called by God to be God's people on the international stage."[37]

Centuries before, any triumphalist version of Christianity was repudiated by Christianized black slaves. As African Americans knew only too well, there was a tragic irony to Americans' claim to be the new Israel—with the reality of an enslaved old Israel in their midst.[38] America had become a New Canaan for whites, but at what cost to blacks? As slaves were exposed to Christian teaching, they embraced and redefined scripture on their own terms. In particular, Exodus-centered spirituals supplied the rudiments of a contextual theology that has informed African American Christianity to this day. God's deliverance of the Hebrews from Pharaoh's grip became the paradigmatic expression of hope that God would also deliver African Americans from slavery. The best-known spiritual, "Go Down Moses," captured this hope, as did other spirituals such as "Let God's Saints Come In" and "Didn't Old Pharaoh Get Los'?"[39] In these songs, the Exodus event functioned as an archetype, enabling slaves to live with the promise of a future when the captives would go free and the righteous would be rewarded.

Although the overwhelming majority of African Americans resigned themselves to their lot under slavery, others concluded that God would avenge the oppressors and liberate the enslaved through human instrumentality just as he had used Moses and Aaron to crush his enemies. Exodus was a double-edged sword, its message adapted to both divine intervention and human initiative. And so the Exodus theme would play a key role in several early nineteenth-century slave insurrections led by black preachers and prophets such as Gabriel Prosser and Denmark Vesey.[40] Moreover, free black radicals in the North such as David Walker and Henry Highland Garnet invoked the Exodus narrative, comparing the conditions of slavery in the United States with Hebrew slavery in Egypt.[41] In the end, however, not a slave rebellion led by a black Moses but another battle led by a white Moses, as Abraham Lincoln was hailed by blacks, ended 250 years of slavery.

In the post–Civil War era, the Exodus theme continued to resonate within the black community. So-called Exodusters left the South for the prairies of Kansas, envisioning themselves as a millenarian community of Israelites bound for the Promised Land. In the Great Migration (1916–18) to the North, blacks viewed their trek as the providential recapitulation of the Exodus event.[42] By the second half of the twentieth century, however, in the context of the civil rights movement and the emergence of black liberation theology, the ancient theme of liberation from oppressive conditions resounded once again throughout the black community. Martin Luther King Jr. occasionally embraced the Moses persona to advance the cause of freedom and equality, but more often he evoked Exodus imagery to describe

FIGURE 1. *Evicted Sharecropper Reading the Bible, Butler County, Missouri, 1939. Courtesy of the Prints and Photographs Division, Library of Congress. LC-USF34-029183-D.*

present-day conditions and possibilities for the deliverance of his people. "The Bible tells the thrilling story of how Moses stood in Pharaoh's court centuries ago and cried, 'Let my people go,'" King wrote. "This was the opening chapter in a continuing story. The present struggle in the United States is a later chapter in the same story."[43]

Growing out of the civil rights era, black liberation theology supplied another iteration of the Exodus motif. In his pathbreaking *A Black Theology of Liberation* (1970), James Cone observed, "By delivering this people [the Israelites] from Egyptian bondage and inaugurating the covenant on the basis of that historical event, God reveals that he is the God of the oppressed, involved in their history, liberating them from human bondage. . . . God, because he is the God of the oppressed, takes sides with black people." And so "Christian theology must become *Black Theology*, a theology that is unreservedly identified with the goals of the oppressed community and seeking to interpret the divine character of their struggle for liberation."[44] The contrast between white and black American Christianities was drawn in sharpest relief. Historically for whites the biblical Exodus has been a narrative of triumph and divine mission; for blacks it has been a story of tragedy and oppression.

As the liberation theology movement expanded (Third World, feminist, "womanist," mujerista) and matured, the indiscriminate appropriation of the Exodus theme gave some theologians pause. Indeed, the Book of Exodus "*is not an innocent text.*"[45] As black feminist theologian Delores Williams pointed out, God liberated some but not others. For example, slavery was not outlawed among the Israelites; God did not object to Hebrew men selling their daughters as slaves.[46] The liberation theme has been even more problematic for Native Americans, "who read the Exodus stories with Canaanite eyes." Yes, there is deliverance, but there is no Promised Land without conquest: the indigenes are to be destroyed. Robert Warrior queries, "With what voice will we, the Canaanites of the world, say, 'Let my people go and leave my people alone?'"[47]

Bible Wars
The Public School

The contested place of the Bible's iconic status is perhaps no better seen than in the nation's public schools. Parents, religious leaders, educators, school boards, legislators, and courts have argued, fought, and litigated over the place of the Bible in the classroom. The conflict has revealed the fault lines that define America's cultural landscape. Indeed, the battle over the Bible is a microcosm not only of American Christianities but also of a polarized culture whose combatants struggle to define America's identity. Played out initially in local school districts and at the state level, the issues surrounding the Bible's role in the classroom would eventually reach the U.S. Supreme Court in the 1960s. What or whose version of the Bible should be read? For what purpose and to what end? Who is properly qualified to teach the Bible? What of sectarian biases? Should the Bible be taught at all?[48]

These questions were seldom raised during the colonial and early national periods. The Bible was *the* book of Americans, first in the home and the church and then, by extension, in the schools. Colonial education was conducted primarily by clergy, be they Puritan in New England, Presbyterian, Lutheran, Quaker, and Mennonite in the middle colonies, or Anglican in the southern colonies. Grammar schools of the colonial period and their successor "common" and then public schools remained nurseries of Protestant piety. The *New England Primer* (ca. 1690), Noah Webster's *American*

Spelling Book (1783 and on), McGuffey's readers (1836 and on), and other similar kinds of instructional literature for Quakers, Lutherans, and Anglicans ensured that successive generations of American youth were familiar with the basic content of the Bible—biblical figures, events, and instruction. (Students were often required to memorize the Ten Commandments and the Lord's Prayer.)

What is crucial for understanding debates over the Bible in public schools is that the origins of public education preceded the separation of church and state. Thus in spite of the establishment clause in the First Amendment, which prohibited not only a national religion but the government giving preferential treatment to one religion over others, the ethos of public education throughout the nineteenth century and well into the twentieth century remained thoroughly Protestant. Public schoolteachers prayed Protestant prayers and read primarily from the Protestant Bible, the King James Version (KJV).

However, as religious pluralism increased, so did challenges to the assumed Protestant character of public education. The first of what became a familiar pattern in disputes over Bible reading occurred in the context of Catholic immigration in the 1830s and 1840s. Seldom are such disputes about one thing only—in this case, the Bible. A variety of related issues—assimilation, minority rights, political power, "Americanism," and the nation's moral fabric—came together in the battle for the Bible between Protestants and Catholics.

During the antebellum era of Protestant crusading and nativism, verbal and physical conflicts over Bible reading erupted in Philadelphia, New York, and Cincinnati. As Irish Catholics (and to a lesser extent German Catholics) grew in numbers and political clout, they objected to compulsory reading of the KJV in the public schools. Protestants responded that the KJV was nonsectarian—that it did not favor a particular *Protestant* sect, whereas Catholics argued that Protestants misconstrued the meaning of sectarian and hence denied them the very religious toleration Protestants claimed to uphold. Catholics used a different Bible, the Douay-Reims Version (or just Douay). This early seventeenth-century English translation of the Latin Vulgate (which included the Apocrypha, a body of writings rejected by Protestants as noncanonical) was subsequently revised in the mid-eighteenth century by London bishop Richard Challoner, who also added notes. The Douay remained the standard version for English-speaking Catholics from the Revolution through the nineteenth century.

In America, the KJV and Douay versions symbolized centuries-old conflict going back to the religious revolutions and wars of the sixteenth and seventeenth centuries. On the Catholic side, the Council of Trent (1545–63) affirmed that the "holy Mother Church" was the sole arbiter "of the true meaning and interpretation of Sacred Scripture."[49] As for Protestants, the original preface in the KJV denied the authority of the Catholic Church and accused it of concealing the truths of scripture from its people. To Catholics, not only did the KJV mistranslate important Catholic dogma, but the Protestant principle of *sola scriptura* opened up the inevitable subjective and heretical interpretation of the Bible. "This weird notion of 'the Bible and the Bible only,'" wrote Hugh Pope in 1928, "is more particularly the child of the Reformation which elevated it to the rank of a dogma, yet it has been the hallmark of all heresies."[50]

Catholic leaders prohibited laity from the individual reading of Bibles without authoritative notes from the Catholic perspective—something only a Catholic Bible could offer. Thus, beginning in the early nineteenth century and into the last half of the century, when American Protestant Bible distribution came to exceed a million copies annually, popes and other church authorities repeatedly condemned Bible societies.[51] Not only did the circulation of vernacular Bibles abet heresy, but, argued Catholic apologists, Bible societies were unbiblical! Amid the whirl of Protestant Bible distribution in the second half of the nineteenth century, Catholics responded: "The commandment which the Catholic Church received from Christ was, 'Go into all the world and preach the Gospel,' not 'Go, distribute Bibles.'"[52] Before the invention of the printing press, all that existed were manuscript Bibles—proof positive "that Christ never meant men in all classes, rich and poor, educated and uneducated alike, to read the Bible, still less to find in it alone the way to salvation."[53]

Obviously this kind of response only reinforced the Protestant canard that the Catholic Church was anti-Bible—Catholic objections such as the following notwithstanding: "*Does the Catholic Church condemn the Bible and forbid her people to circulate and read it?*" asked the author in an 1868 article in the *Catholic World*. "We answer, NO!"[54] In his best-selling *The Faith of Our Fathers* (1876), James Cardinal Gibbons made abundant footnoted references to scripture in his explicit effort to counter the Protestant critique and convert the "separated faithful [Protestants] . . . who generally accept the Scripture as the only source of authority in religious matters." "Be assured," he wrote, "that if you become a Catholic you will never be forbidden to read the Bible. It is our earnest wish that every word of the Gospel may be imprinted on your memory and on your heart."[55]

However much American Catholic leaders urged their people to read and treasure the Bible, it is clear that Catholics were not devoted to reading their Douay Bible in the same way that Protestants were devoted to their KJV.[56] Like Episcopalians, who encountered the Bible through the Book of Common Prayer, Catholics primarily learned their Bible through the mass, the breviary, the missal, and other rituals and teachings of the Catholic Church—sans the proof-texting that was so common among Protestants. Individual Bible reading was largely regarded as a Protestant pursuit. Before Pope Pius XII's 1943 encyclical *Divino afflante Spiritu*, which opened up a new era in Catholic biblical studies, "there was virtually no scriptural scholarship and consequently, very little attempt to revitalize the spiritual life of the faithful with the Bible."[57] Among female religious before the 1960s, few had any familiarity with scripture.[58] The Second Vatican Council (1962–65) gave renewed impetus to biblical studies, not only among scholars, clergy, and religious, but also among laypeople, with the hope that the reading and studying of the Bible would revive the spiritual life of the Catholic Church.[59] This hope, however, in the minds of some Catholics has yet to be fulfilled: "We Catholics," wrote Gerald Sloyan in 1986, "are not a people who have reclaimed the Bible as the book of the church."[60] Of the estimated 100,000 American Catholics who become evangelical Protestants each year—a biased group to be sure—most report that they had never read the Bible for themselves while in the Catholic Church.[61]

Such are the convictions and developments that have resulted in very different Protestant and Catholic approaches toward the Bible. In the nineteenth-century public school controversies, when it became apparent that Protestant school authorities would not relent in reading the KJV (or in some cases, alternating with the Douay Version), Catholic archbishops asked that Bible reading in the public schools cease. Better no Bible than the biased KJV. For Protestants, this action was one more proof of the Catholic hierarchy's ploy to keep the Bible from its members. Of course, they refused to acknowledge that the fundamental issue for Catholics was not Bible reading per se but the correct translation.

The upshot of these conflicts over the place of the Bible in the public schools (which by the 1870s also involved Jews, other non-Protestant religious minorities, and freethinkers) resulted in a series of state court rulings. In a landmark decision in 1872, the Ohio Supreme Court voted to remove the Bible from the public school curriculum. From 1880 to 1920, courts in four states rendered similar decisions, ruling that because the Bible was viewed as the word of God, it was a sectarian ("religious") book and therefore its presence in the public classroom violated the establishment clause.[62] Opposing educators and state legislators argued that education and morality and thus Bible reading were inseparable. Between 1913 and 1930, ten states passed laws mandating Bible reading in public schools.[63] But much of this reading was perfunctory, without comment, done before the class day began, and amounted to little more than an act of civic piety, and by mid-century, the Bible "was reduced to a largely symbolic role."[64]

Still, symbols retain a powerful hold, especially those that evoke transcendent meaning. When challenged, the fallout is predictable: a storm of protest ensues. Such was the case in the U.S. Supreme Court's *Abington v. Schempp* decision (1963), which allegedly "took God out of the classroom" by outlawing the devotional reading of the Bible. Before the *Schempp* ruling, thirty-seven states required, permitted, or condoned Bible reading in their public schools. Now in this unprecedented case—unprecedented not because it secularized education (indeed by 1900 that was so) but because all previous decisions about Bible reading in public schools had been made at the state level—the highest court in the land ruled that the Bible (it did not specify which version) could not be read or taught for devotional purposes.[65] The most vociferous objections came from Christian conservatives, but even mainstream Protestants voiced their displeasure, linking the absence of Bible reading with crime and a general decline in morals.[66]

The Court made a critical point that often got lost in the heated rhetoric. It did not rule against the *study* of the Bible. In his concurring opinion, Justice Arthur Goldberg made the distinction between the teaching *of* religion (which the Court banned) and the teaching *about* religion (which it permitted). The Court's decision "secularized" the Bible. What to most Americans was a uniquely sacred text was now to be treated in the classroom as a book of ancient history or literature worthy of study in its own right alongside other influential books of Western culture.

It is one thing to announce a distinction between the teaching of and about religion, or to affirm, as Justice Tom Clark did in his majority opinion, that public schools can teach the Bible "when presented objectively as part of a secular program of education," but it is another to implement these distinctions.[67] The case of *Herdahl v. Pontotoc County Board of Education* (1996) illustrates the problem. In the mid-1990s, Lisa Herdahl, a devout Pentecostal mother who had recently moved to Mississippi, challenged the legality of the kind of "objective" Bible teaching that Clark had optimistically endorsed. Herdahl protested that a public school was not the place to teach the Bible to her children and also alleged that the content and teaching of the

Bible was not only religious but favored a particular Protestant perspective. School officials contended that the Bible was taught "objectively" as history and literature—that is, as a historical, objective, and accurate report of the truth (for example, that Jesus' miracles and resurrection happened as narrated). In keeping with the *Schempp* decision, the U.S. District Court ruled against Bible teaching that reflected "the community's Protestant beliefs." It did uphold the right of the district to offer secular courses that used the Bible among other texts.[68]

Is it possible to teach *about* the Bible in the public school classroom without controversy? If the reaction to two recent privately funded projects is indicative, the answer is clearly no. The Bible Literacy Project (BLP) and the National Council on Bible Curriculum in Public Schools (NCBCPS) represent two efforts to introduce the teaching about the Bible in the public schools. The BLP, observes one biblical scholar who has studied both curricula extensively, generally "succeeds in avoiding the sectarian assumptions often exhibited in public school Bible courses," but the NCBCPS curriculum "is legally and academically problematic."[69] The BLP's text, *The Bible and Its Influence* (2005), was supported by conservative and liberal Christians alike, given moderate endorsement by Jewish organizations, and relied upon the expertise of biblical scholars and educational professionals. The NCBCPS curriculum, however, was a product of the Protestant Christian Right and was "filled with factual errors, tabloid scholarship, and plagiarism, as well as religious claims and presuppositions" that placed it in legal jeopardy.[70] Yet, according to the NCBCPS website, as of mid-March 2010 its curriculum "has been voted into 532 school districts (2,035 high schools) in 38 states."[71] Where its legality was challenged (in Lee County, Florida), the federal district judge ruled against the teaching of its New Testament component.[72]

In 2006, state representatives in Alabama, Georgia, Missouri, and Tennessee sponsored bills endorsing elective Bible courses in public high schools. Some of the bills either stipulated or recommended a textbook—the BLP's *The Bible and Its Influence* or the NCBCPS's KJV (the text for students is the Bible—only teachers have access to the curriculum). The selection of the textbook broke down along party lines. Democrats initially supported the BLP and Republicans the KJV (which amounts to an endorsement of the NCBCPS). One Republican representative labeled *The Bible and Its Influence* a "liberal textbook."[73] The book was also denounced by leaders on the Christian Right as "anti-biblical" and "a masterful work of deception, distortion, and out-right falsehoods."[74] On a local level, Mark Chancey's recent study of the school district dispute in Odessa, Texas, over the two competing curricula offers a window into the Bible course controversies across the nation.[75] As in earlier Bible classroom controversies, these latest episodes expose cultural tensions about American identity, status, and power in a nation of competing Christianities and religious pluralism.[76]

Of the Making of Bibles There Is No End
Translation Controversies

The Bible is the world's most translated and revised book. In order to make the Bible accessible and relevant, American Christians have contributed mightily to the translation and revision enterprise, whether for English-speaking audiences in America or for non–English speaking audiences at home and abroad. John Eliot's translation of the Bible into Algonquian (1663) was the first non-English translation on American soil. No English versions were published in America for nearly two centuries thereafter, however, because printing rights to the KJV were restricted to those authorized by the British crown. Following the American Revolution, all that would change. Beginning with Charles Thompson's first American English translation in 1808, editions in the thousands and revisions, translations, and paraphrases in the hundreds churned from the presses—a reflection of the democratization of the Bible and the multiplication of Christianities in the new nation. By the 1860s, the American Bible Society—the largest of its kind—was distributing 1 million volumes annually. By 1880, nearly 2,000 different editions (mostly of the KJV) were available, with 60 percent of these including some kind of extended commentary (annotations, for example).[77] By 1957, over 2,500 different English language editions of the Bible had been published. A half century later, hundreds of editions continue to roll off the press. The largest Bible publisher in the world, Thomas Nelson Publishers, now prints Bibles for kids, charismatics, and Calvinists, to name a few in what has become a huge niche-market publishing industry.[78]

The production of Bibles is one aspect of the making of Bibles; the contents or the books included in the Bible is another. Protestant, Catholic, and Orthodox Christians—to note the historic traditions—have never agreed on what books should be included in the Old Testament. Other groups, notably those minorities "born in the U.S.A.," supplemented and clarified the meaning of the Bible (most often the KJV) with their own divinely inspired extracanonical writings. Indeed, American Christianities are differentiated by their Bibles, whether by the number of books in their Bibles or by the version or translation used. Rarely has translation (and commentary or explanations that often accompany the text) been without theological partisanship. At times, translation controversies have been "family affairs," internal to the life of a particular religious tradition. At other times, conflict has raged between Christian groups, as seen earlier in the Bible wars between Catholics and Protestants in the public schools.

As religious sects and denominations proliferated in the first decades of the nineteenth century, so did translations. A few examples out of many must suffice. Unitarian-Universalist Abner Kneeland sought to correct "some of the monstrous errors [for example, passages making explicit reference to the doctrine of the Trinity] that now exist in the Christian church." He argued correctly that a clause in 1 John 5:7–8, the so-called *Comma Johanneum*, was a later addition to the original manuscript.[79] The verses in the KJV read (with the disputed clause noted in italics): "For there are three that bear record *in heaven, the Father, the Word, and the Holy Ghost: and these three are one. And there are three that bear witness on earth*, the Spirit, and the water, and the blood; and these three agree in one." In his 1823 English translation, which relied on the critical edition of the German biblical scholar Johann Griesbach, Kneeland relegated the old translation to a footnote, and rendered the verse as "For there are three that bear testimony, the spirit, and the water, and the blood, and these three agree in one."[80]

At the other end of the theological spectrum, the champion of adult baptism, Alexander Campbell (founder of the Disciples of Christ), offered a new "immersion" version of the New Testament (1825) focused on the correct translation of the Greek *baptizō* into English, rendering it not to "wash" or "dip" or "baptize" as it appeared in some translations, but "to immerse." For his controversial substitution, Campbell "fired the first shot in what would become the largest bible translation battle in early nineteenth-century America."[81]

Like his contemporary Campbell, Joseph Smith wanted to restore the practices and teachings of the primitive church. For the prophet Smith, however, it was not a matter of correcting an offending word. "We believe," contended the founder of the Church of Jesus Christ of Latter-day Saints, "the Bible to be the word of God as far as it is translated."[82] The problem, of course, was "as far as." So corrupt was the present version of the KJV that it required not merely a revision or new translation from the original Hebrew or Greek but emendations by revelation. The canon of scripture was not closed—how could it be if it was corrupt?—but open to ongoing revelation. The Joseph Smith Translation (the JST, used as a supplement, not as a replacement of the KJV) contained 3,410 verses that varied from their KJV counterparts.[83] In his view of the Bible, Smith differed from evangelicals like Campbell for whom "the Bible alone" was a sufficient guide, from Roman Catholics who appealed to the authority of the church, and from confessional Protestants who hewed to creedal formulation in interpreting scripture. Under divine inspiration, Smith not only corrected the many errors of "ignorant translators, careless transcribers, or designing and corrupt priests" in what became the JST (published in 1867).[84] He also added to the canon of scripture with the Book of Mormon.

Other religious communities in the nineteenth century followed what Stephen Stein calls a "scripturalizing process" of supplementing or explaining the "true" meaning of the Bible.[85] The Shakers published their own Bible in 1843. Following the Civil War, Mary Baker Eddy's *Science and Health with Key to the Scriptures* would assume canonical status among Christian Scientists.[86] Ellen White's prophecies illuminated the meaning of the inspired and infallible Bible for Seventh-day Adventists. Spiritualists, Jehovah's Witnesses, and others would add to this ongoing process of clarifying the meaning of scripture or creating their own Bibles. Nineteenth-century feminists Sarah Grimké and Elizabeth Cady Stanton did not create their own Bibles but relied upon the KJV to explain the "true" meaning of passages used against their cause. Stanton's *The Woman's Bible* (1895, 1898) gave voice to a feminist interpretation of the KJV by focusing on those passages that either oppressed women or uplifted their contributions.

A brief review of two translation controversies among major Protestant groups highlights the perennially contentious issue of whose voice and what authority prevails in translations of the Bible. The first, "the greatest translation controversy in American religious history," erupted with the publication of the Revised Standard Version (RSV) in 1952.[87] A number of translated passages excited debate, but most offensive and controversial to conservatives (including the Catholic hierarchy) was the RSV's translation of the Hebrew word *almah* in Isaiah 7:14 as "young woman" rather than as "virgin"—the traditional English translation. Although the Hebrew word for virgin was *bethulah*, KJV translators, in affirming that predictive prophesy unified the Old and New Testaments, chose "virgin"—the word used in the Greek Septuagint. Thus what was predicted in Isaiah 7:14 was fulfilled in the virgin birth of Jesus (see Matthew 1:23).

To Protestant conservatives, this egregious translation blunder undermined not only the unity of scripture but its self-authenticating divine inspiration. Their reaction was swift and had a strange sense of déjà vu. One pastor burned the offending page containing Isaiah 7:14—shades of the Catholic priest who, during the Protestant-Catholic Bible controversy a century earlier, burned the "unauthorized" KJV given to his parishioners by a Protestant Bible society.[88] Fundamentalists called the National Council of Churches, the authorizing body behind the revision, a "super church." A century before, Protestant Nativists charged that American Catholics were puppets controlled by the power-hungry megachurch in Rome. Now, in the menacing atmosphere of McCarthyism, it was rumored that theologically liberal translators of the RSV were un-American communist sympathizers—again, a charge reminiscent of Protestant attacks on Irish and German Catholic immigrants whose use of the Douay Bible was deemed un-American.[89]

The fallout over the RSV exacerbated the divisions that had emerged earlier in the century between Protestant modernists and Fundamentalists, who, while not fighting over a particular translation of the Bible, fought over the more crucial issue of the historical reliability of scripture. In the minds of Fundamentalists, the RSV was the culmination of a half century's worth of tearing down an infallible, inerrant Bible: a translation that embodied modernist views. Indeed, if a Fundamentalist like John R. Rice wanted to raise doubts about the theological integrity of the evangelical Billy Graham, he need only query, "Does Billy use the Revised Standard Version of the Bible or the King James Version?"[90]

Not all Protestant conservatives sang the same condemnatory song, but many were troubled—troubled enough to propose a new translation and troubled enough to insist that all translators of what became the New International Version (NIV) subscribe to the Evangelical Theological Society's statement on the inerrancy of the Bible. In 1973, the New Testament NIV was published; the whole Bible was published in 1978; and the latest American revision came out in 1984. An "evangelical" Bible now competed with and would eventually overtake the mainline Protestant RSV. Indicative of evangelicalism's resurgence in the last thirty years, the NIV has become America's best-selling Bible (about 40 percent market share) and the most consulted translation by Protestant ministers.[91] A 2004 poll revealed that 31 percent of Protestant ministers prefer the NIV and that only 14 percent prefer the NRSV (the RSV was revised and published as the New RSV [NRSV] in 1990). Amid the contention between the RSV and NIV and the proliferation of other Bibles, the KJV endures: 23 percent of Protestant ministers report relying upon the KJV and 13 percent report relying on an updated version of the KJV, the New KJV.[92]

The second translation controversy emerged as an internecine feud among evangelicals. As popular as the NIV has been, evangelical scholars recognized its deficiencies, one being the lack of gender-inclusive or "gender-accurate" language. The NRSV had been careful to avoid male terms when gender-inclusive ideas were intended—an issue that nineteenth-century biblical feminists had pointed out. However, the NIV (published by Zondervan) made no changes in places where a mixed audience was clearly meant by the biblical writers. For example, the NIV retained "brothers" (instead of "brothers and sisters") and "men" (rather than "human beings"). Today's New International Version (TNIV; New Testament published in 2002; Old Testament published in 2005) addressed the inclusive language issue, though most of the substantive changes involved updating the language and eliminating (or in some cases bracketing) textual variants deemed later insertions.[93]

Predictably, protest erupted from ultraconservative evangelicals, who accused the translators of caving in to a secular, "politically correct" culture, of treating the Bible, as one critic put it, "like Silly Putty."[94] TNIV advocates responded in writing, which quickly grew to book-length treatises on the merits of the TNIV.[95] This latest skirmish in the long history of battles for the Bible in America has, as in previous contests, less to do with the integrity of Bible translation and more to do with the social and political agendas of those who oppose the new version. No one burned the TNIV, but one person blasted an earlier British version with a shotgun and mailed it back to the publisher. In America, opponents drilled holes in the TNIV and returned it to Zondervan. No one was physically assaulted, but one seminary professor involved in the translation project lost his job.[96] R. Albert Mohler, president of Southern Baptist Seminary, summed up the issue in words that resonate through nearly four centuries of American Bible controversies. In his endorsement of a Southern Baptist–published Bible, Mohler declared, "We will have a major translation that we can control."[97]

Admittedly, there are other ways to examine the Bible's place in American Christianities than the approach taken in this essay. I would suggest, however, that the Bible in the context of the three themes discussed tells us something about the importance of the Bible in America. After all, if the Bible did not matter there would be nothing to argue about, nothing to spark controversy. To be sure, the Bible has lost its once-preeminent position in America, for a variety of cultural, legal, social, and political reasons—increasing religious pluralism; competition from other media; a loss of binding authority brought about by secularizing influences and higher criticism; an anti-intellectual strain among evangelical Christians that reduces the Christian message to pious platitudes of "Jesus and me"; an overall decline in reading habits; and a decline in religious education. And, as Paul Gutjahr and others have argued (and as nineteenth-century Catholic critics of Protestant Bible societies suggested), mass production by the millions and in so many versions has had the unintended consequence of making the Bible appear less special.[98] Like inflationary money, the more that bibles were made available, the less value (and less read) they become to their purchaser.

And yet the Bible has not become, as it has in much of Europe, an ancient text relegated to literary and historical inquiry, or a cultural artifact to be displayed in museums, or with all the profound implications notwithstanding, a repository of Western culture.[99] One could argue that even in an increasingly secular America, the Bible retains its hold in supplying the master narrative to a conservative form of civil religion that upholds a biblical faith in the God of history and his covenant with America.[100] Moreover, the recent debates, discussions, and legal decisions over whether or how to display the Ten Commandments tell us something about the Bible as a living symbol. The Bible has not become in America, as Christopher Hill wrote of the Bible in England, "a historical document, to be interpreted like any other." The only place you will find that its "old authority exists," he quipped, is "in dark corners like Northern Ireland or the Bible Belt of the USA."[101] The Bible, whether one or many, no longer has the universal appeal it once had in America, but neither has it become a relic of the past or a book whose influence is limited to a particular region. America's Bibles and the controversies that surround them remain not only past but present testimonies to the manifold expressions of American Christianities.

NOTES

1. "The Battle of the Books," *Economist*, December 12, 2007, www.economist.com/research/articlesBySubject/PrinterFriendly.cfm?story_id=10311 (accessed July 1, 2008).

2. "The Bible Is America's Favorite Book Followed by Gone with the Wind," Harris Poll #38, April 8, 2008, www.harrisinteractive.com/harris_poll/printerfriend/index.asp?PID=892 (accessed June 4, 2008).

3. See Stanley Malless and Jeffrey McQuain, *Coined by God: Words and Phrases That First Appear in the English Translations of the Bible* (New York: W. W. Norton, 2003).

4. For a discussion of the biblical meaning, see Walter Brueggemann, "A Disaster of 'Biblical' Proportions?" www.religion-online.org/showarticle.asp?title=3293 (accessed June 4, 2008).

5. For these and other supporting statistics and anecdotes, see Stephen Prothero,

Religious Literacy: What Every American Needs to Know—and Doesn't (New York: HarperCollins, 2007), chap. 1; Kristin Swenson, "Biblically Challenged: Overcoming Scriptural Illiteracy," *Christian Century*, November 3, 2009, 22–25; and Timothy Beal, *Biblical Literacy: The Essential Bible Stories Everyone Needs to Know* (San Francisco: HarperOne, 2009). For laments about biblical illiteracy from a conservative Protestant perspective, see Woodrow Kroll, *Taking Back the Good Book: How Americans Forgot the Bible and Why It Matters to You* (Wheaton, Ill.: Crossway, 2007); and Michael L. Williams, *Silenced in the Schoolhouse: How Biblical Illiteracy in Our Schools Is Destroying America* (Michael L. Williams, 2008).

6. Nathan O. Hatch and Mark A. Noll, eds., *The Bible in America: Essays in Cultural History* (New York: Oxford University Press, 1982), 4.

7. Ernest R. Sandeen, ed., *The Bible and Social Reform* (Centennial Publications, Society of Biblical Literature; Philadelphia: Fortress Press; Chico, Calif.: Scholars Press, 1982); David Barr and Nicholas Piediscalzi, eds., *The Bible in American Education* (Centennial Publications, Society of Biblical Literature; Philadelphia: Fortress Press; Chico, Calif.: Scholars Press, 1982); Giles Gunn, ed., *The Bible and American Arts and Letters* (Centennial Publications, Society of Biblical Literature; Philadelphia: Fortress Press; Chico, Calif.: Scholars Press, 1983); James Turner Johnson, ed., *The Bible in American Law, Politics, and Political Rhetoric* (Centennial Publications, Society of Biblical Literature; Philadelphia: Fortress Press; Chico, Calif.: Scholars Press, 1985); Allene Stuart Phy, ed., *The Bible and Popular Culture in America* (Centennial Publications, Society of Biblical Literature: Philadelphia: Fortress Press; Chico, Calif.: Scholars Press, 1985); Ernest S. Frerichs, ed., *The Bible and Bibles in America* (Centennial Publications, Society of Biblical Literature; Atlanta: Scholars Press, 1988). This series was part of a larger Centennial Publication series of the Society of Biblical Literature covering biblical scholarship in North America and Canada, the Bible and its modern interpreters, and biblical scholarship in confessional perspective. For a review of the entire series to date (nineteen volumes by 1986), see Mark A. Noll, "Review Essay: The Bible in America," *Journal of Biblical Studies* 6 (September 1987): 493–509. As of March 11, 2008, the series had added fifteen more volumes; see http://www.sbl-site.org/publications/browsebyseries.aspx (accessed March 11, 2011).

8. Paul C. Gutjahr, *An American Bible: A History of the Good Book in the United States, 1777–1880* (Stanford, Calif.: Stanford University Press, 1999).

9. Peter J. Wosh, *Spreading the Word: The Bible Business in Nineteenth-Century America* (Ithaca, N.Y.: Cornell University Press, 1994).

10. Peter J. Thuesen, *In Discordance with the Scriptures: American Protestant Battles over Translating the Bible* (New York: Oxford University Press, 1999).

11. Jerry W. Brown, *The Rise of Biblical Criticism in America, 1800–1870: The New England Scholars* (Middletown, Conn.: Wesleyan University Press, 1969); Mark A. Noll, *Between Faith and Criticism: Evangelicals, Scholarship, and the Bible in America* (San Francisco: Harper and Row, 1986); Gerald P. Fogarty, *American Catholic Biblical Scholarship: A History from the Early Republic to Vatican II* (San Francisco: Harper and Row, 1989).

12. Charles Mabee, *Reading Sacred Texts through American Eyes: Biblical Interpretation as Cultural Critique* (Macon, Ga.: Mercer University Press, 1991).

13. Mark A. Noll, "The Bible and Slavery," in *Religion and the American Civil War*, ed. Randall M. Miller, Harry S. Stout, and Charles Reagan Wilson (New York: Oxford University Press, 1998), 43–73; Mark A. Noll, *The Civil War as a Theological Crisis* (Chapel Hill: University of North Carolina Press, 2006), chap. 3; Stephen R. Haynes, *Noah's Curse: The Biblical Justification of American Slavery* (New York: Oxford University Press, 2002).

14. Gary Scott Smith, *Faith and the Presidency: From George Washington to George W. Bush* (New York: Oxford University Press, 2006), addresses the role of the Bible in the lives of eleven presidents. For a journalistic analysis of the Bible in the most current context, see Jacques Berlinerblau, *Thumpin' It: The Use and Abuse of the Bible in Today's Presidential Politics* (Louisville: Westminster John Knox, 2008).

15. Philip L. Barlow, *Mormons and the Bible: The Place of the Latter-day Saints in American Religion* (New York: Oxford University Press, 1991); M. Eugene Boring, *Disciples and the Bible: A History of Disciples Bible Interpretation in North America* (St. Louis: Chalice Press, 1997); Terryl L. Givens, *By the Hand of Mormon: The American Scripture That Launched a New World Religion* (New York: Oxford University Press, 2002).

16. Robert E. Brown, *Jonathan Edwards and the Bible* (Bloomington: Indiana University Press, 2002).

17. The literature is large and ever-growing. For representative examples, see Vincent L. Wimbush, ed., *African Americans and the Bible: Sacred Texts and Social Textures* (New York: Continuum, 2000); Allen Dwight Callahan, *The Talking Book: African Americans and the Bible* (New Haven: Yale University Press, 2006); and Mary F. Foskett and Jeffry Kah-Jin Kuan, eds., *Ways of Being, Ways of Reading: Asian American Biblical Interpretation* (St. Louis: Chalice, 2006).

18. For helpful dictionary- and chapter-length treatments of the Bible in America, see Mark A. Noll, "The Bible in American Culture," in *Encyclopedia of the American Religious Experience*, 3 vols., ed. Charles H. Lippy and Peter W. Williams (New York: Scribner's, 1988): 3:1075–88; Edwin S. Gaustad, "Bible in America," in *Mercer Dictionary of the Bible*, ed. Watson E. Mills et al. (Macon, Ga.: Mercer University Press, 1990), 109–12; Scott M. Langston, "North America," in *The Blackwell Companion to the Bible and Culture*, ed. John F. A. Sawyer (Malden, Mass.: Blackwell, 2006), 198–216; and Mark A. Noll, "Bible and American Culture," in *Dictionary of Christianity in America*, ed. Daniel G. Reid et al. (Downers Grove, Ill.: InterVarsity Press, 1990), 134–36.

19. Sacvan Bercovitch, "The Biblical Basis of the American Myth," in Gunn, *The Bible and American Arts and Letters*, 223.

20. Quoted in Prothero, *Religious Literacy*, 75.

21. Richard S. Dunn and Laetitia Yeandle, eds., *The Journal of John Winthrop, 1630–1649*, abridged ed. (Cambridge: Belknap Press of Harvard University Press, 1996), 197–98.

22. For Puritan biblical support for and against violence, see James P. Byrd Jr., *The*

Challenge of Roger Williams: Religious Liberty, Violent Persecution, and the Bible (Macon, Ga.: Mercer University Press, 2002).

23. John Winthrop, "A Model of Christian Charity," in *The American Puritans: Their Prose and Poetry*, ed. Perry Miller (Garden City, N.Y.: Doubleday Anchor, 1956), 83. Winthrop is referencing Matthew 5:14.

24. Hector Avalos, "Columbus as Biblical Exegete: A Study of the *Libro de las profecías*," in *Religion in the Age of Exploration: The Case of Spain and New Spain*, ed. Bryan F. Le Beau and Menachem More (Omaha, Nebr.: Creighton University Press, 1996), 69, 71.

25. Arnulf Camps, "The Bible and the Discovery of the World: Mission, Colonization, and Foreign Development," in *The Bible as Cultural Heritage*, ed. Wim Beuken and Sean Freyne (London: SCM Press, 1995), 65–66. Much of Las Casas's defense of the Native American is rooted in appeal to the writings of church fathers and canon law. For references to following Christ's example, see Bartolomé de Las Casas, *In Defense of the Indians*, trans. and ed. Stafford Poole (DeKalb: Northern Illinois University Press, 1992), 92–97, 175–81.

26. Jaroslav Pelikan, *The Emergence of the Catholic Tradition (100–600)*, vol. 1 of *The Christian Tradition: A History of the Development of Doctrine* (Chicago: University of Chicago Press, 1971).

27. On the Bible and the Civil War, see Noll, *The Civil War as a Theological Crisis*, chap. 3.

28. Werner Sollors, *Beyond Ethnicity: Consent and Descent in American Culture* (New York: Oxford University Press, 1986), 43.

29. Kerby A. Miller et al., *Irish Immigrants in the Land of Canaan: Letters and Memoirs from Colonial and Revolutionary America, 1675–1815* (New York: Oxford University Press, 2003), 5.

30. Leng Leroy Lim, "'The Bible Tells Me to Hate Myself': The Crisis in Asian American Spiritual Leadership," *Semeia* 90–91 (2002): 319.

31. Callahan, *Talking Book*, 38, 40.

32. Albert J. Raboteau, "The Black Experience in American Evangelicalism: The Meaning of Slavery," in *African-American Religion: Interpretive Essays in History and Culture*, ed. Timothy E. Fulop and Albert J. Raboteau (New York: Routledge, 1997), 101.

33. Winthrop, "Model of Christian Charity," 83.

34. Quoted in Sollors, *Beyond Ethnicity*, 43.

35. Abiel Abbot, "Traits of Resemblance in the People of the United States of America to Ancient Israel," in *The American Republic and Ancient Israel* (New York: Arno Press, 1977), 6.

36. Smith, *Faith and the Presidency*, 229, 363.

37. Jeffrey Siker, "President Bush, Biblical Faith, and the Politics of Religion," SBL Forum, June 2006, http://www.sbl-site.org/Article.aspx?Articled=151 (accessed July 16, 2008). See also Bruce Lincoln, "Bush's God Talk," *Christian Century*, October 5, 2004, 22–29.

38. On expansionism, see Ernest Lee Tuveson, *Redeemer Nation: The Idea of America's Millennial Role* (Chicago: University of Chicago Press, 1968), chaps. 4, 5. On tragic irony, see Albert J. Raboteau, "African-Americans, Exodus, and the American Israel," in *African-American Christianity*, ed. Paul E. Johnson (Berkeley: University of California Press, 1994), 9 (citing Harding).

39. Dena J. Epstein, *Sinful Tunes and Spirituals: Black Folk Music to the Civil War* (Urbana: University of Illinois Press, 1977), appendix 3, 363, 365; William Francis Allen et al., comp., *Slave Songs of the United States* (1867; Baltimore: Clearfield, 1992), 76; James Weldon Johnson, ed., *The Book of American Negro Spirituals* (New York: Viking Press, 1925), 60–61.

40. Vincent Harding, "Religion and Resistance among Antebellum Negroes, 1800–1860," in *Religion in American History: Interpretive Essays*, ed. John M. Mulder and John F. Wilson (Englewood Cliffs, N.J.: Prentice-Hall, 1978), 270–87.

41. On Walker, see Peter P. Hinks, *To Awaken My Afflicted Brethren: David Walker and the Problem of Antebellum Slave Resistance* (University Park: Pennsylvania State University Press, 1997). On Garnett, see Sterling Stuckey, *Slave Culture: Nationalist Theory and the Foundations of Black America* (New York: Oxford University Press, 1987), chap. 3.

42. Nell Irvin Painter, *Exodusters: Black Migration to Kansas after Reconstruction* (New York: Alfred A. Knopf, 1977).

43. James M. Washington, ed., *A Testament of Hope: The Essential Writings and Speeches of Martin Luther King, Jr.* (New York: HarperCollins, 1986), 619.

44. James H. Cone, *A Black Theology of Liberation* (Philadelphia: J. B. Lippincott, 1970), 18–19, 26, 11.

45. David Tracy, "Theological Reflections," in *Exodus—A Lasting Paradigm*, ed. Bas van Iersel and Anton Weiler, Concilium, vol. 187 (Edinburgh: T. & T. Clark, 1987), 120.

46. Delores W. Williams, *Sisters in the Wilderness: The Challenge of Womanist God-Talk* (Maryknoll, N.Y.: Orbis, 1993), 6 (see also 144–48 for a direct critique of traditional liberation theology).

47. Robert Warrior, "Canaanites, Cowboys, and Indians," *Union Seminary Quarterly Review* 59 (2005): 3, 8.

48. Important treatments of the Bible in public schools are Donald E. Boles, *The Bible, Religion and the Public Schools* (Ames: Iowa State University Press, 1965), which treats court cases up to the *Schempp* decision; and the more recent Joan DelFattore, *The Fourth R: Conflicts over Religion in America's Public School* (New Haven: Yale University Press, 2004). As the title suggests, DelFattore's work extends beyond the Bible to other religious issues (for example, prayer) and updates court rulings post-*Schempp*. Also helpful is Kent Greenawalt, *Does God Belong in Public Schools?* (Princeton: Princeton University Press, 2005).

49. "The Creed of the Council of Trent" (1564), in *Creeds of the Churches*, rev. ed., ed. John H. Leith (Atlanta: John Knox, 1973), 440.

50. Hugh Pope, *The Catholic Church and the Bible* (New York: Macmillan, 1928), 58.

51. Dr. (Constantin) Chauvin, *The Catholic Church and the Bible*, trans. J. M. LeLeu (St. Louis: B. Herder, 1904), 77–80; Pope, *Catholic Church and the Bible*, 86–88.

52. G. Dershon, "The Catholic Church and the Bible," *Catholic World* 7 (August 1868): 668. See also James Cardinal Gibbons, *The Faith of Our Fathers*, rev. ed. (Baltimore: John Murphy, 1917), 78; [Thomas F. Hopkins], "Novena of Sermons on the Holy Ghost in His Relationship to the World" (1901), in *Devotion to the Holy Spirit in American Catholicism*, ed. Joseph P. Chinnici (New York: Paulist, 1985), 186.

53. Pope, *Catholic Church and the Bible*, 95.

54. Dershon, "Catholic Church and the Bible," 657. My thanks to Mark A. Noll for his email correspondence (November 22, 2008) pointing to Catholic sources, especially in his own work, "The Bible, Minority Faiths, and the American Protestant Mainstream, 1860–1925," in *Minority Faiths and the American Protestant Mainstream*, ed. Jonathan D. Sarna (Urbana: University of Illinois Press, 1998), 191–231.

55. Gibbons, *Faith of Our Fathers*, vii, 94. For the larger context of *Faith of Our Fathers*, see James Emmett Ryan, "Sentimental Catechism: Archbishop James Gibbons, Mass-Print Culture, and American Literary History, *Religion in American Culture* 7 (Winter 1997): 81–119.

56. Virginia L. Brereton, "The Public Schools Are Not Enough: The Bible and Private Schools," in Barr and Piediscalzi, *Bible in American Education*, 64.

57. Gerald P. Fogarty, "The Quest for a Catholic Vernacular Bible in America," in Hatch and Noll, *The Bible in America*, 174–75.

58. Carole Garibaldi Rogers, *Poverty, Chastity, and Change: Lives of Contemporary American Nuns* (New York: Twayne, 1996), xiii.

59. "Dogmatic Constitution on Divine Revelation," chap. 6: "Sacred Scripture in the Life of the Church," numbers 22, 25, 26, http://www.cin.org/v2revel.html (accessed December 17, 2008). See also John R. Donahue, "The Bible in Roman Catholicism since *Divino Afflante Spiritu*," *Word and World* 13, no. 4 (Fall 1993): 404–13. For recent popular treatments of Catholic views of the Bible, see Daniel J. Harrington, *How Do Catholics Read the Bible?* (Lanham, Md.: Rowman and Littlefield, 2005); and Pope Benedict XVI (Joseph Ratzinger), *Jesus of Nazareth* (San Francisco: Ignatius, 2008).

60. Gerald S. Sloyan, "The Bible as the Book of the Church," *Worship* 60, no. 1 (January 1986): 17. For a recent similar conclusion, see David Gobson, "A Literate Church: The State of Catholic Bible Study Today," *America: The National Catholic Weekly*, December 8, 2008, http://www.americamagazine.org/content/article.cfm?article_id=11270 (accessed December 30, 2008).

61. Scot McKnight and Hauna Ondrey, *Finding Faith, Losing Faith: Stories of Conversion and Apostasy* (Waco, Tex.: Baylor University Press, 2008), 177, 138.

62. Charles R. Kniker, "New Attitudes and New Curricula: The Changing Role of the Bible in Protestant Education, 1880–1920," in Barr and Piediscalzi, *Bible and American Education*, 126.

63. Tracy Fessenden, "The Nineteenth-Century Bible Wars and the Separation of Church and State," *Church History* 74 (December 2005): 807.

64. Peter S. Bracher and David L. Barr, "The Bible Is Worthy of Secular Study: The Bible in Public Education Today," in Barr and Piediscalzi, *Bible and American Education*, 166.

65. On secularization of the curriculum by 1900, see Warren A. Nord, *Religion and American Education: Rethinking a National Dilemma* (Chapel Hill: University of North Carolina Press, 1995), 63–97, especially his conclusion: "Education was secularized not as a result of direct attacks by militant secularists. Instead, as with modern civilization generally, secular values and ways of thinking gradually . . . acquired power in the hearts and minds of people" (96).

66. Boles, *Bible, Religion, and the Public Schools*, 281.

67. *Abington v. Schempp*, http://supreme.justia.com/us/374/203/case.html (Goldberg distinction, p. 306; Clark quote, p. 225) (accessed June 9, 2008).

68. For the Herdahl case, I have relied on DelFattore, *The Fourth R*, 236–48.

69. Mark A. Chancey, "Bible Bills, Bible Curricula, and Controversies of Biblical Proportions: Legislative Efforts to Promote Bible Courses in Public Schools," *Religion and Education* 34 (Winter 2007): 3. See also Mark A. Chancey, "Lesson Plans: The Bible in the Classroom," *Christian Century*, August 23, 2005, 18–21; and Luke Timothy Johnson, "Textbook Case: A Bible Curriculum for Public Schools, *Christian Century*, February 21, 2006, 34–37.

70. Mark A. Chancey, "A Textbook Example of the Christian Right: The National Council on Bible Curriculum in Public Schools," *Journal of the American Academy of Religion* 75 (September 2007): 555.

71. See http://www.bibleinschools.net/Where-This-Has-Been-Implemented (accessed March 17, 2010).

72. On the Lee County case and teaching the Bible in Florida, see David Levenson, "University Religion Departments and Teaching about the Bible in Public Schools: A Report from Florida," www.sbl-site.org/publications/article.aspx?articleId=198 (accessed June 9, 2008).

73. Chancey, "Bible Bills," 7.

74. Ibid. Chancey quotes D. James Kennedy and John Haggee.

75. Mark A. Chancey, "The Bible, the First Amendment, and the Public Schools in Odessa, Texas," *Religion and American Culture* 19 (Summer 2009): 169–205.

76. The contentions over curricula are currently being addressed by two of the world's largest academic organizations in the field of religion, the American Academy of Religion and the Society of Biblical Literature. A Religion in the Schools Task Force is presently drafting "AAR Guidelines for Teaching about Religion in K-12 Schools" as a complement to existing guidelines put out by the National Council for the Social Studies and the National Council for Teachings of English. See http://www.aarweb.org/Public_Affairs/Religion_in_the_Schools/default.asp (accessed March 17, 2009). The Society of Biblical Literature has published a number of classroom resources, including the pamphlet "Bible Electives in the Public Schools: A Guide." For more teacher resources, see www.sbl-site.org/educational/teachingbible.aspx (accessed March 11, 2011).

77. Gutjahr, *An American Bible*, 35, 37.

78. For example, see Paul C. Gutjahr, "The Bible-zine *Revolve* and the Evolution of the Culturally Relevant Bible in America," in *Religion and the Culture of Print in Modern America*, ed. Charles L. Cohen and Paul S. Boyer (Madison: University of Wisconsin Press, 2008), 326–48.

79. Gutjahr, *An American Bible*, 99.

80. Harold P. Scanlin, "Bible Translation by American Individuals," in Frerichs, *The Bible and Bibles in America*, 46–47.

81. Gutjahr, *An American Bible*, 103.

82. Quoted in Kent P. Jackson, "The Sacred Literature of the Latter-day Saints," in Frerichs, *The Bible and Bibles in America*, 104.

83. Barlow, *Mormons and the Bible*, 50. See also Kevin L. Barney, "The Joseph Smith Translation of Ancient Texts of the Bible," in *The Word of God: Essays on Mormon Scripture*, ed. Dan Vogel (Salt Lake City: Signature Books, 1990), 143–60.

84. Quoted in Jackson, "The Sacred Literature of the Latter-day Saints," 166.

85. Stephen J. Stein, "America's Bibles: Canon, Commentary, and Community," *Church History* 64 (June 1995): 178.

86. See Robert Peel, "Science and Health with Key to the Scriptures," in Frerichs, *The Bible and Bibles in America*, 193–213.

87. Thuesen, *In Discordance with the Scriptures*, 4.

88. Fogarty, "The Quest for a Catholic Vernacular Bible in America," 165.

89. Thuesen, *In Discordance with the Scriptures*, 102–4.

90. Quoted in Garth M. Rosell, *The Surprising Work of God: Harold John Ockenga, Billy Graham, and the Rebirth of Evangelicalism* (Grand Rapids, Mich.: Baker, 2008), 157.

91. John Dart, "TNIV Bible Braves Gender-Inclusive World," *Christian Century*, February 13–20, 2002, 10.

92. Ellison Research, http://www.ellisonresearch.com/ERPS%20II/release%209%20versions.htm (accessed July 21, 2008).

93. For a helpful analysis of differences between the NIV and the TNIV, see Craig Blomberg, "Today's New International Version: The Untold Story of a Good Translation," Dialogue on Contemporary Issues, Denver Seminary, http://denverseminary.edu/article/todays-new-international-version-the-untold-story-of-a-good-translation (accessed July 21, 2008).

94. Dart, "TNIV Bible Braves Gender-Inclusive World," 10.

95. See D. A. Carson, *The Inclusive-Language Debate: A Plea for Realism* (Grand Rapids, Mich.: Baker, 1998); Mark L. Strauss, *Distorting Scripture? The Challenge of Bible Translation and Gender Accuracy* (Downers Grove, Ill.: InterVarsity Press, 1998).

96. John G. Stackhouse Jr., "The Battle for the Inclusive Bible," *Christianity Today*, November 15, 1999, 84.

97. "Southern Baptists Blast TNIV," *Christianity Today*, August 5, 2002, 17.

98. Gutjahr, *An American Bible*, 176; Swenson, "Biblically Challenged," 22 (cites Tony Campolo).

99. Jonathan Sheehan, *The Enlightenment Bible: Translation, Scholarship, Culture* (Princeton: Princeton University Press, 2005), 259–60.

100. See Christopher Collins, *Homeland Mythology: Biblical Narratives in American Culture* (University Park: Pennsylvania State University Press, 2007), chap. 7.

101. Christopher Hill, *The English Bible and the Seventeenth-Century Revolution* (London: Penguin Books, 1994), 428.

Space, Time, and Performance
Constitutive Components of American Christian Worship

Christianity in America is profoundly physical, material, and performative. Many Christians have only a rudimentary understanding of the theological or conceptual foundations of their beliefs and instead experience their religious commitment in religious practices. These practices might include such home-based rituals as prayer, saying grace at meals, reading the Bible or other devotional materials, collecting prayer cards or other objects, creating home shrines, displaying religious art, or watching Christian television. Many participate in Bible study groups or other church-based organizations, proselytize door to door, or operate food shelves. Some groups have even conceived of everyday work as a form of worship. The most widely shared, and certainly most public, American Christian practice is attending church services; yet even these community worship events differ widely from denomination to denomination.

Despite this diversity, all worship practices participate in and generate religious meaning. Christianity in America exists within and grows out of all of these worship experiences, whether they are performed publicly in groups or privately by individuals. The meanings generated by these worship practices, as we shall see, flow from the physical actions performed by participants as well as from the temporal and spatial contexts in which the actions take place. Yet the spatial and temporal contexts, the focus of this essay, are often undervalued. Those who study Christianity have generally approached these aspects as simply the *setting* of worship, the background against which the more important work of Christian expression takes place. The Communion service, for instance, requires an altar or table, and although the choice of one over the other may signal a specific theological meaning embedded in the action, the space in which the altar or table sits is generally understood as a functional component of the service, not a constitutive one. Similarly, although some of the ways in which the service portends a connection between the congregants and an event that occurred more than two millennia ago are understood as relevant to the service, the spanning of time is rarely examined as an inherent dimension of it. By examining these contexts of time and space, however, we can learn a great deal about institutional and personal understandings of Christianity in America.

If we think about worship practices as *performative* in character—that is as behaviors performed by both clergy and congregation—we can more clearly see how the contexts in which worship performances take place are in fact integral to their meaning. The actions of worship re-create and signify certain repeated meanings, but, even more important, they creatively generate dynamic new understandings and meanings for the individuals who participate in them. In Catherine Bell's terms, worship performances carry both "ontological and analytic" value.[1] Much of that value derives from the physical relationships, both literal and figurative, that spatial and temporal contexts foster or inhibit, and it is by so doing that these components play central, constitutive roles in the generation of meaning. To explore the role of spatial and temporal elements in the generation of religious meaning in worship, this essay focuses on three performances central to Christian church services: baptism, Communion, and the sermon.[2]

Baptism

Baptism is a sacramental ritual that signifies the entry of the individual into the Christian faith. It consists of the use of water to symbolically mark a transformation in the individual, generally understood as the believer's union with Christ, and is based on biblical precedents found in the books of Matthew and Acts and in several letters of Paul.[3] Baptism is performed by an ordained clergy member, who immerses the individual in water, pours water over the individual's head from a small bowl or cup (a practice called affusion), or sprinkles water on the individual's head (aspersion).[4] Whichever method is used, the action is repeated three times by Trinitarian Christians, invoking the Father, the Son, and the Holy Ghost.

The space in which baptisms take place is determined by both the form they take (immersion, affusion, or aspersion) and the requirements of the participants. Many baptisms are congregational events involving several people: the minister, the individual who is baptized, his or her parents and/or other witnesses (sometimes called sponsors or godparents), and, often, a congregation, which witnesses the act and welcomes the new Christian into the church. The earliest spaces used for baptism were outdoors, along the

FIGURE 1. *A Southern Baptism, Aiken, South Carolina. Detroit Publishing Company, ca. 1905. Baptisms often took place outside in the early twentieth century. Reenacting Jesus' baptism in the River Jordan, this African American woman is about to be immersed by her pastor. Courtesy of the Prints and Photographs Division, Library of Congress. LC-USZ62-107755.*

banks of rivers or lakes, which could accommodate both the full immersion of the individual and substantial numbers of witnesses. The Book of Matthew recounts the Christian prototype, the immersion baptism of Jesus in the River Jordan by John the Baptist, which is reenacted by many congregations. The outdoor performance of this ritual is often a very powerful experience—both for the individual, usually an adult, who is physically submerged in water, and for the gathered community, who together feel a strong communion with nature and the divine. In the United States, outdoor baptisms have been favored by evangelical and charismatic groups, which seek this kind of palpable communion with the divine.

Indoor baptisms have also been common throughout Christian history and have usually been performed in church buildings or separate buildings designed specifically for the ritual.[5] During the American colonial period, for instance, Puritans used a modest bowl placed on a table beneath the pulpit at the front of the meetinghouse for the sprinkling baptism of infants, removing the bowl to storage when not in use. This practice continues to the present day among many Reformed congregations. Episcopalians, who usually practice affusion, have generally placed a stone font holding water near the church entry. Roman Catholics, who also have favored aspersion or affusion, have most often reserved a small room called a baptistery, located near the entry of the church and outfitted with a stone font, for baptisms. Each of these locations—the front of the church, the entry, or a small separate room—places the individual in a distinctive relationship to the congregation and underscores the role of that congregation within the performance—as witnesses, as gathered welcomers, or, in the case of small baptisteries that accommodate few witnesses, as of peripheral importance. In this way, the spatial setting of baptism contributes to the meanings that worshippers attribute to the ceremony.

For the Baptist denomination, the ritual of baptism is the central theological component and the most important worship performance of the faith. As their practice requires the full immersion baptism of adults, Baptist congregations historically conducted baptisms out of doors in a nearby river or lake. In the late nineteenth century, however, they began incorporating shallow baptismal pools into the fronts of their churches, just behind the central pulpit. Contemporary versions of this use of space appear in several suburban megachurches around the United States, including Grace Church in Eden Prairie, Minnesota, which contains a unique, elevated pool placement. In this church, a large stage with several rows of ranked seating for the choir dominates the front of the auditorium-style worship room. Built into the back wall of the stage, behind and above the choir, is the transparent baptismal pool, whose glass front and dramatic lighting allow the congregation to clearly observe the immersion of the individual. This visually captivating spatial arrangement contributes significantly to the meaning of the baptism ritual. Although the public character of baptism and emphasis on the role of the witnessing congregation has always been significant for Baptists, the elevation and lighting of the immersion pool in this church intensify the visual spectacle of the performance, just as a dramatic theatrical set and lighting intensify a secular performance. Baptisms in spaces like this visually unite the congregants and the individual, underscoring the central importance of the ritual's impact on everyone present.

Similar in practice but quite different in location and meaning from this front-of-the-auditorium performance is the immersion baptism that has been adopted in recent years by some Catholics. These groups, who view a full-immersion reenactment of Christ's baptism as more biblically authentic than Catholicism's traditional practice of affusion, have constructed indoor immersion pools for both adult and infant baptisms, but unlike the Baptist practice, the pools are located not within the public worship room but in separate baptisteries similar to those that have housed Catholic fonts for centuries. The immersion pool in the new and widely acclaimed Cathedral of Our Lady of Angels in Los Angeles, for example, is a broad but shallow pool of about two feet, with stairs leading down into it from one side. During baptism, adult initiates are partially submerged, and the priest pours water over the individual's head and shoulders. For infant baptisms, the priest carries the child down the steps into the water, followed by the parents and sponsors, who also stand in the water as he partly immerses the child and pours water over the child's head. In either case, witnesses, usually family members, gather around the pool, but the baptistery does not provide sufficient space for an entire congregation. The intimacy of this baptistery underscores the personal responsibility taken on by the family members, witnesses, and the church itself in raising the infant—a set of meanings quite different from those conveyed by the vast public setting and visual spectacle of adult baptisms in churches like Grace Church.

In all of these instances, a substantial part of the meaning of baptism is connected to the physical relationships among the participants fostered by the spaces. Whether family members or congregational witnesses are close to the action, even in the water, or merely watching from across a room, the spaces that accommodate their presence shape the relationships and thus the meanings that participants express through and discover within the performance.[6]

The distinctive meanings associated with baptismal performances are also influenced by different understandings of the temporal contexts of baptism. Emphasis on the biblical precedent of immersion baptism and the inclusion of immersion pools in churches collapse the temporal distance between the first century and the present by replicating and restoring the practices of Jesus' time. Those so baptized, then and now, are understood to share the new state of existence that baptism bestows, a transformation often understood theologically as analogous to a death and resurrection experience—the descent into the water signifying death (tomb imagery is common around immersion pools) and the emerging from the water signifying rebirth in Christ. Paralleling Jesus' resurrection, baptism can telescope into an instant the two millennia since his lifetime.

Alternatively, churches that use sprinkling and affusion—Lutheran, Episcopalian, Presbyterian, Methodist, United Church of Christ, and others—tend to emphasize entry into the Christian community rather than reenactment as the primary meaning of baptism. For these denominations, baptism is usually performed on infants, and it underscores the role of the congregation in welcoming, educating, and supporting children and other new members in the faith. This understanding of baptism and the placement of the font at the front of the church signify the centrality of the congregation to the performance and its new relationship with the baptized, underscoring the present and future of the church as a living institution.

Communion

The second worship practice we will examine is the Communion service, also called the Eucharist service or the Lord's Supper, which is understood variously as a ritual reenactment of Christ's physical sacrifice and atonement for human sin, a memorial remembrance of his salvation-giving sacrifice, a community-acknowledging meal, and a celebration of oneness in Christ. Communion is performed in response to Jesus' directive during the Last Supper, a Passover meal he shared with his disciples shortly before his death. According to the Gospels, Jesus first gave thanks for the wine and then told the disciples to share the cup among themselves, explaining that "this cup . . . is the new covenant in my blood." He then gave thanks for the bread, broke it, and gave it to them saying, "This is my body, which is given for you. Do this in remembrance of me" (Luke 22:17–22). In Christian liturgical terms, these commands are known as the Words of Institution.

The temporal context of Communion thus telescopes past, present, and future for congregations performing the ceremony. The repeated gestures of taking bread in hand, breaking it, eating it, and taking a sip of wine— or in some cases, simply watching as others do this—constitutes a physical reminder of the ancient roots of the Christian faith. By responding to Christ's command, Christians create a connection to his actions, now over two millennia in the past, collapsing time to bring the past into the present. For some groups, participation in Communion also connects them to the future. Many evangelicals, for instance, understand scripture as indicating that the Last Supper pointed toward the future, to the completion of Jesus' mission to "fulfill the kingdom of God" (Luke 22:16). Thus through these performances of Communion, some believers remind themselves not only of Jesus' sacrifice in the past but also of his promised return in the future. For many Christian congregations, the shared meal also embodies the communion or shared faith of those present, signaling an ongoing connection among Christians.

Just as the meanings of this sacrament vary widely among Christians, so too do the frequency of the ritual, the forms it takes, and the settings in which it is performed. For Catholics, the sacrament of the Eucharist is the centerpiece of every mass. Within this ecclesiastical (clergy-based) institutional structure, the Eucharist service is a highly formalized performance in which the priest performs the actions and recites the words set out in a written manual called the missal. His ritualized activity, performed at an altar, is believed to instigate the miracle of transubstantiation, through which the substance of the wine and bread are converted into the substance of the blood and body of Christ, though the physical elements themselves remain. This understanding of the performance and its use of an altar—historically, a stone platform upon which ritual sacrifices were made—place the ritual in a theological context that emphasizes the sacrifice of Jesus Christ to atone for the sins of humanity. To consume the transubstantiated body and blood of Christ is to participate in that sacrificial atonement.

For centuries, this powerful mystical transformation was performed exclusively by fully ordained priests and could be witnessed only by clergy, other religious, and imperial elites. Ordinary worshippers were granted only a brief view of the consecrated elements. Consequently, church space from the Byzantine period onward was organized to maintain physical separation among these groups. In the popular basilica plan, consisting of an oblong nave flanked by two or more aisles and terminating in an apse housing the sanctuary, the separation is indicated by a rise in the floor, which places the sanctuary two or three steps above the nave, and by an altar rail. In Eastern Orthodox churches, this separation is more dramatically signaled by a full-length iconostasis. Worshippers approach the sanctuary and kneel at the rail to receive the Eucharistic elements. This spatial separation between clergy and laity contributes a powerful set of meanings to the Eucharist service, demonstrating the extraordinary character of the ritual and expressing the relationship among congregants and between congregants and clergy.[7]

Many American Catholic churches also provide added layers of meaning to the worship experience through the inclusion of ornament—statuary, iconography, and other imagery—and auxiliary space, which, in many cases carry both traditional and distinctive (or even idiosyncratic) meanings for the individual congregation. A good example of this is seen in the Cathedral of St. Paul, in St. Paul, Minnesota, a Renaissance-style cruciform building in which the crossing is topped by a massive central dome. Surrounding the crossing are large statues of the four evangelists, Matthew, Mark, Luke, and John, the traditional witnesses to Christ's life. In the sanctuary, several steps higher than the main floor, a marble altar where Communion is performed is covered with an elaborate canopy or baldachin supported by six black-and-gold marble columns and featuring statues of St. Paul and two angels atop its latticework canopy. Reminiscent of the elaborate baldachin in the Basilica of St. Peter in Rome, the institutional home of the pope, this canopy not only underscores the sacredness of the altar and the mass performed at it but also visually connects the performance directly to the spiritual heart of the Roman Catholic church, linking the present, local performance of the mass with the early church and the institutional church—thus, past and present merge. This dual set of meanings has special import in the region, for the Cathedral of St. Paul was erected by Archbishop John Ireland, who urged his immigrant flock to Americanize as quickly as possible, contradicting the position of Pope Leo XIII, who urged Catholics in the United States to remain true to the teachings of the church by keeping separate from the worldly American culture. Thus, although the American congregations and clergy may have had theological or social differences with the church authority in the Vatican, spatial and visual reminders within this church have kept visible the ties between the United States and Europe, the New World and the Old. The Eucharist sacrament, performed in the context of these rich and overlapping meanings, similarly ties past to present.

American Catholic Church spaces also exhibit experimentation with other meanings, including many pertaining to the significance of the mass with respect to congregational identity in a more secular sense. The Cathedral of St. Paul is again illuminating because the building also houses, in addition to the main sanctuary, the Shrine to the Nations, consisting of six chapels located in a semicircle around the apse and accessible by an ambulatory, each dedicated to the patron saint of an immigrant group that settled in Minnesota in the nineteenth century: the Italian St. Antony of Padua, the French and Canadian St. John the Baptist, the Irish St. Patrick, the German St. Boniface, the Slavic St. Cyril and St. Methodius, and St. Therese, the protector of all missions. On these saints' days, private masses held in the chapels connect the participants present with their European and regional past and heritage. Such inclusion of regionally distinctive features in churches is common across the United States. Immigrant congregations erected churches that featured distinctive elements traditional in or reminiscent of their homelands. Similarly, mission churches built by Spanish priests in Texas, New Mexico, and California often include images of flowers, maize, and sunbursts, which were meaningful within the indigenous traditions in those areas. Through the arrangement of space and ornamentation, then, Catholics have used church space in creative ways to add multiple layers of meanings to the performance of Communion in their churches.

Such creativity among American Catholics was particularly evident in mid-twentieth-century modifications in one of the most fundamental features of their traditional church spaces, the separation of the clergy and the laity during the Eucharist. Efforts to move the altar closer to the people and to shift the priest's position so that all those gathered could see his actions were undertaken in the 1950s by the Benedictine monks at the Abbey of St. John in Collegeville, Minnesota. Their Abbey Church, designed in 1958 by Marcel Breuer, featured an altar surrounded by lay seating on three sides and seating for the abbey brothers on the fourth. This arrangement profoundly transformed the space in which the Eucharist was celebrated, allowing all congre-

gants to easily witness the mass, physically collapsing the distance between clergy and laity, and symbolically collapsing the distance between Christ and Christians. A few years later, the Second Vatican Council recommended that altars be moved closer to communicants in all Catholic churches, resulting in many new and sometimes controversial arrangements. In cruciform and longitudinally oriented oblong churches with terminal apses, such as the Cathedral of St. Paul, altars were simply moved out from the rear wall of the apse to a location within the crossing. In newer churches, the altar is often housed on a slightly elevated platform, surrounded by seating on three or even four sides. Idiosyncratic spaces also appeared, such as a short-lived Native American Catholic church in Minneapolis dedicated to Kateri, the Algonquian candidate for sainthood, in which a buffalo robe placed on the floor served as the altar and congregants kneeled around it as the mass was performed.

In contrast to these Catholic examples, many Reformed Protestant congregations understand Communion not as a reenactment of Christ's sacrifice but as a ceremony of memory and cohesion of the Christian community. Such groups generally perform Communion less frequently, twelve or fewer times a year. In many Protestant churches, the bread and wine are placed on a table at the front of the church, rather than on an altar, symbolizing the congregants' sharing of the holy meal, the Lord's Supper. The minister says the Words of Institution over the elements and then the communicants approach the table to receive a small wafer or piece of bread and a sip of wine (from a common cup or an individual glass, or in some cases by dipping the bread into the wine, a practice known as intinction). In some cases, the bread and wine is taken from the table by ushers and passed through the congregation, which is seated in the pews. The organization and use of the space, including the presence of the table and the ability of congregation members to move close to it, set up specific interactions and relationships within the congregation and between congregants and clergy, thereby contributing important spatial meanings to the performance itself. Although these actions are understood to reference those performed by the early followers of Jesus and thus carry a distinctive temporal component, they constitute less a telescoping of time than an acknowledgment of a long, continuous history of the community of believers itself.

Sermon

The third worship performance to be examined here is the sermon, an oratorical performance that is the centerpiece of most Protestant services. Yet the sermon does not stand alone. It always takes place within a host of other worship activities, many of which require significant participation by the congregation. Consequently, the spatial contexts of Protestant worship have been indelibly influenced by the needs of the minister delivering the sermon and by those of the congregation that listens to it and participates in other activities during the service. The resulting spatial and temporal components contribute significantly to the meaning of worship by, again, shaping the relationships among those who participate in the performance.

The sermon as a worship performance derives from belief in scripture as God's primary revelation, the revealed Word of God. For many Protestants, understanding the Bible is the primary means of understanding God. The sermon, an exposition on a biblical passage or theme, has been the principal means through which Protestant laypeople could learn how to interpret the Bible. Yet a great deal of variety exists across theological understandings of the Bible and, consequently, in understandings of the sermon. Some Protestants have believed that the sermon is directly influenced by God—that is, that God assists the minister in his explication of scripture. As Martin Luther suggested, "When the preacher speaks, God speaks!"[8] Theologically conservative Protestants, such as Jehovah's Witnesses and Southern Baptists, who view the Bible as the revealed Word of God, understand the sermon as a human oration on spiritual, moral, or social issues in which the Word infuses the questions raised as well as the answers presented. Sermon performances on this theologically conservative end of the spectrum can be highly emotional, with significant congregational participation in the form of spontaneous shouts of affirmation, derived in part from African American call-and-response patterns. In fact, since the late eighteenth century, African American preachers have developed unique oratorical practices and styles aimed primarily at encouraging enthusiastic congregational participation in the sermon. For such groups, divine revelation—of a different quality than that contained in the Bible but still influenced by the Holy Spirit—occurs during the preacher's performance. On the other end of the spectrum, theologically liberal groups, such as Unitarian Universalists and United Church of Christ, view the Bible as a human creation that provides historical information about Jesus, a Nazarene Jew who preached uniquely insightful moral lessons. Consequently, their sermons generally focus on ethical questions of contemporary import. Many groups, including Presbyterians, Methodists, and Lutherans, embrace some middle territory along this spectrum.

Spatially, sermons can be delivered almost anywhere, indoors or outdoors, but in church buildings they are invariably delivered from the front, usually from a platform elevated above the main floor, and frequently from a pulpit or large podium. Because sermons must be heard and the minister seen by everyone present, many of the spatial features of Protestant churches are designed to enhance acoustics and sightlines to the pulpit. Historically, the standard Protestant worship space, often termed a "preaching hall," has been a rectangular room oriented longitudinally, with an elevated area housing the pulpit at one end of an axis with the door at the other and a center aisle lined with pews, side windows, and, in some cases, galleries. Literally thousands of examples, erected by a wide variety of denominations, exist, including the many Federalist-style churches that dot the East Coast and modest Gothic churches seen across the country.

In such churches, denominations that emphasize both the Word and Communion, such as Episcopalians and Lutherans, place an altar in the raised area and locate the pulpit to the side. Sermon-oriented denominations, however, such as Baptists and Presbyterians, place the pulpit near the center, marking its significance, and may not have other liturgical sites (such as a table or a font) visible at all. The spaces of these churches underscore the importance and authority of the minister and contribute to the centrality of the sermon to worship. Many a famous divine in the eighteenth and nineteenth centuries established his reputation from aloft an impressive pulpit located high above the main floor. Congregants, essentially motionless in their pews, had little option but to attend to the oration of the powerful authority figure above them. Nevertheless, many denominations include visual elements to enhance Word-centered services. In Christ Church Lutheran in Minneapolis, designed by Eliel and Eero Saarinen, for instance, the simple but dramatic movement of sunlight across the large cross mounted on the front wall of the sanctuary contributes considerable meaning to the service.

A new spatial design, the auditorium church, was ushered in by the evangelical revivalism of the nineteenth century, which featured emotional preaching aimed at converting large groups of people to Christianity. Taking a cue from emerging theater arrangements of the period, these churches feature a large and comfortable audience area with balcony and main floor seating that curves around and slopes down to a stage, which typically houses a pulpit or, more frequently, a modest lectern. This arrangement provides exceptional acoustics and direct sightlines to the preacher from each seat in the room, but it also redefines the physical relationships between the clergy and the congregation. The minister pacing the stage is visually and physically more akin to a theatrical performer, a celebrity, with the congregation occupying a physical context like that of an audience gathered to be entertained, in this case by the minister's oration, a musical performance, or another activity. Given the emphasis on theater in these physical spaces, it is not surprising that a host of new practices emerged, including the use of projected visual images, and later films, and performance of theatrical skits.

In the late twentieth century, this arrangement was adopted for large-scale megachurches, such as evangelical minister Robert Schuller's well-known Crystal Cathedral in Garden Grove, California, and Grace Church mentioned above, both of which accommodate several thousand congregants at one time. In these buildings, the celebrity character of ministers is enhanced by video systems that project their images onto huge screens flanking the stage. But the congregations' situation is also transformed in these massive auditoriums, which cater to their needs even more than to clerical ones, offering comfortable seats, embedded video screens for easy viewing, and a host of amenities such as cafeterias or food courts, bookstores, and exercise centers. The result can be sometimes paradoxical experiences and meanings for worshippers. For instance, auditorium spaces allow and encourage congregants to view one another during worship, a feature that fosters a feeling of shared enterprise or fellowship among congregants, even as the enormous spaces of megachurches also allow congregants to feel fairly anonymous. Similarly, even though the stage and the use of a modest lectern—or sometimes no podium at all—by the preacher might be understood to undermine his or her authority, the larger-than-life images of the preacher projected on video screens counteract any such diminishment, even fostering a near-celebrity status.

As central as the sermon is to Protestant services, it is invariably prefaced and followed by a variety of other performances, many of which are carried out by the congregation itself. Liturgical elements surrounding the sermon may include an opening segment such as an introit and processional (particularly in congregations with a formalized liturgy, such as Lutherans and Episcopalians) or a musical performance (particularly in less-formalized denominations, such as Baptists or Presbyterians). Following this, a greeting and announcements by the minister or another congregation leader and an invitation to greet one's fellow congregants by "sharing the peace" are common. Many congregations will sing the Gloria Patria or the Doxology during these opening elements. The congregation might then recite the Apostles' or Nicene Creed and in more liturgically oriented churches respond in unison to specific prompts offered by the minister. Scripture reading is also presented prior to the sermon, usually a "lesson" from the Hebrew Bible (Old Testament) or the New Testament and a "gospel" from one of the evangelists. Additional music, such as congregational hymn singing or a performance by the choir, organist, or other musicians, may occur, and in some churches worshippers may present personal testimony or exhortations. Following the sermon, more musical selections, a hymn sung by the congregation, another long prayer, the offertory, and a benediction or other closing words are common.[9]

Some groups, however, eschew these "formalist" elements in favor of more spontaneous activity. Quaker worship, for instance, consists of a quiet gathering of people, who sit awaiting impetus from the Inner Light to speak. Among evangelicals, congregational performance can include singing and listening to music performed by the choir or other musicians, offering spontaneous vocal responses to clerical prompts, invoking the presence of the Holy Spirit through chanting and raised arms, and responding to that presence through vocalizations and physical movements. Altar calls urging those who are struggling with their consciences to come forward are common. Charismatic and Pentecostal groups will invoke the Holy Spirit with shouts and chanting and respond to its perceived presence by speaking in tongues or through physical movement. Participants may approach the front of the church to receive the blessing of a ministerial or congregational laying on of hands to heal an ailment or to be "slain in the Holy Spirit" (a ritual in which the minister lays hands on the head of the individual and symbolically pushes him or her over into the waiting arms of spotters, who gently lower the person to the floor). In all of these cases, congregants gather close to one another, moving chairs out of the way and creating a caring, human setting in which individuals may experience both the divine and a strong feeling of *communitas.*

Understandings of the Bible, the sermon, and congregational worship performances also carry with them temporal components, particularly for those who believe that the sermon is closely tied to God's revelation. For congregations that take this view, worship time during services is "extraordinary time," a period in which the "ordinary" elements of life are suspended and one experiences the divine. Pentecostal and charismatic congregations focus their services on this encounter with the Holy Spirit during this time-out-of-time. Even for congregations that do not embrace the idea of ongoing revelation, the Sunday sermon and worship service often punctuate the week of everyday activities with a Sabbath period—perhaps a full day, perhaps just an hour—devoted to spiritual matters and rest. That this time, no matter how brief, is important to American Christians is demonstrated as they flock to their churches week after week.

A comprehensive understanding of worship among American Christians requires that we pay attention not only to the diversity of actions that constitute it, whether performed according to scripted guides or extemporaneously, but also to the diversity of spatial and temporal components of worship. For it is through the combination of these components—spatial, temporal, and performative—that the creative energy and significance of the congregational and personal encounter with God is developed. In large measure, the inspiration of worship is linked to the human relationships fostered in space and across time, which are then acted upon through an array of performances. In constructing diverse spaces to accommodate worship, congregations articulate their respective understandings of transcendent power and human authorities, their values—religious, social, and even political in some cases—their community identities, and their ideas about the past, present, and future. For those who seek to understand how American Christians worship, attention to these aspects challenges the static perception that the meanings embedded in worship exist apart from the actual performances of people and are merely "expressed" by rituals that might take place anywhere or at any time. Instead, analysis of the spatial and temporal contexts of worship provides a deeper, more comprehensive perspective on how religious meaning is situated in and developed through the performance of faith.

NOTES

1. Catherine Bell, "Performance," in *Critical Terms for Religious Studies*, ed. Mark C. Taylor (Chicago: University of Chicago Press, 1998), 211.

2. For other discussions of the spatial setting of Christian worship, see James F. White, "The Spatial Setting," in *The Oxford History of Christian Worship*, ed. Geoffrey Wainwright and Karen B. Westerfield Tucker (New York: Oxford University Press, 2006), 793–816; and James F. White, *Protestant Worship and Church Architecture: Theological and Historical Considerations* (New York: Oxford University Press, 1964).

3. A concise overview of meanings ascribed to baptism over time is found in the "Baptism" entry in *The Oxford Dictionary of the Christian Church*, 3rd ed., ed. E. A. Livingstone (Oxford: Oxford University Press, 1917), 150–52. The quotation appears on p. 150.

4. The term "immersion" can mean the full submersion of the individual or it can mean partial immersion followed by the pouring of water over the head and shoulders.

5. The earliest Christian building known to scholars, the Dura-Europos domus ecclesiae in Syria, for instance, contains a small baptistery. See Jeanne Halgren Kilde, *Sacred Power, Sacred Space: An Introduction to Christian Architecture and Worship* (New York: Oxford University Press, 2008), 27–28.

6. On the importance of personal relationships to religious experience, see Robert Orsi, "Abundant History: Marian Apparitions as Alternative Modernity," in *Historically Speaking* (September/October 2008): 14, available at http://www.bu.edu/historic/_hs_pdfs/abundant_history_orsi_shaw.pdf (accessed April 10, 2009).

7. These distinctions are also marked by ritual actions, special vestments and objects, and music.

8. Quoted in Fred W. Meuser, "Luther as Preacher of the Word of God," in *The Cam-*

bridge Companion to Martin Luther, ed. Donald K. McKim (Cambridge: Cambridge University Press, 2003), 136. Jesus' Sermon on the Mount is the prototype sermon for many Christians.

9. An overview of Protestant worship appears in Karen B. Westerfield Tucker, "North America," in *Oxford History of Christian Worship*, 586–632.

Spreading the Gospel in Christian America

On Sunday, October 5, 1913, New Yorkers waited in long lines at a Harlem rail station to file through a railroad car refashioned as a Catholic Church and sidelined for a few days in Manhattan to showcase Catholic evangelism. Billed as the longest car in the world, St. Peter's chapel was built to order by the Barney & Smith Car Company of Ohio, one of the nation's premier suppliers. Its oversized copper roof and attractive interior provided appealing space for "bring[ing] the gospel to the churchless." St. Peter's followed the nation's rails wherever opportunity beckoned, crisscrossing especially remote regions of the West. Staffed by Father William D. O'Brien, chaplain, and George Hennessey, organist, St. Peter's came fully equipped with an altar rail that folded into a confessional, the stations of the cross, and seating for seventy-four, plus living quarters for its staff. One of three Catholic chapel cars (the others were St. Anthony's and St. Paul's), its priests competed for souls along the nation's thousands of miles of track with three Episcopalian and seven Baptist chapel cars with names like Evangel, Good Will, and Glad Tidings.[1]

By 1913, Catholic gospel cars had an impressive track record. St. Anthony, a refurbished Pullman coach, began its journeys in 1907. In Oregon alone, its chaplain, Father H. D. McDevitt, planted forty-three missions in the archdiocese of Portland and forty-one in the archdiocese of Baker. By the time the car was retired in 1919, twenty of these missions had evolved into congregations housed in permanent buildings. Baptists, meanwhile, rode the rails in the interests of their denominations and cooperated as well with the railroad YMCA to provide religious services for transient railroad men.[2] Episcopalian cars served remote settlements in northern Michigan and the Dakotas.

In the early twentieth century, gospel railroad cars took their place in a long list of novelties Americans used to spread the gospel at home. Evangelism stood at the core of Christian identity, but Americans knew that telling the good news and recruiting others to believe was not only a biblical com-

FIGURE 1. *Aimee Semple MacPherson (1890–1944), founder of the Foursquare Church. American Christians have always found creative ways to spread the gospel. In this photo, MacPherson poses in front of a "gospel car" with leaflets in hand. Courtesy of the Foursquare Church.*

mand and a Christian obligation. It had a self-serving side, too. Sharing the gospel both expressed and assured lively faith. "The more gospel we give," one nineteenth-century pundit explained, "the more we have for ourselves."

By law, America's unique combination of democracy and religious freedom permitted every religious group to thrive if it could. Competition for souls encouraged entrepreneurs to devise creative strategies to win and retain converts and enlist them in public causes that promoted the common good. Revivals, camp meetings, and voluntary associations supplemented regular preaching. Protestant, Catholic, and Mormon benevolent societies churned out resources to support evangelism and nurture faith. At every turn—in outreaches to Native Americans, immigrants, African Americans—they confronted each other as well as outsiders. Their commitments to exclusive truth meant that spreading the good news entailed heated competition.

Proclaiming the gospel in the United States was not merely a religious endeavor: enthusiasts wove their understandings of the gospel into their visions for the nation. Protestants intended to shape the national culture, Catholics wanted religious freedom, and Mormons sought a promised land. In the nineteenth century, sheer numbers gave evangelical Protestants pride of place. For them, genuine Christianity began with the new birth and manifested itself in activities that promoted the coming of God's kingdom. They took the Bible as their authority and saw the world as their destiny. They held that the nation enjoyed God's special favor: democracy and freedom were blessings attended by obligations as much as rights to be enjoyed. The first notable survey of American Christianity, published by Robert Baird in 1844, estimated that evangelical religion influenced fully five-sixths of the nation's 18 million citizens. "Unevangelicals" constituted a numerically insignificant mix of Catholics, Mormons, and Unitarians that Baird dismissed in a few pages.[3]

Such triumphalist Protestant generalizations seemed far less lofty "on the ground," where competition got nasty when Protestants rubbed shoulders with Catholics and Mormons, who were equally exclusivist about their own beliefs. In the mid-nineteenth century, partisans of each group insisted that only like-minded people could hope for eternal salvation. Outsiders were fair game since they simply were not "true" or "full" Christians. Protestant-Catholic-Mormon rivalry proceeded without a nod to the view that they might be different tribes of the same clan, and it tested the limits of civility and freedom. Catholics and Mormons asserted their constitutional rights amid sharp resistance from the dominant Protestant culture—resistance rooted in a combination of religious zeal and patriotic aspirations. At stake were incompatible views of the marks of genuine Christianity and rival views of national destiny. Protestants insisted that they found the pure gospel in the pages of the New Testament. It consisted of a new birth manifested in a holy life. Catholics countered that true Christianity resided in the accumulated traditions and teachings of the Roman Catholic Church. Latter-day Saints insisted that they preached the authoritative message of God's restored truth. Led by a prophet whose inspired utterances supplemented scripture and sustained by a strong sense of peoplehood, they demonstrated God's power by exercising spiritual gifts and persevering against great odds. In the mid-nineteenth century, these three groups contended with each other for American souls. The stakes were high: for individuals, eternal salvation; for the gospel, the vindication of truth; for the nation, a test of the limits of religious freedom and civil discourse.

Protestant Mobilization

At the outset, Protestants had a clear upper hand. They gave their message solid institutional expression in denominations and voluntary associations that resulted in massive endeavors at home and abroad. Protestants believed that the nation's well-being depended on its fidelity to true Christianity. They cared about foreign missions, but they directed much of their early collective efforts toward Christianizing and civilizing the West. In their minds, evangelical religion fostered the common good, and the republic would thrive only if biblical values prevailed. Only the dominance of evangelical religion (synonymous with true Christianity) could assure that the United States would fulfill its God-given destiny to advance God's kingdom. Evangelicals controlled much of the media, and so they set the tone for public religious discourse. Since the government was religiously neutral, evangelicals took on the task of "forming a virtuous citizenry"—proselytizing their neighbors.

The West presented them with a challenge of the first magnitude. East Coast Protestants worried about anarchy, irreligion, and Roman Catholics on the expanding frontier. Their forebears arrived in colonial America with deep-seated antagonism toward the Catholic Church. In the eighteenth century, Enlightenment rhetoric heightened anti-Catholicism: everywhere, political liberals denounced the Catholic Church as the archenemy of liberty and progress, a bastion of superstition. Nineteenth-century Protestants agreed in general that Romanism imperiled the nation's march toward its destiny. Sinister Jesuit plots afoot in the West demanded prompt decisive action. Anti-Catholicism was so pervasive in nineteenth-century evangelicalism that for a time it wove itself into the movement's essential fabric. Authors of sensational exposés and students of biblical prophecy saw opposing Catholicism as part of a cosmic spiritual battle. In 1858, the Mortara Affair, a much-publicized Catholic Church–condoned removal of a secretly baptized Jewish child from his family in Italy received wide coverage in the American press because it supported the common wisdom: the Roman Catholic Church considered itself above the law and stopped at nothing to achieve its ends.[4]

Even as Protestants mobilized to save the West, Catholics poured into eastern cities. Over 1 million arrived before 1840, and by 1860, thanks to Irish and German immigration, Catholics totaled 37 percent of the population of the Protestant empire. As Catholic numbers increased, Protestant conspiracy theories flourished. Protestant missionaries redoubled their efforts, since converting Catholics amounted to saving the republic. In 1826, the Home Missionary Society assured supporters, "We are doing the work of patriotism no less than Christianity."

Evangelicals believed that upholding true Christianity demanded much more than converting individuals. Their benevolent empire included voluntary associations designed to address social needs, reform and extend public education, promote cultural opportunities, improve prospects for the physically challenged, and encourage literacy. Many believed that the struggle for America's soul required strategically placed permanent institutions to perpetuate the twin blessings of true Christianity and democracy, and so competition with Catholics contributed to the rationale for Christian higher education in the West. A band of Yale graduates (the first of several such groups from eastern colleges) enlisted in the cause in 1829, and one enduring result was Jacksonville College near Springfield, Illinois. Missionaries from Connecticut founded Western Reserve University in Cleveland in 1826, followed in the 1830s by Oberlin College in Ohio, Hanover and Wabash colleges in Indiana, Grinnell College in Iowa, Illinois College and Knox College in Illinois, and Adrian College in Michigan. Methodists established DePauw in Indiana, while Baptists supported Franklin College in Indiana and Denison College in Ohio.[5]

The legendary Lyman Beecher justified this determined gospel-driven rush westward. In a famous published lecture, *A Plea for the West* (1834), Beecher argued passionately that "the religious and political destiny of our nation is to be decided in the West."[6] Catholics were already there, and Catholic religion was "hostile to civil and religious liberty." Beecher cited Catholic reports to show that Catholic schools were essentially missions in which many children already "embraced the Catholic religion" while other pupils carried favorable impressions of the Catholic faith "into the bosom of their families."[7] A writer for the Catholic *Quarterly Register* reported from Cincinnati in 1832 that "a great number of persons" were under instruction "in the true religion."[8] In 1856, Boston pastor Edward Norris Kirk added his own observations to the Protestant sense of urgency:

> There, brethren, our great battle with the Jesuit, is to be waged. We must build college against college. If the musty atmosphere of a Jesuit school suits the free born western youth; if the repetition of scholastic modes of discipline can captivate the child of the prairies, then we may fail in the contest. But all experience has confirmed our anticipation, that America is a field on which the open, manly, Christian discipline

of a Protestant college must annihilate the rival system of Jesuitical instruction.[9]

Protestants looked with special concern toward St. Louis, a Jesuit hub where at mid-century one-third of the population was Roman Catholic. St. Louis University came under Jesuit control in 1829, and by 1850 it enrolled 160 students. Five Catholic academies served the surrounding towns. To the east, St. Mary's College, established in 1821 near Bardstown, Kentucky, by the Irish missionary priest William Byrne, became a focus of Protestant concern in 1833 when Byrne passed control of the school to the Jesuits. By then, the school had educated at least 1,200 Kentucky youths. Together, the dioceses of St. Louis and New Orleans had one hundred priests, ten convents, two colleges, and two theological seminaries that enrolled six hundred. A dozen churches and a cathedral served a Catholic population in Cincinnati, which grew by conversions as well as through immigration.[10] Evangelicals united to resist such "bids of defiance to Protestantism" through agencies like the Society for the Promotion of Collegiate and Theological Education at the West (founded in 1843) and the Ladies' Society for the Promotion of Education in the West (founded in Boston in 1847). In 1849, evangelicals formed the American and Foreign Christian Union to convert the "papal population at home and abroad." In 1851, its seventy home and thirty foreign missionaries (whose slogan was "the love of Christ constraineth us") reported "encouraging success."[11] Presbyterian activist Robert Baird told the Evangelical Alliance in 1851 that Protestants were learning to approach Catholics in a spirit of "kindness, love, and perseverance"—in marked contrast to the tone of most public discourse at home. The American and Foreign Christian Union took a two-pronged approach to Catholic evangelism: "direct antagonism against the errors, superstitions, mummeries, and absurdities of Romanism, as a system" and "love and amity towards the souls in bondage to such a system."[12] A generation later, eighty-four American Protestant missions were at work in 1,546 mission stations among Roman Catholics in Europe and Latin America.[13]

Home missionaries used alarmist anti-Catholic literature to advantage. Annual home missionary society conventions regularly featured speakers who denounced Catholic intrigue against both the gospel and the nation. Eloquent enthusiasts declared that "the supremacy of Popery" in the American West would "sound the death knell of Protestantism everywhere." When resident Catholics professed ignorance about conspiracies against the United States, their denials merely confirmed evangelical allegations that the

Catholic Church was fundamentally un- and anti-American—the "design and ultimate control" of popish plots "remained abroad." In the second half of the nineteenth century, the assertion of papal infallibility, the conservatism of Vatican I, and the Catholic Church's expectations of members abetted evangelical antipathy for what they called "the whore of Babylon."

Evangelicals mustered a broadly united front against the institution of the Catholic Church, but individual Protestants and Catholics sometimes got along surprisingly well. Bishop John England of the missionary diocese of Charleston, South Carolina, for example, regularly ministered to his scattered flock in Protestant church buildings. In 1826, England became the first Catholic priest to address Congress. An overflow audience heard England rebut the view (advanced by President John Quincy Adams, who sat in the audience) that Catholic intolerance for other religions made the Catholic Church incompatible with republican institutions. England insisted that he would not "allow to the Pope, or to any bishop of our church, the smallest interference with the humblest vote at our most insignificant balloting box." His public embrace of the separation of church and state and his enthusiasm for his adopted land defied the common wisdom that Catholicism inherently opposed American values. He carried on a lively correspondence with contemporaries who vilified the Catholic Church and patiently explained to the public the church's customs.

But the Catholic Church grew most dramatically through immigration, and Nativists harped on its foreign character. And Catholics did not always act in their own best interests. In November 1850, John Hughes, recently elevated to archbishop of New York, delivered a sermon in St. Patrick's Cathedral entitled "The Decline of Protestantism and Its Causes." "There is no secret about this," Hughes declared. "The object we hope to accomplish in time is to convert all pagan nations, and all Protestant nations. . . . Everybody should know that we have for our mission to convert the inhabitants of the United States."[14]

A startling blend of fear-filled alarmism and standard evangelical "love for the lost" bolstered evangelical responses to such assertions. It produced enough converts to alarm American Catholic leaders. Meanwhile, a trickle of native-born American Protestants converted to Catholicism and served the church in highly visible ways. Mother Elizabeth Seton, founder of the Sisters of Charity, was reared an Episcopalian. The one-time Methodist Isaac Hecker founded the Paulist Fathers in 1858 and the *Catholic World* in 1865. He preached, lectured, and wrote with the goal of converting American Protestants to the true faith.

Catholic Missions

The American Catholic Church was itself a mission until 1908, when Pope Pius X removed it from the jurisdiction of the Society for the Propagation of the Faith. As a mission-receiving church, American Catholics welcomed clergy and religious from abroad. Soon after the announcement of the church's changed status, the Vatican named two American cardinals to serve alongside Baltimore's lone Cardinal Gibbons, and church officials reported the pope's satisfaction with the progress of the church "in this land without a concordat to bind state and church."[15]

Catholic missionary work within the United States focused on education and other forms of direct evangelism. Religious orders devoted attention to Native Americans and African Americans, as well as to orphans and the poor. American-founded orders like the Paulists (1858), the Sisters of Charity (1805), and Katherine Drexel's Sisters of the Blessed Sacrament for Indians and Colored People (1891) figured prominently in evangelization efforts. The Paulists introduced missions to non-Catholics in the diocese of Cleveland in 1894. To train and support the work, the Catholic Missionary Union came into being. Directed by bishops, seminary faculty, and parish leaders, it continues to enlist priests and laypeople for missions to non-Catholics in the United States. The Apostolic Training House at Catholic University in Washington, D.C., opened in 1904. Paulist publications included tracts and pamphlets for distribution to Protestants and promoted faithfulness among baptized Catholics, too. Other Catholics countered Protestant revival meetings with a form of Catholic revivalism modeled after European parish missions. Itinerant Catholic preachers appealed to the affections and urged people to convert. In contrast to Protestant conversions, Catholic conversion was completed in the church with participation in the sacraments, and evangelists stressed loyalty to the church and its clergy more than did their Protestant counterparts.[16] Catholic urban missionaries countered Protestant evangelism by attempting to strengthen immigrant religious identity. Their home missionary labors had the dual goals of retention and growth.

An expatriate Canadian priest, Father Francis Kelley, shaped the Catholic Church Extension Society, founded in Chicago in 1905, around distinct evangelistic goals:

- To develop the missionary spirit in the clergy and people of the Catholic Church in the United States.
- To assist in the erection of parish buildings for poor and needy places.

- To support priests for neglected or poverty-stricken districts.
- To send the comfort of religion to pioneer localities.
- In a word, to preserve the faith of Jesus Christ to thousands of scattered Catholics in every portion of our own land, especially in the
  country districts and among immigrants.

A skillful entrepreneur, Father Kelley paid close attention to strategies that worked for Protestants and put them to use for the Catholic Church. At the St. Louis World's Fair in 1904, he learned that railroads pulled chapel cars without charge and decided that Catholics should borrow a Protestant idea. In 1909, Father Kelley was a leading spirit behind the first Catholic Missionary Congress, a massive meeting at Chicago's Holy Name Cathedral where evidences of lay as well as clerical interest in the church's well-being in the United States gratified organizers. "The fear of saying too much," Kelley admitted in his address to the congress, "has kept us for a long time from recognizing the great Missionary needs of the American Church."[17] Real Catholicism was "missionary and zealous in every fiber," he insisted, before turning to the vexing problem of massive Protestant resources and successes.[18] First on his list was the Student Volunteer Movement, its enthusiasts visible on every major campus to energize and enlist young people to evangelize the world. Yale students supported a particular Chinese mission and sent "her sons" to staff it. Missions figured prominently in Protestant seminary education, and the idea of missions, Kelley pointed out, "galvanized a life into a decaying Protestantism." Why did Protestant religion refuse to die? "Because an unselfish spirit is driving its really sincere young ministers into the lanes and byways to compel men to come in."[19] "Our separated brethren" flooded the West with missionaries, colporteurs, and settlers on a mission and, in the absence of priests and religious, Protestants easily raided the ranks of the Catholic faithful. The scandal of ethnic dissension and preoccupation with European politics too often diverted American Catholics from evangelism. Protestants lavished funds on their denominational and purpose-driven agencies, while Catholics, Kelley regretted, threw only pennies at the church, developed "the social and selfish" sides of Catholic community (parish dances came up here), and overlooked "the poor and neglected of Jesus Christ."[20]

Kelley had done his homework. A survey of Protestant pastors produced numbers to confirm his observations that Protestant congregations prioritized missions, gave generously, and understood that missionary giving benefited the giving congregations.

Catholic evangelism in the United States, then, proceeded against enormous odds. Millions of new arrivals overwhelmed Catholic resources. Catholic immigrants were often poor, and they came from places where Catholicism was privileged: lay Catholics did not readily share the Protestant eagerness to evangelize. Those who moved beyond cities often moved as well beyond the regular reach of the Catholic Church. Protestants had money, organization, media, the Bible, energized lay evangelists, and a clear sense of Catholic errors. Catholics were hard-pressed to compete.

Mormons and the Good News

Mormons, on the other hand, employed Protestant strategies against Protestants from the outset. Organized around Joseph Smith's revelations and the Book of Mormon, Latter-day Saints learned from the Book of Mormon that they were a restoration of true Christianity in the last days. They anticipated an end-time ingathering of God's Israel, and they prophesied dire calamities for those who spurned their gospel. Their version of the good news came unfiltered through a European lens: the Americas figured directly in their sacred history. The Church of Jesus Christ of Latter-day Saints organized formally in 1830, but its missionary work began in the 1820s, as soon as Joseph Smith shared his revelations. Believers went door-to-door and talked freely with their neighbors about the words from God they heard directly through God's prophet, Joseph. Waves of recent Protestant revivals made religion a popular subject; competition among revivalist groups lent a certain appeal to assertions of a direct and authoritative word from God. Curious and religiously unsettled people became the first converts to this small group in upstate New York, even before the Book of Mormon was published. In 1829, for example, Joseph Smith prophesied to his brother Hyrum, using words familiar to readers of the King James Version of the Bible: "The field is white unto harvest; . . . reap while the day lasts."[21] Small-town newspapers prepared the way by arousing curiosity about the "Golden Bible" and mocking its unlikely translator. Mormons went town-to-town as well as house-to-house, announcing public meetings and preaching in the open air. Persecution only heightened their ardor.[22]

Mormons blended the familiar and the novel. Their first hymnal featured many standard Protestant songs alongside new lyrics composed by insiders. Early Mormon worship was charismatic—speaking in tongues and prophecies were commonplace and presented as indicators of God's immediate direction of God's chosen people. Since God still spoke through prophets, Mormons freely supplemented scripture. Spiritual gifts not only testified to the Spirit's presence—they also directed the growing constituency's formal activities.

Joseph Smith prophesied over people by name, directing them where to carry his restored gospel.[23] Mormons were instructed to be straightforward, not to "sing lullabies to a slumbering world."[24] They were warned of impending judgment, and foreign and home missions proceeded simultaneously. In the late 1830s, two groups of prominent Mormon men heeded Smith's instructions and undertook missionary trips to Britain. They won thousands of converts and enlisted some to migrate to the United States. Within ten years, one in three Latter-day Saints was British.[25] The first Mormon missionaries were males, and sometimes their missions took them away for indefinite periods, leaving their families to survive as they could. Their journals chronicled sacrifices, opposition, and successes.

The vast majority of the first Mormon converts were Protestants. As Mormon numbers grew, Protestant media mocked their claims and mobilized to curtail Mormon influence.[26] Converts who jumped ship published exposés that confirmed Protestant worries, and Mormons ran afoul of the dominant culture. They saw themselves as a people; outsiders were gentiles, insiders, saints. An early exposé, *Mormonism Unveiled* (1834) quoted a prediction by Martin Harris, Joseph Smith's early collaborator, that confirmed outsiders in their opposition: "I do hereby assert and declare that in four years from the date hereof, every sectarian and religious denomination in the United States, shall be broken down, and every Christian shall be gathered unto the Mormonites, and the rest of the human race shall perish. If these things do not take place, I will hereby consent to have my hand separated from my body."[27]

Mormons followed an autocratic prophet who claimed to speak for God but preached a bewildering message at odds with Christian orthodoxy. In 1838, Mormon leader Parley Pratt told the group's critics that within fifty years, all "unbelieving gentiles" would be gone from North America. Within ten years, he opined, they would be "greatly scourged."[28] A succession of revelations (including one instituting plural marriage), nasty rumors about Joseph Smith, ridicule of the Book of Mormon, and the devastating collapse of a Mormon-controlled bank during the Panic of 1837 brought early Mormons squarely into the sights of the Protestant home missionary movement. When the main group of Latter-day Saints followed Brigham Young to Utah in 1846, home missionaries were not far behind. Sensational literature abetted the missionary cause with vivid allegations of sinister goings-on in Utah. The Mountain Meadows Massacre in 1857 reinforced popular hostility (a Mormon militia executed 125 Arkansans bound for California with 800 head of cattle, left their remains exposed, and confiscated the pioneers' goods, distributing their children among the Mormons).[29] Describing Mormons as "degraded" and "deluded," Congregationalist missionaries, for example, alleged that Mormonism "cast its shadow of shame and reproach upon our American Christianity." Patience might bear fruit. "Some men must acquire intelligence," one Protestant observed. "This will extend, and it is not in the nature of man to submit to such absolute tyranny as is exercised by the Mormon rulers."[30]

Nonetheless, Mormons persisted in asserting that "Babylon, literally understood, is . . . the Roman Catholics, Protestants, and all that have not had the keys of the kingdom."[31] Occasional "vandalism and discourtesy" toward home missionaries reminded Protestants that Mormons considered outsiders a nuisance, an interruption to the progress of the Zion. Missionaries typically began their reports about Mormon evangelism with details of Mormon resistance to the gospel—even declaring the impossibility of a breakthrough—but they generally moved on to describe modest evidences of progress. They found homesick Utah settlers and dissident Mormons ripe for the gospel, and a few Mormon families enrolled children in Protestant schools. Utah statehood raised feelings on both sides to a fever pitch. Detractors focused attention on Mormon "otherness" and stoked unease about Mormon beliefs and designs.

Toward the end of the nineteenth century, debates about polygamy and its implications for Utah statehood raged. During one week in 1886, two Manhattan ministerial associations discussed Mormons in terms that mirrored the popular view. Baptists heard Joseph Smith described as a "rank fraud." Methodist preachers were treated to a description of Mormonism as "treasonable"—not merely un-Christian but "utterly hostile" to the United States. Mormons intended to control the world through their priesthood, and the "ignorant" rank and file looked forward to the day when they would rule the earth.[32] Methodists' indignation prompted New York clergy to draft a resolution asking the federal government to place Utah in the hands of officials who were not "slaves and dupes of an autocratic priesthood" using "republican forms of government to disguise their real objectives." Mormon bashing did not end with statehood. When the Utah legislature elected Mormon apostle Reed Smoot to the Senate in 1902, the public response (which took the form

of much-publicized drawn-out hearings about the full range of Mormon beliefs) revealed a persistent and profound distrust of Latter-day Saints.

In the course of such nineteenth-century confrontations, people clarified
what they believed about themselves and others. In the twenty-first century,
the anxieties about faith and nation that once nurtured acrimonious competition among Protestants, Catholics, and Mormons seem remote. It is easy
to find evidence of change over time—the popularity of the Mormon Tabernacle Choir, the participation of both Protestant and Catholic clergymen in
both inaugurations of Dwight D. Eisenhower, and the emergence of annual
conversations among Mormons and evangelicals. Catholics, Protestants, and
Mormons seem more willing to trust each other's visions for the nation and
to partner on issues of common concern. They still evangelize one another,
perhaps more as people eager to commend their versions of truth than as
devotees of the exclusive truth for eternal salvation. The legacy of their early
turbulent confrontations remains strong: they sharpened their own senses of
the content of "true Christianity," borrowed each other's strategies, tested the
limits of religious freedom, clarified religious rights, shaped a stronger sense
of the meaning of America, and helped fashion public space where religious
discourse could flourish.

NOTES

1. See http://query.nytimes.com/mem/archive-free/pdf?res=9902E3D6163DE633A25
755C0A9669D946296D6CF. See also "This Church Is on Wheels," http://www.chapelcars
.com.

2. Wilma Rugh Taylor and Norman Taylor, *Gospel Tracks through Texas: The Mission
of the Chapel Car Good Will* (College Station: Texas A&M University Press, 2005); Wilma
Rugh Taylor and Norman Taylor, *This Train Is Bound for Glory: The Story of America's
Chapel Cars* (Valley Forge, Pa.: Judson Press, 1999).

3. Robert Baird, *Religion in America* (New York: Harper, 1844).

4. "Abduction a Christian Duty," *New York Times*, November 18, 1858, 4. Forty years
later, this child, Mortara, by then a priest, arrived in New York to evangelize among Italian immigrants. "Strange Story of a Priest," *New York Times*, December 13, 1897.

5. See Timothy L. Smith, "Protestant Schooling and American Nationality, 1800–1850,"
Journal of American History 53, no. 4 (1967): 143–52; Melvin I. Urofsky, "Reforms and
Response: The Yale Report of 1858," *History of Education Quarterly* 5, no. 1 (1965): 53–67;
James Findlay, "The SPCTEW and Western Colleges: Religion and Higher Education in
Mid-Nineteenth-Century America," *History of Education Quarterly* 17 (1977): 31–62.

6. Lyman Beecher, *A Plea for the West* (Cincinnati: Truman and Smith, 1835), 11.

7. Ibid., 102; *Quarterly Register* 3 (1831): 98.

8. Beecher, *A Plea for the West*, 112; *Quarterly Register* 2 (1830).

9. Edward Norris Kirk, *The Church and the College* (Boston, 1856), 108.

10. Robert Baird, *View of the Valley of the Mississippi* (Philadelphia: Henry Tanner, 1834), 329.

11. Robert Baird, *The Progress and Prospects of Christianity in the United States* (London: Partridge and Oakey, 1851), 38; Robert Baird, *The American Home and Foreign Christian Union*, 1857, http://books.google.com/books?id=mQHPAAAAMAAJ&dq=American+and+Foreign+Christian+Union&printsec=frontcover&source=bl&ots=LPeFtuahIh&sig=dbP9nL2BOZIIeoKosLig5s28u_E&hl=en&ei=rOnMScWXLqTrlQfu2N3MCQ&sa=X&oi=book_result&resnum=3&ct=result#PPA279,M1.

12. Baird, *American Home and Foreign Christian Union*, 281.

13. "Progress of Romanism and Protestantism," *Christian World* (January 1884): 16.

14. "The Decline of Protestantism and Its Causes," *The Complete Works of Archbishop John Hughes* (New York: Lawrence Kehoe, 1866).

15. *American Yearbook* (1912): 733.

16. Jay Dolan, *Catholic Revivalism: The American Experience, 1830–1900* (Notre Dame: University of Notre Dame Press, 1978).

17. Francis Kelley, "The Church Extension Society," in *Proceedings of the First American Catholic Missionary Congress*, ed. Francis Clement Kelley (Chicago: J. S. Hyland, 1909), 96, http://books.google.com/books?id=rVdJ3E7ECiwC&printsec=frontcover&dq=Catholic+missionary+congress&ei=AQ3MSaLsJqTGzQSJkqTVCQ#PPA96,M1.

18. Ibid., 100.

19. Ibid., 100, 101.

20. Ibid., 105.

21. The *Doctrine and Covenants* 11: 3. For a complete edition of The Doctrine and Covenants, "a book of scripture containing revelations from the Lord to the Prophet Joseph Smith and to a few other latter-day prophets," see http://lds.org/study/topics/doctrine-and-covenants?lang=eng (accessed March 28, 2011).

22. See, for example, Parley P. Pratt, "Shameful Outrage Committed by a Part of the Inhabitants of the Town of Mentor upon the Person of Elder Parley P. Pratt," April 7, 1835, http://olivercowdery.com/texts/Prat1835.htm#p01.

23. *Doctrine and Covenants* 31:1–5.

24. Grant Underwood, *The Millenarian World of Early Mormonism* (Urbana: University of Illinois Press, 1993), 49.

25. Ibid., 127.

26. Women's home missionary societies united to complain to Congress about Mormon evangelism. See, for example, 1897 *Annual Report of the Board of Managers of the Methodist Woman's Home Missionary Society*, http://books.google.com/books?id=dYMPAAAAIAAJ&pg=PA187&dq=%22Methodist++home+missionary%22&client=safari#v=onepage&q=Mormon&f=false.

27. Parley Pratt, *Mormonism Unveiled* (New York: O. Pratt and E. Fordham, 1838), 14; in a similar vein, Samuel Williams, *Mormonism Exposed* (Pittsburgh: self-published, 1842); both http://www.solomonspalding.com/docs/1834howc.htm#pg011a).

28. Pratt, *Mormonism Unveiled*, 16.

29. *New York Times*, July 7, 1859, 2; "Mountain Meadows: The Story of the Mormon Massacre," *New York Times*, July 24, 1875.

30. "The Future of Mormonism," *Home Missionary*, 1868, http://www.archive.org/stream/homemissionary06socigoog/homemissionary06socigoog_djvu.txt.

31. Quoted in Underwood, *Millenarian World of Early Mormonism*, 44, http://books.google.com/books?id=qkw3ZPP6UioC&pg=PA188&lpg=PA188&dq=Baptist+home+missionary+society+%2B+mormons&source=bl&ots=ZffeYEVUpa&sig=5V69y_9J8Kx ToFB2YSszDDCH8zs&hl=en&ei=57rCSfX-LdzimQe4gdHvCw&sa=X&oi=book_result &resnum=9&ct=result#PPA44,M1.

32. See http://query.nytimes.com/mem/archive-free/pdf?_r=1&res=9903E6D81F30 E533A25755C1A9679D94679FD7CF.

PART III
Christianity and American Culture

When Alexis de Tocqueville visited the United States in the early 1830s, the Christian character of American culture surprised him. Although he had expected to find religion and democracy at odds, the reverse turned out to be true. Unlike in Europe, where people often resented Christian churches because of their formal ties to the government, Americans saw religion and democracy as inseparable, and they expected Christianity to influence virtually every aspect of American life. As Tocqueville remarked in his 1835 book *Democracy in America*, "There is no country in the world where the Christian religion retains a greater influence over the souls of men than in America."[1]

Part III of *American Christianities* examines some of the ways that Christianity has interacted with the cultural forms and institutions that make up American civil society, including capitalism, consumerism, sexuality, science, the media, and literature. In contrast to older understandings of "culture" as artistic or intellectual cultivation or refined taste, we define it in modern terms as "the way of life of a people, including their attitudes, values, beliefs, arts, sciences, modes of perception, and habits of thought and activity."[2] In some cases, the reciprocal relationship between Christianity and American culture has been obvious, especially in explicit debates over such matters as evolution or homosexuality, but in most cases the relationship has been more subtle and difficult to disentangle.

For example, when Tocqueville searched for the right language to describe the American spirit, he coined a new word, "individualism," which he defined as "a calm and mature feeling, which disposes each member of the community to sever himself from the mass of his fellows and to draw apart with his family and his friends, so that after he has thus formed a little circle of his own, he willingly leaves society at large to itself."[3] But it would be misleading to declare Tocqueville's "individualism" to be exclusively a

275

secular or a religious characteristic of nineteenth-century Americans. Certainly, throughout the century, numerous Americans identified one of the principal sources of individualism as popular Protestantism. Many Protestants were happy to take credit for this connection; other Christians, especially Catholics and Social Gospel Protestants, were quick to ascribe blame. Nonetheless, by some symbiosis of religion, politics, and economics, the ideology of individualism deepened and extended its influence throughout the developing nation. Partly because of economic developments, the rise of mass media, and the growing popularity of psychological theories, this individualistic spirit has only grown stronger since Tocqueville's time, and it has influenced how American Christians have viewed everything from religious institutions to sexuality. The historical emergence of capitalism and consumer culture not only transformed the economy—it also conveyed a tacit theory of human nature that celebrated individual preferences, free expression, and the fulfillment of personal desire. Meanwhile, new forms of media encouraged American Christians to view themselves as autonomous individuals in search of personal spiritual transformation, and the rise of psychology changed the way people thought about the self.

As Mark Noll points out, it would be a mistake to argue that American Christians are uniquely individualistic or populist, when many other Christians around the world share the same impulses, especially in Latin America, Asia, and Africa. (When Tocqueville claimed that "no country in the world" was more Christian, he could not have foreseen the future.) Yet it is clear that American Christians have been particularly successful at adapting Christianity, a religion founded in the first century, to the demands of a modernizing, capitalist, and individualistic culture, and as Stewart Hoover explains, they have used the media to spread their ideas around the globe.

American culture and Christianity have thus left their imprints on one another, not in the sense of narrowly defined religious or legal doctrines but instead as vivid, yet capacious, narratives of human personhood, national destiny, or freedom of opportunity. At this broad level of conviction and value, the interconnection of American culture and Christianity serves to expand the diversity of interpretations, through cultural debates, changing contexts, artistic imagination, and the differing interests of ethnic and economic groups. Diverse examples of this mutual influence appear below in essays about the surprising connections between Christianity and consumer culture and the long shadow of the Puritan captivity narrative in later American literature. And Rebecca Davis describes how the Protestant minister, therapist, and media celebrity Norman Vincent Peale joined liberal

Protestantism and psychiatry to fashion an influential vision of heterosexual marriage and "mature" personhood that framed mid-twentieth-century understandings of homosexuality.

Historians have often debated over whether the United States has become more or less "Christian" since Tocqueville's time. Some have pointed to rising church membership figures between the eighteenth century and the present, but others have argued that Americans have drifted away from institutional expressions of Christianity in favor of a more generalized "spirituality." Yet whatever the depth of people's personal religious commitments, there is no doubt that Christianity and American culture have been intertwined ever since the founding of the first British, Dutch, French, and Spanish colonies in the seventeenth century.

NOTES

1. Alexis de Tocqueville, *Democracy in America* (1835; New York: Knopf, 1945), 1:314.

2. "Culture," *The Oxford Dictionary of Philosophy*, ed. Simon Blackburn (Oxford, UK: Oxford University Press, 2008); *Oxford Reference Online* (Oxford, UK: Oxford University Press), June 14, 2010, http://www.oxfordreference.com/views/ENTRY.html?subview=Main&entry=t98.e800.

3. Tocqueville, *Democracy in America*, 2:104.

The Perils of Prosperity
Some Historical Reflections on Christianity, Capitalism, and Consumerism in America

The United States is one of the most Christian countries in the world, with more than 80 percent of the American people identifying themselves as Christian. It is also one of the most capitalist countries in the world, with an economy built on a seemingly endless desire for consumer goods. Throughout much of American history, these two identities—the United States as a Christian nation and the United States as a capitalist, consumerist one—have been in tension. On the one hand, American Christians have depended on the profits earned in a capitalist economy to finance new churches, social service agencies, and community outreach programs, and they have often borrowed commercial techniques in order to spread the gospel. Like religious freedom, capitalism has been a crucial reason for the remarkable vitality (and variety) of Christianity in America. Yet on the other hand, American Christians have also been ambivalent about capitalism and consumerism, and ever since the eighteenth century they have criticized American culture for being shallow, covetous, and materialistic.

Christians have not always been able to articulate their concerns about capitalism and consumerism beyond simply expressing their fear of loving the world more than God, but several issues seem to be involved. Although many critics treat consumer society as fundamentally different from Christianity, there are eerie similarities between the endless consumer desire for fulfillment and the endless Christian desire for God. As theologian Vincent J. Miller has pointed out, Christian commitment is like a train that can easily be misdirected if believers seek fulfillment in material goods rather than in God. Christians have also worried that a consumer mentality has reduced everything, even religion, into yet another thing to sell. As Americans have unconsciously brought their consumer practices into their religious lives, they have tended to pick and choose among religious beliefs and practices—mixing a little Mother Teresa with some Rick Warren, the Dalai Lama, and yoga—in the same way that they pick and choose among consumer goods. In a consumer culture that has little tolerance for complexity, religious beliefs and practices have often been stripped of their deeper meanings. Although the majority of Americans today continue to describe themselves as Christian, the commodification of the Christian tradition has meant that many have only a shallow understanding of it.[1]

Lying underneath these concerns about the power of consumer desire and the commodification of religion is a deeper concern about what it means to live a Christian life. Capitalism has resulted in greater social mobility and economic opportunities and an increased standard of living, but it is based on a positive view of self-interest and personal agency that poses significant challenges to the traditional Christian emphasis on self-denial. How much agency do people have to shape their own destinies? Is the individual self fundamentally good or is it flawed by original sin? Are people free to pursue their own individual interests or should they devote themselves to serving the common good? These questions have always loomed large in the Christian tradition, but they have become more urgent in a capitalist, consumer society that is deeply committed to the values of freedom and choice.

This essay examines how three Christian groups in American history responded to both the challenges and the opportunities offered by capitalism and consumerism: eighteenth-century evangelicals, Catholics at the turn of the twentieth century, and the late twentieth-century Word of Faith movement, more popularly known as the "prosperity gospel." Each of these groups responded differently to the rise of a capitalist economy, but they all recognized that something deeper was at stake than simply money or the obligations of stewardship. The fundamental issue, as they saw it, was the implicit model of selfhood that formed the bedrock of a capitalist economic system—a model of selfhood that exalts individualism, freedom, self-interest, and material happiness as the highest goods in life. Although their conflicting ideals of Christian selfhood probably did not reflect how real people actually lived, their "ideal types" of the self reveal what they feared—and also what they admired—about capitalism and consumerism.

Ye Cannot Serve God and Mammon
Eighteenth-Century Evangelicals

Few religious groups in modern America have been as enthusiastic about free-market capitalism as evangelicals. Not only did members of the Christian Right help to elect Ronald Reagan in 1980, but they insisted that his economic policies (known as Reaganomics) were sanctioned by the Bible. Writing in 1980, Jerry Falwell, the founder of the Moral Majority, insisted that "the free-enterprise system is clearly outlined in the Book of Proverbs in the Bible. Jesus Christ made it clear that the work ethic was a part of His plan for man. Ownership of property is biblical. Competition in business is biblical."[2]

In the eighteenth century, however, during the religious revivals that led to the rise of the evangelical movement, evangelical leaders were far more critical of the economic changes that were reshaping everyday life. Instead of celebrating competition and upward mobility, they condemned the avarice, pride, and selfishness that had been unleashed by the market. George Whitefield, the "Grand Itinerant," who preached to thousands of people in America, Scotland, and England, protested that many so-called Christians cared about their "pleasures" more than about God. "If they can but indulge their sensual appetite, please and pamper their bellies, satisfy the lust of the eye, the lust of the flesh, and the pride of life," they would forget who had created them.[3] Jonathan Edwards worried that a spirit of self-interest had replaced a commitment to the common good. "How many unjust things are done for the sake of worldly gain," he asked his congregation in Northampton, Massachusetts. "Men will be guilty of oppression; they will play little tricks to deceive their neighbors, to advance their own interest. How many men are there that one cannot trust in and depend upon; how few are there that are altogether just or that observe that rule of doing to others [as they would have them do unto them]?"[4] Repulsed by the brutishness of economic life, Edwards even toyed with the idea that the government should regulate prices—this, despite his fear that magistrates would not be any less rapacious than individual merchants. (New England Puritans had regulated both prices and wages in the 1630s, but they eventually abandoned their experiment because of their inability to control people's economic ambitions.) "In many countries," Edwards explained to his congregation, "[prices are] fixed by the civil magistrate. [This is often] a good rule . . . and it may perhaps more generally be followed." Far from sanctioning a free market, Edwards called for greater regulation.[5]

Evangelicals echoed a long Christian tradition of condemning avarice and luxury, but they seem to have sensed that there was something new about economic life in the eighteenth century that went beyond the age-old problem of greed. During the 1740s and 1750s, British manufacturers flooded the colonies with consumer goods, which quickly became associated with status, pleasure, and refinement. China, clothing, ribbons, jewelry, books—all were for sale in cities like Boston and Philadelphia, and even in rural areas people could buy merchandise from itinerant peddlers. This "consumer revolution," as historians have called it, transformed the character of everyday life. Never before had so many goods been available for sale in the marketplace, and never before had the lower and middling sorts enjoyed so many choices about how to spend their money. Between 1750 and 1773, the American market for consumer items rose by an astonishing 120 percent.[6]

Fueling the acceleration of the consumer economy was mercantile capitalism—a form of capitalism characterized by strong government control of trade, the accumulation of wealth, and profit-oriented production instead of subsistence. As the economy of the Anglo-American world shifted in the late seventeenth and eighteenth centuries, increasing numbers of farmers and merchants embraced the opportunities offered by intercolonial and international trade. By taking advantage of the new markets opened up by the Spanish, French, and British empires, merchants amassed vast surpluses of capital. Although they reinvested some of it in order to generate even more wealth, they also spent enormous sums of money on fashionable consumer goods. From the beginning, capitalism and consumerism went hand in hand.[7]

As the intellectual heirs of John Calvin and Martin Luther, who had rejected the asceticism of the Catholic Church during the Protestant Reformation, evangelicals did not object to wealth, and in fact, they saw money as one of the good things of the world, a sign of God's love for his creation. When Jonathan Edwards searched for an image that would capture the joy of being part of a revival, he compared it to a "market day," a day of "great opportunity and advantage."[8] As long as people did not worship money as an idol, they could savor the pleasure of shopping for new things. The challenge was to approach money in a spirit of stewardship, not ownership. Like everything else in the world, money ultimately belonged to God, and those who had been blessed with prosperity were supposed to use it for the common good.

What troubled evangelical leaders was not wealth but the abuse of stewardship—the single-minded pursuit of luxury over concern for those in need. Although the standard of living seems to have risen in the mid-eighteenth century, the gap between the richest and the poorest grew wider, especially in cities. In 1693, for example, the top 5 percent of taxpayers in Philadelphia owned 33 percent of the wealth; by 1774, they owned 55.5 percent of the wealth.[9] In response to growing numbers of vagrants and poor laborers, local governments not only built almshouses and workhouses but they also forced parents to indenture their children and "warned out" transients who were not legal residents. (Under the "warning out" system, colonial governments sent poor people back to their last place of legal settlement in order to avoid giving them poor relief.)[10] While merchants flaunted their wealth by purchasing imported clothing, expensive furniture, and African slaves (perhaps the most precious commodity in the eighteenth century), a growing class of landless poor crowded into cities in search of work.

Besides being concerned about the plight of the poor, evangelical ministers seem to have sensed that the rise of both mercantile capitalism and the consumer revolution undermined their theological commitments. The first evangelicals in America traced their heritage back to the Puritans, and they were Calvinists who saw humans as utterly sinful, or as *The Westminster Catechism* described them, "utterly indisposed, disabled, and made opposite unto all that is spiritually good, and wholly inclined to all evil." Echoing this language, laypeople often portrayed themselves in stark imagery as corrupt or polluted. Hannah Heaton, a farmwife from Connecticut, wrote in her diary that she longed to "fly out of this blind withered naked sore stinking rotten proud selfish self love into the arms of a lovely jesus."[11] The point of her self-abasement was not to wallow in the ugliness of sin but instead to magnify the distance between herself and God. In contrast to humans, who were inherently sinful, God was good, all-powerful, and majestic.

Given their dark view of human nature, evangelicals were troubled by the positive view of the self that lay underneath a capitalist and consumer economy. They believed that they were supposed to "crucify" themselves— to empty themselves of self-love in order to be more like Christ—but in the marketplace they were urged to gratify their desires instead of repressing them. Although advertising was still in its infancy, merchants tried to tempt people into their shops by promising the "best," most beautiful, and most fashionable goods. "Best English Soles," a merchant advertised in the *Boston Evening Post*. Others promised "choice good Chocolate," "choice Bohea and Green Teas," and "superfine" cloth "of a most beautiful Colour."[12] Even if customers did not actually need a piece of ribbon or an imported set of china, they were urged to pamper themselves with the best that money could buy. The self, as merchants suggested, was not tainted by sin but was essentially good and worthy of indulgence.

Capitalism, too, was implicitly predicated on a positive view of the self. Merchants rarely articulated their understanding of human nature, but in practice they did not act as if there was anything problematic about their self-interest. In the seventeenth century, merchants had fixed prices and wages in order to avoid "grinding the face of the poor," but by 1776, when Adam Smith published *The Wealth of Nations*, most seem to have accepted his bold defense of self-interest as a positive good. "It is not from the benevolence of the butcher, the brewer, or the baker, that we expect our dinner," Smith wrote, "but from their regard to their own interest."[13]

Eighteenth-century Americans not only bought "choice" goods, but because of the expansion of the market they also made more extensive choices about their everyday lives, and it was this second meaning of "choice" that alarmed evangelicals. The market encouraged people to imagine themselves as free agents who could fashion their identities however they pleased. Of course, not everyone could afford the tempting wares that were displayed in shop windows or in peddlers' packs, but even the lower-middling sorts bought small consumer items like penknives or ribbons, and they seem to have welcomed the chance to display their taste. They did not view consumer goods simply as goods, but as extensions of their identity. Those who bought books, for example, drew attention to their erudition, while those who bought imported china or furniture displayed their refinement. Many viewed shopping as a form of self-expression, a way to create a new self-image.[14]

Evangelicals, in contrast, were troubled by this celebration of self-fashioning, especially when it involved women. Because of their conviction that God had created the world according to hierarchical principles, they urged women to cultivate the "feminine" traits of modesty, humility, and submissiveness. Even though eighteenth-century men as well as women were avid consumers, evangelical ministers focused much of their ire on "proud" women who had forgotten their subordinate place in the social order. As Harry Stout has pointed out, Whitefield often criticized young women for their "lust," "Worldliness," and "idolatry," but "rarely did he level similar charges against young men."[15]

Evangelicals assumed that selfhood was bestowed, not chosen. There were limits to human freedom—limits to the way individuals could construct their own identities.[16] Theologically, they believed that humans were so dependent on God's grace that they could do nothing to earn their salvation. Even before the foundation of the world, a sovereign God had decided who would be saved and who would be damned. Although humans were free to decide how to act at any particular moment—for example, whether to churn the butter or milk the cow—they were not free in a deeper, moral sense. A person who had been predestined to damnation would always make the free choice to sin. "'Tis entirely in a man's power to submit to Jesus Christ as a Savior, if he will," Jonathan Edwards explained, "but the thing is, it never will be that he should will it, except God works it in him." No matter how hard they tried, humans could not make the correct moral choices without God's grace.[17]

The consumer revolution chipped away at evangelicals' understanding not only of the self, but also of God. Although evangelicals imagined God as a loving father, they also feared him as a forbidding judge who sentenced sinners to eternal damnation. When Sarah Gill, a minister's daughter, asked herself whether it was just for God "to punish us in hell with out the Least hope of Mercy forever," she answered, "Yes, Yes, Yes." Because evangelicals believed that God had created the world to demonstrate his glory, not to make humans happy, they accepted the existence of hell as part of his plan. Yet as people gained greater access to new material goods that increased their pleasure and comfort, it became harder to believe in a vengeful God. Influenced by new, enlightened ideas as well as a rising standard of living, a small group of Protestant liberals questioned the doctrine of eternal damnation, suggesting that God had created the world to promote human happiness, not to demonstrate his power. As the Reverend Charles Chauncy argued, "A more shocking idea can scarce be given of the *Deity*, than that which represents him as *arbitrarily dooming the greater part of the race of men to eternal misery*. Was he wholly destitute of goodness, yea, positively *malevolent* in his *nature*, a worse reputation could not be well made of him."[18] In a world of increasing material abundance, it seemed hard to imagine a God who wanted people to suffer.

Self-interest, freedom, choice, the pursuit of happiness—all of these were celebrated in the marketplace, and as evangelicals seem to have sensed, all of these subtly undermined Calvinist assumptions about God and human nature. Even though evangelicals did not believe that there was anything wrong with buying and selling goods in the market, the model of selfhood that lay underneath an emerging consumer economy troubled them. The self was not free, they insisted, but dependent on God's grace; not good, but vile; not worthy of indulgence, but in need of discipline. An unconverted person, preached the Reverend Gilbert Tennent, was like a corrupt tree that could bring forth nothing but bad fruit—a tree that a wrathful God would cut down.[19]

Troubled by the market's challenge to their theology, evangelicals defended their beliefs in deliberately extreme language. Besides rejecting the claim that God had created the world to make humans happy, they thundered out a message of hellfire that made listeners tremble and cry out with fear. Although judgments about style are hard to quantify, their sermons sounded harsher than those delivered by earlier generations of Puritans. "My Brethren," warned the Reverend Gilbert Tennent, "can the momentary Pleasures and perishing Profits of Sin balance the everlasting Racks of the Damned in Hell for it? Is there any Comparison between the immortal God, and your temporary Profits? . . . *Haste ye, escape for your Lives* to Christ, and be espoused to him, otherwise ye shall surely perish in the Burnings of his unquenchable Vengeance."[20] Although Tennent condemned more than just greed when he criticized the desire for "temporary profits," his choice of language underlined the dangerous temptations of mercantile capitalism.

Besides defending the doctrine of divine sovereignty and the reality of hell, evangelicals also attacked the growing acceptance of self-interest, choice, and free will. They lost their most prominent theologian when Jonathan Edwards died in 1758, but several of his disciples, especially Joseph Bellamy and Samuel Hopkins, took up his mantle. Derided as "New Divinity" men because of their challenges to traditional Calvinist theology, they took Edwards's demand for self-denial to an extreme, equating true holiness with an almost complete renunciation of the self. According to Samuel Hopkins, self-love could never be anything other than selfishness: "Self-love is, in its whole nature, and in every degree of it, enmity against God." Besides insisting that true Christians should be willing to renounce "personal good, for the sake of the whole," he made the controversial assertion that true Christians should be willing to be damned for the glory of God.[21] It is hard to imagine a stronger rebuke to those who defended self-interest as a positive good.

Eighteenth-century evangelicals never directly challenged either the rise of capitalism or the growth of a consumer economy. They did not turn their backs on the modern world in order to create separate religious communities; nor did they offer a serious plan for economic regulation or the redistribution of wealth. Instead they crafted a theology that stood in direct opposition to the values of self-interest, free agency, and self-fashioning that was enshrined by the market. If New Divinity theology sounds extreme to Christians today, it is because evangelical ministers felt as if their most cherished beliefs were under siege—as if people had forgotten that they were neither free nor good, but sinners in the hands of an angry God. Although the purely self-interested, autonomous self of their fevered imaginations may not have actually existed, they were afraid that the consumer revolution had the potential to destroy what they most valued about Christianity.

In the early nineteenth century, evangelicals softened their language of human depravity and helplessness. Most historians have explained this transformation by pointing to the influence of the American Revolution. The "self-made" men who had won a war against the British empire, the world's greatest military power, seem to have found it hard to believe that they were helpless to save themselves from damnation. Yet even though political developments certainly affected evangelical theology, it would be a mistake to overlook the pressures created by economic change. Evangelicals expanded their understanding of human agency not only because of the American Revolution, but also because of the challenges posed by the rise of mercantile capitalism and consumerism.[22]

Evangelicals continued to protest against the language of self-interest, choice, and freedom into the twentieth century, but they eventually narrowed the terrain of their resistance from the capitalist economy to the individual body. On the one hand, modern-day evangelicals insist that people should be able to make free choices in the marketplace, but on the other, they vehemently reject the idea that people should also be able to make choices about gender, sexual orientation, and childbearing. Perhaps because they no longer object to the self-interest enshrined by the consumer marketplace, their focus on the body has become especially intense. By arguing that humans cannot make "choices" about homosexuality or abortion, they have tried to preserve their faith in God's sovereignty over the self.

The Common Good
Late Nineteenth-Century Catholics

Not all Christians in American history responded to the rise of capitalism and consumerism in the same way. But since many Christian leaders articulated their fears about the future of religion in relationship to economic change, their diverse reactions resemble the results of a Rorschach test. When early American evangelicals looked at the economy, they saw a dangerous celebration of self-interest and choice, and in response, they magnified their beliefs in human sinfulness, divine judgment, and limited freedom. In contrast, later generations of Catholics saw something else— an individualistic spirit that threatened to break down the moral authority of the church—and they responded by affirming their commitment to the common good. For Catholics at the turn of the twentieth century, the problem with capitalism could be summed up in a single word: individualism.

The closing decades of the nineteenth century were marked by both industrial growth and labor unrest. With the help of technological break-throughs, like the discovery of electricity, the development of steel, and the extension of railroads, manufacturers expanded their markets and increased their productivity. Merchant capitalism had been replaced by industrial capitalism, an economic system that was characterized by factory production, the division of labor, routinization, and the private ownership of the means of production. During the 1870s, finance capitalism began to emerge as well, a form of capitalism that subordinated production to the circulation of money. As investors bought stock in corporations with the hope of earning profits, industrialists like Andrew Carnegie, Cornelius Vanderbilt, and John D. Rockefeller built corporate empires that turned into monopolies. Many people amassed huge fortunes in this new corporate economy, and overall the standard of living improved. But for ordinary workers, the times were bleak. Laborers were paid poor wages, forced to work in unsafe and unsanitary conditions, and expected to toil ten to twelve hours a day. Steelworkers at Andrew Carnegie's Homestead plant worked twelve hours a day, seven days a week. Industrialists were so hungry for cheap labor that they even employed large numbers of children in their factories, many under the age of ten.[23]

The Catholic Church took a special interest in the plight of suffering workers and their families because so many of them were Catholic immigrants. Catholic sisters in particular responded with an outpouring of charity, founding hospitals and orphanages to care for the poor. In 1869, in New York City, for example, the Sisters of Charity established the Foundling Asylum, an institution that cared for thousands of orphaned and abandoned children. In 1875, when the New York State legislature passed a law mandating that needy children be cared for by people who belonged to the same religion as their parents, Catholic sisters seized the opportunity to obtain state funding for their work. By 1885, they were caring for more than 19,000 Catholic children at the state's expense. Although some of these children were permanent wards of the state, others lived in Catholic institutions only temporarily while their parents struggled to find stable employment. Motivated by their desire to preserve families, Catholic sisters created a vast network of charity that laid the foundation for the welfare state.[24]

Catholics were a minority in the late nineteenth century, and because of their allegiance to the pope, they were often accused of being undemocratic and un-American. Members of the American Protective Association, a secret society, took oaths to exclude Catholics from political office. Yet Catholic leaders refused to be cowed by the threat of nativism. Pointing out the weaknesses in American society, they criticized capitalism, consumerism, and a host of other ills that they lumped together under the rubric of "liberalism." Liberalism, as defined by *The Catholic Encyclopedia* of 1910, was a dangerous ideology that privileged individual freedom over obedience to God's commandments:

> The most fundamental principle asserts an absolute and unrestrained freedom of thought, religion, conscience, creed, speech, press, and politics. The necessary consequences of this are, on the one hand, the abolition of the Divine right and of every kind of authority derived from God; the relegation of religion from the public life into the private domain of one's individual conscience; the absolute ignoring of Christianity and the Church as public, legal, and social institutions; on the other hand, the putting into practice of the absolute autonomy of every man and citizen, along all lines of human activity, and the concentration of all public authority in one "sovereignty of the people."[25]

Liberalism was supposedly responsible not only for the violence of the French Revolution but also for the evils of socialism, communism, anarchism, atheism, and one its most pernicious "isms," capitalism. Just as political liberals acted as if there was no god above the self, economic liberals acted as if individual desires were more important than the common good. In 1888, a writer in the *American Catholic Quarterly Review* argued that "the modern economic system, un-Christian in its essence, and more so still in its application, has wrought havoc in all countries, whether Catholic or not. No government escaped the scourge of Liberalism, and of what Liberalism necessarily entails, 'capitalism.'" Likening capitalism to a "big worm" that "gnaws on the intestines of every nation," the author argued that only Christianity (by which he meant the Catholic Church) could save people from "the tyranny of Liberalism, capitalism, and mammonism."[26]

To make their argument against capitalism, Catholics cited many of the same biblical texts as eighteenth-century evangelicals had used. They read different versions of the Bible (evangelicals used the King James Version and Catholics used the Douay-Reims translation), but they were drawn to the same texts about the dangers of wealth: for example, the parable of the rich man who suffered eternal torment in hell after turning away Lazarus. Because of their belief in original sin, Catholics also agreed with evangelicals that most people could not be trusted to use their wealth for the common good and that the only real solution to economic exploitation was conversion.

Yet despite these shared Christian convictions, Catholics viewed the problem of capitalism through the lens of their own distinctive tradition and theology. Besides citing scriptural injunctions against greed, they used Saint Thomas Aquinas's concept of natural law to argue that all people had the right to share in the earth's bounty. As the *Catholic Encyclopedia* explained in 1917, "the natural law is the rule of conduct which is prescribed to us by the Creator in the constitution of the nature with which He has endowed us."[27] God revealed his will in nature as well as in the Bible, and people could identify universal law by using their reason. According to Aquinas, humans are rational beings, and practical reason teaches that "the supreme principle, from which all the other principles and precepts are derived, is that good is to be done, and evil avoided."[28] Applying this universal principle to late nineteenth-century economic life, Catholic leaders argued that the greed and exploitation that accompanied capitalism were clearly evil. It was rationally evident that God had created the earth for all of humanity, and although it was natural that some people would use their talents to amass greater fortunes than others, God did not want the rich to oppress the poor.[29]

Natural law, according to Catholics, also taught that there should be limits to human freedom. Like eighteenth-century evangelicals, Catholics objected to the exaltation of individual choice that was embedded in both capitalism and consumerism, but on different theological grounds. Early evangelicals had worried that the market seduced people into believing they were free, but Catholics insisted that humans *are* essentially free. The *Baltimore Catechism*, for example, taught that "our free will was not entirely taken away by Adam's sin, and that we have it still in our power to use our free will in doing good or evil."[30] Yet despite their belief in free will, Catholics insisted that it was sinful to elevate the value of individual autonomy over the common good. Freedom, they argued, must always be subordinate to justice. According to Pope Leo XIII, "The true liberty of human society does not consist in every man doing what he pleases." On the contrary, genuine freedom "supposes the necessity of obedience to some supreme and eternal law."[31] In the case of the market, this meant that people could not use their God-given freedom to exploit or impoverish others.

In 1891, Leo XIII issued his papal encyclical *Rerum Novarum*, one of the most influential encyclicals ever written. Troubled by the gap between "the enormous fortunes of some individuals, and the utter poverty of the masses," Leo lamented that "working men have been surrendered, isolated and helpless, to the hardheartedness of employers and the greed of unchecked competition." Many Catholic workers were attracted to socialist ideas, but Leo condemned socialism as an evil that subordinated the individual to the secular state. And he was equally withering in his treatment of capitalism. "A small number of very rich men," he protested, "have been able to lay upon the teeming masses of the laboring poor a yoke little better than that of slavery itself." Although people had the right to own private property, they were morally obligated to share their excess with others. "It is one thing to have a right to the possession of money and another to have a right to use money as one wills," he wrote. Quoting Thomas Aquinas, he argued that "man should not consider his material possessions as his own, but as common to all, so as to share them without hesitation when others are in need."[32]

Rerum Novarum was a groundbreaking document that laid the foundation for modern Catholic social thought, but at the time it was published, many Catholic leaders chose to emphasize its conservatism over its call for economic justice. Concerned about the growing popularity of socialism, they highlighted the parts of the encyclical that condemned socialist remedies to the problem of poverty. The socialist movement, Leo protested, was "manifestly against justice. For, every man has by nature the right to possess property as his own." According to a writer in the *American Catholic Quarterly Review*, the most important conclusion of the encyclical was that the principle of private property must be defended.[33]

Yet a small but vocal group of Catholic leaders and laypeople used *Rerum Novarum* to make the more radical argument that economic individualism was sinful. Leo never used the word "individualism" in his encyclical, but he clearly rejected liberal notions of individual autonomy. Although Catholics defended the dignity of the individual, they condemned what they perceived as the extreme individualism of American culture, a failing that they ultimately traced back to the errors of the Protestant Reformation. By elevating individual conscience over the external authority of the church, Protestants had unleashed a dangerous spirit of selfishness. The economic version of individualism was free-market capitalism, a system that valued individual profit more than the common good. Joseph Husslein, a Jesuit professor at St. Louis University, condemned capitalism as a form of "economic rationalism" that requires "the subordination of all the interests connected with production to the one consideration of personal gain." His verdict was stark: capitalism was "antagonistic to the entire spirit of Christianity."[34]

Like many other Catholic thinkers of the time, Husslein argued that Catholic workers had been treated better in the Middle Ages than they were in the modern world. His ideal was the medieval guild system, in which associations of craftsmen regulated prices, hours, and wages on behalf of the common good. He believed that guilds were superior to the capitalist system because they honored workers' obligations to their families and to God. For example, medieval guilds prohibited labor on Sundays and on saints' days and provided for the needs of widows and orphans. Although Husslein admitted that greed had always existed, he insisted that medieval guilds had been more Christian than a capitalist market that explicitly legitimated avarice and selfishness. He wrote angrily, "A man may grind and crush the poor, paying starvation wages to labor and exacting starvation prices for his products, and yet stand justified by the principles of this system. He may even, if he chooses be crowned as a philanthropist and public benefactor, should he desire to satisfy his craving for publicity. Such a code was impossible in the Middle Ages. It could never be tolerated while the Church exercised her power over the people."[35] In contrast to medieval guilds, which had treated individuals with compassion, capitalism stripped them of their dignity by reducing them to the sum of their labor. As a writer in the *American Catholic Quarterly Review* complained, capitalism treated the worker like a thing, "the absolute slave of the employer."[36]

Catholic leaders argued that employers should not treat workers simply as individuals but as members of families. Free-market capitalism "makes the individual the unit of society," a writer in the *Catholic World* complained. But "the true unit of society is the family."[37] Since the family was part of the natural order created by God, employers had a moral responsibility to pay wages that were high enough to support more than an individual worker. As Leo XIII explained in *Rerum Novarum*, "It is a most sacred law of nature that a father should provide food and all necessaries for those whom he has begotten." The employer's right to make free contracts was subordinate to the worker's right to support a family.[38]

Pope Leo's emphasis on the father's role as breadwinner was typical of Catholic thought. Although Catholics encouraged single women to get jobs in order to help their families, they argued that in an ideal world women would remain at home to care for the house and family. In their eyes, one of the greatest evils of capitalism was that it violated natural law by pushing women into the workplace. God had created women to be mothers, not wage earners.

Despite their fear of being associated with the socialist movement, several prominent Catholic leaders eventually concluded that the state should intervene to protect workers from exploitation. Joseph Husslein argued that the state regulation of capital should be a "last resort," but he also insisted that "the State is called upon to act wherever the general welfare of the community or the just interest of any particular class is imperiled." The state should regulate hours and working conditions, enforce a family wage, prohibit child labor, and guarantee a day of rest on Sundays so that workers were free to worship.[39]

Because the state was slow to act, many Catholic leaders, including Bishop John Lancaster Spalding, the bishop of Peoria, Illinois, also supported the labor movement. Unions were controversial because of their resemblance to secret societies and their ties to the socialist movement (Archbishop John Ireland feared that their real goal was to wage a "war against property"), but Catholic workers joined them in large numbers. The Knights of Labor counted 700,000 members in 1886, and according to their leader, Terence Powderly, two-thirds of the membership was Catholic.[40] (Powderly himself was a Catholic who tried to convince the church hierarchy that the labor movement was motivated by a Christian vision of economic cooperation.) "Labor priests," as they were known, supported striking workers, and many Catholic journals and newspapers printed sympathetic stories about the struggle for a just wage. The *Pilot*, a Catholic newspaper published in Boston, featured a weekly column that reported on the conflicts between capital and labor. "The consolidation of huge blocks of capital has rendered possible the subjection of millions of workmen," the newspaper declared. "And it is by counter-organization that the latter can regain the lost ground."[41]

The most influential Catholic critic of the American economy in the early twentieth century was Father John Augustine Ryan (1869–1945), a professor at the Catholic University of America. In 1906, influenced by *Rerum Novarum*, he published a book entitled *A Living Wage: Its Ethical and Economic Aspects*, a defense of the worker's natural right to a minimum wage. Besides publishing books and giving speeches across the country, he wrote the Bishops' Program of Social Reconstruction in 1919, a plan that called for a minimum wage, affordable health care, the creation of cooperative stores, the right to unionize, the prohibition of child labor, and higher taxes on the wealthy. In 1934, Franklin Delano Roosevelt appointed Ryan to the Industrial Appeals Board of the National Recovery Administration.[42]

Because of Ryan's close relationship with Roosevelt (he gave the invocation at two of Roosevelt's inaugurations), he was nicknamed the "Right Reverend New Dealer," but it would be a mistake to link him too closely to political liberals. Although Ryan was willing to work with progressives on particular reforms, especially minimum-wage legislation, he rejected their emphasis on individual rights. For example, he not only condemned capitalism but also contraception. Like employers who exploited their workers, couples who tried to limit their families cared more about "material goods" and "self-indulgence" than God's will. Individual freedom could never take precedence over natural law. As John McGreevy has explained, "This mistrust of individualism in all spheres led to Catholics' favoring the minimum wage *and* barriers to divorce, economic planning *and* film censorship." Catholic alliances with political liberals were usually based on pragmatism, not shared principles.[43]

Catholic leaders were among the most vocal critics of capitalism in the early twentieth century, but most believed that the economic system should be reformed, not dismantled. On the one hand, their ideas sounded radical at the time: minimum wage legislation, the right to unionize, and even the prohibition of child labor were all controversial issues in the early 1900s. On the other hand, they took pains to distance themselves from socialists, and they upheld the right to private property as the cornerstone of a just economic order. Speaking at a lay Catholic congress in Baltimore in 1889, Peter Foy, a journalist, condemned the exploitation of poor workers, but he still affirmed that capitalists held "the keys of the workingman's paradise— permanent, remunerative, invigorating employment." If the system could be reformed, the laboring classes would enjoy a virtual "paradise." Similarly, Joseph Husslein distinguished between capitalism as a single-minded desire to maximize profits and capitalism as "private ownership in the means of production."[44] The first was unchristian because it placed "personal gain" over all considerations, but the second could lift the masses out of poverty and dependence. Although Catholic leaders feared that most people were too sinful to be trusted with their wealth, they were hopeful that the state could regulate wages and working conditions and, if necessary, raise taxes on the rich in order to serve the poor. Faithful Catholics, they claimed, had to resist the American spirit of individualism on behalf of the common good.

Prosper and Be in Health
The Late Twentieth-Century Word of Faith Movement

By the closing decades of the twentieth century, capitalism had entered a new stage in its development. A "Fordist" economy (named after Henry Ford), based on mass production and standardization, was replaced by a more specialized "post-Fordist" economy, characterized by globalization, niche production, and the rise of service industries. When Ronald Reagan became president in 1980, he hoped to extend the benefits of capitalism to as many Americans as possible, but historians have disagreed over whether his economic policies—including tax cuts and deregulation—helped lower- and middle-class Americans as much as the wealthy. What is clear, however, is that Americans increasingly viewed prosperity as their right.

At the same time as these economic developments were reshaping the American economy during the 1980s, a new Christian movement emerged in the United States that repudiated almost everything that earlier genera- tions of Christians had said about the dangers of capitalism and consumer- ism. The Word of Faith movement, also known as the "prosperity gospel," enshrines individualism, free choice, personal agency, and happiness as the very heart of Christianity.[45] Instead of preaching on the biblical texts that decry greed, the movement focuses on John 10:10, "I have come that they may have life, and that they may have it more abundantly," and on 2 Corin- thians 8:9, "Yet for your sakes he became poor, that you through his poverty might become rich." As portrayed by Word of Faith ministers, Christian- ity and capitalism are virtually the same thing: both involve free individu- als trying to maximize their profits in this world. Kenneth Copeland, one of the most popular Word of Faith preachers, announces on his website, "Throughout the Word, God plainly shows that His will is for His covenant people to have a surplus of prosperity. He promised to make Abraham rich, and the promise of Abraham is ours today (Galatians 3:13–14 and Genesis 17:6). God's will is prosperity for you—spirit, soul and body."[46] Other Word of Faith ministers have published best-selling books with titles like *Prosper- ity: Good News for God's People* and *Answered Prayer: Guaranteed.* Fusing Christianity with capitalism, the Word of Faith movement claims that indi- viduals have the power to create their own destinies—if, that is, they have faith.

The Word of Faith movement is organized around three major organiza- tions: the International Convention of Faith Ministries, founded in 1979 in Arlington, Texas; the Rhema Ministerial Alliance International, founded in 1985 in Tulsa, Oklahoma; and the Fellowship of Inner-City Word of Faith Ministries, founded in 1990 in Los Angeles. Trinity Broadcasting Network, originally founded in 1973 by Paul and Jan Crouch with Jim and Tammy Faye Bakker, broadcasts Word of Faith programs to thousands of network and cable channels across the world. According to a recent study, "The Word of Faith Movement consists of between 2,300–2,500 churches, ministries, or television networks in the United States and in more than 60 countries abroad," including countries in Africa, Europe, and South America. Many

Word of Faith churches in the United States have enormous memberships. For example, Frederick K. C. Price's church in Los Angeles—the Crenshaw Christian Center—currently has between 16,000 and 20,000 members. Creflo Dollar's church in College Park, Georgia—World Changers International Ministries—has approximately 20,000 members.[47] Most Word of Faith churches are located in the South, with another constellation in California, and the movement includes both white and black congregations. The leaders of the movement are almost all men, but a few women preside over large congregations and host television programs as well, including Joyce Meyer and Paula White.

The Word of Faith movement represents the fusion of several strands of American Christianity, including Pentecostalism, the nineteenth-century faith cure, the Holiness movement, and New Thought. Almost all the ministers in the movement trace their ideas back to Kenneth Erwin Hagin Sr. (1917–2003), popularly known as "Dad" Hagin. Hagin was a Southern Baptist turned Pentecostal who borrowed many of his ideas from E. W. Kenyon, a popular radio evangelist during the 1920s and 1930s who mixed Pentecostal beliefs in the baptism of the spirit and speaking in tongues with New Thought ideas about the divinity of humans and the power of positive thinking. Although Hagin denied it, he plagiarized several of Kenyon's books, and his "revelations" included Kenyon's claim that Christians could conquer poverty and illness by "speaking faith."[48]

Hagin founded the Rhema Bible Training Center in 1974, where he passed on his ideas to a new generation of ministers like Kenneth Copeland and Frederick Price, but it was not until the mid-1980s that the Word of Faith movement exploded in size and popularity. Millmon Harrison, one of the few scholars to have studied the movement, argues that it was fueled by lower-class Christians who wondered why they did not share the prosperity of Ronald Reagan's America. As they watched television shows like *Dynasty* and *Dallas* or read magazine stories about wealthy bankers on Wall Street, they felt as if they had been left behind by the Reagan revolution. When they heard Word of Faith preachers insisting that they, too, could be rich, they flocked to the movement in droves. Influenced by the American faith in personal agency, they did not attribute their problems to government policies or structural inequalities but only to their own individual failings. Why were they poor? Word of Faith ministers had the answer: because they lacked faith.

The Word of Faith movement does not have a single creed or statement of faith, but the leaders of the movement share four common beliefs about

God and humanity. First, they believe that humans have enormous religious power to influence the world around them. According to their reading of the creation story in the Bible, Adam was not created as a mere human but as a god who was supposed to rule over the earthly world. As Kenneth Hagin Sr. explained, "Adam was the god of this world."[49] In a sermon that he delivered in 1989, Kenneth Copeland argued that God created Adam as a "reproduction of Himself," an exact copy:

> He [Adam] was not a little like God. He was not almost like god. He was not subordinate to God, even. Now this is hard on the human mind, but I'm telling you what the Bible said. The Bible said, "Let us make man in our image and give him dominion." . . . And Adam is as much like God as you could get—just the same as Jesus when He came into the earth. He [Jesus] said, "If you've seen Me, you've seen the Father." He wasn't a lot like God; he's God manifested in the flesh! And I want you to know something—Adam in the Garden of Eden was God manifested in the flesh! He was God's very image, the very likeness. Everything he did, everything he said, every move he made was the very image of Almighty god. . . . You see, Adam was walking as a god. Adam walked in the gods class. Adam did things in the class of gods."[50]

In another sermon, Copeland claimed to have seen the creation of Adam in a vision, and God and Adam looked like twins: "I mean, man, they looked just exactly alike. You couldn't tell one of them from the other."[51] (The logical implication of Copeland's "vision" is that God has a physical body, an assertion that most Christians deny.) If Adam had not committed treason against God by allowing Satan to rule the world, he would have remained a god himself, and the world would have been a paradise.

Adam's treason brought poverty and illness into the world, but according to Word of Faith preachers, Christ's resurrection ended Satan's dominion over the world and restored humanity's godlike powers. Satan is still at work in the world, however, and he has infiltrated Christian churches to deceive people about who they really are. For more than 2,000 years, Christians have been duped into seeing themselves as flawed and sinful, but in reality they are the incarnations of God as much as Jesus was. "Don't tell me you have Jesus," Benny Hinn scolded his television viewers in 1993. "You are everything he was and everything he is and ever shall be."[52] In a statement that shocked many mainstream Christians, Kenneth Copeland said on television, "And I say this with all respect, so that it don't upset you too bad, but

I say it anyway: When I read in the bible where He says, "I AM," I just smile and say, 'Yes, I AM too."[53] (He was echoing Jesus' words from the Gospel of John.) Humans are just like Jesus, and if they have faith, they can do anything that Jesus did, including perform miracles. This is a much more positive image of the self than the one embraced by eighteenth-century evangelicals, who described themselves as "corrupt" and "polluted," and the one of late nineteenth-century Catholics, who insisted that self-interest must be subordinated to the common good.

Besides their shared conviction that humans have godlike powers, Word of Faith preachers are also linked together by their belief in "positive confession." According to their interpretation of the Bible, God used his faith to create the world and he literally spoke it into existence. (The two key texts for them are Hebrews 11:3: "By faith we understand that the worlds were prepared by the word of God, so that what is seen was not made out of things which are visible. God created the world through his faith"; and Genesis 1:3: "And God said, 'Let there be light.'") Most mainstream Christians argue that God does not "have faith," only humans do, but Word of Faith preachers claim that God set a model for joining faith to speech. As Frederick Price has explained, "God believed in His heart that what he said with His mouth would come to pass, and He dared to say it. . . . If our Father is a faith God, then we must be faith children of a faith God."[54] Just as God spoke the world into creation, Christians can create their own reality through speech. Because words are so powerful, Christians must be very careful about what they say. As Paula White explains on her website, "Do you realize that you can deceive yourself into thinking you are in poverty . . . and you will create poverty in your life? You might be thinking, 'Oh come on, Paula . . . are you actually saying that just because my mouth says it, that makes it true?' Well, I am here to tell you, yes, that's just what I'm saying: *your words create your world.*"[55] One should never admit out loud to being poor, unhappy, or ill.

"Positive confession" involves speaking one's desires out loud in order to change the world. Since God has given Christians abundant life, they do not need to pray for health or prosperity, but only to have faith that they already possess everything that they want. If people want to be healthy or rich, all they need to do is to "name it and claim it" and it will be theirs. "It's time to step up to God's dining table," Joel Osteen writes in his best-selling book, *Your Best Life Now.* "God has prepared a fabulous banquet for you, complete with every good thing imaginable. And it has already been paid for. God has everything you need there—joy, forgiveness, restoration, peace, healing—

whatever you need, it's waiting for you at God's banquet table if you'll pull up your chair and take the place He has prepared for you." God has made a contract with Christians that he is required to honor. "As a believer, you have a right to make commands in the name of Jesus," Kenneth Copeland has explained. "Each time you stand on the Word, you are commanding God to a certain extent because it is His Word. Whenever an honest man gives you his word, he is bound by it."[56] God is not a forbidding judge, as he was for both early American evangelicals and nineteenth-century Catholics, but an indulgent father whose sole concern is human happiness. He can be "commanded" to shower blessings on the faithful.

The third belief that is broadly shared in the Word of Faith movement is known as "seed-faith," a term that was originally coined by Oral Roberts. Roberts argued that if Christians make free offerings to God, they should expect great returns. Building on this idea, ministers in the Word of Faith movement quote a text from Mark to argue that Christians will receive a hundredfold blessing in return for their donations to the ministry, and they also insist that God has required people to tithe.[57] (Tithing involves giving the church 10 percent of one's yearly income.) If believers disobey God by refusing to tithe they will be cursed with poverty, but if they give in the right spirit of faith they will be abundantly rewarded. The more they give, the better. "I thank God every day that God will bring finances to you, members of Rhema Bible Church," Kenneth Hagin Jr. said to his congregation, "because I want you to have finances, but second, I want you to give money to Rhema Bible Church."[58] Church members are not only expected to make regular donations but also to buy their pastors special gifts: cars, Rolex watches, cruise vacations, even private jets. Consumer goods are not perceived as a source of spiritual temptation but as a tangible sign of God's blessing. Indeed, Word of Faith preachers flaunt their wealth as a sign of divine favor. Kenneth Copeland, for example, owns four jets (including one that cost 20 million dollars) and lives in an 18,000-square-foot mansion.[59]

The fourth belief that links together the Word of Faith movement is known as "rhema," or direct revelation. (Millmon Harrison explains that "the Greek word transliterated as 'rhema' is frequently used among movement insiders and is defined in Thayer and Smith's *Greek Lexicon* as 'that which is or has been uttered by the living voice, thing spoke, word.'")[60] Ministers argue that humans are trichotomous—they are composed of body, soul, and spirit—and God speaks *only* through the spirit, not the soul or the body. Since the intellect is supposedly located in the soul, people cannot learn about Christianity through reason but only through direct revelation.

The movement is strongly anti-intellectual, and those who question ministers' grasp of the Bible are accused of being agents of Satan.

Coupled with the demand for tithes, the insistence that Christians should not rely on their reason has created an environment ripe for abuse, and some Word of Faith preachers have exploited their congregations. In 1991, ABC aired an investigative report revealing that Robert Tilton's ministry emptied the money out of prayer envelopes and threw away the prayer requests.[61] Since churches are tax-exempt, Word of Faith ministers do not have to report the details of their financial transactions, but there have been widespread reports of church funds being misused. In 2007, Senator Charles Grassley of Iowa launched an investigation of six prosperity preachers because of his concern that they had violated their churches' tax-exempt status.

Word of Faith ministers have been widely criticized by other Christian leaders, especially African American pastors who see them as a threat to the progressive black Christianity forged during the civil rights movement. Robert Franklin, the president of Morehouse College, has decried the prosperity gospel for elevating the individual pursuit of wealth over social, political, and economic reform. In his book *Crisis in the Village*, he argues that the prosperity gospel poses the single greatest danger to the prophetic identity of black churches.[62]

The Word of Faith movement has also been condemned by feminists. The movement portrays humans as free agents who can determine their own destinies, but leaders have often been ambivalent about extending this freedom to women. Although ministers like Kenneth Copeland and Kenneth Hagin Jr. encourage their wives to join them in the pulpit, they also insist that women must occupy a subordinate position in the family. Since God is literally a man with a physical body, women must submit to their husbands.[63]

Why do people join these churches? Based on a small number of in-depth interviews with members of a Word of Faith church in Sacramento, Millmon Harrison has argued that people are drawn to these churches because they offer a sense of empowerment. As an African American woman in her mid-thirties explained, "I feel like I have more control over what happens in my life, you know? I can look at the scriptures and I can find scriptures within the bible and know that there are things that I can create for myself." Yet there is also a dark side to this sense of agency. When Harrison asked another African American woman in her thirties to talk about prosperity, she blamed herself for her poverty. "Five years ago they were asking for a thousand dollars, so I gave a thousand dollars. . . . I didn't get a lump sum like they say you're supposed to get, you know. And they say if you sow seed—if you sow finances—that's what you get back! Well, I haven't gotten that back, you know? If I put a thousand dollars in, I should be able to get ten thousand back, or something—I haven't even gotten *two* thousand back, you know what I'm saying?" But instead of leaving the church, she questioned the depth of her faith. "Well, maybe it's because I don't pay my tithes consistently, you know? So maybe that's why I'm not receiving the blessings because I'm not applying the principles—I'm not doing what God tells me to do in order for me to get it."[64] Because she believes that she has the power to create her own reality, she blames herself when she becomes sick or cannot pay her bills.

In many ways, the Word of Faith movement is the embodiment of what eighteenth-century evangelicals and late nineteenth-century Catholics most feared about capitalism and consumerism. Rather than trying to preserve an ethic of the common good against a spirit of self-interest, the Word of Faith movement has redefined the meaning of Christianity to fit a capitalist economy. Although the purely self-seeking individual imagined by the movement may not actually exist, believers are urged to conform their lives to the ideal type. In the consumer empire of videos, books, CDs, mugs, posters, T-shirts, and television programs that enrich Word of Faith preachers, Christianity is not about charity, self-sacrifice, human finitude, community, or the sovereignty of God. Instead, it is about freedom, choice, and the sovereignty of the individual. Or, as Creflo Dollar announces on a commercial for his video series, it is about getting what is "rightfully yours"—health, wealth, and happiness. "I want my stuff—RIGHT NOW," a man on the commercial declares.[65]

Ending with the Word of Faith movement might suggest that the narrative of Christianity, capitalism, and consumerism should be written as a narrative of decline—or at least accommodation. But I have chosen to focus on this movement because it is such a compelling illustration of the pressures that all American churches face in a capitalist economy. Christianity has shaped American culture, but American culture has also shaped Christianity. Even though most American Christians have not followed the example of the Word of Faith movement, none have been immune to the challenges posed by the marketplace.

Since most Christians today have a relatively positive understanding of individual freedom, few have responded to the pressures of a capitalist, consumer society by returning to the solutions offered by eighteenth-century evangelicals, who emphasized the utter depravity of the self, or by late nineteenth-century Catholics, who understood individualism in almost purely negative terms. Instead, most have struggled to nurture a different model of selfhood than the one sanctified in the market—an understanding of the self that recognizes the modern values of individualism, freedom, and choice but that also honors the historic Christian commitment to sacrifice, generosity, and the common good.

NOTES

1. On these themes, see Vincent J. Miller, *Consuming Religion: Christian Faith and Practice in a Consumer Culture* (New York: Continuum, 2004).

2. Jerry Falwell, *Listen America* (Garden City, N.Y.: Doubleday, 1980), 13. Falwell did not list the specific verses in Proverbs that he had in mind.

3. George Whitefield, *The Folly and Danger of Parting with Christ for the Pleasures and Profits of Life* (London: C. Whitefield, 1740), 30. On the emergence of evangelicalism in the eighteenth-century Atlantic world, see Mark A. Noll, *The Rise of Evangelicalism: The Age of Edwards, Whitefield, and the Wesleys* (Leicester, UK: InterVarsity Press, 2004).

4. Jonathan Edwards, "Sin and Wickedness Bring Calamity and Misery on a People" (Proverbs 14:34), 1729, p. 18, in *Works of Jonathan Edwards Online*, ed. Harry S. Stout, Kenneth P. Minkema, and Caleb J. D. Maskell, 2005–, http://edwards.yale.edu/ref/13226/e/.

5. Jonathan Edwards, "The Sin of Extortion" (Ezekiel 22:12), 1747, in *Works of Jonathan Edwards Online*; Mark Valeri, "The Economic Thought of Jonathan Edwards," *Church History* 60, no. 1 (1991): 52–53.

6. T. H. Breen, "'Baubles of Britain': The American and Consumer Revolutions of the Eighteenth Century," *Past and Present* 119 (May 1988): 78. See also T. H. Breen, *The Marketplace of Revolution: How Consumer Politics Shaped American Independence* (New York: Oxford University Press, 2004).

7. Stephen A. Mrozowski, *The Archaeology of Class in Urban America* (New York: Cambridge University Press, 2006).

8. Jonathan Edwards, "Having No Part in the Saving Influences of God's Spirit" (Acts 8:21), 1735, p. 7, in *Works of Jonathan Edwards Online*.

9. Gary B. Nash, "Urban Wealth and Poverty in Pre-Revolutionary America," *Journal of Interdisciplinary History* 6, no. 4 (1976): 549.

10. See Ruth Wallis Herndon, *Unwelcome Americans: Living on the Margin in Early New England* (Philadelphia: University of Pennsylvania Press, 2001).

11. *The Larger Catechism; First Agreed Upon by the Assembly of Divines at Westminster* (Boston: J. Draper, 1745), 10. The *Westminster Confession of Faith* was originally drafted in 1646. Barbara E. Lacey, ed., *The World of Hannah Heaton: The Diary of an Eighteenth-*

Century New England Farm Woman (DeKalb, Ill.: Northern Illinois University Press, 2003), 56.

12. *Boston Evening Post*, January 3, 1743.

13. Adam Smith, *The Wealth of Nations* (1776), in *The Portable Enlightenment Reader*, ed. Isaac Kramnick (New York: Penguin Books, 1995), 507.

14. On the accessibility of consumer goods, see Breen, *The Marketplace of Revolution*; and Richard L. Bushman, *The Refinement of America: Persons, Houses, Cities* (New York: Knopf 1992).

15. Harry S. Stout, *The Divine Dramatist: George Whitefield and the Rise of Modern Evangelicalism* (Grand Rapids, Mich.: Eerdmans, 1991), 163.

16. D. Bruce Hindmarsh, *The Evangelical Conversion Narrative: Spiritual Autobiography in Early Modern England* (New York: Oxford University Press, 2005).

17. Thomas A. Schafer, *The "Miscellanies"* (entries A–Z, Aa–Zz, 1–500), ed. Harry S. Stout and John E. Smith, in vol. 13 of *The Works of Jonathan Edwards* (New Haven: Yale University Press, 1994), 238–39.

18. Sue Lane McCulley and Dorothy Zayatz Baker, eds., *The Silent and Soft Communion: The Spiritual Narratives of Sarah Pierpont Edwards and Sarah Prince Gill* (Knoxville: University of Tennessee Press, 2005), 25; Charles Chauncy, *The Benevolence of the Deity* (1784), quoted in Edward M. Griffin, *Old Brick, Charles Chauncy of Boston, 1705–1787* (Minneapolis: University of Minnesota Press, 1980), 112–13.

19. Gilbert Tennent, *A Solemn Warning to the Secure World, from the God of Terrible Majesty* (Boston: S. Kneeland and T. Green, 1735), 47.

20. Gilbert Tennent, *The Espousals: or, A Passionate Perswasive to a Marriage with the Lamb of God* (Boston: Thomas Fleet, 1741), 45.

21. Samuel Hopkins, *An Inquiry into the Nature of True Holiness* (Newport, R.I.: Solomon Southwick, 1773), 28.

22. On nineteenth-century evangelical attitudes toward capitalism and consumerism, see Stewart Davenport, *Friends of the Unrighteous Mammon: Northern Christians and Market Capitalism, 1815–1860* (Chicago: University of Chicago Press, 2008); and Mark A. Noll, ed., *God and Mammon: Protestants, Money, and the Market, 1790–1860* (New York: Oxford University Press, 2002).

23. For a view of this transformation through the eyes of a Protestant female reformer, see Kathryn Kish Sklar, *Florence Kelley and the Nation's Work* (New Haven: Yale University Press, 1995), 45.

24. Maureen Fitzgerald, *Habits of Compassion: Irish Catholic Nuns and the Origins of New York's Welfare System, 1830–1920* (Urbana: University of Illinois Press, 2006).

25. Hermann Gruber, "Liberalism," in *The Catholic Encyclopedia* (New York: Robert Appleton, 1910), vol. 9, http://www.newadvent.org/cathen/09212a.htm (accessed February 22, 2009).

26. "The Year 1888—A Retrospect and a Prospect," *American Catholic Quarterly Review* 14, no. 53 (January 1889): 117, APS Online.

27. James Fox, "Natural Law," *The Catholic Encyclopedia* (New York: Robert Apple-

ton, 1910), vol. 9, http://www.newadvent.org/cathen/09076a.htm (accessed February 22, 2009).

28. Thomas Aquinas, *Summa Theologica* I–II, Question 94, Article 2, http://www.newadvent.org/summa/2094.htm#article1 (accessed February 22, 2009).

29. Thomas E. Woods, *The Church Confronts Modernity: Catholic Intellectuals and the Progressive Era* (New York: Columbia University Press, 2004), 119–42; Stephen J. Pope, "Natural Law in Catholic Social Teachings," in *Modern Catholic Social Teaching: Commentaries and Interpretations*, ed. Kenneth R. Himes (Washington, D.C.: Geo9rgetown University Press, 2005), 49–50.

30. The *Baltimore Catechism (1885)*, Question 262, available electronically at Google Books, http://books.google.com (accessed March 28, 2011).

31. *Libertas* (1888), in *The Papal Encyclicals, 1878–1903*, ed. Claudia Carlen, I.H.M. (Raleigh, N.C., 1981), 172, quoted in John T. McGreevy, *Catholicism and American Freedom: A History* (New York: W. W. Norton, 2003), 37.

32. Leo XIII, *Rerum Novarum (1891)*, available electronically at http://www.papalencyclicals.net/Leo13/l13rerum.htm (accessed March 3, 2009).

33. Leo XIII, *Rerum Novarum*; "The Encyclical 'Rerum Novarum,'" *American Catholic Quarterly Review* 16, no. 63 (July 1891).

34. Joseph Husslein, "The System of Capitalism," *America* 18, no. 1 (October 13, 1917): 9–10.

35. Ibid., 10.

36. "The Year 1888—A Retrospect and a Prospect," 117.

37. Quoted in Woods, *The Church Confronts Modernity*, 131.

38. Aaron Ignatius Abell, *American Catholicism and Social Action* (Garden City, N.Y.: Hanover House, 1960), 88.

39. Joseph L. Husslein, "The State and Labor," *America* 18, no. 24 (March 23, 1918): 595–96.

40. Abell, *American Catholicism and Social Action*, 86; Jay Dolan, *The American Catholic Experience* (New York: Doubleday, 1985), 330.

41. "The Workman's One Way to Protect Himself," *Pilot*, August 14, 1886, quoted in Abell, *American Catholicism and Social Action*, 56.

42. On the Bishops' Program, see Joseph Michael McShane, *Sufficiently Radical: Catholicism, Progressivism, and the Bishops' Program of 1919* (Washington, D.C.: Catholic University of America Press, 1986).

43. McGreevy, *Catholicism and American Freedom*, 161, 154. On Ryan, see ibid., 140–44; and Francis L. Broderick, *Right Reverend New Dealer* (New York: Macmillan, 1963).

44. *Souvenir Volume Illustrated: Three Great Events in the History of the Catholic Church in the United States* (Detroit: William H. Hughes, 1889), 36–38, quoted in Abell, *American Catholicism and Social Action*, 107; see also Husslein, "System of Capitalism," 9–11.

45. On the Word of Faith movement, see Robert M. Bowman, *The Word-Faith Controversy: Understanding the Health and Wealth Gospel* (Grand Rapids, Mich.: Baker,

2001); Millmon F. Harrison, *Righteous Riches: The Word of Faith Movement in Contemporary African American Religion* (New York: Oxford University Press, 2005); and Stephanie Y. Mitchem, *Name It and Claim It? Prosperity Preaching in the Black Church* (Cleveland: Pilgrim Press, 2007).

46. See http://www.kcm.org/real/index.php?p=finances teachings_01 (accessed March 28, 2011).

47. Harrison, *Righteous Riches*, 18, 132, 44.

48. On Kenyon, see Bowman, *The Word-Faith Controversy*, 37, 43–84. Kirk R. MacGregor suggests that the Word of Faith movement may also have been influenced by the Nation of Islam and Mormonism. See Kirk R. MacGregor, "The Word-Faith Movement: A Theological Conflation of the Nation of Islam and Mormonism?" *Journal of the American Academy of Religion* 75, no. 1 (2007): 87–120.

49. Kenneth E. Hagin, *New Thresholds of Faith* (Tulsa: Kenneth Hagin Ministries, 1972), 53–54, quoted in Bowman, *The Word-Faith Controversy*, 125.

50. Kenneth Copeland, "Following the Faith of Abraham," tape #01–3001 (Fort Worth: Kenneth Copeland Ministries, 1989), cited in Bowman, *The Word-Faith Controversy*, 126.

51. Kenneth Copeland, "Authority of the Believer," tape #1, cited in Bowman, *The Word-Faith Controversy*, 126.

52. Benny Hinn, "Our Position in Christ #2—The Word Made Flesh," audiotape (Orlando: Orlando Christian Center, 1993), cited in MacGregor, "The Word-Faith Movement," 100.

53. Kenneth Copeland, Trinity Broadcast Network, August 9, 1987, cited in Bowman, *The Word-Faith Controversy*, 183.

54. Frederick C. Price, *How Faith Works* (Tulsa: Harrison House, 1976), 93, quoted in Bowman, *The Word-Faith Controversy*, 106.

55. See the article "Understanding the Power of Words over Your Money," http://www.paulawhite.org/content/view/172/88888897/ (accessed October 18, 2008).

56. Joel Osteen, *Your Best Life Now: 7 Steps to Living at Your Full Potential* (New York: Warner Faith, 2004), 84; Kenneth Copeland, *Our Covenant with God* (Fort Worth: Kenneth Copeland Publications, 1987), 40–41, quoted in Bowman, *The Word-Faith Controversy*, 196.

57. The text is, "Truly I say to you, there is no one who has left house or brothers or sisters or mother or father or children or farms, for My sake and for the gospel's sake, but that he will receive a hundred times as much now in the present age, houses and brothers and sisters and mothers and children and farms, along with persecutions; and in the age to come, eternal life."

58. Quoted in Sarah Posner, *God's Profits: Faith, Fraud, and the Republican Crusade for Values Voters* (Washington, D.C.: PolipointPress, 2008), 47.

59. "Copeland Ministries' CEO Responds to Investigation," *CBS 11 News* (Dallas), June 2, 2008, http://cbs11tv.com/local/Kenneth.Copeland.Ministries.2.738990.html; see

also "Fleecing the Flock," *Good Morning America*, ABC, November 11, 2007, http://abc news.go.com/GMA/Story?id=3850403&page=1.

60. Harrison, *Righteous Riches*, 7.

61. *Primetime Live*, ABC, November 21, 1991. This episode is available at http://www .youtube.com/watch?v=fdSP9La5slw.

62. Robert M. Franklin, *Crisis in the Village: Restoring Hope in African American Communities* (Minneapolis: Fortress Press, 2007).

63. Kenneth E. Hagin, *The Woman Question* (Greensburg, Pa.: Manna Christian Outreach, 1975). See also the discussion of T. D. Jakes, in Shayne Lee, *T. D. Jakes: America's New Preacher* (New York: New York University Press, 2005), 130, 134. For a critique of the movement's patriarchalism, see Mitchem, *Name It and Claim It.*

64. Harrison, *Righteous Riches*, 25, 72.

65. Ibid., 131–32.

A Wilderness Condition
The Captivity Narrative as Christian Literature

The possibilities for a single essay on Christianity and literature in America are endless. One could take up Christianity, literature, and social activism, exemplified by *Uncle Tom's Cabin*, written by Harriet Beecher Stowe, the "little woman who started this big war," as Abraham Lincoln is supposed to have greeted her.[1] One could interrogate the ways the seventeenth-century Puritan plain style extended beyond its moment, influencing modernism's spare style. One could turn to individual authors like Flannery O'Connor, Madeleine L'Engle, or John Updike, who weave together faith and fiction. Then there is popular literature and Christianity. Stephen King termed his 1978 novel *The Stand* "this long tale of dark Christianity." Anne Rice has abandoned her Vampire chronicles and completed the second in her life-of-Christ novels. And the *Left Behind* series, which followed characters "left behind" after the Rapture, was enormously popular in the 1990s and early 2000s.[2]

Among the myriad of choices, this essay focuses on the Indian captivity narrative, a form that was meant to spur social reform, with an aesthetic that has been amazingly influential on later writers, making up a genre that has proved to be immensely popular from colonial times to the present day. In New England, colonial captivity narratives, accounts of settlers—most often women—captured by Native people, were developed in the seventeenth century "*to declare the Works of the Lord*, and His wonderfull Power in carrying us along, preserving us in the *Wilderness*."[3] This choice is driven by the scholarly reception of the form as "a natural, spontaneous product of the New World experience" and as "the single narrative form indigenous to the New World."[4] Inspired by biblical tropes drawn from the Book of Exodus, Indian captivity narratives have their roots in Christian martyrologies—both Catholic and Protestant—in Jeremiad sermons, and in Puritan confession narratives. Indian captivities were used to Americanize Romantic, domestic, and gothic fictions that otherwise were inspired by European forms. Their influence persists to the present day, in science fiction abduction stories, in prisoner of war stories, and even in grocery-store romance novels marked by lurid cover art of Indian "braves" embracing disheveled but beautiful white women. The colonial Indian captivity has been directly referenced or reprised in fiction by Sherman Alexie and Bharati Mukherjee, in poetry by Louise Erdrich and Mary Ann Samyn, in films such as *The Searchers* and *The Missing* and even, quite recently, *Avatar*.[5] Additional examples abound. Once you start looking for Indian captivity plots and tropes in contemporary literature, you cannot help but stumble over them. Although both its primacy and its indigeneity have been challenged, there is no denying that the captivity narrative has exerted a forceful influence on American literature and letters, giving shape to autobiographies, poetry, fiction, and film from the seventeenth century until the present.

American captivity narratives began as stories of Europeans taken captive by Native Americans, captives who were returned to their communities after having endured numerous physical and spiritual trials in the "wilderness." These individuals' stories were often published with introductions or commentary by ministers about the stories' significance to the community as a whole. For example, and this narrative will be a touchstone for my analysis, Mary Rowlandson's narrative of her eleven weeks in captivity among Narragansetts was published in 1682, sandwiched between a preface most likely written by Puritan minister Increase Mather and a transcript of her minister husband's last sermon before his death.[6]

The explanatory texts that surround the primary narrative are intended to make clear to the reader that Rowlandson's experience should be seen as an example for the community; her captivity is to be understood as the affliction sent by God that will fall on all of New England for its sins; her return to her family is meant to stand in for God's recovery of a properly repentant people. The form of such contextual materials is that of the Jeremiad, a sermon type based on the pattern of the biblical prophet Jeremiah's thundering accusations that the nation of Israel had turned away from God and risked terrible punishment.[7] Rowlandson was a prominent woman—a minister's wife—who was captured in Lancaster, Massachusetts, a small town at the edge of English settlement, in February 1676 by Nipmuc, Narragansett, and Wampanoag forces. Those who took her captive were part of a significant pan-Indian force opposed to English settlers (and their Native allies) in a conflict that came to be known as King Philip's War, after Metacom, the Wampanoag leader, who was called Philip by the English. She traveled with her captors for eleven weeks, returning to the English after being ransomed for a modest sum. She published her account of captivity in 1682, organizing

A

NARRATIVE

OF THE

CAPTIVITY, SUFFERINGS AND REMOVES

OF

Mrs. *Mary Rowlandſon,*

Who was taken Priſoner by the INDIANS with ſeveral others, and treated in the moſt barbarous and cruel Manner by thoſe vile Savages : With many other remarkable Events during her TRAVELS.

Written by her own Hand, for her private Uſe, and now made public at the earneſt Deſire of ſome Friends, and for the Be- nefit of the afflicted.

BOSTON:

Printed and Sold at JOHN BOYLE's Printing-Office, next Door to the *Three Doves* in Marlborough Street. 1773,

1773

her experience by a series of "removes," the steps she journeys with her captors that mark her increasing distance—primarily physical, but also spiritual and cultural—from her home in Lancaster. For Rowlandson, "removal" from English settlements metaphorically reflected her distance from God; removal was a just affliction for her sins. Her physical return to Boston and to her husband was a metaphor for her spiritual salvation by God.

Rowlandson's story is an eyewitness account that is used by the clergymen who comment on it as proof of their Jeremidical analysis of divine providence, and it is the juxtaposition of the eyewitness testimony and the Jeremiad that is the focus of this essay. In order to understand the legacy of this Christian literature, we must differentiate between the literature that is the generic descendant of the individual's experience of captivity and the literature that is the love child of the Jeremiad. In other words, if we take Rowlandson's narrative as a starting point, two trajectories emerge. Historians of American literature, led by Richard Slotkin in his influential book *Regeneration through Violence*, have persuasively argued that the captivity narrative develops the energies of the Jeremiad into a vigorous, masculinist literature of the frontier, a largely secular literature. Following this thesis, we can see that Rowlandson's encounter with the wilderness develops in the eighteenth and nineteenth centuries into tales of frontier heroes in which physical trials test the hero's strength and courage. But too close a focus on the frontier adventure as the captivity narrative's descendant misses the significance of American literature that developed along different lines, literature that preserved and extended the original narratives' Christian ideology into personal accounts of spiritual and emotional trials, and into accounts of a quieter kind of heroism.

This essay focuses on the captivity tradition in English colonial literature published in New England. But there is no single origin of the genre, and its form has proven to be protean. The captivity narrative transcends standard national and colonial boundaries. Setting aside European antecedents such as fairy tales of girls lost in the woods and beset by ravenous beasts or even stories of crusaders imprisoned in the Holy Land, there are multiple colonial origins for the captivity narrative, including Cabeza de Vaca's account of Spanish conquistadores shipwrecked and wandering the Southwest and Jesuit accounts of martyrdom in present-day Canada.[8]

It is even more important to acknowledge the ways that the European-colonial captivity narrative overwrites the mistreatment of Native peoples by Europeans. As a genre focused on the experiences of invaders, traders, and settlers, the captivity narrative does not inscribe the counter story of Euro-

pean violence against religious, ethnic, and racial others. The case of Pocahontas is perhaps the best-known example of this neglect. The capture and
redemption of John Smith by the Powhatans has become a national myth,
but the fact that Pocahontas was kidnapped and held for ransom before she
was baptized and married to English colonist John Rolfe goes largely unre-
marked. Or consider John Underhill's account of the Pequot War, in which
he describes first the captivity and return of two Puritan girls and then in detail the English attack on the Pequots' fort at Mystic, in which English troops
set fire to the fort, burning hundreds of women and children alive, an unbe-
lievably violent act that he explains as a necessary action in a defensive war.
He does not describe the treatment of survivors, who were kept as servants
in New England or sold into slavery in the West Indies and elsewhere.[9] As
Pauline Turner Strong argues, regarding Pocahontas's story, consideration of
captivity narratives must include Native as well as colonial victims, because
"it is in large part through the suppression of the complexity of captivity as
a practice—and particularly the suppression of the colonists' role as captors
of Indians—that the selective tradition of captivity has gained its ideological
force."[10]

Wilderness Condition

Thus it is the white minister's wife Mary Rowlandson and not the Mystic fort
survivors or Pocahontas who has come to occupy the center stage of the captivity narrative. Whatever the injustice of Rowlandson's place in American
mythology and literary history, there is no denying her narrative's rhetorical
and emotional power. She begins her story with chaos, noise, smoke, blood,
and fear:

> At length they came and beset our own house, and quickly it was the
> dolefulest day that ever mine eyes saw. . . . Now is the dreadful hour
> come, that I have often heard of (in time of war, as it was the case of
> others), but now mine eyes see it. Some in our house were fighting for
> their lives, others wallowing in their blood, the house on fire over our
> heads, and the bloody heathen ready to knock us on the head, if we
> stirred out. Now might we hear mothers and children crying out for
> themselves, and one another, "Lord, what shall we do?"[11]

Bleeding and grieving, Rowlandson stumbled out of her house at a cold
dawn in 1676, carrying her six-year-old daughter, Sarah, who had been shot

through the wrist and stomach with the same bullet that had wounded Mary in the side. She describes her state and the child's over the next several days during several "removes," until Sarah dies, nine days into the ordeal. As she describes her grief, she feels God's presence: "I cannot but take notice how at another time I could not bear to be in the room where any dead person was, but now the case is changed; I must and could lie down by my dead babe, side by side all the night after. I have thought since of the wonderful good-ness of God to me in preserving me in the use of my reason and senses in that distressed time, that I did not use wicked and violent means to end my own miserable life." Her child is dead, and she is required to leave the body and continue traveling:

> I went to take up my dead child in my arms to carry it with me, but they bid me let it alone; there was no resisting, but go I must and leave it. When I had been at my master's wigwam, I took the first opportu-nity I could get to go look after my dead child. When I came I asked them what they had done with it; then they told me it was upon the hill. Then they went and showed me where it was, where I saw the ground was newly digged, and there they told me they had buried it. There I left that child in the wilderness, and must commit it, and my-self also in this wilderness condition, to Him who is above all.[12]

She leaves her child in the wilderness and commits herself to a "wilder-ness condition"—she commits herself to God. For Puritans, the notion of the "wilderness" was derived from biblical stories and imagery: the post-Exodus wanderings of Israel before they reached Canaan and the forty-day temptation of Christ. Rowlandson uses the intensifying word "condition" in the phrase "wilderness condition" to apply the biblical stories to her own sit-uation. Her experience is not a simple physical trial; rather, her physical suf-fering points to a more important spiritual testing. Whatever happens to her body, to emerge from her spiritual "wilderness condition" she must identify and repent of her past sins and renew her covenant with God.[13] Although the Exodus narrative and the gospel descriptions of Christ's temptation end with a return "home"—to the promised land, back to daily life, attended by angels—as Rowlandson wanders in the wilderness she has no guarantee of such a homecoming. Thus, it is essential that in the midst of the descriptions of her child's suffering and death and of her own despair, she finds reasons to explain why she and her family are faced with this trial. Four or five days into her captivity, she comes to the town of Wenimesset and notes that it is Sunday eve, which sparks in her memories of "how careless I had been of

God's holy time; how many Sabbaths I had lost and misspent, and how evilly I had walked in God's sight. . . . It was easy for me to see how righteous it was with God to cut off the thread of my life and cast me out of His presence forever. Yet the Lord still showed mercy to me, and upheld me; and as He wounded me with one hand, so he healed me with the other."[14]

This is a moment that knits together the "individual captive" and the "Jeremiad" pieces of the narrative. Around and beneath the details of suffering that consume the captive, Rowlandson weaves a theological explanation: Her child has died in her arms. She is wounded, bewildered. Her very sanity is threatened. Why? Because she has transgressed. Yet God still knows her and is merciful. Her proper response to this realization is to throw herself entirely on the mercy of God, a response best represented by the scriptural refrain of Rowlandson's and later captivity narratives: "Be still and wait upon the Lord."

The consequences for the community as a whole of this explanation are profound. The place of divine "affliction" in the Puritan belief system on the one hand sustained individuals in the face of horrific events. On the other, it enabled the community, in this case the Massachusetts Bay Colony, to imagine catastrophes like widespread war, or even more local events like fires or deaths, as a means to a triumphant end. That is, a covenanted community, a community of God's chosen, might suffer calamity, but such suffering was, paradoxically, a mark of God's favor—God would only punish—and then redeem—those he most loved. As Sacvan Bercovitch, author of *The American Jeremiad*, the most influential study of the form, describes it, the Jeremiad's function was to push "an imperiled people of God toward the fulfillment of their destiny, to guide them individually toward salvation, and collectively toward the American city of God."[15]

It is a short step in the history of American literature, some critics argue, from believing that affliction in the wilderness was a mark of God's favor to believing that Americans should seek out the wild, should recognize that their power and energy comes out of their existence as a people on a frontier. In other words, whereas the early authors of captivity narratives labeled the wilderness as frightening, a place of horrific trial, later writers embraced it. They assumed that by entering the wilderness they had achieved the promised land, not entered into a period of testing and preparation for a spiritual homecoming. Henry David Thoreau proclaimed, "In Wildness is the preservation of the world," and many certainly believed more specifically that the frontier was the preservation of America and later the United States.[16]

We can see this later American literary embrace of wilderness and wildness even in Rowlandson's narrative. Many readers especially revel in this passage in which she becomes the savage in order to survive: "There came an Indian to them at that time with a basket of horse liver. I asked him to give me a piece. 'What,' says he, 'can you eat horse liver?' I told him, I would try, if he would give a piece, which he did, and I laid it on the coals to roast. But before it was half ready they got half of it away from me, so that I was fain to take the rest and eat it as it was, with the blood about my mouth, and yet a savory bit it was to me."[17]

Her grief over her lost child, her savage satisfaction in a bit of bloody meat—this is the Rowlandson who many readers today see as most deserving of historical and cultural recovery. They approve of the Rowlandson who should be credited with inventing the "first" American literary form, not of the woman who decides passively to "wait on the Lord."[18]

Indeed, scholars have argued that her text has a double voice, that of "the redeemed captives themselves and the ministers who propagated the captives' histories for didactic purposes of their own," assuming that the woman who strives to survive her ordeal is the authentic Rowlandson and that the ministers are imposing on her their desire for a passive, resigned response to her situation.[19] Given this split, it has seemed natural and necessary for critics to listen carefully, even primarily, to that first voice, or at least to investigate ways that voice resisted the controlling minister's voice. This approach to Rowlandson's text sees orthodox theological overtones and the passive injunction to "wait on the Lord" as instances of clerical manipulation rather than as expressions of a deep and personal faith.

Yet the impulse to parse out two voices in Rowlandson's text revisits the tactics of her ministerial editors. However careful critics are to reconnect these voices, the effect is to isolate and control those elements of the text that seem most dangerous to the project of literary recovery: moments or impulses that seem least empowering or most conventional from our worldview. The effect is to remove Rowlandson from her own text, or at least—by assuming that there is an authentic voice lurking outside the text, underneath it, waiting to be recovered—to run the risk of dismissing the words she does give us. The approach leaves Rowlandson's—or indeed any historical woman writer's text—vulnerable. If one aspect of the text is considered more "authentic" or important than another, what happens when our understanding of that voice undergoes a shift—for example, if we turn our attention to hearing still other voices "muffled" by the text's more dominant voices, such as that of Weetamoo, the Wampanoag "mistress" Rowlandson repeatedly criticizes?[20] Or, as Judith Fetterly asks in her study of nineteenth-century women writers, "how do we keep criticism . . . from working at cross purposes by in effect eroding any possibility for a recuperation of the very texts we are struggling to reevaluate?"[21]

A partial answer is to change tactics—yes, there are different agendas inscribed in Mary Rowlandson's text, and yes, ministers authorized its printing. They tried to control its effects (and that of other captivity narratives) by embedding the first-person accounts in their own prefaces and sermons. But it is entirely possible, even likely, that Rowlandson and other early writers of the captivity could hold paradoxical beliefs simultaneously, if in tension. Because her clerical sponsors did not experience captivity firsthand, their writings can be read as much more unambiguously Jeremidical—their hopeful emotional register is clear. Whereas Rowlandson's hope, as real as it is to her, is matched by other emotions.

Consider the conclusion to the preface to her story, most likely written by minister Increase Mather: "How evident is it that the Lord hath made this Gentlewoman a gainer by all this affliction that she can say 'tis good for her, yea better that she hath been, than that she should not have been, thus afflicted.'" Although she does indeed say this, at the end of her narrative she also famously describes bouts of insomnia: "When others are sleeping mine eyes are weeping." And her "celebration" of affliction in captivity seems somewhat more ambiguous:

Before I knew what affliction meant, I was ready sometimes to wish for it. When I lived in prosperity, having the comforts of the world about me, my relations by me, my heart cheerful, and taking little care for anything, and yet seeing many, whom I preferred before myself, under many trials and afflictions, in sickness, weakness, poverty, losses, crosses, and cares of the world, I should be sometimes jealous least I should have my portion in this life, and that Scripture would come to my mind, "For whom the Lord loveth he chasteneth, and scourgeth every Son whom he receiveth" (Hebrews 12:6). But now I see the Lord had His time to scourge and chasten me. The portion of some is to have their afflictions by drops, now one drop and then another; but the dregs of the cup, the wine of astonishment, like a sweeping rain that leaveth no food, did the Lord prepare to be my portion. Affliction I wanted, and affliction I had, full measure (I thought), pressed down and running over. Yet I see, when God calls a person to anything, and through never so many difficulties, yet He is fully able to carry them through and make them see, and say they have been gainers thereby.

And I hope I can say in some measure, as David did, "It is good for me that I have been afflicted."[22]

The sense is the same in both versions, but the emotional impact is very different.

Thus the captivity narrative tradition as exemplified in Mary Rowlandson's narrative is representative of the individual's experience of captivity. As such it is various and nuanced, embracing the heroic and the timid, the despairing and the salvific. In particular, it articulates self-denial, self-sacrifice, service, and even doubt or unbelief, while the collective, Jeremidical meaning on which its interpreters insisted (and the key interpreter was, very often, the captive herself) employed a more positive emotional register. In other words, as a Jeremiad, the captivity narrative taught that God only afflicts those who are most deserving of His love and attention, and at times it approached self-righteousness, self-aggrandizement, and ambition. These qualities gave way more readily than that of the captivity itself to secular sensationalism, perhaps because they were farthest from the Christian ideals of humility before God's omnipotence, from which the Jeremiad is meant to derive (that is, it is God, not man, who makes possible the triumph over affliction).[23] Thus the colonial Indian captivity narrative gave rise to frontier stories of wilderness heroism. But as a story of individual affliction, the captivity narrative continued to speak as well to suffering individuals, whose hopes were directed toward Christian salvation rather than worldly success.

Whither the Captivity

The captivity narrative took two directions in American literary history, both Jeremidical and individual. Although most scholars locate the persistence of the captivity narrative in secular frontier tales derived from the Jeremiad, the ideological force of the individual's captivity narrative as exemplified by Mary Rowlandson's personal account is a significant one—persistent and flexible in both secular and Christian literature for some 400 years of American literary history.

James D. Hartman argues that the captivity narrative, because of its "exotic characters and settings," "quickened the rate of secularization in providence narratives," a Christian literary form that he argues predates the captivity in America.[24] Richard Slotkin, whose work has been foundational to early Americanists' understanding of the captivity genre, of the frontier in

American culture, and of the place of the wilderness and violence in the American identity, traces the central images of the captivity narrative to later literature in which the frontiersman, rather than fearing the wilderness and resisting transculturation, revels in it and mediates between the savage and the civilized. He cites the stories of Daniel Boone, published in the 1780s, as the culmination of the American mythology of the wilderness, introduced but not embraced by the captivity narrative.[25] From Boone, if we follow Slotkin's lead, we can trace a literary genealogy (even a mythos) that extends to Davy Crockett, John Wayne, Ronald Reagan, and perhaps even the Presidents Bush.

For other examples of the shift, we might turn to James Fenimore Cooper's character David Gamut from his novel *The Last of the Mohicans*, who is described as a man who sings—especially psalms—at the most inopportune times, surely a spoof of the reliance of earlier captives (including Rowlandson) on psalms to survive their ordeals. In the literature of the early United States, captivity narratives often turn away from overtly religious messages toward themes that Gordon Sayre describes as "consistent with the ideals of the Revolution," in that "captivity was figured less as a conversion or test of faith and more as a violation of the individual's rights of freedom and self-determination."[26] Throughout the eighteenth and nineteenth centuries, countless straightforward stories of European Americans being captured by Indians were published and read, not for any spiritual lesson but for their sensational entertainment value.

How did the literature make this transition? How do we get from Rowlandson's *Sovereignty and Goodness of God* to a title such as *An Authentic and Thrilling Narrative of the Captivity of Mrs. Horn* (1839)? Slotkin proffers Benjamin Church's account of King Philip's War as a linchpin. Church, a contemporary of Rowlandson, was an enthusiastic frontier settler and a militia leader. The account of his exploits was prepared for the press by his son, apparently working from his father's diary and correspondence.[27] Few literary critics have taken his work up, but it merits closer attention. Church has been neglected, perhaps, because his text has seemed so much more transparent than Rowlandson's, so much more a direct account of the events as they transpired. There is no doubt that Church participates in the formal transition from the spiritual to the sensational that has been seen as the hallmark of later captivity narratives. As Slotkin notes, neither Church's title page nor the text makes direct biblical reference.[28] And Church's title, *Entertaining Passages Relating to Philip's War*, certainly seems to place his experiences among later, more sensational accounts rather than among seventeenth-century pious publications. But in terms of the genre, his text consciously invokes and overturns its precedents. Church deliberately bucks conventions established by Rowlandson and her ministerial sponsors. That is, the literary thread that leads to Daniel Boone is not simply a "natural" evolution of the form from sacred to secular. Rather, it results from the choices of Church and others.

One moment in particular seems a direct response to Rowlandson's well-known account, a passage in which Church describes his decisions as head of his family rather than as head of his militia. In the midst of his description of military decisions and actions, the narrative digresses to domestic decisions and actions. We learn that Church has decided to move his family to Rhode Island, fearing that the frontier settlement of Duxbury, Massachusetts, was indefensible. Pragmatically, this move seemed a good decision—more on that issue in a moment. Spiritually, however, he was proposing to move his family to Rhode Island, a colony that Puritan clergy considered a refuge for religious error, hardly the right move if one believed, Jeremiah-like, that the war and even personal affliction reflected a neglect of God's ordinances. Consider that Rowlandson understood her tragedies as spiritually productive (and even merited) once she took notice of "how careless I had been of Gods [sic] holy time: how many Sabbaths I had lost and misspent."[29]

Moreover, Church's wife was about to give birth, and her parents urged her to stay in a fortified house close to home, not to go wandering outside of the settlement. Her situation was exactly that of countless female captives on the frontier, whose narratives stressed their physical vulnerability in settlements distant from the center of English colonization as a metaphor for their spiritual vulnerability. Such women were often captured soon after giving birth or with young children in their arms.[30] This time, however, Church's decision saved his family. Indeed, "Twenty-four hours or there abouts, after their arrival at *Rhode-Island*, Mr. *Clarks* Garrison that Mr. *Church* was so much importuned to leave his Wife and Child at, was destroyed by the Enemy."[31] Thus Church countered the message of earlier narratives: his decision as head of his household to leave home, to "remove" his heavily pregnant wife from the protection of Bay Colony church and family, saved her from captivity or worse. It is no use waiting on the Lord in Benjamin Church's world. Heroes save themselves and their loved ones.

Though Church's narrative certainly seems to confirm the "frontier" account of the later captivities, a problem remains. An account of the genre that follows the tradition through secularization, to wildness and the development of a hero of the wilderness, leaves out several key elements of the genre. It assumes a direct linear progression from Rowlandson to Boone, Cooper, and beyond. But the print history of the captivity narrative, and of Rowlandson's publication in particular, is not nearly so tidy.

In fact, Church's story and those inspired by his example did not displace Rowlandson's. Her narrative continued to be read, though as times changed, her tale was repackaged—not surprisingly—as a story of Indian savagery and intrepid female survival. Visual images of Rowlandson and new titles for later editions of her text map onto the secular-hero thesis easily. Indeed, one argument for her enduring popularity is that the captivity narrative's nuances lend themselves to a variety of readings. If the themes of Puritan spirituality did not appeal, the text's more salacious elements, descriptions of cruelty, accounts of Indian customs, and exotic foods could take its place. The pious singer of psalms could be replaced by an image of Rowlandson as a strong woman who survives great hardships (see figure 1). And indeed, Rowlandson's text remained popular. Her story, first printed in Boston and London in 1682, was a best seller. Few copies of the original survive because, as it was passed from reader to reader, it was literally read to pieces. The first edition sold out almost instantaneously, and five editions were published between 1682 and 1720. It was reissued in 1770 and has remained available to readers ever since.[32] But as Barbara E. Lacey argues with regard to the frontispiece image of the 1773 edition, which depicts Rowlandson as a musket-wielding defender of the home, an emphasis on the Rowlandson as wilderness hero "belies both the spirit and the letter of the text."[33]

In other words, the title pages conform to certain marketplace demands, but the content of her narrative—unchanged since its original publication—also remained popular. The persistence of the captivity narrative can be attributed to the works of writers like Charles Brockden Brown, James Fenimore Cooper, and others who revitalized the genre and made it speak in new ways to eighteenth- and nineteenth-century political and cultural concerns.[34] But Rowlandson's particular vision of personal spiritual suffering—her account of a different kind of heroism—must have resonated with American readers as well, or else why repackage her account when so many other contemporary adventures were available to publishers and readers alike?

Although narratives that described acts of physical prowess on the frontier were extremely popular, interest nevertheless remained in the kind of tentative, hesitant, even self-contradictory personal account of regeneration through affliction that Rowlandson inscribed in her narrative. Hers is an account of the kind of Christian heroism possible for the relatively powerless, of triumph over one's sinful nature, of learning to place trust in God rather than relying on limited human strength.[35] If we acknowledge the continuing power of the idea of personal regeneration through affliction, even against the story of physical survival, we will be able to construct a fuller American literary history, one that includes and acknowledges not only well-known novels such as *The Last of the Mohicans* and figures from Daniel Boone to Davy Crockett, but also neglected publications and more obscure people.

Consider, for example, Abigail Abbott Bailey's memoir, published in 1815. Bailey was a devout Christian, but she married unhappily. Generally, her work is classified as a conversion narrative; certainly that is the way her minister treated her story. But the captivity form marks it at least as strongly. Her husband, Asa Bailey, was abusive—both verbally and physically. He regularly had adulterous affairs and even attempted a rape of one of their servants. Despite these troubles, Abigail Bailey endured the marriage and had fourteen children with him. She separated from him only after finding out that he had sexually abused their oldest daughter. Eventually she sought a divorce. In response, her husband separated her from her children and kidnapped her in an attempt to remove her from a supportive community and retain control of both her person and her property.

This part of the narrative in particular bears all the marks of a captivity narrative and can serve as a case study of the ways that many conventions of the captivity continued with little alteration into the nineteenth century, however much the marketing (from saintly to sensational), the central character (from female captive to frontier male hero), and even the genre (from nonfiction to fiction) had changed in more popular publications. In her memoir, Bailey details her Christian conversion, but its continued interest to critics today lies (like that of Rowlandson's own account) in the narrative she inscribes. Although the text has not garnered a lot of attention, it is important to the history of the captivity narrative because it gives us a good sense of the kinds of readers who continued to make publication of the original American captivity narratives lucrative. However much frontier hero tales caught the public's imagination, at home and abroad, Bailey's journal provides insight into the beliefs and experiences that kept overtly Christian narratives like Rowlandson's popular.

When Asa Bailey tricks her into going into New York State with him, in effect kidnapping her, she represents their travel in terms similar to Rowlandson's removes—and like Rowlandson, the most troubling aspect of her captivity is the separation from her children: "I had every day moved on with a heavy heart. . . . I was going every day farther and farther from my dear little children."[36] When her husband "threw off the mask" and told her his plans to separate her from the support of family and friends, she declares to him, "I knew no better way than to submit to him as a captive. . . . I would yield as a captive to his violent hands, till the Lord should see fit to deliver me." Just a few pages later, she writes, in sentimentally inflected language, which is nonetheless a clear echo of Rowlandson: "I must wait,—I must wait a captive in the cruel hands of my oppressor, till God in his mercy should see fit to open some door of escape."[37] Like Puritan captives of Indians, she even invokes biblical scenes of slavery and captivity to make sense of her situation. In her May 26, 1774, entry, she likens her suffering in marriage to the slavery of Israel in Egypt. When the couple put up for the night with a settler family, her husband told her "to wash my face, and go into the house, and appear cheerful. . . . These things brought to my mind the case of the captive Jews. 'By the rivers of Babylon,' etc."[38]

Although I have as yet found no evidence that Abigail Bailey ever read Rowlandson (or indeed any other captivity narrative), her journal reveals her to be the kind of reader who would find personal spiritual solace in Mary Rowlandson's captivity narrative regardless of its Jeremidical importance for New England as a whole. There is little in Bailey's text to suggest that she saw her sufferings as exemplary for her community. Rather, this is an intensely personal story of captivity and redemption. But like earlier captivity narratives, it tells a story not of action and violence but of personal suffering—both spiritual and physical—and finds triumph in the individual's ability to rely on God to see her through her trials. It is in this register that the captivity narrative is carried forward as a Christian genre.

This essay has traced two trajectories for the captivity narrative genre: that of the wilderness hero, a direction well documented by literary historians and charted by Benjamin Church, and that of the individual's affliction and salvation in the wilderness, represented by Abigail Abbot Bailey's memoir. A full accounting of the genre and its relationship to Christianity in America would need to discuss other directions as well. In particular, the slave narratives of the eighteenth and nineteenth centuries build on Indian captivity narratives, and we can see the extension of some of their themes into contemporary literature: for example, Toni Morrison's 2008 novel A Mercy traces the lives of African American, Native American, and European American women who were captured, enslaved, or otherwise displaced from their homes.[39] The limits of the captivity narrative as Christian literature would need to be considered as well. As the example of the slave narrative exemplifies, the form has proven to be amazingly flexible and useful for immigrant writers—whether that immigration was voluntary or forced. Colonists and slaves alike wrote themselves into American versions of the Exodus story, with Puritan settlers in the role of enslaved Israelites or white slavers as "modern day Egyptians."[40]

But as Robert Allen Warrior has asserted, the liberating promise of this biblical story for oppressed peoples in colonial America and in the United States is not universal. The Exodus narrative cannot easily be extended to Native peoples, who are represented in the biblical story by the Canaanites, indigenous residents of the land of milk and honey displaced by the freed nation of Israel.[41] His reading presents a challenge to the captivity narrative as American Christian literature, a challenge that may be particularly relevant today. What happens to this genre when its roles are reversed—when the captors are Christian and the victims are not?[42] The next important variation on the American captivity narrative may come not from U.S. citizens or from Christians but from Muslims held captive by the United States. What form will the stories of released Guantánamo Bay prisoners take? What imagery will convey their experiences to the Americans who imprisoned them?

This essay began with the claim that once we start looking for descendants of the Indian captivity narrative, we find them everywhere. At the risk of being too presentist, or perhaps too Jeremidical, this essay ends with the claim that although the Indian captivity narrative has followed several trajectories in American literary history, the Puritan aesthetic of the Jeremiad with its connotations of communal righteousness—the godliness of the congregation, the colony, the nation—continues its strong influence. Its power is evident even to those newly introduced to the genre. In September 2001, when I was teaching an undergraduate early American literature class, my students could not help being struck by the strong Jeremidical language of so many commentators—religious and secular alike—in response to the attack on the World Trade Towers. Again, following the devastation of Hurricane Katrina on the Gulf Coast, and even more recently after the devastating earthquake in Haiti, there have been invocations of Jeremiah's dire prophecies. These are but the latest instances of a pattern that dates back to the earliest British-American settlements. For Americans, a close look at our own literary history may give us the tools and courage to refuse the moral certitude that leads to national sin—to refuse to allow the nation easily to claim righteousness based on the affliction of individuals, as tragic as it may be, but rather to let the individuals claim and interpret their experiences for themselves. For others, it is important that their "outsider" perspective is brought to bear on these texts to help those enmeshed in their legacies to read them carefully, sensitively, and critically.

NOTES

1. Joan D. Hendrick, *Harriet Beecher Stowe: A Life* (New York: Oxford University Press, 1994), vii.

2. Stephen King, *The Stand: Complete and Uncut* (New York: Knopf, 1990). The first book in Rice's series is *Christ the Lord: Out of Egypt* (New York: Knopf, 2005). The *Left Behind* series starts with Tim LeHaye and Jerry B. Jenkins, *Left Behind: A Novel of the Earth's Last Days* (Colorado Springs: Tyndale House Publishers, 1995).

3. Mary Rowlandson, *The Sovereignty and Goodness of God, with Related Documents*, ed. Neal Salisbury (New York: Bedford, 1997), 82.

4. Richard Slotkin, *Regeneration through Violence: The Mythology of the American Frontier, 1600–1860* (Middletown, Conn.: Wesleyan University Press, 1973), 95; Annette Kolodny, *The Land before Her: Fantasy and Experience of the American Frontiers, 1630–1860* (Chapel Hill: University of North Carolina Press, 1984), 6.

5. See Sherman Alexie, *Indian Killer* (New York: Warner Books, 1996); Bharati Mukherjee, *Holder of the World* (New York: Knopf, 1993); Louise Erdrich, "Captivity," in *Original Fire: Selected and New Poems* (New York: HarperCollins, 2003); Mary Ann Samyn, *Captivity Narrative* (Columbus: Ohio State University Press, 1999); *The Searchers*, DVD, directed by John Ford (1956; Burbank, Calif.: Warner Home Video, 1997); *The Missing*, DVD, directed by Ron Howard (2003; Culver City, Calif.: Columbia Tristar Home Entertainment, 2004); and *Avatar*, DVD, directed by James Cameron (2009; Beverly Hills, Calif.: 20th Century Fox Home Entertainment, 2010). Alexie has also written a poem, "Captivity," that, like Erdrich's, references Mary Rowlandson's captivity: see *First Indian on the Moon* (New York: Hanging Loose Press, 1993).

6. To list all useful studies and compilations of captivity narratives in the New England tradition is impossible here. A few key titles include Alden T. Vaughan and Edward W. Clark, eds., *Puritans among Indians: Accounts of Captivity and Redemption, 1676–1724* (Cambridge: Belknap Press of Harvard University Press, 1981); Christopher Castiglia, *Captivity, Culture-Crossing, and White Womanhood from Mary Rowlandson to Patty Hearst* (Chicago: University of Chicago Press, 1996); Michelle Burnham, *Captivity and Sentiment: Cultural Exchange in American Literature, 1682–1861* (Hanover, N.H.: University Press of New England, 1997); Kathryn Zabelle Derounian-Stodola, ed., *Women's Indian Captivity Narratives* (New York: Penguin, 1998); Pauline Turner Strong, *Captive Selves, Captivating Others: The Politics and Poetics of Colonial American Captivity Narratives* (Boulder: Westview, 1999); and Gordon Sayre, ed., *American Captivity Narratives* (Boston: Houghton Mifflin, 2000). For a good, brief overview of the genre, see Lorrayne Carroll, "Captivity Literature," in *The Oxford Handbook of Early American Literature*, ed. Kevin J. Hayes (Oxford, UK: Oxford University Press, 2008), 143–68.

7. For a book-length study of the form, see Sacvan Bercovitch, *The American Jeremiad* (Madison: University of Wisconsin Press, 1980).

8. These narratives are accessible in new editions. See Alvar Núñez Cabeza de Vaca, *The Narrative of Cabeza de Vaca*, trans. Rolena Adorno and Patrick Charles Pautz (Lincoln: University of Nebraska Press, 2003); and Allan Greer, ed., *The Jesuit Relations: Natives and Missionaries in Seventeenth-Century North America* (Boston: Bedford, 2000).

9. John Underhill, *Newes from America* (1638; Digital Commons, University of Nebraska–Lincoln, *Electronic Texts in American Studies*, 2007, http://digitalcommons.unl.edu/etas/37/ [accessed April 4, 2008]).

10. Strong, *Captive Selves, Captivating Others*, 3.

11. Rowlandson, *Sovereignty and Goodness of God*, 68.

12. Ibid., 75.

13. Critics have focused as well on Rowlandson's physical survival—she learns to fit into the culture and economy of her captives' community; she learns to eat the starvation diet that she shares with the Algonquians with whom she travels. But it is clear that for Rowlandson, physical survival is (or ought to be) secondary to spiritual salvation. For instance, she records the story of Goodwife Joslin, who was captured with her and is about to give birth. Joslin implores her captors to release her and confides in Rowlandson that she plans to run away with her young child. Rowlandson convinces her that she cannot survive the trek home on her own, but she is soon put to death by her captors. What might be seen as a simple tragedy or an indictment of Indian cruelty is also portrayed in Rowlandson's account as a spiritual victory. When Joslin keeps making complaints to her captives, they publicly execute her and her young child, but eyewitnesses testify that "she did not shed one tear, but prayed all the while."

14. Rowlandson, *Sovereignty and Goodness of God*, 74.

15. Bercovitch, *The American Jeremiad*, 9.

16. "Walking," in *The Norton Anthology of American Literature*, ed. Nina Baym, 5th ed. (New York: W. W. Norton, 1998), 1:1964. See Frederick Jackson Turner's articulation of the "frontier thesis," "The Significance of the Frontier in American History," in *Proceedings of the State Historical Society of Wisconsin*, December 14, 1893.

17. Rowlandson, *Sovereignty and Goodness of God*, 81.

18. Rowlandson directly quotes Psalm 27, "Wait on the Lord, Be of good courage, and he shall strengthen thine heart, wait I say on the Lord," at the end of the third remove, as she is counseling Goodwife Joslin to stay with their captors rather than attempt to run away. Joslin was nine-months pregnant at the time.

19. Tara Fitzpatrick, "The Figure of Captivity: The Cultural Work of the Puritan Captivity Narrative," *American Literary History* 3 (1991): 2.

20. See Laura Liebman, "'Now . . . Didn't Our People Laugh?' Female Misbehavior and Algonquian Culture in Mary Rowlandson's 'Captivity and Restauration,'" *American Indian Culture and Research Journal* 21, no. 4 (1997): 1–28.

21. Judith Fetterly, "Nineteenth-Century American Women Writers and the Politics of Recovery," *American Literary History* 6, no. 3 (Autumn 1994): 607.

22. Rowlandson, *Sovereignty and Goodness of God*, 112.

23. In his excellent article, "Mary Rowlandson and the Invention of the Secular,"

Bryce Traister points to the "text's simultaneous commitment to both representative and personal orders of suffering's relation to meaning" and suggests that this doubling "anticipates the relational structure of secular and religious identity in Western modernity." *Early American Literature* 42, no. 2 (2007): 325. I find his thesis provocative, and to a large degree I agree with it, but here I am interested in following the continued Christian resonances at both the individual and the communal levels.

24. James D. Hartman, *Providence Tales and the Birth of American Literature* (Baltimore: Johns Hopkins University Press, 1999).

25. Slotkin, *Regeneration through Violence*; see especially chap. 9.

26. Sayre, *American Captivity Narratives*, 347.

27. For an introduction to the narrative, see Richard Slotkin and James K. Folsom, eds., *So Dreadfull a Judgment: Puritan Responses to King Philip's War, 1676–1677* (Hanover, N.H.: Wesleyan University Press, 1978), 370–91.

28. Slotkin, *Regeneration through Violence*, 159.

29. Rowlandson, *Sovereignty and Goodness of God*, 74.

30. Consider, for instance, Hannah Duston, who had given birth just a week before her capture, a fact emphasized in the many retellings of her story. Cotton Mather's version of her experiences is included in an appendix to the Neal Salisbury edition of Mary Rowlandson's narrative.

31. Benjamin Church, "Entertaining Passages Relating to Philip's War," in Slotkin and Folsom, *So Dreadfull a Judgment*, 420.

32. For Rowlandson's publishing history, see Salisbury's introduction to Rowlandson, *Sovereignty and Goodness of God*, 51; see also Kathryn Zabelle Derounian, "The Publication, Promotion, and Distribution of Mary Rowlandson's Indian Captivity Narrative in the Seventeenth Century," *Early American Literature* 23, no. 3 (1988): 239–61.

33. Barbara E. Lacey, *From Sacred to Secular: Visual Images in Early American Publications* (Newark: University of Delaware Press, 2007), 153.

34. Brown's 1799 novel *Edgar Huntly* features Indian captivity and wilderness adventure. James Fenimore Cooper's *The Last of the Mohicans* (1831) is perhaps the best known, containing several Indian captivity narratives that present a vision of the eighteenth-century frontier as one in which white men rescue captive women, earning their place in the American wilderness as Native peoples "inevitably" pass away.

35. Although I am not arguing that this direction in the captivity narrative traditions spoke exclusively to women, certainly many women would have found reprints of Rowlandson's narrative attractive. In her influential study of the frontier in women's writings, Annette Kolodny argues that captivity narratives offered women readers an allegory of their own despair and anger as they followed their husbands west to seek their fortunes, in which Indian captors represented their husbands. See Kolodny, *The Land before Her*, 33.

36. Abigail Abbot Bailey, *Religion and Domestic Violence in Early New England: The Memoirs of Abigail Abbot Bailey*, ed. Ann Taves (Bloomington: Indiana University Press, 1989), 121.

37. Ibid., 129, 132.

38. Ibid., 138.

39. The many published anthologies of slave narratives include Henry Louis Gates, ed., *The Classic Slave Narratives* (New York: Signet Classics, 2002); and William L. Andrews, ed., *Six Women's Slave Narratives* (Oxford, UK: Oxford University Press, 1989). For earlier African American writings, see Joanna Brooks and John Saillant, eds., *Face Zion Forward: First Writers of the Black Atlantic, 1785–1798* (Boston: Northeastern University Press, 2002); and Vincent Carretta, ed., *Unchained Voices: An Anthology of Black Authors in the English-Speaking World of the Eighteenth-Century* (Lexington: University Press of Kentucky, 2003). See also Toni Morrison, *A Mercy* (New York: Knopf, 2008).

40. The phrase is used by African American poet Phillis Wheatley in a 1774 letter to Samson Occom, a Mohegan writer and Methodist minister. In Phillis Wheatley, *Complete Writings*, ed. Vincent Carretta (New York: Penguin, 2001), 152.

41. Robert Warrior, "Canaanites, Cowboys, and Indians: Deliverance, Conquest, and Liberation Theology Today," in *Native and Christian: Indigenous Voices on Religious Identity in the United States and Canada*, ed. James Treat (New York: Routledge, 1996), 93–104. This anthology also includes several responses to Warrior's thesis.

42. I do not mean to suggest that Native Americans are not Christian or that no Native writers found the captivity genre useful. See, for example, my arguments about the Christian convert Ponampam's application of Christ's temptation in the wilderness to his experience in colonial New England, in *Dry Bones and Indian Sermons: Praying Indians in Colonial America* (Ithaca, N.Y.: Cornell University Press, 2004), 76–83.

Science and Christianity in America
A Limited Partnership

During the past several decades, historians have devoted a great amount of attention to the history of the relationship between science and Christianity. Although this attention has unquestionably led to a more nuanced view of that history, it may have unwittingly fostered an exaggerated view of the importance of science in shaping Christian thought. Christian theology consists of a broad complex of ideas concerning God, human nature, and the dynamics of the divine-human encounter. The interaction of Christians with the natural world has doubtless played a role in determining the formulation of those ideas, but that role has rarely been central. Moreover, even on those occasions when Christians have given sustained attention to nature, they have typically drawn on a variety of approaches—providential, biblical, occult, and aesthetic, as well as scientific—in developing their ideas of its meaning. My hope in this essay, which traces the responses of Christians in America to scientific inquiry, will be to avoid exaggerating the spiritual and theological significance of that inquiry.[1]

Colonial North America

Throughout the colonial period, New England Protestants dominated discussions of both theology and the natural world in British North America. The absence of commentary from Catholics or even from most Protestants in the English colonies hinders us from knowing what those Christians thought about the theological implications of the natural world. During the seventeenth century, New England Protestants emphasized that the created order served as a vehicle of divine revelation by attesting to the existence, wisdom, and power of its Creator. Puritan poets like Anne Bradstreet and Edward Taylor valued nature as a fertile source of "illustrations" of the "goodness, wisdom, glory, light" that "dwells on high." For their part, Puritan clergy expressed confidence that contemplation of "the fabrike of the world" would lead one inexorably to the conclusion that "an infinite wisdom, and an almightie power hath been here."[2]

The conviction that the creation attested to its Creator prompted some Puritans to play an active role in appropriating and disseminating knowledge gleaned from natural philosophy. As early as the 1640s, seniors at Harvard were receiving some instruction in astronomy, and tutors filled the blank pages of the almanacs printed annually at the college with essays on a variety of topics relating to nature—comets, meteorology, even Copernican heliocentrism. Although some Puritans who were exposed to novel scientific ideas remained committed to the more traditional views associated with Aristotle and Ptolemy, their resistance was motivated more by the counterintuitive nature of the newer approaches than by concern about their theological implications.[3]

Puritans in the New World rarely actively resisted natural philosophy, but few appear to have cherished the knowledge that it yielded. There were several reasons for this. First, they were convinced that the evidences of God's glory in nature were so apparent that it was virtually impossible to avoid them. Accordingly, they saw little reason to invoke the results of scientific investigation in discussing the wonders of creation. Second, their belief that every event was utterly contingent on the will of a sovereign Deity undermined their confidence in the stability of the uniform regularities revealed by natural philosophy. Finally, the providentialism that constituted the conceptual framework within which most Protestants in seventeenth-century British North America understood the natural world was predicated not only on a theocentric view of divine governance but also on a human-centered interpretation of divine purpose. Persuaded that God had "made this world to be a mappe and shadow of the spirituall estate of the soules of men," those believers ascribed significance to nature primarily because it served as the site for a cosmic drama featuring the ongoing interaction of God and human beings. Exemplifying this anthropocentric orientation, a Boston clergyman interpreted a mouse killing a snake allegorically: "The snake was the devil, the mouse was a poor contemptible people which God had brought hither, which should overcome Satan here and dispossess him of his kingdom."[4]

Providentialism also prompted Protestants to find special spiritual edification in the numerous unexpected and irregular natural events that deviated from the "ordinary wayes and means" that God used to govern the universe. Those events were sometimes awe-inspiring—earthquakes, floods, eclipses, meteors, and comets—but they could also be less dramatic, such as infestations of caterpillars, or more narrowly confined to smaller groups or individuals, such as "monstrous" births. The "lore of wonders" generated in the New World frequently bore only a tenuous connection to formal Christian doctrine, but it played an important role in reinforcing the idea that the cosmos was, as one historian has put it, "unpredictable and communicative."[5]

Another factor serving to limit the interest of many seventeenth-century Protestants in scientific investigation was their conviction that given humanity's fallen state, any knowledge derived from empirical observation and reason was "unsafe and obscure" compared to the "more evident and *certain*" knowledge provided in the Bible. That view prompted John Cotton, a Massachusetts Bay clergyman and prominent Puritan theologian, to suggest that although Christ did not "mislike the study of nature," it was doubtful that such study was sufficiently important to one's spiritual state "as that a man should busie himselfe with the observation of it." Indeed, some Puritans expressed concern that an overweening preoccupation with the things of this world might well lead to indifference to the more important spiritual realm. Others, sensitive to the distinctiveness of and sometimes even tension between nature and grace, emphasized that although the natural world sometimes illustrated truths expressed in scripture, it was necessary to look to the Bible for a complete, infallible, and sufficient guide to the essential truths concerning God's redemptive activities.[6]

During the late seventeenth and eighteenth centuries, many educated Protestants in America began to express greater confidence in the capacities of the mind. That confidence, coupled with increasing knowledge of the natural world, convinced some believers to examine the subject matter subsumed within scientific investigation for truths concerning God's governance of the universe. Cotton Mather, whose understanding of the natural sciences was unequalled by any other clergyman in British North America, held that a careful examination of the universe would do much to enhance appreciation of the divine handiwork. His most ambitious exposition of this position, *The Christian Philosopher* (1721), drew on works ranging from the philosophers of classical antiquity to more recent natural philosophers and "physico-theologians," in a sustained attempt to "exhibit" the glories of God throughout the created order. By 1756, John Winthrop IV, a gifted astronomer and the Hollis professor of mathematics and natural philosophy at Harvard, was sufficiently confident of the theological value of investigation of nature to assert that "the consideration of a DEITY is not peculiar to *Divinity*, but belongs also to *natural Philosophy*."[7]

In their fascination with scientific inquiry, Mather and Winthrop were hardly typical of even the well-read Christians of their day. A number of other Protestants in British North America did share their conviction, however, that theological lessons could be derived from scientific investigation. Many, for example, inferred from the increasing success of natural philosophers in using "second causes" to describe the activities of natural phenomena that God had typically chosen to use such causes in governing the created order. Some Protestants described the events associated with those second causes as dispensations of God's "general" providence, while reserving use of the term "extraordinary" providence for those numerous "*Reserved cases*"—the meteors, comets, earthquakes, and "whatever else shall happen that is prodigious"—in which God chose to intervene directly within the natural order. Others eschewed such distinctions in favor of simply ascribing all events to divine agency. Boston clergyman Thomas Prince, for example, maintained that matter was by its nature passive and therefore required the agency of the "wise, mighty, and constant operations of God" to sustain its activity. Jonathan Edwards emphasized that the continued existence of all things from moment to moment was the result of the "immediate power" of a sovereign Deity; indeed, he asserted, the entire "*course of nature*" should be seen as "an *arbitrary constitution*" that "depends on nothing but the divine will."[8]

As in the early seventeenth century, most Protestant commentators in the period between 1680 and 1800 remained committed to an anthropocentric vision of cosmic processes. As a result, they were much more interested in the providential purposes informing natural events than the precise apparatus that the Deity employed in realizing those purposes. When an earthquake struck New England in 1727, the issue that obsessed most of the Christians who discussed the event was not whether natural agencies were at work in causing the event, for they simply took it for granted that such "*Causes* are still under the Government of HIM that is the GOD *of Nature*." Rather, they believed that the really compelling question was what message God was sending them by visiting their region with that dramatic event.[9]

The conviction that God was attempting to convey messages to human beings in cosmic events cut across theological lines. It prompted Jonathan Edwards to assert that "the material world, and all things pertaining to it, is by the Creator wholly subordinated to the spiritual and moral world," but it also led one of Edwards's most influential antagonists, the clergyman Charles Chauncy, to insist that God manipulated secondary causes in order to impart theological lessons to His children. During the controversy that erupted in Boston over smallpox inoculation in 1721–22, providentialist assumptions not only moved Boston physician William Douglass to justify his demand that the clergy cease meddling in medical affairs by insisting that they rely on "the *all-wise Providence* of God Almighty," but they also led his clerical antagonists to respond by insisting that their efforts to prevent or cure disease were quite "consistent with a humble trust in our Great preserver, and a due Subjection to His All-wise Providence." A commitment to providentialism underlay charges that supporters of lightning rods were guilty of interfering with the will of God, but it was no less prominent in claims made by supporters of those rods that the devices were akin to the "means" that God had provided for preventing or curing diseases.[10]

Also continuing to inhibit interest in scientific investigation during the late seventeenth and eighteenth centuries was the widespread conviction that knowledge gleaned through such investigation was inferior in quality to the spiritual insights disclosed in the scriptures. After all, Protestants believed, the natural world itself revealed only God's "back-parts." For this reason, natural philosophy could never become anything more than a "*Hand-maid* unto Divinity." Harvard College president Samuel Langdon thus admonished students in 1776 to beware of allowing the spiritual truths derived from a study of nature "to vie with the honor of divine revelation."[11]

Prior to 1800, few Christians in North America expressed concern that scientific inquiry was yielding ideas that were irreconcilable with the scriptures. Although most believers assumed in the absence of any evidence to the contrary that the Bible accurately depicted the natural events it described, their belief that in dealing with natural phenomena the biblical authors had employed language adapted to the intellectual capacities of the common people gave them some flexibility in interpreting scriptural texts. Commentators also agreed that an accurate interpretation of God's works would never conflict with an accurate rendering of God's Word. For some Protestants, this suggested that "the Book of the *Creatures*" could serve as an aid to understanding "the Book of the *Scriptures*." Many others, however, lauded the Bible as "the interpreter of the book of nature" on the grounds that it provided the clearest disclosure of "those spiritual mysteries that are indeed signified or typified in the constitution of the natural world." The "Catholick" Congregational clergyman Benjamin Colman thus concluded that "after all this fine Doctrine in our *New Philosophy*, concerning the *Centripetal Forces* of the Sun and Planets; a plain Christian is much more edified by the simply and vulgar Account which the sacred Pages give us of this mysterious Thing."[12]

During the first two-thirds of the nineteenth century, lectures, lyceums, museums, published works, and the activities of educational institutions made the results of scientific investigation increasingly available to Americans within the "learned culture." For many Christian participants in that culture, science became an important source of cultural authority. Accordingly, those believers found themselves devoting a good deal of energy to the task of assessing the theological implications of scientific inquiry. After about 1830, books and articles addressing the relationship between science and Christian thought became a staple of American literature.[13]

Many authors of those publications emphasized the value of science for Christian thought. Convinced that the natural world was "as truly a manifestation from Heaven as the Scriptures," a growing number of defenders of the faith concluded that "the calm investigation of science, stamped with the seal of Christian charity," provided compelling grounds for belief in the existence of a rational and benevolent Deity. In elaborating that argument, some apologists maintained that in revealing the ubiquitous presence of order and intelligibility in the natural world, science provided proof of the *"personal, universal, and continual presence of the Almighty"* within the natural world. Others called attention to the fossil record, which seemed to show that the organisms that had lived on the planet throughout its history were "contrived" for adaptation to the conditions of their existence. The fact that those organisms had periodically changed in accordance with alterations in the environment led proponents of this argument from design to affirm that there had been "direct interposition, often repeated and distinctly visible, of the same almighty power, which originated the whole design at first."[14]

Protestant and Catholic apologists were most likely to invoke direct supernatural intervention for events in realms that resisted scientific explanation. If natural scientists subsequently succeeded in arriving at plausible natural explanations for events in those realms, Christians continued to affirm the possibility of "the free intervention of God in the affairs of the universe he has himself created" but typically were willing to alter their interpretations to include those explanations. For example, during the first half of the nineteenth century, it was not unusual for Christians to regard cholera as, in the words of one Presbyterian clergyman, a "rod" employed by God to "promote the cause of righteousness" by eliminating the "filth and scum which contaminate and defile human society." When the medical community developed efficacious means of dealing with the disease, however, few Christian thinkers persisted in ascribing cholera to special providential intervention.[15]

Not all Christians were enamored of the use of data from the natural world in defending the tenets of their worldview. John L. Girardeau, a professor at Columbia Theological Seminary in South Carolina, held that "the oracles of nature are dumb in response to the most pressing demands of the human soul. We ask them for knowledge as to the gracious willingness of God to pardon and accept the sinner, and they answer—not a word." James Marsh, president of the University of Vermont, derided the notion that arguments based on nature constituted "the strong ground of our conviction of theism." Most Mormon thinkers assumed that divine revelation was sufficient to establish God's existence and nature and thus proved indifferent to natural theology. Roman Catholic essayist Orestes Brownson insisted that "without the principles which are given us only by divine revelation," the cosmos would appear to be little more than "a vast assemblage of inexplicable phenomena."[16]

Lack of enthusiasm for natural theology was only one of the reasons why many Christians found scientific inquiry spiritually unedifying. A sizable number of them, convinced that the instrument through which humanity encountered the divine was the heart rather than the head, believed that humanity's bondage to sin, the glory of salvation through Christ, and the imperative of establishing a personal encounter with God were the urgent issues of life, and they regarded scientific descriptions of the natural world as utterly irrelevant to those concerns. Many also tended to dismiss scientific accounts of the regular occurrences within the natural order because they were much more forcibly struck by the pervasive presence of a host of mysterious and sometimes sinister forces encountered through dreams, apparitions, disembodied voices, or even divine emissaries, as in the case of Mormon prophet Joseph Smith's interactions with the angel Moroni. For Christians living in such "enchanted" environments, it seemed obvious that God was inclined to intervene directly, momentously, and suddenly in the order of nature as well as in the order of grace.[17]

The issue that generated the most discussion among Christians who addressed the relationship between science and religion in the period between 1800 and 1870 was how to square many of the ideas scientists were embracing—ideas such as the nebular hypothesis of the origin of the solar system, the periodic appearance and disappearance of species, the almost unimaginable antiquity of the earth, phrenology, and ethnology—with understandings of natural history derived from the Bible. Some believers—one

commentator's estimate in 1852 was "perhaps one half of the Christian public"—held that the biblical narrative of creation was "to be taken literally, in
its obvious sense." Those believers, aware that the investigation of nature was
the work of "imperfect and fallible men," reasoned that "revealed religion, as
understood by the church of Christ, is entitled to a high pre-eminence over
the theories of science." Other Christians believed that scriptural language
was "elastic enough" to permit reinterpretation to bring the Bible into line
with the latest conclusions of modern science. Some accommodationists
suggested that men of science could provide an improved understanding
of scriptural passages relating to nature. Others held that since the purpose
of the scriptures was to reveal the essential truths relating to the scheme
of redemption rather than to teach science, it was entirely appropriate that
scientists investigate the natural world without regard to biblical discussions
of natural history.[18]

Serious tension between Christian thought and modern science also
arose in the wake of efforts by men of science in one discipline after another
to use only "secondary" causes and natural processes in accounting for the
history, structure, and operation of natural phenomena. Actually, those efforts began long before 1800 in certain disciplines like celestial mechanics,
but they intensified after about 1830, when the range of phenomena that
scientists could describe naturalistically widened significantly. The work of
Charles Darwin, who ascribed the origin of new species to the work of natural agencies and denounced alternatives to that procedure as unscientific,
constituted an apt symbol of the triumph of "methodological naturalism"
within the scientific community. In the aftermath of Darwin's work, a growing number of scientists, including many who remained devout Christians,
came to believe that, as one Wesleyan University natural historian put it, "it
is the aim of science to narrow the domain of the supernatural, by bringing all phenomena within the scope of natural laws and secondary causes."
Indeed, scientists increasingly maintained that the only descriptions of the
natural world meriting designation as "science" were those that employed
naturalistic norms of discourse and explanation.[19]

1870–1917

During the late nineteenth and early twentieth centuries, the scientific community's insistence on detaching its investigations from biblical considerations, coupled with its growing commitment to a naturalistic methodologi-

cal norm, triggered the emergence of a series of important new divisions within American Christianity. Many believers, who regarded the scriptures as the vehicle by which a gracious and merciful God had provided a fallible and sinful humanity with a complete, inerrant, and clear account source of religious knowledge, repudiated scientists' efforts to exclude biblical testimony from their assessments. Those believers appealed to the "plain sense" of the scriptures as the standard for evaluating the legitimacy of all "decrees, opinions and doctrines of men." It was absurd, they declared, to confer the kind of infallibility on the sciences that "alone belongs to the theology of the Bible."[20]

Many Protestants and Catholics alike also took umbrage at the efforts scientists were making to describe all things in terms of natural agencies and processes. Their awareness that doctrines as central to the Christian worldview as the Incarnation and the Resurrection, the plenary inspiration of the scriptures, and the efficacy of prayer were predicated on the idea that God had periodically intervened directly within the natural order convinced those believers that "Christianity is supernatural—from above nature, or it is nothing." From this perspective, they ascribed the strictures that scientists were placing on their discourse and explanations to a desire, in the words of a prominent Pentecostal clergyman, "to rule God out entirely, or to leave us only a vague, mysterious, impersonal God." A similar view prompted Brownson to complain in 1873 that "the scientific theories in vogue are all atheistic, or have at least an atheistic tendency." Although proponents of methodological naturalism such as John William Draper and Andrew Dickson White doubtless overstated the case when they asserted the existence of long-standing "warfare" between science and religion, tension between science and traditional formulations of Christian faith did become one of the most conspicuous features of the American cultural landscape during the late nineteenth and early twentieth centuries.[21]

Christians who combined a muscular view of biblical authority with a vigorous supernaturalism did not hesitate to assail ideas put forward by members of the scientific community when those ideas seemed irreconcilable with their worldview. Beginning in the last quarter of the nineteenth century, the theory of organic evolution evoked especially vociferous expressions of outrage. That theory, many believers asserted, was not only "intended to eliminate the idea of God from the creation," but it was also "radically and irreconcilably antagonistic" to "the whole system of truth, for the revelation of which the Scriptures were given to men."[22]

Some proponents of the idea that supernaturalism played a central role in Christianity did not attack science head-on. They chose instead simply to call attention to the frequent instances of direct divine interpositions that they believed were occurring within the natural order. For numerous believers, ranging from Catholics and Christian Scientists to theologically conservative evangelicals from mainline, Holiness, and Pentecostal churches, the boundary line between the natural and the supernatural remained quite permeable. Those Christians not only held that God intervened within the created order to redeem sinners but insisted that the Deity also acted in "direct and supernatural" ways to heal mind and body alike. In addition, the doctrine of "entire sanctification" central to the Holiness movement and the Pentecostals' concept of the "latter rain" implied a supernaturalistic conception of divine activity that was inconsistent with the notion that all phenomena can be described in terms of natural agencies. Some Christians also cited God's responses to petitionary prayer as evidence that the Deity acted directly in the natural order without the mediation of natural laws and processes.[23]

During the late nineteenth and early twentieth centuries, Christians who occupied positions on the liberal end of the theological spectrum typically sought to make peace with ideas endorsed by the scientific community. Those believers, who regarded scientists as the most reliable arbiters of ideas concerning the natural world, expressed concern that opposition to their conclusions would drive literate men and women away from Christianity. From their perspective, it seemed obvious that "the future of Religion would be vastly more sure and prosperous if she could make science an ally instead of a rival."[24]

Believers committed to reconstructing theological formulations to bring them into line with the disclosures of modern science commonly insisted that the scriptures did not convey scientific truths. Even as they were thus imposing limits on the scope of biblical authority, however, many of those Christians also found themselves championing a concept of revelation that was broadened to include "everything that makes God known to men, and everything that is made known of him." Making use of that broadened concept, they asserted that nature served as a vehicle of divine revelation and that scientific inquiry played an important role in bringing that revelation to light.[25]

Americans intent on establishing harmony between Christian thought and the results of scientific investigation employed a variety of strategies in attempting to show that the naturalistic processes described by scientists were compatible with belief in an active, providential Deity. Some affirmed that God created and sustained the "mediate" causes that served as the object of scientific inquiry. Although that position was consistent with the idea that second causes could account for all activity within the natural world, many of its proponents refused to assume that God *always* worked through natural agencies. Rather, they retained the categories *natural* and *supernatural* and held that some events—in particular, the origin of matter, life, and mind— were the result of immediate divine infusions of "fresh creative energy."[26]

Most Christians who expressed allegiance to the tenor of modern science adopted a different approach. They regarded the impressive advances that scientists had made in expanding the realm of naturalistic discourse as a signal that it was time to repudiate the idea that divine activity within the natural world was limited to events that remained outside that realm. They chose instead to embrace a radical formulation of the doctrine of divine immanence that identified God's will and power as "the only real forces in nature." From that perspective, they reasoned that "the natural and supernatural are not two mutually exclusive spheres"—although science might well eventually be able to *describe* all phenomena in terms of natural processes, those phenomena could only be *explained* by appealing to the activity of an immanent Deity.[27]

Christians sympathetic to scientific inquiry made it clear that they were determined to interpret the results of that inquiry in ways that minimized their threat to important tenets of their worldview. For example, an unwillingness to abandon the conviction that human beings had been created in God's image prompted most believers who accepted an evolutionary interpretation of human origins to insist that humans possessed a variety of mental attributes—self-consciousness, the ability to reason, a moral sense, and the capacity for free will—that were different in kind from those found in other creatures. Similarly, Christian evolutionists commonly insisted on interpreting the theory of evolution in ways that left ample room for the kind of altruistic impulses that they associated with the teachings of Jesus.[28]

By the early twentieth century, many liberal Protestants were adopting a more chastened view of the theological usefulness of science and even the natural world. Their reading of German theologians such as Albrecht Ritschl did much to convince them that a sharp distinction existed between the realm of nature and the realm of the spirit. They emphasized that whereas the sciences were "disinterested" cognitive enterprises centered on discovering facts relating to natural phenomena and formulating theories based on those facts, religion dealt with the realm of human experience and employed the feelings and the will as well as the intellect in making "independent value judgments." Science and Christian theology were therefore complementary rather than overlapping enterprises. The relatively few liberal Catholics in America who commented on the relationship between science and Christianity also sought to detach the realm of theology from the realm of the natural sciences.[29]

1917–1960

The claim that science deals with the interaction of natural phenomena while religion centers on the private, more subjective realms of meaning and value continued to dominate discussions of liberal theology in America for much of the twentieth century. Nor were liberals alone in denigrating the theological value of science. Proponents of Protestant neo-orthodoxy, an important theological position in the United States between 1930 and 1960, devoted little attention to science, preferring instead to focus on God's redemptive activity as revealed through the person of Jesus and the pages of scripture. For their part, Catholic neo-scholastics, though embracing a theological perspective quite different from either the liberals or the neo-orthodox, expressed similar indifference to the idea of appealing to science in validating the claims of philosophical theology.[30]

Not all Christians ignored science. In the period after World War I, a few liberal Christians in the United States made concerted efforts to bring theology into closer alliance with the spirit of scientific inquiry. The dean of the University of Chicago Divinity School, Shailer Mathews, described the modernist theological project itself as "the use of the methods of modern science to find, state and use the permanent and central values of inherited orthodoxy in meeting the needs of a modern world." The desire to make the theological enterprise more "genuinely scientific" prompted Yale theologian Douglas Clyde Macintosh to espouse an "empirical theology" that employed the insights gleaned through religious experience to ascertain the characteristics that could be ascribed to God, whom Macintosh described as the "religious Object" of that experience.[31]

Many liberal Christians in the interwar period, however, made it clear that not every idea put forward in the name of science would receive their support. For example, their allegiance to the sanctity of personality led most liberals to reject deterministic psychological theories such as behaviorism, because of both their "indubitably materialistic tint" and their dismissive attitudes toward those aspects of human nature most closely associated with human selfhood. Similar concerns convinced many liberals to resist many of the claims associated with psychoanalysis.[32]

Christians who coupled allegiance to biblical inerrancy with affirmations of ongoing divine interventions within the created order charged that the naturalistic ideas put forward by the scientific community were fostering the growth of infidelity. In substantiating that charge, they appealed to statistical evidence that appeared during World War I indicating that the incidence of unbelief was considerably higher among scientists and the college students exposed to their ideas than it was among members of the population as a whole. Although proponents of biblical inerrancy and supernaturalism repeatedly insisted that they remained committed to the legitimacy of science, they made it clear that their understanding of science conformed to the dictionary's definition of it as knowledge based on inductively ascertained and verified facts and principles. Armed with that definition, they concluded that some events that took place within the natural world lay beyond the purview of scientific inquiry.[33]

During the period after World War I, a growing number of conservative Christians joined William Jennings Bryan in blaming the theory of evolution for both inspiring German militarism and undermining the faith of the nation's youth. More broadly, many regarded the increasing resonance of evolutionary ideas within mainline churches, secondary schools, colleges, theological seminaries, and other institutions as an especially apt symbol of the increasingly secular tenor of American culture and society. During the 1920s, such concerns led more than twenty state legislatures to debate laws expressing opposition to evolution, and three states actually succeeded in passing laws banning the teaching of human evolution in the public schools. Contrary to the view often popularized in American history textbooks, the Scopes trial did little to diminish the enthusiasm with which conservative Christians assailed evolution. Although by the end of the 1920s those believers had become less intent on seeking legislative action to ban the theory, they enjoyed a great deal of success thereafter in convincing publishers to minimize discussions of the subject in textbooks, removing works espousing evolutionary ideas from school libraries, and harassing teachers who introduced the theory in their classes.[34]

Not all Christians of conservative theological inclinations expressed interest in the religious implications of scientific ideas. It is noteworthy, for example, that prior to the furor associated with the Scopes trial, most members of the jury in that trial had been unaware that evolution was the object of theological controversy. It is also significant that although the General

Holiness Convention in the 1920s asserted that "the Holiness Movement *uniformly* believes that man is the product of God's immediate creation," it admonished its members to concentrate on "the battle for immediate salvation" rather than on the antievolutionary campaign. In this spirit, Nazarene theologian E. P. Ellyson warned his readers against excessive devotion to the scientific laboratory, lest they give insufficient attention to "the laboratory of Pneumatology and the development of the higher spiritual and immortal powers."[35]

Since 1970

In recent years, discussions of the relationship between science and religion have generated a great deal of interest, at least in part because the issue has become a focal point in the "culture wars." An increasing number of Christians who acknowledge the legitimacy of scientific inquiry have moved beyond the fact-value distinction in an effort to show that a theological "reading" of the natural world can plumb dimensions of reality deeper than those reached through scientific analysis. Georgetown University theologian John F. Haught, for example, has maintained that such a reading will not conflict with science but will yield a more profound understanding of the "cosmic purpose" informing nature than science is capable of providing. Conservative Protestants, operating from a theological perspective quite different from that of Haught, have denounced the naturalistic animus underlying scientific investigation. Those conservatives have emphasized that methodological naturalism constitutes an arbitrary and unjustifiably narrow conception of legitimate explanations for natural phenomena. Focusing primarily on what they see as the inadequacy of evolution, proponents of that view have advocated a variety of positions, ranging from the establishment of a balanced treatment of "evolution science" and "creation science" to the inclusion of explanations employing "Intelligent Design" in public school science classes. So far, at least, proponents of those positions have run aground of the courts, which have interpreted the teaching of both creationism and Intelligent Design as unlawful attempts to use the classroom to promote religious views. Court rulings, however, have not prevented many Christians from placing pressure on individual school districts, science teachers, and school board members, either to encourage the advocacy of alternatives to evolution in discussions of natural history or to teach the strengths and weaknesses of evolutionary theory.[36]

Although it seems doubtful that the scientific community will abandon naturalism as its methodological norm, it is quite clear that many Americans do not believe that this norm enables science to account for all events. Gallup Polls since 1982 have consistently revealed that somewhere between 43 percent and 47 percent of Americans believe that "God created human beings pretty much in their present form at one time within the past 10,000 years or so." In the "U.S. Religious Landscape Survey," a document compiled by the Pew Forum on Religion and Public Life, which appeared in 2008, 55 percent of Christians in "mainline churches," 62 percent in evangelical churches, 72 percent in historically black churches, and 54 percent in Catholic churches affirmed that they had received a "definite answer to a specific prayer request." Anywhere from a quarter to slightly over half of the Christians in those various groupings reported that they had "witnessed a divine healing of an illness or injury" at least several times a year. In June 2008, the *Washington Post* reported polling data that indicated that almost 80 percent of all Americans believe in the occurrence of miracles. These data strongly suggest that even in an age that quite clearly values scientific inquiry, belief in divine supernatural intervention within the natural order remains quite robust.[37]

NOTES

I wish to thank Ronald L. Numbers for his critical reading of the manuscript and Sara Georgini and Patricia Peknik for their assistance with the research on which parts of this paper are based. In addition, I continue to be grateful to Sharon Roberts (ILYS), Jeff Roberts, and Laura Roberts for their love and support.

1. Exemplary recent works treating the relationship between science and religion from a historical perspective include David C. Lindberg and Ronald L. Numbers, eds., *God and Nature: Historical Essays on the Encounter between Christianity and Science* (Berkeley: University of California Press, 1986); David C. Lindberg and Ronald L. Numbers, eds., *When Science and Christianity Meet* (Chicago: University of Chicago Press, 2003); and John Hedley Brooke, *Science and Religion: Some Historical Perspectives* (Cambridge: Cambridge University Press, 1991).

2. Perry Miller, *The New England Mind: The Seventeenth Century* (New York: Macmillan, 1939), 216–17, 224; Edward Taylor quoted in Robert Daly, *God's Altar: The World and the Flesh in Puritan Poetry* (Berkeley: University of California Press, 1978), 180; Anne Bradstreet quoted in ibid., 118; Thomas Hooker quoted in E. Brooks Holifield, *Theology in America: Christian Thought from the Age of the Puritans to the Civil War* (New Haven: Yale University Press, 2003), 33.

3. Samuel Eliot Morison, "The Harvard School of Astronomy in the Seventeenth

Century," *New England Quarterly* 7 (1934): 8–14, 16; Sara Schechner Genuth, "From Heaven's Alarm to Public Appeal: Comets and the Rise of Astronomy at Harvard," in *Science at Harvard University: Historical Perspectives*, ed. Clark A. Elliott and Margaret W. Rossiter (Bethlehem, Pa.: Lehigh University Press, 1992), 28–29, 32; Samuel Eliot Morison, *The Intellectual Life of Colonial New England* (New York: New York University Press, 1956), 246–47; Holifield, *Theology in America*, 72.

4. Genuth, "From Heaven's Alarm," 32 (includes quotation from John Cotton [1641]); Miller, *New England Mind*, 437–38; Keith Thomas, *Religion and the Decline of Magic* (1983; New York: Oxford University Press, 1996), 79; Gary B. Deason, "Reformation Theology and the Mechanistic Conception of Nature," in Lindberg and Numbers, *God and Nature*, 174; Michael P. Winship, *Seers of God: Puritan Providentialism in the Restoration and Early Enlightenment* (Baltimore: Johns Hopkins University Press, 1996), 10–15; David D. Hall, "A World of Wonders: The Mentality of the Supernatural in Seventeenth-Century New England," in *Seventeenth-Century New England*, ed. David D. Hall and David Grayson Allen (Boston: Colonial Society of Massachusetts, 1984), 251; John Winthrop, entry for July 1632, in *The Journal of John Winthrop, 1630–1649*, ed. Richard S. Dunn, James Savage, and Laetitia Yeandle (Cambridge: Belknap Press of Harvard University Press, 1996), 72.

5. John Cotton quoted in Holifield, *Theology in America*, 37; Hall, "World of Wonders," 239, 241, 251 (quotation on 241); "Extracts from John Eliot's Records of the First Church of Roxbury, Massachusetts (1643–1646)," in *Remarkable Providences, 1600–1760*, ed. John Demos (New York: George Braziller, 1972), 375–76; David D. Hall, *Worlds of Wonder, Days of Judgment: Popular Religious Belief in Early New England* (Cambridge: Harvard University Press, 1989), 73; Winship, *Seers of God*, 2.

6. John Morgan, "The Puritan Thesis Revisited," in *Evangelicals and Science in Historical Perspective*, ed. David N. Livingstone et al. (New York: Oxford University Press, 1999), 56, 58–59; John Cotton (1641) quoted in ibid., 57; John Cotton (1641) quoted in Theodore Hornberger, "Puritanism and Science: The Relationship Revealed in the Writings of John Cotton," *New England Quarterly* 10 (1937): 507.

7. Mark A. Noll, "The Rise and Long Life of the Protestant Enlightenment in America," in *Knowledge and Belief in America: Enlightenment Traditions and Modern Religious Thought*, ed. William M. Shea and Peter A. Huff (New York: Woodrow Wilson Center Press and Cambridge University Press, 1995), 88; Holifield, *Theology in America*, 59–83; Cotton Mather, *The Christian Philosopher*, ed. Winton U. Solberg (1721; Urbana: University of Illinois Press, 1994), 17; John Winthrop IV quoted in Charles Edwin Clark, "Science, Reason, and an Angry God: The Literature of an Earthquake," *New England Quarterly* 38 (1965): 353.

8. Maxine Van de Wetering, "Moralizing in Puritan Natural Science: Mysteriousness in Earthquake Sermons," *Journal of the History of Ideas* 43 (1982): 425; Thomas Prince (1749) quoted in Theodore Hornberger, "The Science of Thomas Prince," *New England Quarterly* 9 (1936): 36–37; Increase Mather, *Remarkable Providences Illustrative of the Earlier Days of American Colonisation* (originally entitled *An Essay for the Recording*

of Illustrious Providences) (1684; London: John Russell Smith, 1856), preface; Thomas Prince (1750) quoted in John E. Van de Wetering, "God, Science, and the Puritan Dilemma," *New England Quarterly* 38 (1965): 501, 498; Jonathan Edwards, *Original Sin* (1758), in *The Works of Jonathan Edwards*, vol. 3, ed. Clyde A. Holbrook (New Haven: Yale University Press, 1970), 400, 402–3 (quotations on 400, 403); Jonathan Edwards, "Things to Be Considered an[d] Written Fully About," in *Scientific and Philosophical Writings*, in *The Works of Jonathan Edwards*, vol. 6, ed. Wallace E. Anderson (New Haven: Yale University Press, 1980), 241–42.

9. Winship, *Seers of God*, 94; Holifield, *Theology in America*, 72; William D. Andrews, "The Literature of the 1727 New England Earthquake," *Early American Literature* 7 (1973): 282, 287, 283 (Cotton Mather quotations on 283).

10. Jonathan Edwards, "Images of Divine Things," in *Typological Writings*, vol. 11 of *The Works of Jonathan Edwards*, ed. Wallace E. Anderson et al. (New Haven: Yale University Press, 1993), 61; Edward M. Griffin, *Old Brick: Charles Chauncy of Boston, 1705–1787* (Minneapolis: University of Minnesota Press, 1980), 104–5; William Douglass quoted in Ronald L. Numbers, "Science without God: Natural Laws and Christian Beliefs," in Lindberg and Numbers, *When Science and Christianity Meet*, 270; Cotton Mather and five other clerics quoted in ibid.; I. Bernard Cohen, *Benjamin Franklin's Science* (Cambridge: Harvard University Press, 1990), 141–43.

11. Samuel Willard, *A Compleat Body of Divinity: In Two Hundred and Fifty Lectures on the Assembly's Shorter Catechism* (Boston: B. Green and S. Kneeland for B. Eliot and D. Henchman, 1726), 43; John Barnard (1738) quoted in Theodore Hornberger, *Scientific Thought in the American Colleges, 1638–1800* (Austin: University of Texas Press, 1946), 84; Samuel Langdon quoted in Harry S. Stout, *The New England Soul: Preaching and Religious Culture in Colonial New England* (New York: Oxford University Press, 1986), 297.

12. Donald Fleming, "The Judgment upon Copernicus in Puritan New England," in *L'aventure de l'esprit: Mélanges Alexandre Koyré*, 2 vols. (Paris: Hermann, 1964), 2:161; Mather, *Christian Philosopher*, 17–18; Edwards, "Images of Divine Things," 106; Benjamin Colman quoted in Theodore Hornberger, "Benjamin Colman and the Enlightenment," *New England Quarterly* 12 (1939): 233.

13. Noll, "Rise and Long Life," 88.

14. [Orville Dewey], "Diffusion of Knowledge," *North American Review* 30 (1830): 312; anonymous review of *The Indications of the Creator*, by George Taylor, *Knickerbocker* 39 (1852): 85; [John Price] Durbin, "On the Omnipresence of God," *Methodist Magazine and Quarterly Review* 2 (1831): 48 (italics in original); L. W. Green, "The Harmony of Revelation and Natural Science: With Especial Reference to Geology," in *Lectures on the Evidences of Christianity Delivered at the University of Virginia, during the Session of 1850–1* (New York: Robert Carter, 1851), 463; Jon H. Roberts, *Darwinism and the Divine in America: Protestant Intellectuals and Organic Evolution, 1859–1900* (Notre Dame: University of Notre Dame Press, 2001), 7–13; Jon H. Roberts and James Turner, *The Sacred and the Secular University* (Princeton: Princeton University Press, 2000), 23–24.

15. Orestes A. Brownson, *The Convert: or, Leaves from My Experience* (1857), in *The Works of Orestes A. Brownson*, collected and arranged by Henry F. Brownson, 20 vols. (1882–87; New York: AMS Press, 1966) 5:139; Charles E. Rosenberg, *The Cholera Years: The United States in 1832, 1849, and 1866* (Chicago: University of Chicago Press, 1962), esp. 5, 43, 220–21 (quotation from Gardiner Spring on 43).

16. John L. Girardeau, "The Glorious Gospel of the Blessed God" (1860), in *Sermons*, ed. George A. Blackburn (Columbia, S.C.: State Company, 1907), 200; James Marsh to Richard Henry Dana, August 21, 1832, in James Marsh et al., *Coleridge's American Disciples: The Selected Correspondence of James Marsh*, ed. John J. Duffy (Amherst: University of Massachusetts Press, 1973), 140; Erich Robert Paul, *Science, Religion, and Mormon Cosmology* (Urbana: University of Illinois Press, 1992), 27, 37; Brownson, "Spiritism and Spiritists" (1869), in *Works of Orestes A. Brownson*, 9:340.

17. Horace Bushnell, *Nature and the Supernatural, as Together Constituting the One System of God* (New York: Charles Scribner, 1858), 20; Richard Rabinowitz, *The Spiritual Self in Everyday Life: The Transformation of Personal Religious Experience in Nineteenth-Century New England* (Boston: Northeastern University Press, 1989), 153–216; Christine Leigh Heyrman, *Southern Cross: The Beginnings of the Bible Belt* (New York: Alfred A. Knopf, 1997), 61–62; Leigh Eric Schmidt, *Hearing Things: Religion, Illusion, and the American Enlightenment* (Cambridge: Harvard University Press, 2000), 38–77.

18. William B. Hayden, *Science and Revelation: or, The Bearing of Modern Scientific Developments upon the Interpretation of the First Eleven Chapters of Genesis* (Boston: Otis Clap, 1852), 77; [James Read Eckard], "The Logical Relations of Religion and Natural Science," *Biblical Repertory and Princeton Review* 32 (1860): 580; James A. Lyon, "The New Theological Professorship of Natural Science in Connection with Revealed Religion," *Southern Presbyterian Review* 12 (1859): 191; Heman Lincoln, "Development versus Creation," *Baptist Quarterly* 2 (1868): 257–58 (quotation on 258); R[ufus] P. S[tebbins], "The Religion of Geology," *Christian Examiner and Religious Miscellany*, 4th ser., 18, no. 53 (1852): 59.

19. Numbers, "Science without God," 272–79; W. N. Rice, "The Darwinian Theory of the Origin of Species," *New Englander* 26 (1867): 608; Roberts and Turner, *Sacred and the Secular University*, 25–29.

20. Edward D. Morris, "The Religious Consciousness Viewed as a Help and Test in Belief," *Presbyterian and Reformed Review* 1 (1890): 606; Henry Darling, "Preaching and Modern Skepticism," *Presbyterian Review* 2 (1881): 763–64 (quotation on 764).

21. J. Macbride Sterrett, "Apologetics—Its Proper Attitude at the Present Time," *American Church Review* 43 (1884): 143; William H. Durham (1910?) quoted in Douglas Jacobsen, *Thinking in the Spirit: Theologies of the Early Pentecostal Movement* (Bloomington: Indiana University Press, 2003), 142; Brownson, "Essays in Refutation of Atheism" (1873–74), in *Works of Orestes A. Brownson*, 2:1; John William Draper, *History of the Conflict between Religion and Science* (1874; New York: D. Appleton, 1875); Andrew Dickson White, *A History of the Warfare of Science with Theology in Christendom*, 2 vols. (New York: D. Appleton, 1896).

22. George B. Cheever, "The Philosophy of Evolution," *Presbyterian Quarterly and Princeton Review* 4 (1875): 130; John A. Earnest, "Evolution and the Scriptures," *Lutheran Quarterly* 12 (1882): 105; John T. Duffield, "Evolutionism, Respecting Man and the Bible," *Princeton Review*, 4th ser. (1878): 173–74.

23. A. J. Gordon quoted in Heather Curtis, *Faith in the Great Physician: Suffering and Divine Healing in American Culture, 1860–1900* (Baltimore: Johns Hopkins University Press, 2007), 98; Robert Bruce Mullin, *Miracles and the Modern Religious Imagination* (New Haven: Yale University Press, 1996), 58–220; Grant Wacker, *Heaven Below: Early Pentecostals and American Culture* (Cambridge: Harvard University Press, 2001), 92–93; Richard Ostrander, "Proving the Living God: Answered Prayer as a Modern Fundamentalist Apologetic," *Fides et Historia* 28, no. 3 (Fall 1996): 69–89.

24. James T. Bixby, *Similarities of Physical and Religious Knowledge* (New York: D. Appleton, 1876), 10–11 (quotation on 11).

25. William Rupp, "The Theory of Evolution and the Christian Faith," *Reformed Quarterly Review* 35 (1888): 162–63 (quotation on 162); John W. Chadwick, "The Revelation of God," *Unitarian Review* 27 (1887): 495; Roberts, *Darwinism and the Divine*, 146–56.

26. M. H. Valentine, "The Influence of the Theory of Evolution on the Theory of Ethics," *Lutheran Quarterly Review* 28 (1898): 218; Roberts, *Darwinism and the Divine*, 136.

27. B. F. Cocker, *The Theistic Conception of the World: An Essay in Opposition to Certain Tendencies of Modern Thought* (New York: Harper, 1875), 175; George T. Ladd, "The Origin of the Concept of God," *Bibliotheca Sacra* 34 (1877): 35; Roberts, *Darwinism and the Divine*, 137–43.

28. Roberts, *Darwinism and the Divine*, 175–79, 184–92.

29. Albrecht Ritschl, *The Christian Doctrine of Justification and Reconciliation: The Positive Development of the Doctrine*, ed. H. R. Mackintosh and A. B. Macaulay, 3 vol., 3rd ed. (New York: Charles Scribner's, 1900) 3:16, 398, 205, 225; J. L. Spalding, *Lectures and Discourses* (New York: Catholic Publication Society, 1890), 54, 59.

30. Ian G. Barbour, *Issues in Science and Religion* (Englewood Cliffs, N.J.: Prentice-Hall, 1966), 116–19; Langdon Gilkey, *Naming the Whirlwind: The Renewal of God-Language* (Indianapolis: Bobbs-Merrill, 1969), 82–91; William M. Halsey, *The Survival of American Innocence: Catholicism in an Era of Disillusionment, 1920–1940* (Notre Dame: University of Notre Dame Press, 1980), 156–59.

31. Shailer Mathews, *The Faith of Modernism* (New York: Macmillan, 1924), 23; Douglas Clyde Macintosh, *Theology as an Empirical Science* (New York: Macmillan, 1919), 5, 25–27.

32. George A. Coe, "What Constitutes a Scientific Interpretation of Religion?" *Journal of Religion* 6 (1926): 233; Jon H. Roberts, "Psychoanalysis and American Religion, 1900–45," in Lindberg and Numbers, *When Science and Christianity Meet*, 225–44.

33. James H. Leuba, *The Belief in God and Immortality: A Psychological, Anthropological, and Statistical Study* (Boston: Sherman, French, 1916), 177, 187–218, 250, 277–79; Jon H. Roberts, "Conservative Evangelicals and Science Education in American Col-

leges and Universities, 1890–1940," *Journal of the Historical Society* 5 (2005): 304, 308–9, 312; Michael Lienesch, *In the Beginning: Fundamentalism, the Scopes Trial, and the Making of the Antievolution Movement* (Chapel Hill: University of North Carolina Press, 2007), 61–68.

34. Ronald L. Numbers, *The Creationists: From Scientific Creationism to Intelligent Design*, expanded ed. (Cambridge: Harvard University Press, 2006), 55–57; Roberts, "Conservative Evangelicals," 301; George M. Marsden, *Fundamentalism and American Culture*, 2nd ed. (New York: Oxford University Press, 2006), 148–49, 170, 179; Lienesch, *In the Beginning*, 61–71, 82, 171–72, 176–78, 204–5; Judith V. Grabiner and Peter D. Miller, "Effects of the Scopes Trial," *Science* 185 (1974): 832–37.

35. Jeffrey P. Moran, "The Scopes Trial and Southern Fundamentalism in Black and White: Race, Region, and Religion," *Journal of Southern History* 70 (2004): 99; General Holiness Convention (1923) quoted in Ronald L. Numbers, "Creation, Evolution, and Holy Ghost Religion: Holiness and Pentecostal Responses to Darwinism," in Ronald L. Numbers, *Darwinism Comes to America* (Cambridge: Harvard University Press, 1998), 117–18; E. P. Ellyson quoted in ibid., 124.

36. John F. Haught, *Deeper Than Darwin: The Prospect for Religion in the Age of Evolution* (Boulder: Westview, 2003), 17, 25, 45; Numbers, *Creationists*, 208–85, 373–98; Lienesch, *In the Beginning*, 209–16, 219–25, 231–34.

37. Pew Forum on Religion and Public Life, "U.S. Religious Landscape Survey," http://www.gallup.com/poll/21814/Evolution-Creationism-Intelligent-Design.aspx?version (accessed December 16, 2008), 187–88; Jacqueline L. Salmon, "Most Americans Believe in Higher Power, Poll Finds," in Washingtonpost.com, http://www.washingtonpost.com/wp-dyn/content/article/2008/06/23/AR2008062300813_p (accessed October 2, 2008).

"My Homosexuality Is Getting Worse Every Day"

Norman Vincent Peale, Psychiatry, and the Liberal Protestant Response to Same-Sex Desires in Mid-Twentieth-Century America

The Reverend Dr. Norman Vincent Peale famously urged Americans to engage in "positive thinking" to rid themselves of guilt, pain, and insolvency. That message of healing through faith and optimism captured the imaginations of millions of Americans who read his best-selling self-help books (most famously, the 1952 blockbuster hit *The Power of Positive Thinking*), tuned in to his radio programs, and listened to his sermons from his pulpit at the Marble Collegiate Church in New York City. Less understood has been Peale's unlikely role as a spokesman for postwar liberal Protestant understandings of same-sex desire. In December 1956, Peale used his regular advice column in *Look* magazine, a popular biweekly, nationally distributed, family magazine, to reprint and respond to a young man's agonized query about homosexuality. The published exchange exposed *Look*'s readers to theories about the psychological sources—and possible "cure"—of same-sex desire that had been circulating among psychiatrists and among some liberal Protestant clergy who found such theories appealing. Theological liberals like Peale gravitated toward psychiatry's definition of homosexuality as a psychological disorder rather than a sin or a criminal proclivity, at a time of growing public hostility toward gay and lesbian people. The man's letter, Peale's printed advice, and the unpublished letters that Peale received in response reveal how the liberal Protestant appropriation of psychiatry created a normative vision of heterosexual marriage and "mature" personhood that framed mid-twentieth-century understandings of homosexuality.

Among American believers, liberal Protestants were, like Reform Jews and other theologically modernist denominations, especially inclined to interpret their faith according to the insights of science. Liberal Protestant leaders, according to one historian, "saw great possibility in science, particularly its promise to alleviate human suffering."[1] Faith in science buttressed the liberal Protestant belief in an immanent God, one who acted through human beings and whose rewards could accrue in human history. The Social Gospel of the late nineteenth and early twentieth centuries found liberal Protestants endeavoring to solve broad, systemic problems like poverty using tools from the social sciences; by the 1940s, much of that energy had turned inward, applying Freudian theory to resolve individuals' psychological and interpersonal conflicts. Pastoral counseling, a movement to help ministers become more psychologically sophisticated and therapeutically adept, epitomized this mid-twentieth-century liberal Protestant proclivity for therapeutic treatments. Peale propelled the liberal Protestant ethos of human and spiritual progress to new heights of optimism. He promised unlimited happiness for people who believed in a benevolent God, followed his recommendations for "positive thinking," and attained a psychologically "mature" adulthood. Pastoral counselors' conversations about same-sex desire, psychology, and religion had been limited to the narrow confines of professional publications and conferences until Peale, an artful popularizer of psychologically oriented Protestantism, used his column in *Look* to advise a young gay man.

Thanks to Peale's ability to bring esoteric discussions about homosexuality and pastoral counseling to a general audience, mid-century Americans who read his column learned that they might view homosexual desires as symptoms of psychiatric disorders that interfered with an individual's chances for a happy marriage. Peale and other liberal Protestant pastoral counselors defined marriage as the apex of social and spiritual maturity—and thus worried that homosexuality constituted a stubborn impediment to both psychological health and moral progress. Pastoral counselors were worried about helping members of Protestant congregations develop successful marriages at a time when Americans more broadly were idealizing the nuclear family—mother, father, and children—as the basis of a stable, moral Cold War society.[2] Liberal Protestants such as Peale embraced the secular celebration of the postwar nuclear family wholeheartedly. The liberal Protestant appropriation of psychiatry shaped this national preoccupation with marriage by framing the pursuit of marital happiness as a path to emotional, spiritual, and psychological well-being—and conversely characterizing homosexuality as a psychological illness that impaired a person's ability to attain (hetero)sexually "mature" relationships. The absence of sin from liberal Protestant interpretations of homosexuality attested to the extent to which Peale and others relied on psychiatric theories to explain their moral universe. It left unresolved the question of how Christians should reconcile psychiatric definitions with biblical texts, a dilemma that theologically conservative Protestants would take up with zeal later in the twentieth century.

Peale, *Look*, and Positive Thinking

By the time this column appeared in *Look* in the mid-1950s, Peale had become one of the most recognizable ministers in the United States, well known for promoting the connections among body, mind, and spirit. He was born in 1898 in Bowersville, Ohio, a small town an hour's drive from Cincinnati. Peale attended the theological seminary at Boston University, but his religious philosophy owed as much to a long American tradition of probing the powers of the mind as it did to any formal religious training. During the nineteenth century, Ralph Waldo Trine, the father of the New Thought movement, had portrayed God as "an immanent force, pervading the universe, reflected in human higher consciousness, and potentiating in power, energy, and growth . . . ever ready to bestow health, peace, and well-being" on those who tuned in. Peale adapted New Thought principles of mental healing and coached his congregants to cultivate the spiritual power of the mind. He had already built a reputation for dynamic preaching, which emphasized "personal religion" and its practical effects, when he accepted a ministerial position at Marble Collegiate Church in New York City in 1932. With a substantial endowment and a tiny congregation, Marble Collegiate Church offered the ambitious preacher the resources and spare time he needed to bring his message of personal spiritual healing to a wider audience. Over the next two decades, Peale's ministry expanded from the pews of Marble Collegiate Church to America's living rooms. During the 1930s, the National Broadcasting Company carried his first radio program, *The Art of Living*, and he published his first "inspirational books," *The Art of Living* (1937) and *You Can Win* (1938). Peale described religious faith as a "power channel," through which the "spiritual Christ" would flow, using language that encouraged millions of Americans to believe that hard work and prayer could help them attain the joy, health, and material comforts they desired.[3]

Peale's fame skyrocketed in 1952 with the publication of *The Power of Positive Thinking*, a self-help guide that promised its readers "new life, new power, increased efficiency, [and] greater happiness," if they followed an eclectic strategy of personal prayer and "new thought patterns."[4] *The Power of Positive Thinking* established Peale as the preeminent expositor of Christian popular psychology. The book showcased his seamless—if often non-sensical—interpolation of psychosomatic medicine, New Thought theology, and moralism. Peale promised Christian rewards such as redemption, grace, and heavenly approval for men and women who learned how to discipline their minds and experience God's power. He described a world riddled with psychological as well as theological traps: the wise reader would learn to abjure both anxiety and sin. At points, the book elided distinctions between psychological and spiritual issues entirely; Peale often characterized anxiety and guilt as "sinful" attitudes. More rigorous theologians and intellectuals blasted Peale's book for its inconsistencies and accused the author of popu-larizing vacuous distortions of both Protestantism and psychology. A typi-cal critique of Peale's wildly popular theology came from the Reverend Dr. Paul Calvin Payne, a Philadelphia-area minister who oversaw the Christian education activities of both the National Council of the Churches of Christ in the U.S.A. and the Presbyterian Church in the U.S.A. By the time Payne criticized Peale, in February of 1955, for promulgating "easy optimistic senti-ments" and ignoring the Christian ethic of sacrifice, *The Power of Positive Thinking* had already spent 118 weeks on the *New York Times'* best-seller list.[5] Regardless of the qualms Peale's colleagues had about his interpreta-tions of Protestant theology, millions of Americans looked to him for advice about faith, health, and success.

Look magazine afforded Peale another opportunity to showcase the bene-fits of positive thinking when it introduced his column on June 29, 1954. "Norman Vincent Peale Answers Your Questions" featured readers' ques-tions on topics ranging from financial debt to crises of faith. Every two weeks, from June 1954 until March 1959, *Look* printed excerpts from four to eleven of those letters (and also, most likely, questions that Peale and the editors concocted—could it be that a sixteen-year-old wrote to Peale, "I . . . would like a few pointers on the problems I shall have to face when I go on my first date"?).[6] Among the more than 800 questions that Peale answered, topics ranged from vocational advancement to communism to the efficacy of prayer. The vast majority of the questions pertained to marital conflicts, vocational problems, and teenage angst (including young people complain-ing about myopic parents and about the sexual pressures of dating). An all-purpose clearinghouse for common sense, "Norman Vincent Peale Answers Your Questions" promised its readers that nearly any problem, from fear of nuclear attack to grief over a young child's death to paralyzing shyness, could be overcome.

Peale therefore had a well-established reputation as an authority on morality and on mental health when *Look*, in its December 11, 1956, issue, carried his answer to a nineteen-year-old who, his excerpted letter explained, feared that he was homosexual. The author, an anonymous college student, articulated his frustration with his sexual nonconformity: "I am homosexually inclined. I want to be like other boys. I have tried hard to be like them, but there is just something missing. I simply can't get interested in girls, but I can in boys. I am 19 now and will be a sophomore in college this fall. This problem has been bothering me for a long time. Now that I am getting older, I want to know what I can do about it. I hate being this way and want to do something about my problem if I can."[7]

Uncharacteristically, Peale made no pretences about the efficacy of positive thinking when he answered this question about same-sex desire. Instead, he referred the young man directly to psychiatric help:

> If you want to get over your trouble and [if you] have the will to follow directions, I feel sure you can become a normal person. You are suffering from an emotional sickness. Incidentally, I have received many letters through this page relative to this problem. Depth psychology has worked out effective methods of treatment for such trouble. Consult a good psychiatrist. If you prefer, the American Foundation of Religion and Psychiatry in New York, where psychiatrists and ministers work together, will be glad to help you, or any reader of *Look*, regarding any personal problems free of charge.[8]

By directing the young man and other readers to the American Foundation of Religion and Psychiatry (AFRP), the clinic that he and the Freudian-trained psychiatrist Smiley Blanton had cofounded, Peale identified homosexuality as a mental health ailment that competent, religiously sensitive counseling could treat. Peale thus endorsed and helped publicize a therapeutic definition of same-sex desires.

Homosexuality and American Religion at Mid-Century

Peale appropriated psychiatry to explain (and, he hoped, to cure) homosexual desires at a moment when homosexuality was more visible, but also more vigorously scrutinized, than at any prior point in U.S. history. Since the colonial era, Americans have equivocated over whether same-sex desire permeated a person's character or reflected transitory lust that might be eliminated by prayer, medical treatments, or some combination of the two.[9] Scientists had created the terms "homosexuality" and "heterosexuality" in the late nineteenth century to describe discrete categories of psychological pathology.[10] Defining and controlling those categories of sexual desire became one of the hallmarks of "modern" sexuality, which one historian encapsulates as "the twentieth-century redefinition of sexuality as a means of self-realization rooted in pleasure and unconnected to reproduction." Attempts to clarify who—and what—constituted homosexuals tended, however, to confuse lawyers, physicians, social purity reformers, and government officials. Their limited categories of "normal" and "deviant" sexual behaviors obscured the multivalent desires and practices of men who had sex with men and women who had sex with women.[11] Gay and lesbian identities emerged within vibrant urban subcultures at the turn of the twentieth century, independent of scientists' attempts to develop a taxonomy of sexual deviance.[12] By the 1920s, "the homosexual" had emerged not only as a medical type but also as a general term for a rich array of sexual identities and desires.

Americans' attitudes toward homosexuality—and toward "homosexuals" as a distinct class of people—grew increasingly hostile in the 1930s and into the early Cold War years. When police officers raided gay bars and bathhouses in the name of saving Americans from "sexual psychopaths," they forced the nascent gay subculture underground and taught the American public to regard same-sex desire as a malicious contagion.[13] Medicalizing and pathologizing homosexuality became official government policy during World War II, when the U.S. military began to screen all enlistees for homosexuality and instituted a policy of discharging suspected homosexuals.[14] The U.S. government continued to label, isolate, and ostracize homosexuals during the 1940s and 1950s as part of its official Cold War foreign policy. According to historian David K. Johnson, during the "Lavender Scare" of the 1950s and 1960s, "approximately 1,000 persons were dismissed from the Department of State for alleged homosexuality"; the federal government pilloried homosexuals as a deviant subset of Americans who were prone to subversion, betrayal, and crime. The military, meanwhile, policed homosexual "tendencies" among women who served in its ranks.[15] American popular culture reflected this homophobic attitude; films and pulp fiction novels portrayed gay men and lesbians as psychotic killers. By the time Peale's reply to the homosexual college student appeared in Look in the mid-1950s, gay and lesbian Americans had adopted secrecy as a survival tactic.[16]

American professionals addressing the "homosexual problem" in the postwar period could not agree upon precisely what homosexuality was or what caused it, but Peale adopted the most popular explanation of the day: homosexuality was a curable psychiatric disorder, a symptom of psychosexual immaturity.[17] Although a few progressive voices within the psychiatric profession advised tolerance of and sympathy for the homosexual patient, a conventional wisdom rapidly coalesced around the idea that homosexuality might be responsive to intensive psychiatric therapy. As the influential psychoanalyst Irving Bieber taught, children who identified too closely with an opposite-sex parent often failed to develop mature heterosexual desires, until developmental obstructions grew into sexual pathologies. Given enough psychoanalytic treatment, Bieber wrote, "every homosexual is a latent heterosexual."[18] Liberal Protestants such as Peale who were interested in pastoral counseling recapitulated psychoanalytic theories of homosexuality throughout the 1950s. Dr. Roy A. Burkhart, who led the First Community Church in Columbus, Ohio, and authored books on premarital and marital counseling, described heterosexuality as the apex of emotional and sexual adjustment in *The Freedom to Become Yourself* (1957): "Heterosexuality is right and follows naturally. . . . If father and mother are well-adjusted and love each other, the child will catch the spirit of it." As he explained in an undated premarital counseling pamphlet, "When two people are mature, they are heterosexual."[19] Smiley Blanton, Peale's colleague at the AFRP, informed Peale's views of homosexuality most profoundly. Blanton encapsulated his theories of sexual desire in the self-help guide he coauthored with Peale, *Faith Is the Answer* (1955). "Such an impulse in people [toward sexual intercourse with someone of the same sex]," Blanton explained in one of his chapters, "is obviously due to an early, childish relationship for which they are not to blame." Psychiatrists could treat people who suffered from "an undue degree of love for persons of the same sex," but "a great many conferences are always necessary to change this condition."[20] Peale and other liberal Protestant pastoral counselors were especially amenable to the work of psychiatrists like Bieber and Blanton who promised that homosexuals could be "cured" and thus could ultimately overcome their sexual immaturity to enjoy happy marriages.

When the topic of homosexuality surfaced within pastoral counseling literature it was portrayed as a mental disorder that obstructed individuals' capacity for a "normal" life, defined as the enjoyment of heterosexual marriage. *Pastoral Psychology*, a journal for liberal Protestant (and some Reform

Jewish) clergy interested in pastoral counseling, occasionally featured discussions of homosexuality as part of the journal's mission to help ministers become more therapeutically sophisticated counselors. In a regular feature called the "Minister's Consultation Clinic," the journal published questions submitted by ministers from around the country and responses from both secular and religious authorities. One minister asked for advice about how to deal with two hand-holding women in his church: "I have come to realize there is a situation of 'unnatural affection' here. . . . It is believed that [the women's] constant association is characterized by one acting as a man and the other as a woman." Seeking confirmation of whether "unnatural affection" was even possible between two women as he knew it to be between two men, the minister asked, "Does holding hands in church, sleeping together, and constant companionship indicate a possibility?" A psychiatrist instructed the minister (and readers of the journal) to view homosexuals empathically as sufferers of a serious, but treatable, condition: "This phenomenon can be regarded as a kind of mental illness and not as a willful perversity. . . . The minister should hope to exploit any opportunity to get either party into competent psychiatric hands." Seward Hiltner, a highly regarded liberal Protestant educator and advocate of pastoral counseling, urged ministers to view these women as homosexual individuals with stunted psychological developmental processes: "Both these women have been unable to reach the kind of maturity in which the most deeply-sought love object is fundamentally different from oneself, of the other sex."[21] The emerging liberal Protestant understanding of homosexuality defined it as a mental illness or as the consequence of a deep-seated psychological conflict. According to this paradigm, homosexuality rendered its sufferers emotionally incapable of heterosexual marriage unless they could get help from a psychiatrist.

Liberal Protestants' relatively progressive stance toward homosexuality contrasted sharply with how most Christians discussed same-sex desire at mid-century—that is, when they discussed it at all. In a memoir about his Fundamentalist Protestant upbringing, marriage, and eventual coming-out, Mel White described the silence that engulfed all aspects of sexuality but that especially concealed homosexuality. White, who was born in 1940, learned during his early adolescent years that his religion abhorred homosexuality, and he grappled with glaring omissions in his religious sexual education: "I can't recall one sermon on homosexuality in all my early years of church and Sunday school attendance. In fact, I hardly remember anyone, including my loving parents, mentioning sex at all."[22] Evangelicals rejected liberal Protestants' (and psychologists' and psychiatrists') conceptualizations of sexuality as something constructed, contingent, and changeable; the extant printed record suggests that they avoided discussions of homosexuality almost entirely.

Instead, Fundamentalist and evangelical Protestants focused their ruminations about marriage and sexuality on the importance of two distinct, discrete, and complementary sexes that were essential for the survival of moral Christian family life.[23] In that, they shared with theological liberals like Peale an overriding concern about heterosexual marriage, but conservative Protestants took a much different view of the appropriate roles of men and women. John R. Rice, a popular Fundamentalist Baptist preacher and author, published books in the 1940s that interpreted passages from the New Testament (and particularly from Ephesians) as rubrics for wifely submission and manly household headship. In *Bobbed Hair, Bossy Wives, and Women Preachers* (1941), he railed against women who pretended to assume masculine roles. In *Home—Courtship, Marriage, and Children* (1945), he taught readers how to achieve "Christian" ideals of biblically based gender complementarity in their own families.[24] Far more preoccupied with the dangers of gender equality than with sexual perversions, conservative Protestants endeavored to maintain a complementary gender hierarchy that adhered to what they believed to be a divinely ordained, moral mandate for male-female gender differences.

Peale, by contrast, equated rigid gender roles with "immaturity" in his frequent discussions of marital conflict in *Look*. He answered more questions about marital difficulties than about any other subject in his *Look* column, invariably urging husbands and (more often) wives to reconcile after betrayals or disappointments. In a special column on September 16, 1958, "How to Make Marriage Work," he devoted his page to describing the gender ideals that he believed led to marital conflicts. Too many men, Peale wrote, expected to become "lord and master of the home, handling the money, doling out an allowance, while the wife supposedly has the business sense of the babe in the woods." Women suffered under comparable delusions. He explained: "Many women consciously or unconsciously seem to regard themselves as art objects to be taken care of by a father substitute in the form of a husband. This immature, infantile un-grown-up state of mind assumes as the wifely right that the woman is to be made 'happy.'" Instead, he encouraged couples to view marriage "as a team relationship," which he believed resembled God's plan for unity between man and woman. (True to form, Peale then enumerated ten steps to achieve marital harmony.)[25]

Peale's message of treatment and cure also contrasted with the response of some Protestant leaders to the "sex panics" of the 1950s. In cities and towns across the United States, police officers and clergy joined forces to protect American youth from supposedly predatory homosexuals. As historian John Howard has shown in his study of postwar Atlanta, when public officials and law enforcement officers stepped up their surveillance of sex between men in public restrooms and parks during the mid-1950s, religious leaders were instrumental in shaping their intolerant attitudes toward homosexuality. The presiding judge in one notorious case involving sex in a public library restroom even ordered several of the men who had been caught by the vice squad (all of whom pleaded guilty) to have evangelical Protestant ministers supervise their probation.[26] In the mid- to late 1960s, a Baptist deacon and "former head of the Miami vice squad," adamant that he would "rather see any of my children dead than homosexual," similarly combined recitations of scriptural prohibitions against sodomy with a defense of the need to criminalize sex between men.[27] But avoidance rather than vitriol may have typified the conservative Protestant attitude toward homosexuality during the 1950s. Although much more research remains to be done about how liberal and conservative Protestants understood homosexuality in the post–World War II years, these scattered examples suggest that perhaps most Protestants, when they felt forced to confront it, associated homosexuality with sinful desires and criminal behaviors.

Nevertheless, Peale's decision to print the young man's letter about same-sex desires and the sin-free language he used to address the issue illuminate the complexity and diversity of Protestant understandings of homosexuality in the mid-twentieth century. By the 1940s and 1950s, historian Heather White explains, liberal Protestant pastoral counselors had begun to agree that "homosexuality must be approached as a developmental and not a moral issue."[28] Peale's therapeutic approach to homosexuality suggested a third option: that Protestant clergy might view homosexuality as a psychological stumbling block on the path to self-improvement. At the same time, Peale tiptoed around his chosen subject matter, employing euphemisms and elisions to address his correspondent's concerns. Despite Peale's claim that he had received multiple letters expressing anxiety about same-sex desires, this exchange represented the first and the last time that the word "homosexual" (in the phrase "homosexually inclined") appeared in his column. Notably, Peale himself dared not speak its name. His response referred to the young man's same-sex desires elliptically as "emotional sickness," "this problem," and "such trouble."

"The Secret of My Heart"
Readers Respond to Peale

The relative dearth of religious voices discussing homosexuality sympatheti-cally in the public sphere helps explain why Peale's answer struck a chord among *Look*'s readers. All together, 130 letters survive of men and women from throughout the United States and Canada who wrote to Peale express-ing hope, confusion, and desperation about same-sex desires. Individuals who suspected or knew that they had homosexual desires wrote the bulk of these letters (10 from women, 108 from men), but a few mothers and fathers sought help for their children. Only one correspondent objected to Peale's advice. Dozens of men wrote that the boy's story in *Look* might have been their own. Unable to "cure" themselves (and several noted that they had tried), they seized upon Peale's offer of psychiatric help. Peale's corre-spondents largely accepted his description of homosexuality as a disease and found hope in the prospect of a cure. As G.A., a man from Arizona, explained in a letter to Peale, "I wonder Dr. if you can help me [by] sending me some information on how to stop this terrible disease. I can't live any longer this way. I am 29 years of age and my homosexuality is getting worse every day. I really want to stop, and lead a normal life."[29] This pursuit of the normal life was Peale's stock-in-trade: his ethos of positive thinking prom-ised that a life full of emotional, material, and spiritual rewards was within the grasp of every earnest striver.

Respondents to Peale's column accepted his description of homosexu-ality as an ailment, describing how their condition isolated them within their home communities, where homosexuality was rarely, if ever, discussed. One nineteen-year-old from Montana asked for the AFRP's address so that he could find relief: "To be cured would make me the happiest person in the world."[30] This man and several others expressed their fear of seeking help in their hometowns and having their sexuality discovered by family and friends. Three men and one woman confessed to Peale that he was the first person they had ever told about their sexual desires. One of the men, who was studying to become a minister, described his sexual longings as "the se-cret of my heart."[31] Articulating those secrets in letters to Peale offered these men and women a rare opportunity to acknowledge their desires and ideally receive some empathy for their predicaments.

The cure that many of these men and women sought centered on the attainment of marriage and children, a desire that reflected the ethos of the postwar Baby Boom generation that glorified middle-class family life. As one Nebraska man expressed it, "I am 29 now and am wondering if it is too late for me to correct this most depressing situation. To me life is meaningless unless I can be cured as I want a home and family."[32] None of these writers recognized any possibility for family life within a homosexual framework. For all of them, family formation demanded heterosexuality. "More than anything," wrote E.P., a sophomore at a college in Alabama, "I want to fall in love with a wonderful girl, marry her and be a father someday." If he could not marry and become "a respectable citizen," E.P. wrote, he might reach a terrible end: "I cannot live with this guilt and fear which has kept me from having even the smallest degree of self-confidence, and which I know could ruin my life. Sir, I beg you from the bottom of my heart to help me. I am appealing to you for my very life. Please, please help me."[33] Whether E.P. feared that he would be the victim of gay-bashing or crime, or whether he worried that his despair might lead him to suicide, his letter suggested that the attainment of a happy marriage signified for him the ultimate proof of his worth as a person. A twenty-four-year-old man from Lubbock, Texas, explained that he had been attracted to boys since junior high: "It has become so worrisome that it now haunts me continually, for above everything else in this world, I want to have a wife and as many children as I can afford. . . . I know that in order to have a happy home complete with a loving wife and children I must stop having tendencies (in the wrong way) toward boys, and that these tendencies must be channeled in the right direction." Now in his senior year of college, he kept his sexual feelings secret from all of his friends and family members. "Truthfully, I am at my wit's end. Something has to be done."[34]

Correspondents who described prior attempts to benefit from psychiatric treatment did not share Peale's optimism about psychiatry's power to cure homosexuality. T.J., a man from Montana, explained that he had consulted a psychiatrist in Denver and contacted a California hospital "that specializes in the treatment of sexually maladjusted people." A cure had eluded him, and now he found himself unable "to follow through as far as treatment" was concerned.[35] E.C., a twenty-two-year-old man in New Jersey, wrote that his parents had already taken him to see Dr. John Money at Johns Hopkins University Hospital. During the 1950s, Money was building a national reputation as an expert on "gender role" development and intersexuality. He tended to disagree with psychoanalysts about the causes of homosexual desires. Money developed a behaviorist model, in which people learned throughout their lives the "language" of gender, and he asserted that gender roles had no bearing on mental health. Homosexuality, according to Money, represented an organic development of a person's lifetime experiences, not a pathology. Indeed, E.C. wrote, "I have been advised by [Money] that there is no hope, only in exceptional cases, of a cure. I was advised that seeing a psychiatrist would be only necessary if I found I could not adjust to accepting what I am."[36] When psychiatric efforts to cure homosexuality were obtained, they could lead to depression. A woman wrote to Peale about her twenty-year-old son, who had been discharged from the army for being homosexual and had subsequently sought psychiatric care. Since then, her son "says that he doesn't feel that way any longer, but he isn't interested in girls and is very listless most of the time."[37] For another person, psychiatric care remained financially unfeasible.[38] The very solution Peale offered had not, in the experiences of these correspondents, achieved its intended result.

The absence of religion and prayer from Peale's published reply puzzled other correspondents. Several asked Peale how he reconciled biblical passages that seemed to condemn homosexuality with a psychiatric assessment of sexual disease. One mother in Illinois described her confusion over how to decipher the religious and psychological sources of same-sex desire. After she "accidentally" discovered her son's sexual inclinations, her son moved to San Francisco and ceased contact with his family. The mother turned to psychiatrists at the University of Iowa, where she learned that her son had probably received "too much Mom" and "too little Dad" during his childhood—a diagnosis in keeping with how most postwar psychiatrists traced men's same-sex desires to their mothers' behaviors. Her subsequent quest for information about homosexuality led her to Freud, the Bible, and frustration with conflicting explanations. She reacted to Peale's description of homosexuality as a sickness with evident exasperation: "Yes I know that's the theory, but what about I Corinthians 6:9? In my Revised Standard Version it says 'Do you not know—Do not be deceived—Neither, nor homosexuals will inherit the kingdom of God? And such were some of you. . . .' I can only say that these conflicting statements, have caused much anxiety and grief to me. If the experts can't agree, how can the layman expect to draw conclusions or get any help?"[39] A sophomore at the University of Iowa likewise wrote: "This matter causes me considerable concern and frustration. I have approached my problem from so many different angles, including the principles set forth in *The Power of Positive Thinking*, without much help. Always in the back of my mind is I Corinthians 6:9."[40] Craving instructions for reconciling psychiatry's definition of homosexuality with their Christian faith, these writers complained that Peale's brusque response had skirted central theological issues.

Letters attest to the extent to which Americans trusted Peale to advise them about sexual matters, but they also reveal the unresolved tension that many of Peale's readers perceived between his reliance on psychiatric treatment and his role as a minister. Because Peale evidenced no compunction about expounding upon the moral implications of anxiety, doubt, or premarital petting, his silence on the moral dimensions of same-sex desire baffled, and in some instances irked, readers for whom the issue was of paramount concern. Although Peale had tried, through his collaboration with Blanton, to integrate liberal Protestantism and psychiatry throughout his professional endeavors, his response to the young man's question about homosexuality marks an instance in which he appeared to cede authority to scientific theory. Peale's deference to psychiatric expertise failed to provide his readers with a theological framework for interpreting the origins or implications of same-sex desires.

The Pursuit of Heterosexual Happiness

The exchange between Peale and his readers offers a rare opportunity to witness how mid-twentieth-century Americans responded to liberal Protestant ideas about sexuality, marriage, and mental health—and reveals how much weight liberal Protestants like Peale gave to heterosexual marriage when they pondered the psychological and spiritual fortunes of the people they counseled. Ultimately, Peale deferred to psychiatry on the question of same-sex desire because the mental illness model of homosexuality fit his theological worldview. In his invariably optimistic assessment of human nature, Peale preached that each human being possessed the potential for happiness and love. For Peale, as for his readers, that happiness required marriage and a family. Marriage met all of Peale's criteria for personal, spiritual, and social success: happily married couples complemented one another, and together they could "handle situations with real effectiveness." The emotionally balanced couple would attain "that profound oneness, that spiritual union, that God must surely have intended when He created man and woman." By satisfying an individual's basic need "of being needed," marriage formed the nexus of the spiritual-psychological universe that Peale's theology inhabited.[41] For positive thinking to work, it needed to build upon a heteronormative foundation. Heterosexuality, in other words, formed a necessary precondition for the kind of spiritual growth that Peale believed he could help people achieve. Psychiatric diagnosis enabled Peale to classify homosexuality as an admittedly serious medical condition, acknowledge how difficult men and women found the task of "curing" themselves, and maintain his faith in the possibility of heterosexual perfection.

The parameters of personal happiness, however, remained malleable and subject to shifting social, scientific, and religious trends. Over the ensuing decades, liberal Protestants' therapeutic faith would be tested, as a growing number of gay Americans demanded that God, love, mental health, and same-sex desire find a way to coexist. Indeed, in the years immediately following the publication of Peale's column in *Look*, liberal Protestant leaders increasingly aligned themselves with researchers and activists who debunked the disease model of homosexuality. At a 1961 conference on marriage and the family, sponsored by the National Council of the Churches of Christ in the U.S.A., attendees heard from Evelyn Hooker, the pathbreaking researcher who demonstrated that no discernible difference existed between the mental health of "homosexual" men and that of "heterosexual" men. The conference report endorsed tolerance of homosexuality.[42] Starting in the 1960s, increasing numbers of liberal Protestant clergy partnered with gay and lesbian activists to protest discriminatory policing practices and antisodomy laws. A few ministers established gay-friendly congregations, like the Metropolitan Community Church in Los Angeles, which opened in 1968.[43] By the time that the American Psychiatric Association removed homosexuality from its compendium of pathologies in 1973, many leaders of liberal Protestantism were already allies of the nascent gay rights movement and preached acceptance of homosexuals, rather than the cure of homosexuality.

As liberal Protestants, following the psychiatric mainstream, began to walk away from the sickness/treatment paradigm, evangelical and Pentecostal Christians marched in the opposite direction, championing the disease model of homosexuality—and preaching the possibilities of therapeutic cures. But unlike liberal Protestants, theologically conservative Christians incorporated a robust theology of sin into their antigay therapies. In 1973, evangelical Christians founded Love in Action, one of the first ministries devoted to "converting" homosexuals to heterosexuality through a combination of prayer and therapy. "Curing" homosexuality became a high-profile cause for evangelical leaders. When Anita Bryant launched her Save Our Children campaign in 1977 to overturn Miami–Dade County's antidiscrimination employment law, she proposed the creation of a counseling center for the homosexual teachers who she believed were infecting the public school system and "recruiting" innocent children. Peale and other liberal Protestant ministers had advised gay men and women to understand same-sex desires as symptoms of a psychiatric illness and thus to rely on mental health professionals for a cure; therapists within the evangelical "ex-gay" movement discussed therapy as a form of repentance and described the outcome as a conversion.[44] Whereas theologically liberal clergy had prided themselves on staying in step with the most current trends in professional psychiatry and psychology, evangelicals rejected mainstream mental health opinion, often relying on the same psychoanalytic theories, first popularized in the 1950s, that the APA had just renounced.

Religious leaders like Peale helped shape the public debate about homosexuality because of—not in spite of—their appropriation of psychiatric and other scientific theories. Peale, an especially significant figure in the history of how twentieth-century American religious leaders promoted a therapeutic model of personal betterment, promulgated psychiatric theories of homosexuality to an eager American public. When the dominant paradigms of homosexuality were sin and criminality, Peale urged his readers to think about same-sex desire as a form of mental illness—a view hardly progressive by today's standards but one that aligned Peale with mainstream psychiatrists and sexual progressives of his day. The responses his column elicited suggest how readily some Americans adopted psychiatric models of sexual identity and how relieved many of Peale's readers were to find that he spoke the language of diagnosis and cure. The legacy of those conversations has endured in the decades since in impassioned debates over the connections among faith, sexuality, and mental health.

NOTES

The author wishes to thank Sarah Hammond, Heather R. White, Catherine Brekus, and W. Clark Gilpin for improving this essay with their keen historical insights, Jennifer Fang for research assistance, and Mark B. Hoffman for his careful reading and comments.

1. Christine Rosen, *Preaching Eugenics: Religious Leaders and the American Eugenics Movement* (New York: Oxford University Press, 2004), 13. See also Richard Wightman Fox, "The Culture of Liberal Protestant Progressivism, 1875–1925," *Journal of Interdisciplinary History* 23, no. 3 (1993): 641.

2. For further discussion of these issues, see Rebecca L. Davis, *More Perfect Unions: The American Search for Marital Bliss* (Cambridge: Harvard University Press, 2010), 136–75.

3. Carol V. R. George, *God's Salesman: Norman Vincent Peale and the Power of Positive Thinking* (New York: Oxford University Press, 1993), 46, 55–69, 86–87.

4. Norman Vincent Peale, *The Power of Positive Thinking* (New York: Prentice-Hall, 1952), ix.

5. George Dugan, "Educator Describes Dr. Peale's Views," *New York Times*, February 8, 1955, 25.

6. "Norman Vincent Peale Answers Your Questions," *Look*, January 25, 1955, 32.

7. "Norman Vincent Peale Answers Your Questions," *Look*, December 11, 1956, 132.

8. Ibid.

9. Richard Godbeer, *Sexual Revolution in Early America* (Baltimore: Johns Hopkins University Press, 2002), 104–15; Thomas A. Foster, *Sex and the Eighteenth-Century Man: Massachusetts and the History of Sexuality in America* (Boston: Beacon, 2006), 156–74.

10. Jonathan Katz, *The Invention of Heterosexuality* (New York: Dutton, 1995), chap. 2.

11. Sharon R. Ullman, *Sex Seen: The Emergence of Modern Sexuality in America* (Berkeley: University of California Press, 1997), 3 and passim; George Chauncey, "Christian Brotherhood or Sexual Perversion? Homosexual Identities and the Construction of Sexual Boundaries in the World War One Era," *Journal of Social History* 19, no. 2 (1985): 189–211.

12. George Chauncey, *Gay New York: Gender, Urban Culture, and the Making of the Gay Male World, 1890–1940* (New York: Basic Books, 1994), chap. 5.

13. Estelle B. Freedman, "'Uncontrolled Desires': The Response to the Sexual Psychopath, 1920–1960," *Journal of American History* 74, no. 1 (1987): 83–106; Chauncey, *Gay New York*, 331–42.

14. Allan Berube, *Coming Out under Fire: The History of Gay Men and Women in World War Two* (New York: Free Press, 1990), chap. 6.

15. David K. Johnson, *The Lavender Scare: The Cold War Persecution of Gays and Lesbians in the Federal Government* (Chicago: University of Chicago Press, 2004), 76 and passim; Margot Canaday, *The Straight State: Sexuality and Citizenship in Twentieth-Century America* (Princeton: Princeton University Press, 2009), chap. 5.

16. John D'Emilio, *Sexual Politics, Sexual Communities: The Making of a Homosexual Minority in the United States, 1940–1970*, 2nd ed. (Chicago: University of Chicago Press, 1998), chap. 3; Lillian Faderman, *Odd Girls and Twilight Lovers: A History of Lesbian Life in Twentieth-Century America* (New York: Columbia University Press, 1991), chap. 6.

17. Jennifer Terry, *An American Obsession: Science, Medicine, and Homosexuality in Modern Society* (Chicago: University of Chicago Press, 1999), 192, 215, 286–87; Henry L. Minton, *Departing from Deviance: A History of Homosexual Rights and Emancipatory Science in America* (Chicago: University of Chicago Press, 2002), 33–57.

18. Bieber quoted in Ronald Bayer, *Homosexuality and American Psychiatry: The Politics of Diagnosis* (Princeton: Princeton University Press, 1987), 30; see also 28–34.

19. Roy A. Burkhart, *The Freedom to Become Yourself* (Columbus, Ohio: Community Books, 1957), 104; Roy A. Burkhart, "A Church's Program of Education in Marriage and the Family" (Columbus, Ohio: First Community Church, n.d.), 1–2, 8.

20. Smiley Blanton and Norman Vincent Peale, *Faith Is the Answer: A Pastor and a*

Psychiatrist Discuss Your Problems, rev. ed. (Englewood Cliffs, N.J.: Prentice-Hall, 1955), 198–200.

21. Article reprinted in Simon Doninger, *The Minister's Consultation Clinic: Pastoral Psychology in Action, a Selection of Questions Submitted by Ministers to the Magazine* Pastoral Psychology, *and Answered by a Board of Psychiatrists, Psychologists, Social Scientists, and Clergymen* (Great Neck, N.Y.: Channel Press, 1955), 263–68.

22. Mel White, *Stranger at the Gate: To Be Gay and Christian in America* (New York: Simon and Schuster, 1994), 13.

23. Brenda E. Brasher, *Godly Women: Fundamentalism and Female Power* (New Brunswick, N.J.: Rutgers University Press, 1998), chap. 5.

24. John R. Rice, *Bobbed Hair, Bossy Wives, and Women Preachers: Significant Questions for Honest Christian Women Settled by the Word of God* (Wheaton, Ill.: Sword of the Lord Publishers, 1941); John R. Rice, *The Home—Courtship, Marriage, and Children: A Bible Manual of Twenty-two Chapters on the Christian Home* (Wheaton, Ill.: Sword of the Lord Publishers, 1945).

25. "Norman Vincent Peale Answers Your Questions: How to Make Marriage Work," *Look*, September 16, 1958, 62.

26. John Howard, "The Library, the Park, and the Pervert: Public Space and Homosexual Encounter in Post–World War II Atlanta," *Radical History Review* 62 (1995): 171, 180–82. See also Johnson, *The Lavender Scare*, chap. 2.

27. Sara Harris, *The Puritan Jungle: America's Sexual Underground* (New York: Putnam, 1969), as quoted in Jonathan Ned Katz, *Gay American History: Lesbians and Gay Men in the U.S.A.* (New York: Harper and Row, 1985), 123.

28. Heather Rachelle White, "Homosexuality, Gay Communities, and American Churches: A History of a Changing Religious Ethic, 1944–1977" (Ph.D. diss., Princeton University, 2007), 27, 33.

29. Letter from G.A. to Norman Vincent Peale (hereafter, NVP), December 12, 1956, Norman Vincent Peale Papers, series II C, box 1, Folder: "Clinic Corres. 1957," Special Collections and Research Center, Syracuse University, Syracuse, New York.

30. Letter from R.L. to Doctor, February 3, 1957, ibid.

31. Letters from G.C. to NVP, December 5, 1956; L.M. to NVP, November 27, 1956; E.M. to NVP, December 7, 1956; and M.L. to NVP, December 17, 1956; all ibid.

32. Letter from H.J. to NVP, December 8, 1956, ibid.

33. Letter from E.P. to NVP, December 11, 1956, ibid.

34. Letter from P.F. to NVP, December 4, 1956, ibid.

35. Letter from T.J. to NVP, November 26, 1956, ibid. See also Letter from B.G. to NVP, November 26, 1956, ibid.

36. Letter from E.C. to NVP, December 1, 1956, ibid.; Joanne J. Meyerowitz, *How Sex Changed: A History of Transsexuality in the United States* (Cambridge: Harvard University Press, 2002), 114–15.

37. Letter from Mrs. G.S. to NVP, November 27, 1956, Norman Vincent Peale Papers,

series II C, box 1, Folder: "Clinic Corres. 1957," Special Collections and Research Center, Syracuse University, Syracuse, New York.

38. Letter from R.K. to NVP, n.d., ibid.

39. Letter from Mrs. O.P. to NVP, December 1, 1956, ibid.

40. Letter from K.A. to NVP, December 26, 1956, ibid.

41. Peale, "How to Make Marriage Work," 62.

42. Elizabeth Steel Genné and William Henry Genné, eds., *Foundations for Christian Family Policy* (New York: Department of Family Life, National Council of the Churches of Christ in the U.S.A., North American Conference on Church and Family, 1961), 166–74, 254. For a further discussion of Hooker's influence on psychology's understanding of homosexuality, see Ellen Herman, *Psychiatry, Psychology, and Homosexuality* (New York: Chelsea House, 1995), 56–61. On liberal Protestant sexual toleration at mid-century, see R. Marie Griffith, "The Religious Encounters of Alfred C. Kinsey," *Journal of American History* 95, no. 2 (2008): 349–77.

43. White, "Homosexuality, Gay Communities, and American Churches," chaps. 2, 4.

44. Herman, *Psychiatry, Psychology, and Homosexuality*, 108–10; Tanya Erzen, *Straight to Jesus: Sexual and Christian Conversions in the Ex-Gay Movement* (Berkeley: University of California Press, 2006), 27–42.

STEWART M. HOOVER

Christianity and the Media
Accommodation, Contradiction, and Transformation

The relationship between Christianity and "the media" is more profound than is often appreciated by clerical, scholarly, or lay observers. It has been convenient to think in rather simple and straightforward terms, but upon closer investigation a complex history of interaction is revealed. In this essay, I will argue that such a close reading shows that there are important ways in which the mediation of Christianity makes such profound sense that it is hard to think of the movement without its media. Even though this is particularly obvious from the perspective of the twenty-first century, there are important ways that this situation has roots as deep as the Reformation itself, extending as well into the development of the American brand of Christianity. It is also important to understand that neither "Christianity" nor "the media" are hermetic in these regards—that there are ways that each has been changed by their interaction.

It almost goes without saying that all religions are mediated. Religions—and indeed all human interactions—require contexts and languages of expression and shared meaning. From the most "primitive" religions and rituals for which we have records (and indeed the records are evidence of this), humans have found ways to express, share, and document their explorations of religion and spirituality. The history of Christianity is likewise a history that is in important ways typified by, and is certainly known by, its representation and expression, first through the words of Jesus and the apostles, secondarily (but more importantly) through the written records of the Gospels and Epistles, and finally through an extensive scholarly and lay record in written, visual, and material-culture forms. Christianity is a religion of these various "texts."

Processes of mediation have also played important roles in the history of the Christian movement, nowhere more so than in the Reformation. Our received understanding of the Reformation connects writing and publishing to it in a rather fundamental way. The medium of print, the process of movable-type publishing, and the spread of literacy were each essential to the realization of Luther's universal priesthood. The importance of print, publishing, and reading to Protestant movements led many of them to commit to ambitious literacy programs (such as in Scandinavia) and resulted in higher rates of literacy overall in areas dominated by Protestantism.[1]

The story is more complex than this. It is advisable to look at a wider range of factors and implications in order to more helpfully historicize the relationship between Christianity and the media. I argue that these relations are not rooted in any essentialized notions of either "Christianity" or "the media." We cannot explain the mediation of Christianity if we assume that the media simply transmits received ideas of the faith. In the case of the Reformation, for example, Elizabeth Eisenstein has shown that Gutenberg's revolution was not only about the reproduction and distribution of words. It was, more fundamentally, about markets and industries. Simply put, Eisenstein argued that it was the distribution of *publishers* more than of *books* that explains printing's more profound effects.[2] The fact that printing could become an industry with its own entrepreneurs and markets gave it an autonomy and a reach that far outstripped any particular implications for the spread of knowledge.

The autonomy of publishing is what we experience today as "the media." Printing and the historical context of the early modern period thus ushered in a new force in culture and politics, one that has come to contest church, state, and other institutions for authority. This role of the media—their prominence in public life—is but one valence of a more complex definition of the situation. The implications of publishing (and lately of the media) for Christianity are today coming to a kind of fulfillment that has destabilized and reordered the way we have understood religion in modernity.

This more expansive and nuanced view thus must take account of "the media" as an institutional and cultural force, but even that profile for the media resides elsewhere, in a complex and layered set of conditions that deserve careful attention. Among these conditions are the role of technology; the phenomenon of commodification; the so-called democratic religious impulse that can be said to define American religion; the particular modes of expression within Christianity and such things as the mandate for evangelism; the place of the religious voice in the public sphere; the increasing importance of popular expression and popular culture; and the power of "the media" to frame and define religious symbols. In these pages, I hope to explore each of these areas in more detail.

The Mediation of Modern Christianity

It is important for relations between Christianity and the media to be seen as part of a larger set of conditions in media and religion. We tend to think of "religion" and "the media" as separate spheres. There are a number of dimensions to this. First, perhaps, is the fact that such an assignment preserves autonomous spheres of influence for religious institutions and authorities. It has been convenient for clerical leadership to assume certain prerogatives over its role in relation to culture and society and to assume that there are clearly demarcated geographies in which it is active. Journalism, as a practice, necessarily contests this as it seeks to look behind the barriers of sacred reservations. Second, a kind of Durkheimian view of the demarcation of the realms of the "sacred" and the "profane" has tended to see the media sphere as profoundly secular and thus profane in its intentions and effects. Third, again owing to Émile Durkheim and others in classical social thought, we tend to think of religion in essentialized terms as something that is categorically "authentic" and that the "artificial" media are necessarily a threat to this authenticity. Fourth, theological and intellectual leaders in the field of religion have tended to de-emphasize, even derogate, popular pieties in favor of more legitimated modes of religious exploration and expression. Thus, certain kinds of media are favored over others. The legitimate media of theological enquiry are the book, the sermon, and elite arts such as academic visual arts, literature, and even cinema. The popular media of television, theatrical film, popular music, and so on, are necessarily suspect.[3]

The structured relations between "religion" and "the media" typical of the situation in the United States at mid-century were clearly demarcated by these assumptions. This was most obvious in commercial broadcasting, where the major commercial networks and all local television and radio stations offered free airtime to religion as part of their public service obligations.[4] In practice, this meant that preferential treatment was given to the major branches of American religion, identified by Will Herberg.[5] This institutionalism was determined in many ways by the assumptions of Protestantism and by the tacit assumption that there was a Protestant establishment. This situation was not without its criticisms and stresses and strains, but it remained a settled issue well into the 1970s. As Michele Rosenthal demonstrates, the structural relations of this time implied a position of authority over media culture on the part of Protestant and Catholic clerical and academic authorities, a position that these leaders used to level vibrant critiques against what they saw to be the profane, secular, and problematic media.[6]

This positioning of media in relation to religion also had implications for media practice. Defining religion as a matter of public service encouraged media managers and producers to assume the other side of the "sacred/profane" model, accepting that the media bore essentially no obligation to give much profile to religion in entertainment and news content.[7] A derivation of the secularization hypothesis held sway, in which it was thought that religion was either fading as a major dimension of modern life or was so much a private matter that extensive treatment of it would be inappropriate.[8] This meant that what religion existed in mainstream media was of the "public service" variety or, in relatively rare circumstances, involved news of major religious groups or controversies that would find its way to the air.

The situation began to change in the 1970s, when a new form of religious television, what we now know as "televangelism," began to appear on the national scene. This emergence resulted from changes in technology and regulation. Up until that time, domestic reception of satellite signals had been strictly limited, but once satellites were deregulated, a whole host of new media channels began to emerge, feeding their signals to the newly constructed cable television systems via satellite distribution. Among the earliest adopters of these technologies were Christian evangelicals like Pat Robertson.[9] Robertson was among the first to realize that this new system offered nearly unlimited audience access for relatively little financial investment, and he and others soon set up prodigious Christian television channels largely supported by individual evangelicals as a kind of mission effort.

The effects on both the evangelical and the nonevangelical Christian establishments were profound. Catholic and mainline Protestant leaders saw this new kind of religious broadcasting as a threat to membership, influence, and giving. And there was reason to be concerned, because unlike earlier religious broadcasting, these new programs were slick, sophisticated, attractive, and much like the entertainment media that surrounded them.[10] Later research nuanced these effects substantially, showing that televangelism was largely influential within certain evangelical communities, but the general sense among religious authorities and the wider culture continued to hold that this phenomenon was radically rebalancing the power relations in Protestantism.[11] Mainstream Catholicism felt the effects, too, with independent, parachurch broadcasters like Mother Angelica offering a similar challenge to institutional authority via new media.

Media and the Restructuring of American Christianity

But more profound changes were afoot that have more substantially altered the relationship between religion and the media. These were both changes in "religion" and changes in "the media." In religion, it is becoming increasingly obvious that the prospects and prerogatives of institutional religion are no longer the central issue. Sociologists have long observed a "restructuring" of American religion, in which the terms of religious commitment and identification have been shifting.[12] These changes have had major implications for religious practice, where a kind of autonomy of the self has begun to hold sway, described by scholars like Wade Clark Roof as "seeking."[13] The result has been a decline in the profile and authority of religious institutions and structures and a rise in the profile and the authority of individuals, as they construct their own imbrications of "the religious" or "the spiritual." These shifts in practice have further been recognized by a shifting of paradigms in the study of religion, described by Stephen Warner as a shift away from religion "as ascribed" to religion "as achieved."[14]

This has meant that in important ways religion could begin to look more volitional, more individualized, and more subjective than the formal, received view. In the case of religion or spirituality, the overall project comes to resemble the more general situation described by Anthony Giddens as the reflexive project of the self.[15] In Giddens's view, late modern social subjects are motivated by the desire to perfect a self that makes sense in the maelstrom of modern life. Individuals today arrogate to themselves the responsibility to locate themselves, and the conditions of what he calls "late modernity" have made them increasingly reflexive in the way they think about the social order. Where once they might have ceded certain fields of responsibility to social authorities of various kinds, today (largely due to the rise of media culture, according to Giddens) they "see behind the curtain" and understand the nature and sources of power and authority (or at least think and act as though they do).

This increasingly individualized and autonomous approach to religion has coincided historically with changes in the media sphere. From the 1970s onward, we have seen a proliferation of media sources and channels. This is true across media, but is most obvious in the case of the "screen media" of television and film. The development of cable and satellite television and home video (VCRs and DVDs) has brought hundreds of channels into the home. This contrasts with the pre-1970s period, when the number was in the tens. New channels of the digital sphere such as YouTube and Hulu have added to this mix. Other entertainment media, from Internet- and web-based services to digital gaming to personal media like MP3 players to the "social media" of IM-ing, Facebook, and Twitter, have added to the range of places and sources where we get our mediated culture.

This proliferation has had direct effects on religion and spirituality. In the period during which the Protestant and Catholic establishments are thought to have enjoyed their greatest power and influence—the 1950s—the range of media was limited compared to today. The rather easy relationship between religion and media in those days that resulted in public service religion in broadcasting and a kind of benign neglect in journalism has given way to a situation where the media marketplace is acting more and more like a "marketplace."[16] The concentrated channels of the earlier era had little time or space for specialized and particularized messages. That has all changed. As the media have proliferated, so has media content, and among the changes this has brought has been an increase in the amount of religious and spiritual material that is available in commercial media markets.[17] It is simply more possible today for religious and spiritual programming to find space in commercial media markets and for religious and spiritual themes to appear in otherwise "secular" programming. A signal example was the network television program *Touched by an Angel*, which ran from 1993 to 2004 to high ratings. *Touched by an Angel* opened the door for more and more such programming, substantially lowering whatever barriers to religion might have existed before.

As the result of these two trends—the rise of the religiously autonomous individual and the diversification of the media (both in structure and in ownership)—"religion" and "media" can be said to be converging. What were once thought to be independent spheres are now coming together. Evidence of this abounds from both "sides." There are more and more media today that are aimed at religious and spiritual concerns. Looking at the digital realm alone, we can see a plethora of websites, chat groups, online communities, and programs emerging. "The media," lodged as they are in the commercial marketplace, have now thoroughly realized the promise that Gutenberg's invention offered to publishers as a commercial class six centuries ago: they have become a socially and politically independent force in the forming and shaping of cultures, including religious cultures. In the case of digital media, this was made most obvious when the prominent religion website Beliefnet was acquired by Rupert Murdoch's News Corporation in 2007.

In the world of religion, there is widening recognition that to exist today, religions must exist in the media, and all major faith groups (and especially minor ones) have moved to establish their presence in the screen media, on-line, and in other media venues. The Vatican, for example, has an expanding media presence, including sophisticated media-based marketing campaigns as well as public relations efforts born under a very media-savvy Pope John Paul II. Evangelicals have long been focused on media, and both denominational and nondenominational institutions are actively engaged in media. Most megachurches are typified by their media engagement, and the demographically focused "emerging church" and "post-Christian" movements are often more "media" than not.

Yet the broader context of media and commodities remains determinative of the meaning of Christianity, its various practices and its various projections and readings of symbols. I have already suggested an economic and structural explanation for this: the media today are primarily commercial, and their position in the capitalist marketplace gives them an autonomy in social and political spheres. But I have also hinted at another dimension of this, the rise of the autonomous individual religious "seeker" and his or her self-generated quest for religious knowledge. To the extent that these quests are pursued outside the bounds of received framings by authority, doctrine, or tradition, the symbolic marketplace where they take place becomes the determinative framework for them. Evidence suggests that even those who remain denominationally identified do so with an eye to a broader framework of seeking and quest and pay less attention to authority and discipline than their parents or grandparents did. This was most striking in a 2008 report of the Pew Religious Landscape Survey, which found, among other things, that even religiously identified Americans believe that "there are many paths to God."[18]

This also influences the way that audiences look at media. Audience studies of religiously framed viewing have found a wide range of screen entertainment qualifying as "religious" or "spiritual." It is not just *Touched by an Angel*, but things as varied as *Lost, The X-Files, Star Trek, Walker, Texas Ranger, Braveheart*, and *Monty Python and the Holy Grail*.[19] The point is that the symbolic frames and terms have shifted, and that people are now finding religion and spirituality in all kinds of places in media culture. And it is the very indeterminancy of this that is destabilizing both the authority of religions in general and Christianity in particular—and the terms through which we have come to think about religion.

All of this is to an extent true of all religions. The mullahs in Iran share with Protestant and Catholic authorities in the United States a discomfort with the way that media culture has interposed itself between institution and believer.[20] However, there are ways that the American Christian case is both unique and probative in that much of what we see in the relationship between media and religion globally is rooted in the U.S. context. These roots owe both to the global profile and reach of American culture and American religious culture and to the technical fact of the dominance of American media forms, from Hollywood to the World Wide Web, in the global media landscape. Thus, what happens in the United States matters a great deal outside the United States, and although there is rightly much postcolonial resistance to this situation, it remains.

Media and Evangelism in the United States

Turning to the U.S. case, then, the interactions between media and Christianity are complex and layered. They have deep roots that are most obvious in the nineteenth century and the frontier evangelism of the second and third Great Awakenings. The Methodist and Campbellite movements, for example, were active publishers of books, tracts, and other print and pictographic materials, and they purveyed Bibles through complex commercial systems involving itinerant agents.[21] Religious publishing had been at the core of what became the American publishing industry, but the experience of the frontier forever changed the way at least these branches of Protestantism thought about media and mediation. Simply put, it became conventional for Christians to think of media and mediation as central to evangelism, at least in the form of the book, the spiritual tract, or later the Sunday school lesson and thus as integral to Christian witness.

In light of what we have been observing about issues of individualism and autonomy in relation to religious authority, it is important to note another dimension of the nineteenth-century Protestant experience. Nathan Hatch has persuasively argued that this period established a "democratic" sensibility in American Protestantism.[22] Thus the individualism we have identified in contemporary religion in general has deeper roots in the American Protestant experience, which is arguably the definitive religious motif in the United States.[23] For Hatch, this "democratic" impulse arose in movements that intended to empower individual believers with mastery of their own religious and spiritual lives. Media and mediation were central to this project. Thus, it could be argued that the media have assumed a place of centrality in Protestantism that, while contested (as we will see), linked media to this important branch of Christianity.

This place for media in Protestantism proved even more important after the turn of the twentieth century, with the rise of the Fundamentalist movement. Fundamentalism was—and remains—extensively mediated and media-friendly. The major voices in Fundamentalism as early as the 1920s were radio voices. And, as Joel Carpenter points out, radio was an essential component of the revival of mass evangelism in the early part of the twentieth century as well.[24]

An even more significant connection between media and religion came at mid-century with what we today know as the neo-evangelical movement. Billy Graham's centrality in the development of evangelicalism was partly rooted in his potential as a media figure. As George Marsden has described the rise of Graham and the wider movement, there was a clear intention on the part of evangelical leaders to find and promote a figure who could help develop a new, more modern form of Protestant Fundamentalism—and media were clearly thought to be essential to this project.[25] The Graham organization moved quickly to develop this potential, pursuing ambitious publishing, music, television and film-production efforts.[26] Graham became a media figure, linking these media production efforts with an extensive public relations and promotion enterprise supporting his public "revival" appearances across the United States. He became a national, even global "pastor" (at least to the right bank of Protestantism), a position from which he ascended to significant political profile by the 1970s. Thus, the mediation of Billy Graham was central to his development as the defining figure of evangelical Protestantism, arguably the definitive branch of American Christianity during the latter half of the century.

It should be obvious that I am arguing that the evangelical movement became the central dynamic of Protestantism, and even of Christianity in general, in the United States in the latter part of the twentieth century, and that media and mediation were central to evangelicalism. There is evidence to support it, but I do not want to make this claim overbroad. The rise of media and mediation in American Christianity was not unproblematic, and media's achievement of the kind of accommodation I am describing depended on the resolution of a series of contradictions that were—and remain—important.

First, media and mediation make sense for Christians to the extent that the evangelical impulse is important to them. Thus, it is easiest for the Christian mind to think about modern media as valid in relation to their ability broadly and efficiently to realize the Great Commission of Matthew 28. The second condition, then, is the acceptance that the primary function of media is what media theorists call their "instrumental" purpose: that is, that media are primarily instruments for the intentional transmission of messages.[27] Broader cultural or ritual functions of media are downplayed. The third condition that explains relations between Christianity and the media is that which obtained at the time of the Reformation: the idea of the "priesthood of believers" and a concomitant commitment to provide to them the (largely mediated) resources necessary for them to exercise that right. Centuries ago, this was primarily a question of print publishing and the provision of Bibles. Today this impulse easily extends (for most Protestants and for many Catholics) to other media and other media genres.

In fact, most of these conditions apply equally well to Catholic, Protestant, and Orthodox Christians today. There would be little disagreement that media have a kind of natural fit with the way Christians think of themselves and of their faith and witness. Thus, it is arguable that a kind of easy consonance exists between "Christianity" and media on a general level.

There are some further conditions of this relationship that are more particular to Protestantism, though, which are worth noting. For many Protestants, the widespread acceptance of media and mediation depended on confronting a major cultural issue: a general distaste among them—particularly in the American Midwest and among Northern European immigrants—for entertainment and popular culture.[28] For them, the Calvinist impulse to work hard as a sign of grace extended into a generalized disapproval of leisure, and popular entertainments were thus necessarily antithetical to the well-lived life. And such opprobrium could extend to popularized religious media, such as that produced by the Graham organization and others.[29]

These questions came to a head with the rise of the evangelical television ministries of the 1970s and after. Vibrant debates raged within evangelicalism and beyond it about the appropriateness of genres that so obviously borrowed from the forms of popular and entertainment media.[30] As noted above, one of the issues was practical and pragmatic: were television ministries drawing members and support away from conventional churches? But on a more profound level, questions arose about the cultural appropriateness of these programs. Were they more than just trivial entertainment? A general distaste for popular culture among Protestant academic and clerical elites found specific focus here as well.[31] These are far from settled issues today, in spite of the fact that most Christians seem generally to accept the notion that mass media are a logical, even sought-after context for faith exploration and expression.

Observers of the early debates over televangelism noted another layer in these debates as well. It seemed that some proponents of these forms assumed a kind of mystical power in the media beyond their mere instrumentality. Historians have noted in regard to a range of technologies of the modern era a tendency for some people to invest them with almost mystical or transcendent power.[32] For some Protestants, it became possible to overcome resistance to the use of modern media with what one observer of the time called a new "mythos" of mediated evangelicalism.[33]

Finally, the accommodation between media and conservative Protestantism at the time of the rise of televangelism relied for some on the sense that these new media ministries had a symbolic power to confer a new status and credibility on the neo-evangelical movement as a whole. In the 1970s, evangelicals still labored to throw off the stereotypes of their Fundamentalist roots. For many supporters and followers of the televangelists, the fact that Pat Robertson or Oral Roberts or Jimmy Swaggart or Jim and Tammy Bakker were present in the media sphere was symbolically important. It signified a kind of cultural ascendancy for the movement. In fact, this may well have been the single most important effect of televangelism.[34]

There is little doubt that for most Christians in the twenty-first century, modern media of communication are significant and relatively unproblematic. Yet Protestants vary in their attitudes toward the media sphere. The recently ascendant evangelical establishment has important roots in the media sphere, as we have seen. Its political successes in the Reagan and Bush years owed much to its comfortable relationship with media. For mainline Protestants, media remain more problematic. Some denominations have begun prominent public relations and promotion campaigns in mass media, but clerical and academic authorities among the mainline churches remain skeptical of media. This skepticism is not particularly shared by people in the pew. Both mainline and evangelical Protestants are happy and active members of the general media audience.[35]

The Catholic Church has had a more troubled relationship to mass media. At mid-century, Catholic ascendancy in American culture was in fact symbolized in television, in the person of Bishop Fulton J. Sheen, who presided over a popular, network-aired weekly program.[36] At the same time, Catholic authorities were expressing their view of popular culture through efforts like the Legion of Decency, founded in 1933 to rate films, broadcasting, and other media and accused of exercising a kind of censorship over film and television. These efforts continue today with organizations like the Catholic League, which has done public battle against such films as *The Da Vinci Code* in 2006 and *Angels and Demons* in 2009.

American Catholicism also experienced the power of media—in this case journalistic media—in a series of scandals over priestly behavior beginning in the 1990s.[37] But a charismatic Pope John Paul II also served to give an accessible media face to Catholicism during his years in office, generating much goodwill and media expectation for his successor. In terms of their informal and private media behaviors, however, Catholics share much in common with mainline Protestants.[38]

Other histories exist within the general relationship of media to Christianity. Pentecostalism, for example, shares some features with evangelicalism but has not shared its aspirations in relation to ascendancy in the public arena. The rise of the modern Pentecostal movement owed much to mass media, with local newspapers giving a great deal of coverage to the early meetings at Azusa Street in Los Angeles.[39] The modern megachurch movement is also heavily mediated in some very important ways.[40] Megachurch pastors like Rick Warren and Joel Osteen not only use media in their own institutions and ministries but they have become public media figures in their own right, assuming a mantle first donned by Billy Graham sixty years ago.

But we must turn again to reflect on the nature of contemporary media and how religions in general are being transformed by the media age. Each of the above relations to "the media" assume a media paradigm that is of fading importance as we move further into the twenty-first century. Thinking about how Christian denominations and groups relate to the media depends on the view that media marketing theorists call "push media"—that is, the assumption that the media function as instruments of dissemination and that what matters is what kinds of messages, symbols, and values are sent out or "pushed" on audiences. Although most media were once assumed to be "push" media, recent changes in the media marketplace have changed these conditions. The diversity of channels and sources, along with the increasing cultural and social autonomy of audiences, has resulted in a situation that is increasingly one of "pull" media. Audiences and users now have the momentum in their favor, and what they achieve through media is of most importance.

But a new paradigm shift is also under way, toward what is known as the interactive world of "Web 2.0." In this realm, more and more media are interactive and user-generated. For religion and spirituality, this means that audiences and consumers are not only selecting media symbols, resources, and values from a broad marketplace of media supply but they are also creating their own religiously and spiritually meaningful media through You-Tube, Facebook, and the so-called social media more generally. As with earlier evolutions of media, Christians are active in exploring this new way of mediating faith.

The fact that the media sphere is also fundamentally involved in globalization is also significant. It is no longer possible to have a private conversation, and the worlds of Christianity are increasingly mediated worlds across national and regional boundaries. To mention only one example, the rise of neo-Pentecostal movements and megachurches in West Africa has been accompanied by a vibrant mediation in both religious and secular popular culture in Africa. At the same time, global media mean that transnational media networks link those developments to Pentecostal groups, churches, and interests in the United States and across the globe.[41]

To understand the breadth and depth of the implications of media for Christianity, we thus need to move outside the received framing, the "emic" vision of religions and religious institutions and authorities as they encounter and grapple with the media, to an "etic" framework where we see the media as important ritual forms in their own rights.[42] We further need to understand the extent to which these media forms now control the expression of religion, 1) through their framing and representation of religion in journalism and in entertainment; 2) through control of the channels and contexts of public communication; and 3) through new technological arrangements that are rapidly remaking the meaning of community, authority, and practice.

What can we expect from all of this for the foreseeable future? There are some implications worth considering. First, the nature of contemporary religious practice as autonomous individual "seeking" within a symbolic marketplace of supply necessarily implies a kind of horizontalization or flattening of religious symbols and values. A more generalized kind of consensual Christianity will necessarily result and will further undermine authority. Second, within these structures of practice in the emerging cultural/media marketplace, particularized expressions of Christianity will find their place. Particular and specific churches, leaders, and symbols will continue to be salient, not as part of larger systems or structures, but instead as focused representations of the faith. Finally, this situation will encourage new local, national, and even global syncretisms to emerge. The marketplace of Christian symbols within the larger marketplace of religious and spiritual supply, when encountered by autonomous seekers, will provide links to new imbrications and combinations. None of this, of course, will be orthodox in any sense. Instead, this picture is one of emergent and reforming heterodoxies.

At the same time, it is surely premature to suggest that any of this will soon lead to fundamental redefinitions of the nature and meaning of Christianity or of its movements. However, change is under way, and has been for at least a century, as media culture, media industries, and new processes of mediation have interacted with Christian institutions, communities, and practices. Christianity has already been remade in important ways by these trends. Both academic and clerical authorities have been slow to catch on, but it is never too late to come to grips with its implications.

NOTES

1. Richard Venezky, "The Development of Literacy in the Industrialized Nations of the West," in *Handbook of Reading Research*, vol. 2, ed. Rebecca Barr et al. (New York: Lawrence Erlbaum Associates, 1995), 61.

2. Elizabeth Eisenstein, *The Printing Press as an Agent of Change* (New York: Cambridge University Press, 1978).

3. Sally Promey, "Interchangeable Art: Warner Sallman and the Critics of Mass Culture," in *Icons of American Protestantism: The Art of Warner Sallman*, ed. David Morgan (New Haven: Yale University Press, 1996).

4. Michele Rosenthal, *Satan and Savior: American Protestants and the New Medium of Television* (Hampshire, UK: Palgrave Macmillan, 2004).

5. Will Herberg, *Protestant-Catholic-Jew: An Essay in American Religious Sociology* (Chicago: University of Chicago Press, 1995).

6. Rosenthal, *Satan and Savior.*

7. Stewart M. Hoover and Douglas K. Wagner, "History and Policy in American Broadcast Treatment of Religion," *Media, Culture, and Society* 19, no. 1 (January 1997).

8. Stewart M. Hoover, *Religion in the Media Age* (London: Routledge, 2006).

9. Peter Horsfield, *Religious Television: The American Experience* (Boston: Longman Press, 1984); Stewart Hoover, *Mass Media Religion: The Social Sources of the Electronic Church* (London: Sage, 1988).

10. Jeffrey Hadden and Charles Swann, *Prime-Time Preachers: The Rising Power of Televangelism* (New York: Addison-Wesley, 1981).

11. Horsfield, *Religious Television*; Hoover, *Mass Media Religion*; Janice Peck, *The Gods of Televangelism* (Cresskill, N.J.: Hampton Press, 1993).

12. Robert Wuthnow, *The Restructuring of American Religion* (Princeton: Princeton University Press, 1990).

13. Wade Clark Roof, *Spiritual Marketplace: Baby Boomers and the Remaking of American Religion* (Princeton: Princeton University Press, 1999).

14. R. Stephen Warner, "Work in Progress toward a New Paradigm for the Sociological Study of Religion in the United States," *American Journal of Sociology* 98, no. 5 (March 1993): 1044–93.

15. Anthony Giddens, *Modernity and Self-Identity* (Stanford: Stanford University Press, 1991).

16. Stewart M. Hoover, *Religion in the News: Faith and Journalism in American Public Discourse* (London: Sage, 1998); Mark Silk, *Unsecular Media: Making News of Religion in America* (Champaign: University of Illinois Press, 1998).

17. Lynn Schofield Clark, *From Angels to Aliens: Teenagers, the Media, and the Supernatural* (New York: Oxford University Press, 2003); Hoover, *Religion in the Media Age*.

18. "More Have Dropped Dogma for Spirituality in U.S.," *USA Today*, July 2, 2008, http://www.usatoday.com/news/religion/2008-06-23-pew-religions_N.htm (accessed April 14, 2009).

19. Stewart M. Hoover, Lynn Schofield Clark, and Diane F. Alters, with Joseph G. Champ and Lee Hood, *Media, Home, and Family* (New York: Routledge, 2004).

20. Stewart M. Hoover, "Surprises and Earnings from the Tehran Conference," Special Issue, "Media and Religion in Iran," *Journal of Media and Religion* 7, nos. 1 and 2 (2008): 100–102.

21. David Morgan, *Protestants and Pictures: Religion, Visual Culture, and the Age of American Mass Production* (New York: Oxford University Press, 1999); David Paul Nord, *Faith in Reading: Religious Publishing and the Birth of Mass Media in America* (New York: Oxford University Press, 2004).

22. Nathan Hatch, *The Democratization of American Christianity* (New Haven: Yale University Press, 1989).

23. Kathleen Sands, "Feminisms and Secularisms," in *Secularisms*, ed. Janet Jakobsen and Anne Pellegrini (Durham: Duke University Press, 2008), 313.

24. J. Harold Ellens, *Models of Religious Broadcasting* (Grand Rapids, Mich.: Eerdmans, 1974); Ben Armstrong, *The Electric Church* (Nashville: Thomas Nelson, 1979); Joel Carpenter, "Tuning in the Gospel: Fundamentalist Radio Broadcasting and the Revival of Mass Evangelism, 1930–45," paper delivered to the Mid-America American Studies Association, University of Illinois, Urbana, April 13, 1985.

25. George Marsden, "Preachers of Paradox," in *Religion and America: Spiritual Life in a Secular Age*, ed. Mary Douglas and Steven Tipton (Boston: Beacon, 1993).

26. Heather Hendershot, *Shaking the World for Jesus: Media and Conservative Evangelical Culture* (Chicago: University of Chicago Press, 2004).

27. James W. Carey, "A Cultural Approach to Communication," *Communication* 2, no. 2 (1975): 1–25.

28. Morgan, *Protestants and Pictures*; Promey, "Interchangeable Art."

29. Hendershot, *Shaking the World for Jesus*; Hoover, *Religion in the Media Age*.

30. Armstrong, *The Electric Church*; Hoover, *Mass Media Religion*; Peck, *The Gods of Televangelism*.

31. Promey, "Interchangeable Art"; Rosenthal, *Satan and Savior*.

32. Carolyn Marvin, *When Old Technologies Were New: Thinking about Electric Communication in the Late Nineteenth Century* (London: Oxford University Press, 1990); Patrice Flichy, *Understanding Technological Innovation: A Socio-Technical Approach* (Cheltenham, UK: Edward Elgar Publishing, 2007), 130.

33. Quentin Schultze, "The Mythos of the Electronic Church," *Critical Studies in Mass Communication* 4, no. 3 (1987): 245–61.

34. Hoover, *Mass Media Religion*; Jeffrey Hadden and Anson Shupe, *Televangelism: Power and Politics on God's Frontier* (New York: Henry Holt, 1989).

35. Hoover, *Religion in the Media Age*; Hendershot, *Shaking the World for Jesus*; Bill Carter, "Many Who Voted for 'Values' Still Like Their Television Sin," *New York Times*, November 22, 2004, A1.

36. Everett C. Parker, David W. Barry, and Dallas W. Smythe, *The Television-Radio Audience and Religion* (New York: Harper's, 1955).

37. Frances Forde Plude, "The U.S. Catholic Church Sexual Abuse Scandal: A Media Case Study," in *Belief in Media*, ed. Peter Horsfield, Mary Hess, and Adan Medrano (London: Ashgate, 2004), 179–93.

38. Hoover, *Religion in the Media Age*.

39. Grant Wacker, "Searching for Eden with a Satellite Dish: Primitivism, Pragmatism, and the Pentecostal Character," in *Religion and American Culture*, ed. David G. Hackett (London: Routledge, 1995), 440.

40. Stewart M. Hoover, "The Cross at Willow Creek: Seeker Religion and the Contemporary Marketplace," in *Religion and Popular Culture in America*, ed. Bruce D. Forbes and Jeffrey H. Mahan (Berkeley: University of California Press, 2000).

41. Birgit Meyer, "Impossible Representations: Pentecostalism, Vision, and Video Technology in Ghana," in *Religion, Media, and the Public Sphere*, ed. Birgit Meyer and Annelies Moors (Bloomington: Indiana University Press, 2005), 290–312.

42. Carey, "A Cultural Approach to Communication."

What Is "American" about Christianity in the United States?

Debates about whether the United States is "exceptional" are usually less productive than considerations about what has been "distinctive" in American experience. For religious history, claims about American "exceptionalism" are often confusing precisely because they elide results of empirical research with assertions about the United States' uniqueness in the plans of God. The difference between asserting "exceptionalism" and assessing "distinctives" can be illustrated when considering claims that God intervened in the American Revolution to ensure the victory of the patriotic cause. In terms of "distinctives," fruitful investigation results when such claims are compared with similar claims made by religious believers in other nations about climactic events in their own experiences (as Calvinists in Holland, Orthodox in Russia, Catholics in Poland, Muslims in Saudi Arabia). But if such claims are advanced to argue for the uniqueness under God of American experience, difficulties abound. During the American War for Independence, many patriots did profess to see God at work for their cause, which would certainly count as an "exceptional" interpretation. But many who also thought the Revolution was "exceptional" interpreted "exceptionalism" very differently. Thus, African American slaves liberated by the British thought that God was specially at work for King George III; Loyalists in the United States and Britain sometimes saw the devil specially active in using patriots for his evil ends; and still other observers, with attention fixed on terrestrial causes and effects, have concluded that politics, trade, and geography, rather than the work of heavenly beings, determined what took place. For defining the ultimate truth about the American Revolution in "exceptional" terms, point of view is just as important as the assessment of evidence.

American Distinctives

In this essay, by contrast, judgments about American "distinctiveness" rely on empirical comparisons, open to believers of all types and nonbelievers, rather than on prescriptive theological insights. On these terms, foreign observers have often described Christianity in America as incorporating aspects of "modernity" that traditional Christianity in Europe mostly combated—with modernity understood as movement toward individualism, liberalism, and democracy, along with a willingness to accept market relationships in most spheres of life. The most famous early statements of this view came from Alexis de Tocqueville after his tour of the United States and Canada in the early 1830s. As he wrote in *Democracy in America*, "On my arrival in the United States it was the religious aspect of the country that first struck my eye." Yet it was not simply widespread religiosity that impressed Tocqueville, but rather religion taking a particular form and exerting a particular influence: "As I prolonged my stay, I perceived the great political consequences that flowed from these new facts. Among us, I had seen the spirit of religion and the spirit of freedom almost always move in contrary directions. Here I found them united intimately with one another: they reigned together on the same soil."[1]

A distinguished German historian, Hartmut Lehmann, has tried to analyze more specifically why over the last two centuries the churches of the United States have remained relatively full while in Europe they have emptied. By emphasizing how different histories produce different results, Lehmann carries Tocqueville's assessment one step farther: "In the United States factors such as voluntarism, revivalism, and pluralism created a cultural climate which favored the growth of religion and in which religious activism could easily be related to matters of justice and social reform. In Germany, factors such as the close cooperation between state and church, the suppression of nonconformism, and the domestication of active Christian groups produced a cultural climate in which religion was tainted with conservatism and with opposition to 'progress.'"[2]

The contemporary French sociologist Sébastien Fath uses a different historical assessment to underscore Lehmann's conclusions. In Fath's view, "A particularly Protestant heritage has profoundly shaped contemporary American society and the way in which Americans practice their social relationships." But in turn, "the social impact of a culture defined by choice" has decisively shaped the character of American Protestantism.[3] Along with American commentators, Fath believes that the resultant "civil religion" is not the same as the Christianity confessed by the churches but that it everywhere interacts with that Christianity. This civil religion he views as compounded of "the mythic events of the foundation of . . . white Anglo-Saxon Protestant . . . religious culture"; a public "accent on faith and prayer"; the strongly individualist shape of American religious instincts; the tendency to regard the United States as "supported by a prophetic and messianic special mission"; and an optimistic approach ("admirable from one angle but insufferable from another") to the American role in the world.[4] The ease with which specific forms of Christianity coexist with such a civil religion is, for Fath, a strong American distinctive.

Many of the recent efforts to define the particular character of American Christian experience have been driven by perceptions of the growing gap between public religious practice in the United States and in Europe. Since at least the 1960s, that gap has become noticeable on many fronts, with Americans much more likely to attend church, to claim religious membership, to profess belief in God, and to hold traditional Christian convictions. As one gauge of the international differences, the Angus Reid Group in 1997 conducted a multinational survey in which it asked respondents four different religious questions: whether they attended church, whether they prayed, whether they felt religion was important in their lives, and if they were "converted" Christians.[5] The United States, with 35 percent answering positively to all four items, registered a considerably higher result than Italy (27 percent), Poland (22 percent), Greece (20 percent), Spain (17 percent), and Canada (15 percent)—and a much higher result than Switzerland (9 percent), Ukraine (8 percent), Britain (7 percent), Germany (7 percent), Netherlands (7 percent), Norway (6 percent), Czech Republic (4 percent), Belgium (4 percent), Finland (3 percent), Sweden (3 percent), France (1 percent), and Russia (1 percent). Significantly, however, when compared with non-Western nations instead of with European countries, the U.S. response rate was not unusual—the Philippines (38 percent), South Africa (33 percent), South Korea (26 percent), and Brazil (25 percent).

Careful students of international trends have raised proper cautions about interpreting such survey results.[6] These cautions rightly draw attention to the fact that religious practices vary greatly by American region (some parts of the American Northeast and of the West Coast being almost as unconcerned about religion as much of Europe), that some sectors of American culture are just as secular as much of Europe (especially media and higher education), and that the American churches' much more accommodating attitude toward popular culture (rather than intrinsic religious differences) explains polling differences with Europe.

Yet with proper qualifications in place, what foreign visitors from Alexis de Tocqueville to Sébastien Fath have isolated as the special character of American Christianity remains convincing. They have suggested that the special circumstances of American history have encouraged special traits in American churches. These observations usually stress that the American character of American Christianity pertains first to Protestant traditions, but then with only slightly less force to Catholics as well as to adherents of other Christian traditions and of non-Christian religions as well.

They see a tendency toward individual self-fashioning instead of communal identification. They have observed much talk about personal free choice alongside language of received limits and personal responsibility. They have identified a strong American willingness to embrace commercial images and forms. They see religious institutions depicted as voluntary bodies organized for action instead of inherited institutions organized for holding fast. They emphasize that American approaches to scripture prize personal interpretations over inherited or hierarchical interpretation. And they find the center of religion in the bourgeoisie middle classes instead of in traditional elites or peasant masses.

Put most generally, this picture of American distinctiveness stresses the adaptations of traditional Christian forms to American society, defined, as one student of American exceptionalism has put it, by "populism and individualism at the personal level, democratization and market-making at the institutional level."[7] Some of the adaptations may have come pragmatically from adjustment to the religious pluralism that always characterized American settlement, first among Christian traditions and then among world religions in general. Some arise from the singular events of American history acting to mold a singular shape for American Christianity. Significantly, most of these perceptive accounts come from European perspectives. The case studies that follow bear out the wisdom of the foreign observers when focused on Europe. Another story emerges when the world as a whole comes into view.

Comparative Instances

Scottish and American Presbyterians

As Presbyterian churches developed in the American colonies, they shared much in common with Presbyterian and Reformed churches in Europe. Parallels were especially close with Scottish Presbyterians, the direct ancestors of Presbyterian churches in the New World. The great impetus for the founding of Presbyterian churches in the British Atlantic colonies was the desire of Scottish people, migrating directly from the mother country or with a stopover in the north of Ireland, for religion as they had known it at home. Beginning in 1707, the congregations and presbyteries that immigrant leaders like Francis Makemie, James Anderson, and George Gillespie established were marked by the standard practices and convictions of churches in the homeland. They were eager to employ well-educated ministers, committed to organization by congregation–presbytery–general assembly, and engaged actively with wider social and political concerns. Like the Presbyterians of Scotland, they were also interacting with many of the era's transnational and transdenominational movements.

Thus, these New World offshoots, like their Scottish progenitors, were open to the quickening currents of revival, and they were also dabbling in the oppositional politics of the day, known variously as republicanism, civic humanism, or Real Whiggery. And Presbyterians on both sides of the Atlantic were still joined by substantially similar practices, doctrines, assumptions, and convictions about politics and society.

Yet even in the earliest periods, local conditions were obviously pushing development in different directions. In Scotland, revival energies were mostly contained within the established church—the itinerant George Whitefield preached at Cambuslang in 1742 to immense crowds, but under the authority of authorized ministers of the Church of Scotland. In America, by contrast, revival split the church, with revival-favoring New Sides divided from revival-threatened Old Sides during the years from 1741 to 1758. For the long term, it would be significant that the popular energies of revival—either accepted or opposed—exerted a greater influence in America than in Scotland.

Again, in Scotland, oppositional politics were contained within one element of the church, while the Scottish Kirk as a whole maintained its traditional loyalty to the British crown and Britain's aristocratic body politic. In America, by contrast, oppositional politics flowed freely between church and society, with the result that most Presbyterians supported the American Revolution. Conversely, the move toward national independence made the church a more republican institution. When the American church organized its own General Assembly in 1789, more authority was ceded to synods, presbyteries, and particular congregations than had been the case in Scotland. This willingness to increase the democratic element and decrease the aristocratic, in response to the American political circumstances, permanently marked Presbyterian experience on this side of the Atlantic.

One other matter from the colonial period also pointed toward American distinctives—a pluralism that, though limited by later standards, was extensive for its own day. In the early decades of the eighteenth century, the newly formed American presbytery reached out to former Congregationalists from New England, incorporated immigrants from both Scotland and Northern Ireland, and then added a few individuals of Dutch and German extraction. The path was thus marked for an accommodation to diversity that would later make room for Hungarians, Slovaks, Mexicans, Koreans, Africans, and more.

In 1789, American Presbyterians also accommodated themselves to the radical new idea that church and state should be separated. This notion was not accepted in Scotland until the late nineteenth century, if even then. But the first American General Assembly, without pausing for a second thought about abridging a founding constitutional document, changed the original Westminster Confession of 1646 to eliminate references of help provided by magistrates to the churches. In addition, the Americans added a complete new paragraph to explain how governments were responsible for keeping the peace but were to do nothing positive for the churches except ensure that all "ecclesiastical persons" enjoyed "full, free, and unquestioned liberty."[8]

By taking their stand *against* Old World patterns of church-state establishment, American Presbyterians took their stand *for* what would become the United States' more democratic and more individualistic market in religion. Whether Presbyterians fully comprehended what they were getting into by welcoming an ecclesiastical landscape where *persuasion* replaced *coercion* is not entirely clear. Differentiation from Europe was still modest, but the trend was evident. Through a process of interaction with American events and ideas, Presbyterians in the new United States were becoming American Presbyterians.

Canada, Mexico, and the United States

A different comparative perspective comes from examining the three main nations of the North American continent—Mexico, the United States, and Canada. Broad historical comparisons among these three nations are rare for all subjects except cross-border trade, but such analysis offers much to religious history by showing how both founding circumstances and later events molded characteristic distinctives. Those distinctives, not surprisingly, are just as strong for Canada and Mexico as for the United States.

The common origin of North American Christianity was the ferment of Reformation and Counter-Reformation in sixteenth-century Europe. Yet the type of sixteenth-century Christianity exported to North America, and the manner of its planting, led to three very different Christian expressions in the New World. At its outset, Mexico was stamped by the comprehensive Roman Catholicism of Southern European regimes from the late Renaissance and the Catholic Counter-Reformation. Canada, by contrast, developed under the necessity of accommodating two Old World patterns in one nation: French Quebec, a traditional Old World society with church and state joined together organically, and the English Atlantic provinces with Upper Canada (Ontario), which were shaped by a British Protestantism that was more liberal politically than anything in Catholic Europe. For its part, the United States carried Protestant tendencies toward voluntary action and democratic polity to their logical conclusions (and sometimes beyond).

The European Christianity brought to Mexico attempted to absorb the Native Indian population. In Canada and the United States, by contrast, Native populations were mostly shunted aside, if they were not wiped out altogether by European diseases, loss of land, and warfare. Canadian Christian outreach to Native populations was marginally more extensive than in the United States, but the result in both countries was destruction for Natives.

Protestantism did not exist in Mexico before the mid-nineteenth century, and it was then only a small factor during the next century. At the start of the twenty-first century, though the number of Protestant adherents and the diversity of Protestant churches are both growing rapidly, Protestants still play a relatively small role in public life.[9] In the United States and in English Canada, Catholics learned to survive as a minority, while the Catholic majority in Quebec has always had to take account of the surrounding Protestant dominance of the United States and English Canada.

Comparatively observed, Christianity in Canada has been a force for calming or avoiding civil strife. To be sure, the historical picture is not entirely tranquil. Religious issues were not absent during the American invasions of 1775–76 and 1812–14, Canada's aborted revolutions of 1837–38, and the Fenian incursion of 1866.[10] Catholic-Protestant violence leading to fatalities attended the lectures of the Italian ex-priest Alessandro Gavazzi in 1853.[11] The tragic career of Louis Riel also precipitated a violent crisis thoroughly imbued with religion.[12] When Riel, a Catholic Métis, led uprisings in Manitoba (1870) and Saskatchewan (1885), he was judged more harshly by Protestants than by Catholics. When he was executed after the second uprising, bitter conflict simmered between Catholic Quebec and the rest of Canada for a decade, until Canada's first Catholic prime minister, Wilfrid Laurier, successfully assuaged both sides.

Taken as a whole, however, the religious contribution to civil strife in Canada has been much less than what religion has done to inflame violence in the United States and Mexico. The establishmentarian Catholicism of Catholic Quebec and the moderate, proprietary, and institutional nature of Canadian Protestantism worked in the settings of the New World to restrain violence. By contrast, the kind of social tensions that Canadian religious institutions moderated were in the United States and Mexico exacerbated by religious forces—in Mexico by the inherited strength of institutions and in the United States by the relative weakness of institutions.

In sharp contrast to the Canadian situation, the history of Christianity in Mexico is a history of ongoing institutional conflict.[13] The Mexican drive for independence early in the nineteenth century was led by priests—a creole, Miguel Hidalgo y Costilla, and a mestizo, José María Morelos—who were executed by the Spanish imperial authorities. To indicate how religious-political perceptions charged this early conflict, Hidalgo and Morelos were accused of fomenting Lutheran heresy, they were stripped of their clerical offices, and they became the last two individuals condemned to death by the Mexican Inquisition.

Once Mexico succeeded in securing its independence, reformist and more politically liberal forces clashed repeatedly with conservative forces strongly identified with the Catholic Church. Mexico represented a European Christendom transferred to the New World. Instead of the pluralism and institutional laissez-faire that came to characterize the United States and that was substantially present in Canada as well, Mexico experienced ongoing struggles for hegemony that had almost no parallels in the rest of North America. These struggles resembled much more the nineteenth-century French conflict of republican *laïcité* versus traditional Catholicism or the twentieth-century Spanish conflict between republicans and communists, on the one side, and Falangists, monarchists, and Catholics, on the other. The basic struggle was between the ideal of Catholicism as an effective agent of social cohesion for a racially and regionally diverse nation opposed to an ideology of liberal republicanism that sought separation between church and state.

Repeatedly, Mexican governments took extreme actions against institutional Catholicism, which led to predictable resistance—as in the 1830s when all bishoprics were vacated, or in the Revolutionary constitution of 1917 when churches lost all property rights and were prohibited from running schools. The overwhelming Catholic allegiance of Mexico's lower classes, and of considerable numbers from the middle and upper classes, fueled resistance to such measures. That resistance contributed to civil violence—in the War of the Reform (1857–59), the invasion sponsored by European powers that made Archduke Maximilian of Austria the emperor of Mexico (executed in 1867 by resurgent Mexican constitutionalists), the conflicts surrounding the Mexican Revolution of 1910–17, and the Cristero War of 1926–29, when Catholics opposed the draconian, anticlerical measures of the Revolutionary constitution. Normalization of relations between the Catholic Church and the Mexican state occurred only in the early 1990s. But by then, violence had broken out in the southern state of Chiapas between rapidly growing groups of Pentecostal Protestants and peasant Catholics resentful of Protestant disregard for traditional ritual practices.

The religious history of Mexico is distinctive in North America for how tensions between political liberalism and traditional Catholicism replicated a European pattern. Historical state-church ties were so close that political initiatives or religious innovations generated violent struggles for authority. Much of Mexico's religious history has been as nonviolent as that of the United States or Canada. But where religious tension has flared into violence, the inherited shape of Mexican Christianity and the singular character of Mexican experience have made that violence distinctive in a North American context.

In the United States, the Civil War was manifestly a religious war as well as a conflict over republican rights and sectional autonomy.[14] From the 1830s, the biblical defense of slavery exerted a nearly complete sway over the white South, even as it won over substantial segments of the North. In opposition, biblical and more generally Christian attacks on slavery fueled both northern immediate abolitionists and the more moderate forces behind gradual emancipation. During the war itself, appeals to God for military victory inspired troops and home fronts in both sections of the country.[15] After the war, active religious support and passive religious acceptance sanctioned the violence that stripped African Americans in the South of the civil rights granted by the post–Civil War amendments to the Constitution. When, in the 1950s and 1960s, the civil rights movement, which was driven by the strong Christian faith of its main supporters, finally succeeded, that success only took place after surmounting violent opposition, which was sometimes supported by other expressions of Christian faith.

The American history of slavery, race, sectional conflict, civil rights, and violence has always been a complex Christian history as well.[16] The success of populist, democratic, and individualistic forms of Christianity in gaining the allegiance of Americans from all regions, in all economic classes, and among all races virtually guaranteed that political violence would be religious. Christian warrants would justify conflict, Christian consolation would comfort the abused, and Christian rationalization would defend the antagonists.

When comparing the history of religion-connected violence in Canada, Mexico, and the United States, American Christianity is clearly distinctive, but not in a morally exceptional sense. Rather, it is distinctive for how the populist, individualistic, and institutionally flexible form of its dominant American expressions gave Christianity special prominence in conflicts, movements, and social tensions that emerged in a populist, individualistic, and institutionally flexible social milieu.

America and the World

American Christianity appears most distinctive when the focus is on how New World circumstances modified patterns of worship, organization, self-conception, and connection to government inherited from Christian Europe. When, however, perspective shifts, American distinctiveness appears in a new light. In fact, what makes American Christianity distinctive in a European or North American setting is precisely what makes it less distinctive when compared with the rest of the world.

The insights of Scottish missiologist Andrew Walls are especially important for this kind of broad world comparison.[17] Walls has suggested that the nineteenth century witnessed two developments that were of extraordinary significance for later history. First was the successful adaptation of traditional European Christianity to the liberal social environment of the United States. Second was the emergence of the voluntary society as the key vehicle for Protestant missionary activity. The American turn in the late eighteenth and early nineteenth centuries to voluntary, self-directed organization as the dominant means for carrying on the work of the church was immensely important.[18] Increasingly, American believers practiced the faith by forming their own churches and religious agencies, generating their own financial support, and taking responsibility themselves for guiding the faith. For the most part, voluntarism became the pattern for all churches in America— first for Europe's Dissenting traditions (Baptists) and the newer Protestant movements of the modern period (Methodists, Disciples, independents of many varieties), but then also for the older European state-churches (Catholics, Episcopalians, Presbyterians, Lutherans, English Puritans). This pattern of self-starting, self-financing, and self-spreading Christianity was not in itself new, for it had appeared among some earlier monastic and Pietist movements. But the voluntary pattern came into its own when American believers used the powerful resources of a liberal democracy to establish and support their churches.

Historically, Eastern Orthodox, Catholic, and the major European Protestant denominations had differed substantially among themselves, but almost all assumed that Christianity required Christendom—which meant taking for granted formal cooperation between church and state as well as a prominent place for the churches in the formal legal life of a society. It also meant that great weight was given to historical precedents—how things should be done depended as much on previous patterns as upon assessments of current opportunities. In short, Christendom meant that society was intended to function as an organic whole, with comprehensive public acknowledgment of God and comprehensive religious support for the nation.

The new American pattern did not abandon the Christendom ideal entirely, but it nonetheless embodied a much more informal Christianity and pushed consistently for ever-more-flexible institutions and ever-newer innovations in responding to spiritual challenges. A great deal of traditional European faith survived, especially among the Lutherans, Episcopalians, Roman Catholics, Eastern Orthodox, and some of the Calvinistic denominations that valued their European roots. But even in these groups, the voluntary principle worked with unprecedented effects. In many Christian traditions—among African Americans, for Holiness and Pentecostal movements, in contemporary megachurches—it became completely dominant.

As these adjustments of Old World Christianity to the voluntary democracy of the New World took place, the results were dramatic. From 1815 to 1914, the U.S. population grew very rapidly (from 8,400,000 to 99,100,000). Yet over the same century, Christian adherence grew even faster, from under one-fourth of the population to over two-fifths of the population, that is, from something around 2 million to something around 40 million.

This American expansion may have been the most rapid in the entire history of Christianity—until, that is, the even more rapid expansion on the continent of Africa over the last century and (perhaps) in China over the last half century. To notice where, and under what circumstances, these later expansions have taken place is to approach from a new angle the question of American Christian distinctiveness.

It has become a truism to note that Christianity in various forms is now advancing rapidly in parts of the world where the instincts of ancient Christendom are largely absent. Not coincidentally, such expansion often takes place where societies are marked by at least some characteristics similar to what developed in the nineteenth-century United States. These characteristics are especially obvious in the burgeoning cities of the Global South and in the rural areas worldwide that are being reshaped by global economic forces. These newer societies tend to be competitive and not deferential, open to Christian witness but not officially Christian, allowing space for entrepreneurial activity while not restricting religious expression too drastically. To the extent that these conditions have developed, it is not surprising that styles of Christianity that flourished in North America's competitive, market-oriented, rapidly changing, and initiative-rewarding environment would also flourish when other environments begin to look more like nineteenth-century America than fifteenth-century Europe.

Examples multiply from around the world. Catholic charismatics flourish in the chaotic social systems of Nigeria and the somewhat more controlled social flux of Brazil. Protestant megachurches blossom in South Korea alongside the fruits of aggressive entrepreneurial capitalism. Lay-led base communities and lay-led Bible study fellowships have developed throughout Latin America, among both Catholics and Protestants and especially in regions where natural disasters, urbanization, or Protestant missionary efforts have undercut the once-hegemonic character of Latin Catholicism. Most remarkable has been the dramatic rise of a great variety of Christian movements in China, which has taken place *after* the expulsion of Western missionaries, *despite* a full generation of intense persecution, and *alongside* the turn to commercial and industrial development.

In a word, forms of conversionistic and voluntaristic Christianity seem to be flourishing where something like nineteenth-century American social conditions have come to prevail—where, that is, the Christian message is active in situations marked by social fluidity, personal choice, the need for innovation, and a search for anchorage in the face of vanishing traditions exist. For such comparisons, it is still possible to observe much that is different in the United States, where wealth, local traditions, political connections, and forms of religious pluralism remain untypical. But viewed from a long historical perspective, similarities are just as striking as differences.

Is American Christianity distinctive? A well-rounded theological answer would require close attention to the quality of Christian observance, the life-transforming power of the Christian gospel, and the nature of Christian influence on surrounding cultures. In historical terms, the simple, but accurate, answer is—definitely, when compared with Europe, Western societies like Canada and Mexico, or elsewhere where the heritage of European Christianity remains strong. The answer for comparisons with the rest of the world is—not so much.

NOTES

1. Alexis de Tocqueville, *Democracy in America*, ed. and trans. Harvey Claflin Mansfield and Delba Winthrop (Chicago: University of Chicago Press, 2000), 282.

2. Hartmut Lehmann, "The Christianization of America and the Dechristianization of Europe in the 19th and 20th Centuries," *Kirchliche Zeitgeschichte* 11 (1998): 12.

3. Sébastien Fath, "Protestantisme et lien social aux États-Unis," *Archives de Sciences Sociales des Religions* 108 (October–December 1999): 6.

4. See Sébastien Fath, "American Civil Religion and George W. Bush," in *Religion and American Politics: From the Colonial Period to the Present*, ed. Mark A. Noll and Luke E. Harlow, 2nd ed. (New York: Oxford University Press, 2007), 393–400, which summarizes Sébastien Fath, *Dieu bénisse l'Amérique: La religion de la Maison-Blanche* (Paris:/ editions du Seuil, 2004).

5. "Faith in the Modern World," *Angus Reid World Monitor* 1 (January 1998): 33–42; personal correspondence, Andrew Grenville (of Angus Reid) to Mark Noll, November 26, 1997.

6. See especially Hugh McLeod, *The Religious Crisis of the 1960s* (Oxford, UK: Oxford University Press, 2007), 249–55.

7. Byron E. Shafer, "What Is the American Way?" in *Is America Different: A New Look at American Exceptionalism*, ed. Byron E. Shafer (Oxford, UK: Clarendon, 1991), 223.

8. *The Constitution of the Presbyterian Church (U.S.A.): Part I, Book of Confessions* (Louisville: Office of the General Assembly, 2002), 147.

9. Lindy Scott, *Salt of the Earth: A Socio-political History of Mexico City Evangelical Protestants, 1964–1991* (Mexico City: Editorial Kyrios, 1991).

10. George A. Rawlyk, ed., *Revolution Rejected, 1775–1776* (Scarborough, Ont.: Prentice-Hall, 1968). On the War of 1812, see David Mills, *The Idea of Loyalty in Upper Canada, 1784–1850* (Montreal: McGill-Queen's University Press, 1988), 25–28; Colin Read and Ronald J. Stagg, eds., *The Rebellion of 1837 in Upper Canada* (Ottawa: Carleton University Press, 1985); and Allan Greer, *The Patriots and the People: The Rebellion of 1837 in Rural Lower Canada* (Toronto: University of Toronto Press, 1993), 233–39.

11. D. G. Paz, "Apostate Priests and Victorian Religious Turmoil: Gavazzi, Achilli, Connelly," *Proceedings of the South Carolina Historical Association* (1985): 57–69.

12. Thomas Flanagan, *Louis "David" Riel: Prophet of the New World*, rcv. ed. (Toronto: University of Toronto Press, 1996).

13. See Jean Pierre Bastian, *Protestantismo y sociedad en México* (Mexico City: Casa Unida de Publicaciones, 1983).

14. Mark A. Noll, *The Civil War as a Theological Crisis* (Chapel Hill: University of North Carolina Press, 2006).

15. Harry S. Stout, *Upon the Altar of the Nation: A Moral History of the Civil War* (New York: Viking, 2006).

16. Mark A. Noll, *God and Race in American Politics: A Short History* (Princeton: Princeton University Press, 2008).

17. Andrew Walls, "The American Dimension of the Missionary Movement" and "Missionary Societies and the Fortunate Subversion of the Church," in Andrew Walls, *The Missionary Movement in Christian History: Studies in the Transmission of Faith* (Maryknoll, N.Y.: Orbis, 1996), 221–40, 241–54; and Andrew Walls, "The Missionary Movement: A Lay Fiefdom?" in Andrew Walls, *The Cross-Cultural Process in Christian History: Studies in the Transmission and Appropriation of Faith* (Maryknoll, N.Y.: Orbis, 2002), 215–35.

18. See especially Nathan O. Hatch, *The Democratization of American Christianity* (New Haven: Yale University Press, 1989).

PART IV
Christianity and the American Nation

"Congress shall make no law respecting an establishment of religion, or prohibiting the free exercise thereof."

The First Amendment to the Constitution, passed in 1791, prohibited the creation of an established national church and defended the principle of religious freedom. Few documents in American history have been as celebrated, as revolutionary—or as controversial. Most colonial Americans had assumed that government could not survive without strong religious foundations, and nine of the original thirteen colonies had required people to pay taxes to support an established church. In the new republic, however, Americans would be able to worship—or *not* worship—as they pleased. Under Article Six of the Constitution—"No religious test shall ever be required as a qualification to any office or public trust under the authority of the United States"—even the nation's highest elected officials were not compelled to profess any religious belief.

Yet even though the Founders severed the formal connection between church and state, they also guaranteed the "free exercise" of religion, and Christians quickly learned how to rely on persuasion rather than coercion to influence the nation. In the nineteenth century, they relied on voluntary mobilization to influence public attitudes toward the most pressing issues of the day, including slavery, civil war, temperance, and women's rights, and although they lamented their declining influence in the twentieth and twenty-first centuries, Christians continued to make their voices heard in political elections, the civil rights movement, and public debates over capital punishment, abortion, feminism, homosexuality, health care, and the meaning of the First Amendment. Even though the U.S. government is supposed to be religiously neutral, Christian language, ideas, and symbols have always been an integral part of national life.

Part IV of *American Christianities* examines the profound influence of Christianity on American national identity. As the essays in this section reveal, Christians have often argued over what an ideal nation should look like, and in the jostle of democratic politics they have disagreed about national purpose and policy. Abolitionists and slaveholders, pacifists and generals, isolationists and secretaries of state—all have used Christian language to support their causes. During the 1970s, for example, Methodists and Latter-day Saints argued over whether the Equal Rights Amendment would raise women to their natural Christian status as men's equals or whether it would destroy the traditional Christian family. American Christians have also argued over whether violence can ever be morally justified, whether they should concentrate on saving individual souls or transforming the social order, whether religion should be a matter of private conscience or public discourse, and which political party best represents their religious ideals. All of these debates have contributed to the fractiousness of American public life.

In the midst of these disagreements, however, American Christians have also joined together to promote a common faith in the nation's exceptionalism. Ever since John Winthrop, a Puritan leader, described America as a "city on a hill" in his 1630 sermon, "A Model of Christian Charity," religious leaders and politicians have insisted that the United States has a special destiny. Drawing on biblical imagery, they have described America as a "new Israel," a "redeemer nation," or in Abraham Lincoln's phrase, "the last best hope of earth." Although not all Christians have invested the nation with religious meaning, many have conflated the flag with the cross, justifying even violence and warfare in the Christian language of "sacrifice." The image of the United States as a "city on a hill" has become so common that it no longer strikes many Americans as particularly religious, but it is ultimately rooted in the Bible. Whether or not Americans have always recognized it, they have drawn on Christian language and ideas to create a common national identity.

Over the past half century, a distinguished series of books has emphasized the powerful influence of Christianity on American national identity, an influence well conveyed in the titles: *Redeemer Nation* by Ernest Lee Tuveson, *Righteous Empire* by Martin Marty, *A Christian America* by Robert Handy, and *God's New Israel* by Conrad Cherry. This section of *American Christianities* contributes to that distinguished interpretive project by focusing on how American Christians have contributed to national conversations about public schooling, political parties, women's citizenship, warfare, social reform, and the First Amendment.

Christianity, National Identity, and the Contours of Religious Pluralism

> As to religion, I hold it to be the indispensable duty of every government, to protect all conscientious professors thereof, and I know of no other business which government hath to do therewith. . . . For myself, I fully and conscientiously believe, that it is the will of the Almighty, that there should be a diversity of religious opinions among us: it affords a larger field for our Christian kindness. — Thomas Paine, *Common Sense*

In his 2009 inaugural address to the nation, President Barack Obama affirmed that "our patchwork heritage is a strength, not a weakness. We are a nation of Christians and Muslims, Jews and Hindus—and nonbelievers."[1] The new president's salutary nod to America's religious variety differed from those of his recent predecessors in extending the scope of recognition beyond the so-called Abrahamic faiths of Judaism, Christianity, and Islam. But the pride of place Obama gave to religious pluralism among America's strengths was not itself new. In the founding documents and in the speeches of statesmen, presidents, and policymakers, the nation's vaunted commitment to protect the religious rights of all has served as a kind of shorthand for the more general freedoms that Americans purportedly enjoy to a degree equaled by no other nation on earth.

Such celebrations typically ground religious freedom and pluralism in the constitutional separation of church and state. The sanctity of individual conscience affirmed by the First Amendment's framers and their denominationalist supporters constituted religion as *inherently* free, a matter of private conviction rather than civil allegiance, and as such beyond the reach of government or other powers. To this view, national unity grounded in the principle of religious freedom would do what no established church could do, which was to secure national identity not through government interference in belief but through collective opposition to government interference in belief. The policy of legal noninterference in the religion of citizens, so a long-standing version of this story goes, both nurtures and protects the religious pluralism that goes to making *e pluribus unum* in a resiliently diverse United States.

As the editors of *American Christianities* point out, however, what distinguishes religion in the United States from religion in other industrialized countries is not how diverse it has become under the First Amendment's safeguards, but instead how Christian it remains. Even Thomas Paine, whose harsh words for Christianity are routinely quoted by those at pains to insist that America was founded as a secular nation, nevertheless imagined the religious diversity protected by church-state separation to flourish within a Christian frame. "Careful listening" to invocations of religious pluralism as a good, observes religious historian Martin Marty, "would reveal that 'pluralism' implies and involves a polity, a civic context which provides some 'rules of the game,' refers to an ethos, and evokes response."[2] In the U.S. context, the "rules of the game" set by the civic context of church-state separation would nevertheless seem to be Christian. At the very least, the U.S. model of separation between religion and government emerges from historically Protestant formulations of religion as a matter, foremost, of private conscience. "I do not believe in the creed professed by the Jewish church, by the Roman church, by the Greek church, by the Turkish church, by the Protestant church, nor by any church that I know of," Paine wrote in *The Age of Reason*. "My own mind is my own church."[3] This way of understanding religion allows for the flourishing of potentially as many religions as there are individual minds, but at the cost of making religion a matter of what both Paine and Thomas Jefferson famously called "opinion."[4]

The subtly prescriptive nature of appeals to religious pluralism as a shining achievement in America also conceals a messier history. In the United States, a dominant Protestant presence in government, law, schools, and other civic institutions has shaped and enforced the meanings of both "religion" and "pluralism" over against competing models of what either might entail, a process more often marked by bitter and even violent divides than the resulting narrative of America's religious development has been able or willing to register.[5] As this volume's editors observe, moreover, what also tends to go missing in normative accounts of religion in the United States is the long history of disagreement internal to Christianity itself. Throughout American history, they note, a vast majority of men and women have identified themselves as Christian even as they have differed sharply in theology and practice—not to mention politics, ethics, and the conduct of their day-to-day lives.

Against this immense and often conflictual variety, instances of apparent consensus deserve attention as less than self-explanatory. When and why have members of a diverse population of adherents to a variety of faiths banded together under the unified heading of "Christians" in America? This essay focuses on three such moments, poised across three centuries of religious and political practice: the responses of Anglo-American colonists to the British Parliament's passage of the 1774 Quebec Act, which legalized the practice of Roman Catholicism in the formerly French colony; mid-nineteenth-century conflicts between Protestants and Catholics over the reading of the King James Bible in public schools; and the political maneuverings and party realignments by which the nonchurchgoing presidential candidate Ronald Reagan came to wrest the self-identified Christian vote (both Protestant and Catholic) from the more overtly pious Jimmy Carter in 1980.

What unites these otherwise disparate examples is that in each a particular understanding of Christianity made far-reaching claims to legitimacy as a *national* and not only a religious identity. In none of the three examples, however, was American identity conceived as Christian identity in defiance of emerging or entrenched conceptions of the separation of church and state. On the contrary, the fusing of religious and national identity was made in each case to serve the American ideals of religious freedom, pluralism, and tolerance, with Christianity specifically invoked to safeguard these ideals. Confronted with the political challenge of Quebecois religious otherness, the 1774 Continental Congress enduringly cast the Protestantism of the lower colonies not as a party to the religious differences the emerging democratic polity would need to address, but instead as the frame within which those differences could best be accommodated. When mid-nineteenth-century Catholics objected that the centrality of the King James Bible to the curriculum made U.S. public schools into instruments of a de facto Protestant establishment, school boards, courts, and the national press insisted that both schools *and* the Protestant Bible were religiously neutral, and that Catholic claims for redress were themselves a sectarian imposition that violated the separation of church and state. In the 1980 presidential election, finally, Ronald Reagan's signature stances against communism and in favor of states' rights and free markets carried the day in part by tagging him as more "Christian" and so more capable of leading the nation than his earnestly devout Southern Baptist opponent. After considering each of these examples, I briefly trace the career of what critic Gil Anidjar has called "(Christian) politics as usual"[6] into more recent presidential administrations and revisit Obama's inaugural address in the context of this history.

The Quebec Act

Anxieties about religious variety and Protestant-Catholic difference in particular belong centrally to the emergence of democratic governance in the United States and to American notions of liberty more generally. When Harriet Beecher Stowe compared the plight of slaves to the tortures of the Inquisition or when Lyman Beecher, in a different register, charged the Catholic Church with bringing "debasement and slavery to those who live under it,"[7] both signaled their debt to an Anglo-American narrative of freedom that set Protestantism, the Hanoverian succession, and love of liberty against Catholicism, the Jacobites, and "slavery," a noun that enjoyed a long career in America as a metaphor for endangered self-government at a time when few colonists went on record as being troubled by racial bondage. "Slavery" could be seen, for example, in the Roman Catholic doctrine of transubstantiation, which elicited Jonathan Mayhew's defense of "the common rights of seeing, hearing, touching, smelling, tasting; all which popery attacks and undermines . . . and would take . . . from us, as a means of making us dutiful sons, or rather wretched slaves of the church."[8]

Mayhew's concern for the integrity of the senses against the rapacious designs of Rome was motivated by the 1763 Treaty of Paris, which ceded Quebec to the British and included a provision for the protection of Catholic practice in the formerly French colony. To colonists on the cusp of rebellion, accommodation of the religious rights of Canadian Catholics under the British crown was a double assault, at once "unfriendly to the protestant cause," as the Continental Congress would put it, "and inimical to liberty."[9] The perceived danger was that the monarchy and the Catholic Church would prove mutual allies in unjust rule: in 1774, the closing of Boston Harbor by the British in retaliation for the Boston Tea Party the previous year brought forth an advertisement for the *Master-Key to Popery*, a book deemed "highly necessary to be kept in every Protestant family in this country; that they may see to what a miserable state the people are reduced in all arbitrary and tyrannical governments, and be thereby excited to stand on their guard against the infernal machinations of the British ministers, and their vast *host* of tools, emissaries, etc., etc., sent hither to propagate the principles of Popery and Slavery, which go hand in hand as inseparable companions."[10]

In 1774, Britain's George III also signed the Quebec Act into law, codifying the conditions agreed to in the Treaty of Paris. The section of the act concerning the "Free Exercise of Religion of the Church of *Rome*" explicitly limited Catholic practice to the "Boundary of the Province of *Quebec*" and subjected it "to the King's supremacy."[11] The act nevertheless renewed unease among Anglo-Protestants in the thirteen lower colonies, where newspapers appealed to the colonists to unite against "*Popish* Superstition and *French* Tyranny" and to "vindicate . . . our Protestant Religion and our *British* Liberties."[12] The Continental Congress responded to the Quebec Act in its 1774 *Address to the People of Great Britain*, which argued that when dangerously cosseted by an "Administration, so friendly to their religion," Canadian Catholics "might become formidable to us, and on occasion, be fit instruments in the hands of power, to reduce the ancient free Protestant Colonies to the same state of slavery with themselves."[13]

This framing of the Quebec Act as an affront to liberty in the lower colonies was fraught with contradictions, among them the fact that to repeal it would be to retract the religious liberty conditionally granted to the Quebecois or the fact that the condemnation of Catholic "slavery" was made in the early documents of a nation that would long harbor race slavery within its borders. In its address to the British overseas, the Continental Congress warned of the evil designs of an "Administration" that indulged Catholic practice even as this same administration—a Protestant monarchy with an established Anglican Church—governed both the British colonial subjects, who complained of its "Romish business,"[14] and the citizens of Great Britain, with whom, for the purpose of opposing Catholicism, they here made common cause.

More than a catalyst for revolt against a "Protestant Popish King," however, the Quebec Act forced the uniting colonies to confront the very real challenge of incorporating a variety of religions within an emerging democratic polity that would need to mediate their divergent, perhaps powerfully conflicting, claims. Rather than engage religious pluralism as a site of ongoing negotiation and struggle, the nation's Founders elected instead to present Protestantism, one party in the face-off, as the *answer* to the problem of pluralism and the source of a coherent national identity in the face of religious difference.

In this sense, the Founders grafted their nascent experiment in democracy to the more long-standing Protestant emphasis on the sanctity of conscience, an emphasis that developed from the Protestant Reformers' insistence that the relationship between God and the individual soul was not to be mediated by government or ecclesiastical authorities. In implicit opposition to Catholic understandings of religious identity as sanctioned by apostolic authority and bound to communities of practice, this view made religion a matter of private conviction rather than corporate allegiance, and as such beyond the power of either civil or ecclesiastical bodies to compel. "And what is offered to you by the late Act of Parliament," the Continental Congress would ask in an overture to the Quebecois, inviting them to send their own delegation to Philadelphia. "Liberty of conscience in your religion? No. God gave it to you."[15] To this view, government protection for religious freedom could proceed only through official acknowledgment of that freedom's a priori nature.

In protesting the Quebec Act as "inimical to liberty," the Continental Congress sought simultaneously to portray Catholicism as incompatible with democracy *and* to extend the promise of religious liberty to Catholics within the new nation. Rather than grant official protection for their Catholic practice, union with the rebelling colonies—in the majority of which formal Protestant establishment in fact remained in force—would instead safeguard for the Quebecois the more diffuse but fundamental liberty of conscience, the alleged basis of both religious freedom and representative government. In inviting them to join in opposing the British monarchy that offered formal protection for their rights as Catholics, the Continental Congress offered the Quebecois membership in a democratic polity where all rights flow from the "first grand right," which is "that of the people having a share in their own government by their representatives chosen by themselves, and, in consequence, being ruled by *laws*, which they themselves approve, not by *edicts* of *men* over whom they have no control."[16]

The formulation of religious freedom given by the Continental Congress in 1774 carried over into the rhetoric that shaped the religious clauses of the First Amendment. Since "the duty which we owe to our Creator and the manner of discharging it, can be directed only by reason and conviction," James Madison argued in 1785, so the religion "of every man must be left to the conviction and conscience of every man."[17] Such a view protects religious pluralism by giving primacy to a particular understanding of religion as individual rather than collective, believed rather than performed or embodied, and voluntary rather than rote or compelled. "Believing with you that religion is a matter which lies solely between Man & his God," Jefferson famously wrote in his 1802 letter to the Danbury Baptists, "that he owes account to none other for his faith or his worship, that the legitimate powers of government reach actions only, & not opinions, I contemplate with sovereign reverence that act of the whole American people which declared that *their* legislature should 'make no law respecting an establishment of religion, or prohibiting the free exercise thereof," thus building a wall of separation between Church & State."[18]

In arguing against official legal support for Christianity at the federal level, Madison warned that such support would be viewed as a cautionary "Beacon on our Coast," warning all who suffer the "cruel scourge" of religious intolerance "in foreign Regions" to "seek some other haven."[19] The constitutional protections for religious liberty that Madison helped to craft offered however only limited relief to sufferers of religious intolerance at home. The establishment clause of the First Amendment—"Congress shall make no law respecting the establishment of religion"—was understood to preclude *dis*establishment as well, and Protestant establishment in fact survived in Vermont, Connecticut, and Massachusetts until the early nineteenth century. Moreover, many of the eighteenth-century state constitutions that precluded religious establishment also specified that no Catholic, Jew, or nonbeliever was eligible to hold legislative office; some stipulated further that only Protestant teachers could count on the support of the state. More subtly, the grounding of the right to religious freedom in privacy enduringly constrains its legal applications, particularly among those whose understandings of religious identity and practice lie at some distance from the Protestant model.

Christians who, against secularists, have wished to claim a Protestant, Christian imprimatur for America's founding principle of religious liberty do not entirely misread its sources, even if they fall short of identifying its limitations. Those who contributed to this Protestant model of religious freedom in America need not themselves have formally embraced a particular strand of Protestantism, as Thomas Jefferson, James Madison, Thomas Paine, and many others did not. As literary historian Elizabeth Fenton argues, their view of religion reveals less their theological disposition or commitment to Protestant flourishing than it does "the extent to which a post-Reformation logic permeated early U.S. notions of liberty."[20]

Subsequent appeals to a Christian America would move away from this post-Reformation logic, even as they often maintained its signature flourishes and residual assumptions. Among these is the assumption that when lifted away from its institutional contexts, the language of Protestant Christianity is also the language of religious neutrality, and so the language most conducive to safeguarding religious freedom and pluralism. As Andover Seminary professor Bela Bates Edwards put it in 1848, "Perfect religious liberty" does "not imply that the government of th[is] country is not a Christian government," thanks to the "real, though indirect association between the State and Christianity."[21]

The Bible Wars

In the middle decades of the nineteenth century, American Catholics would come to challenge the spirit of "Christian government," even when and often because this spirit was given as one of tolerance and accommodation. In populous cities like Boston, New York, Cincinnati, and Philadelphia, their challenge came to center on the compulsory reading in public schools of the King James Bible, often presented as the antidote to their religious and cultural foreignness. The "son of an Irishman, a Frenchman, or Italian is an American," wrote Princeton Theological Seminary trustee Nicholas Murray, "and he will not be a Romanist. We have a mill, of which the common school is the nether, and the Bible and its institutions the upper stone; into this mill let us cast the people of all countries and all forms of religion that come here, and they will come out in the grist Americans and Protestants. And the highest wisdom of our country is to keep this mill in vigorous operation."[22]

In Philadelphia, Protestant-Catholic conflicts over Bible reading in public schools that had begun in the 1830s escalated by the summer of 1844 into a series of violent confrontations in which churches and homes were burned to the ground and more than a dozen rioters were killed. The Philadelphia Bible riots have usefully been cast as class and ethnic conflicts, but little attention has been paid to Catholic objections to compulsory Bible reading as a political critique, namely, an indictment of the exclusionary nature of civil protections for religion within a de facto Protestant state. "We rejoice in the progress of civil liberty," declared the Philadelphia Baptist Association in 1796, "because [it is] so intimately related to the liberty with which Christ has made us free."[23] Such views primed Nativist Protestants in the Philadelphia conflict to detach "Christianity" from both denominational affiliation and privately held belief and to tether it all the more securely to national symbols, including the Constitution and the American flag, which were then invoked as the mantle of "freedom of religion," whose fabric Catholic claims to free exercise of religion could only be figured as rending in pieces.

On March 21, 1839, an editorial in the *Philadelphia Catholic-Herald* under the pen name "Sentinel" voiced the objections of Catholic parents whose children were compelled to take part in Protestant devotional exercises and subjected to partisan religious sentiments in textbooks that purported to teach general knowledge. The writer called for a "legal provision" that would "permit no books to be used in the schools, save of a literary or scientific character," and would "allow no religious exercise or instruction whatever." No such provision arrived. Rather than limit their efforts to the identification of objectionably partisan lessons and religious exercises, Catholics who continued to protest against the Protestant character of public schooling came over the next several years to argue with increasing force that the schools' central, common textbook—the King James Bible—was a sectarian one, and therefore that the entire curriculum required revision. As "Sentinel" put it in a November 25, 1841, *Philadelphia Catholic-Herald* editorial,

> The union of Church and State is virtually effected as soon as public education has become sectarian, or received a sectarian bias: which is the case the moment the Protestant principle of the Bible as the sole rule of faith is adopted by its introduction into the public schools, as the source of religious instruction to the pupils. Protestants cannot conceive that such education should be styled sectarian, as long as it is not professedly in the hands of a sect: but if it assume not the hue of any particular sect of Protestants, it will necessarily be Protestant in its character.

Bishop Francis Kenrick of Philadelphia, meanwhile, shrewdly appealed to Catholics' rights of conscience in urging the Philadelphia Board of Controllers to allow Catholic pupils to be excused from compulsory participation in Protestant religious observance. "We offer up prayers and supplications to God for all men," Kenrick wrote; "we embrace all in the sincerity of Christian affection, but we confine the marks of religious brotherhood to those who are of the household of the faith. Under the influence of this conscientious scruple, we ask that the Catholic children be not required to join in singing hymns or other religious exercises."[24] This the Board of Controllers grudgingly granted, over complaints lodged by the American Protestant Association that Kenrick's objections to the sectarian nature of Protestant hymns constituted a "grotesque phantom of the brain" and that his objections to compulsory prayer "disparages and dishonors its source."[25]

In ensuing exchanges in the Philadelphia press, Protestants and Catholics alike saw themselves as victims of sectarian persecution. The *Episcopal Recorder* of March 9, 1844, urged that "Protestant Christians,—American Christians, awake to the crisis and consider the duty which is before them." "Are we to yield our personal liberty, our inherited rights, our very Bibles, the special, blessed gift of God to our country, to the will, the ignorance, or the wickedness of these hordes of foreigners . . . thrown upon our shores, and sheltered here with a kindness the most tolerant and confiding?" On February 15, 1844, the *Catholic-Herald* had warned its readers, meanwhile, that the "Protestant Association will take charge of our youth, and provide them with a Bible, hymns, and prayers, according to their judgment, and we must sit down contented, and be silent, if not grateful. They may afterwards provide us with a national religion, when we shall have been prepared for the blessing, by means of a National Protestant Education."

Those who were unwilling to distinguish Protestantism from religious neutrality were also unwilling to distribute the meaning of "American" and "Christian" across a broader spectrum of religious difference, even as they claimed for Americans and Christians the privilege of extending religious tolerance. According to a leader of Philadelphia's Native American Party, a man "may be a Turk, a Jew, or a Christian, a Catholic, a Methodist or Presbyterian, and we say nothing against it," but "when we remember that our Pilgrim fathers landed on Plymouth rock to establish the Protestant religion, free from persecution, we must contend that this was and always will be a Protestant country."[26] Writing about the Philadelphia conflict a decade later, a nativist chronicler of the period vested the principle of religious freedom in the very text that Catholic pupils were forced to read against their families' religious scruples, finding in the Bible's pages "the Divine authority for the rights of man, as well as for the separation of church and state, on which depends so essentially the pursuit of happiness and freedom of conscience."[27]

In early May 1844, scuffling between Protestant and Catholic crowds in the working-class Kensington section of Philadelphia gave way to gunfire that took the life of a young Protestant rioter. The first casualty in the skirmishes that followed, the victim was widely hailed in the Protestant press as a martyr for "defending the American flag." Over the next several days, Catholic homes and churches were burned as Protestants marched through the streets carrying flags and open Bibles. A placard carried by one Protestant flag waver proclaimed that this was "the FLAG that was trampled UNDERFOOT by the IRISH PAPISTS."[28]

What is noteworthy is not the vehemence of Protestant outrage—Protestant lives lost in the continuing conflicts exceeded Catholic ones—but the associations it fixes between "Protestant" and "American." After the quelling of a second wave of riots that broke out in the wake of Fourth of July demonstrations by Protestant nativists, the *Christian Observer* of July 19, 1844, magnanimously extended the blessings of American liberty to Catholics in precisely the language they had rejected in refusing conversion to a "national religion" by means of a "National Protestant Education": "We wish them [the Roman Catholics] to enjoy the same religious liberty, the same protection, that we enjoy. . . . But when they come to our shores, we wish them to . . . have their minds imbued with *American* principles. We wish them to be *Americanized*, if we may use that term, instead of . . . act[ing] over again, scenes of turmoil in which they have too often been prominent in the old world."[29]

Such imputations to Catholics of the propensity to incite "turmoil" in their efforts to claim religious rights in the United States figured graphically in the response of liberal political cartoonist Thomas Nast to revivals of the "Bible Wars" in several American cities over the next two decades. A Nast cartoon in the February 19, 1870, issue of *Harper's Weekly* juxtaposed two images. In the first, titled "Europe," Queen Victoria and other monarchs and statesmen righteously preside over the tearing of a banner into halves marked "church" and "state"—no matter that Victoria herself was titular head of an established national church—while a caricatured assembly of disgruntled Catholic leaders cowers in one corner. In the second image, "United States," a crowd of unruly priests and bishops dip their hands into bags marked "public school money," while the figure of Liberty (shackled to a ballot box marked "fraudulent votes") looks helplessly on and a coarse-looking woman in a cross-emblazoned dunce cap stitches the severed pieces of a banner marked "church" and "state" back together. Although the haphazardly mended banner in the second image looks like the severed banner of the first, closer inspection reveals it to be a makeshift map of the United States, on which the cities of New York, Cincinnati, and San Francisco are imprecisely aligned on the tear along which "church" and "state" are awkwardly rejoined. If the cartoon suggests that these are cities in which Constitution-defying Catholic immigrants stand to win the balance of power, it also hints that a mangled United States can only be the result if the reconstruction of the Union proceeds on terms that favor them.

That a Catholic-Protestant divide might stand in for other axes of difference was suggested by a second Nast cartoon that appeared in the same magazine a week later. This cartoon aligns three images in a vertical display. The uppermost image ("Our Common Schools as They Are") depicts children of assorted, visually representable races, religions, and nationalities—a black child, a Chinese child, a child in tartan plaid—who join hands in a circle on the grounds of a building marked "Common School." The image at the bottom of the page ("Our Common Schools . . . as They May Be") depicts a similarly diverse group of children now at violent odds—swar-

FIGURE 1. *"Church and State,"* by Thomas Nast. Harper's Weekly, February 19, 1870. Courtesy of Harpweek.

thy Jewish and Irish boys exchanging blows, a black boy pulling a Chinese boy's queue—against a backdrop of tenement-like buildings marked "Methodist school," "Episcopal school," "Low Church school," "High Church school," "Jewish school," "Roman Catholic school," "African school," "Chinese school," "German school," and "French [school]." In the image dividing these two, the blindfolded figure of Justice stands mute as a public school's coffers are emptied to enrich the Roman Catholic school just opposite.

In fact, the African American, Native American, and immigrant children pictured in the image of "Our Common Schools as They Are" were unlikely to have been in public schools in 1870; they were more typically on waiting lists because of overcrowding in urban schools, in parochial or racially segregated schools, or truant because of pressure on them to work. As the Continental Congress had depicted the "*free* Protestant Colonies" as able on that basis to accommodate the religious difference of the Catholic Quebecois, however, so the Nast image of "Our Common Schools as They Are" figures a Protestant America uniquely equipped to value religious and racial diversity. Nowhere in Nast's idealized public school is the Catholic child represented with other Catholics, the Jewish child with other Jews, and so on; each child appears instead as part of expansive and assimilative Protestantism. At the same time, no child appears to be menaced by the divided loyalties or fractious isolation he might plausibly be expected to feel as one severed from the collective life of a particular tradition. Instead, this state of alienation obtains only *outside* the circle of Protestant solicitude, where those who continue to assert communal identities other than American and Protestant are represented as rejecting the extension of community on democratic terms.[30]

Catholic Assimilation and the Christian Vote

In the earlier twentieth century, anti-Catholicism would assume familiar forms ranging from scandalized popular accounts of the Catholic Church's tyrannical ambitions to the more sober warnings of secular intellectuals who distinguished Catholic authoritarianism from Protestant freedom in matters of education, government, and trade. What united these discourses was their commitment to making America a model of liberty and framing as dangerously *un*-American either the Catholic Church or the constraints on individual freedom it was made to represent. The 1928 presidential campaign of the Democratic nominee Alfred E. Smith, a Catholic, was derailed by both popular and elite prejudice, prompting members of the church hierarchy to

FIGURE 2. *"Our Common Schools as They Are and as They May Be,"* by Thomas Nast. Harper's Weekly, *February 26, 1870. Courtesy of Harpweek.*

convene a National Conference on Apologetics in 1929 to improve the Catholic Church's image in the United States. Part of the public relations work undertaken by U.S. Catholics over the next several decades would be to join in the symbolic construction of a "Judeo-Christian" America built on the values allegedly held in common among Protestants, Catholics, and Jews.

Foremost among these values was respect for individual liberty, private property, and the democratic process. The Temple of Religion at the 1939–40 World's Fair, for example, was sponsored by a coalition of New York business and civic leaders that included Protestants, Catholics, and Jews. The Temple of Religion's motto, engraved on its entablature and seen by all who entered, was "For All Who Worship God and Prize Religious Freedom." Welcoming all who, in their view, worshiped God, the Temple of Religion's managers excluded from participation those they deemed (not insufficiently theistic but) "not decidedly American," a category that included Muslims, Buddhists, and other practitioners of "foreign" religions as well as those with dissident political views. Catholic and Jewish leaders, meanwhile, used invited appearances at the Temple of Religion to argue for their place under the erstwhile exclusionary mantle of Americanism.[31] In this and like venues, the Catholic Church in the United States came to wave the ideological flag of a "Judeo-Christian" America, presenting itself as an enemy of foreign tyranny, a champion of religious freedom, and a benign steward of capital.

This last emphasis marked a relatively recent shift. At the end of the nineteenth century, when American Protestant elites were openly hostile to workers' demands as restraints on free trade, the Catholic Church had stood for the rights of labor and condemned unrestricted capitalism. "Free competition," wrote the Italian Jesuit Matteo Liberatore, "is a terrible weapon, most effectual to crush the weak and reduce whole populations to economic slavery."[32] The 1891 papal encyclical *Rerum Novarum* insisted that "wages ought to be sufficient to support a frugal and well-behaved wage-earner. If through necessity or fear of a worse evil the workman accept harder conditions because an employer or contractor will afford him no better, he is made the victim of force and injustice."[33]

Whatever the Catholic Church's hospitality to workers' rights at the end of the nineteenth century, however, the encyclical was an attempt to mediate between capitalism and socialism, not an endorsement of the latter. Its depiction of a "well-behaved" labor force, moreover, appealed even to Protestants hostile to both the Catholic Church and workers' movements. As European immigrants to America flocked to Catholicism and to organized labor in growing numbers, the Church yielded to pressures from the Protestant establishment to lead the faithful in the ways of democracy as Protestants defined it. By the late 1930s, historian John McGreevey contends, "the most obvious legacy of early Catholic involvement in the union movement was not the development of Catholic social thought but Catholic leadership in the struggle" against the foreign menaces of socialism, fascism, and communism.[34]

This Catholic purchase on historically Protestant notions of American freedom smoothed the paths of assimilation by which U.S. Catholics sought full participation in American economic, political, and civil-religious culture later in the century. Thus sociologist Robert Bellah, in his classic essay on the American civil religion, found in the 1962 inaugural speech of America's only Catholic president, John F. Kennedy, an exemplary instance of the "motivating spirit" of the Protestant Framers.[35] By the time Pope Paul VI expressed his support for economic redistribution and Latin American bishops meeting in Medellín, Colombia, in 1968, condemned "liberal capitalism" and articulated a "preferential option for the poor," even these departures from the American model of democracy were insufficient to revive older fears of Rome as the evil empire. *Humanae Vitae*, the 1968 papal encyclical that reiterated the Catholic Church's prohibition of artificial contraception, distanced many American Catholics from the church, weakening its presence in American life. At the same time, the church's teachings on birth control, homosexuality, and abortion contributed to a strengthened conservative Christian bloc in the United States by allying those Catholics who accepted these teachings more closely than ever with socially conservative Protestants, who later welcomed Pope John Paul II on his 1979 visit to America nearly as warmly as did their Catholic counterparts.

During this time, conservative Protestants were pursuing in the political realm a particular "freedom" agenda, to which a large part of the Catholic electorate would transfer its allegiance for decades to come. In her study of the affluent white Orange County, California, activists who helped to put Ronald Reagan in the governor's mansion and eventually in the White House, historian Lisa McGirr notes that although these conservatives' fears of deteriorating family and community life were very much responses to the "growth of large-scale institutions and the concentration of economic and political power that are part of the functioning of a free-market economy," their "strong stakes in this capitalist order" led them to argue that it was *deviations* from the free market and not its dynamics that most threatened their deeply held values.[36] Thus entrepreneurs who relied on small business loans railed against challenges to free competition; homeowners with FHA mortgages condemned social spending; and defense industrialists with lucrative standing contracts blasted government handouts.

For these staunch individualists, who lived in gated enclaves separated by freeways and strip malls, a surge of evangelical and Fundamentalist churches, bookstores, and media supplied the social and spiritual connectivity they missed, while at the same time articulating a vision of Christian life that supported their atomized politics. Enemies to their way of life appeared to this conservative Christian culture as the assaults of secularism, homosexuality, feminism, and social welfare policies that overrode the autonomy of individuals and families—and tied to each of these, the evil of communism. The southern California–based Christian Anti-Communist Crusade enlisted the talents of then-governor Ronald Reagan to narrate its film series "The Truth about Communism." The elaborately nurtured discourse of communist threat to which such projects contributed likewise played a prominent role in Reagan's path to the White House and in the conduct of his presidency.

The white Christian South, meanwhile, shared the social conservatism of this new, powerful cadre of California Republicans. Reliably Democratic for most of the century following Reconstruction, white Southerners who enrolled their children in the makeshift "Christian academies" that sprang up in the wake of civil rights victories to shelter them from newly integrated schools now increasingly lined up behind the Republican Party. The dynamics of party realignment in the South were not lost on Reagan's campaign strategists, who had their candidate announce his run for the presidency at the Neshoba County Fair in Philadelphia, Mississippi, where civil rights workers had been brutally slain just fifteen years earlier and where Reagan now pledged his support for "states' rights"—the mantra of the "Dixiecrats," whose alienation from the national Democratic Party on civil rights issues and whose racist appeals to the plight of poor whites would eventually deliver most of the white South to the GOP.[37]

Reagan, divorced and not a churchgoer, nevertheless appealed to self-described Christian voters across the United States by a wide margin over the committed Southern Baptist Jimmy Carter, whose morally exacting and theologically literate piety did not as neatly map onto the rhetoric of God-given freedom that propelled his opponent's political career. Reagan did not offer prayers in the White House, host religious services there, or attend church as president because, he claimed, his relationship with God was a private matter. He was not a student of the Bible, but he did believe in the battle of Armageddon and discussed it often as an event he might live to witness.[38]

Reagan's self-taught American religiosity—"I have always believed that there was some divine plan that placed this great continent between two oceans to be sought out by those who were possessed of an abiding love of freedom," he said in his famed "City upon a Hill" speech[39]—proved capacious enough to accommodate Catholics as well as Protestants. In the 1980 election, many erstwhile Catholic Democrats made common cause with Christian Republicans on issues of sexuality and abortion. Some working-class white Catholics, disenchanted with civil rights initiatives, notably busing, used the election to lay belated claim to white privilege, joining those southerners whose support Reagan had cemented with his appeal to states' rights. Newly affluent Catholics shared many of the concerns of Orange County's conservative Christian activists and may have recognized in the latter's vigorous defense of free-market capitalism a chapter in their own history of assimilation. Catholic defections from the party they had long supported produced the enduring electoral category of "Reagan Democrats," who would go on to support the self-styled evangelical George W. Bush over the Catholic candidate John Kerry in 2004.

McGirr refers to the Republican activists she studies as "ordinary men and women,"[40] and, indeed, in both his successful bids for the presidency Reagan was perceived by a safe majority of voters as championing the causes of "ordinary" Americans, concerned to safeguard their families, neighborhoods, religious values, and purses. Like the alleged neutrality of the Protestant position in the Bible wars or the self-evident nature of religious freedom as formulated by the Framers, however, the category of "ordinary" citizens in Reagan's America was as much exclusionary as inclusionary, fraught with contradiction, and yet made in its construction and use to appear natural, normal, and uncontestable.

The making of Reagan's big-tent Christianity as a simple fact of American life, for example, was the work in part of politically savvy evangelicals, who made it the role of churches to provide an ever-widening array of services—schools and child care facilities, counseling offices, theaters, exercise centers, cafés, and so on. This responsiveness to the quotidian needs and wants of members fostered the growth of congregations, producing the megachurch phenomenon, and made participation in church activities less separable from everyday life. The transformation of churches into centers of 24/7 activity, meanwhile, brought their members into a welter of government regulations affecting zoning, education, child care, employment practices, and the like. This forced a confrontation between the interests of the state in regulating business development and the provision of social services, on the one side, and on the other the churches' claims to immunity under the free-exercise clause of the First Amendment—or in the shorthand of "ordinary" Christians, between big government and religious freedom.[41]

The Christian Right triumphed as a political force in the Reagan years by likewise framing its social and policy agenda in the language of rights, equality, and opportunity: school prayer, proselytization, and the public display of religion became issues of free speech; the legal status of abortion became a matter of equal protection for the rights of the unborn. The military death squads the Reagan administration trained and supported in Latin America with the blessing of conservative Christian leaders, meanwhile, were hailed as Freedom Fighters in the war against godless communism. What made Americans "ordinary" was also what made America extraordinary, qualities given in both cases in the most stripped-down yet sacrosanct rhetoric of America distinctiveness, the rhetoric of freedom.

(Christian) Politics as Usual?

Just as Reagan's city-on-a-hill exceptionalism was not new to American policy and self-perception, so it did not disappear when he left office. During the Clinton administration, the claim of American exceptionalism, tacitly given as Christian and deployed through the language of freedom, found concentrated expression in the International Religious Freedom Act (IRFA). Passed unanimously in both houses of Congress and signed into law by President Bill Clinton in 1998, IRFA put into play a complex regulatory machinery that empowers the U.S. government to monitor religious freedom and punish violations in every nation of the world *except* the United States.

The text of IRFA asserts that "freedom of religion undergirds the very origin and existence of the United States." Stopping just short of identifying the First Amendment as the source of that protection worldwide, the act continues: "Many of our Nation's founders fled religious persecution abroad, cherishing in their hearts and minds the ideal of religious freedom. They established in law, as a fundamental right and as a pillar of our Nation, the right to freedom of religion. From its birth to this day, the United States has prized this legacy of religious freedom and honored this heritage by standing for religious freedom and offering refuge to those suffering from religious persecution."[42] As legal scholar Winnifred Fallers Sullivan suggests, this story belongs to a particularly resilient myth of America's genius, one that—like Reagan's "City on a Hill" speech—conflates the Puritans who sought refuge from religious persecution with the Founders who wrote religious freedom into law. What the myth obscures in turn is the fact that the United States has repeatedly denied religious freedom to citizens and subjects within its own borders, including Catholics, Mormons, Native Americans, and slaves, among others, and turned away asylum seekers persecuted for their religion, including Jewish refugees from Nazi Germany.[43]

Critics of IRFA in the United States and abroad charge that the act creates a hierarchy of human rights, with religious freedom at the top: rights violations come in for censure under the act only if religious freedom is at issue, thus potentially draining support for human rights protections for which no such international instruments exist, or whose instruments the United States has elected not to sign. IRFA has also drawn criticism for its formulation of religious freedom in an exclusively American way. Although predecessor versions of the act that targeted only the persecution of Christians abroad were amended to include all violations of religious freedom, the very definition of religious freedom championed by IRFA, its interpreters, and enforcers—U.S. commissions appointed by U.S. elected officials—inevitably emerges from the historical experience of Protestant dominance and church-state separation in the United States. The act's mechanisms for protecting religious freedom in every country *except* the United States further implies that religious freedom enjoys robust legal protections in the United States and that the soundness of its own jurisprudence in religion cases is what authorizes the United States to adjudicate religious freedom violations worldwide. In this sense, IRFA can be said not only to privilege religious freedom above other rights but to privilege some kinds of religion over others, namely those forms of religion already legally recognized in America as deserving of protection.

Enforcement of IRFA has been uneven on other grounds. The United States has refused to act against its economic or strategic allies, even when IRFA's monitoring bodies present evidence of egregious violations of religious freedom. The act's implicit assertion to the international community that the concern of the U.S. government for religious freedom exceeds its concern for other human rights potentially gives cover to the neglect of "lesser" human rights beyond and within U.S. borders. For all of these reasons, critics charge, IRFA does less to promote religious freedom in the abstract than it does to advance particular U.S. interests.[44]

In the George W. Bush administration, religious liberty, refracted through the experience of Christian dominance in the United States, likewise tacitly underwrote more general appeals to "freedom" to win support for particular strategic interests. Bush had begun his first, contested term with an unprecedented overture to American Christians in the form of the Faith-Based and Community Initiative (FBCI). Defeated in Congress but signed into law by executive order in January 2001, the FBCI allowed religious organizations to compete on a "level playing field" with nonreligious organizations for federal funds. The FBCI thus removed what some Christians saw as an impediment to their enjoyment of full religious freedom, namely, the operative understanding among federal agencies that government funding for religious groups was prohibited by the establishment clause of the First Amendment.[45]

Narrowly elected to a second term despite the electorate's growing misgivings about the conduct of wars in Afghanistan and Iraq, Bush proclaimed in his 2005 inaugural address that "from the day of our founding," America has stood for the conviction "that every man and woman on this earth has rights, and dignity, and matchless value, because they bear the image of the maker of heaven and earth." Bush's nod to religious pluralism later in the speech—the "edifice of character is built in families, supported by communities with standards, and sustained in our national life by the truths of Sinai, the Sermon on the Mount, the words of the Qu'ran, and the varied faiths of our people"—recognized the diversity of faiths in America only to the degree that these take the form of "good" religion, compatible with the national civic order. The presumptive support of "good" religion for the interests of American power continues in the next-to-last paragraph of the speech:

> We go forward with complete confidence in the eventual triumph of freedom . . . not because we consider ourselves a chosen nation; God moves and chooses as He wills. We have confidence because freedom is the permanent hope of mankind, the hunger in dark places, the longing of the soul. When our Founders declared a new order of the ages; when soldiers died in wave upon wave for a union based on liberty; when citizens marched in peaceful outrage under the banner "Freedom Now"—they were acting on an ancient hope that is meant to be fulfilled. History has an ebb and flow of justice, but history also has a visible direction, set by liberty and the Author of Liberty.

Like the text of the International Religious Freedom Act, this passage makes liberty both America's project and divinely ordained, even as it (barely) sidesteps the notion that America was chosen by God to spread its brand of freedom across the globe. The "mission that created our nation," Bush continued, is now the "urgent requirement of our nation's security, and the calling of our time. . . . The best hope for peace in our world is the expansion of freedom in all the world."[46]

This sentiment returns to Reagan's "City on a Hill" speech, with its framing of America as "the last best hope of man on earth," and subtly echoes Bush's earlier case for preemptive war in Iraq. There is arguably nothing Christian in the Bush doctrine of aggressive unilateralism or the means of its deployment. Still, the Bush administration's language of freedom as a universal right conferred by the God of Christian revelation succeeded, at least for a time, in consecrating a most situational definition of freedom and modes of pursuing it that, critics of his administration argue, have left myriad human rights abuses in their wake.

President Barack Obama's renewal of support for Bush's policy on faith-based organizations, which significantly favored evangelical Christian perspectives and groups, together with his choice of California megachurch celebrity pastor Rick Warren to deliver the invocation at his inauguration ceremony, have raised concerns that Obama's depiction of a religiously inclusive America in his inaugural address—"a nation of Christians and Muslims, Jews and Hindus—and nonbelievers"—portends only more of the same: a continuation of city-on-a-hill exceptionalism that uses the language of religious pluralism, freedom, and tolerance to advance an agenda shaped by America's history of Christian dominance. That the acknowledgment of American Muslims in particular came between references to terrorism, in a speech blessed at both ends by the prayers of Protestant clergy, opened Obama to suspicions that his administration no less than his predecessors' would continue what Gil Anidjar describes as a politics of fear, divisiveness, and military aggression "barely disguised as the politics of love."[47]

Like Bush's speeches, Obama's inaugural address moved smoothly back and forth between invocations of the nation's founding documents, recognition of America's religious variety, and references to Christian scripture. New elements in the speech, however, suggested at least the promise of a departure from "(Christian) politics as usual." An immediate difference between Obama's familiar references and his predecessors' is the context of struggle in which they appeared. Enumerating in unsparing detail the challenges America faces at the beginning of his administration—war against "a far-reaching network of violence and hatred," a shattered economy, failing education and health care, and an imperiled environment—Obama then paraphrased in quick succession both 1 Corinthians and the Declaration of Independence: "We remain a young nation, but in the words of Scripture, the time has come to set aside childish things. The time has come to reaffirm our enduring spirit; to choose our better history; to carry forward that precious gift, that noble idea, passed on from generation to generation: the God-given promise that all are equal, all are free and all deserve a chance to pursue their full measure of happiness." As Bush had, Obama links God (specifically the God of Christian revelation) with freedom, understood in the language of the Founders. What's new is that Obama invokes this freedom as a burden to be taken up in order to repair a broken nation—a point reinforced by his electing to take the presidential oath on Abraham Lincoln's Bible. Obama spoke of freedom and equality not as God-given "rights" but as each a "God-given promise," thus subtly acknowledging that the nation's formal commitment to freedom and equality has been imperfectly and unevenly fulfilled.

Obama's positioning of Muslims within America's patchwork religious heritage came in the foreign policy section of the speech, immediately after a stare-down to would-be terrorists and just before his invitation to the Muslim world to forge a new path of "mutual interest and mutual respect," an extension of the hand predicated on the willingness of hostile leaders and states to unclench their collective fist. These audible linkages between terrorism and the Muslim world came nevertheless in a speech remarkable for its powerful if oblique criticisms of the conduct of George W. Bush's War on Terror. If Bush's speeches invoked the nation's founding documents to muster support for a go-it-alone war, pursued in disregard for the Geneva Conventions and the rule of law, Obama did so to call the excesses of the Bush administration into view and redress them:

> As for our common defense, we reject as false the choice between our safety and our ideals. Our founding fathers . . . faced with perils we can scarcely imagine, drafted a charter to assure the rule of law and the rights of man, a charter expanded by the blood of generations. Those ideals still light the world, and we will not give them up for expedience's sake. And so to all the other peoples and governments who are watching today, from the grandest capitals to the small village where my father was born: know that America is a friend of each nation and every man, woman, and child who seeks a future of peace and dignity, and that we are ready to lead once more.

As noted earlier, Obama's naming of Hindus along with Christians, Jews, and Muslims extends the scope of religious pluralism in America beyond either the so-called Judeo-Christian or the Abrahamic traditions. More subtly, his inclusion of nonbelievers on a longer list of religious possibility puts religion and the secular on a different standing in relation to one another than the deeply entrenched, binary logic of either church-state or private-public divisions would ordain. Obama's framing of the nonreligious not as the default position in American public life but instead as one class of Americans alongside Jews, Christians, Hindus, and Muslims suggests that religion is now both public—there is no putting the genie back into the bottle—and plural, not simply Protestant.[48] Christianity retains the predominant share in this religious mix, but it is now one share among many, and not the accommodating frame.

Nor is religious variety given as the unalloyed ornament of American distinctiveness. No longer the shining beacon-to-the-world of the nation's exemplary tolerance and accommodation, religious pluralism in Obama's speech belongs instead to a far more complex network of affiliation and difference, one marked as much by conflict, bitterness, and yet-to-be-realized flourishing as by tolerance or common cause: "We are a nation of Christians and Muslims, Jews and Hindus, and nonbelievers. We are shaped by every language and culture, drawn from every end of this Earth; and because we have tasted the bitter swill of civil war and segregation, and emerged from that dark chapter stronger and more united, we cannot help but believe that the old hatreds shall someday pass . . . and that America must play its role in ushering in a new era of peace." Even as it might serve as a model for overcoming other divisions, the story of America's religious variety, in Obama's speech, belongs as much to the nation's darker history as to its brightest. This is not a facile understanding of religious pluralism. Its ends are promissory but uncertain.

Obama ended his address by quoting Thomas Paine, whose stirring words General Washington had read to dispirited troops in a war waged in part over challenges to American Protestant notions of what religious freedom should—and should not—entail. "Let it be told to the future world," wrote Paine, "that in the depth of winter, when nothing but hope and virtue could survive . . . that the city and the country, alarmed at one common danger, came forth to meet [it]." For Paine, the "danger" was political tyranny embodied in the British monarch, whose extension of religious tolerance to non-Protestant subjects in Quebec had fomented a war undertaken on behalf of liberty of conscience, a formulation that enduringly tied both religious freedom and representative government to the sovereign rights of individuals. If the invocation of Paine in Obama's inaugural address is meant to elicit devotion to the "Protestant" America the Founders created, the perils spelled out elsewhere in the speech nevertheless include not only potential assaults to this legacy, but also its blind spots and excesses. Shortly before the inaugural, in an essay whose salient points would all be heard in Obama's speech, Robert Bellah remarked on the challenges faced by the president-elect. "American exceptionalism is often interpreted to mean how exceptionally good we are," Bellah wrote; but "it is important to remember also how exceptionally bad we are" at a long list of things too, a dual legacy of the "fundamental individualism . . . rooted in the earliest and most pervasive religious culture in America, Protestantism." Many of the national crises Obama would detail in his first address as president are those that Bellah here lays squarely at the feet of America's Protestant inheritance of "radical individualis[m]."[49] In the context of this speech, fittingly, religious freedom and pluralism are at once desiderata and sites of struggle, less benedictions on the nation than challenges to be addressed with historical awareness and humility to the task.

NOTES

I wish to thank Catherine Brekus, Elizabeth Fenton, and Clark Gilpin for their readings of earlier drafts of this essay, parts of which draw on material presented in my *Culture and Redemption: Religion, the Secular, and American Literature* (Princeton: Princeton University Press, 2007).

1. The full text of the speech is available at http://www.whitehouse.gov/the_press_office/President_Barack_Obamas_Inaugural_Address/ (accessed March 28, 2011).

2. Martin Marty, "Pluralisms," *Annals of the American Academy of Political and Social Science* 612 (2007): 16. I am indebted to Courtney Bender and Pamela Klassen for this reference.

3. Thomas Paine, *The Age of Reason*, in *Collected Writings*, ed. Eric Foner (New York: Library of America, 1995), 666.

4. See Thomas Paine, *Common Sense*, in ibid., 43; and Thomas Jefferson, *Letter to the Danbury Baptist Association*, January 1, 1802, in *Jefferson: Political Writings*, ed. Joyce Appleby and Terence Ball (New York: Cambridge University Press, 1999), 397.

5. This point is made by Courtney Bender and Pamela Klassen in the introduction to their edited volume, *After Pluralism: Reimagining Models of Religious Engagement* (New York: Columbia University Press, 2010).

6. Gil Anidjar, "So, What About the Christian Lobby?" *The Immanent Frame*, http://www.ssrc.org/blogs/immanent_frame/2009/01/31/so-what-about-the-christian-lobby/ (accessed March 28, 2011).

7. Harriet Beecher Stowe, *Uncle Tom's Cabin*, in *Three Novels* (New York: Library of America, 1982), 403–4; Lyman Beecher, *A Plea for the West* (1835; New York: Arno Press, 1977), 131.

8. Jonathan Mayhew, *Popish Idolatry, a Discourse Delivered in the Chapel of Harvard-College in Cambridge, New-England, May 8, 1765* (Boston: R&S Draper, 1765), 49.

9. Continental Congress, *Address to the People of Great Britain*, October 21, 1774, in *Journals of the American Congress from 1774–1788*, 4 vols. (Washington, D.C.: Way and Gideon, 1823), 1:27. My reading of the Quebec Act is indebted to Elizabeth Fenton's "Birth of a Protestant Nation: Catholic Canadians, Religious Pluralism, and National Unity in the Early U.S. Republic," *Early American Literature* 41, no. 1 (2006): 29–57.

10. From an advertisement reprinted in Martin Ignatius Joseph Griffin, *Catholics and the American Revolution* (Ridley Park, Pa.: by the author, 1907), 7.

11. Adam Shortt and Arthur Doughty, eds., *Documents Relating to the Constitutional History of Canada, 1759–1791*, 2 vols. (Ottawa: J. de L. Taché, 1918), 1:572; as quoted by Fenton, "Birth of a Protestant Nation," 34.

12. From a 1755 sermon reprinted in the *Pennsylvania Gazette*, no. 2390, October 12, 1774, submitted by L.S. "for the Amusement of your Readers, leaving them to judge how applicable they [these words] may be to that [Quebec] Bill, as well as to the several Acts of Parliament passed in the late and present Reign for enslaving and taxing *America*."

13. Continental Congress, *Address to the People of Great Britain*, 30.

14. "On Return from 'Executing the Romish Business' with Quebec[,] the King Was Greeted with Cries of 'No Popery! No French Laws! No Protestant Popish King!'" *New York Journal*, August 25, 1774; quoted in Charles H. Metzger, S.J., *The Quebec Act: A Primary Cause of the American Revolution* (New York: U.S. Catholic Historical Society, 1936), 43.

15. *To the Inhabitants of the Province of Quebec*, in *Journals of the American Congress*, 1:42.

16. Ibid., 1:41.

17. James Madison, *Memorial and Remonstrance against Religious Assessments*, in *Selected Writings*, ed. Ralph Louis Ketcham (Indianapolis: Hackett, 2006), 22.

18. Jefferson, *Letter to the Danbury Baptist Association*, 397.

19. Madison, *Memorial and Remonstrance*, 25.

20. Fenton, "Birth of a Protestant Nation," 31.

21. Bela Bates Edwards, *The Influence of the United States on Other Nations*, in *Writings*, 2 vols. (New York, 1852), 2:489; quoted by John R. Bodo, *The Protestant Clergy and Public Issues, 1812–1848* (Princeton: Princeton University Press, 1954), 35.

22. "Kirwan" [Nicholas Murray], *Romanism at Home: Letters to the Hon. Roger B. Taney* (New York: Harper, 1852), 249–50.

23. Circular Letter by Rev. William Staughton, in *Minutes of the Philadelphia Baptist Association from 1707 to 1807*, ed. A. D. Gillette (Springfield, Mo.: Particular Baptist Press, 2002), 319.

24. Francis Patrick Kenrick, Letter to the Philadelphia Board of Controllers of Public Schools, November 14, 1842, reprinted in the Philadelphia paper the *Christian Observer*, January 27, 1843. The *Christian Observer* remarked: "The Bishop is, no doubt, well aware that our institutions are most intimately connected with the religion taught by the Bible. Christianity forms a most important part of what is called the "Common Law" of our

country. . . . Hence its introduction into our public schools without note or comment, that our youth may imbibe from this pure fountain the great principles of truth, equity, and liberty, on which our institutions are founded. . . . The bishop's letter is nothing less than an attempt to impair confidence in the principles which form the *basis* of our rights and privileges."

25. Rev. Walter Colton, "The Bible in Our Public Schools: A Reply to the Allegations and Complaints Contained in the Letter of Bishop Kenrick to the Board of Controllers of [Philadelphia] Public Schools," *Quarterly Review of the American Protestant Association* 1 (January 1844): 17.

26. *Public Ledger*, June 8, 1844; quoted by Michael Feldberg, *The Philadelphia Riots of 1844: A Study of Ethnic Conflict* (Westport, Ct.: Greenwood, 1975), 95.

27. John Hancock Lee, *The Origin and Progress of the American Party in Politics: Embracing a Complete History of the Philadelphia Riots in May and July, 1844* (1855; Freeport, N.Y.: Books for Libraries Press, 1970), 246.

28. *Native American* (May 7, 1844); quoted by Vincent P. Lannie and Bernard C. Diethorn, "For the Honor and Glory of God: The Philadelphia Bible Riots of 1840," *History of Education Quarterly* 8 (Spring 1968): 73. Feldberg, *Philadelphia Riots*, 109.

29. *Christian Observer* (July 19, 1844).

30. I am here indebted to Gauri Viswanathan's discussion of William James's *Varieties of Religious Experience* in her *Outside the Fold: Conversion, Modernity, and Belief* (Princeton: Princeton University Press, 1998), 84–85.

31. I draw gratefully here on J. Terry Todd's presentation of this material in "The Temple of Religion and the Politics of Pluralism," in Bender and Klassen, *After Pluralism*, 201–22.

32. Matteo Liberatore, *Principles of Political Economy* (New York: Benziger, 1891), 194; quoted by John T. McGreevey, *Catholicism and American Freedom: A History* (New York: Norton, 2003), 131.

33. *Rerum Novarum: Encyclical of Pope Leo XIII on Capital and Labor*, http://www.vatican.va/holy_father/leo_xiii/encyclicals/documents/hf_l-xiii_enc_15051891_rerum-novarum_en.html (accessed March 28, 2011).

34. McGreevey, *Catholicism and American Freedom*, 144.

35. Robert Bellah, "Civil Religion in America," in *The Robert Bellah Reader*, ed. Steven M. Tipton (Durham: Duke University Press, 2006), 229.

36. Lisa McGirr, *Suburban Warriors: The Origins of the New American Right* (Princeton: Princeton University Press, 2001), 163.

37. See Joseph Crespino, *In Search of Another Country: Mississippi and the Conservative Counterrevolution* (Princeton: Princeton University Press, 2007).

38. On Reagan's religious faith, see Gary Scott Smith, *Faith and the Presidency from George Washington to George W. Bush* (New York: Oxford University Press, 2006), 326–38.

39. "We Will Be as a City upon a Hill," speech of Governor Ronald Reagan to the Conservative Political Action Conference, Washington, D.C., January 25, 1974, http://reagan2020.us/speeches/City_Upon_A_Hill.asp (accessed March 28, 2011).

40. McGirr, *Suburban Warriors*, 12.

41. See Peter Beinart, "Battle for the 'Burbs,'"> *The New Republic*, October 19, 1998, pp. 25–29. I am indebted to Bryan F. le Beau for this reference.

42. The text of the 1998 International Religious Freedom Act is available at http://web.archive.org/web/20070608190937/http://usinfo.state.gov/usa/infousa/laws/major law/intlrel.htm (accessed March 28,2011).

43. Winnifred Fallers Sullivan, "Exporting Religious Freedom," *Commonweal*, February 26, 1999, 10–11.

44. See Eugenia Relaño Pastor, "The Flawed Implementation of the International Religious Freedom Act of 1998: A European Perspective," *Brigham Young University Law Review* 3 (2005): 711–46; Matthew L. Fore, "Shall Weigh Your God and You: Assessing the Imperialistic Implications of the International Religious Freedom Act in Muslim Countries," *Duke University Law Journal* 52 (2002): 423–53; and Sullivan, "Exporting Religious Freedom."

45. See Winnifred Fallers Sullivan, "Waking Up to Still Being a Faith-Based Nation," *The Immanent Frame*, http://www.ssrc.org/blogs/immanent_frame/2009/01/22/waking-up-to-still-being-a-faith-based-nation/ (accessed March 28, 2011).

46. The text of Bush's second inaugural address is available at http://www.npr.org/templates/story/story.php?storyId=4460172 (accessed March 28,2011). My reading of this speech and of Obama's speech in the context of his predecessors is indebted to Jerome E. Copulsky, "God in the Inauguration: JFK, Bush, and Obama," *Religion Dispatches*, http://www.religiondispatches.org/archive/atheologies/1029/god_in_the_inauguration%3A_jfk%2C_bush%2C_and_obama (accessed March 27, 2011).

47. Anidjar, "So, What About the Christian Lobby."

48. Eight years after the passage of George Bush's Faith-Based and Community Initiative, Winnifred Sullivan, in "Waking Up to Still Being a Faith-Based Nation," suggests that "understanding Americans to be fundamentally religious is now deeply embedded in government and in our public culture. That is the default position. Not secularism."

49. According to Bellah, "It is our radical individualistic culture that allows us to tolerate a level of poverty higher than any other advanced nation, a degree of income polarization that would be unacceptable in most advanced nations, a health system that leaves tens of millions without insurance, that is the most expensive in the world but leaves the health of our citizens only slightly above that of many third world nations, an environmental policy that has not only failed to lead the world to greater sustainability but actually stood in the way of the things which almost all the other advanced nations have tried to do, and these are only the most obvious of the many ways we have differed for the worse from most of the advanced world." Robert Bellah, "This Is Our Moment, This Is Our Time," *The Immanent Frame*, http://blogs.ssrc.org/tif/2009/01/12/this-is-our-moment-this-is-our-time/ (accessed March 28, 2011).

Beyond Church and Sect
Christian Movements for Social Reform

Christian efforts to reform the social order have roots as deep as the prophets and the gospels. Amos's call to "let justice roll down like waters" (Amos 5:24) and Jesus' promise to fulfill Isaiah's prophecy by "proclaiming release to the captives" (Luke 4:18) resonate in Saint Francis's call to gospel simplicity, John Calvin's reorganization of public charity in Geneva, and Menno Simons's creation of a nonviolent Christian community. The same impulses arrived in North America with the earliest European settlers and missionaries. They appear in the "holy commonwealths" created by Pilgrims and Puritans in New England, by Quakers in Pennsylvania, and by Catholics in Maryland. The Christian social reform spirit took on a more radical form when newly Christianized African Americans glimpsed their own predicament in the Exodus story and began a centuries-long struggle against slavery. And by the end of the colonial period, both the evangelicals of the Great Awakening and their liberal rivals came to identify the cause of national independence with God's millennial plan to remake all human societies.

As these examples suggest, Christian social reform has never been the monopoly of a single theological or denominational tradition, and it cannot be traced to a single source or starting point. Social reformers have always been a diverse lot, and on more than one occasion—whether the struggle over Sabbath observance in the early nineteenth century or the contemporary abortion debate—activist Christians have lined up on both sides of a contentious issue. In many activist movements, moreover, Christians have worked alongside freethinkers, Spiritualists, Marxists, humanists, and adherents of the full spectrum of world religions, sometimes blurring the boundaries between "religious" and "secular" reform and sometimes drawing a sharp distinction between the two. But in almost every case, the distinctly American experience of Christian social reform has been inseparable from the American experiment with religious disestablishment.

Disestablishment was decisive for social reform because it allowed Christian communities to break free of the rigid dichotomy of "church" and

427

"sect" that had prevailed during the colonial period.[1] Under establishment, "churches" were concerned for the well-being of the entire society, but they were so closely tied to the political power structure that they rarely advocated substantive changes in the social order. Marginalized "sects," on the other hand, were free to experiment with new social arrangements within the bounds of their own congregations, but they lacked the power (and, in many cases, the will) to transform the larger society. The Bill of Rights, and the subsequent disestablishments at the state level, largely eliminated state power over the churches while leaving religious groups free to engage in political and social activism. (By contrast, liberal regimes in Europe and Latin America typically expanded state power at the expense of religious organizations.)

The change liberated all sorts of Christian communities to engage the larger society from a position that was distinct but not separate: they could "speak truth to power" without risking either persecution or loss of privilege. Disestablishment also made it difficult for non-Christian reformers to rely on the sort of broad-brush attacks on church power that were popular with European radicals, leading them instead toward strategies of coalition and cooperation. Still, the reformers' position between "church" and "sect" was inherently unstable. Reform movements that succeeded in changing society could become quasi-establishments, identifying so closely with the new regime that they failed to see emerging injustices. More radical or "ultra" reformers, on the other hand, moved close to the sectarian fringe when they prized personal purity over broad social change. And for those Christians who were less passionate about reform, disestablishment encouraged a privatized spirituality in which a "personal relationship with Jesus" had no consequences for one's social or political relationships. Indeed, many social reformers found they had to combat privatized religion just as fiercely as they struggled against slavery, war, and economic injustice.

The diversity, intensity, and hybrid character of Christian social reform can be illustrated through three case studies spanning the past two centuries of U.S. history. The abolitionist movement of the early nineteenth century is notable for both its transformative impact on American society as a whole and the countercultural intensity of its most radical adherents, who transformed their own habits of eating, dress, child rearing, and devotion in pursuit of what they called "ultra" reform. The Catholic Worker movement of a century later has been equally countercultural in its practice of voluntary poverty, hospitality to the stranger, and direct resistance to war, but it has also embraced the "churchly" vision of Roman Catholicism and cooperated with a wide range of Marxists, anarchists, and other non-Christian radicals. Aptly described as a "sect within a church," the Worker illustrates the freedom with which American religious groups can practice counter-cultural spiritualities while maintaining low social boundaries.[2] Finally, the tradition of "congregation-based community organizing" inspired by Saul Alinsky has transformed America's religious diversity into a vital resource for social transformation, blending the organizational strengths of white, black, and Latina/o Christian communities in its campaigns for affordable housing, worker rights, and community development.

Abolitionism

The abolitionist movement traced its roots to two religious communities that had already begun to transcend the church-sect divide in the colonial period: the Society of Friends and the independent African American churches. The Quakers were the dominant religious community in colonial Pennsylvania, but from the beginning they refused to act as a traditional "establishment." They welcomed Anabaptists and other persecuted sects to their colony, respected both the religious and the political autonomy of Native American communities, and largely withdrew from positions of political power rather than participate in the French and Indian Wars. Even as Quakers renounced the political privileges of establishment, they continued to express their concern for society as a whole by speaking out on behalf of enslaved Africans. Beginning in 1746, John Woolman (1720–72) remonstrated with hundreds of slave owners during his travels around the colonies, while Quaker teacher Anthony Benezet (1713–84) incorporated enslaved and free African Americans into his classes and founded the Society for the Relief of Free Negroes Unlawfully Held in Bondage, the first American antislavery society. When the Philadelphia Yearly Meeting forbade its members from holding slaves in 1776, it set a standard that other denominations would emulate only slowly.

The black church was born in the moment when enslaved Africans discovered the liberatory message at the heart of their oppressors' religion. The God who had heard the cries of the Israelites in Egypt would also hear their cries, and the Christian ritual of baptism—often blended with West African practices of spirit possession—meant incorporation into a new community of freedom. By the end of the eighteenth century, independent congregations had formed, both among southern slaves and among newly freed African Americans in both the North and the South. These religious communities had a churchly sensibility insofar as they identified with the entire black community, but their experience of racial prejudice and violence meant that they had few investments in the larger social status quo. From the beginning, they sought to change society by uplifting members of their own community—through literacy and economic self-help—and by challenging the white power structure with petitions, protests, and both violent and nonviolent acts of resistance.

Other Christians began gravitating toward social reform around 1818, when the state of Connecticut withdrew the privileges of legal establishment from the Congregational churches. Though most other states (with the exceptions of Massachusetts and New Hampshire) had already followed the example of the federal government and dismantled their own establishments, Connecticut's decision symbolized the end of the Puritan theocracy that had dominated New England for almost two centuries. Lyman Beecher (1775–1863), speaking for many heirs of the Puritans, at first believed that "the injury done to the cause of Christ . . . was irreparable."[3] But he soon saw an opportunity. The churches could create their own "voluntary societies" that would impress Christian values on society without the intermediary of the state.

The emergence of voluntary societies also reflected theological changes. In the first decades of the nineteenth century, the dominant Calvinist theology of the colonial period faced a twofold challenge. On the one hand, the revivalists of the Second Great Awakening challenged Calvin's notion that humans were so bound by sin that only a mysterious interposition of divine grace could free them. It was possible, asserted Methodist circuit riders and such frontier Presbyterians as Charles Grandison Finney (1792–1875), to "work up" revivals through human means, to choose to renounce sin, and—by extension—to overthrow even the most venerable injustices. At the same time, the nascent Unitarian, Universalist, and Hicksite Quaker movements offered a more sweeping critique of Calvinism, insisting that humans were not merely capable of renouncing sin but were virtually unlimited in their capacity to emulate the divine benevolence. Both the Enlightenment optimism of these liberals and the emotional fervor of the revivalists opened the door to radical, institution-shaking styles of reform, even as the Calvinists—themselves heirs to a noble tradition of social concern—continued to pursue the more conservative, institution-preserving approach.

Calvinists, liberals, and revivalists mingled, cooperated, and contended with one another in the local and national "societies" that began to be formed in the first decade of the new century. The earliest of these were not concerned with social reform at all but with evangelization. Bible, tract, Sunday school, and home mission societies were all charged with functions that would have had state sponsorship under establishment. Most were ecumenically Protestant—actively concerned for Christian unity but also worried about the spread of Roman Catholicism and of various forms of Enlightenment religion, including Unitarianism and Universalism. Typically, they were managed by boards of directors with substantial clerical involvement; they hired "agents" who fanned out across the countryside to recruit members; and they hosted annual "anniversary meetings" in which a broad constituency came together in a revival-like environment.

The first "social" causes taken on by these voluntary societies were conservative. As early as 1803, Lyman Beecher organized a local society to take on blasphemy, Sabbath-breaking, dueling, and intemperance.[4] The American Temperance Society, founded at the national level in 1826, drew substantial support from wealthy employers who believed they could achieve higher profits with a sober workforce. As temperance gained the largest constituency of any nineteenth-century reform movement, however, it revealed a more radical side. The sentimental writers who penned hundreds of "temperance tales" typically portrayed both alcoholics and their families as innocent victims of heartless "rumsellers" and the callous social drinkers who subjected them to temptation. In 1840, the alcoholics organized themselves into a "Washingtonian" movement whose members affirmed that "the universal boundary of human sympathy" included even the most hardened drunkard "in its cheering circle."[5] Occasionally, Washingtonians aligned themselves with radical peace and antislavery movements. But temperance also attracted xenophobes, who readily identified the scourge of alcohol with Irish and German Catholic immigrants. As political historian James Morone has pointed out, temperance activists could perceive alcoholics either as good neighbors fallen on hard times or as demonic outsiders to be suppressed.[6]

The antislavery movement was similarly divided between those who saw enslaved Africans as oppressed fellow Christians and those who wished only to preserve a homogeneous community of free whites. The American Colonization Society, founded in 1816, blended antislavery sentiment with overt racism in its call for the repatriation of freed slaves to Africa, on the grounds that they were unsuited for full participation in American society. From the beginning, such black activists as James Forten (1766–1842) protested against colonization on the grounds that it would divide families and renew "all the heart-rending agonies which were endured by our forefathers when they were dragged into bondage from Africa."[7] When this complaint was taken up by Forten's white ally, William Lloyd Garrison (1805–79), the antislavery community was abruptly polarized.

Garrison's *Liberator* newspaper, launched in 1831, began by attacking the Colonization Society, demanding the immediate emancipation of all slaves, and calling for the repeal of any legislation (such as the antimiscegany laws common in northern states) that would limit their full participation in American society. "I am in earnest," thundered Garrison. "I will not equivocate—I will not excuse—I will not retreat a single inch—and I will be heard."[8] Raised a Baptist in Newburyport, Massachusetts, he blended the fervent style of Second Great Awakening revivalism with the older reform traditions of Quakers and the black church. During a brief stay in Baltimore, he had been mentored by Benjamin Lundy, Quaker editor of the *Genius of Universal Emancipation*, and by the free African Americans who constituted most of its subscribers. The *Liberator* provided the first venue for such African American writers as Maria Steward, and Garrison portrayed even the apocalyptically tinged violence of Nat Turner as a sign of the divine judgment that would come if America did not soon repent of the sin of slavery. Garrison also forged an especially strong alliance with Quaker feminists Lucretia Mott and Abby Kelley, as well as with Unitarian activists Samuel Joseph May, Lydia Maria Child, and Maria Weston Chapman.

Garrison himself would soon repudiate all formal religious institutions, but his "immediatism" struck a chord with many evangelicals, both the relatively conservative admirers of Lyman Beecher who dominated the New York–based voluntary societies and the more radical westerners influenced by Charles Grandison Finney. In New York, the brothers Lewis (1788–1863) and Arthur Tappan (1786–1865) played key roles in establishing a New York Anti-Slavery Society in 1831 and, with the Garrisonians and a large group of Philadelphia Quakers, the American Anti-Slavery Society in 1833. At Cincinnati's Lane Seminary, Theodore Weld (1803–95) and other zealous evangelical students befriended the fugitive slaves who had just crossed the Ohio River and called on President Lyman Beecher to commit the school to the abolition of slavery. When Beecher refused, they defected to Oberlin, Ohio, and Oberlin College (then led by Finney himself) and began recruiting an "apostolic" band of lecturers to spread the antislavery word to other frontier communities.

The Anti-Slavery Society proved remarkably fruitful for new approaches to antislavery agitation, as well as for entirely new reform movements. Frederick Douglass (1818–95) began lecturing for the society as a twenty-three-year-old fugitive just three years removed from slavery; he soon pioneered both the "fugitive slave narrative" as an effective form of abolitionist propaganda and tactics of civil disobedience (such as riding on segregated railway cars) that anticipated later civil rights strategies. When Sarah (1792–1873) and Angelina Grimké (1805–79) were trained as antislavery lecturers by Theodore Weld, they forced other abolitionists to consider whether women could be full participants in a movement committed to the full participation of African Americans in society. The preoccupation of abolitionists with the violence meted out on enslaved Africans led many of them to repudiate both military violence and all participation in governments that relied on force. And the claims of slave owners that their slaves ate better than northern factory workers forced at least a few abolitionists to embrace either the trade union movement or the communitarian socialism found at Brook Farm, Hopedale, Northampton, and dozens of Fourierist "phalanxes."

Ultimately, the uneasy alliance between Garrisonians, Tappanites, and western evangelicals could not hold. By 1840, the *Liberator* was the organ not only for antislavery but for virtually every "ultra" reform conceivable, and its sensibility infected the publications and activities of the Anti-Slavery Society itself. Exasperated, the Tappan brothers and their New York allies left the society. The immediate cause of the split was a dispute over whether women could serve on the society's executive committee, but the New Yorkers were also distressed by Garrison's nearly anarchist repudiation of political action and his attacks on clerical and biblical authority. By excluding women leaders and maintaining close ties to the "benevolent empire" of evangelical reform, the new American and Foreign Anti-Slavery Society affirmed its desire to stay close to the "churchly" mainstream. Meanwhile, the Garrisonians increasingly used the Anti-Slavery Society and the New England Non-Resistance Society (formed after an 1838 schism in the American Peace Society) as purified alternatives to traditional Christian congregations.

Western abolitionists were caught in the middle: they sympathized with the Garrisonians' feminism and their opposition to existing political and religious institutions, but they were not willing to repudiate institutions altogether. So they created both a new political party—the Liberty Party—and an array of abolitionist congregations and denominations. These new religious bodies, dubbed the "church reform" movement by historian Douglas Strong, broke new ground by installing African American Samuel Ringgold Ward (1817–ca. 1866) as pastor of a predominantly white congregation in 1841 and by ordaining Antoinette Brown (1825–1921) in 1853. Paradoxically, the institutions of western abolitionism could gravitate in either a churchly or a sectarian direction: while the Liberty Party prefigured the new Republican Party that would dominate American politics for eighty-five years, in close alliance with the emerging Protestant "mainline," such abolitionist denominations as the Free Methodists gravitated to the fundamentalist margin by the beginning of the twentieth century.[9]

Antoinette Brown herself left the pulpit within a year, becoming a women's rights lecturer and writer, as well as an occasional preacher in Unitarian churches. This shift of religious allegiance was typical of many within the radical wing of Christian social reform. Though William Lloyd Garrison never renounced his identity as a Christian, his repudiation of religious institutions and vehement attacks on the clergy, the Sabbath, and even the Bible branded him as an apostate in the eyes of most conventional Christians. Frederick Douglass gravitated from his Methodist roots to a vaguely defined humanism; by 1870 he could declare that it was only through his fellow activists that he could "get any glimpses of God anywhere."[10] Elizur Wright (1804–85), an evangelical opponent of Garrison in 1840, was an outright atheist by the postwar years. The most significant defection, though, was to the Spiritualist movement of the 1850s. Spiritualism was strongest in the areas most influenced by abolitionism and communitarian socialism, and the messages conveyed by Spiritualist mediums often echoed the rhetoric of radical reformers. Though a few activists, notably Adin Ballou (1803–90), were adamant that one could be both a Christian and a Spiritualist, most adherents wound up leaving Christian churches. Others—including Theodore Weld and Angelina Grimké—eventually affiliated with Unitarian congregations that were themselves moving beyond Christianity and toward a liberal religion of humanity.

Those abolitionists who refused to break with the Christian mainstream experienced a painful triumph in the 1850s and 1860s. First the mainline Protestant denominations and then the nation as a whole split between North and South, and as a consequence the abolitionist goal of emancipation (though not of full social and political equality for African Americans) was achieved. The immediate postwar years were quiet ones for reformers. Some abolitionists worked diligently to build up black schools and colleges in the South (notably through the American Missionary Association, founded by the Tappans), but the major abolitionist organizations disbanded on the questionable ground that their work was complete. Christian pacifism was marginalized by the seemingly self-evident justice of the Union cause, and consistent commitment to women's rights was largely limited to the Spiritualist movement and the Unitarian and Universalist fringe of Christianity.

In the decades after the Civil War, the social reform tradition was gradually reborn within the mainline Protestant churches. The temperance movement was revived by the Women's Christian Temperance Union, described by one ally as "the feminine Congress of the United States." Its long-serving president, Frances Willard (1839–98), sought not only to protect her members' homes from the scourge of alcohol but "to make the whole world HOMELIKE" by "doing everything"—exercising moral suasion, lobbying Congress, and even struggling to gain women the right to vote.[11] In urban centers, increasing economic inequality and a rising labor movement caught the attention of middle-class Protestants, who served their neighbors through settlement houses and "institutional churches," articulated a "Social Creed" emphasizing labor rights, and declared a new gospel of "social salvation." Serving an overwhelmingly working-class community, Catholic leaders were equally outspoken advocates of a "living wage" for every worker. Indeed, American bishops, including John Ireland of St. Paul and James Cardinal Gibbons of Baltimore, played a central role in prodding Pope Leo XIII and his successors to articulate the principles of "Catholic social teaching."

Dorothy Day and the Catholic Worker Movement

When the Great Depression hit in 1929, socially concerned Christians could thus draw on an exceptionally wide range of reforming traditions. The Catholic Worker movement took in virtually all of them, integrating in its potent stew the communal structures of Benedictine monasticism, the anarchism of the Industrial Workers of the World, the Catholic philosophy of Emmanuel Mounier and Jacques Maritain, the direct action of Mohandas Gandhi, and the mystical literature of Tolstoy and Dostoyevsky. It was born on May Day in 1933, when ex-socialist Dorothy Day (1897–1980) and vagabond immigrant Peter Maurin (1877–1949) unveiled the first issue of a newspaper intended to introduce Catholic social teaching to the nation's suffering workers. As Communist Party agitators in New York's Union Square shouted, "Read the *Daily Worker*!" their new Catholic rival countered with "Read the *Catholic Worker* daily!" Those who accepted the invitation soon built up a national network of urban houses of hospitality, "agronomic universities" that sought to return workers to the land, and "roundtable discussions" welcoming "Communists, radicals, priests, and laity."[12]

Though Dorothy Day always gave first credit to her mentor Peter Maurin, whom she saw as the Saint Francis of the twentieth century, both the endurance and the diversity of the movement reflect her personality. Raised in a religiously nonobservant family, Day launched her career as a socialist journalist in the 1910s and 1920s. According to her own recollection, she became a socialist for essentially religious reasons, believing that "the poor and oppressed were going to rise up, they were collectively the new Messiah, and they would release the captives." But she also became a Catholic for reasons that reflected her socialist commitments. Drawn closer to God by the "natural happiness" she felt after the birth of her daughter, she chose to join the Catholic Church because it "claimed and held the allegiance of the masses of people in all the cities where I had lived."[13] Under Maurin's tutelage, she became committed to a decentralized variant of Catholic social teaching that drew on the "personalism" of Emmanuel Mounier, the "distributism" of Eric Gill, and the Thomism of Jacques Maritain but that also had strong affinities with the indigenous American anarchism of the Industrial Workers of the World.

Day's personal spirituality has been described as conservative Catholic, as Jansenist, as sectarian, and even as centered on "self-dissolution," and there is some truth to all these characterizations.[14] Her diaries reveal a woman who was, at times, obsessed with the practice of "see[ing] every man as better than oneself."[15] She treasured the intense retreats that Father John Hugo sponsored for the Catholic Workers and stood by Hugo when he was disciplined for excessive asceticism. Though she had participated in the pre–Vatican II liturgical movement, which called for greater lay participation in the mass, she was troubled by the casual style of worship that swept through American Catholicism after Vatican II's embrace of the vernacular. She loved the saints, even the seemingly passive Thérèse of Lisieux, and consistently respected the authority of the bishops—marking a sharp contrast to the liberal, future-oriented style of the Protestant Social Gospelers. She stands today as a clear reminder that no single theological or ecclesial tradition has a monopoly on Christian social reform.

At the same time, Day built a movement that itself incorporated much of the Christian (and interfaith) diversity present in the United States. Drawing on the Catholic tradition of recognizing Christ in the stranger, she consistently encouraged and affirmed the diverse individuals who found their way to the Catholic Worker, whether they were her former socialist comrades, guests struggling with mental illness and homelessness, or idealistic young Catholics. As a result, the movement became a seedbed for a wide range of others. John Cort (1913–2006), an early Worker who admired Day but was frustrated by her anarchism and agrarianism, launched the Association

FIGURE 1. *Dorothy Day Picketing Civil Defense Drill in New York City, 1959. Courtesy of the Department of Special Collections and University Archives, Marquette University Libraries.*

of Catholic Trade Unionists to support the burgeoning industrial unions formed during the Depression. Ammon Hennacy (1893–1970), a latter-day Garrisonian who made antiwar civil disobedience an integral part of the Catholic Worker program, converted to Catholicism under Day's influence but subsequently declared himself a "non-Church Christian" devoted to waging a "one man revolution" against war and capitalism. Michael Harrington (1928–89) joined the Catholic Worker movement because it was "as far left as I could go and still be in the church" but soon repudiated both Catholicism and Day's utopianism to become an architect of the Great Society and a leader in the Democratic Socialists of America.[16] And Philip (1923–2002) and Daniel Berrigan (1921–) worked closely with Catholic Workers to create both a mass movement against the Vietnam War and, subsequently, a radical network of "resisters" who oppose warmaking through civil disobedience and symbolic sabotage of weapons systems.

Dorothy Day died in 1980, the same year that Ronald Reagan was elected. As Reagan slashed funding for low-income housing and launched proxy wars in Central America, the Catholic Worker movement grew exponentially, sponsoring houses of hospitality in cities both large and small and participating actively in the "overground railroad" for Central American war refugees. Embodying the religious freedom guaranteed by the First Amendment, some Catholic Worker houses accepted government funds for low-income housing, while others refused any cooperation with the bureaucratic state. Some aligned themselves closely with bishops or religious orders, some engaged in civil disobedience against the church as well as the state, and some incorporated Buddhist, Quaker, or Wiccan practices into their spiritual lives. A few asserted their independence by identifying themselves not as "Catholic Workers" but as "in the Catholic Worker tradition," while Protestant admirers of Day launched sister communities such as the Open Door in Atlanta and Sojourners in Washington, D.C. Today there are at least 150 Catholic Worker houses spread across the nation and the world, and Dorothy Day's practice of radical hospitality is an inspiration for thousands of Christians beyond the movement.[17]

Saul Alinsky and Community Organizing

Day's influence on twentieth-century social reform was matched by that of an eclectic activist who was never personally a Christian. Saul Alinsky (1909–72) was perhaps the least likely personality ever to play a major role in church history. Raised by Orthodox Jewish parents on the tough streets of Chicago, Alinsky venerated the Deist Thomas Paine as the prototypical American "radical," styled himself as the Machiavelli of the masses, and opened one of his books by praising Lucifer as "the first radical known to man who rebelled against the establishment and did it so effectively that he at least won his own kingdom."[18] But he could also quote Saint Francis and the Hebrew prophets, and he exchanged dozens of letters over a twenty-five-year period with the Catholic Thomist philosopher Jacques Maritain.[19] Alinsky mentored countless urban ministers, priests, and activists and was a hero to Christian reformers, ranging from the evangelical Jim Wallis to the Roman Catholic cardinal Joseph Bernardin.[20]

Alinsky's distinctive approach to social reform was shaped by his study of urban sociology at the University of Chicago, where he was initiated into a practice of close neighborhood observation that was indebted to the Social Gospel heritage of Hull House, Chicago Commons, and other settlement house communities. While working as a researcher on juvenile delinquency during the Depression, he encountered organizers sent by John L. Lewis (1880–1969) of the Congress of Industrial Organizations to build a union of Chicago's meatpackers. Attracted to Lewis's method of organizing workers by industry rather than by trade, Alinsky wondered if it could be taken a step further. Instead of simply focusing on the workplace, why not treat "the worker as a living man who votes, rents, consumes, breeds, and participates in every avenue of what we call life?"[21] In Chicago's Back of the Yards neighborhood, Alinsky tested this approach by building a neighborhood council representing bowling clubs, union locals, the American Legion, and, above all, Roman Catholic parishes. He found a steady ally in Auxiliary Bishop Bernard J. Sheil, who introduced him to most of the priests in the neighborhood and, eventually, the city. Just two days after the founding of the Back of the Yards Council in July 1939, Alinsky arranged a joint appearance of Bishop Sheil and John Lewis at a rally for the Packinghouse Workers Union. Convinced that they could not stand up against a coalition of unions and churches, the packing companies acceded to the union's demands and avoided what might have been a bitter and violent strike.[22]

Catapulted into national prominence by this turn of events and generously funded by bishops, unions, and the heir to Chicago's Marshall Field's department store, Alinsky began exporting the Back of the Yards model to other cities. In South St. Paul, Minnesota, and Kansas City, Missouri, his Industrial Areas Foundation organized meatpacking neighborhoods much like Back of the Yards, though the latter was more Protestant than Catholic. By 1945, he had launched a much more ambitious project to bring together the Mexican American, African American, and European American communities of Los Angeles. Bishop Sheil persuaded his Los Angeles counterpart to recommend Alinsky to all the local pastors, and Alinsky hired Fred Ross (1910–92) as lead organizer. Like Alinsky himself, Ross was a sociological researcher who had begun organizing the neighborhoods while doing research. Their relationship would be replicated dozens of times over the years, as Alinsky trained organizers who would in turn train additional organizers. Among those trained by Ross were César Chávez (1927–93) and Dolores Huerta (1930–). After helping to build the Community Service Organization in southern California, Chávez and Huerta would take Alinsky's eclectic religious style back into the labor movement, incorporating devotion to both Our Lady of Guadalupe and the Gandhian nonviolence of the civil rights movement into the organizing of the United Farm Workers. By the middle of the 1960s, Chávez had evolved into something of a "living saint" in the tradition of Mexican folk Catholicism. During his celebrated fasts, visiting supporters would sometimes approach him on their knees or conduct masses using vestments cut from his flag. But Chávez was also eclectic enough to carry banners depicting the Star of David alongside the Virgin of Guadalupe, "because we ask the help and prayers of all religions."[23]

Alinsky, meanwhile, made his vision more broadly available in 1946 by publishing *Reveille for Radicals* as a manual for community organizers. In its pages, he declared himself a "radical" in a pragmatic, American key, indebted more to Tom Paine, Tom Jefferson, the abolitionists, and the unionists than to doctrinaire socialism. A radical, Alinsky explained, "is that person to whom the common good is the greatest personal value . . . who genuinely and completely believes in mankind" and "is so completely identified with mankind that he personally shares the pain, the injustices, and the sufferings of all his fellow men."[24] The radical's goal was simply to give power to the people, and the path to that goal was to organize existing community organizations (churches, above all) and mobilize them around attainable goals. This vision held enormous appeal for Roman Catholic bishops and priests who were wary of socialism but eager to implement the "common good" vision of Catholic social teaching. In the 1950s, Alinsky's foremost clerical ally was Monsignor John O'Grady, the long-serving leader of the National Conference of Catholic Charities. Concerned especially about rising racial tensions in northern cities, the two men launched projects in St. Louis, Buffalo, New York City, and back in Chicago.

Many of these projects failed, but in Chicago Alinsky worked closely with Monsignor John Egan to build up a coalition of neighborhood organizations—Back of the Yards, the Organization for Southwest Chicago, the Woodlawn Organization, the Northwest Community Organization—that represented a wide array of religious and racial groups. Alinsky's methods sparked more controversy in democratically organized Protestant congregations than in priest-directed Catholic parishes, and the liberal Protestant *Christian Century* conducted a five-year polemic against Alinsky that insinuated first that he was an agent of racist Catholics and later that he hoped to spark a Peasant's Revolt in American cities.[25] But Alinsky used both persistence and humor to bring diverse groups together—on one occasion he suggested to a Catholic censor that instead of banning the Martin Luther movie he should have it shown backward so that "Luther ends up being a Catholic"[26]—and when he organized the African American Woodlawn neighborhood, he did so with both Presbyterian and Catholic support. By 1964, Protestants took the lead in inviting Alinsky to promote racial reconciliation after urban riots in Rochester, New York—a job that Martin Luther

King's Southern Christian Leadership Conference had declined.[27] The success of the FIGHT (Freedom, Independence, God, Honor, Today) organization established Alinskyite organizing as a viable middle path between the Black Power movement and the backlash of white Christians who feared movement militancy.

That middle path proved enormously appealing to Catholic and Protestant denominational executives in the late 1960s. The "urban crisis" of rioting before and after the assassination of Martin Luther King Jr. persuaded them that they needed to do something, but James Forman's 1969 Black Manifesto—which demanded half a billion dollars in reparations to support black nationalist cooperatives, radio stations, and universities—was anathema to most of their donors. Watching the chaotic effects of the Manifesto in Protestant denominations, the Catholic bishops pledged 50 million dollars to a new Catholic Campaign for Human Development and placed responsibility for distributing the money in the hands of a cluster of activist priests with close ties to Alinsky. The Catholic Campaign for Human Development, which today describes its mission as "address[ing] the root causes of poverty in America through promotion and support of community-controlled, self-help organizations and through transformative education," has channeled funds to dozens of Alinskyite groups since 1969, and most mainline Protestant denominations have followed suit.[28]

Most of the projects receiving this money have adapted Alinsky's model to place even more emphasis on local congregations. Although Alinsky's early organizations typically aligned congregations with roughly equal numbers of unions and community groups, projects today typically include seven congregations for every one other group and incorporate intensive theological reflection into the training they offer activists. This new model was pioneered by Communities Organized for Public Service, a San Antonio project that was developed in 1974 with strong support from Bishop Patricio Flores—the first Mexican American to serve as a bishop in the United States—and PADRES, the national organization for Hispanic priests. In recruiting activists, Communities Organized for Public Service organizer Ernesto Cortes Jr. built on people's concrete commitment to their parishes rather than on their abstract commitment to social change, and this style of "relational organizing" resulted in a movement that rapidly changed the racial power structure in San Antonio, culminating in the 1981 election of Henry Cisneros as the city's first Mexican American mayor since the Mexican American War.[29]

By the end of the 1970s, the relational, congregational approach became the norm among projects not only organized by the Industrial Areas Foundations but also by three rival national networks that drew heavily on denominational funding. Together, the Pacific Organization for Community Organization (founded in 1974 by Jesuit John Baumann and strongest in California), the Gamaliel Foundation (founded in Chicago in 1968 but primarily oriented to community organizing since 1986), and Direct Action, Research and Training (which grew out of a senior citizens organization in Miami funded by the United Church of Christ) maintain more than 150 affiliates in most major metropolitan areas. Projects associated with these or other networks have worked for "living wage" legislation (an idea first promoted by Father John Ryan at the beginning of the twentieth century), for fair housing, and for neighborhood revitalization; they have pioneered new organizing techniques, including "one-on-one" encounters between new activists and organizers and the "asset mapping" of a neighborhood's strengths rather than its liabilities. They have raised up prominent Hispanic and African American leaders, such as the Bronx's Johnny Youngblood, and in many places they bring together Catholic, mainline Protestant, and black church congregations in roughly equal numbers.[30] They have also influenced some of America's most prominent leaders: Hillary Clinton wrote her undergraduate thesis on Saul Alinsky, and Barack Obama became a Christian while working for a Gamaliel affiliate in Chicago. Though his name is largely forgotten today, Alinsky's legacy of congregation-based organizing may be the most powerful expression of Christian social reform at the beginning of the twenty-first century.

In some ways, Alinskyite community organizing and the Catholic Worker represent the opposite poles of Christian social reform. Alinskyites are intensely pragmatic, committed to broad coalitions and achievable victories; Catholic Workers espouse a radical vision but disavow "success, as the world determines it."[31] A casual observer might categorize the Catholic Worker as "sectarian" and Alinskyite community organizing as "churchly"—yet both movements refuse either to withdraw completely from society or to identify fully with existing institutions. Both make confident use of religious freedom while rejecting the privatized religiosity that others see as the American way. Both draw deeply on classical Christian theology, but also on socialist and unionist traditions that are usually understood as secular.

By charting this middle path between church and sect, Alinskyites and Workers stand in the social reform tradition of the abolitionists and alongside a wide range of movements that might well have been featured in this essay: the social justice lobbying sponsored by mainline Protestant denominations, the sanctuary and solidarity movements concerned with international justice, evangelical activism that repudiates conventional boundaries of "left" and "right," and the rising tide of Christian work for ecojustice. Christian social reformers also stand alongside Buddhist environmentalists, neo-pagan feminists, and Native American fighters for cultural integrity, just as their ancestors worked hand in hand with Spiritualists, Theosophists, and Jewish socialists. Freed by the First Amendment, reformers of all these traditions have effectively blended the broad concern of the "church" with the zeal of the "sect." Thomas Jefferson's "wall of separation," paradoxically, has opened many doors for those prophetic souls who strive to change the world.

NOTES

1. My use of the terms "church" and "sect" reflects the typology developed in Ernst Troeltsch, *The Social Teaching of the Christian Churches*, trans. Olive Wyon, 2 vols. (New York: Macmillan, 1931), 2:993.

2. Elizabeth Flynn, "Catholic Worker Spirituality: A Sect within a Church" (master's thesis, Graduate Theological Union, 1974).

3. Lyman Beecher, in *The Autobiography of Lyman Beecher*, ed. Barbara M. Cross, 2 vols. (Cambridge: Belknap Press of Harvard University Press, 1961), 1:252.

4. Robert H. Abzug, *Cosmos Crumbling: American Reform and the Religious Imagination* (New York: Oxford University Press, 1994), 39–56.

5. John Bartholomew Gough, *An Autobiography* (1845), in *Drunkard's Progress: Narratives of Addiction, Despair, and Recovery*, ed. John W. Crowley (Baltimore: Johns Hopkins University Press, 1999), 160. For more on temperance narratives, see Dan McKanan, *Identifying the Image of God: Radical Christians and Nonviolent Power in the Antebellum United States* (New York: Oxford University Press, 2002), 102–26.

6. James A. Morone, *Hellfire Nation: The Politics of Sin in American History* (New Haven: Yale University Press, 2003), 281–317.

7. *Resolutions and Remonstrances of the People of Colour against Colonization to the Coast of Africa* (Philadelphia, 1818), cited in C. Peter Ripley, ed., *Witness for Freedom: African American Voices on Race, Slavery, and Emancipation* (Chapel Hill: University of North Carolina Press, 1993), 32.

8. William Lloyd Garrison, "To the Public," *Liberator*, January 1, 1831.

9. Douglas M. Strong, *Perfectionist Politics: Abolitionism and the Religious Tensions of American Democracy* (Syracuse, N.Y.: Syracuse University Press, 1999); Timothy L. Smith, *Revivalism and Social Reform: American Protestantism on the Eve of the Civil War*, rev. ed. (Baltimore: Johns Hopkins University Press, 1980).

10. Frederick Douglass, "A Reform Absolutely Complete," April 9, 1870, in *The Frederick Douglass Papers* (New Haven: Yale University Press, 1979–92), ser. 1, 4:264.

11. Gaines M. Foster, *Moral Reconstruction: Christian Lobbyists and the Federal Legislation of Morality, 1865–1920* (Chapel Hill: University of North Carolina Press, 2002), 50; Ruth Bordin, *Woman and Temperance: The Quest for Power and Liberty, 1873–1900* (Piscataway, N.J.: Rutgers University Press, 1990), 95.

12. Dorothy Day, *Loaves and Fishes*, new ed. (Maryknoll, N.Y.: Orbis, 1997), 26, 23.

13. Dorothy Day, *The Long Loneliness* (New York: Harper, 1952), 45, 139.

14. James T. Fisher, *The Catholic Counterculture in America, 1933–1962* (Chapel Hill: University of North Carolina Press, 1989), 47.

15. Dorothy Day, *The Duty of Delight: The Diaries of Dorothy Day*, ed. Robert Ellsberg (Milwaukee: Marquette University Press, 2008), 102.

16. Cited in Rosalie Riegle Troester, *Voices from the Catholic Worker* (Philadelphia: Temple University Press, 1993), 120.

17. Dan McKanan, *The Catholic Worker after Dorothy: Practicing the Works of Mercy in a New Generation* (Collegeville, Minn.: Liturgical Press, 1998).

18. Saul Alinsky, *Rules for Radicals* (New York: Random House, 1971), ix.

19. Bernard Doering, ed., *The Philosopher and the Provocateur: The Correspondence of Jacques Maritain and Saul Alinsky* (Notre Dame: University of Notre Dame Press, 1994).

20. Sanford D. Horwitt, *Let Them Call Me Rebel: Saul Alinsky, His Life and Legacy* (New York: Knopf, 1989).

21. Saul Alinsky, *Reveille for Radicals* (1946; New York: Vintage, 1969), 35.

22. P. David Finks, *The Radical Vision of Saul Alinsky* (New York: Paulist, 1984), 13–18.

23. Stephen R. Lloyd-Moffett, "The Mysticism and Social Action of César Chávez," in *Latino Religions and Civic Activism in the United States*, ed. Gaston Espinosa, Virgilio Elizondo, and Jesse Miranda (New York: Oxford University Press, 2005), 42; Luís D. León, "César Chávez and Mexican American Civil Religion," in ibid., 60–61.

24. Alinsky, *Reveille for Radicals*, 15.

25. Finks, *Radical Vision of Saul Alinsky*, 127–28, 141–43.

26. Ibid., 122.

27. Stephen C. Rose, "Rochester's Racial Rubicon," *Christianity and Crisis*, March 22, 1965, 55–59.

28. Lawrence J. Engel, "The Influence of Saul Alinsky on the Campaign for Human Development," *Theological Studies* 59 (1998): 636–61.

29. Mark R. Warren, *Dry Bones Rattling: Community Building to Revitalize American Democracy* (Princeton: Princeton University Press, 2001), 40–71.

30. Richard L. Wood and Mark R. Warren, "A Different Face of Faith-Based Politics: Social Capital and Community Organizing in the Public Arena," *International Journal of Sociology and Social Policy* 22, nos. 11 and 12 (Fall 2002): 6–54; Richard Wood, *Faith in Action* (Chicago: University of Chicago Press, 2002); Samuel G. Freedman, *Upon This Rock: The Miracles of a Black Church* (New York: HarperCollins, 1993).

31. "Aims and Means of the Catholic Worker Movement," available at www.catholicworker.org/aimsandmeanstext.cfm?Number=5.

Shifting Sacrifices
Christians, War, and Peace in America

It is a first-class human tragedy that peoples of the earth who claim to
believe in the message of Jesus who they describe as the Prince of Peace
show little of that belief in actual practice. . . . If even one great nation were
unconditionally to perform the supreme act of renunciation, many of us
would see in our lifetime visible peace established on earth. — Mohandas
Gandhi, "Answer to *The Cosmopolitan*," Harijan, June 18, 1938

"Love your enemies." This simple imperative attributed to Jesus in the Gospel of Matthew has been ignored, interpreted, and applied in often startling
ways by Christians in America. American Christians have not, by and large,
had a difficult time identifying enemies. What it has meant to love them, in
contrast, has repeatedly been more difficult for followers of Jesus in America
to discern. Much of the difficulty has centered, over the centuries, in the
shifting ways that discourses and practices of "sacrifice" have been understood and applied. For many Christians in America, the central act of Jesus'
life—his death on the cross—has consciously or unconsciously been conflated with the death of soldiers or the killing of enemies in battle on behalf
of the nation or its predecessor communities. And, just as Jesus' death produced new life, so too have Christians in America interpreted the crucible
of warfare as promising a triumph in which blood sacrifice proved redemptive, as soldiers and citizens shared in the providential spoils of victory. And
yet, especially in the late twentieth and early twenty-first centuries, but with
roots much earlier, an alternative notion of "sacrifice" as the self-critical and
nonviolent participation of Christians in democratic processes emerged. In
this notion of "sacrifice," which is not dissimilar to Gandhi's notion of renunciation in the epigraph to this essay, people of faith sought to disentangle
spiritual or religious power from physical force and effectively united Christians in peacemaking efforts across expanding networks of ecumenical and
interfaith allies.

This essay will track how American Christians identified a wide variety of
enemies to "love" over the centuries and the shifting meanings of "sacrifice"

at play in four historical episodes: the Pequot War of 1637, the Civil War, the World Wars of the first half of the twentieth century, and the conflicts against "godless, atheistic communists" and "extremist Muslim terrorists" in the late twentieth and early twenty-first centuries. Although Christians in America were among the architects of the First Amendment's separation of church and state, in practice Christians have repeatedly blurred allegiance to the Christian God with allegiance to America. These blurred loyalties have produced violence in a pattern that I have called elsewhere "innocent domination" and an "empire of sacrifice."[1] This empire, built on a Protestant foundation, diffused as the nation expanded to enlist any number of different believers in shifting "sacrifices" against a similarly shifting array of enemies. Coinciding with the emergence of this empire were various efforts to turn Christianity toward peacemaking and nonviolence, and away from Constantinian efforts to prop up state power, but these have been piecemeal and reactive. Such efforts have, however, expanded allegiances both across Christian communities and in interreligious movements. That these Christian peacemakers arose alongside the astonishing military prowess, economic expansion, and arsenal of weapons of mass destruction developed by citizens of the United States in the late twentieth and early twenty-first centuries marks the history of American Christianities in relationship to violence, war, and peace with an ambivalent legacy, at best.

The Pequot "War" and Providential Conquest

It was not inevitable that Christians and Native Americans would clash. Yet in 1637, the first major armed conflicts between Europeans and Indians in New England broke out. The murders of two European traders, including John Oldham, provided the pretense for an English attack on the Pequots (even though Oldham's killers were, in all likelihood, Niantics). The attack occurred on May 26, 1637, when ninety English soldiers, led by Captain John Mason and supported by several hundred Native allies, attacked the Pequot village at Mystic, Connecticut, and set it ablaze. The fire killed between 300 and 700 Pequots—most of them women, children, and the elderly.[2]

The attack quickly took on the significance of a providentially directed sacrifice of God's enemies, in several senses. It began, according to eyewitness and participant Captain Roger Clap (1609–91), when "God permitted Satan to stir up the Pequot Indians to kill divers English Men, [such] as Mr. Oldham . . . which put us upon sending out Souldiers . . . whom God prospered in their Enterprizes, until the Pequot People were destroy'd." The Reverend Thomas Prince (1687–1758), in his introduction to Clap's *Memoirs*, reinforced Clap's theological judgment by contrasting the heathenish wilderness of this "hideous land" to the "mighty Spirit of Love to God" exhibited by patriarchs like Clap, who were, obviously, rewarded for their piety by their providential victory.[3]

Most English observers had little difficulty construing the slaughter of the Pequots as a sacrifice, but the meaning of the sacrifice was gradually spiritualized over the decades. Commander of the attack John Mason described the event in bluntly physical terms shortly afterward, claiming that God "laughed his Enemies and the Enemies of his People to scorn making them as a fiery Oven. . . . Thus did the Lord judge among the Heathen, filling the Place with dead Bodies!"[4] A few decades later, Nathaniel Morton imagined the scene in equally vivid terms. After adding a suitable expression of disgust at the carnage, he asserted how pleased God must have been with this "loving" action. It "was a fearful sight to see [the Pequots] thus frying in the Fire, and the streams of Blood quenching the Same; and horrible was the stink and scent thereof," Morton recalled. "But the Victory seemed a sweet Sacrifice, and they gave praise thereof to God, who had wrought so wonderfully for them, thus to enclose their Enemies."[5] By 1677, Increase Mather directly attributed this glorious victory to the sacrifice of prayer, theologically linking the literal fire at Mystic to the metaphorical fire of the Holy Spirit, and all but completing the spiritualization of a military massacre.[6] The ironic inversion reached full circle when in 1725 Roger Wolcott could poetically imagine a Pequot sachem envisioning the "sacrifice" of Mason on the eve of the conflict, only to be surprised when the sacrificial victim turned out to be the sachem and his people.[7]

Along with discourses that expressly described the killing of Pequots as sacrifices in loving service to God, these early American Christians also established an economy of sacrificial practices through which they claimed power for themselves by taking offerings from the Mohegans and Narragansetts. Such offerings demonstrated to the Christians (as they imagined it) the subordination of indigenous peoples to English sovereignty, if not necessarily to the sovereignty of God—although the two could be easily confused. More prosaically, the Christians called for, and received, the severed hands and heads of Pequots from Narragansetts and Mohegans. Such "godly butchery," in the words of English jurist Sir Edward Coke, was a well-established means by which English Christians demonstrated power and illustrated righteousness, all as acts of loving one's enemies, of course.[8]

Thus, when Mohegan sachem Uncas delivered "five Pequeats heads" to the English at Fort Saybrook in early 1637, "this mightily encouraged the hearts of all," recalled Captain John Underhill, another participant in the slaughter at Mystic. After that massacre, Commander Lion Gardiner of nearby Fort Saybrook was understandably worried about retaliation, so he recruited Long Island sachem Waiandance by promising him: "If you will kill all the Pequits that come to you, and send me their heads," then "you shall have trade with us." Pequot heads (and, eventually, hands as well) began arriving in such a number to the English across New England that Massachusetts governor John Winthrop could casually record that "still many Pequods' heads and hands [coming] from Long Island and other places." And lest the theological point be lost, namely that requesting and collecting enemy body parts could be an act of sacrificial love, William Bradford of Plymouth Plantation opined that "cutting off [Pequot] heads and hands, which [Natives] sent to the English, [was] a testimony of their love and service."[9]

Of course, all of this high-flown theological rhetoric of love and sacrifice had more base motives.[10] Thus, in the Treaty of Hartford of 1638, the Indians and the English also split up the Pequots' corn harvest, divvyed up their land, and established terms by which any serviceable Pequot could be "branded on the shoulder" and sold into slavery in colonial households or on plantations.[11] As it turned out, the Pequots did not make good slaves. They tended to run away, and some of them found refuge among the Mohegans and Narragansetts, who quickly discovered good reasons to distrust the Christians, when their sacrifices of heads and hands were not reciprocated with good-faith trading practices and peaceful relations.[12]

Blood Sacrifice and the Nation in the Civil War

By the mid-nineteenth century, the enslavement of Africans on American plantations and in American households was a well-established feature of economic and cultural life.[13] That slavery had religious dimensions has not always been appreciated by historians but was recognized very early by Frederick Douglass, who famously contrasted the "pure, peaceable, and impartial Christianity of Christ" with the "corrupt, slaveholding, women-whipping, cradle-plundering, partial and hypocritical Christianity of this land."[14] This distinction was not only a rhetorical device for Douglass.[15] It was an early attempt to disentangle Christianity—and Christians in America—from violence.

FIGURE 1. *Sunday Morning Mass. Camp of 69th N.Y. SM (New York State Militia). In both North and South during the Civil War, Christian ministers argued that God was on their side. Courtesy of the Prints and Photographs Division, Library of Congress. LC-DIG-cwpb-06586.*

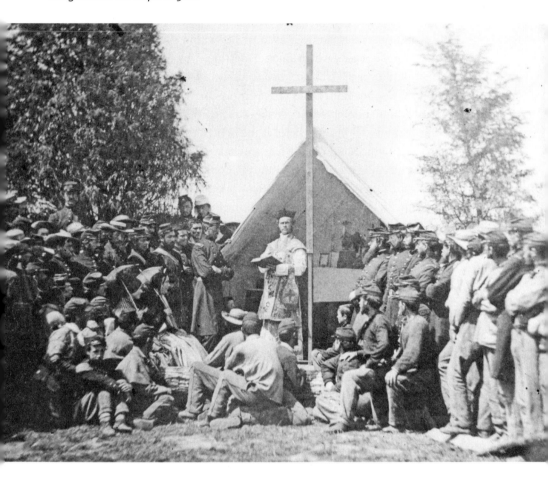

That effort coincided with the massive violence of the Civil War, which both sides interpreted in Christian terms of sacrifice. Both sides, as Abraham Lincoln put it so clearly in his Second Inaugural Address, "read the same Bible and pray to the same God, and each invokes His aid against the other."[16] Such sacrifices of prayer and invocations of God's providence were matched by deaths on the battlefield, which Americans across the North and the South framed as sacrifices. In the North, the famous lines of "The Battle Hymn of the Republic" clarified the logic: "As he died to make men holy, let us die to make men free."[17] Massachusetts's abolitionist senator Charles

Sumner put it more prosaically in 1863 when he argued that "all who die for country now, die also for humanity. Wherever they lie, in bloody fields, they will be remembered as the heroes through whom the republic was saved and civilization established forever."[18] In the South, in the early days of the conflict, the *Richmond Daily Dispatch* offered up a positively romantic interpretation of the sacrifices in war. "War . . . has within it," the essay contended, "seeds of good, seeds which must be fertilized by blood to bring forth a harvest of blessings."[19] Thus, when Confederate general Stonewall Jackson died from wounds inflicted by "friendly fire" in May 1863, Virginia attorney general John Randolph Tucker could extol how "Christianity may well cherish the memory of this holy hero, as the noblest example . . . that the devout conscience of the South, in the fear and love of God, is constrained to yield up life, a bleeding sacrifice, upon the altar of its country's independence."[20] Once again, love of God for American Christians had come to mean killing and death. As Harry S. Stout concludes, by the end of the war "the language of martyrdom and sacrificial altars was instinctual and, through sheer repetition, [was] forming a national consensus and literally incarnating a powerful new religion of patriotism."[21] This new religion of sacrifice emerged from the prayers, fasts, and funerals that were celebrated in town after town across the North and the South.

Such a "religion of patriotism" was informed by white, Protestant Christian piety, but it morphed into hybrid forms capable of being associated with distinctions or enemies defined along the lines of region, race, age, class, gender, and nation. It had a great deal of work to do in the years after the Civil War. "Sacrifice and the state became inextricably intertwined," as Drew Gilpin Faust has put it, in ways that diffused the (il)logic of Christian sacrifice across American cultural institutions and practices. "Shared suffering," Faust writes, "would override persisting differences about the meanings of race, citizenship, and nationhood to establish sacrifice and its memorialization as the ground on which North and South would ultimately reunite."[22]

An Empire of Sacrifice Emerges

If the North won the military battles of the Civil War, the South won the culture war. As Christine Leigh Heyrman has suggested, a patriarchal ideal of southern living merged ideals of masculinity with Christian faith so that "men of God were men of honor, initiates into the mysteries of competition, combat, and mastery."[23] In the years following the Civil War, this southern code of masculine honor led many Christians to sacrifices in conflicts against a range of enemies.

Most notably, throughout the late nineteenth century, Christians in America were still occupied on the "home front" with conflicts against Native Americans. Many indigenous children were torn from their communities of origin in the nineteenth and early twentieth centuries and sent to boarding schools, where they were taught to assimilate various versions of Christian "civilization." Following the earlier policy of removals, by which indigenous peoples from the eastern seaboard were largely relocated to reservations, the late nineteenth century witnessed conflicts between federal troops and a wide variety of tribal groups west of the Mississippi. The battles culminated in two attacks that have been preserved in memory for very different reasons. The first occurred at Little Big Horn, Montana, on June 25–26, 1876, where the Lakota and Cheyenne wiped out the U.S. 7th Cavalry under George Armstrong Custer. The second occurred at Wounded Knee, South Dakota, on December 29, 1890, when the revived 7th Cavalry retaliated against the Lakota and massacred roughly 300 men, women, and children. Only the first battle entered into American national mythology, however, as Edward Tabor Linenthal has recorded. "Veneration of Custer and the martyrs of the 7th Cavalry," Linenthal wrote, "began almost immediately after the battle. . . . By killing the enemy in a sacred cause, these men had preserved the life of the nation; indeed, the blood spilled during their redemptive sacrifice made possible the formation of a new world," what General William T. Sherman called a few years later a "great wave of civilization."[24]

This "wave" of sacrifices eventually extended in foreign affairs to battles against "papist" enemies in the Spanish-American War, but it was World War I and World War II that produced the most vivid new enemies around which Christians could mobilize sacrifices, notably the Germans and the Japanese.[25] Coinciding with President Woodrow Wilson's engagement of the United States in World War I, "Baseball Evangelist" Billy Sunday expressed the popular consensus by scapegoating "the Kaiser" in a sermon preached at Carnegie Hall in 1918. The war pitted "Germany against America, hell against heaven," Sunday suggested, thus describing national conflict in theological terms.[26] Such a spiritual conflict would of course require sacrifice—a rhetoric President Woodrow Wilson had invoked in his War Message to Congress just months prior to Sunday's sermon. "We seek no indemnities for ourselves, no material compensation for the sacrifices we shall freely make," Wilson urged. And yet "there are, it may be, many months of fiery trial and sacrifice ahead of us," he went on. The conclusion to his speech linked such sacrifices with other typical American ideals, and eventually to God's will: "The right is more precious than peace, and we shall fight for the things which we have always carried nearest our hearts—for democracy. . . . To such a task we can dedicate our lives and our fortunes, everything that we are and everything that we have, with the pride of those who know that the day has come when America is privileged to spend her blood and her might for the principles that gave her birth and happiness and the peace which she has treasured. God helping her, she can do no other."[27] Subtly invoking the classic language attributed to the reformer Martin Luther, President Wilson here took his stand for war as sacrifice, on an unmistakably Christian foundation.[28]

In World War II, Germans again became enemies, but it was the bombing of Pearl Harbor on December 7, 1941, that led President Franklin Delano Roosevelt to invoke a rhetoric of sacrifice to mobilize the American people to another war, this time against the Japanese. In a speech bearing the title "A Call to Sacrifice," Roosevelt first equivocated, preferring the phrase "self-denial" for his programs that called for higher taxes and lower salaries: "'Sacrifice,'" the president intoned on April 28, 1942, "is not exactly the proper word with which to describe this program of self-denial. When, at the end of this great struggle, we shall have saved our free way of life, we shall have made no 'sacrifice.'" And yet, by the end of his speech, Roosevelt dropped the equivocation and appealed directly to the now-conventional term. After telling the stories of several military "heroes" fighting against Japan, Roosevelt urged Americans "here at home" to "contemplate our own duties, our own responsibilities": "Our soldiers and sailors are members of well-disciplined units. But they're still and forever individuals—free individuals. They are farmers and workers, businessmen, professional men, artists, clerks. They are the United States of America. That is why they fight. We too are the United States of America. That is why we must work and sacrifice. It is for them. It is for us. It is for victory."[29] This sacrifice for the sake of victory would exact its most direct cost among the Japanese. As many as 120,000 men, women, and children of Japanese descent were interred in military camps under Executive Order 9066, issued by President Roosevelt on February 19, 1942.[30] Roosevelt's rhetoric invoked self-denial and echoed Gandhi's idea of renunciation. But Roosevelt's rhetoric was put into practice through the legalized imprisonment of noncombatant citizens and was eventually accompanied by the mobilization of the "arsenal of democracy," with attendant "sacrifices" of many kinds, cutting across systems of church and state.

Shifting Enemies, Expanding Allies

In the years after World War II, as the United States mobilized to achieve hitherto unimagined prowess, an ideology of anticommunism emerged to replace antifascism as a consensus around which sacrifices were required. "Containment" of Communism as a doctrine was an ideological exclusion, a sacrifice by discourse, of the "godless."[31] Such service to God helped warrant the social "sacrifice" of communists, homosexuals, and fellow travelers inside the United States during the McCarthy era.[32] It also justified the military "sacrifice" of U.S. soldiers on battlefields in Korea and Vietnam. The durability of this rhetoric, and its ability to shift easily to different enemy-objects, can become apparent through a brief examination of how the Vietnam conflict (1959–75) has been memorialized in American history.

The United States entered Vietnam for the express purpose of "containment" of communism.[33] The conflict eventually led to the deaths of 58,000 Americans and as many as 2 million Vietnamese. As is well known, the original model for the official Vietnam Veterans Memorial on the Mall in Washington, D.C., was a simple black granite wall of names, descending into a hillock on the Mall. The wall, designed by Yale undergraduate Maya Ying Lin, emerged in 1981 from a competition underwritten by financier H. Ross Perot. The wall would list the names of all Americans who died in the war, in chronological order, etched in reflective black granite. After Lin's design emerged, Perot and some veterans' groups protested that the memorial was not "heroic" enough.[34] As a result, compromises to Lin's simple design began to emerge. Such compromises have increased over the decades, and all of them involved various efforts to cloak the war, and Lin's simple design, in sacrifice.

The first compromise was a dedicatory "inscription," or Epilogue, which was added to the wall over Lin's objections. It reads: "Our nation remembers the courage, sacrifice, and devotion to duty and country of its Vietnam Veterans. This memorial was built with private donations from the American people." A second compromise was the "three men" statue designed by sculptor Frederick G. Hart that was added to the memorial shortly before groundbreaking in 1982, to appease Secretary of the Interior James Watt and other conservatives who threatened to stall its construction. Hart described his intent in creating the statue: "The [three soldiers] wear the uniforms and carry the weapons of warriors. They are young. The contrast between the innocence of their youth and the weapons of war underscores the poignancy of their sacrifice. There is about them the physical contact and sense of unity that bespeaks the bonds of love and sacrifice that is the nature of men at war."[35] Again, an odd conjunction of love and sacrifice emerged in association with war in American history.

Not surprisingly, "sacrifice" also became a key theme in the effort to build a "Vietnam Women's Memorial" on the Mall. The statue that emerged from this process—designed by sculptor Glenna Goodacre—was dedicated on the memorial site after a long controversy in 1993. The official National Park Service web page for the memorial suggests that the statue of three women coming to the aid of a soldier "recalls the courage and sacrifice of all women who served."[36] The visual imagery of the sculpture is even more overt. It depicts a wounded (or dead) young male soldier lying across the lap of a female soldier, presumably a nurse. It is, in short, a Pietá—a depiction of the dead Christ cradled by his loving and grieving Mother. Here, an American soldier displaces Christ as a "sacrifice" to save the nation.

In an earlier essay, published in 1996, I contended that the memorial could serve to diffuse the process of scapegoating that led to the deaths of the 58,000 soldiers.[37] Competing targets of blame, and competing targets of devotion, I suggested, made the wall a democratic and pluralistic sacred place whose meaning could not be contained in any one version of sacrifice. I believe this is still true, but efforts have clearly increased to control the meanings of the memorial and to subsume the diverse experiences of the veterans under the category of sacrifice for the nation, no matter the enemy.[38] In November 2003, President George W. Bush signed legislation to build a visitor's center at the Vietnam Memorial to "educate future generations about patriotism and sacrifice." Cosponsor of the House bill Congressman Jim Gibbons (R-Nev.), who is himself a Vietnam veteran, contended that "the sacrifices made by the soldiers and their families during the Vietnam War must never be forgotten. The Visitor Center will give every American generation the opportunity to gain a better understanding and greater respect for the sacrifices our soldiers made during this war."[39] And lest the context of this statement and its rhetoric of sacrifice be missed, Rep. Gibbons clarified: "As our servicemen and women are engaged in a war against a brutal tyrant and an oppressive regime in Iraq, there is no better time to recognize the efforts and sacrifices of our veterans."[40]

Now it may indeed be apt to describe the death of a soldier on a battlefield as a "sacrifice," and I do not at all want to belittle the difficulties faced by military families and the grief that the loss of a loved one can bring. But the ubiquitous use of a religious term to refer to national policy ought to be subject, at least, to some critical scrutiny.[41] At one level, of course, the euphemism of "sacrifice" for death in war has become so conventional as to be banal. But as Hannah Arendt long ago showed, it is precisely this banality that renders violence plausible to the human conscience.[42] Calling the death of a soldier in war a "sacrifice" makes *war* a religious phenomenon. This pattern of justification has proved to be remarkably durable in American history.

Of course, there have always been those who protested against such sacrifices and sought to join Frederick Douglass's early effort to disentangle Christianity from them. Perhaps the most wide-ranging and significant of the organizations to emerge on behalf of religious nonviolence in the United States was the Fellowship of Reconciliation (FOR),[43] founded in 1915.[44] World War I was the catalyst. As war broke out in Europe, two Christians—Henry Hodgkin, an English Quaker, and Friedrich Sigmund-Schultze, a German Lutheran—pledged to find a way to collaborate despite the conflict between their countries.[45] Out of their pledge came the FOR, an interreligious movement that by 2009 had branches on every continent and groups in over forty countries.[46] The FOR has sponsored programs such as nonviolence education and training for congregations and communities, including many during the civil rights era; Muslim-Jewish peace walks around the world and interfaith dialogues in Israel; agitation and activism for racial justice in U.S. policies and prisons; and most recently, a "campaign of conscience for the people of Iraq."[47]

The year 1917 saw the emergence of the American Friends Service Committee (AFSC).[48] The Friends, or Quakers, who traced their roots to George Fox in the seventeenth century, decided early on that "there is that of God in everyone" and that they could not, in good conscience, participate in warfare against any enemy. Soon Quakers like Mary Dyer were proclaiming the existence of an "inner light" in every human, and the New England Puritans whipped, branded, ear-cropped, and hanged them for it.[49] On one level, the hangings backfired badly and the Quaker "Lamb's War" won out over the Puritan war of force, for soon an entire Quaker colony was established in Pennsylvania. Gradually, however, even Pennsylvania was overrun by Protestants who were unconvinced that nonviolence would really work with Natives and heretics. By 1917, when the nation entered World War I, Quaker pacifists were a decided minority in the United States. The AFSC was organized as a way to engage Friends who conscientiously objected to the war by providing them with opportunities to provide relief service near the trenches.[50] Since then, the AFSC has won a Nobel Peace Prize for its work in rescue and refugee services during World War II and has been a tireless advocate of peace education. "We regard no person as our enemy" is one AFSC mantra.[51]

Out of another stream of the "peace churches," among the Mennonites, came the Mennonite Central Committee (MCC) in 1920.[52] The roots of this organization go back even further than the Quakers, to the sixteenth century and the interesting figure of Menno Simons. Simons never forgot the bloodletting he saw during the Peasants' War in Germany. Observing how various "prophets," who claimed immediate inspiration from God, briefly took over a town and its political system by force and who just as quickly were slaughtered themselves, Simons renounced the use of force as a vehicle for building God's kingdom.[53] Today, on the global scene, the MCC has been involved in projects to improve health care and agriculture, mediate conflict, and provide relief in war zones or after natural catastrophes, among other things. In North America, the MCC has been especially active in immigration and refugee assistance, job creation, work with indigenous peoples, and programs of restorative justice for offenders and victims of crime.[54]

Since 1945, a rather remarkable, and largely unrecognized, flourishing of grassroots groups of Christians committed to active religious nonviolence has appeared, following patterns established by the more venerable organizations and often building directly on Gandhi's notion of sacrifice as renunciation. Pax Christi is the most prominent such organization to emerge among Roman Catholics.[55] It was founded in France in 1945 by Marie-Marthe Dortel Claudot and was established in the United States in 1972, primarily at the instigation of laypeople.[56] The organization has behind it in its quest for peace many statements by the late Pope John Paul II and the U.S. Catholic bishops and the examples of individuals such as Dorothy Day, Oscar Romero, and Daniel and Philip Berrigan.[57]

Just as Roman Catholics developed a peace movement, so did Protestant evangelicals.[58] In the early 1970s, a group of students at Trinity Evangelical Divinity School in Deerfield, Illinois, began to meet to talk about how their faith connected to politics and especially to the escalation of the Vietnam War. They began publishing a journal, initially called the *Post-American*, which became *Sojourners* in 1975. As of 2011 the journal had a circulation of roughly 35,000, with over 200,000 subscribers to Sojomail, which included links to articles from the magazine.[59] Under the leadership of Jim Wallis, the intentional Christianity community has moved from Chicago to Washington, D.C., and now has become an ecumenical movement on a solid evangelical root.[60] The official Sojourners Statement of Faith, entitled "Our Life at the Foot of the Mountain," accurately connects the Sojourners to many historic Christian movements in the past, from monks to mystics, reformers and radicals, abolitionists and civil right agitators.[61]

The list could go on. Lutheran Peace Fellowship traces its roots to 1941 and was especially active during the Vietnam War.[62] Presbyterian Peace Fellowship goes back to 1973, when the Witherspoon Society was formed. The organization named itself after John Witherspoon—the first moderator of the Presbyterian General Assembly, in 1789, and the only clergyperson to sign the Declaration of Independence.[63] Episcopal Peace Fellowship was founded in 1939 on the eve of World War II as the Episcopal Pacifist Fellowship. In 1966, it took its current name and became a broader peace and justice movement at the same time that it named its first executive director.[64] And, finally, from within the Protestant fold—and this list is by no means comprehensive—is the Baptist Peace Fellowship of North America, founded in 1984, but with roots in twelve different Baptist peace organizations dating back to 1941.[65]

So these developments of the last fifty years represent a very different tale than the militant pieties of sacrifice so common in American history.[66] It might even be said that the emergence of active nonviolence across religious traditions represents their actual "coming of age."[67] Yet with the attacks on the World Trade Towers and the Pentagon on September 11, 2001, a new enemy emerged to channel the "love" of some American Christians. "Terrorists" replaced communists, and a "New Cold War" was launched, which eventually became a "Global War on Terror" with two primary fronts—Afghanistan and Iraq.[68] Just as Islamist martyrs sacrificed themselves in suicide bombings around the globe, President George W. Bush (and a veritable army of cultural commentators) consistently invoked religious language, and especially the language of "sacrifice," to justify military activity in Iraq.[69] During his remarks at the National Cathedral on the National Day of Prayer on September 14, 2001, the president claimed that his response to the terrorist attacks would be to "rid the world of evil." What it would take to accomplish this modest goal became clearer later in the address, when he linked "our national character" to "eloquent acts of sacrifice."[70] The "sacrifices" he meant, at the time, were those of firefighters and police. Soon, however, they would include soldiers. Thus, in an address on Monday, October 7, 2002, in Cincinnati, shortly before the invasion of Iraq, the president first demonized or scapegoated Saddam Hussein and then claimed repeatedly that Hussein possessed chemical and biological weapons and sought nuclear weapons. He then asserted that Americans would sacrifice, in war if necessary, but ideally such "sacrifices" would be made "for peace": "I hope this will not require military action, but it may. . . . If we have to act, we will take every precaution possible. We will plan carefully. We will act with the full power of the United States military. We will act with allies at our side, and we will prevail.

As Americans, we want peace. We work and sacrifice for peace. But there can be no peace if our security depends on the will and whims of a ruthless and aggressive dictator. I'm not willing to stake one American life on trusting Saddam Hussein."[71] Instead, he would sacrifice thousands.

The president himself called these deaths in Iraq "sacrifices." In a speech on September 7, 2003, Bush claimed that "these months have been a time of new responsibilities, and sacrifice, and national resolve and great progress." Later in the same speech, the president reiterated again that the war "will take time and require sacrifice."[72] Then, in a speech at the U.S. Naval Academy on November 30, 2005, President Bush asserted more generally that "a time of war is a time of sacrifice," thus baptizing war yet again in the religious language of sacrifice. Invoking the Revolutionary War legacy, the president claimed further that "advancing the ideal of democracy and self-government is the mission that created our nation." Here, too, the religious language of "mission" could not be a coincidence. Indeed, this mission entailed a "calling," yet another significant religious term, "of a new generation of Americans," thus implicating the young men and women in a future of "sacrifice." Throughout the buildup to and waging of war in Iraq, in short, President Bush cloaked deaths-by-policy in the innocence of religious discourse. He could thereby assert a future of American dominance: "We will answer history's call with confidence—because we know that freedom is the destiny of every man, woman and child on this earth."[73] As Kelly Denton-Borhaug concludes, for George W. Bush "the rhetoric of sacrifice was shaped in a purposefully strategic fashion so as to coincide with perceived American cultural values and expectations. . . . Spotlighting sacralized military sacrifice has had the intended consequence of veiling, discouraging or mystifying hard questions."[74]

Throughout American history, then, American Christians have identified enemies on whom to vent violence and wage war. At times, such acts have been explicitly identified as works of love, but more often the violence has been cloaked under religious discourses of sacrifice. From the Pequot War in the seventeenth century, to the Civil War in the nineteenth century, down to the Global War on Terror in the twenty-first century, American Christians have used "sacrifice" in association with various forms of violence. At the same time, and especially since 1945, but with roots in the historic peace churches, different forms of American Christianity—across traditions—have emerged. Such non-Constantinian Christianities, committed to nonviolence and the rule of law, might actually make loving one's enemies more than a platitude, and make America something other than an empire of sacrifice.

NOTES

1. Jon Pahl, *Empire of Sacrifice: The Religious Origins of American Violence* (New York: New York University Press, 2010).

2. See Alfred A. Cave, *The Pequot War* (Amherst: University of Massachusetts Press, 1996).

3. Captain Roger Clap, *Memoirs of Capt. Roger Clap, Relating Some of God's Remarkable Providences to Him* (Boston: B. Green, 1731), i.

4. John Mason, *A Brief History of the Pequot War* (Boston: S. Kneeland and T. Green, 1736), 9–10.

5. Nathaniel Morton, *New-Englands Memoriall* (Cambridge: S.G. and M.J. for John Usher of Boston, 1669), 101.

6. Increase Mather, *A Relation of the Troubles Which Have Hapned in New-England, by Reason of the Indians There . . . Together with an Historical Discourse Concerning the Prevalency of Prayer Shewing That New Englands Late Deliverance from the Rage of the Heathen Is an Eminent Answer of Prayer* (Boston: John Foster, 1677).

7. Roger Wolcott, *Poetical Meditations* (New London, Conn.: T. Green, 1725), 64–71.

8. Andrew Lipman, "A Meanes to Knit Them Together": The Exchange of Body Parts in the Pequot War," *William and Mary Quarterly* 65 (January 2008): 1–18.

9. Ibid.

10. Jon Pahl, *Paradox Lost: Free Will and Political Liberty in American Culture, 1630–1760* (Baltimore: Johns Hopkins University Press, 1992).

11. Michael L. Fickes, "'They Could Not Endure That Yoke': The Captivity of Pequot Women and Children after the War of 1637," *New England Quarterly* 73 (March 2000): 58–81.

12. Ronald Dale Karr, "'Why Should You Be So Furious?': The Violence of the Pequot War," *Journal of American History* 85 (December 1998): 876–909.

13. Jon Butler, *Awash in a Sea of Faith: Christianizing the American People* (Cambridge: Harvard University Press, 2000).

14. William L. Andrews and William S. McFeely, eds., *Narrative of the Life of Frederick Douglass, An American Slave, Written by Himself* (New York: W. W. Norton, 1997), 75.

15. In fact, Douglass continued, selectively, to support Christian churches throughout his life. Unless one is willing to disregard both this fact and his own language here and in many of his speeches on religion, that this distinction is more than merely a rhetorical ploy must be acknowledged. See William L. Van Deburg, "Frederick Douglass and the Institutional Church," *Journal of the American Academy of Religion* 14 (June 1977): 515–37. Van Deburg concludes that Douglass was "selective in his attendance" and "only those religious bodies which had attempted to remove both spiritual and physical fetters received his approbation."

16. See Library of Congress, *Primary Documents in American History*, "Abraham Lincoln's Second Inaugural Address," http://www.loc.gov/rr/program/bib/ourdocs/ Lincoln2nd.html (accessed February 9, 2009).

17. Julia Ward Howe, "The Battle Hymn of the Republic," *Atlantic Monthly* 9 (February 1862): 10, online at http://www.theatlantic.com/issues/1862feb/batthym.htm (accessed February 9, 2009).

18. Charles Sumner, *Emancipation! Its Policy and Necessity as a War Measure for the Suppression of the Rebellion* (Boston, 1862), 23, as cited by Harry S. Stout, *Upon the Altar of the Nation: A Moral History of the Civil War* (New York: Viking, 2006), 175.

19. *Richmond Daily Dispatch*, May 21, 1862, as cited by Stout, *Upon the Altar of the Nation*, 131.

20. John Randolph Tucker, *The Southern Church Justified in Its Support of the South in the Present War* (Richmond, 1863), 17, as cited by Stout, *Upon the Altar of the Nation*, 228.

21. Stout, *Upon the Altar of the Nation*, 341.

22. Drew Gilpin Faust, *This Republic of Suffering: Death and the American Civil War* (New York: Knopf, 2007), xiii.

23. Christine Leigh Heyrman, *Southern Cross: The Beginnings of the Bible Belt* (Chapel Hill: University of North Carolina Press, 1997), 207.

24. Edward Tabor Linenthal, *Sacred Ground: Americans and Their Battlefields* (Champaign: University of Illinois Press, 1993), 131.

25. See Orlando Patterson, *Rituals of Blood: Consequences of Slavery across Two American Centuries* (Washington, D.C.: Civitas/Counterpoint, 1993), 173, 231.

26. "Billy Sunday Fires Hot Shot at Kaiser," *New York Times*, February 19, 1918.

27. Woodrow Wilson, *War Messages*, 65th Cong., 1st Sess., Senate Doc. No. 5, Serial No. 7264, Washington, D.C., [April 2] 1917, online at *The World War I Document Archive*, http://wwi.lib.byu.edu/index.php/Wilson%27s_War_Message_to_Congress (accessed February 7, 2009).

28. Allen J. Frantzen, in *Bloody Good: Chivalry, Sacrifice, and the Great War* (Chicago: University of Chicago Press, 2003), has traced the roots and role of this rhetoric and its depiction across media in Germany and England during the same conflict. In the United States, see Richard J. Gamble, *The War for Righteousness: Progressive Christianity, the Great War, and the Rise of the Messianic Nation* (Wilmington, Del.: ISI Books, 2003), especially chap. 7, "Soldiers of the Cross."

29. Franklin D. Roosevelt, "A Call for Sacrifice," April 28, 1942, online at Paul Halsall, *Internet Modern History Sourcebook*, http://www.fordham.edu/halsall/mod/1942roosevelt-sacrifice.html (accessed February 7, 2009).

30. "Transcript of Executive Order 9066: Resulting in Relocation of the Japanese," online at http://www.ourdocuments.gov/doc.php?flash=false&doc=74&page=transcript (accessed February 7, 2009).

31. See William Inboden, *Religion and American Foreign Policy, 1945–1960: The Soul of Containment* (Cambridge: Cambridge University Press, 2008).

32. See Donald F. Crosby, *God, Church, and Flag: Senator Joseph R. McCarthy and the Catholic Church, 1950–1957* (Chapel Hill: University of North Carolina Press, 1978).

33. See Marvin E. Gettleman et al., eds., *Vietnam and America: A Documented History* (New York: Grove Weidenfeld, 1985).

34. See Jan C. Scruggs and Joel L. Swerdlow, *To Heal a Nation: The Vietnam Veterans Memorial* (New York: HarperCollins, 1985).

35. At one time, this rhetoric was evident on the official Vietnam Veterans Memorial website and also in a brochure distributed to visitors, sponsored by the National Park Service. Hart's language endures with the help of Wikipedia. See "The Three Soldiers," http://en.wikipedia.org/wiki/The_Three_Soldiers (accessed February 11, 2009).

36. The official language of the National Park Service suggests that the memorial can be effective at "deliberately setting aside the controversies of the war." See http://www.nps.gov/vive/ (accessed February 9, 2009).

37. Jon Pahl, "A National Shrine to Scapegoating? The Vietnam Veterans Memorial, Washington, D.C.," in *Contagion: Journal of Violence, Mimesis, and Culture* 2 (Spring 1995): 165.

38. As Jeffrey F. Meyer has noted, the Vietnam Memorial is, in its earthy simplicity, "like no other in Washington, its statement the opposite of every other architectural statement made in this city of dominant white memorials." See *Myths in Stone: Religious Dimensions of Washington, D.C.* (Berkeley: University of California Press, 2001), 191. Meyer documents in vivid detail how this imperial city is "a fusion of the secular and sacred, a uniquely modern blend of politics and religion that is nevertheless grounded in the archaic past" (8).

39. "Gibbons Statement on Introduction of Vietnam Veterans Memorial Visitor Center Legislation," at http://www.vietnamwar.com/vietnamveteransmemoriallegishouse.htm (accessed February 11, 2009). The plans for the new center have proceeded to site evaluation, with the most likely location being directly north and west of the memorial, near the street, which means visitors are likely to go through the visitor's center prior to experiencing the memorial. This suggests that many visitors' experiences of the wall—with its somber reminder of the cost of war in the lives of individuals—are likely to be preempted by an "official" interpretation of the wall, which is, in all probability, likely to reinforce the rhetoric of "sacrifice" so prominent in the legislation promoting it. The site analysis for the visitor's center has as its epigraph an anonymous poem: "Read the Names, Remember them All; Sacrifice, Courage, They answered the Call." See "Vietnam Veterans Memorial Center, Site Selection Study Environment Analysis, Public Comment Draft," at http://www.vvmf.org//attachments/VVMCenter_SiteAnalysis.pdf (accessed February 11, 2009).

40. Ibid. It is not my aim to develop an alternative to the euphemism of "sacrifice" for death in war, but I find helpful the commentary of Daniel Pick, *War Machine: The Rationalisation of Slaughter in the Modern Age* (New Haven: Yale University Press, 1993), who contends that "the most productive accounts of war . . . are those which recognise, precisely, the unavoidable roughness of the outcome, the lacunae, the inconsistencies

of the execution, the questionable nature of the very enterprise," and that instead "call into question some of the cliches of our current discourse, the platitudes which still have their purchase today, their numbing and exonerating effect" (10–11).

41. For the problems this link between sacrifice and the nation can bring, see Frantzen, *Bloody Good*; Ivan Strenski, *Contesting Sacrifice: Religion, Nationalism, and Social Thought in France* (Chicago: University of Chicago Press, 2002); and Carolyn Marvin and David W. Engle, *Blood Sacrifice and the Nation: Totem Rituals and the American Flag* (Cambridge: Cambridge University Press, 1999).

42. Hannah Arendt, *Eichmann in Jerusalem: A Report on the Banality of Evil* (New York: Penguin, 1994).

43. Pacifism, if not active nonviolence, is not unknown in Christianity prior to the modern era. See Peter Brock, *The Roots of War Resistance: Pacifism from the Early Church to Tolstoy* (Nyack, N.Y.: Fellowship of Reconciliation, 1981); and Roland H. Bainton, *Christian Attitudes toward War and Peace: A Historical Survey and Critical Reevaluation* (New York: Abingdon, 1960). See, for a survey, W. Michael Slattery, *Jesus the Warrior? Historical Christian Perspectives and Problems on the Morality of War and the Waging of Peace* (Milwaukee, Wis.: Marquette University Press, 2007).

44. See, for selections from Fellowship of Reconciliation leaders, Walter Wink, ed., *Peace Is the Way: Writings on Nonviolence from the Fellowship of Reconciliation* (Maryknoll, N.Y.: Orbis, 2000).

45. The war was a turning point for many pacifists in the United States and elsewhere. See Scott H. Bennett, *Radical Pacifism: The War Resisters League and Gandhian Nonviolence in America, 1915–1963* (Syracuse, N.Y.: Syracuse University Press, 2003).

46. The official history is Jim Wallis, *Valiant for Peace: A History of the Fellowship of Reconciliation, 1914–1989* (London: Fellowship of Reconciliation, 1991).

47. See the home page of the group, at http://www.forusa.org (accessed February 9, 2009). The in-house history is Paul R. Dekar, *Creating the Beloved Community: A Journey with the Fellowship of Reconciliation* (Scottdale, Pa.: Herald Press, 2005).

48. No major historical publication traces the history of this organization, whose home page is http://www.afsc.org (accessed February 11, 2009). Two dissertations provide glimpses: Patricia Faith Applebaum, "The Legions of Good Will: The Religious Culture of Protestant Pacifism" (Ph.D. diss., Boston University, 2001); and Jane K. Webb, "The American Friends Service Committee: A Quaker Experiment in Social Change and Organizational Innovation—A Study in Value Conflict" (Ph.D. diss., Boston College, 1975).

49. See Ruth Talbot Plimpton, *Mary Dyer: A Biography of a Rebel Quaker* (Boston: Branden Publishing, 1994); and Eve LaPlante, *American Jezebel: The Uncommon Life of Anne Hutchinson, the Woman who Defied the Puritans* (San Francisco: HarperSanFrancisco, 2004).

50. A helpful pamphlet on the early years is J. William Frost, *Our Deeds Carry Our Message: The Early History of the American Friends Service Committee* (Haverford, Pa.: Friends Historical Association, 1992).

51. See the organization's home page, at http://www.afsc.org (accessed February 9, 2009).

52. A fine documentary history has been published: Cornelius J. Dyck, ed., with Robert S. Kreider and John A. Lapp, *The Mennonite Central Committee Story: Documents*, 5 vols. (Scottdale, Pa.: Herald Press, 1980–88). A history of the early years can be found in Mary Jane Heisey, *Peace and Persistence: Tracing the Brethren in Christ Peace Witness through Three Generations* (Kent, Ohio: Kent State University Press, 2003). Countering accusations that the Mennonite Central Committee and similar organizations are "top-down" bureaucratic approaches to peacemaking is Cynthia Sampson and John Paul Lederach, eds., *From the Ground Up: Mennonite Contributions to International Peacebuilding* (New York: Oxford University Press, 2000).

53. For an overview of Simons's place in the history of theology, see Sjouka Voolstra, "Menno Simons," in *The Reformation Theologians: An Introduction to Theology in the Early Modern Period*, ed. Carter Lindberg (Oxford, UK: Blackwell, 2002), 363–78. For learned essays on the legacy of the man, see Gerald R. Brunk, ed., *Menno Simons, a Reappraisal: Essays in Honor of Irvin B. Horston* (Harrisonburg, Va.: Eastern Mennonite College, 1992). Simons's works are available in a scholarly edition, *Complete Writings*, trans. Leonard Verduin, ed. John Christian Wenger, with a biography by Harold S. Bender (Scottdale, Pa.: Herald Press, 1966).

54. The home page of the organization is http://www.mcc.org (accessed February 11, 2009).

55. See the group's home page at http://www.paxchristi.net (accessed February 11, 2009). See the U.S. chapter at http://www.paxchristiusa.org (accessed February 11, 2009). The organization's periodical, *Catholic Peace Voice*, has been published continuously since 1975.

56. Typical of the spirit and leadership of the group is Mary Lou Kownacki, *The Nonviolent Moment: Spirituality for the 21st Century* (Erie, Pa.: Pax Christi USA, 2002).

57. See, for a sample of John Paul II's frequent statements on peace, his annual addresses on World Peace Day, at http://www.vatican.va/holy_father/john_paul_ii/messages/peace/documents/hf_jp-ii_mes_20031216_xxxvii-world-day-for-peace_en.html (accessed February 11, 2009). For bishops' statements, for instance on Iraq, go to http://www.usccb.org/bishops/iraq.shtml (accessed February 11, 2009). Pax Christi has published a biography of Romero and a collection of Daniel Berrigan's writings. See John Dear, *Oscar Romero and the Nonviolent Struggle for Justice* (Erie, Pa.: Pax Christi USA, 1991); and John Dear, ed., *Selections from the Writings of Daniel Berrigan, SJ* (Erie, Pa.: Pax Christi USA, 1991). Day has been widely anthologized and remembered by historians. See, for one stellar example, William L. Miller, *Dorothy Day: A Biography* (San Francisco: Harper and Row, 1982).

58. Evangelicals often get stereotyped as right-wingers. In fact, a significant left wing of evangelicalism has existed throughout the history of the movement. See Donald W. Dayton, *Discovering an Evangelical Heritage* (New York: Harper and Row, 1976).

59. The home page of the community, linked to the journal, is http://www.sojo.net (accessed February 11, 2009).

60. See Jim Wallis, *The Soul of Politics: A Practical and Prophetic Vision for Change; with a Foreword by Garry Wills; and a Preface by Cornel West* (New York: Orbis, 1994).

61. See the official history at http://www.sojo.net/index.cfm?action=about_us.history (accessed February 11, 2009).

62. See Steven Schroeder, *A Community and a Perspective: Lutheran Peace Fellowship, 1941–1991* (Lanham, Md.: University Press of America, 1993); *Peace Notes: Newsletter of Lutheran Peace Fellowship*, 1984–; and the group's home page, http://members.tripod.com/~lutheran_peace (accessed February 11, 2009).

63. See Eugene TeSelle, "A Network of the Concerned: The Witherspoon Society and Its Challenge to the Church," historical pamphlet available from the Witherspoon Society, 1418 Clarendon Dr., Wayzata, MN 55391. See also the group's home page, http://www.witherspoonsociety.org (accessed February 11, 2009). The group publishes *Network News: Witherspoon Society of Presbyterians*, at a rate of ten per year since 1984.

64. See Nathaniel W. Pierce and Paul L. Ward, *The Voice of Conscience: A Loud and Unusual Noise? The Episcopal Peace Fellowship, 1939–1989* (Washington, D.C.: The Fellowship, 1989). Its publication, the *EPF Newsletter*, ran continuously from 1966 to 2002 but has been replaced by *Episcopal Peace Notes*.

65. See http://www.bpfna.org (accessed February 11, 2009). In the interest of ecumenical fairness, I should point out that Methodists have also been active in nonviolence. See David Scott Cooney, "A Consistent Witness of Conscience: Methodist Nonviolent Activists, 1940–1970" (Ph.D. diss., Iliff School of Theology, 2000); and Michael Hughes, *Conscience and Conflict: Methodism, Peace, and War in the Twentieth Century* (Peterborough, UK: Epworth, 2008).

66. Scholars and citizens have begun to take note. In the American Academy of Religion, http://www.aarweb.org (accessed February 11, 2009), I co-chair the study group Religions, Social Conflict, and Peace, and Congress established the United States Institute of Peace in 1984, which has an active working group on religious peacebuilding. See, for instance, the report "Religious Contributions to Peacemaking: When Religion Brings Peace, Not War," ed. David R. Smock, *Peaceworks* 55 (January 2006), http://www.usip.org/publications/religious-contributions-peacemaking-when-religion-brings-peace-not-war (accessed March 17, 2011).

67. See, for another representative sampling, Roger S. Gottlieb, ed., *Liberating Faith: Religious Voices for Justice, Peace, and Ecological Wisdom* (Lanham, Md.: Rowman and Littlefield, 2003).

68. See Mark Juergensmeyer, *A New Cold War? Religious Nationalism Confronts the Secular State* (Berkeley: University of California Press, 1994).

69. See Paul Christopher Johnson, "Savage Civil Religion," *Numen* 52 (2005): 289–324, for a provocative argument about how Bush's language of sacrifice accomplished "symbolic hijacking" to mobilize public support for war.

70. "Transcript of President Bush's Prayer Service Remarks," at http://www.opm.gov/guidance/09-14-01gwb.htm (accessed January 22, 2009).

71. "President Bush Outlines Iraqi Threat," at http://www.cfr.org/iraq/president-bush-outlines-iraqi-threat/p8352 (accessed March 17, 2011).

72. "President Addresses the Nation," September 7, 2003, at http://transcripts.cnn.com/TRANSCRIPTS/0309/07/se.04.html (accessed January 22, 2009).

73. "Transcript: President Bush's Speech on the War on Terrorism, Delivered at the U.S. Naval Academy in Annapolis, Maryland," at http://www.washingtonpost.com/wp-dyn/content/article/2005/11/30/AR2005113000667.html (accessed January 22, 2009).

74. Kelly Denton-Borhaug, "The Language of 'Sacrifice' in the Buildup to War: A Feminist Rhetorical and Theological Analysis," *Journal of Religion and Popular Culture* 15 (Spring 2007), at http://www.usask.ca/relst/jrpc/art15-langsacrifice.html (accessed January 22, 2009).

Women, Christianity, and the Constitution

The Reverend Maria Bliss, a homemaker and mother of three in North Carolina, combined her call to ministry with leading her state's campaign to ratify the Equal Rights Amendment (ERA) to the U.S. Constitution. Still a relative rarity as an ordained woman in the early 1970s, Bliss joined a fast-growing cohort of Methodist women clergy. As a United Methodist, she belonged to the denomination with one of the nation's largest and strongest women's organizations—religious or secular. Her sense of responsibility for elevating women's status through political activism grew out of a vision of social Christianity deeply embedded in the work of United Methodist Women, the most recent name of the denomination's women's missionary association.[1]

For a century, Methodist women had acted on the belief that Christianity held the surest path to emancipation for women by taking "women's work for women" as their special purview, raising their daughters on heroic stories of women missionaries who sacrificed to improve conditions of women in distant lands. The ERA, which, if ratified, would have guaranteed American women "equality of rights under the law," was a natural extension of these historic commitments. The amendment was utterly uncontroversial in religious or secular circles when the U.S. Senate passed it with an eighty-four to eight vote in 1972. Endorsed by both major political parties and by all recent sitting presidents, it had been ratified by thirty-five of the thirty-eight states needed when it was introduced into the North Carolina legislature. The thirty-five legislatures that ratified the amendment viewed it as a logical next step in advancing the democratic principles launched at the founding of the republic.

The ERA failed in North Carolina, and in the nation, due in no small part to the political mobilization of Christian women who came to view the amendment as a threat to their roles as wives and mothers and to the teachings of their churches. Both the legalization of abortion in the Supreme Court's *Roe v. Wade* decision in 1973 and the increasing visibility of feminist organizations attracted the attention of activists, who began to raise questions about the ERA's compatibility with Christianity. Although the ERA had no direct legal bearing on the legality of abortion, the two issues were linked in the public mind both by proponents and by opponents. In North Carolina, opposition to the ERA galvanized around the leadership of Phyllis Schlafly, a Catholic attorney from Illinois whose national organization STOP ERA played a key role in the amendment's defeat.

Schlafly embraced a view dating back to the early republic that the success of democracy rested on the nurturing of moral citizens within the family. She viewed the ERA as undermining democracy by encouraging women to enter public life on the same basis as men rather than embrace special responsibility for children and the home. Equality under the law, in her view, diminished women's welfare by eliminating legislation designed to protect their distinctive roles as mothers and homemakers. Schlafly, together with Protestant and Mormon opponents of the ERA, was far more successful than Bliss and her coworkers in mobilizing church networks, Bible study groups, and prayer groups toward a public political agenda. In so doing, they affected the practice of both American Christianity and citizenship, incorporating political rallies, lobbying efforts, and letter-writing campaigns as acts of piety beyond the walls of the churches.[2]

The success of ERA opponents in making their views a vehicle for the expression of Christian faith represents only one moment, although an important one, in the complicated interplay between religiously based assertions about women's nature and the evolving concept of equality informing definitions of U.S. citizenship. Although Christians have consistently asserted the spiritual equality of men and women, they have engaged in heated debates about the meaning and extent of equality. Advocates for women's legal and social equality as well as advocates for distinctive gender roles or hierarchies (sometimes the same people) base their positions on biblical texts, Christian principles, and religious experience. The claim that Christianity elevated the status of women figured heavily in multiple constitutional debates: debates about the enslavement of African Americans, about the rights of Native American women who lived outside of U.S. law, about woman suffrage, about the ERA, and about U.S. domestic and foreign policies. Accusations that other faiths, even other versions of Christianity, diminished women's welfare divided Protestants, Catholics, and Mormons from each other, as well as from non-Christian groups.

Attention to gender highlights potential conflicts between Christian virtues and emerging American values. Although the young nation cultivated a spirit of independence and self-reliance in its male citizens, it excluded women, as well as all African Americans and Native Americans, from constitutional rights intended to nurture those qualities by ensuring individual interests in private property and giving property owners a voice in government. While assuming that women would be represented by the votes of their fathers and husbands (or, in the case of enslaved women, their owners), early republicans relied on mothers to inculcate privately in men the public virtues necessary to the functioning of a democracy. Men schooled by republican mothers, they hoped, would learn to reconcile individual political freedoms with the common good.[3]

As American Christianities grew up with the development of the consumer economy, an ideology of separate spheres associated men with a competitive public sphere of the marketplace and women with an idealized private, moral sphere of the home. The legal "death" of married women coupled with their economic dependence harmonized with the Christian endeavor to subjugate one's own will to the will of God, allowing the moral mother to evolve into the model Christian of the nineteenth century.

This essay picks up the intertwining stories of Christian gender systems and U.S. citizenship in the nineteenth century. It looks through the lens of Christianity at the campaigns for and against two amendments to the U.S. Constitution intended to extend the rights of U.S. citizens to women: woman suffrage and the ERA. The campaign to grant women the elective franchise lasted seven decades, stretching from the Seneca Falls Convention in 1848 to the passage of the Nineteenth Amendment in 1920. The unsuccessful campaign for the ERA occupied almost as large a portion of American history, first introduced into Congress in 1923 and failing ratification by the states in 1982.[4] For this essay, three large Christian communities, Catholic, Methodist, and Mormon, will provide three angles of vision on these two formative debates. Although each group of Christians incorporated a diversity of opinions, Methodists contributed disproportionately to support for both amendments; a preponderance of Catholic positions opposed both amendments; and the Church of Jesus Christ of Latter-day Saints actively supported the first amendment and opposed the second. In addition to illustrating distinct perspectives on the relation of Christianity to women's citizenship, each group demonstrates a particular dynamic relating religious practice and political mobilization.

Methodists
"No Sex in Citizenship"[5]

Methodists emerged as America's largest Protestant community by the time woman suffrage became a plank of the platform adopted at Seneca Falls in 1848, and would remain so when the Nineteenth Amendment enfranchised women in 1920. Spread by revivals and itinerant preachers, Methodism was a chief component of the denominational revolution that extended evangelical culture with U.S. territorial expansion and urban growth throughout the period. Although Methodists initially partook of the general evangelical suspicion of innovations in women's roles, they also contributed key leadership in advancing the suffrage cause.[6]

The Wesleyan Methodists of Seneca Falls hosted the first women's rights convention in their chapel, and eleven members signed the Declaration of Sentiments, including Saron Phillips, the minister of the church.[7] But these Methodists, like the Quakers who formed the convention's largest religious group, were dissidents who had formed antislavery branches of both societies. Suffrage was the most controversial proposal at Seneca Falls, due in part to the general suspicion of voting in the Society of Friends. The most impassioned plea that the vote be added to the platform of the convention came from African American Methodist minister Frederick Douglass. Born in slavery, Douglass painted a compelling picture of the risks of disenfranchisement, and the resolution carried.[8]

When Elizabeth Cady Stanton and Lucretia Mott initially called the convention, they invited participants to consider the "social, civil, and religious conditions and rights of woman." They modeled the convention's Declaration of Sentiments closely on the Declaration of Independence. Recognizing that women's civil disabilities paralleled disenfranchisement in Protestant churches, they added attention to religious rights, a category absent from the Declaration of Independence. "He allows her in Church, as well as State, but a subordinate position, claiming Apostolic authority for her exclusion from the ministry, and . . . from any public participation in the affairs of the Church," they declared. Male colonists' grievances against King George were primarily civil and economic, but Stanton and Mott complained that men placed theological impediments in the way of women's full citizenship. "He has usurped the prerogative of Jehovah himself, claiming it as his right to assign for her a sphere of action, when that belongs to her conscience and her God." Extending the abolitionist argument that slaveholding was a sin that jeopardized the soul of the slaveholder, they accused those who subordinated women of breaking the first commandment. In the twentieth century, such idolatry would be called the sin of sexism.

Male headship was enshrined in nineteenth-century Protestantism by tradition and belief. Biblical texts understood to preclude women from speaking in church cast moral doubt on any form of women's public speech. Yet early American critiques of female subordination also used the Bible as the primary basis to argue for women's rights.[9] Indeed, while the small cadre of women's rights activists who began agitation before the Civil War were inspired primarily by their involvement with the movement for the abolition of slavery, a broader swath of nineteenth-century women became active advocates of woman suffrage because of goals inspired by the Bible.

Frances Willard's embrace of woman suffrage as a Christian imperative marked a watershed in locating an expanded public role for women at the heart of an evangelical agenda for the reform of society. As the powerful president of the Woman's Christian Temperance Union (WCTU) from 1879 to 1898, Willard led the country's largest nondenominational women's organization and the largest organization endorsing woman suffrage during those years. The WCTU advocated "the ballot for home protection," so that women could vote for measures ensuring their own and their children's welfare. Women's votes, they hoped, could bring to fruition the ideals of a moral world they heard preached from the pulpit. Willard led the 100,000 women of the WCTU in a broad "do everything" platform, including temperance, suffrage, prison reform, kindergartens, and a host of other social reforms.[10]

Willard recorded the Methodist roots of her religious commitment to woman suffrage in the pages of her private journal. As part of her lifelong effort to conform her character to Christian values and lead a moral life, Willard examined her actions, reflecting on opportunities to discern God's will and to shape her human impulses accordingly. Following a life-threatening bout of typhoid fever at the age of nineteen, she yearned to have her intellectual acceptance of Christ's salvific role affirmed by the palpable assurance of Christ's presence reported by other Methodists. The turning point in her conversion came when she heard a revival sermon reordering the stages of conversion. The preacher "said you might as well tell a frozen person to feel warmth as a frozen heart to melt. First the sinner must commence to do what his reason taught him was best, and in the act of striving for the right, feeling would come." Three days later, Willard answered the altar call to make a public profession of faith. Five months later, she was baptized and formally received into the Methodist Church.[11]

This moderate revival theology governed both Willard's attempt to shape her own character and her hopes for reforming society. All social actors, she believed, should first choose moral actions, committing themselves to temperance, honesty, and justice. Rather than "legislating morality," laws requiring such actions would encourage moral behavior that might be followed by assurance of God's presence. Willard's commitment to woman suffrage connected individual and corporate advancement, offering each American woman the opportunity to develop a moral character by working toward the creation of a moral nation.

Like many WCTU activists, Willard experienced a "conversion" to woman suffrage conforming to Methodist religious practice as well as theology. Alone on her knees in prayer after Bible study on a Sunday morning, she felt a direct prompting from God. "You are to speak for woman's ballot as a weapon of protection to her home and tempted loved ones from the tyranny of drink." Beyond this clear statement, she received "a complete line of argumentation and illustration" for her first speech on the subject in 1876.[12]

Although Willard's religious experience as a Methodist provided both the source of her commitment to woman suffrage and the method for advancing it, exclusion from authority in the Methodist Episcopal Church affirmed her conviction that women needed the vote to have their views represented. In 1880, Willard was prevented from addressing the Methodist General Conference on behalf of the WCTU because there was no precedent for female speakers. "Grave, dignified clergymen who had always been my friends, looked curiously at me as if I were, somehow, a little daft." In other words, church leaders who welcomed women's work in the civic arena still hesitated to permit it within the polity of the church. When Willard's home church elected her as a delegate to the General Conference eight years later, she assumed she would be seated because she had become a nationally recognized figure and the WCTU had become so influential in Methodist circles. She was deeply disappointed when she and four other elected women delegates were refused seats. Following this event, Willard and a few others contemplated starting an interdenominational church centered in the WCTU, in which "the laying on of hands in consecration . . . shall be decreed on a basis of 'gifts, graces and usefulness' irrespective of sex."[13] Willard's loyalty to the church, which had nurtured her faith, prompted her to delay this step. She did not live to see the Methodist Episcopal Church enfranchise women as lay delegates in 1900.

Methodist women resisted the trend away from single-sex voluntary organizations that accompanied the passage of the Nineteenth Amendment and the call for women's equality in mixed organizations in the 1920s. Eager to hold on to the distinctive agenda of women's work as well as the purse strings of their powerful organization, they retained autonomy, even as other Protestant women's organizations merged into lay organizations controlled by male leaders. Simultaneously, they continued efforts dating to the suffrage era for full clergy rights, finally achieved in 1956. But the ordination of women made little impact against the tide of domestic expectations discouraging women's leadership in the 1950s. When Congress passed the ERA in 1972, Methodist women saw a strong resonance with the call for equality in their faith, but little with the leadership structures of their church. Women made up 1 percent of the clergy, and there were no bishops and few denominational lay leaders.

Theressa Hoover provided an unvarnished account of Methodist women's struggles within their denomination in her 1980 book, *With Unveiled Face*.[14] As associate general secretary of the Women's Division of the General Board of Global Ministries of the United Methodist Church from 1968 to 1990, her unwieldy title as the chief church official relating to women suggests the complexity of the issues she addressed. Methodists adopted the term "Global Ministries" in place of "missions," with that term's connotation of cultural imperialism. Hoover, the highest-ranking African American woman in the United Methodist Church, was "associate general secretary" rather than "general secretary" because the women's missionary organization had been placed structurally under the General Board. "General" indicated that the General Board combined previous organizations focusing on domestic and foreign missions, encompassing both men and women, both homemakers and working women. "United" referred to a series of denominational mergers among Methodist bodies in the twentieth century, including the reunification in 1940 of the northern and the southern branches, which had split over slavery a hundred years earlier. Each denominational merger reopened the question of women's rights, often sacrificing them to achieve unification of more and less liberal bodies. The 1940 merger accepted a structure fostering racial segregation, squashing interracial initiatives of both northern and southern Methodist women's groups.[15]

Hoover's outspoken advocacy of women's participation in church leadership incorporated her view that only through a strong, separate organization could women attain an equal voice in the church. Her greatest achievement was the birth of United Methodist Women (UMW) in 1972, an organization that regained the financial and organizational autonomy that Methodist women had kept for most of the century but had lost in a 1964 reorganization of mission work. UMW, she believed, continued the distinctive contribution to Christianity of the women's missionary movement.[16] She described UMW as "unapologetic" about being a separate women's organization. Women's programs deepened and amplified Christian action because of their "alternate vision as outsiders to the true power centers of this country." Women, she wrote, "have been attentive to the needs of the poorest, most helpless and despised." Calls for women's groups to be subsumed into the church, she argued, were based on a false assumption that groups dominated by men constituted "the church" in a way that women's groups did not. "The accusation that our separateness impedes the growth of the community of men and women in the church reveals ignorance or discomfort with genuine female authority. Only *corporately* strong women—determined, mature, loving and naturally supportive—can assist the church to enter its agreements with women seriously and to live them out in good faith."[17]

Hoover's calls for women's separateness and autonomy may seem to contradict the goals of the ERA. But the tone and timing of the struggles she described explain the enthusiasm with which Methodists advocated for an amendment they believed would promote the same goal of justice for women they were trying to advance in their own church polity. A 1969 Women's Division Report, for example, commented on recent restructurings. "Where organized women's groups have been removed from a visible policy-making and power-sharing role . . . male chauvinism increases [and] the status of women declines." The Board of Church and Society endorsed the ERA in 1972, and the Women's Division followed suit in 1974. The statement adopted by the Women's Division condemned the hundreds of federal and state laws discriminating on the basis of sex, arguing that "Jesus made no such distinction between persons." It urged all United Methodists to work toward ratification in their states. The United Methodist Building on Capitol Hill provided a strategic headquarters for ERA supporters during the 1970s and 1980s.[18] And activists like the Reverend Maria Bliss followed the teachings of their church into the public sector.

Catholicism
Sacrifice for the Common Good

Catholic religious congregations brought with them to the United States a strong tradition of women organizing to assist the needy and advance the welfare of society. Beginning with the French Ursulines, who founded an interracial school for girls in New Orleans in 1727, they spawned a network of institutions, including hospitals, orphanages, schools, and agencies attending to every need of the Catholic community. Their efforts "contributed to the extension of democracy by educating the children of America's working poor."[19] Catholic women's orders shared the sense of a special responsibility for women and children expressed by Protestant women reformers. But the deep-seated anti-Catholicism of Protestant culture colored the way nuns' efforts were received, and consequently, the way Catholic women would view efforts like Willard's to enlist women's votes toward public goals. When those goals incorporated an anti-Catholic agenda, Catholic women wanted nothing to do with them.

By the time of the Civil War, American Catholics outnumbered members of any single Protestant denomination, although Protestants, taken as an aggregate, outnumbered Catholics, establishing a religious landscape that persists in the twenty-first century. In general, the Roman Catholic Church has been more concerned with guarantees of equal rights for Catholics as a community of faith in a nation dominated by Protestants than with equal rights for individuals. Catholics often saw assertions of individual rights, including women's rights, as competing with the church's efforts to promote the common good.

Laypeople observed models of the sacrifice of individual wants and needs in favor of the common good in the religious vocations of Catholic women. Nuns' vows of poverty and obedience pulled in a dramatically different direction from the constitutional values of independence and self-reliance presumably reinforced through private property. But it was the nun's vow of chastity that was incomprehensible to Protestant America. Protestants viewed monastic orders as one of the sources of corruption from which they had sought to sever themselves by parting from the Catholic Church during the Reformation.

So thoroughly had Protestant Americans embraced marriage and the family as the locus of salvation that celibate communities evoked fantasies of illicit liaisons between licentious priests and debauched nuns bound to iniquity by vows of obedience to priestly authority. Catholics saw the holiest women in their communities derided in reform rhetoric as well as in sensational exposés. After Lyman Beecher, popular revivalist and prominent anti-slavery reformer, preached three anti-Catholic sermons in Boston in 1834, a mob burned the Ursuline Convent in Charlestown to the ground. Thousands of bystanders watched as the nuns and boarding students shivered in the garden while the mob torched the convent and desecrated the cemetery.

This act of misogyny and of anti-Catholicism anticipated a message Catholic women would learn from many sources through American history: that the church, not the state, offered both protection and resources in the face of hardship or hostility.[20]

Although anti-Catholicism tells us more about the Protestant reform agenda than it does about the content of Catholicism, it nevertheless provides an essential context for consideration of the chilly reception Catholics gave to woman suffrage. Neither the Vatican nor the American bishops took an official position on suffrage because they viewed it as a political issue. "There is no Catholic view of suffrage because it is not a Catholic question," explained the Reverend Elliot Ross of Chicago, himself a supporter.[21] Nevertheless, vocal opposition came from Catholic clerics and publications as well as from lay activists, including women. As Archbishop of Boston John Williams put it, the church "leaves alone" the issue of woman suffrage, but women should eschew politics to secure the family as the nucleus of society. Clerical opposition rested on natural law arguments emphasizing women's roles as mothers and helpmeets and the historical tradition of male supremacy. When Margaret Sanger, founder of the National Birth Control League, suggested that women would need to limit the sizes of their families in order to be active in politics, priests found another reason to oppose woman suffrage.[22]

Boston provided an example of the entanglement of woman suffrage with nativism in 1884 when the school committee reassigned a history teacher for ridiculing church doctrine on indulgences. Having allowed women to vote for school committee in 1879, Boston witnessed the largest female vote ever in support of a nativist ticket running to replace the school committee that reprimanded the teacher. Protestant clergy, as well as the WCTU, the Republican Party, and other nativist organizations, asked women to register and vote to keep Catholic influence out of the public schools.[23] As long as nativism found a place in suffrage coalitions, Catholics would see their own interests elsewhere.

Kathleen Sprows Cummings has linked opposition to woman suffrage with both anti-Catholicism and the fact that American Catholic women had "vastly more opportunities for education and meaningful work" inside church structures than outside of them from the mid-nineteenth to the mid-twentieth centuries. Catholic women's orders built an astounding number of colleges, academies, and schools to promote women's education during the late nineteenth and early twentieth centuries, as well as orphanages, foundling homes, and hospitals to address their needs. Cummings argues that the

Catholic women who built both an educational system and an unparalleled social safety net should be seen as architects of the Progressive Era as much as their Protestant counterparts like Jane Addams, who are so well known for establishing a smaller network of social settlements.[24]

Clerical objections to woman suffrage softened as the Nineteenth Amendment moved toward passage in 1919. Once the amendment was ratified, the Catholic Church viewed suffrage as "a duty which Catholic women should exercise with wisdom and prudence."[25] Voting, it hoped, could now be a vehicle for preserving "marriage, home, parenthood, family life." Not sanguine that Catholic women would use the franchise for this purpose, the bishops warned the pope that the strength of the feminist movement in America threatened Catholicism and required the formation of an organization to counter its impact. The National Council of Catholic Women (NCCW) was founded in 1920 to promote Catholic social goals.[26] It opposed the ERA from its inception, lobbying against it in the 1920s, 1930s, and 1940s.

The NCCW, like most of the women's movement, objected to the ERA as a threat to protective labor legislation that limited women's hours and regulated their working conditions. They joined with two other ERA opponents, the Women's Trade Union League and the Department of Labor's Women's Bureau in advocating for women workers and encouraging their leadership. Pope Leo XIII had critiqued labor conditions as "little better than that of slavery itself" and defended the right to unionize in his *Encyclical on Capital and Labor*.[27] Catholics also supported another constitutional amendment championed by the women's movement to protect vulnerable workers: the unsuccessful Child Labor Amendment.[28]

As both the women's movement and the labor movement came to see the shortcomings of protectionist legislation in the 1960s, the Catholic Church also underwent a dramatic set of transitions. Pope John XXIII called the Second Vatican Council to bring the Catholic Church "up to date." Popularly known as Vatican II, the council urged all Catholics to turn from insular concerns to the promotion of human dignity and human rights, both within and beyond their own communities. Religious congregations, including American nuns, whose population peaked at 125,000 in 1968, were asked to reexamine their missions in light of the gospel and the needs of the modern world.

For women, the Second Vatican Council embodied a host of ironies. A few bishops insisted that women's roles be addressed. "In our age, when woman goes almost to the moon, it is indispensable that she play a more important role in the church," said Cardinal Léon Joseph Suenens of Belgium to the all-male assembly. Meanwhile, the handful of women who had been admitted as auditors sat in enforced silence, permitted on the floor of the assembly only to kneel and bow their heads when they received communion from a male priest.

Vatican II's statements, promulgated by the pope, reflected this double message. Explicit recognition of women's claim to "equity with men before the law and in fact" came in *Gaudium et Spes: The Pastoral Constitution of the Church in the Modern World*, which inspired a generation of Catholic activists for social justice. "Every type of discrimination, whether social or cultural, whether based on sex, race, color, social condition, language or religion," it explained, "is to be overcome and eradicated as contrary to God's intent." Emboldened to see their own liberation from patriarchy as part of "God's intent," laywomen as well as women religious began to incorporate women's equality into a social justice agenda embraced as both duty and vocation. Nuns embarked on political ministries, and an array of Catholic feminist organizations sprang up in the 1960s and 1970s. Invariably their commitment to justice for women was heightened by a sense that the church had failed to live up to its own teachings when it asked disproportionate sacrifices of women, cutting them off from the body of Christ by refusing their service and denying their experience.

Virtually all of the new Catholic women's organizations endorsed the ERA, most notably the Leadership Council of Women Religious, which represented the majority of the 125,000 nuns in American religious communities. Indeed, support for the ERA seemed to be required by *Gaudium et Spes*, when it described discrimination on the basis of sex as "contrary to God's intent." But the same document that condemned sexism also condemned abortion as an "unspeakable crime," including it with murder, genocide, and slavery among a long list of "infamies." American bishops responded to the emphatic support for life, condemning the nuclear arms race, the war in Vietnam, and abortion. But of these concerns, keeping abortion illegal received consistent support on the diocesan level.

The emergence of legal abortion as a key demand of the women's movement seemed to put feminism and Catholicism at odds. Abortion opponents feared that the *Roe* decision reflected an activist Supreme Court that might also find a right to abortion in the ERA. Catholic feminists were now on the defensive to show that abortion and the ERA were "separate and distinct."[29] Sister Ana Ida Gannon, cochair of ERA-Illinois, reported that after every pro-ERA speech she made she was asked how she could support it when the Catholic Church opposed it. She would then explain that the church had no position on the ERA. "As one who has supported the ERA for ten years, and as one who strongly opposes abortion, I took the cochairmanship to prove they are completely separate issues," she told the *Chicago Tribune*. The former president of Mundelein College and a professor of philosophy, Gannon found support for the ERA in both the documents of Vatican II and the Constitution.[30]

But the church's lack of a position on the ERA was overshadowed by its vigorous stand against abortion. The bishops allocated $50,000 to fight efforts to liberalize state laws against abortion in 1967, before anyone dreamed that the Supreme Court would legalize abortion in the *Roe v. Wade* decision of 1973.[31]

The increasing identification of the ERA with legalized abortion prompted Loretto Sister Maureen Fiedler to cofound Catholics Act for ERA, which she cochaired until the ten-year ratification campaign ended in 1982. The last hopes for ratification rested on Illinois, the only non-Mormon state outside the South where the ERA had not been passed. Illinois required a supermajority of three-fifths of both state legislatures for ratification. While Sister Ana Ida Gannon met with legislators inside the state capitol to encourage passage, Sister Maureen Fiedler joined six other women, including Quaker Mary Ann Beall and excommunicated Mormon Sonia Johnson, in announcing a solemn fast for ratification of the ERA. Invoking both the religious meaning of fasting and the dramatic tactics of early twentieth-century suffragists, they hoped to draw attention to women's fidelity in their quest for justice. At the eleventh hour, a month into the fast and twenty-eight days before the final deadline for ratification in 1982, Fiedler announced that twenty-three bishops joined in a public statement of support for the ERA. Citing *Gaudium et Spes*, the bishops, who signed the statement as individuals, called on legislators in unratified states to pass the amendment before the June 30 deadline, calling it a "fundamental issue of justice." But this minority statement also called attention to the silence of the larger official body, the National Conference of Catholic Bishops, who refused to endorse the ERA.

In addition to abortion, another issue complicated the bishops' support for the ERA: the ordination of women. Many of those inspired by *Gaudium et Spes* assumed that encouragement of women to an active apostolate and new roles in the church would result in women's ordination. In 1974, the Leadership Council of Women Religious adopted resolutions affirming that "all ministries in the Church should be open to women" and that women should have "active participation in all decision making bodies in the Church."

For them, the commitment to women's equality required support for both the ERA and the ordination of women. When the first Women's Ordination Conference was held in Detroit the following year, conference organizers expected 600 participants. Over 1,200 showed up, including a few bishops, laying the foundation for a permanent organization that amassed the theological basis for the ordination of women. Before the second large-scale conference could be held in 1978, the Vatican issued a "Declaration on the Question of the Admission of Women to the Ministerial Priesthood," in which the exclusion of women from the priesthood was attributed to "fidelity to the example of the Lord." Many American bishops questioned the novel theological basis of the statement, so much so that the National Council of Catholic Bishops appointed a Committee on Women in Society and in the Church to meet with representatives of the Women's Ordination Conference. "The challenge women offer the institutional church," the bishops acknowledged, "is to recognize that sexism is a sin."[32]

When advance reports indicated that the committee was considering support for the ERA, the bishops were flooded with mail from newly mobilized antiabortion groups that they themselves had helped start. The National Council of Catholic Bishops rejected the pro-ERA statement, fearing that it would conflict with its antiabortion efforts, especially its support for the human life amendment, which was intended to define human life, and therefore constitutional protections, as beginning at conception. Refusing to endorse the ERA also shielded it from attention to questions of gender equity and the ordination of women within the Catholic Church. If passed, the ERA would have heightened the level of scrutiny of professions limited to a single sex—scrutiny that would have further complicated the jobs of bishops charged with interpreting the teachings of Rome for the American faithful.[33]

The Church of Jesus Christ of Latter-day Saints

The women of the Church of Jesus Christ of Latter-day Saints (LDS—commonly known as Mormons) were among the first American women to exercise the right to vote. Two months after the Territory of Wyoming became the first U.S. jurisdiction to enfranchise women, the Utah Territorial Assembly extended suffrage to adults irrespective of sex in 1870. Because Utah's larger population of 17,179 voters so greatly exceeded the 1,000 white women residing in Wyoming, historian Carol Madsen has called Utah "the first major locus of woman suffrage in the United States."[34] Seventeen years

FIGURE 1. *Five Portraits of Voting Mormon Women, ca. 1920–25.
As this postcard reveals, Latter-day Saint women were proud that
Utah had been the third state to give women the vote. Courtesy of
The Schlesinger Library, Radcliffe Institute, Harvard University.*

Five Generations of Voting Mormon Women

MRS. MARY GIBBS-BIGELOW
b. 26 June. 1809 d. 19 April, 1888
Voted 14 Feb. 1870
at Salt Lake City election

MRS. LUCY BIGELOW-YOUNG
b. 3rd Oct. 1830 d. 3rd Feb. 1905
Voted 14th Feb. 1870, election

MRS. SUSA YOUNG GATES
b. 18th March, 1856
Voted Nov. 1872 [was married]

MRS. LEAH D. WIDTSOE
b. 24th Feb. 1874
Voted Nov. 1895

MISS ANNA GAARDEN WIDTSOE
b. 1st April, 1890
Voted 5th Nov. 1920

later, Congress disenfranchised Mormon women as part of the Edmunds-Tucker Act, which outlawed polygamy, disincorporated the Church of Jesus Christ of Latter-day Saints, and appropriated its property. Finally, in 1896, when Utah was admitted to the Union after Mormons disavowed polygamy, women were reenfranchised by the state constitution, making Utah the third state to grant women the vote.

It is easy to dismiss the Mormon embrace of woman suffrage as an attempt to increase the total number of Mormon voters while Utahans campaigned for statehood. Indeed, the story of woman suffrage in Utah cannot be understood without engaging both the Mormon quest for statehood and the interlocking story of polygamy. But Mormon historians argue that support for suffrage was consistent with the place of women in Mormon society. From the time of Mormon settlement of Utah in 1847, LDS women enjoyed rights to property, to conduct a business, and to divorce for incompatibility long before other American women. Though they could not hold ecclesiastical offices, they did vote in local congregations and in the relatively autonomous women's Relief Society.[35]

For the purposes of this essay, the argument of expediency falters because it incorporates the assumption embraced by Protestant reformers that woman suffrage and polygamy reflect inherently contradictory agendas, one extending democratic values, the other defying them. But nineteenth-century Latter-day Saints advocated expanded roles for women in public at the same time that they worked to restore biblical patriarchy. Indeed, polygamy itself challenged the legal death of married women in common law, as the Utah legislature attempted to secure inheritance by plural wives and their children not recognized as legal heirs. Brigham Young, the famously polygamous LDS president, could exemplify patriarchal authority while advocating that women enter law, medicine, and business to "answer the call of their nature" and benefit society by exceeding domestic roles.

Combined support for woman suffrage and for a restored patriarchy reflects the energetic spiritual culture of America's most successful indigenous Christian movement. Those who embraced the new faith answered a call to a dynamic role in building the kingdom of God. The activist movement had no room for notions of ladyhood that kept women out of sight at home, abjuring economic or civic activity. Rather, Mormonism invited women and men to join in an intense communal effort where the labor of each individual was needed to build a society restoring God's order and authority. Viewing God as a material being, faithful Mormons saw Godhead as an attainable goal for humans. Living by the Latter-day revelation and participating in Mormon rituals provided a path of progression toward celestial kingdoms where Mormon patriarchs would reign for eternity surrounded by large families magnifying their exaltation.

Polygamy was the most controversial aspect of the attempt to restore biblical order. In 1843, Joseph Smith's "Revelation on Celestial Marriage" made plural marriage, based on the example of Abraham, Sarah, and Hagar, an essential element of the Mormon path to eternal life. Because Mormon theology includes the "pre-mortal" existence of spirit children waiting to be born so that they can embark on the path to exaltation as part of a patriarchal family, procreation is an urgent religious duty. Polygamy was seen as a moral mandate because it guaranteed that all women could have the opportunity to marry and bear children. Not only did it restore biblical patriarchy, according to its Mormon proponents, it also purified an immoral society in which ostensibly monogamous men sought illicit liaisons and abandoned the resulting offspring, while prostitution flourished.

For women, polygamy was seen both as securing the right to marry and reproduce and as spiritual sacrifice. Placing the duty of bearing offspring above selfish pleasures of romantic love, the doctrine of celestial marriage could have the effect of distancing husbands and wives. Combined with the frontier conditions of Mormon life in the Great Basin Kingdom, polygamy produced an independent cadre of able women committed to faith and family and ready to exercise public leadership.

Polygamy formed the central element of non-Mormon critiques of Mormonism as oppressive to women. The rhetoric of anti-Mormonism reiterated the themes of anti-Catholic literature: authoritarian religious structures victimized women by giving free reign to male licentiousness under cover of religious secrecy. In both cases, the presumed religious oppression of women was likened to slavery and rebellion: anti-Mormons decried polygamy and slavery as the "twin relics of barbarism." In spite of their differences, Catholics and Protestants could agree that polygamy was the most heinous crime against Christian marriage. Pope Leo XIII condemned Mormon polygamy in his *Encyclical on Christian Marriage* in 1880, listing Mormons with first-century heretics and communists among those "who aim at the destruction of Christian marriage."[36] Susan B. Anthony echoed the roots of the suffrage movement in antislavery agitation when she proposed that Congress should pass a law to "enfranchise the women of Utah as the one safe, sure and swift means to abolish polygamy." Indeed, Representative George Julian did submit a bill to Congress giving Utah women the vote as a means of ending polygamy and was surprised to receive support from the Utah delegate. The

Mormon editor of the *Deseret News* congratulated "our ladies upon the unexpected and unsought interest in their welfare felt by congress. . . . VERILY the world progresseth."[37]

When the Edmunds-Tucker Act was appealed to the Supreme Court, most of the arguments centered on the appropriation of the LDS Church's property by Congress. The disenfranchisement of Utah's women was consistent with the practice in other states, and therefore acceptable. Although the Court upheld the act, the church's property was eventually returned after polygamy was abandoned. After forty years of legal resistance and social nonconformity, Mormon commitment to bringing their kingdom into the United States exceeded commitment to celestial marriage. The cost to the kingdom of imprisoned leaders, vilified pregnant women, and alienated property proved too high. In 1890, church president Wilfred Woodruff received a communication from God advising him that the church's survival required an end to polygamy. Utah was admitted as a state in 1896.[38]

Once polygamy moved from the center to the periphery of Mormon practice, Americans could accept the other distinctive aspects of the faith as compatible with citizenship. In other words, concerns that Mormonism degraded women by abandoning a Christian concept of marriage outweighed questions about the separation of church and state in Utah, about secret ceremonies and new prophecies.

According to legal historian Sarah Barringer Gordon, the success of the U.S. government in forcing Latter-day Saints to abandon polygamy as a condition of entering the Union marked the success of Protestants in enshrining their own moral vision into the First Amendment guarantee of freedom of religion.[39] But Mormon accommodation also initiated a century-long transition from outsider status among other Christians to a more general acceptance of the way they had always seen themselves, as stalwart defenders of the Constitution, the republic, and Christian faith. Uniting with their Catholic and Protestant opponents, the LDS found common cause with an emerging conservative political consensus eager to defend a specific view of Christian women's rights by defeating the ERA.[40] Opposition to the ERA would be the vehicle through which Mormons would complete their move into the mainstream.

When the ERA passed the House and the Senate and was ratified by twenty-two states in 1972, it did so with the votes of numerous Mormon legislators, notably those in Hawaii, Idaho, Colorado, and California, where Mormons made up a considerable percentage of voters.[41] Belle Spofford, LDS Relief Society president from 1945 to 1974, was also president of the National Council of Women, which represented 23 million American women, when it endorsed the ERA in 1970.[42] In 1974, a survey by the Mormon newspaper, the *Deseret News*, found that most church members supported passage. But a year later, a strong anti-ERA editorial in the same newspaper indicated that church leaders opposed the amendment. Both the Mormon public and their elected representatives reversed their views. Ratification failed to pass the Utah legislature in 1975, and the prodigious energies of the well-organized LDS church were deployed in the national campaign to defeat ratification.

The convergence of conditions leading to this reversal merits exploration because the Utah constitution had included equal rights for women since passage with full Mormon support in 1890. Indeed, the Utah constitution is unique in echoing the language of Seneca Falls linking women's equality to religious as well as civil rights.[43] Yet Mormon leaders in the 1970s felt that if the same rights were assured by the federal government this would present insurmountable conflicts with the distinctive roles and nature of men and women in Mormon theology. This apparent contradiction reflects the evolution of church teachings away from the emphasis on women's independence so highly valued in pioneer days, toward a focus on maternal obligation and female subordination.

Mormon theology did not change, but the social context in which it was interpreted did. Procreation remained imperative, the path to the celestial kingdom, where those who lived the most deserving lives on earth would dwell together with their families for eternity. Only temple-married couples, sealed forever as man and wife, could attain this highest realm of glory. As women, including Mormons, began to question assumptions about the naturalness of female subservience in the 1960s, male church leaders moved to solidify their authority. The Relief Society lost its autonomy, as part of a program of "Priesthood Correlation" aimed at ensuring uniformity of Mormon teachings and efficiency in Mormon organizations. Just as mergers aimed at denominational efficiencies cost Methodist women dearly in the 1960s, the Relief Society was deprived of financial independence and, perhaps most painfully, of its beloved vehicle of communication, the *Relief Society Magazine*. The 300,000 subscribers received the last, black-bordered issue in 1970. Henceforth, all publication would be under general supervision. The trend away from women's autonomy continued when the church condemned the ERA as a threat to distinctions between men and women that lay at the foundation of Mormon theology. In 1890, the church portrayed women's legal equality as a bolster to Mormonism's distinctive values;

in 1970, equality imperiled gender-based obligations of marriage that lay at the heart of both men's and women's pursuit of holiness.

Church opposition began after Phyllis Schlafly traveled to Utah in November 1974 seeking recruits for STOP ERA, the organization she founded in 1972. Schlafly met with the new Relief Society president, Barbara Smith. Smith recalled telling Schlafly that she doubted church officials would take a stand on the ERA because it was a political rather than a moral issue. Schlafly responded that "the ERA was one of the greatest moral issues of our day and that it would be very destructive to the family." Smith met with church authorities, who began to formulate a position opposing the amendment.[44]

Two days before the Utah legislature voted on ratification, a single editorial in the *Deseret News* handily reversed the anticipated positive outcome. But this was only the beginning of church opposition. In 1976, the LDS leadership designated the ERA a "moral issue," meaning that defeating it was part of the ongoing battle between good and evil through which individual Mormons achieved exaltation.[45] This contrasted with the Catholic position that the ERA was a political issue, therefore not one on which the church should take a stand, while abortion was a moral issue affecting the salvation of the individual as well as human rights. If the ERA were solely a political issue, Mormon interests might have been limited to defeating ratification in the states where they lived. But a moral issue required commitment to defeat ratification nationwide.

The extraordinary influence of the Mormon hierarchy was demonstrated once again at Utah's International Women's Year Conference. The United Nations declared 1975 as International Women's Year (IWY), and President Ford appointed a National Commission for the Observance of IWY, allocating funds for fifty state IWY conferences leading up to a national event in Houston in 1977. The commission formulated sixteen resolutions for discussion at the state conventions, including the ERA, which were enthusiastically endorsed by most state conventions.

Mormons initially encouraged women to stay away from the Utah IWY convention because of its implicit support for the ERA and other feminist issues. But when Barbara Smith learned that LDS women had been excluded from voting at the Idaho IWY convention and refused election as Idaho delegates to the national convention in Houston, she asked LDS president Ezra Taft Benson for help. Benson's response was decisive. He directed that each ward (local LDS church) in Utah send ten women to the IWY conference in Salt Lake City. Further, he charged each local Relief Society president with making sure that participants were fully informed about procedures and schedules for speaking and voting as well as with LDS positions opposing the ERA and other IWY proposals and with identifying at least one woman who could speak from the floor in support of LDS positions.[46]

Near chaos ensued. Organizers, who expected perhaps 2,000 participants, were now faced with the single largest state IWY conference in the nation. Over 13,000 women, most of them Mormon, gathered for two days at the Salt Palace in Salt Lake City, dwarfing the next-largest convention of 6,000 in California, a state with twenty times Utah's population.[47] And they came with a religious mission—they had been personally contacted by their bishop and their Relief Society president.

Most of the women who attended the Utah IWY convention learned about the ERA for the first time when they were called by a church official and told that it imperiled their family and their faith. Those calls introduced the ERA as a threat to women's welfare that would undermine the country's security by weakening families. And they introduced its defeat as an opportunity to serve their church and enact their faith. Armed with trust in religious authority, they loyally answered the call to uphold the values of their church and defend their families.

Maria Bliss and Phyllis Schlafly disagreed about whether the ERA advanced the welfare of women and the goals of democracy, but they agreed that Christian values should mobilize women to political activism. Political historian Neil Young argues that LDS women opposed the ERA not only because they believed it conflicted with their theology but also because it gave them an opportunity to demonstrate their commitment to the celestial kingdom, to themselves, and to each other. Young argues that Mormon women seized power to demonstrate their effectiveness as an asset to the church during the first LDS foray into national politics.[48]

To some extent, Young's argument can be extended to conservative Protestant and Catholic women who, together with their Mormon sisters, defeated ratification. Concerned Women for America, which claimed to be America's largest women's political lobby, began to fight the ERA but soon embraced support of a panoply of conservative issues. Although not affiliated with any specific religious organization, it introduced church women to a feminist agenda as a threat to the family, propelling them from local to national concerns. The Right-to-Life movement, while supported by the Catholic Church, also mobilized church women to political activism. Ironically, opposition to the ERA created a generation of politically engaged women for whom public action was part of their religious role. Most had never heard of the ERA before it was presented to them as a threat to their faith, together with horror stories about sending women to the front lines of military combat and requiring coed bathrooms where women could be raped.

Whenever Americans have disputed the appropriate roles of women, Christianity has figured prominently in the debate. The examples explored here unpack the political potency of intersections of gender and religion in three Christian contexts. In each case, positions on the extension of citizenship rights to women were tied to both fundamental religious beliefs and the historical context of the denomination's relation to the American republic.

Rather than suggesting a Christian perspective on gender, these cases show gender as a point of contention among Christians, with competing groups claiming that their treatment of women illustrates their moral superiority to other Christians as well as to members of non-Christian faiths. Thus, gender norms (or claims about them) police boundaries between religious groups, in particular forming a potent aspect of Protestant anti-Catholicism and anti-Mormonism. In the twenty-first century, rhetoric about the victimization of women once used by Protestants to dispute the "Americanness" of Catholics or Mormons has reappeared to critique Islam.[49] This suggests that whether or not sex is a suspect category in the U.S. Constitution, it should be in the historical analysis of American Christianities.

NOTES

1. Donald G. Mathews and Jane Sherron De Hart, *Sex, Gender, and the Politics of ERA: A State and the Nation* (New York: Oxford University Press, 1990), 74; John Patrick McDowell, *The Social Gospel in the South: The Woman's Home Mission Movement in the Methodist Episcopal Church, South, 1886–1939* (Baton Rouge: Louisiana State University Press, 1982).

2. Donald T. Critchlow, *Phyllis Schlafly and Grassroots Conservatism: A Woman's Crusade* (Princeton: Princeton University Press, 2005).

3. Rosemarie Zagarri, "Morals, Manners, and the Republican Mother," *American Quarterly* 44, no. 2 (June 1992): 192–215; Ruth H. Bloch, "The Gendered Meaning of Virtue in Revolutionary America," *Signs* 13, no. 1 (Autumn 1987): 37–58; Linda K. Kerber, *Women of the Republic: Intellect and Ideology in Revolutionary America* (Chapel Hill: Published for the Institute of Early American History and Culture by the University of North Carolina Press, 1980).

4. Even before time ran out for ratification, the Supreme Court found that gender was a "semi-suspect" category under the equal protection clause of the Fourteenth Amendment. See *Craig v. Boren* (1976). Laws could not include gender classification without a compelling state interest but need not meet the strict scrutiny standard applied to

suspect categories like race. This application of the equal protection clause combined with the passage of equal rights amendments to most state constitutions meets many of the original objectives of the ERA. Occasional efforts to reintroduce the ERA since 1982 have been made by those who believe the symbolic importance of absolute equality merits a constitutional amendment.

5. Frances Elizabeth Willard, *Glimpses of Fifty Years: The Autobiography of an American Woman* (Chicago: Woman's Temperance Publication Association, 1889), 474.

6. Evelyn A. Kirkley, "'This Work Is God's Cause': Religion in the Southern Woman Suffrage Movement, 1880–1920," *Church History* 59, no. 4 (December 1990): 507–22.

7. Judith Wellman, *The Road to Seneca Falls: Elizabeth Cady Stanton and the First Woman's Rights Convention*, Women in American History (Urbana: University of Illinois Press, 2004), 206.

8. Douglass was a licensed preacher in the African Methodist Episcopal Church, Zion.

9. Sarah Moore Grimké, *Letters on the Equality of the Sexes, and Other Essays* (New Haven: Yale University Press, 1988); Elizabeth Wilson, *A Scriptural View of Woman's Rights and Duties: In All the Important Relations of Life* (Philadelphia: W. S. Young, Printer, 1849).

10. The following discussion of Willard is based on the work of Carolyn De Swarte Gifford, including "'My Own Methodist Hive': Frances Willard's Faith as Disclosed in Her Journal, 1855–1870," in *Spirituality and Social Responsibility*, ed. Rosemary Keller (Nashville: Abingdon, 1993), 80.

11. Ibid., 84.

12. Carolyn De Swarte Gifford, "Home Protection: The WCTU's Conversion to Woman Suffrage," in *Gender, Ideology, and Action: Historical Perspectives on Women's Public Lives*, ed. Janet Sharistanian (New York: Greenwood Press, 1986), 109.

13. Willard, *Glimpses of Fifty Years*, 615–22; Mary Earhart Dillon, *Frances Willard: From Prayers to Politics* (Chicago: University of Chicago Press, 1944), 298–307.

14. Theressa Hoover, *With Unveiled Face: Centennial Reflections on Women and Men in the Community of the Church* (New York: Women's Division, General Board of Global Ministries, United Methodist Church, 1983).

15. Ibid., 29, 110.

16. For a survey of this distinctive contribution, see Dana Lee Robert, *American Women in Mission: A Social History of Their Thought and Practice* (Macon, Ga.: Mercer University Press, 1996).

17. Hoover, *With Unveiled Face*, 61, 63.

18. Ibid., 41, 81–82; "The United Methodist Building," website of the General Board of Church and Society of the United Methodist Church, accessed February 10, 2010, http://www.umc-gbcs.org/site/c.frLJK2PKLqF/b.3791391/k.348A/The_United_Methodist_Building.htm#historic.

19. Kathleen Sprows Cummings, *New Women of the Old Faith: Gender and American Catholicism in the Progressive Era* (Chapel Hill: University of North Carolina Press, 2009), 3.

20. Jenny Franchot, *Roads to Rome: The Antebellum Protestant Encounter with Catholicism*, The New Historicism 28 (Berkeley: University of California Press, 1994); Nancy Lusignan Schultz, *Fire and Roses: The Burning of the Charlestown Convent, 1834* (New York: Free Press, 2000).

21. Cummings, *New Women of the Old Faith*, 173.

22. James J. Kenneally, "Catholicism and Woman Suffrage in Massachusetts," *Catholic Historical Review* 53, no. 1 (April 1967): 43–44.

23. Ibid., 47–48.

24. Cummings, *New Women of the Old Faith*.

25. Kenneally, "Catholicism and Woman Suffrage in Massachusetts," 57.

26. James J. Kenneally, "Women Divided: The Catholic Struggle for an Equal Rights Amendment, 1923–1945," *Catholic Historical Review* 75, no. 2 (April 1989): 250.

27. *Rerum Novarum: Encyclical on Capital and Labor*, May 15, 1891.

28. Deirdre M. Moloney, *American Catholic Lay Groups and Transatlantic Social Reform in the Progressive Era* (Chapel Hill: University of North Carolina Press, 2002).

29. Elizabeth Alexander and Maureen Fiedler, "The Equal Rights Amendment and Abortion: Separate and Distinct," *America* 142 (1980): 314–18.

30. Carol Kleiman, "Sister Ana Ida Pushing Spirit of ERA in '76," *Chicago Tribune*, June 24, 1976, B2; cited in Mary J. Henold, *Catholic and Feminist: The Surprising History of the American Catholic Feminist Movement* (Chapel Hill: University of North Carolina Press, 2008), 271.

31. Faye D. Ginsburg, *Contested Lives: The Abortion Debate in an American Community*, updated ed. (Berkeley: University of California Press, 1998), 44.

32. This paragraph and the next are based on Antoinette Iadarola, "The American Catholic Bishops and Woman: From the Nineteenth Amendment to the ERA," in *Women, Religion, and Social Change*, ed. Yvonne Yazbeck Haddad (Albany: State University of New York Press, 1985), 457–76.

33. Mary C. Segers, "Sister Maureen Fiedler: A Nun for Gender Equality in Church and Society," *Religious Leaders and Faith-Based Politics*, ed. Jo Renee Formicola and Hubert Morken (Lanham, Md.: Rowman and Littlefield, 2001), 185–86.

34. Carol Cornwall Madsen, *Battle for the Ballot: Essays on Woman Suffrage in Utah, 1870–1896* (Logan: Utah State University Press, 1997), 6.

35. Thomas G. Alexander, "An Experiment in Progressive Legislation: The Granting of Woman Suffrage in Utah in 1870," *Utah Historical Quarterly* 38 (Winter 1970): 20–30; Madsen, *Battle for the Ballot*.

36. *Arcanum: Encyclical of Pope Leo XIII on Christian Marriage*, February 10, 1880.

37. Lola Van Wagenen, "Sister-Wives and Suffragists: Polygamy and the Politics of Woman Suffrage, 1870–1896" (Ph.D. diss., New York University, 1994), 6, 56.

38. Sarah Barringer Gordon, *The Mormon Question: Polygamy and Constitutional Conflict in Nineteenth-Century America* (Chapel Hill: University of North Carolina Press, 2002), 220.

39. Ibid., 222.

40. The most complete account of LDS involvement with the ERA is Martha Sonntag Bradley, *Pedestals and Podiums: Utah Women, Religious Authority, and Equal Rights* (Salt Lake City: Signature Books, 2005). Other helpful discussions include Neil J. Young, "'The ERA Is a Moral Issue': The Mormon Church, LDS Women, and the Defeat of the Equal Rights Amendment," *American Quarterly* 59, no. 3 (2007): 623–44.

41. Bradley, *Pedestals and Podiums*, 77.

42. Tona Hangen, "Guide to a Generation: Belle Spofford's Latter-day Saint Leadership," in *New Scholarship on Latter-day Saint Women in the Twentieth Century* (Provo, Utah: Joseph Fielding Smith Institute for Latter-day Saint History, 2005), 89.

43. Article IV, section 1, of the Utah Constitution, entitled "Equal Political Rights," reads: "The rights of citizens of the State of Utah to vote and hold office shall not be denied or abridged on account of sex. Both male and female citizens of this State shall enjoy equally all civil, political and religious rights and privileges."

44. Bradley, *Pedestals and Podiums*, 143.

45. Ibid., 149.

46. Ibid., 175–76.

47. Attendees constituted approximately 3 percent of the adult female population of the state, an astounding level of participation when compared to any other state.

48. Young, "The ERA Is a Moral Issue"; Bradley, *Pedestals and Podiums*.

49. Jose Casanova, "Nativism and the Politics of Gender in Catholicism and Islam," in *Gendering Religion and Politics: Untangling Modernities*, ed. Hanna Herzog and Ann Braude (Palgrave Macmillan, 2009), 21–50.

An Enduring Contest
American Christianities and the State

From their beginnings in a new-to-them world, the experience and ideals of British and Dutch North Americans required them to confront the issue of church-state relations. The nature of their response, as a matter of law, varied according to their experiences in their homelands and their purposes in crossing the Atlantic. Initially, all colonists imported religious establishments, of course. No other form of government was conceivable as they mapped their new terrain with old forms. The vast majority of seventeenth-century immigrants were children of the Protestant Reformation, whether British or Continental, and came from societies that had substituted their own religious establishments for Catholic Christendom. Their assumptions about the necessary integrity of church and state were complicated, however, by broad philosophical currents and increasing Protestant sectarianism that raised new concerns about the origins and prerogatives of individual conscience. Moreover, toleration was beginning to be considered a necessary predicate to peace and, among more radical thinkers, a moral good in its own right. Thus, in their intent to maintain a unified moral vision, America's seventeenth- and early eighteenth-century Christianities were overtly establishmentarian. But, in their radical sectarian diversity and dawning sense of human dignity, they carried the seeds of disestablishment with them across the Atlantic.

From Colonial Intolerance to Constitutional Liberty

Even the Puritans wished to separate themselves from the conflation of crown and church that made every English subject a member of the Church of England. These New Englanders believed that old England's use of religion as an instrument of the state had polluted the church with unbelievers. Thus, in their Massachusetts Bay Colony they separated the offices of church from those of their government. Nevertheless, the Puritans, as their name implies, came to New England not for freedom alone, but for the freedom to be righteous. Therefore political rights were tied to religious status, and Puritans were not above using the state as an instrument of the church. In particular, the Puritans' desire for holiness rationalized their invocation of state police powers against their fellow Protestants who did not submit to church order. Local magistrates summarily disciplined heretics, whether defined as reformers from within or proselytizers from without. Anne Hutchinson, who accused her Puritan ministers of damnable works righteousness, was banished from the colony. Quaker missionaries who trod upon the "New England Way" were brutally punished and, if they persisted, executed. Thus, in 1644, Roger Williams founded Rhode Island as a haven for Christian sectarians, religious libertarians, and the otherwise unwelcome religious others, including not only his fellow Baptists and antinomians such as Hutchinson's followers but also Jews. He was the first to make a principled claim for religious liberty—and not merely tolerance. For Williams, "all civil states with their officers of justice, in their respective constitutions and administrations, are . . . essentially civil, and therefore not judges, governors, or defenders of the Spiritual, or Christian, State and worship."[1]

Not least because of their experience with persecution on both sides of the Atlantic, the founding Quakers of Pennsylvania and Catholics of Maryland were more liberal in their efforts to permit religious difference. In 1672, Governor William Penn echoed Roger Williams when he stipulated that in his colony "no Men nor number of Men upon Earth hath power or Authority to rule over mens consciences in religious matters."[2] Similarly, in an attempt to ensure peace and protect Maryland's Catholic minority, Lord Calvert gave liberty to all Christians. Moreover, he required his Catholic coreligionists to treat their faith as a private matter, ordering them to "be silent, upon all occasions of discourse concerning matters of religion."[3] Overrun by Protestants within twenty years, however, Maryland Catholics became subject to legal prohibitions to the practice of their faith and exercise of civil rights, such as through the imposition of test oaths and restraints on the transfer of their property. Not just in Maryland, however, did Protestant establishments oppress Catholics. Even William Penn's "holy experiment" of religious liberty classified them—with atheists—as ineligible for public office.

For other mid-Atlantic Protestants, religious tolerance was a pragmatic solution to a logistical problem, not a philosophical ideal. Long Island's Dutch governor Peter Stuyvesant was reprimanded by the West Indies Company for his efforts at religious conformity: labor in the New World was too precious for such scruples. Strong state establishment was unthinkable in these commercially successful, rapidly diversifying colonies. Even the more cohesive and less market-driven New Englanders could not maintain their religious monopoly very long. Protestant individualism and anticlericalism, coupled with a zeal for holiness, inspired sectarian reformers and nonconformists such as Anabaptists, who bedeviled the Puritans' theocratic hopes for uniformity. Especially in the mid-Atlantic colonies, however, the variety of American Christianities seemed unlimited. By the late seventeenth century, New York's catalog of Christians included not only the expected Anglicans, Catholics, and Dutch Calvinists, but also Singing Quakers, Ranting Quakers, Sabbatarians, Antisabbatarians, Anabaptists, and Independents. In the early eighteenth century, these were joined by Baptists, Congregationalists, Methodists, German and Swiss Moravians, Lutherans, and Scots Presbyterians. Again, however, the détente among the Protestant sectarians in the British colonies was not extended to Catholics, who were variously denied rights to possess and transfer property, train for elite professions, or hold public office.

The strongest Anglican establishment was in the southern colonies. But even in Virginia, the oldest crown colony, scattered plantations, lack of clerical leadership, and the primacy of commercial intentions undermined religious conformity and made the colony susceptible to religious laxity and diversity. As in Massachusetts, civil authority tried with varying degrees of success to enforce its established church, especially against itinerant Baptist and Presbyterian preachers who sought to rescue Anglicans from perceived religious formalism. Virginia sheriffs routinely harassed, whipped, and jailed Baptists for disturbing the peace by holding church meetings or holding forth in public sermons. Nevertheless, state efforts at religious uniformity were frustrated as waves of revivalism strengthened the evangelical churches. Methodists, Baptists, and Presbyterians produced a populist religious ethos and cadre of lay leadership that destabilized southern establishments. Moreover, as religious passions joined revolutionary ones, the traditional British establishments throughout the colonies were openly criticized. Baptist Isaac Backus was quick to inform any who would listen, including the Continental Congress, that being taxed to support a church contrary to one's conscience was as tyrannical as other forms of taxation without representation.[4] The ideals of liberty required that all be overthrown.

Religious liberty's most influential proponents were Virginians Thomas Jefferson and James Madison, who engineered passage of the nation's first state guarantee of religious freedom in 1786. For Jefferson, "Almighty God hath created the mind free" and, therefore, political coercion of the mind was both futile and immoral. Madison, who had been deeply affected by witnessing the persecution of Virginia Baptists, added the ideal of neutrality to Jefferson's judgment of futility. Even to benefit one religion over another, he wrote, "violates equality by subjecting some to peculiar burdens, so it violates the same principle, by granting to others peculiar exemptions."[5] These principles appealed to a broad philosophical and religious constituency and, five years later, were incorporated into the U.S. Constitution. As amended, it forbade test oaths for federal office and also required that "Congress shall make no law respecting an establishment of religion, or prohibiting the free exercise thereof."

The First Amendment was ratified through a political marriage of convenience between two otherwise antagonistic groups: Deists and orthodox Christians. Deists were a small but elite group made up of the most influential of the Constitution's Framers, including the overtly deistic Thomas Jefferson and Benjamin Franklin and the more private James Madison and James Monroe, as well as the nation's first president, George Washington. Deists, as stated by Jefferson in the Virginia statute, believed that the human mind was naturally free and that coercion could not change that fact of creation. Moreover, truth was discernible by humans without divine (or state) aid, and falsehood was best identified through free competition of ideas. Thus, government should remain neutral toward America's churches or, as argued by James Madison, should give no benefit to one church in order not to burden another. This was, he later wrote, "essential to the purity of both" religion and government.[6] On the other hand, orthodox Christians among the Framers, such as Samuel Adams, John Jay, and Elias Boudinot, believed in the superiority of Christianity as revealed truth and assumed the necessity of state reliance on specifically Christian morality. For them, religion—as the expression of God's law—had a special status under human law and was properly exempt from human regulation. This last point did not need to be pressed, since everyone assumed that only false religion would require regulation. Moreover, it was unimaginable that the laws of a moral state would contradict true religion. These assumptions were so deeply held that the non-Christian Deists and the Christian sectarians among the Framers were able to cooperate long enough to overcome opposition to amending the Constitution.[7]

Opposition to the First Amendment was strongest among those who thought that constitutional guarantees were unnecessary, given the "prevailing liberality" of the times. Still others regretted that such liberality treated all conscience alike. "In a Christian country, it would be at least decent," said the delegate from Maryland, "to hold out some distinction between the professors of Christianity and downright infidelity or paganism."[8] Notwithstanding such fears, Americans became the first to remove religion from the machinery of the state. With ratification of the Bill of Rights in 1791, they created a federal government without formal ties to church and one that was prohibited from coercing the human conscience. For Jefferson, this act constituted a "wall of separation," a phrase that would be key to later interpretations of the meaning of the First Amendment.[9] In the meantime, since the religion clauses applied only to the federal government, individual states could freely discriminate on the basis of religion, if they chose. Those that did were largely continuing colonial habit, which they eventually abandoned, however. In 1833, Massachusetts was the last to formally disestablish.[10]

Privileging Protestant Christianity

Churches may have been disestablished, but religious sentiment flourished in the new republic. Both the stability of the government, especially a democratic one, and its ultimate success were believed dependent on a moral citizenry. Though moral sensibilities were increasingly believed by most Americans to be inherent, the church was almost universally believed to be the best instrument for developing those sensibilities. Thus, formal disestablishment of church and state was accompanied by renewed commitment to the spread of Christian influence among the nation's population and its institutions. Throughout the nineteenth century, but especially in the formative years of the nation, it was a given that Christianity should inform American political life, and in fact it did. As stated by no less than the Supreme Court's Chief Justice John Marshall in 1833: "The American population is entirely Christian, and with us, Christianity and religion are identified."[11] Of course, things were much more complicated than that. Not all Americans were Christian; most notably, the nation was made up also of Jews, Indians, and Africans, each with sophisticated belief systems distinct from Christianity.

Moreover, it was a particular kind of Christianity that constituted permissible religion in the new republic. In a letter to Jefferson in 1813, John Adams reflected on the negotiations that underlay the creation of America's constitutional system by men of varied sectarian commitments, including "Roman Catholicks . . . Horse Protestants and House Protestants, Deists and Atheists; and *Protestans qui ne croyent rien*." Their common ground, said Adams, lay in principles of British liberty most obviously but, just as important, in "the general Principles of Christianity, in which all those Sects were united."[12] As with the Congress, so also with the new nation, it was thought. The guarantee of religious liberty and the implied promise of neutrality were applicable to Christianity generally. In practice, however, the sanctioned moral order was invariably Protestant. Catholics remained a suspect population in the new republic. Not only did Protestant Americans bear old resentments and theological prejudices from their European roots in the Reformation. Also, they believed that Catholics were dangerously loyal to a foreign power—and an undemocratic and priestly one at that. To Protestants, Catholics' veneration of the Holy See, not to mention their theocratic history and failure to privilege the Bible over sacraments, made them superstitious and susceptible to manipulation by despots. It was over against the foil of Catholicism that the "general Principles of Christianity"—or Protestant moral concepts of personal behavior and civic duty—were deemed lawfully applicable to the nation at large.

With the ratification of the First Amendment, arguments that had always supported the necessity of Christian establishment were deployed to argue for the necessity of Protestant influence by voluntary, not state, action. Evangelical religion, especially as articulated by perfectionists like Charles Finney, taught that "a higher law than the Constitution was at work in the nation—a law of holiness and freedom that called every citizen to moral action to rid the nation of its sins against justice and love."[13] Thus, although Protestants accepted the idea of separation of any particular church from the state, they insisted that churches were necessary to combat moral threats to the nation. Based on this conviction, religious Americans, especially mainstream Protestants, devised umbrella organizations to give order to their radically democratizing society and give unified expression to their sectarian, but shared piety.

By maximizing their shared piety and minimizing theological differences, Protestant sectarians developed a unique consensus that avoided religious violence among themselves and found common cause in social reform. Sunday schools were organized to teach literacy and "general Christianity" to urban populations, especially ones of non-Protestant foreign immigrants—namely, Catholics and Jews. Moral reform societies railed against such social evils as slavery, prostitution, divorce, profanation of the Sabbath, and drunkenness. Because "the law could [no longer] compel men to support the Gospel," there was, Rev. Lyman Beecher said, "no substitute but the voluntary energies of the nation itself, in associations for charitable contributions and efforts, patronized by all denominations of Christians, and by all classes of the community."[14] Indeed, the pursuit of social benevolence and moral reform allowed Protestantism to cross institutional boundaries in a variety of ways, but especially through intrachurch organizations. The effect was to obtain for American Protestantism a political unity and influence reminiscent of Christendom, but without its creedal demands.

Volunteerism by the churches did not exclude the use of the state as an agent of religion, however. Congress appointed chaplains for itself and for the armed forces; sponsored the publication of a Bible; set aside public lands for the building of churches; and, in times of triumph or threat, declared national days of fasting and prayer. The states enforced Christian codes of conduct by statute and through their courts. Many, with the famous exception of Jefferson, believed that the English common law inherited by the new nation incorporated Christianity, and courts explicitly enforced its principles in such matters as blasphemy, for example.[15] "Temporal and spiritual power were fused," observed one historian, "even while Americans proclaimed to the world that they were the first nation on the earth truly to understand that religious freedom meant the separation of church and state."[16]

Troubling Nonconformity

America's informal fusion of Protestant church and democratic state allowed, for example, the appropriation in 1819 of federal funds to churches for the teaching of agriculture and literacy to Indians. Fifty years later, President Grant's administration turned the management of entire government reservations over to various denominations. An attempt to end corruption among party appointees, Grant's "Peace Policy" gave missionaries from thirteen denominations control over seventy-three government agencies. Catholics were excluded from this largesse, however, notwithstanding their longer history of Indian missions. Like the Indians themselves, Catholics were still a problem population for Protestant America.

Viewed as foreigners still under the sway of the pope, all Catholics—but especially Catholic European immigrants, who arrived in great numbers in the second quarter of the nineteenth century—were deemed at best unprepared for the responsibility of democratic citizenship and at worst a threat to the state. Anti-Catholic activity included riots over Bible reading in public schools; continuing efforts at the national level to keep Catholics from political office, as well as restrict their immigration; and attempts to amend the Constitution to forbid public support of parochial schools. Catholics had to fight for religious liberty and political acceptance for more than a century.

As for the Indians themselves, Grant's Peace Policy did not result in peace. Indian resistance, most notably in the form of the Ghost Dance movement, was empowered by religious beliefs, both Christian and indigenous. Ultimately, the Dancers' aspiration for self-government and millennial expectations were dashed at Wounded Knee in 1890, as well as by government regulation of Indian religious activities.[17] State laws criminalized sacramental use of peyote, and similar bills were introduced in the national legislature. During the first decades of the twentieth century, congressional concerns culminated in investigative hearings. For the next thirty years, a series of federal and state statutes treated peyote as a harmful narcotic and attempted to criminalize its use.

In the same year as the massacre at Wounded Knee, efforts to control another religiously motivated population in the West also came to a head. Rooted in New England restorationism and frontier utopianism, Mormonism had early and always attracted the negative attention of its fellow citizens, but no more so than when it claimed the right to restore Old Testament polygamy. This was clearly not consistent with the "general Principles of Christianity." After the Civil War, Congress passed several antipolygamy statutes that criminalized the Latter-day Saints' marital practices and sent more than a thousand of them to federal prisons, as well as disincorporated their church and confiscated its property. In 1890, the Supreme Court upheld these actions, declaring: "The organization of a community for the spread and practice of polygamy is . . . contrary to the spirit of Christianity and of the civilization which Christianity has produced in the Western world."[18]

A contemporary indictment of Mormonism by a Congregationalist minister was more to the point and equally applicable to Indian religious practices: "Mormonism must first show that it satisfies the American ideas of a church, and a system of religious faith, before it can demand of the nation the protection due to religion. This it cannot do, for it is not a church; it is not religion according to the American idea and the United States Constitution."[19] Ultimately, both Latter-day Saint and Indian efforts to obtain First Amendment protection succeeded only when they conformed their Christian beliefs and institutions to socially accepted and legally recognized forms. Specifically, both groups became liberated under the Constitution only after they acted more like Protestants, not only by accepting consensus

morality but also by adopting a denominational ecclesiology that emphasized moral, not creedal, conformity.

Like religious liberty itself, denominationalism arose from several aspects
of antebellum American life, especially the experience of religious diversity
that undermined confidence in exclusive truth. Further informed by Reformation and Enlightenment convictions regarding the independence and
competency of individual conscience, the denomination made no claim to
exclusive truth among its Protestant coreligionists. Above all, in Lockean
terms, denominations were voluntary organizations. An individual's choosing among them was based on personal proclivities. "The denomination,
unlike the traditional forms of the church," wrote historian Sidney Mead,
"is not primarily confessional, and it is certainly not territorial. Rather it
is purposive. And unlike any previous church in Christendom, it has no
official connection with civil power whatsoever."[20] Thus, denominationalism shaped religion into a form compatible with American disestablishment
(that is, "British liberty") and American morality (that is, "the principles
of General Christianity"). Both these categories, identified by Madison as
the sure foundation for America's social compact, constituted an unforeseen
slippery slope that led to ironic results in the late twentieth century and
changed the relation of church and state, as we shall see. For late nineteenth-
and early twentieth-century Indians and Latter-day Saints, however, mainline Protestantism's values and forms still set the terms for participating in
America's social compact.

Strategic conformity to the norms of American Protestantism began
among the Indians with the arrival of Smithsonian anthropologist James
Mooney to Oklahoma in 1891. Mooney spent several years studying the
Plains Indians and became their advocate in Washington. In reports to supe-
riors, he described peyote rituals as a bona fide religious practice and argued
that they reduced alcohol use, an appealing argument to Protestant reformers. After testifying before Congress in 1918 on Indian religious practices,
Mooney advised the peyote adherents to organize as a religious denomination, even recommending that they call themselves the "Native American
Church." That same year, representatives from a number of tribes convened
specifically to organize a pan-Indian religious organization to protect the
use of peyote as a religious practice. Incorporation documents filed with the
state emphasized the classic aspects of denominationalism: voluntariness
and shared purpose, as well as commitment to Christian moral teachings.
Specifically, they stipulated that the Native American Church was organized
"to promote the religious belief of the several tribes of Indians in the state

of Oklahoma, in the Christian religion with the practice of Peyote Sacrament . . . and to teach the Christian religion with morality, sobriety, industry, kindly charity and right living."[21]

The Latter-day Saints, too, were subject to several congressional investigative hearings during this period. The last and most famous of these was catalyzed by Utah's election of an ecclesiastical officer, Apostle Reed Smoot, to the U.S. Senate.[22] After four years of testimony and thousands of petitions from Protestant churches and reform agencies, the matter was resolved by Senate floor debate. In the end, Senator Albert Beveridge of Indiana summarized, albeit in romantic terms, the criteria by which Mormonism would be judged legitimately religious and, therefore, protected by the First Amendment. "Obedience to law, tolerance of opinion, loyalty to country—these are the principles which make the flag a sacred thing and this Republic immortal. . . . By these principles let us live and vote and die, so that 'this Government of the people, for the people, and by the people may not perish from the earth.'"[23] The Senate galleries burst into applause as he finished his definition of what made a religion safe for the republic and therefore protected by First Amendment restraints on the state. By agreeing to abandon polygamy, the Latter-day Saints had subordinated their truth claims to the laws of the nation. By providing evidence that Protestants were not discriminated against in Utah civil society, the Latter-day Saints proved their tolerance—or that their creedal commitments were not stronger than their commitment to the democratic state. Finally, by demonstrating during the hearings that their church had acted for the common good at times of national crisis, the Latter-day Saints proved its loyalty, even its conformity to the benevolent activity that had been an essential characteristic of American Protestantism.

Disestablishing Religion, Again

During these first years of the twentieth century, it was not just the Native American and Latter-day Saint churches that had figured out how to conform themselves to that particularly American and Protestant type of church, the denomination. Just as important, the U.S. government figured out how to act less like one. After Beveridge spoke, another voice in the Senate debate cautioned his colleagues to distinguish between their political responsibilities and their personal morality, reminding them that the issue "must be approached from the standpoint of practical statesmanship rather than from the standpoint of the religious reformer."[24] Not primarily concerned with inculcating virtue in citizens, the "practical statesman" would not press for moral conformity but would find obedience to law sufficient in the political sphere. As a direct appeal to restraint in matters of substantive morality, this statement suggested that, although the Smoot hearing began as an exercise in nineteenth-century Christian reform, the Senate accepted Smoot on terms more compatible with twentieth-century procedural fairness and substantive neutrality. As a consequence, the Protestants had to abandon their demand that Mormonism be excluded from First Amendment guarantees and settle for federal enforcement of monogamous marriage. This event was, however, only one sign of Protestantism's changed relation to the state.

During the Progressive Era, Protestantism was being reduced from the whole to a part, albeit a big part, of the complex of American religion. Though they still dominated the cultural center, the mainstream churches were losing their exclusive hold and the margins were pressing toward the middle. There were many reasons for the loss of consensus and related loss of political power among the Protestant mainstream. Catholic and Jewish immigration was radically reducing Protestantism's numerical dominance and electoral reach. Higher education and industrialization were challenging virtually all the mainline churches' cultural authority and moral values. Urbanization was eroding Protestantism's traditional base of political organization. Developments in the sciences, both human and physical, were causing conflicts within congregations. Each of these factors had theological consequences that were causing new schisms in the largest denominations. In addition, old splits from the Civil War had not been healed, leaving the mainline churches still fractured. Finally, new religious movements were thriving, such as Christian Science, Jehovah's Witnesses, and Seventh-day Adventists, as well as numerous Pentecostal and Holiness groups. By the 1930s, Protestantism was undergoing what has been called a "second disestablishment," a period when "the voluntary effort to maintain a Protestant America had failed."[25] It was also a period when the state began to interpret its relation to religion through that branch of government most aloof from political pressure, the Supreme Court.

It had taken a century for the Supreme Court to rule, in 1878, on its first religious liberty case, which upheld the constitutionality of federal laws that criminalized the Latter-day Saints' marital practices. Because polygamy was universally abhorred as an unchristian, immoral practice, corrosive of American democracy, no one mourned its death or worried about the First Amendment implications of how it died.[26] Beginning in the 1920s, however, and continuing at an unrelenting pace for the rest of the century, a series of Supreme Court opinions began to tread on matters of immediate interest to many of America's Christians: aid to parochial schools; public school prayer, Bible reading, and school curricula; release time for religious education; zoning laws and tax exemption; proselytizing in neighborhoods and airports; pledges of allegiance and oath taking; Sunday blue laws; religious holiday displays; and, it seemed, every other conceivable intersection of religion and society. Initially, only the interests of marginalized religions were at stake, especially those of Catholics. In 1925, the Court held unconstitutional an Oregon law that effectively prohibited parochial education. Five years later, it upheld Louisiana's grant of textbooks to parochial schoolchildren, and in 1947, it allowed New Jersey to fund transportation to parochial schools.[27] As distressing as these victories may have been to the evangelical majority, the Court's extension of the benefit of the religion clauses to Catholics was of less concern than a series of cases that restricted the activities of the Protestant majority.

In 1948, the Court held that Illinois had violated the First Amendment by allowing public school classrooms to be used for religious education. Reinhold Niebuhr was among those who objected, warning that Protestants "do not seem to realize that if the separation of Church and State is made absolute, education, and indeed our culture in general, must become secular."[28] But the majority of religious Americans were both preoccupied by the nation's mid-century campaign against "godless" communism and reassured by formal acts of government legislating God into a national motto and placing the nation "under God" in the pledge of allegiance. Beginning in the 1960s, however, a series of decisions forbidding prayer and Bible reading in schools captured the attention of religious America.[29] These cases were followed in quick succession by prohibitions against teaching biblical creation in public schools and giving tax support to private schools.[30] The shift in the Court's attention from parochial to private schools paralleled white flight and later Fundamentalist flight from public education. Consequently, not only was explicitly religious activity outlawed in the public schools, but tax benefits to Protestant-identified schools were jeopardized.

During this same period, efforts to display the indicia of Christianity in public spaces were thwarted by the Court. Crèches were deemed legitimate only if included as part of an equally celebrated display of other religious and nonreligious holiday symbols.[31] This was less than well received by those who felt that it both desacralized the crèche and legitimized non-Christian symbols. Just as distressing to those who believed the nation to be "under

God," the Court held that display of the Ten Commandments in public facilities was permissible only if part of a larger display of secular historical documents. No pride of place or inference of divine imprimatur could be given the Ten Commandments.[32] In addition, the right to free exercise was extended not only to less popular religions—proselytizing Jehovah's Witnesses and Seventh-Day Adventists who refused to work on Saturday—but also to the unreligious as well.[33] By the mid-1960s, neither notary publics nor conscientious objectors had to be theist to be protected by the First Amendment.[34] In sum, the application of the First Amendment religion clauses to the states, beginning with *Everson* in 1947, had opened a floodgate of litigation contesting the old assumptions about the relation of "general Christianity" to the nation. By the end of the 1960s, Protestantism was no longer definitive of constitutionally protected religion.

Thus, in the 1970s, a religiously conservative, Christian "Moral Majority" reasserted the reform-oriented, nation-saving agenda of nineteenth-century Protestantism. Shorn of its informal establishment, this new evangelical and Fundamentalist alliance was dedicated to finding its way back into political influence and even control. Evangelical Christianity began to play an increasing role in elections and governance, including Supreme Court appointments and presidential elections.[35] At the 1992 Republican convention, candidate for president Pat Buchanan articulated old assumptions about America's religious character when he said: "There is a religious war going on in our country for the soul of America. . . . The [opposing party's] agenda . . . is not the kind of change we can tolerate in a nation that we still call God's country."[36] That Pat Buchanan was Catholic revealed the sociopolitical realignment of churches in the last half of the twentieth century. American Christianities were divided left and right, liberal and conservative—and not Protestant and Catholic, as they had been in the nineteenth century.

Raising the Walls of Separation

Among the most serious moral reforms sought by conservative churches was a constitutional amendment to ban abortion and, barring that, state and federal regulation to restrict its availability. In the course of these campaigns, Catholics and conservative Protestants elided differences, if not overcame centuries of ill will, and Protestants increasingly turned to Catholic Supreme Court appointments to effect their policy goals. The broadest religious coalition was created in 1993, the year after Buchanan raised his alarm. It included a number of former antagonists on both sides of the left-right axis and church-cult divide. Catholics, Jews, Southern Baptists, Latter-day Saints, and the International Society for Krishna Consciousness, to name a few, joined to lobby Congress for passage of the Religious Freedom Restoration Act. As indicated by the bill's title, the coalition was catalyzed by the shared fear that religious freedom had been lost. The perceived culprit was the Supreme Court, and the offending decision involved an old dilemma: the Native American Church's use of peyote. Only this time, "general Christianity" was on the side of the Indians, if only out of a sense of self-preservation.

Oregon Employment Division v. Smith, like so many cases that resist resolution in lower courts, was driven by an odd set of facts: drug counselors—who had been fired for using drugs—appealed from the state's denial of unemployment benefits. The counselors claimed the denial was unconstitutional because their use of peyote was an exercise of religious conscience and in furtherance of their religious duties as members of the Native American Church. In the end, the Supreme Court ruled against the counselors and established a new First Amendment standard: Otherwise neutral statutes (such as generally applicable antidrug laws) that adversely affect the free exercise of religion are not unconstitutional.[37] In other words, since Oregon's proscription of peyote applied to all citizens, the fact that it burdened some in their religious duties did not violate the First Amendment. This decision found no special constitutional status for religion; it could be, but it was not presumed to be, exempt from otherwise permissible statutes.

This was a shocking reversal for those Americans who believed that the nation had originated in the search for religious freedom and, having found it, had made it a matter of absolute legal right with the words "Congress shall make no law respecting an establishment of religion or prohibiting the free exercise thereof." The history of American Christianities and the state is much more complicated, of course. That complexity is measured in no small part, as we have seen, by the diversity and antagonisms of America's many Christianities, the majority factions of which leveraged the power of the state to impose their moral consensus and sense of right religion on others. When, however, the state withdrew its sponsorship of "the general Principles of Christianity," religious questions were increasingly "approached from the standpoint of practical statesmanship rather than from the standpoint of the religious reformer."[38] This made the state a referee, not a player, among competing religious and social interests. Therefore, in *Smith*, the Court did not question the religious bona fides of peyote use, much less assume it to be irreligious. Long gone were the days when the Court could judge religious practices in terms of conformity to a valorized notion of Christian civilization.[39] In the place of judging the religious merits of the practice at issue, the Court substituted procedural fairness or, in other words, neutrality of application, not result.

Indeed, many feared the actual result of such cases would be unfair because the Court gave legislatures discretion as to whether or not to exempt religion from any given statute. Specifically, the Court provided that, though not constitutionally required to do so, Oregon's legislature could exempt the Native American Church's peyote use from the state's general regulatory scheme, which it subsequently did. For the dissenting justices, such deference to state legislatures was an invitation to discriminate. It enabled the imposition of popular religious prejudices on minority religions by popularly elected officials.[40] But not only the minority religions were alarmed. By declaring religion no longer necessarily exempt from religiously burdensome statutes, *Smith* raised for all of America's churches the specter of governmental regulation through "generally applicable" statutes. These concerns prompted a near-unanimous Congress to attempt to reverse *Smith* by statute. Congress and the anti-*Smith* coalition of religious organizations were frustrated by the same Court that issued *Smith*, however. The Religious Freedom Restoration Act was held unconstitutional, and procedural neutrality remained the law of the land for the foreseeable future.[41]

Coming at the end of a century-long struggle over church-state relations in an increasingly non-Christian nation, *Smith* marked another turning point in America's effort to accommodate a variety of moral orders within a single nation. The twentieth century had begun with the loss of certain political privileges held by majority American Christianities and the denominational reshaping of many nonconformists, allowing greater participation in American polity. At mid-century, the relocation of the religious mainstream and the margins was furthered by the Court's unwinding the informal, but no less privileged, relation of "general Christianity" to America's other public institutions, especially schools. By century's end with *Smith*, American Christianities were themselves generalized with all other American religions and their legal status was equated with that of other social institutions, at least in federal courts. At the beginning of the twenty-first century, state constitutional provisions for religious liberty are poised to become the new locus for religious liberty claims and for defense against legislative establishment of majority religious interests. This is a striking reversal of the historical pattern. If that history tells us anything, however, *Smith*'s neutrality doctrine is not the final word on church-state relations, though it may mark the final disestablishment of American Christianities.

NOTES

1. Roger Williams, *The Bloody Tenent of Persecution, for the Cause of Conscience* (1644), in "The Founders' Constitution," ed. Philip B. Kurland and Ralph Lerner, http://press-pubs.uchicago.edu/founders/documents/amendI_religions4.html.

2. William Penn, *The Concessions and Agreements of the Proprietors, Freeholders, and Inhabitants of the Province of West New-Jersey* (1677), in Kurland and Lerner, "Founders' Constitution."

3. Quoted in Jon Butler, *Awash in a Sea of Faith: Christianizing the American People* (Cambridge: Harvard University Press, 1992), 51.

4. See, for example, Isaac Backus, *Appeal to the Public for Religious Liberty* (Boston: John Boyle in Marlborough Street, 1773), 32–33.

5. *The Virginia Statute* and *Memorial and Remonstrance*, documents 43 and 44, in Kurland and Lerner, "Founders' Constitution."

6. James Madison to the Baptist Churches in Neal's Creek (1811), in *Letters and Other Writings of James Madison, Fourth President of the United States, in Four Volumes, Published by the Order of Congress* (Philadelphia: J. B. Lippincott, 1865), 2:512.

7. Regarding the demise of this coalition of rationalist Deists and pietistic separatists, see Sidney E. Mead, *The Lively Experiment* (New York: Harper and Row, 1963), 38–54.

8. Respectively, Roger Sherman and Luther Martin regarding test oaths, as quoted in Derek Davis, *Religion and the Continental Congress, 1774–1789* (New York: Oxford University Press, 2000), 205–6.

9. "Jefferson's Letter to the Danbury Baptists: The Final Letter, as Sent," *Library of Congress Information Bulletin*, http://www.loc.gov/loc/lcib/9806/danpre.html.

10. For a discussion of colonial laws governing religion, see Thomas J. Curry, *The First Freedoms: Church and State in America to the Passage of the First Amendment* (New York: Oxford University Press, 1986).

11. John Marshall to Jasper Adams, May 9, 1833, in Daniel L. Dreisbach, ed., *Religion and Politics in the Early Republic: Jasper Adams and the Church-State Debate* (Lexington: University of Kentucky Press, 1996), 113.

12. John Adams to Thomas Jefferson, June 28, 1813, in Lester J. Cappon, ed., *The Adams-Jefferson Letters: The Complete Correspondence between Thomas Jefferson and Abigail and John Adams* (Chapel Hill: University of North Carolina Press, 1988), 338.

13. Timothy Smith, "Righteousness and Hope: Christian Holiness and the Millennial Vision in America, 1800–1900," *American Quarterly* 31, no. 1 (Spring 1979): 39.

14. Lyman Beecher, *Lectures on Political Atheism and Kindred Subjects* (New York: J. P. Jewett, 1852), 334.

15. Sarah Barringer Gordon, "Blasphemy and the Law of Religious Liberty in Nineteenth-Century America," *American Quarterly* 52, no. 4 (December 2000): 682–719.

16. William G. McLoughlin, "A Nation Born Again," in *In the Great Tradition: In Honor of Winthrop S. Hudson, Essays on Pluralism, Voluntarism, and Revivalism*, ed. Joseph D. Bana and Paul R. Dekar (Valley Forge, Pa.: Judson Press, 1982), 190.

17. The now-classic but still controversial interpretation of these events is Dee Brown, *Bury My Heart at Wounded Knee* (New York: Henry Holt, 1970). A contemporary account is James Mooney, *The Ghost Dance Religion and the Sioux Outbreak of 1890* (1896; Lincoln: University of Nebraska Press, 1991).

18. *The Late Corporation of the Church of Jesus Christ of Latter-day Saints v. United States*, 136 U.S. 1 (1890), 48–49.

19. Rev. A. S. Bailey, "Anti-American Influences in Utah" (1888), in *Christian Progress in Utah: The Discussions of the Christian Convention* (Salt Lake City, 1888), 17–23.

20. Mead, *Lively Experiment*, 103.

21. Carolyn N. Long, *Religious Freedom and Indian Rights: The Case of Oregon v. Smith* (Lawrence: University Press of Kansas, 2000), 14. As Long notes, four years earlier, in Oklahoma, a group had organized itself under the name "First Born Church of Christ," but it remained local and did not stipulate peyote among its religious practices. Therefore, it appears not to have been organized to defend its use and to create an intertribal organization. For further background on the evolution of the Native American Church and James Mooney's role, see Huston Smith and Reuben Snake, *One Nation under God: The Triumph of the Native American Church* (New Mexico: Clear Light Publishers, 1996), 169.

22. See, generally, Kathleen Flake, *The Politics of American Religious Identity: The Seating of Senator Reed Smoot, Mormon Apostle* (Chapel Hill: University of North Carolina Press, 2004).

23. *Congressional Record*, 59th Cong., 2nd sess., 1907, 41, pt. 4, 3412 (February 20, 1907).

24. Ibid., pt. 2, 1494 (January 22, 1907).

25. Robert T. Handy, *A Christian America: Protestant Hopes and Historical Realities*, 2nd ed. (New York: Oxford University Press, 1984), 184.

26. *Reynolds v. U.S.*, 98 U.S. 145 (1879).

27. *Pierce v. Society of Sisters*, 268 U.S. 510 (1925); *Cochran v. Louisiana State Board of Education*, 281 U.S. 370 (1930); *Everson v. Board of Education*, 330 U.S. 1 (1947). During this same period, the Court extended protection to persons marginalized by their pacifist consciences. See *U.S. v. Schwimmer*, 279 U.S. 644 (1929); and *U.S. v. Macintosh*, 283 U.S. 605 (1931).

28. *McCollum v. Board of Education*, 333 U.S. 203 (1948); Reinhold Niebuhr, "Secularism and Religion in Education," quoted in Robert S. Alley, *School Prayer: The Court, the Congress, and the First Amendment* (New York: Prometheus Books, 1994), 97.

29. *School Dist. of Abington Tsp. v. Schempp*, 374 U.S. 203 (1963) Pa.: "No state law or school board may require that passages from the Bible be read or that the Lord's Prayer

be recited in the public schools of a State at the beginning of each school day." *Engel v. Vitale*, 370 U.S. 421 (1962) N.Y.: "State officials may not compose an official state prayer and require that it be recited in the public schools of the State at the beginning of each school day—even if the prayer is denominationally neutral."

30. *Epperson v. Arkansas*, 393 U.S. 97 (1968), and, twenty years later, *Edwards v. Aguillard*, 482 U.S. 578 (1987), held against religiously motivated efforts to undermine the teaching of evolution. In *Committee for Public Education v. Nyquist*, 413 U.S. 756 (1973), and *Meek v. Pittenger*, 421 U.S. 349 (1975), the Court ruled against aid that did not go directly to the student for specifically nonreligious use and that was susceptible to financially benefiting the private school in general.

31. *Lynch v. Donnelly*, 465 U.S. 668 (1984).

32. *Stone v. Graham*, 449 U.S. 39 (1980), and *McCreary County v. ACLU of Kentucky*, 545 U.S. 844 (2005), thwarted efforts in Kentucky to post the Ten Commandments in public buildings.

33. *West Virginia Bd. of Ed. v. Barnette*, 319 U.S. 624 (1943); *Sherbert v. Verner*, 374 U.S. 398 (1963).

34. *Torcaso v. Watkins*, 367 U.S. 488 (1961); *United States v. Seeger*, 380 U.S. 163 (1965).

35. See, for example, Randall Balmer, *God in the White House, a History: How Faith Shaped the Presidency from John F. Kennedy to George W. Bush* (San Francisco: HarperOne, 2008).

36. Patrick Buchanan, speech delivered at the 1992 Republican National Convention in Houston, Texas, August 17, 1992, http://en.wikisource.org/wiki/Patrick_Buchanan%27s_Speech_to_1992_GOP_Convention.

37. *Employment Div. v. Smith*, 494 U.S. 872 (1990).

38. *Congressional Record*, 59th Cong., 2nd sess., 1907, 41, pt. 2, 1494 (January 22, 1907).

39. *Reynolds v. U.S.*, 98 U.S. 145, 153 (1879); *Davis v. Beason*, 133 U.S. 333, 342 (1890); *The Late Corporation of the Church of Jesus Christ of Latter-day Saints v. United States*, 136 U.S. 1 (1890), 48–49.

40. See Justice O'Connor's dissent to the majority's dictum that "the repression of minority religions is an 'unavoidable consequence of democratic government.'" *Employment Div. v. Smith*, 494 U.S. 872 (1990), 890, 902.

41. In *City of Boerne v. Flores*, 117 S.Ct. 2157 (1997), the Supreme Court held that the Religious Freedom Restoration Act, 42 U.S.C.S. 2000 (1993), was unconstitutional on the grounds that Congress did not have the authority to impose on the Supreme Court a standard of constitutional interpretation.

Contributors

Catherine L. Albanese is J. F. Rowny Professor Emerita in Comparative Religions and research professor in the Department of Religious Studies at the University of California at Santa Barbara. She is the author of numerous articles and books, including *A Republic of Mind and Spirit: A Cultural History of American Metaphysical Religion* (Yale University Press, 2007), *Nature Religion in America: From the Algonkian Indians to the New Age* (University of Chicago Press, 1991), *America: Religions and Religion*, 4th. ed. (Wadsworth, 2007), *Corresponding Motion: Transcendental Religion and the New America* (Temple, 1977), and *Sons of the Fathers: The Civil Religion of the American Revolution* (Temple, 1976).

James B. Bennett is associate professor of religious studies at Santa Clara University. He is the author of *Religion and the Rise of Jim Crow in New Orleans* (Princeton University Press, 2005). He is currently working on a history of religion in the American West.

Edith L. Blumhofer is director of the Institute for the Study of American Evangelicals and professor of history at Wheaton College. She is the author of *Her Heart Can See: The Life and Hymns of Fanny J. Crosby* (Eerdmans, 2005), *Aimee Semple McPherson: Everybody's Sister* (Eerdmans, 1993), *Restoring the Faith: The Assemblies of God, Pentecostalism, and American Culture* (University of Illinois Press, 1993), and *Pentecost in My Soul: Explorations in the Meaning of Early American Pentecostal Experience* (Gospel Publishing House, 1989). She is the coeditor of a number of volumes, including *Pentecostal Currents in American Protestantism* (with Russell Spittler and Grant Wacker, University of Illinois Press, 1999), and has edited *Religion, Politics, and the American Experience* (University of Alabama Press, 2002). She is currently writing *A Short History of Pentecostalism* (Cambridge University Press, forthcoming).

Ann Braude is director of the Women's Studies in Religion Program and senior lecturer on American religious history at Harvard Divinity School. She is the author of *Radical Spirits: Spiritualism and Women's Rights in 19th-Century America* (Beacon Press, 1989) and *Sisters and Saints: Women and Religion in America* (Oxford University Press, 2007). She served as editor of *Transforming the Faiths of Our Fathers: Women Who Changed American Religion* (Palgrave/Macmillan, 2004) and as coeditor of *Root of Bitterness: Documents of the Social History of American Women* (with Nancy F. Cott, Jeanne Boydson, and Lori D. Ginzberg, Northeastern, 1996) and *Gendering Religion and Politics: Untangling Modernity* (Palgrave, 2009).

Catherine A. Brekus is associate professor of the history of Christianity at the University of Chicago Divinity School and a member of the associate faculty in the Department of History. She is the author of *Strangers and Pilgrims: Female Preaching in America, 1740–1845* (University of North Carolina Press, 1998) and *The Religious History of American Women: Reimagining the Past* (University of North Carolina Press,

2007). She is currently working on a book entitled *Sarah Osborn's World: The Rise of Evangelicalism in Early America.*

Kristina Bross is associate professor of English and American studies at Purdue University. She is the author of *Dry Bones and Indian Sermons: Praying Indians in Colonial American Identity* (Cornell University Press, 2004) and is the coeditor of *Early Native Literacies in New England: A Documentary and Critical Anthology* (with Hilary Wyss, University of Massachusetts Press, 2008).

Rebecca L. Davis is assistant professor of history at the University of Delaware. She specializes in the histories of gender, sexuality, religion, and ethnicity in the United States during the nineteenth and twentieth centuries. She received her Ph.D. in 2006 from Yale University and is the author of *More Perfect Unions: The American Search for Marital Bliss* (Harvard University Press, 2010).

Curtis J. Evans is assistant professor of the history of Christianity at the University of Chicago Divinity School. He received his Ph.D. from Harvard University in 2005 and is the author of *The Burden of Black Religion: Representing the Race and Enlisting the Black Churches in the Nation's Racial Struggle* (Oxford University Press, 2008).

Tracy Fessenden is associate professor of religious studies at Arizona State University. She is the author of *Culture and Redemption: Religion, the Secular, and American Literature* (Princeton University Press, 2007) and the coeditor of *The Puritan Origins of American Sex: Religion, Sexuality, and National Identity in American Literature* (with Nicholas F. Radel and Magdalena J. Zaborowska, Routledge, 2001). Her current projects include a study of American violence and its neglect in the synoptic writing of U.S. religious history.

Kathleen Flake is associate professor of American religious history at Vanderbilt Divinity School. She is the author of *The Politics of American Religious Identity: The Seating of Senator Reed Smoot, Mormon Apostle* (University of North Carolina Press, 2004). She is currently writing a book entitled "Mormon Matriarchy: Gendered Power in Antebellum America."

W. Clark Gilpin is Margaret E. Burton Professor Emeritus of the History of Christianity and Theology at the University of Chicago Divinity School. He is the author of *The Millenarian Piety of Roger Williams* (University of Chicago Press, 1979) and *A Preface to Theology* (University of Chicago Press, 1996), editor of *Public Faith: Reflections on the Political Role of American Churches* (CBP Press, 1990), and coeditor of *The Voice from the Whirlwind: Interpreting the Book of Job* (with Leo G. Perdue, Abingdon, 1992). He is currently writing two books: "The Letter from Prison: Testimony and Literary Form in Early Modern England," which analyzes the letter from prison as a genre of religious literature in England during the sixteenth and seventeenth centuries, and "Alone with the Alone: Solitude in American Religious and Literary History."

Stewart M. Hoover is professor in the School of Journalism and Mass Communication and professor adjunct of religious studies and American studies at the University of Colorado. He is the author of *The Electronic Giant* (Brethren Press, 1979), *Mass Media Religion: The Social Sources of the Electronic Church* (Sage, 1988), and *Religion in the*

News: Faith and Journalism in American Public Discourse (Sage, 1998). He has coedited *Religious Television: Controversies and Conclusions* (with Robert Ableman, Ablex, 1990) and *Rethinking Media, Religion, and Culture* (with Knut Lundby, Sage, 1997). He chairs the International Study Commission on Media, Religion, and Culture.

Jeanne Halgren Kilde is director of the Religious Studies Program at the University of Minnesota. She is the author of *When Church Became Theatre: The Transformation of Evangelical Architecture and Worship in Nineteenth-Century America* (Oxford University Press, 2002), *Sacred Power, Sacred Space: An Introduction to Christian Architecture and Worship* (Oxford University Press, 2008), and *Nature and Revelation: A History of Macalester College* (University of Minnesota, 2010) and coeditor of *Rapture, Revelation, and the End Times: Understanding the Left Behind Series* (with Bruce David Forbes, Palgrave/Macmillan, 2004). Her current projects include a study of how religious space participates in the construction of gender and a study of immigrant religious space in Minnesota.

David W. Kling is professor of religious studies at the University of Miami. He is the author of *A Field of Divine Wonders: The New Divinity and Village Revivals in Northwestern Connecticut, 1792–1822* (Pennsylvania State University Press, 1993) and *The Bible in History: How the Texts Have Shaped the Times* (Oxford University Press, 2004) and coeditor of *Jonathan Edwards at Home and Abroad: Historical Memories, Cultural Movements, Global Horizons* (with Douglas A. Sweeney, University of South Carolina Press, 2003). He is an area editor (American Christianity) for the projected thirty-volume *Encyclopedia of the Bible and Its Reception* (de Gruyter, 2009–). He is currently working on a fourth book, "A History of Christian Conversion."

Timothy S. Lee is associate professor of the history of Christianity at Brite Divinity School, Texas Christian University, and director of Brite's Asian (Korean) Church Studies Program. He is the author of *Born Again: Evangelicalism in Korea* (University of Hawai'i Press, 2010) and coeditor of *Christianity in Korea* (with Robert E. Buswell Jr., University of Hawai'i Press, 2006).

Dan McKanan is the Ralph Waldo Emerson Unitarian Universalist Association Senior Lecturer at Harvard Divinity School. From 1998 to 2008, he taught theology and peace studies at the College of Saint Benedict and Saint John's University in Minnesota. He is the author of *Identifying the Image of God: Radical Christians and Nonviolent Power in the Antebellum United States* (Oxford University Press, 2002), *Touching the World: Christian Communities Transforming Society* (Liturgical Press, 2007), and *The Catholic Worker after Dorothy: Practicing the Works of Mercy in a New Generation* (Liturgical Press, 2008). His current project, *Prophetic Encounters: Religion and the American Radical Tradition*, is forthcoming from Beacon Press in October 2011.

Michael D. McNally is professor and chair of the Religion Department at Carleton College. He is author of *Ojibwe Singers: Hymns, Grief, and a Native Culture in Motion* (Oxford University Press, 2000, reissued by Minnesota Historical Society Press, 2009), *Honoring Elders: Aging, Authority, and Ojibwe Religion* (Columbia University Press, 2009), and other books and articles on Native American religious traditions.

Mark A. Noll is Francis A. McAnaney Professor of History at Notre Dame. He is the author of over thirty books, including, most recently, *The Civil War as a Theological Crisis* (University of North Carolina Press, 2006), *The Rise of Evangelicalism: The Age of Edwards, Whitefield, and the Wesleys* (InterVarsity Press, 2004), *Is the Reformation Over? An Evangelical Assessment of Contemporary Catholicism* (with Carolyn Nystrom, Baker, 2005), and *America's God, from Jonathan Edwards to Abraham Lincoln* (Oxford University Press, 2002). Noll's many honors include the National Humanities Medal.

Jon Pahl is professor of the history of Christianity in North America and director of M.A. programs at the Lutheran Theological Seminary in Philadelphia. He is the author of *Paradox Lost: Free Will and Political Liberty in American Culture, 1630–1760* (Johns Hopkins University Press, 1992), *Youth Ministry in Modern America: 1930 to the Present* (Hendrickson, 2000), *Hopes and Dreams of All: The International Walther League and Lutheran Youth in American Culture, 1893–1993* (Wheat Ridge Ministries, 1993), *Shopping Malls and Other Sacred Spaces: Putting God in Place* (Brazos Press, 2003), and *Empire of Sacrifice: The Religious Origins of American Violence* (New York University Press, 2010). He is working on a manuscript entitled "A Coming Religious Peace: The Global Rise and American Development of Religious Peacebuilding."

Sally M. Promey is professor of American studies and professor of religion and visual culture at Yale University, where she is also deputy director of the Institute of Sacred Music. She holds a secondary appointment in the Department of Religious Studies and an affiliation with History of Art. She convenes the Sensory Cultures of Religion Research Group and directs the Initiative for the Study of Material and Visual Cultures of Religion. Current book projects include volumes on the public display of religion, sensory cultures of American Christianities, and relations among religion and art in constructions of Western modernities.

Jon H. Roberts is the Tomorrow Foundation Professor of American Intellectual History at Boston University. He is the author of *Darwinism and the Divine in America: Protestant Intellectuals and Organic Evolution, 1859–1900* (University of Wisconsin Press, 1988) and *The Sacred and the Secular University* (with James Turner, Princeton University Press, 2000). He is currently working on a book dealing with American Protestant thinkers' treatment of the mind from 1840 to 1945.

Jonathan D. Sarna is the Joseph H. and Belle R. Braun Professor of American Jewish History at Brandeis University and chief historian of the National Museum of American Jewish History. He has written, edited, or coedited more than twenty books, including the acclaimed *American Judaism: A History*. Winner of the Jewish Book Council's Jewish Book of the Year Award in 2004, it has been praised as being "the single best description of American Judaism during its 350 years on American soil." His *When Grant Expelled the Jews* will appear in 2011.

Acknowledgments

American Christianities began with a question. As scholars and citizens have become increasingly aware of the amazing religious diversity in the United States, how has that recognition altered understandings of the historically predominant American religion, Christianity? To help us think about that question and its many implications for the study of American religious history, we invited five scholars to the University of Chicago Divinity School for a preliminary conversation. Anthea Butler, Martin Marty, Sally Promey, Sarah McFarland Taylor, and Thomas Tweed generously contributed learning and imagination to that initial shaping of *American Christianities*. It is a better book because of their probing observations about the history, social influence, and relations among the diverse Christianities that make up Christianity in the United States. We thank them.

We also thank two deans of the Divinity School, first, Richard Rosengarten, and now, Margaret Mitchell. From its inception to final production, both have actively supported *American Christianities*, and we are immensely grateful for their interest in this project. We are indebted to Philippa Koch, a Ph.D. candidate in American religious history at the Divinity School, for preparing the index. Finally, our editor at the University of North Carolina Press, Elaine Maisner, has carefully and efficiently guided the review and editing process, and we thank her for the advice she contributed to the final shaping of *American Christianities*.

Index

Abolitionist movement, 428–29, 433–34, 440, 442, 449, 456; and post–Civil War reform, 434; and women's rights movement, 469–70. *See also* Antislavery movement

Abortion, 287, 397, 414, 416–17, 427, 466–67, 477–79, 485, 503

Adams, John, 495

Adams, John Quincy, 265

Adams, Samuel, 494

Addams, Jane, 167, 476

Adventists, 50

African Americans: and Islam, 43–44; and liberation theology, 45, 220–21; and religion, 153, 171, 495

—Christians: Imani Temple movement, 38; Catholics, 38, 44; Baptists, 40, 93, 110–11; missions, 43, 104–5, 138–39, 260, 266; Spiritual Churches, 44; and voodoo, 44; and revivals, 44, 107, 138; Holiness and Pentecostal, 44–45; Garveyites and African Orthodox Church, 45; West African influence on, 105–6, 429; and discrimination and segregation, 108, 110, 113–14, 138; Methodists, 108, 110, 469, 472; African Methodist Episcopal Church, 108–9; in the North, 108–12, 138, 220; political activism of, 109–10; in the South, 110, 113–14, 138–39; feminist theology, 111; women, 111, 114–15, 432; and Great Migration, 111–12, 220; violence toward, 113–14; and televangelism, 115; and ecumenism, 116, 145; and material culture, 193; and science, 341; and voluntarism, 392; ministers, 433, 469

—slavery, 32, 52, 107, 220, 283; and spirituals, 45, 220; and Exodus narrative, 218, 220–21, 427; and insurrections, 220, 432; narratives of, 321, 433; and denial of re-

ligious freedom, 418; and abolition, 429, 431–32; and disfranchisement, 468–69. *See also* Black church; Practice, Christian: African American; Slavery

Afro-Caribbeans: Catholicism, 38, 44; and *santeria*, 44; and *vodou*, 44

Ahlstrom, Sydney, 13, 15–16, 29

Alacoque, Marguerite Marie, 190

Albanese, Catherine, 4, 25, 133

Alexander VI (pope), 133

Alexie, Sherman, 308

Algonquian, 228, 252

Alinsky, Saul, 429, 438–42

Allen, Richard, 108–9

American religious history, academic field of, 11–16, 129; Protestant influence on, 13–16, 29, 261; comparative and theoretical approaches of, 14, 30

American Revolution, 382, 386, 458

Amish, 32, 40

Anabaptists, 429, 493; influence of, 37, 39–40

Anarchists, 429

Anderson, James, 386

Angelica, Mother, 369

Anglicans, 6, 45, 217, 222–23, 403, 491, 493; missions to slaves, 43, 104–5; establishment in southern colonies, 136, 493. *See also* Episcopalians

Anidjar, Gil, 401, 420

Anthony, Susan B., 482

Antisabbatarians, 493

Antislavery movement, 431–33, 474; and colonization, 108–9, 431–32; polarization of, 432; and nonviolence, 433; and woman suffrage, 482. *See also* Abolitionist movement

Antiwar movement, 50, 144, 428, 437. *See also* Peace movement

Apess, William, 72–73

Aquinas. *See* Thomas Aquinas, Saint

Arcanum, 482

Arendt, Hannah, 455

Armenian Apostolic Church, 37

Asbury, Francis, 108

Asian Americans: Christians, 47–48, 77–79, 93; immigration of, 47–48, 78–84, 93; missions to, 47, 78, 80–84, 267; discrimination against, 80–83, 89, 93. *See also* Japanese Americans; Korean Americans

Atheists, 121–22, 434, 492, 495

Austin, Ann, 135

Backus, Isaac, 493

Badillo, David A., 88

Bailey, Abigail Abbott, 320–21

Bailey, Asa, 320

Baird, Robert, 6, 7, 10, 21, 261, 264

Bakker, Jim, 295, 376

Bakker, Tammy Faye, 295, 376

Baldridge, William, 70

Ballou, Adin, 434

Baltimore, Lord (Cecilius Calvert), 136, 492

Baptism, 243–47, 429; and material culture, 203–4; by immersion, 204, 229, 244–47; spatial context of, 244–47

Baptists, 6, 32, 37, 39, 42–43, 47–48, 51, 137, 245–46, 254–55, 270, 355–56, 391, 432, 491, 493–94; Missionary and Anti-Mission division, 39; National Baptist Convention of America, Inc., 40; Landmark movement, 40, 51; African American, 40, 93, 110–11; National Baptist Convention, USA, Inc., 40, 111; and Native Americans, 67; missions, 67, 78, 83–84, 105; Asian American, 78, 83–84; American Baptist Convention, 84; and slaves, 105; and civil rights movement, 110; Women's Convention, 111; Modernist-Fundamentalist controversy, 143; Northern Baptists, 160; railroad missions, 259; and higher education, 263; Danbury, 404; and nativism, 406; and peace movement, 457. *See also* Southern Baptists

Barnes, Albert, 139

Baumann, John, 442

Baxter, Richard, 185

Beall, Mary Ann, 478

Beecher, Lyman, 140, 263, 402, 430–32, 474, 496

Bell, Catherine, 243

Bellah, Robert, 414, 423

Bellamy, Joseph, 286

Benedictines, 250, 435

Benedict XVI (pope), 54

Benezet, Anthony, 429

Bennett, James, 26

Benson, Ezra Taft, 485

Bercovitch, Sacvan, 216, 313

Bernardin, Joseph, 438

Berrigan, Daniel, 437, 456

Berrigan, Philip, 437, 456

Beveridge, Albert, 500

Bible: Scofield Reference, 50; King James Version (KJV), 140, 145–46, 223–25, 227–31, 268, 289, 401, 406–7; Revised Standard Version (RSV), 145, 230–31, 359; New Revised Standard Version (NRSV), 145, 231–32; Gideon, 214; Hebrew (Old Testament), 216, 228; Apocrypha, 223; Latin Vulgate, 223; Douay-Reims Version, 223, 225, 231, 289; Algonquian, 228; translations and versions of, 228–32; Joseph Smith Translation (JST), 229–30; Greek Septuagint, 230; *The Woman's Bible*, 230; New King James Version (New KJV), 231; New International Version (NIV), 231–32; Southern Baptist, 232; Today's New International Version (TNIV), 232

—in American culture, 214–15, 226, 232, 398; and material culture, 205, 207, 214, 233; sales and distribution of, 214–15, 224, 228, 231, 233, 375, 431; and slavery, 215, 218, 390; and politics, 215, 232, 421; and Protestantism, 215–16, 227, 416; in colonial period, 216–17; in public schools, 222–23, 225–27, 233, 401, 406–7; in worship, 253, 255; and science, 329, 331, 333–35, 339; and homosexuality, 349, 356, 359; and gender roles, 355, 467; and social reform, 427; and women, 470

—interpretation of: higher criticism, 52, 143, 233; historical study of, 162–63, 170; controversies over, 215, 217–18, 228, 230–31; feminist and minority, 215, 230, 232; individual, 215, 385; and gender-inclusive language, 232

See also Exodus, biblical theme of

Bieber, Irving, 353

Bigelow, Silas, 188

Black church, 145, 429; as separate from white, 102, 107, 110, 115–16, 138; historiography of, 102–4, 108, 113–14; burden of, 103–4, 108, 112; and political activism, 109–11, 112, 116; critique of Word of Faith ministers, 300; and social reform, 430, 432, 442. See also African Americans

Blanton, Smiley, 351, 353

Bliss, Maria, 466–67, 473, 486

Blum, Edward J., 15

Boone, Daniel, 317–19

Bouchard, James, 81

Boudinot, Elias, 494

Bourdieu, Pierre, 70

Bradford, William, 133–34, 448

Bradstreet, Anne, 327

Brainerd, David, 42

Brainerd, John, 42

Braude, Ann, 19

Brauer, Jerald C., 13–14

Brazier, Byron, 115

Brekus, Catherine, 20

Breuer, Marcel, 250

Brooks, Joanna, 15

Bross, Kristina, 20

Brown, Antoinette, 433–34

Brown, Charles Brockden, 319

Brown, Joseph Epes, 61

Brown, William Adams, 168

Brownson, Orestes, 333, 335

Bryan, William Jennings, 339

Bryant, Anita, 361

Buchanan, Pat, 503–4

Buddhists, 120, 122, 134, 171, 438, 443; as un-American, 413

Burkhart, Roy A., 353

Bush, George H. W., 317, 376

Bush, George W., 219, 317, 376, 416, 418–21, 454, 457–58

Bushman, Claudia Lauper, 35

Bushman, Richard Lyman, 35

Bushnell, Horace, 195

Butler, Jon, 33, 35

Byrne, William, 264

Cabeza de Vaca, Alvar Núñez

Cahensly, Peter Paul, 46

Callahan, Dwight, 218

Calvary Chapel, 34

Calvin, John, 198, 282, 427, 430

Calvinism, 37–38, 133–34, 198, 283, 285–86, 375, 392, 430; Dutch, 493

Campbell, Alexander, 141, 229–30

Campbell, Colin, 197–98

Campbell, James, 103

Campbellite movement, 373

Capitalism, 159, 209, 275–76, 279–80, 282–83, 286–88, 294; model of selfhood, 280, 283–87, 289–95, 301–2

—and Christianity, 279–302, 393, 413–14, 416; ambivalence toward, 279–87, 289, 291, 301–2; different model of selfhood, 280–81, 283–87, 289–93, 300–302; and Word of Faith movement, 295–301; Catholic critique of, 413, 437

See also Consumer Culture; Modernity

Captivity narrative: literary influence of, 276, 307–8, 310–22; and biblical theme of Exodus, 307, 312, 321–22; as Jeremiad, 307–8, 310, 313, 315–16, 318, 321–22; as account of Christian forbearance, 308, 310–21; and secular frontier literature, 310, 313–14, 316–21; and Native Americans, 310–11, 319, 321–22; and clergy, 314–15; and slave narratives, 321; and immigrants, 322

Carey, Patrick W., 16

Carnegie, Andrew, 288

Carpenter, Joel, 374

Carroll, Coleman F., 85

Carter, Jimmy, 9, 219, 401, 415

Castro, Fidel, 85–86

Catholics, 4–5, 11, 32, 34, 53–54, 144, 174, 282, 493, 495; in narratives of American Christianity, 13, 15–16, 261; Dignity movement, 38; Slaves of the Immaculate Heart of Mary, 38; Voice of the Faithful, 38; African American, 38, 44, 110; Black Madonna of Czestochowa, 48; National Polish Catholic Church, 46; Filipino, 48; National Conference of Catholic Bishops, 92, 478–79; and Bible, 216–17, 225, 230; and sacraments, 245–46, 248–52

—and American society, 383, 388; seen as threat to, 6–7, 140, 262–65, 288, 402–4, 406, 409, 411, 496–97; persecution and discrimination in, 121, 136, 140–41, 407, 418, 493; growing acceptance of, 146; and desire for religious freedom, 261, 408, 474, 498, 502, 504; and education, 263, 498, 502, 504; and science, 327, 332, 335–36, 341; and the media, 368–69, 371–73, 375–77; and voluntarism, 391–92; and restrictions on office holding, 405, 493, 498; and assimilation, 413–14, 416

—immigration: and ethnic tensions, 36–38, 45–46; and Cahenslyism, 38, 46; in colonial era, 133, 136–37, 192, 427, 492; influence of, 249–50, 262, 264–68, 288, 496–98; and pressure to Americanize, 249–50, 409, 411

—material culture, 190–91, 193–96, 206, 209; sacred heart devotion, 190–91, 193, 196, 199–200; viaticum cabinet, 194–95; First Communion Remembrances, 199–202, 204, 206

—missions, 32, 42–43, 47, 259–68, 271; to Native Americans, 61, 64–67, 73–74, 266; to Asian Americans, 78, 81, 84, 250; to African Americans, 266

—and modernity, 159–60, 162–63; and critique of individualism, 19, 163, 276, 287, 289–94, 298, 301–2, 411, 474; and Americanist controversy, 46, 163, 223; and neo-scholasticism, 172–73; and capitalism, 280, 287–94, 299, 413–14

—outside United States: in Canada, 388; in Mexico, 388–90; in French Quebec, 388–89, 401–4, 411, 422; in France, 389; in Spain, 389; in Nigeria and Brazil, 393; in Latin America, 414

—and Protestants: cooperation, 118, 146–47, 414, 416, 483, 486, 503; and public schools, 124, 140, 223, 225, 401, 406–8, 411; and gender norms, 141, 474; and Bible controversies, 223–25, 231, 233, 401, 406–9; differences, 264–65, 390, 403–4

—social teaching, 435–36, 440; Catholic Worker movement, 179, 428–29, 435–38, 442; and concern for workers, 288, 290–94, 413–14, 435–36, 476; and socialism, 290–94, 413–14, 436, 440; and women, 292; and family, 292, 294; and unions, 293, 413–14, 436–37, 476; and reform efforts, 427, 431, 435–41, 477; and community organizing, 439–42; and nonviolence, 456

—women: women religious, 38, 91, 141, 190, 225, 265–66, 288, 473–79; and feminist movement, 38, 476; ordination of, 54, 478–79; and birth control, 414; and Equal Rights Amendment, 467, 476–79, 483, 485–86; and suffrage, 468, 475–76; and social welfare, 473–76; and Nativism, 474–75; and family, 475–76; and higher education, 475–76; work within church, 475–76; and labor movement, 476; and Vatican II, 476–78; and abortion, 477–78 See also Latinos—and Catholic Church; Theology, Christian—Catholic

Certeau, Michel de, 70

Challoner, Richard, 223

Chancey, Mark, 227

Chapman, Maria Weston, 432

Charismatics, 228, 244, 256

Charles II (king of England), 135

Chauncy, Charles, 285, 330

Chávez, César, 91, 93, 439–40

Chenu, Marie-Dominique, 173

Cherokee, 42, 70

Cherry, Conrad, 398

Cheyenne, 451

Child, Lydia Maria, 432

Children: and slavery, 107; and material culture, 199–202, 204–5; and baptism, 247; and labor, 283, 288, 476; and Catholic charity, 288, 474; and sexuality, 353, 356–57, 361. *See also* Education

Chinese Americans: immigration of, 47, 78, 81–82; missions to, 47, 78, 267; Baptists, 78; Catholics, 78; Methodists, 78; Presbyterians, 78; discrimination against, 80–82; Disciples of Christ, 81; Chinese Christian Institute, 81–82. *See also* Asian Americans

Choctaw, 67

Christianity outside United States: identified with colonialism, 171; in Africa, 378, 392; in Europe, 383–87, 389, 391–94; in non-Western nations, 384; in Canada, 387–88, 391, 394; in Mexico, 387–91, 394; in China, 392–93; in Brazil, 393; in Latin America, 393; in Nigeria, 393; in South Korea, 393

Christian Right, 53, 227, 280, 417

Christian Scientists, 34, 49, 51, 230, 336, 501; as religious outsiders, 129

Church, Benjamin, 317–18, 321

Churches: architecture, 66, 154; worship setting, 242–43, 245–47, 249–57. *See also* Practice, Christian

Churches of Christ, 39

Church of God in Christ, 45

Church of the New Jerusalem, 34

Church-state issues, 17–18, 417–19; Christianity in the public square, 119–26, 140, 223, 225–27, 401, 417, 492–94, 497, 502, 505; and religious minorities, 121–23, 125–26, 223, 418, 422–23; Old World

models, 134, 383, 387–89, 428–29, 491; in colonial era, 137, 397, 403–5, 428, 430, 491–94; influence of Protestantism on, 383, 400, 403–8, 411, 414, 416, 418, 420, 483, 492–93, 497–98, 501, 503; at state level, 493–94, 503–6

—and U.S. Constitution, 18, 32, 48, 120–21, 196, 261, 406, 494, 505; First Amendment, 7, 126, 142, 223, 397–400, 404–5, 417–19, 443, 446, 483, 494–96, 498, 500–504; and Supreme Court rulings, 14, 125, 222, 226, 483, 495, 498, 501–4; and principle of neutrality, 397, 405, 501, 505–6

See also Disestablishment; United States

Cisneros, Henry, 441

Civil rights movement, 220–21, 390, 397; and academy, 13; precursors to, 50, 433; influence of, 83, 91, 439; in South, 415; nonviolence of, 439, 455

Civil War, 390, 397, 446, 449–51, 458; influence on American Christianity, 25, 39, 51–52, 159, 434–35, 501

Clap, Roger, 446–47

Clark, Elmer T., 29

Clark, Tom, 226

Clarke, William Newton, 162

Clayton, Horace, 112

Clinton, Bill, 417

Clinton, Hillary, 442

Coffin, William Sloane, 9

Coke, Sir Edward, 447

Colman, Benjamin, 331

Columbus, Christopher, 217

Communion, 242–43, 247; and material culture, 204–6; performance of, 248; and transubstantiation, 248–49, 402; and meaning, 248–51; temporal and spatial context of, 248–51

Communism, 446, 453, 457, 502; and Christianity, 231, 401, 414–15, 417, 435

Community organizing, congregation-based, 429, 439–42; and urban race relations, 440–41. *See also* Social reform

Cone, James, 221

Congregationalists, 6, 8, 37, 39, 42, 47, 144, 217, 219, 331, 387, 430, 493, 498; and missions, 69, 80, 138, 270; and Native Americans, 69; and Asian Americans, 80; African American, 110; and Plan of Union, 138–39

Constitution, U.S. *See* Church-state issues—and U.S. Constitution; Women's rights movement

Consumer culture: and religious objects, 206–8; desire for transformation, 208–9; and Christianity, 275, 279–87, 289–90, 299, 301–2; values of freedom and choice, 276, 280, 284–87, 289–90, 301; and commodification of religion, 280; and advertising, 283. *See also* Capitalism; Material culture

Continental Congress, 401, 403–4, 411, 493

Cooper, James Fenimore, 317, 319–20

Copeland, Kenneth, 295–97, 299–300

Copernicus, Nicolaus, 328

Coptic Christians, 37

Copway, George, 72

Corrigan, John, 15–16

Cort, John, 436

Cortes, Ernesto, Jr., 441

Cotton, John, 329

Cox, Harvey, 129

Coyne, John, Jr., 9

Crèvecoeur, Hector St. John de, 76–77, 93

Crockett, Davy, 317, 320

Crouch, Jan, 295

Crouch, Paul, 295

Crummell, Alexander, 109

Cuban Americans: immigration of, 47, 77–78, 84–85; Catholicism of, 47, 85–87. *See also* Latinos

Cummings, Kathleen Sprows, 475

Custer, George Armstrong, 451

Dakota, 61

Darby, John Nelson, 50

Darwin, Charles, 52, 334

Day, Dorothy, 178–79, 435–38, 456

Deists, 6, 18, 121, 438, 494–95

De Lubac, Henri, 173

DeMille, Cecil B., 196, 214

Denominationalism, 41, 134, 138, 148, 158, 229, 262, 499–500, 505; effect of disestablishment on, 41, 499; and voluntarism, 41, 499; decline of, 144; and nonconformists, 500, 505

Denton-Borhaug, Kelly, 458

Dewey, John, 159, 168–69

Disciples of Christ, 39, 51, 141, 229, 391; and Asian Americans, 78, 81–83

Disestablishment: and denominationalism, 41, 499; effect on American Christianity, 41–42, 223, 260, 499; and social reform, 427–28, 430, 442–43; and voluntarism, 496, 499. *See also* Church-state issues

Divino afflante Spiritu, 225

Dolan, Jay, 16, 36, 86

Dollar, Creflo, 296, 301

Dollard, John, 113

Dominicans, 217

Dorchester, Daniel, 7, 10, 15, 21

Dortel Claudot, Marie-Marthe, 456

Dostoyevsky, Fyodor, 435

Douglass, Frederick, 432, 434, 448, 455, 469

Douglass, William, 331

Drake, St. Claire, 112

Draper, John William, 335

Drexel, Katherine, 266

Du Bois, W. E. B., 116, 218

Dunkers, 32

Durkheim, Émile, 368

Dutch Reformed, 31

Dyer, Mary, 137, 455

Eastern Orthodox, 145, 249, 392

Ecumenism, 4, 11, 53, 134, 137–39, 144–48, 158; Federal Council of Churches, 53, 145, 147; and missions, 139; and social reform, 145, 148, 431, 497; National Council of Churches, 145–47, 231, 350, 361; and academy, 147, 158; and peace movement, 445, 456. *See also* Missions, Christian